THE ENGLISH AND THE NORMANS

Ethnic Hostility, Assimilation,
and Identity 1066–*c*.1220

The English and the Normans

*Ethnic Hostility,
Assimilation, and Identity
1066–c.1220*

HUGH M. THOMAS

OXFORD

UNIVERSITY PRESS

OXFORD
UNIVERSITY PRESS

Great Clarendon Street, Oxford OX2 6DP

Oxford University Press is a department of the University of Oxford.
It furthers the University's objective of excellence in research, scholarship,
and education by publishing worldwide in

Oxford New York

Auckland Cape Town Dar es Salaam Hong Kong Karachi
Kuala Lumpur Madrid Melbourne Mexico City Nairobi
New Delhi Shanghai Taipei Toronto

With offices in

Argentina Austria Brazil Chile Czech Republic France Greece
Guatemala Hungary Italy Japan South Korea Poland Portugal
Singapore Switzerland Thailand Turkey Ukraine Vietnam

Published in the United States
by Oxford University Press Inc., New York

© Hugh M. Thomas 2003

British Library Cataloguing in Publication Data

Data available

Library of Congress Cataloging in Publication Data

Data applied for

ISBN 0–19–925123–1
ISBN 0–19–927886–5 (Pbk.)

1 3 5 7 9 10 8 6 4 2

Typeset by Regent Typesetting, London
Printed in Great Britain
on acid-free paper by
Biddles Ltd,
King's Lynn, Norfolk

À minha amada esposa, Patricia

Acknowledgements

THIS BOOK WOULD not have been possible without the assistance and support of many institutions and individuals. The University of Pennsylvania provided me with a Mellon Fellowship for the years 1993–4 which allowed me to carry out extensive research. The National Endowment for the Humanities provided funding for a preliminary summer of comparative and theoretical reading and, with the American Council of Learned Societies, funded a year at the National Humanities Center in 1999–2000. The National Humanities Center itself provided a wonderful atmosphere in which to work and especially to write. Above all, the University of Miami has been very generous, providing a number of summer fellowships for research and writing, providing benefits during my Fellowships, and granting me a Sabbatical for work on this project. Like any faculty member, I consider it my right, even my duty, to advise (i.e. complain to) administrators about a variety of academic shortcomings, but I will say that when it comes to my own research, the University of Miami has put its money where its mouth is.

The staffs of the Van Pelt Library at the University of Pennsylvania, the British Library, the Bodleian Library, the Cambridge University Library, the Spaulding Gentleman's Club, the Institute of Historical Research, and above all of Richter Library at the University of Miami have all provided the resources needed for this project. Jean Houston and Eliza Robertson, librarians at the National Humanities Center, were particularly helpful, and special thanks must go to Don Carreau at the Richter Library for consistently enthusiastic help and support since I arrived in Miami.

Many scholars have contributed to this project and to my thinking on ethnicity, assimilation, and identity more generally. The graduate students in my courses on Ethnicity, Race, and Nationalism in a Comparative Context have provided many insights and tested my own ideas. Two other graduate students, Ruben Valencia and Jarbel Rodriguez, wrote papers that contributed to my thinking about ethnic relations after the Norman Conquest, and Jarbel was invaluable in helping to set up a database on English landholders in Domesday Book. The participants in the 'Place as an Analytical Concept' seminar at the National Humanities Center, organized by Karen Wigen, helped me to think in new ways about places and peoples, and Susan Crane and Sherry Ortner, who were also fellows during my time at the National Humanities Center, helped me work through specific issues relating to the project. Ann Williams and Hirokazu Tsurushima, who have both produced their own work on relations between the English and their conquerors, have helped stimulate my thinking in conversations as well as through their admirable publications. Michelle Warren helped improve my translations from Old French, and Tom

Goodman has critiqued some translations from Latin. Emily Albu, Ruth Karras, Felice Lifshitz, Bruce O'Brien, Ed Peters, Guido Ruggiero, Leah Shopkow, and Bob Stacey have all read one or more chapters of this work, and John Gillingham has read the whole thing. Their criticisms and suggestions have improved this work immeasurably. Any remaining errors and shortcomings remain my own responsibility.

Karen Carroll at the National Humanities Center helped clean up those parts of the manuscript that were finished by the time I left there, and helped improve my fairly dismal command of copy-editing rules. Jeff New had the unenviable task of shifting the typescript from American to British or at least mid-Atlantic usage, and greatly furthered the process of cleaning it up. My editor at OUP, Ruth Parr, has been extremely supportive and has helped me make some tough but important decisions about the organization of the final project. Anne Gelling and Kay Rogers have also been very helpful.

Finally, I would like to thank my family, both nuclear and extended, for support during the long period it took to complete this project. My greatest debt is reflected in the dedication to my wife, who has served as a pillar of support, an intellectual partner, and a great source of inspiration.

Table of Contents

Abbreviations

AASS	*Acta Sanctorum.*
AHR	*American Historical Review.*
ANS	*Anglo-Norman Studies*: vols. 5–11 (1983–9), ed. R. Allen Brown. Vols. 12–16 (1990–4), ed. Marjorie Chibnall. Vols. 17–22 (1995–2000), ed. Christopher Harper-Bill. (Woodbridge.)
ASC	*Two of the Saxon Chronicles Parallel*, ed. Charles Plummer, John Earle, and Dorothy Whitelock, rev. edn., 2 vols. (Oxford, 1952).
Becket Materials	James C. Robertson and J. B. Sheppard, eds., *Materials for the History of Thomas Becket*, 7 vols. (London, 1875–85).
BL	British Library.
CJW	*The Chronicle of John of Worcester*, ed. P. McGurk, vol. 3 (Oxford, 1998).
CRR	*Curia Regis Rolls*, 18 vols. to date (London, 1922–).
DB	Domesday Book.
EEA	*English Episcopal Acta*: vol. 1, *Lincoln, 1067–1185*, ed. David M. Smith (1980); vol. 2, *Canterbury, 1162–1190*, ed. C. R. Cheney and Bridget E. A. Jones (1986); vol. 3, *Canterbury, 1193–1205*, ed. C. R. Cheney and E. John (1986); vol. 4, *Lincoln, 1186–1206*, ed. David M. Smith; vol. 5, *York, 1070–1154*, ed. Janet E. Burton (1988); vol. 6, *Norwich, 1070–154*, ed. Christopher Harper-Bill (1990); vol. 7, *Hereford, 1079–1234*, ed. Julia Barrow (1992); vol. 8, *Winchester, 1070–1204*, ed. M. J. Franklin (1993); vol. 10, *Bath and Wells, 1061–1205*, ed. Frances M. R. Ramsey (1995); vol. 11, *Exeter, 1046–1184*, ed. Frank Barlow (1996); vol. 12, *Exeter, 1186–1257*, ed. Frank Barlow (1996); vol. 14, *Coventry and Lichfield, 1072–1159*, ed. M. J. Franklin (1997); vol. 15, *London, 1076–1187*, ed. Falko Neininger (1999); vol. 16, *Coventry and Lichfield, 1160–1182*, ed. M. J. Franklin (1998); vol. 17, *Coventry and Lichfield, 1183–1208*, ed. M. J. Franklin (1998); vol. 18, *Salisbury, 1078–1217*, ed. B. R. Kemp (1999). (Oxford.)
EETS	Early English Text Society.
EHOV	Orderic Vitalis, *The Ecclesiastical History of Orderic Vitalis*, ed. Marjorie Chibnall, 6 vols. (Oxford, 1969–80).
EHR	*English Historical Review.*
EYC	William Farrer and Charles Clay, eds., *Early Yorkshire Charters*, 13 vols., Yorkshire Archaeological Society Record Series, extra series (Edinburgh and Wakefield, 1914–65).
Fasti	John le Neve and Diana E. Greenway, *Fasti Ecclesiae Anglicanae 1066–1300*, 6 vols. (London, 1968–99).
GCO	Gerald of Wales, *Giraldi Cambrensis Opera*, ed. J. S. Brewer, J. F. Dimock, and G. F. Warner, 8. vols., Rolls Series (London, 1861–91).
GGWP	William of Poitiers, *The* Gesta Guillelmi *of William of Poitiers*, ed. R. H. C. Davis and Marjorie Chibnall (Oxford, 1998).
GND	*The* Gesta Normannorum Ducum *of William of Jumièges, Orderic*

	Vitalis, and Robert of Torigni, ed. Elisabeth M. C. van Houts, 2 vols. (Oxford, 1992–5).
HCY	James Raine, ed., *Historians of the Church of York*, 3 vols., Rolls Series (London, 1879–94).
HHHA	Henry, Archdeacon of Huntingdon, *Historia Anglorum*, ed. Diana Greenway (Oxford, 1996).
HN	Eadmer, *Historia Novorum in Anglia*, ed. M. Rule, Rolls Series (London, 1884).
LDE	Symeon of Durham, *Libellus de exordio atque procursu istius, hoc Dunhelmensis, ecclesie*, ed. David Rollason (Oxford, 2000).
Mon. Ang.	William Dugdale, *Monasticon Anglicanum*, rev. edn., 6 vols. in 8 (London, 1846).
PBC	*Proceedings of the Battle Conference on Anglo-Norman Studies*: vols. 1–4 (1979–82), ed. R. Allen Brown. (Woodbridge.)
Pipe Roll	*Magnus Rotulus Scaccario de Anno tricesimo-primo regni Henrici Primi*, ed. Joseph Hunter (London, 1833); *The Great Roll of the Pipe for the Second, Third, and Fourth Years of the Reign of King Henry the Second*, ed. Joseph Hunter (London, 1844); *The Great Rolls of the Pipe* (Pipe Roll Society, 1884–present).
PL	J. P. Migne, ed., *Patrologia cursus completus: series Latina*, 221 vols. (Paris, 1844–66).
RCR	*Rotuli Curiae Regis*, ed. Francis Palgrave, 2 vols. (London, 1835).
Rot. Litt. Claus.	*Rotuli Litterarum Clausarum in Turri Londinensi Asservati*, vol. 1, ed. Thomas Duffus Hardy (London, 1833).
Rot. Litt. Pat.	*Rotuli Litterarum Patentium in Turri Londinensi Asservati*, vol. 1, pt. 1, ed. Thomas Duffus Hardy (London, 1835).
RRAN	*Regesta Regum Anglo-Normannorum*, 4 vols. (Oxford, 1913–69): vol. 1, ed. H. W. C. Davis; vol. 2, ed. Charles Johnson and H. A. Cronnne; vol. 3, 1135–54, ed. H. A. Cronne and R. H. C. Davis.
SMO	Symeon of Durham, *Symeonis Monachi Opera Omnia*, ed. Thomas Arnold. 2 vols., Rolls Series (London, 1882–85).
TRHS	*Transactions of the Royal Historical Society.*
VCH	*Victoria History of the Counties of England* (1900–).
Williams, ENC	Ann Williams, *The English and The Norman Conquest* (Woodbridge, 1995).
WMGP	William of Malmesbury, *De Gestis Pontificum Anglorum*, ed. N. E. S. A. Hamilton, Rolls Series (London, 1887).
WMGR	William of Malmesbury, *Gesta Regum Anglorum*, ed. R. A. B. Mynors, R. M. Thomson, and M. Winterbottom, vol. 1 (Oxford, 1998).
WNHA	William of Newburgh. *Historia Rerum Anglicarum*. In vols. 1–2 of *Chronicles of the Reigns of Stephen, Henry II and Richard I*, Richard Howlett, ed. Roll Series (London, 1884–5).
VW	*The Vita Wulfstani of William of Malmesbury*, ed. Reginald R. Darlington, Camden Society, 3rd ser., 40 (London, 1928).

PART I

Theory and Background

1

Introduction

ON CHRISTMAS DAY, 1066, large crowds of English and Normans gathered for the coronation of William the Conqueror. Though William had gained his crown by force, he claimed to be the legitimate successor to Edward the Confessor, and sought to have that claim reinforced and symbolized by a traditional coronation, which included a call for acclamation and assent from the people gathered. The call was duly read out, both in French and English, and both Normans and English responded dutifully. At that point, however, William's carefully planned propaganda coup met disaster. A nervous guard of Norman knights posted outside Westminster Abbey, unfamiliar with the traditional ceremony and unable to understand what the English were shouting, mistook the ceremonial acclamation for the beginnings of an attack and reacted by setting fire to the houses surrounding the abbey.[1]

William's coronation was indeed a powerful symbol, but not of the unity he hoped to achieve. Instead, it showed the cultural and linguistic gulf between his Continental followers and English subjects and foreshadowed the renewed warfare and hostility to come. In the years following the coronation revolt followed upon revolt and the Normans countered with savage reprisals, including the deliberate devastation of wide swaths of countryside.[2] Hostility dominated the relationship between the ethnic groups and even shattered the tranquillity of monastic life when the new Norman abbot of Glastonbury sought to introduce Continental innovations in the liturgy and his monks reacted forcefully. The abbot sent in troops, and during the resulting massacre, in the words of the Anglo-Saxon Chronicle, 'blood ran from the altar onto the steps and from the steps onto the floor'.[3] Peace between English and Norman aristocrats proved unattainable and within twenty years of the conquest the Normans had slaughtered, exiled, or dispossessed almost all of the most powerful pre-conquest landholders.[4] The bitterness between the English and Normans lingered well into the twelfth century.

Yet by the end of the twelfth century this hostile state of affairs was altered beyond recognition.[5] Ethnic distinctions had broken down to the point that one could not

---

[1] *GGWP* 150.
[2] For an excellent recent account of the revolts and warfare after the conquest, see Williams, *ENC* 14–70.
[3] *ASC* E 1083.
[4] I provide the most recent discussion of this process in 'The Significance and Fate of the Native English Landholders of 1086', *EHR*, forthcoming, 2003.
[5] For the chronology, see below, Chaps. 5 and 6.

know who was English and who was Norman. Although Norman French continued to be spoken, at least as a second language, until the fourteenth century, and though English society absorbed a tremendous amount of Continental culture, the aristocracy of England, descended in large measure from the conquerors, came to identify itself firmly as English. By the time of the Magna Carta revolt, rebels and then royalists attempted to use anti-foreign and especially anti-French sentiment as a rallying cry, and there remained a strong pro-English, xenophobic streak throughout thirteenth-century English politics. Despite the bitter warfare and deep hostility that marked relations in the decades immediately following the conquest, the two peoples merged quite quickly. Despite Norman victory and the concentration of power and wealth in the hands of the conquerors, English identity triumphed. These are the processes with which this book is concerned.

Interest in relations between the English and Normans is hardly new. In the early nineteenth century Sir Walter Scott captured the public's imagination with his romantic account of those relations in *Ivanhoe*. At the end of that century Edward A. Freeman devoted parts of his monumental history of the Norman Conquest to a more historical, albeit still romantic and nationalist, discussion of the subject.[6] Modern historians and their readers have been no less fascinated by the topic, though far less romantic or nationalist about it. Almost every overview of the Norman Conquest or the Anglo-Norman period devotes some attention to relations between the peoples. Rüdiger Fuchs has written a comprehensive work on ethnic groups after the conquest, which also explores the nature of ethnicity in the period.[7] Ann Williams has made a detailed examination of the English after the Norman Conquest, which inevitably deals extensively with their relations with the Normans and with assimilation.[8] Other scholars have written articles on specific aspects of English and Norman interaction.[9] The subject of ethnic or national identity has also received attention, particularly in recent years. R. H. C. Davis, G. A. Loud, Cassandra Potts, and Claude Carozzi have studied Norman identity, before and after the conquest.[10] More attention has been paid to identity in

---

[6] This work is badly flawed by many biases but nonetheless contains unparalleled detail and some insightful observations: Edward A. Freeman, *The History of the Norman Conquest of England*, 3rd edn., 6 vols. (Oxford, 1877).

[7] Rüdiger Fuchs, *Das Domesday Book und sein Umfeld: zur ethnischen und sozialen Aussagekraft einer Landesbeschreibung im England des 11. Jahrhunderts* (Stuttgart, 1987).

[8] Williams, *ENC*.

[9] e.g., F. M. Stenton, 'English Families and the Norman Conquest', *TRHS*, 4th ser., 26 (1944), 1–12; Eleanor Searle, 'Women and the Legitimization of Succession at the Norman Conquest', *PBC* 3: 159–70, 226–9; George Garnett, '"*Franci et Angli*": The Legal Distinctions Between Peoples After the Conquest', *ANS* 8: 109–37; C. P. Lewis, 'The Domesday Jurors', in *Haskins Society Journal*, 5, ed. Robert B. Patterson (Woodbridge, 1993), 17–44; H. Tsurushima, 'The Fraternity of Rochester Cathedral Priory about 1100', *ANS* 14: 313–37.

[10] R. H. C. Davis, *The Normans and their Myth* (London, 1976); G.A. Loud, 'The *Gens Normannorum*—Myth or Reality?' *PBC* 4: 104–16, 204–9; Cassandra Potts, '*Atque unum ex diversis gentibus populum effecit*: Historical Tradition and the Norman Identity', *ANS* 18: 139–52; id., *Monastic Revival and Regional Identity in Early Normandy* (Woodbridge, 1997); Claude Carozzi, 'Des Daces aux Normands: Le mythe et l'identification d'un peuple chez Dudon de Saint-Quintin', in *Peuples du Moyen Âge: Problèmes d'identification*, ed. Claude Carozzi and Huguette Taviani-Carozzi (Aix-en-Provence, 1996), 7–25. See

England before rather than after the conquest, but both John Gillingham and Ian Short have visited the latter topic.[11] Though I differ with some individual arguments in these recent works, my debt to the excellent work that has preceded my own will quickly become apparent. But assimilation and the eventual triumph of English identity after the conquest are vast topics, and I do not believe that current scholarship has yet fully explained these processes, nor revealed their true complexity. My aim is therefore to substantially expand our understanding of ethnic fusion and changing identity after the Norman Conquest.

Moreover, the history of the English and Normans needs to be placed more firmly within the context of the growing literature on ethnic encounters throughout the Middle Ages. Three areas of research are particularly important in recent historiography. Scholars have long been interested in ethnic relations during the period in which central control collapsed in the western half of the Roman Empire, and recently this area has been dominated by the ethnogenesis school. The scholars of this school argue (to oversimplify) that ethnic groups were tremendously fluid in the post-Roman period, with peoples frequently disintegrating and new ones (sometimes with old names) forming around an existing *Traditionskern* made up of a powerful leader and his group of warriors. Many aspects of the ethnogenesis school's picture of late antique and early medieval ethnicity will no doubt remain controversial, and I myself have reservations about the level of ethnic fluidity and discontinuity some works describe. Nonetheless, this school has done medieval studies a signal service in emphasizing and publicizing what anthropologists have long known and many historians have intuited, namely that ethnic groups are socially constructed, flexible, and subject to change over time.[12]

The second area of fruitful research has been into the relations of peoples divided by religion, particularly in the Iberian Peninsula and the Crusader States. Recent work has greatly undermined older pictures of *convivencia* in Spain and similar tolerance in other regions, showing the depths of hostility that so often existed. Scholars have also demonstrated how strong ethnic/religious barriers could be maintained over generations in the face of frequent interaction and cultural interchange. In addition, researchers in this area have demonstrated what a large difference the subordination of one group to another made and have shown the importance of power and oppression in ethnic relations. The absence of any major

---

also, David Bates, *Normandy Before 1066* (London, 1982), pp. xiv–xviii; Eleanor Searle, *Predatory Kinship and the Creation of Norman Power, 840–1066* (Berkeley, 1988), 1–2, 124–5, 240–6.

[11] John Gillingham, *The English in the Twelfth Century: Imperialism, National Identity and Political Values* (Woodbridge, 2000), 123–60; Ian Short, '*Tam Angli quam Franci*: Self-definition in Anglo-Norman England', *ANS* 18: 153–75. Works on pre-conquest identity will be discussed in Ch. 2.

[12] Some important works not noted elsewhere are Reinhard Wenskus, *Stammesbildung und Verfassung. Das Werden der frühmittelalterlichen Gentes* (Cologne, 1961); Herwig Wolfram, *History of the Goths*, trans. Thomas J. Dunlap (Berkeley, 1988); id., *The Roman Empire and Its Germanic Peoples*, trans. Thomas J. Dunlap (Berkeley, 1997); id. and Walter Pohl (eds.), *Typen der Ethnogenese unter besonderer Berücksichtigung der Bayern*, 2 vols. (Vienna, 1990); Patrick Geary, 'Ethnic Identity as a Situational Construct in the Early Middle Ages', *Medieval Perspectives*, 3 (1988), 1–17. See also the important discussion of ethnicity in Patrick Amory, *People and Identity in Ostrogothic Italy, 489–554* (Cambridge, 1997), 13–42.

religious difference between the English and Normans weakens but does not nullify
the comparability of post-conquest England with these situations, and it is worth
cautiously drawing on the lessons provided by the relevant studies.[13]

A third area has to do with the expansion of what Robert Bartlett has called
colonial aristocracies, and the conquest or settlement of Slavic and Celtic regions by
people from the core areas of Catholic Europe.[14] Scholars exploring the expansion,
like those focusing on religious difference, have shown the importance of imbalances of power and explored the maintenance of ethnic hostility over long periods.
They have also been concerned with the relations of culture, ethnicity, and identity.
Particularly important for the study of relations in England is the growing amount
of work on ethnic relations in other parts of the British Isles, pioneered by Bartlett,
R. R. Davies, and Robin Frame among others. As British Studies have exploded in
recent decades, our knowledge of ethnicity in what is now Scotland, Wales, and
Ireland has expanded dramatically. Historians of those countries have created their
own sophisticated and complex understanding of the nature of ethnicity and provided useful case studies of ethnic interaction. Such studies are particularly useful
for an understanding of post-conquest England, because they involve some of the
same actors and cultures. Thus this study, though it focuses on English history, is
designed to be placed in the context of British history, and of medieval European
history as a whole.

Within this scholarly context, a study of assimilation is somewhat unusual.[15]
Partly this is a matter of historiography. For various reasons ethnic difference and
hostility have come to dominate the scholarly agenda. The fall-out of colonialism,
the persistence of ethnic conflicts throughout the world, and the dashing of earlier
hopes for growing harmony have led scholars worldwide to place their attention on
ethnic conflict. In the United States, questioning of the old melting-pot ideal has
further fueled this tendency. In England, immigration and resulting ethnic tensions
have likewise contributed to this historiographic trend, and throughout the British
Isles the growing debate about Irish, Welsh, Scottish, and English identity has
played an important role as well. Scholarship, as it so often does, and indeed as it
ought to do up to a point, has reflected current concerns and anxieties. But it is
worth bringing assimilation back into the picture. Though it is important to understand why ethnic divides often persist, it is also important to study how and why
they sometimes break down, though in the process one must be careful to avoid

[13] Important works not cited elsewhere include Robert I. Burns, *Muslims, Christians, and Jews in the
Crusader Kingdom of Valencia* (Cambridge, 1984); Thomas F. Glick, *Islamic and Christian Spain in the
Early Middle Ages* (Princeton, 1979); David Nirenberg, *Communities of Violence: Persecution of Minorities
in the Middle Ages* (Princeton, 1996).

[14] Robert Bartlett's *The Making of Europe: Conquest, Colonization and Cultural Change, 950–1350*
(Princeton, 1993) is a key work in this area.

[15] Traditional historians of the early Middle Ages have been interested in assimilation, and ethnogenesis by its nature involves assimilation, though in general the ethnogenesis school has focused more
on identity than on assimilation. For some accounts of early medieval assimilation, see Lucien Musset,
The Germanic Invasions: The Making of Europe A.D. 400–600, trans. Edward and Columba James
(Philadelphia, 1975), 149–51, and Chris Wickham, *Early Medieval Italy: Central Power and Local Society,
400–1000* (Totowa, 1981), 67–70.

anachronistically romanticizing assimilation as automatically being the product of high-minded, tolerant, liberal behavior.

Assimilation stands out not just for historiographic reasons but also because ethnic hostility was so common in the Middle Ages. There is a certain complacency in past scholarship about the inevitability of assimilation after the Norman Conquest. Yet during the very period in which the conquering Norman elite assimilated with the English, members of that elite began incursions into Wales and Ireland that created enduring ethnic divides. Though the descendants of the invaders absorbed much Celtic culture (one earl of Desmond even became a Gaelic poet), they continued to retain a separate English identity, and hold themselves distinct from the Welsh and Irish for centuries.[16] In general, it was quite common for the conquering elites in central Europe and the Mediterranean, and even the lesser folk who accompanied them, to maintain themselves apart from subject peoples during the central Middle Ages.[17] There are, of course, obvious differences between Anglo-Norman England and the other cases, and one can obviously point out examples of assimilation outside England, for instance in Scotland and the Norman kingdom of Sicily. The point here is simply that assimilation is not automatic, and one should therefore not treat assimilation as the norm and enduring hostility as the exception. The realization that assimilation in England needs to be explained every bit as much as ethnic hostility elsewhere should prompt us to ask more probing questions about why it did occur after the Norman Conquest.

There is an even greater complacency about the inevitable emergence of Englishness as the identity of the assimilated people.[18] On the rare occasions when scholars address the reason why the identity of the conquered people triumphed, they generally ascribe it to the difference in numbers.[19] Numbers alone, however, cannot tell the full story, a point Bryan Ward-Perkins has made forcefully in his recent article on why the Anglo-Saxons did not become British despite the superior numbers of the latter.[20] To take other examples, the Romans, Arabs, and Franks (or French—there is no distinction in the Latin) started out as conquering elites. Not only did their identities remain intact but they also eventually filtered down to many of their subjects. The processes involved were complex, gradual, and incomplete, and brought about shifts in the nature of the identities in question, but the fact remains that the spread of identities from politically dominant to subordinate

[16] For the earl of Desmond who was a Gaelic poet, see J. F. Lydon, *The Lordship of Ireland in the Middle Ages* (Dublin, 1972), 184–5.

[17] See e.g. Eric Christiansen, *The Northern Crusades: The Baltic and the Catholic Frontier, 1100–1525* (Minneapolis, 1980), 210–18; James M. Powell (ed.), *Muslims under Latin Rule, 1100–1300* (Princeton, 1990), 171–2; Hans Eberhard Mayer, 'Latins, Muslims and Greeks in the Latin Kingdom of Jerusalem', *History*, N.S. 63 (1978), 175–92.

[18] But see *Words, Names and History: Selected Papers of Cecily Clark*, ed. Peter Jackson (Woodbridge, 1995), 37.

[19] See e.g. David Bates, 'The Rise and Fall of Normandy, c. 911–1204', in *England and Normandy in the Middle Ages*, ed. David Bates and Anne Curry (London, 1994), 27; Adrian Hastings, *The Construction of Nationhood: Ethnicity, Religion and Nationalism* (Cambridge, 1997), 44.

[20] Bryan Ward-Perkins, 'Why Did the Anglo-Saxons Not Become More British?' *EHR* 115 (2000), 513–33.

groups is fairly common. Indeed, a central idea in the ethnogenesis school, as noted earlier, has been that identity can spread from a small military core, the *Traditions-kern*, to create new peoples. This model clearly applies in the case of Normandy. Though there may have been extensive Norse settlement in some areas of the duchy, in others the Normans were simply a ruling elite.[21] Yet despite the adoption by the descendants of the conquerors of the French language and much French or Frankish culture, the new Norman identity, centred on the conquering elite, remained dominant.[22] In England after 1066, by contrast, the ethnogenesis model falls flat. *Normanitas*, the identity of the ruling dynasty and its chief warriors, eventually ceded to the Englishness of the conquered people. Who, if anyone, made up the *Traditionskern* of Englishness? More generally, the triumph of English identity should not be viewed as automatically preordained by population ratios alone.

Indeed, in some ways the emergence of Englishness as the dominant identity is surprising. Nobles continued to take pride in their (sometimes fictitious) Norman roots throughout the Middle Ages and occasionally up to the present day.[23] Not only the French language but also many aspects of Continental culture remained prestigious in England throughout the twelfth century and beyond. Nobles travelled to the Continent to prove themselves in war and tournaments, while scholars moved to Paris and other Continental towns to gain the latest learning.[24] Despite all this, an aristocracy of predominantly Continental descent, at least in the male lines, adopted an English identity. Where their ancestors had largely abandoned Scandinavian culture but maintained a Scandinavian identity in Normandy, the conquerors of England maintained much Continental culture but largely abandoned a Continental identity. Why they did so requires a complex answer. Exploration of identity after the Norman Conquest will therefore provide an important case study for understanding ethnicity, not only because of the wealth of surviving evidence, but also because it constitutes an unusual example of the identity of the conquered absorbing the allegiance of the dominant elite. In sum, there are a number of reasons why the subject of ethnic relations after 1066 should be explored more fully.

Having described the rationale for a new look at an old subject, I need first to address the issue of terminology, then to describe my theoretical approach to ethnicity, and finally to outline some important controversies that impinge on this study. As Marjorie Chibnall has remarked, no single English word adequately conveys the meaning of the medieval terms *gens* or *natio*, which should

[21] In Normandy, as in most conquered areas in the early Middle Ages, there is debate about the extent of immigration. For overviews of the question, see Bates, *Normandy Before 1066*, 16–20; Lucien Musset, 'Naissance de la Normandie', in *Histoire de la Normandie*, ed. Michel de Bouard (Toulouse, 1970), 103–6.
[22] For works on Norman identity, see above, n. 10. See below, p. 35 n. 18, for the question of acculturation.
[23] For fictitious Norman ancestry, see below, pp. 134–5.
[24] This was not only because of the cultural inheritance of the invaders, but also because French culture was so important throughout Western Europe as a whole. But this very prestige, one might think, would help keep the descendants of the invaders focused on the Continental identity.

form the starting point for discussions of medieval ethnicity.[25] The term 'people' comes closest, and I will therefore use it frequently. Indeed, when I speak of an ethnic group, I basically mean the same as when one speaks of a people. The advantages of the term 'ethnic group' are that it has a more restricted meaning than the term 'people', and that one can employ the related terms 'ethnic' and 'ethnicity', for which no equivalent terms based on 'people' exist. I generally avoid the terms 'nation' and 'national', which raise the vexed question of whether one can speak of nationalism in the pre-modern world, an issue I will discuss below. More important, they are best used for ethnic identities that are closely tied to a specific political entity. This work concerns a period when a single state, England, was divided between two major peoples, along with a number of other groups. In this context the term 'ethnic group' is more useful, though this is a usage that will probably seem more natural to American readers, who are accustomed to using the phrase for subgroups within the United States, than it will to British readers. A term that I have consciously rejected, though it is still sometimes used, particularly by British scholars, is 'race'. 'Race' can be used in British English simply as a synonym for people, or nation, or ethnic group. In this context the tradition of speaking of the English and Norman races is not inherently invalid. However, the term 'race' has a pseudoscientific pedigree linking it to flawed and harmful theories of biology that are extremely problematic in general, and particularly so for an analysis of assimilation and shifts in identity.[26] Moreover, the construct of race, which still has great cultural impact despite the discrediting of its supposed scientific basis, generally involves differences in physical characteristics, at least in an American setting, and thus it is very odd to an American ear to hear the English and the Normans described as races. Therefore, I will stick to 'peoples' and 'ethnic groups'.

My theoretical approach to the study of ethnic groups, ethnicity, and ethnic relations is a complex one. I would argue that to avoid conceptual confusion and fully understand the complicated nature of identity and assimilation it is necessary to approach these subjects on three levels, that of the human bearers of ethnicity, that of the cultural, and that of the construct. The first level recognizes the simple fact that ethnic groups are made up of people and owe their existence to the willingness and desire of humans to belong to them, and to acknowledge themselves as part of a particular group. Any complete exploration of ethnic interaction must explore the interaction of individuals. The second level acknowledges that cultural similarities play an important role in the formation of ethnic identities and that cultural differences can foster ethnic divides. Medieval thinkers were as able to think of ethnicity along these lines as modern ones. In the eleventh century the

[25] Marjorie Chibnall, '"Racial" Minorities in the Anglo-Norman Realm', in *Minorities and Barbarians in Medieval Life and Thought*, ed. Susan J. Ridyard and Robert G. Benson (Sewanee, 1996), 49. For discussion of the Latin terminology, see Fuchs *Domesday Book*, 40, 156; Loud, '*Gens Normannorum*', 109–11; Susan Reynolds, *Kingdoms and Communities in Western Europe, 900–1300*, 2nd edn. (Oxford, 1997), 254–6; Karl Schnith, 'Von Symeon von Durham zu Wilhelm von Newburgh. Wege der englischen "Volksgeschichte" im 12. Jahrhundert', in *Speculum Historiale; Geschichte im Spiegel von Geschichtsschreibung und Geschichtsdeutung*, ed. Clemens Bauer (Munich, 1965), 254.
[26] See also Reynolds, *Kingdoms and Communities*, 254–5.

author of the *Encomium Emmae Reginae*, writing for a queen of England, could speak of King Canute dominating many peoples 'differing greatly in way of life, customs, and, moreover, language', and similar statements can be found in other medieval sources.[27] The third level is based on the argument that ethnic groups have no independent Platonic reality but exist only because people say they do. All three levels are fundamentally important to an understanding of ethnicity and ethnic relations.

Indeed, one cannot fully understand any single case of ethnic interaction unless one explores it at all three levels. To say that ethnic groups are made up of people does not get one very far. It does not explain how individual groups were created, and why individual people belong to one group or another. People in traditional societies have sometimes (though less often than many modernists believe) posited a primordial origin for their own or other ethnic groups, with membership coming through birth. Racist thinkers of the modern period fostered similar ideas, and argued that ethnic or racial divisions had biological origins, which also made birth the crucial factor. Though descent obviously matters in the transmission of ethnic identity, a point to which I will return later in the book, both of the above beliefs about the nature of ethnicity are untenable, not only because of badly flawed science in the latter case, but because neither can explain the creation and dissolution of ethnic groups, nor the ability of people to change ethnic allegiance, as the Normans did in becoming English. Many thinkers, both modern and pre-modern, have therefore turned to culture, in the broad, anthropological sense, as an explanation for ethnicity.

The problem with viewing ethnicity only through the lens of culture is that there is no precise correlation between cultural groupings and ethnic ones. Anthropologists have discovered that individuals with quite different cultures can belong to the same ethnic group, whereas distinct ethnic groups can have identical or nearly identical cultures. Moreover, the specific phenomena that create unity and coherence vary from group to group, and the key differences that divide different groups also vary from situation to situation.[28] Among some modern nationalists, language was held up as an overarching, somehow natural, factor in sorting out groups, but the shared use of the English language has not prevented English, Americans, Jamaicans, and other English-speaking groups from going their own ways, nor did the continuing cultivation of French by the Normans prevent them

---

[27] Alistair Campbell (ed.), *Encomium Emmae Reginae* (London, 1949), 34. See also Fuchs, *Domesday Book*, 23, n. 59; Patrick Geary, *Aristocracy in Provence: The Rhône Basin at the Dawn of the Carolingian Age* (Philadelphia, 1985), 108; Reynolds, *Kingdoms and Communities*, 257.

[28] Fredric Barth (ed.), *Ethnic Groups and Boundaries: The Social Organization of Culture Difference* (Boston, 1969), 9–38; Pierre Castile and Gilbert Kushner (eds.), *Persistent Peoples: Cultural Enclaves in Perspective* (Tucson, 1981), pp. xvi–xviii; George De Vos and Lola Romanucci-Ross, 'Ethnic Pluralism: Conflict and Accommodation', in De Vos and Romanucci-Ross (eds.), *Ethnic Identity: Cultural Continuities and Change* (Palo Alto, 1975), 9–18; Thomas Hylland Eriksen, *Ethnicity and Nationalism: Anthropological Perspectives* (London, 1993), 10–12, 33–4; Manning Nash, *The Cauldron of Ethnicity in the Modern World* (Chicago, 1989), 5–16; Walter Pohl, 'Telling the Difference: Signs of Ethnic Identity', in Walter Pohl and Helmut Reimitz, eds., *Strategies of Distinction: The Construction of Ethnic Communities, 300–800* (Leiden, 1998), 17–69.

from becoming English. There is no objective way to classify ethnic groups or assign individuals to particular groups by a standard set of cultural factors. One must turn instead to the subjective ways people define themselves or are defined by others.

This subjectivity is what makes ethnic groups constructs. But construct and culture interact. To describe ethnic groups as constructs is not to state that they have nothing to do with objectively observable phenomena such as shared languages, customs, or physical features. In fact such phenomena are fundamentally important, more so, I think, than some scholars fascinated with the artificiality of nations and ethnic groups allow.[29] Thus, construct depends on culture. But, once created, constructs can take on lives of their own. Moreover, because people filter reality through expectations created by existing ideas about the world around them, constructs can influence how cultural differences or similarities are interpreted. Equally, constructs are subject to change or disappearance when they conflict too heavily with reality.[30] Thus the level of construct can no more stand alone than can the level of culture.

Both of these levels must also be studied in conjunction with that of the individuals involved. Because people are shaped by the cultures in which they live, and influenced by the constructs current in their culture, culture and constructs will strongly affect how individuals interact with others from their own group and those from other groups. But humans are, of course, the bearers and creators of culture and constructs rather than pre-programmed robots, unable to deviate from the cultures and beliefs that shaped them. Thus, they can assess and test cultural practices and beliefs against the world around them, and make changes that they deem useful. Such assessing is particularly likely when cultures and peoples come into contact. Therefore, when exploring shifts in culture and identity resulting from cultural contacts, it is especially important to look at interaction between individuals 'on the ground', to borrow an anthropological term.

Because the idea of construct is somewhat foreign to the historiography of medieval Britain, and because discussion of it sheds further light on my methodology, I will explain further what I do and do not mean by it. Some scholars of the modern period tend to reduce the construction of identity to a tool of politics, power, and economics, most frequently used by the elites.[31] This is emphatically *not* what I mean. The construction of identity did get bound up with politics in medieval England, but there is no evidence of any effort by kings or political elites to impose English identity. Instead, it moved upwards, and the kings were the last to become thoroughly English after 1066. Nor is there evidence for anyone else consciously creating Englishness. In my own use of the term 'construct' I do not mean anything radically different from what R. H. C. Davis intended when he used the

---

[29] A similar point is made in Eugene Roosens, *Creating Ethnicity: The Process of Ethnogenesis* (Newbury Park, Calif., 1989), 156.

[30] Marshall Sahlins makes similar points in his discussion of structures and history: *Historical Metaphors and Mythical Realities: Structure in the Early History of the Sandwich Islands Kingdom* (Ann Arbor, Mich., 1981), 3–8, 67–72.

[31] Umut Özkirimli, *Theories of Nationalism: A Critical Introduction* (New York, 2000), 109–16; Eriksen, *Ethnicity and Nationalism*, 45–6.

term 'Norman myth' in discussing a very real people.[32] I use the term 'construct' because it has gained widespread acceptance in various fields, but one problem is that it can give an impression of conscious 'creation' that can be misleading. Though modern politicians and others do sometimes try to consciously construct or build up national or ethnic identities, this can provide only a partial understanding of the creation even of modern, let alone medieval, identities. How, then, does the construction of identity work in the absence of conscious efforts?

To understand how ethnicity worked in the pre-modern period (and to some degree still works today), scholars of the subject must partially lay aside their own expertise and try to place themselves in a less theoretically structured framework. Modern scholars interested in ethnicity, nationalism, and race spend a great deal of time systematically analysing these concepts, but medieval scholars did not (and this is true of most modern people as well). People raised in a particular group or nationality tend to take their identity for granted. Those who move to another group or interact extensively with one may think more deeply about the issue, but even those who shift identities may be hard pressed to describe what exactly constituted the shift. There are sometimes rituals to mark passages. But when my wife was recently sworn in as a citizen of the United States, she did not feel a sudden and radical shift in identity as a result of the ceremony, nor did most others, judging by the cheers as those presiding over the ceremony listed various countries from which people had immigrated. Because identities are complex, most shifts in identity take place gradually. Moreover, I would argue that though some aspects of the creation of ethnic identities, or shifts between group identities, can be consciously made, these processes take place in large measure on a subtle, even subliminal level. The fact that people, especially those with a mixed identity or choices between groups, often speak of 'feeling', say, English or Pakistani or somewhere in between illustrates this point. Identity is generally experienced at a level other than one of rational choice or objective acknowledgment of a set of cultural facts. I would argue that this was particularly true in the shift of the Normans to English identity, which involved no formal or ritualistic changes or choices, and took place in gradual steps.

In exploring both the maintenance and propagation of ethnic identities, it might be useful to think about how advertising works. This is so even though advertising campaigns are conscious efforts, for advertising rarely appeals to conscious decision-making. Advertising is not, of course, a comparison that normally springs to mind when thinking about ethnicity, but it can help modern readers conceptualize aspects of the process of assimilation in terms that we are familiar with. Though sometimes advertising introduces to people a new or patently improved product, more frequently it is designed to raise brand recognition and shape an image of a product. Just as advertisers will show the same advertisement over and over to instil familiarity and an image, so a broader ethnic or national identity requires constant reminders to keep people's attention and allegiance focused on it. This is why, in the modern world, both nationalists and rulers or politicians using

---

[32] Davis, *Normans and Their Myth*, 15–17.

nationalism as a tool have often sought to create or deepen national identity (even when they believe it already exists in some natural, latent form), through a range of symbols and minor rituals. They create flags, anthems, and pledges of loyalty to build a consciousness of national identity in the minds of citizens or subjects, and try to instil this consciousness through constant exposure to and repetitious use of these nation-building tools. Few people look at a flag or sing an anthem and consciously decide to become ardent nationalists, but over time these tools and practices can play an important role in shaping and strengthening group identity. They also maintain such identities over time. There was nothing like these modern nationalist 'advertising' campaigns in post-conquest England, but I will argue that certain institutions and social practices served the same purpose without any directing force.

A strong and at least partly positive image of the English was also important to ensure the survival of Englishness after the conquest. The shaping of images through advertising is a subtle process. Few people are so naive as to consciously believe that good-looking potential sex partners will automatically be attracted to them because they use a certain toothpaste or smoke a certain cigarette, but clearly advertisers work to associate sexual appeal or other positive attributes with their product. There was no formal campaign after the conquest to protect and promote the image of the English in order to attract Norman allegiance, and even if there had been, no Norman was likely to consciously decide to become English because of the image. But, as we shall see, writers who associated themselves with the English were concerned with that people's image, and in defending it, they helped make Englishness a subtly more attractive identity for the Normans.

Obviously the comparison of the construction of ethnicity with the practice of advertising has limitations beyond the fact that advertising campaigns are conscious attempts to influence how people think about invented products. Though constructed, ethnic identities, and to a lesser degree national ones, are most effective if they seem a natural or divinely ordained part of the social landscape. Moreover, ethnic and national identities have to be able to command a special kind of allegiance to be effective. Some individuals might oppose or even make fun of a patriotic call to fight or die for their people or nation, but it does not seem inherently ridiculous in the same way that a call to die for Crest toothpaste or Rolls Royce cars would be, no matter how effective the advertising. Peoples and nations are not products but groups or, to use Benedict Anderson's evocative phrase, 'imagined communities'.[33] By this he means any group large enough that its members do not know each other, but still feel they have a shared bond. (Note that the phrase is not 'imaginary community'. The failure of Harold and his army to successfully defend their *patria* at Hastings had dire consequences not just for the fighters and those they knew, but also for people throughout the imagined community of the English.) To be effective, groups have to be special in some way. As

---

[33] Benedict Anderson, *Imagined Communities: Reflections on the Origin and Spread of Nationalism*, rev. edn. (London, 1991), 6.

Anderson points out, the idea of dying for the Labour Party or the American Medical Association does not have the same resonance as that of dying for the *patria*.[34] One of the reasons why ethnicity and nationality are so often linked to common ancestry is that the widespread belief in fighting for one's kin can be extended to the broader group (association with kinship ties can also make larger groups seem more natural). But since most English nobles after the conquest did not believe their ancestors came over with the Germanic invaders, as in Bede's origin myth, but with William the Conqueror, the idea of common ancestry could not make the nobles English.

There are, then, several tasks required to explain the triumph of English rather than Norman identity. One must search for the institutions, cultural factors, and written works that promoted awareness and a positive image of the construct of Englishness. This is not an investigation to uncover some conscious programme to promote English identity, but rather an attempt to see what made becoming English seem an obvious or natural choice to descendants of the Normans. One must also look for the qualities that made the English once again a special group, worth fighting and dying for, even for nobles of real or fictitious Norman ancestry.

The above considerations about the nature of ethnicity and ethnic change, and about the character of our task, have methodological implications. Because ethnicity worked on such a subtle, subliminal level, very few writers talked about their own identity or that of others explicitly, and when they did address the subject they did so only allusively or in passing. There were no explicit discussions of why individuals shifted to an English identity, and only the occasional indirect reference to the source of ethnic allegiance. Because intellectuals of the time did not think systematically about ethnicity, moreover, one will find no discourse on the attractions of Englishness or the nature of *Normanitas*. What the researcher must do is to look at what factors writers mentioned in passing when they did refer to ethnicity, and to look at the contexts in which ethnicity, and more specifically *Normanitas* or Englishness, appeared. When one finds, for instance, an expression of Englishness or English pride, one is generally seeing the *effects* of strong English identity. But because of the subtle operations of ethnicity, the effects of strong Englishness are also the cause of the maintenance and propagation of that identity. When Englishness is linked to an institution, that institution then fosters Englishness. When an individual expresses English pride, it could prompt others to think along the same lines. Though one cannot hope to find explicit descriptions of why people became English, one can quite clearly map out the context in which Englishness came to seem first a possible choice, then an inevitable or even 'natural' choice for the descendants of the invaders.

My theoretical approach also involves treating ethnic identity as a process as well as a thing.[35] At any moment in time, ethnicity *is* a thing, or, more precisely, a com-

---

[34] Benedict Anderson, *Imagined Communities*, 144.

[35] Walter Pohl has noted that the Russian ethnologist Shirokogoroff wrote in the 1930s that we can describe 'ethnos' as a process: 'Conceptions of Ethnicity in Early Medieval Studies', *Archaeologia Polona*, 29 (1991), 41.

plex concept, whether in the mind of an individual or in a society's world-view. But when one adds in a temporal dimension, ethnicity becomes a process of interaction between the levels of the individual, cultural, and construct. This is not only true of the period in which a people is created, but also for the maintenance of their identity over time and the adaptation of that identity to new circumstances. Another reason for thinking of ethnic identity as a process is that it adds a temporal element to the relational aspect of ethnicity that is stressed by many anthropologists. By relational aspect, I mean the fact that ethnic identity is often shaped by reference to other peoples, and the contrast between them and one's own people. For a time, English identity was defined by contrast against *Normanitas*, but obviously this relationship changed as assimilation proceeded. At the same time, the way Englishness was defined in relation to other surrounding ethnic identities also changed. These changes will be important themes of several chapters of the book, and to think of them as parts of the process of ethnicity will be useful. Finally, thinking of ethnicity as a process will allow the reader to focus on its dynamic rather than static attributes.

In general, I wish to pursue a multifaceted approach to relations between the English and Normans. It is all too easy to focus on a few obvious factors such as intermarriage or the imbalance of population to explain the two historical developments of assimilation and the triumph of English identity after the Norman Conquest. Such factors were important, but they must be seen in the context of, and as part of, an extremely complicated web of causation. The two peoples assimilated and the Normans became anglicized through a wide range of personal relationships and through the interplay of many diverse elements of culture and construct. Throughout this book I discuss many factors, but in every case one could point to a similar phenomenon in another case study in which the outcome was that an ethnic divide proved durable, or the conquered accepted the identity of the conquerors. It is the precise interaction of all the factors together that in the end determined the outcome. It would, in many ways, be more satisfying to list the three or five main causes of assimilation and the triumph of English identity, but I would argue that the very complexity of these processes is worth emphasizing. In pursuing this complexity, I also hope to blend together and to some degree reconcile old and new approaches to ethnicity, emphasizing both a traditional prosopographical approach, and newer concepts such as the construction of identity.

Before turning to the body of the work, it is important to address two major historiographic traditions that complicate the study of ethnic or national identities in the medieval period. The first was the habit of nationalist historians of the nineteenth and early twentieth centuries to draw on medieval evidence to illustrate and 'prove' their own theories, Freeman being an excellent example for our purposes.[36] All too often this nationalism was intertwined with the influential racist theories of the period and with an ugly xenophobia. Since World War II (and in some cases, before), scholars have rightly been suspicious of the ways in which nationalist

---

[36] Rees Davies, *The Matter of Britain and The Matter of England* (Oxford, 1996), 17–22.

theories and longings can distort the interpretation of medieval evidence, and create teleological readings of the past. There has therefore been a strong ideological resistance to any interpretation of the evidence that might seem to mirror nationalist ideology. As Barrow commented in 1980: 'The last two generations of medieval scholars . . . have been so anxious to correct the false romantic nationalism of the nineteenth century that the very idea of nationalism in the middle ages has become one of our most rigidly observed taboos.'[37] Discussions of the medieval identities of peoples who were not powerful in the modern period, such as the Irish, are less affected by the taboo, but investigation of any identity that could be related to a powerful modern nation state has become politically problematic. This is particularly true of any sort of German identity. It is no accident that the ethnogenesis school, which seeks to disrupt any sort of continuity within Germanic identity, thereby undermining one of the pillars of Nazi thought and of north-western European racism more generally, had its origin in German-language scholarship, since the need to come to grips with the legacy of romantic, racist nationalism is most obvious in Germany and Austria. But English identity is implicated in some of the same dynamics.[38] I applaud the widespread repudiation of the xenophobic racist nationalism of earlier scholars, and I believe that criticism of their theories was one of the most admirable facets of late twentieth-century historiography. But in the case of England at least, nationalist historians were not making up the evidence for English identity in the medieval period, even if they sometimes exploited it for their own ends. Instead of turning aside from this evidence because of its unsavory modern associations, it is time to explore it again with a fresh and more critical approach, one informed by the anthropological and sociological work of recent decades as well as by the vast amount of historical work on medieval England.

The second historiographic (and social science) tradition that raises important questions and problems for the medievalist is the modernist approach which argues that one cannot speak of nations and nationalism in the pre-modern period.[39] The differences between modern nations and nationalism and the polities and concepts that preceded them are so great that the question of whether they existed before the modern period is a perfectly legitimate one. Medievalists and other students of the pre-modern period have divided on the issue.[40] Certainly the medieval English

---

[37] G. W. S. Barrow, *The Anglo-Norman Era in Scottish History* (Oxford, 1980), 148.

[38] When I gave a paper on the triumph of English identity after the Norman Conquest at Kalamazoo during the war in Kosovo, some members of the audience were upset by what they apparently perceived as a kind of chauvinistic approach (despite the fact that I am blatantly American), and one scholar even came up afterwards and compared what I was doing with Slobodan Milosevic's manipulation of Serb history.

[39] e.g. Anderson, *Imagined Communities*; Ernest Gellner, *Nations and Nationalism* (Ithaca, NY, 1983). For a good overview of the debate over the modernity of nationalism, see Özkirimli, *Theories of Nationalism*, 64–189. In Özkirimli's typology, I would count myself as an ethno-symbolist of the constructivist variety.

[40] For some useful discussions by medievalists, see Robert Bartlett, *Gerald of Wales, 1146–1223* (Oxford, 1982), 10–12; Lesley Johnson, 'Imagining Communities: Medieval and Modern', in *Concepts of National Identity in the Middle Ages*, ed. Simon Forde *et al.* (Leeds, 1995), 1–19; Reynolds, *Kingdoms and*

polity was so different from the modern one that it is hard to identify them as the same phenomenon, and the nature of English identity has changed markedly over time. Moreover, nationalism as a theoretical approach to politics, with the belief that each people should have its own state, did not exist in any organized way in the Middle Ages.[41] It is therefore legitimate and useful for modernists to draw distinctions between broader modern and medieval identities.

But to discuss broader medieval identities simply by reference to modern ones seems to me a trap for medievalists. As Davies has argued, modernists are certainly entitled to define nations and nationalism in temporally specific ways. Nonetheless, there is no reason why medievalists should be bound to interpret their evidence *only* by reference to modern theories based upon nineteenth- and twentieth-century models, as if Western societies in those centuries are the only benchmark for studying broad social identities. As Davies suggests, the peoples of the Middle Ages ought to be studied on their own terms.[42]

Moreover, though pre-modern identities were radically different from modern ones, there has been a strong degree of continuity between the two in many cases, emphatically including Englishness, and on this subject I must take issue with the modernists, or at least many of them. There is a certain cult of medieval alterity among modernists, who use assumptions about the Middle Ages that are sometimes inaccurate to emphasize and exaggerate changes brought by various modern phenomena. In the case of nationalism, they are often motivated by a laudable desire to delegitimize the xenophobic nationalistic identities that have created such horrors in the modern period. That their motives are good, however, does not mean that their arguments are always correct. For instance, Benedict Anderson, a specialist in South-East Asia whose broader theoretical work on nationalism has been very influential, can say that the barons who imposed Magna Carta on King John 'had no conception of themselves as "Englishmen"', which, as we shall see, is wrong, and that William the Conqueror spoke no English, 'since the English language did not exist in his epoch', a claim that would have come as a great shock to eleventh- and twelfth-century writers who often referred to *englisc*, the *lingua anglica*, or some variation thereof.[43] It is easy for specialists to take potshots at scholars who tackle large theoretical topics, and I will therefore add that I greatly admire Anderson's work. Nonetheless, there *is* a link between medieval and

---

Communities, 251–3; C. Leon Tipton (ed.), *Nationalism in the Middle Ages* (New York, 1972); Karl Ferdinand Werner, 'Les Nations et le sentiment national dans l'Europe médiéval', *Revue Historique*, 244 (1970), 285–304. For a broader discussion of the debate, Anthony D. Smith, *The Ethnic Origins of Nations* (Oxford, 1986), 6–18; id., *National Identity* (Reno, 1991), 1–70; and id., 'National Identities: Modern and Medieval?' in *Concepts of National Identity in the Middle Ages*, ed. Simon Forde *et al.* (Leeds, 1995), 21–46, are particularly useful.

[41] Smith has made a useful distinction between this kind of nationalism and what he calls national sentiment, namely feelings of attachment to a people or country, which certainly could exist in earlier periods; 'National Identities', 24–5. See Özkirimli, *Theories of Nationalism*, 229–30, for the importance of the modern 'Discourse of Nationalism'.

[42] Davies, 'Identities', 4.

[43] Anderson, *Imagined Communities*, 118, 201. Orderic Vitalis explicitly tells us that William tried but failed to learn the *Anglica locutio*: *EHOV* 2: 256.

modern English identity. This is not to argue for some essentialist or perennialist view of English identity that traces it back to the mists of time and links it to some notion of biological destiny or historical inevitability. Englishness was a construct, and one whose development and survival was historically contingent. But it was a construct that was created in the early Middle Ages, not in the modern period. On this issue, as with so many others, the entrenched and deeply reified line between modern and medieval, or modern and pre-modern, needs to be more aggressively challenged from both sides.[44]

The key to reconciling my acceptance of modernist arguments about the great gap between medieval and modern identities with my insistence on continuity is the protean nature of Englishness (and of other broad identities as well). Here again the idea of ethnicity as process can play a role, for Englishness has constantly changed over time. Medieval Englishness is not only radically different from modern Englishness, but also from early modern Englishness. To take one obvious example, Protestantism, and an accompanying antipathy to Catholicism, was central to English identity in the early modern period in a way it is not today, and could not possibly have been before the Reformation. Colin Kidd has investigated the intellectual framework of ethnic or national identities in the British Isles in the period from 1600 to 1800, and this framework seems to me nearly as strange from my perspective as a medievalist as it is from my point of view as a person living on the cusp of the twenty-first century.[45] Even within the time covered by this book, there were important changes. Most importantly, Englishness shifted from a widespread and entrenched identity embraced by the elites, to an embattled one associated with the peasantry, and then back again. During the middle period Englishness could have a double meaning, referring to the natives as opposed to the conquerors in some cases, and to anyone associated with England in others, showing that Englishness could be a polyvalent concept even within a single period.[46] In general, Englishness has been a very fluid concept that has changed radically over time.

The fluidity of the concept of Englishness deserves to be emphasized, but so too does its continuity. Historians tend to stress too much the dichotomy between continuity and change, and are especially fond of radical revolutions. For some issues a gradualist approach is more useful. Today's Englishness is obviously quite different from Bede's Englishness, to take the earliest major source for its existence, but it is hard to point to any sudden and sharp period of change that created an overwhelming rupture with the past. Here I not only differ from many modernists but would also suggest some limitations to the ethnogenesis school, with its emphasis on periodic recreations of peoples. The ethnogenesis approach may well work for the late antique period, with its tremendous upheavals, though even here it has encountered criticism. But the denial of links between early medieval identities and

---

[44] For a similar argument, see Johnson, 'Imagining Communities', 14.

[45] Colin Kidd, *British Identities Before Nationalism: Ethnicity and Nationhood in the Atlantic World, 1600–1800* (Cambridge, 1999).

[46] See below, pp. 74–5, 97.

modern ones which, for instance, Pohl has made, goes too far.[47] One might rightly say that the English and French today bear hardly any resemblance to the early medieval Angles and Franks, which is why the distinction between the modern and medieval groups has been projected onto the medieval terminology. But an analogy may be useful to suggest the coexistence of continuity with this radical change. London in the Anglo-Saxon period, with its tiny size, small and flimsy buildings, and lack of industry, was a completely different entity from the city that exists today. Indeed, by most modern standards it was not even a city. Yet no one would deny an essential continuity between Anglo-Saxon and modern London. So too, gradual but cumulatively radical change could coexist with continuity in the ethnic process we know as Englishness. Englishness is not so much an 'invented tradition' of the modern period, as one that has been continuously reinvented over the space of many centuries.[48] One must be extremely wary of the teleological approach of nationalist historians who worked backwards to enhance the political claims of modern nationalist groups while ignoring the claims of others as merely local or invalid despite pre-modern origins.[49] Nonetheless, where continuity exists it is worth studying.

Speculation about alternative histories is generally entertaining rather than help-ful, but in this case the reader, by taking a few moments to imagine what English history might have been like had assimilation not occurred so rapidly or not occurred at all, can quickly appreciate just how different it would have been, and therefore how crucial was the fusion of English and Normans. Long-standing ethnic hostility would have completely altered the course of English political, economic, social, and cultural history. Likewise, a simple exercise of imagining what English history would have been like if Norman or French rather than English identity had triumphed should convince the reader of how important that process was. If nothing else, one would probably not even be talking about *English* history, and the whole history of relations between England and the Continent, particularly with the possessions there of William the Conqueror, Henry II, and their succes-sors, might have been quite different. This book does not seek to follow 'what ifs', but it does seek to reveal more fully the reasons why the English and Normans did in fact assimilate into a single people that eventually considered itself English.

[47] Walter Pohl, 'The Barbarian Successor States', in *The Transformation of the Roman World AD 400–900*, ed. Leslie Webster and Michelle Brown (Berkeley, 1997), 47; Pohl and Reimitz, *Strategies of Distinction*, 14.

[48] The phrase is from Eric Hobsbawm and Terence Ranger (eds.), *The Invention of Tradition* (Cam-bridge, 1983).

[49] See also Reynolds, *Kingdoms and Communities*, 251–2; Smith, 'National Identities', 32–3; Carl-richard Brühl, *Deutschland–Frankreich. Die Geburt zweier Völker* (Cologne, 1990), 268–302.

2

English Identity Before the Norman Conquest

A BRIEF OVERVIEW of Englishness and of ethnic interaction before 1066 is necessary to understand the fate of that identity and the nature of relations between English and Normans after the conquest. A key factor in the survival of Englishness after 1066 is the strength of that identity before. An exploration of the various factors that upheld English identity in the Anglo-Saxon period can help explain its strength and will also allow the reader to see both change and continuity in that identity in the generations following 1066. A study of how the English dealt with important pre-conquest minorities can set the stage for understanding their inter-action with the Normans. The Norman Conquest brought much change, but did not create a *tabula rasa*, and no study of ethnicity in England after 1066 can ignore what went on before.

The construct of Englishness was well in place before the Norman Conquest. By the eleventh century the idea that the English (*Angli, Englisc, Angelcynne*) formed a distinct and unified people had gained widespread currency. This was a people, moreover, in which pride might be taken, a 'celebrated people' according to Ælfric of Eynsham, a 'glorious and splendid people' according to the scribe of a charter from Canute's reign.[1] Their land, widely known as *Engla Lond*, was a unified king-dom sometimes described with the emotive term, *patria*, translated into Old English as *eard*.[2] To contemporary writers it was a land worth fighting or dying for, as when Byrhtferth of Ramsey depicted Ealdorman Byhrtnoth fighting for the *patria* against the Vikings at the battle of Maldon. Similarly, the Old English poem about that battle has Byhrtnoth say to a Viking messenger: 'Tell your people . . . that

---

[1] *Aelfric's Lives of Saints, Being a Set of Sermons on Saints' Days Formerly Observed by the English Church*, ed. Walter W. Skeat, vol. 1 (London, 1881), 2; Edward Edwards, *Liber Monasterii de Hyda* (London, 1866), 324.

[2] For translating *patria* into *eard*, see Ælfric's glossary in William Somner, *Dictionarium Saxonico-Latino-Anglicum* (1659, repr. Menston, 1970), 76 (separate pagination for Ælfric's section). Both words had a variable meaning, but for instances from the late Anglo-Saxon period in which the terms clearly apply to the English kingdom as a whole, see A. J. Robertson, ed., *The Laws of the Kings of England from Edmund to Henry I* (Cambridge, 1925), 76; J. M. Kemble, *Codex Diplomaticus Aevi Saxonici*, vol. 3 (London, 1845), 265, 358; William Stubbs, ed., *Memorials of Saint Dunstan Archbishop of Canterbury* (London, 1874), 6; Frank Barlow, ed., *The Life of King Edward Who Rests at Westminster*, 2nd edn. (Oxford, 1992), 12; Pauline Stafford, 'Political Ideas in Late Tenth-century England: Charters as Evidence', in *Law, Laity and Solidarities: Essays in Honour of Susan Reynolds*, ed. Pauline Stafford *et al.* (Manchester, 2001), 76.

here stands a noble with his band, who will defend this land, the *eard* of my lord Æthelræd.'[3] Indeed, for Ælfric of Eynsham and Archbishop Wulfstan of York, defending the *patria* or the *eard* was the chief duty of warriors.[4] Ernst Kantorowicz and Gaines Post showed how in the twelfth and thirteenth centuries medieval writers and legal thinkers took the exhortations of classical writers to fight or die for the *patria* and increasingly applied them to the kingdoms of their own day, but in England this had begun well before the Norman Conquest.[5]

In recent decades a number of scholars, whose work I rely on heavily in this chapter, have begun to lay bare the process by which Englishness emerged as the predominant identity in what is now England.[6] The identity as it existed in the eleventh century was centuries in the making, with figures such as Bede, Alfred, Alfred's aggressive descendants, participants in the late Anglo-Saxon monastic reform movement, and countless others all helping to shape, preserve, and promote the concept of Englishness. Various factors supported English identity before the conquest. Language sharply distinguished the English from their neighbours in Britain. Undoubtedly there were also other cultural differences that the English saw as distinguishing themselves from the Galwegians, Scots, and Welsh, though these are less easy to detect than in the fuller later sources.[7] Geographically, the sea formed a powerful divide from groups outside the island, including those with whom the English had originally been linked, and though this is an obvious point, its importance should not be overlooked.

The English also had a strong tradition of history and a powerful origin myth.[8] Patrick Wormald has emphasized Bede's importance not only in popularizing the term English over Saxon but also in the development of what might be called the 'English myth', and in the creation of an ideological model of English history based on the Old Testament and focusing on sin, redemption, and the relationship between the English people and God.[9] Drawing on the earlier British moralist

[3] *HCY* 1: 456; Elliot van Kirk Dobbie, ed., *The Anglo-Saxon Minor Poems* (New York, 1942), 8.

[4] *Aelfric's Lives of Saints* 2: 122; S. J. Crawford, ed., *The Old English Version of the Heptateuch*, EETS os 160 (Oxford, 1922; repr. 1969), 72; D. Whitelock *et al.*, eds., *Councils and Synods: With Other Documents Relating to the English Church*, vol. 1, pt. 1 (Oxford, 1981), 252; Wulfstan, *Die 'Institutes of Polity, Civil and Ecclesiastical'*, ed. Karl Jost (Bern, 1959), 56.

[5] Ernst H. Kantorowicz, 'Pro Patria Mori in Medieval Political Thought', *AHR* 56 (1950–1): 472–92; Gaines Post, 'Two Notes on Nationalism in the Middle Ages', *Traditio* 9 (1953), 281–96; id., *Studies in Medieval Law and Thought: Public Law and the State, 1100–1322* (Princeton, 1964), 435–53.

[6] For some works not cited elsewhere, see Eric John, *Orbis Britanniae and Other Studies* (Leicester, 1966), 1–63; James Campbell, 'The United Kingdom of England: The Anglo-Saxon Achievement', in *Uniting the Kingdom? The Making of British History*, ed. Alexander Grant and Keith J. Stringer (London, 1995), 31–47; Sarah Foot, 'The Making of *Angelcynn*: English Identity before the Norman Conquest', *TRHS* 6th ser., 6 (1996), 25–49; Timothy Reuter, 'The Making of England and Germany, 850–1050: Points of Comparison and Difference', in *Medieval Europeans: Studies in Ethnic Identity and National Perspectives in Medieval Europe*, ed. Alfred P. Smyth (New York, 1998), 53–70.

[7] See below, pp. 53–5, 310–15.

[8] See Susan Reynolds, 'Medieval *Origines Gentium* and the Community of the Realm', *History*, 68 (1983), 375–90; Davis, *Normans and their Myth*, 15–16, and John A. Armstrong, *Nations Before Nationalism* (Chapel Hill, 1982), 7–9, for the importance of history and origin myths.

[9] Patrick Wormald, 'Bede, the *Bretwaldas* and the Origins of the *Gens Anglorum*', in *Ideal and Reality in Frankish and Anglo-Saxon Society*, ed. Patrick Wormald *et al.* (Oxford, 1983), 120–2; id., 'Engla Lond:

Gildas, Bede viewed the conquests by the Germanic invaders as part of the divine plan, with the subsequent conversion of the invaders causing, in Wormald's words: 'The "*gens Anglorum*" too [to become] a people of the Covenant.' I might add to Wormald's arguments, though this is based more on Bede's followers than Bede, that in looking back to a biblical model, the English faced a choice between the ethnically particularist vision that dominated the Old Testament and the vision in the New Testament of Christianity crossing and indeed transcending ethnic boundaries. They finessed this by emphasizing, with biblical and other support, that Christ and his apostles came to the *peoples*, and envisioning Christendom as being divided into distinct peoples, of whom the English were one.[10] This allowed the English to be *a* chosen people, though not *the* chosen people, a point with obvious implications for their relations with other Christian peoples such as the Normans. In any case, Bede was an extremely prestigious intellectual, coming to be known as the teacher of the English (*doctor Anglorum* in Latin, *Engla þeode lareow* in Old English) by way of comparison with the most important Christian intellectual of all, Paul, the teacher of the peoples (*doctor gentium* and *þeoda lareow*).[11] Bede's influence alone ensured that his vision of English history continued to hold sway and gave Englishness a powerful ideological and moral foundation. Later works of history, most notably the works known collectively as the Anglo-Saxon Chronicle, helped to preserve and spread knowledge of English history, thereby undergirding English identity.[12]

The institutions of secular government also strengthened English identity. Bede's Englishness was based on cultural, religious, and historical unity, but the English (and Saxons and others) were divided into a number of kingdoms until the ninth century, when the Viking invasions finished off most of the kingdoms still in existence. Alfred the Great, however, preserved Wessex and established a powerful foundation for his descendants to create a kingdom with boundaries that were broadly coterminous with the culturally English and insular Saxon regions. Though this state started out as West Saxon, and occasionally one finds analogues to the modern term Anglo-Saxon, by the end of the tenth century it was basically

---

The Making of an Allegiance', *Journal of Historical Sociology*, 7 (1994), 10–18. See also Michael Richter, 'Bede's *Angli*: Angles or English', *Peritia* 3 (1984), 99–114; Reynolds '*Origines Gentium*', 382–3; Robert W. Hanning, *The Vision of History in Early Britain from Gildas to Geoffrey of Monmouth* (New York, 1966), 63–90; Nicholas Howe, *Migration and Mythmaking in Anglo-Saxon England* (New Haven, 1989), 49–71, for Bede's importance.

[10] See e.g. Ælfric, *The Homilies of the Anglo-Saxon Church: The First Part Containing the Sermones Catholici, or Homilies of Aelfric, in the Original Anglo-Saxon with an English Version.*, ed. Benjamin Thorpe, vol. 1 (London, 1844; repr. 1971), 32, 198, 301, 538; *Homilies of Aelfric: A Supplementary Collection*, ed. John C. Pope, 2 vols, *EETS* os 259–60 (London, 1967–8), 1: 360; 2: 583; *Heptateuch*, 57.

[11] For places in which Bede was given this title, see Whitelock *et al.*, *Councils and Synods* 1: 445; Ælfric, *Catholic Homilies*, 2: 132, 348; A. J. Robertson, *Anglo-Saxon Charters* (Cambridge, 1956), 100. For Bede's reputation in the late Anglo-Saxon period, see Antonia Gransden, 'Bede's Reputation as a Historian in Medieval England', *Journal of Ecclesiastical History*, 32 (1981), 399–402.

[12] Janet Thormann, 'The *Anglo-Saxon Chronicle* Poems and the Making of the English Nation', in *Anglo-Saxonism and the Construction of Social Identity*, ed. Allen J. Frantzen and John D. Niles (Gainesville, Fla., 1997), 60–85.

seen as English.[13] When Æthelweard, one of Alfred's descendants, translated the Anglo-Saxon Chronicle into Latin, he was so intent on systematically changing Saxons to English that at one point he even turned fighting between West Saxons and Angles into a civil war by making an early West Saxon king who in the original fought against Angles (*Angel cynn*) fight against 'his own people' in the translation![14]

Not only did Alfred and his descendants create a unified state, but they also created what was, for the time, an unusually sophisticated government.[15] By modern standards its ability to affect people and reshape society was severely limited, and my own view is that this was also true in comparison with twelfth-century English government. Nonetheless, through military power, coinage, taxation, and judicial control, the government of the English kings, once it had become fully developed, would have had an impact on virtually all those kings' subjects, and therefore could influence how their subjects thought about their identity. Two tools of government may have been particularly important in fostering a national unity focused upon the newly created English state, not only among the elites, who had the most contact with the king, but possibly also among the population as a whole. The first is coinage, which circulated the images of the English kings and, from Edgar's reign on, frequently included the title *rex Anglorum* or some abbreviation thereof.[16] Because kings allowed only their own coins to circulate in England, people had to be able to distinguish the images on an English coin from those on a non-English one even if they could not read. Domesday Book and other sources indicate that England was already a fairly monetized economy, and almost everybody would have periodically used coins. Common people might well have handled few coins in any given year, but that may have made them pay all the more attention to them; it is striking that several miracle stories from the twelfth century turn on people being able to recognize *individual* coins that had been stolen or lost.[17] Thus coinage could have served as a constant reminder to people that they lived in England and served an English king. The other tool of government that was important for identity was the oath. As Wormald has noted, English freemen were expected to pledge their loyalty at the age of 12 from at least the early eleventh century and perhaps from

[13] Alfred was described as king of the West Saxons in his law code, for instance; F. L. Attenborough, ed., *The Laws of the Earliest English Kings* (Cambridge, 1922; repr. New York, 1963), 62. For a discussion of the term 'Anglo-Saxon' and its use, see Susan Reynolds, 'What Do We Mean by "Anglo-Saxon" and "Anglo-Saxons"?', *Journal of British Studies*, 24 (1985), 395–414.

[14] *The Chronicle of Æthelweard*, ed. A. Campbell (London, 1962), pp. li, 18; ASC AE 597; Fuchs, *Domesday Book*, 90.

[15] For recent work on English government in the late Anglo-Saxon period, see James Campbell *et al.*, *The Anglo-Saxons* (London, 1982), 168–81; Pauline Stafford, *Unification and Conquest: A Political and Social History of England in the Tenth and Eleventh Centuries* (London, 1989), 134–49; James Campbell, 'Observations on English Government from the Tenth to the Twelfth Century', *TRHS* 5th series 25 (1975), 39–54; id., 'The Late Anglo-Saxon State: A Maximum View', *Proceedings of the British Academy*, 87 (1994), 39–65.

[16] Herbert A. Grueber and Charles Francis Keary, *A Catalogue of English Coins in the British Library: Anglo-Saxon Series*, vol. 2 (London, 1893), 168–474.

[17] *Becket Materials* 1: 288–9; Reginald of Durham, *Libellus de Admirandis Beati Cuthberti Virtutibus* (London, 1835), 275–7.

earlier still. The importance of loyalty oaths in instilling and reinforcing English national identity needs no explanation.[18]

The English kings managed to develop an ideology of loyalty partly to themselves and partly to the English people or nation, however vaguely defined, by the end of the tenth century.[19] The kings, of course, viewed loyalty to themselves, to the people, and to the *patria* as parts of a single package, a point of view best seen from the law codes, especially those of Æthelræd and Canute. These frequently express solicitation for the good of the people and *eard*, but also call on the people to love and support the king. The various elements are brought together in V Æthelræd, which states: 'And let us loyally support one royal lord, and all of us together defend our lives and our country.'[20] The link between king and country is also found elsewhere. For instance, the D version of the Anglo-Saxon Chronicle states that Eadric Streona, when he fled from the battle of Ashingdon, 'betrayed his royal lord and the whole people'.[21]

What is even more interesting is that loyalty to the English people or land could appear independently of loyalty to the king and could even be used to justify actions counter to the royal will. The best example of the ability of people to separate allegiance to national well-being from obedience to the king's desire was the political pressure placed on Edward the Confessor to avoid civil war in 1051 and 1052 when he was locked in conflict with Earl Godwine. In 1051, according to the D version of the Anglo-Saxon Chronicle, the king had gathered large forces to attack his enemies, but many of the king's supporters argued that it was foolish to engage in battle, for 'the noblest men of England were gathered on the two sides' and conflict would therefore 'leave the land open to enemies'. Godwine and his sons subsequently fled to avoid a trial but returned the next year. They gathered forces and marched against the king but, according to two versions of the Chronicle, 'it was hateful for men to fight their own kin, for there were few with any power on either side except *Englisce* and they did not want to leave the *eard* open to foreigners by slaughtering each other'. As a result, Edward was forced to accept the full re-instatement of Godwine and his sons, and the agreement was accompanied by the promise of good laws for the whole people (*eallum folce*).[22] The germ of the later idea that a king might act against the good of his people, which played so large a role in political struggles from the thirteenth century on, already existed in the Anglo-Saxon period, and so potentially strong was loyalty to England and the English people that it could transcend loyalty to the kings. Thus, allegiance to England

---

[18] Wormald, '*Engla Lond*', 6–10. See also Campbell, 'Late Anglo-Saxon State', 49–52, for the participation of free men in the government.

[19] Stafford, 'Political Ideas in Late Tenth-century England', 68–82.

[20] Robertson, *Laws*, 90 (V Æthelræd 35): '& uton ænne cynehlaford holdlice healdan & lif & land samod ealle werian'. See also ibid. 22, 52, 108, 128, 130, 154; Wulfstan, *Institutes of Polity*, 152, 165. For a discussion of the nature of these laws and their ideological nature, see Patrick Wormald, *The Making of English Law: King Alfred to the Twelfth Century*, vol. 1, *Legislation and its Limits* (Oxford, 1999), 416–65.

[21] *ASC* D 1016.

[22] *ASC* CDE 1051–2; see also Barlow, *Life of King Edward*, 28–44. For overviews of the dispute involved, see F. M. Stenton, *Anglo-Saxon England*, 3rd edn. (Oxford, 1971), 561–9; Frank Barlow, *Edward the Confessor* (Berkeley, 1970), 104–26; Stafford, *Unification and Conquest*, 89–93.

could survive the temporary displacement of the traditional royal house by Canute and his sons and the permanent supplanting of that dynasty by the Norman Conquest.

Of course, to argue that an ideology of loyalty to the English kings, England, and the English people existed in the late Anglo-Saxon period is not to argue that it always triumphed over self-interest or other loyalties. Godwine and his family plundered and harried their own countrymen in 1052 before the agreement noted above, and they were far from unique in Edward the Confessor's reign.[23] Moreover, ideology could be manipulated. The earliest, anonymous, biographer of Edward the Confessor, who was a supporter of Queen Edith and her family, and who began the work before the Norman Conquest destroyed that family's ambitions, used the language of national allegiance to put her father, Earl Godwine, in the best possible light in his descriptions of the 1051–2 conflict. Earl Godwine, according to this account, was revered as a father by all the English, and his flight was considered the ruin of the English people and the whole *patria*. The biographer stated that almost all the natives of the country (*indigeni patrie*) urged him to return. Whatever one thinks of Earl Godwine, this was clearly propaganda.[24] But no ideology has ever completely overcome self-interest, and its manipulation only underscores its importance.

Another factor buttressing Englishness was the English church, which was closely linked to the English nation in people's minds, and in the later Anglo-Saxon period with the government as well.[25] The links can be most copiously illustrated through the figure of Dunstan, the monastic reformer who became archbishop of Canterbury, 'the chief see of the English', in the late tenth century. A letter to Dunstan depicts him as an advocate before God for the English people. Dunstan's first biographer opens his *vita* with the conversion of England, which occurred some 400 years before his subject was active, thus placing him in the context of English national history along Bede's lines. He goes on to describe Dunstan as the first or foremost abbot of the English nation (*Anglica natio*), and writes about how he filled the English land with his teachings.[26] In addition to reinforcing English identity, members of the English church also supported the English state. In writings from the wars against the Vikings of Æthelræd's reign, Ælfric defined just war as defence against pirates or other invaders of the *eard*, and elsewhere he speaks of translating the story of Judith to encourage men to take up arms to defend the *eard*.[27] More routinely, litanies from the Anglo-Saxon period, some of them written in the context of the Viking invasions, routinely call upon God and the saints to save 'our king and princes', or more specifically to save 'the king of the English and his army' or even 'King Aethelred and the army of the English'. Such litanies were

[23] *ASC* CDE 1052. For other nobles raiding, see *ASC* CD 1049, CDE 1055, CDE 1065.

[24] Barlow, *Life of King Edward*, 40.

[25] For the close relationship between the English Church and government see Frank Barlow, *The English Church 1000–1066: A Constitutional History* (Hamden, Conn., 1963), 96–153.

[26] Stubbs, *Memorials of St. Dunstan*, 5–6, 25, 50, 372; see also 56, *HCY* 1: 462.

[27] *Aelfric's Lives of Saints*, 2: 114; *Heptateuch*, 48.

formulaic, but the very routine of repeating them would have reinforced allegiance to the king and strengthened English identity, in the same way that singing national anthems and similar routine rituals do today.[28]

Another contribution of the church was the development of specifically English saints' cults. One tends to see saints' cults as existing in either a very local context or in the context of Christendom as a whole, but a startling number of hagiographic works linked saints to the English people. Saints had tremendous prestige in medieval society, and it is not surprising that writers proud of their own English identity would brag about the Englishness of saints. Moreover, saints were believed to act not only as intermediaries between God and individuals but between God and entire peoples. Dunstan's connection with the English nation continued in his posthumous incarnation as a saint; a prayer to him calls on him to save the *patria*, and a hymn describes him as the light of the English people. Ælfric, in his translation of Abbo's life of St Edmund, boasts that 'the English are not deprived of the Lord's saints since in England lie such as this holy king, the blessed Cuthbert and saint Æthelthryth at Ely'. Wulfstan of Winchester wrote in his life of St Swithun that God granted miracles through the merits of St Swithun to 'his English', and bragged, in a marvellous piece of ethnic one-upmanship, that since the English were the only people who had converted without killing their missionaries and thus had no martyrs, God had given them other saints.[29] The English saints could be envisioned as a distinct group; there were lists of the burial-places of saints in England, setting out the holy geography of that country and demonstrating how many saints it had.[30] Hagiographic works both expressed and reinforced English pride, thus strengthening English identity.

A variety of cultural practices, institutions, and beliefs thus served to strengthen the construct of Englishness, particularly among the political and intellectual elites, but one must ask how far down the social scale English identity and allegiance had penetrated, especially since the elites were most vulnerable to the effects of the Norman Conquest. Scholars of modern nationalism have often doubted peasant allegiance to national identities in the pre-modern period, and Rodney Hilton has

---

[28] Michael Lapidge, ed., *Anglo-Saxon Litanies of the Saints* (Woodbridge, 1991), 225, 233, 239, 264; see also 127, 147, 151, 177, 180, 185, 201, 217, 268, 287, 299.

[29] Stubbs, *Memorials of St. Dunstan*, 440–1 (see also 369–70); *Aelfric's Lives of Saints*, 2: 332; Alistair Campbell, ed., *Frithegodi Monachi Breviloquium Vitae Beati Wilfredi et Wulfstani Cantoris Narratio Metrica de Sancto Swithuno* (Zurich, n.d.), 65, 81 (see also 73, 76, 82, 112, 117, 135, 149, 167, 169). See also David Rollason, *The Mildrith Legend: A Study in Early Medieval Hagiography in England* (Leicester, 1982), 126; Rosalind C. Love, ed., *Three Eleventh-century Anglo-Latin Saints' Lives* (Oxford, 1996), 50, 54, 66; Wulfstan of Winchester, *Life of St Aethelwold*, ed. Michael Lapidge and Michael Winterbottom (Oxford, 1991), pp. cxv, cxxvii; George Herzfeld, ed., *An Old English Martyrology*, EETS os 116 (London, 1900), 18, 86, 178, for other connections between saints and England or the English. For royal cults and the relations of kings to cults, which have an obvious relevance here, see Susan J. Ridyard, *The Royal Saints of Anglo-Saxon England: A Study of West Saxon and East Anglian Cults* (Cambridge, 1988); David Rollason, 'Relic-Cults as an Instrument of Royal Policy c. 900–c. 1050', *Anglo-Saxon England*, 15 (1986), 91–103; id., *Saints and Relics in Anglo-Saxon England* (Oxford, 1989), 133–63

[30] David Rollason, 'Lists of Saints' Resting-Places in Anglo-Saxon England', *Anglo-Saxon England*, 7 (1978), 61–93.

specifically raised the question for Englishness in the medieval period.[31] Unfortunately, it is impossible to provide a satisfactory answer because the sources simply provide no direct information about the ethnic self-identity, or any other kind of self-identity, of peasants. Certainly common people were considered by others to have an English identity. An ordinance of King Æthelstan ordered each of his reeves to provide food for one poor *Engliscmon*, and Canute in 1027 issued a proclamation to 'all the English people, both nobles and plebeians'.[32] As seen earlier, there were political factors that could help foster widespread Englishness and saints' cults could also have helped spread English identity far down the social scale. Though certainty is impossible, I suspect that English identity was quite widespread. Whether it mattered much to peasants and slaves, and whether they accepted any ideology of loyalty to the English nation, however, is a different matter, about which I am more sceptical. Archbishop Wulfstan recorded that slaves were running off to join the Vikings, and who can blame them?[33] The degree of Englishness among survivors at different social ranks is a subject I will continue to pursue throughout the book. Here, what I want to suggest is that readers should keep an open mind, but be both open to the possibly widespread existence of English identity at the lower reaches of society and sceptical about its strength.

More generally, Englishness had no monopoly on group identities in England, for other ethnic and geographic groupings existed there in the decades before 1066. Because the relationship between Englishness and various regional identities was similar before and after the conquest, I will reserve discussion of the latter identities for Chapter 15. Rival ethnic identities need to be investigated here, however, since discussion of ethnic relations in England before the conquest can shed light on those afterwards. There were several distinct ethnic groups in England before 1066: Scandinavians, French who had immigrated before 1066, Welsh along the border with Wales, and Cornish. In this chapter I will focus on two of these groups, the Scandinavians and the French, who had a more central role in English society and about whom there is fuller information than the others.

The Scandinavians originally came as enemies, and to some degree formed the Other that social scientists are so fond of talking about, thereby helping to create unity and cement Englishness among those who opposed them. English writers portrayed them as cruel and evil, and the sources were filled with atrocity stories.[34] They were frequently described as barbarians.[35] Even in Æthelræd's reign, when Christianity was penetrating Scandinavia, the English sources continued to depict an oversimplified struggle between English Christians and Viking pagans who

[31] Rodney Hilton, 'Were the English English?', in *Patriotism: The Making and Unmaking of British National Identity*, vol. 1, *History and Politics*, ed. Raphael Samuel (London, 1989), 39–43.

[32] Attenborough, *Laws of the Earliest English Kings*, 126; Robertson, *Laws*, 146.

[33] Wulfstan, *Sermo Lupi ad Anglos*, ed. Dorothy Whitelock (New York, 1966), 58–9.

[34] Abbo of Fleury, 'Life of St. Edmund', in *Three Lives of English Saints*, ed. Michael Winterbottom (Toronto, 1972), 71–3, 79–80; *Aelfric's Lives of Saints*, 2: 316; HCY 1: 455–6; David Dumville and Michael Lapidge, eds., *The Annals of St Neots with Vita Prima Sancti Neoti* (Cambridge, 1984), 124–30.

[35] *Chronicle of Aethelweard*, 46, 52, 54; Barlow, *Life of King Edward*, 14; Kemble, *Codex Diplomaticus*, 3: 319, 339; Dumville and Lapidge, *Annals of St Neots*, 125, 126, 130.

could not even get their own religion right, at least in the eyes of scholars who treated paganism as a unitary religion with the Roman version as orthodox.[36] This propagandistic image, of course, only emphasized what the Christian, doctrinally sound, 'civilized' English had in common, and what made them superior to their enemies.

Yet the first wave of Viking invasions brought settlers as well as raiders, and immigration may have been quite high, though this is a subject of fierce debate and the more recent scholarship is sceptical about earlier claims of settlement on a large scale.[37] Merchants and others continued to come into England through the tenth century, and Canute established many aristocratic and military followers in the country in the eleventh. Naturally enough, Scandinavian immigrants tended to retain a Scandinavian identity for some time, and there are references to Danes as late as 1065, when several of Earl Tosti's Danish followers were killed during a revolt against him.[38] Equally naturally, there were cultural boundaries that could keep the peoples separate. The most important of these, at least until Canute threw his weight behind Christianity, was religion, along with the cultural practices that religion entailed.[39] The Danes also, from the English point of view, dressed differently, sported odd haircuts, and had names, such as Orc, that were as distinctive to eleventh-century English people as they are to us.[40] Scandinavians formed, at least at first, a people apart in England.

Not surprisingly, given the hostility generated by years of warfare, even peaceful Scandinavians were the objects of English hostility. In 1002 King Æthelræd unleashed a pogrom against the Danes on St Brice's Day, and a vivid account survives, in one of the king's own charters, of how the Danes in Oxford fled into a monastery

[36] *Aelfric's Lives of Saints*, 1: 294; Pope, *Homilies of Aelfric*, 521–2; *Heptateuch*, 416–17; Wulfstan, *Sermo Lupi ad Anglos*, 47–67; Robertson, *Laws*, 110; Dobbie, *Anglo-Saxon Minor Poems*, 8, 12; Kemble, *Codex Diplomaticus*, 3: 285, 339. As Wormald points out, the Viking invasion underscored the biblical and Bedan messages: '*Engla Lond*', 1, 16–17. For criticisms of the Vikings as poor pagans, see Pope, *Homilies of Aelfric*, 2: 683–4, and Dorothy Bethurum, ed., *The Homilies of Wulfstan* (Oxford, 1957), 223–4.

[37] Stenton, *Anglo-Saxon England*, 513–25; P. H. Sawyer, 'Conquest and Colonization: Scandinavians in the Danelaw and in Normandy', in *Proceedings of the Eighth Viking Congress*, ed. Hans Bekker-Nelsen *et al.* (Odense, 1981), 123–31; Niels Lund, 'The Settlers: Where Do We Get Them From—And Do We Need Them?', in ibid. 147–71; Peter Sawyer, *The Age of the Vikings* (London, 1962), 145–65; H. R. Loyn, *The Vikings in Britain* (New York, 1977), 113–37; Pauline Stafford, *The East Midlands in the Early Middle Ages* (Leicester, 1985), 115–21; D. M. Hadley, '"And They Proceeded to Plough and to Support Themselves": The Scandinavian Settlement of England', *ANS* 19: 69–75; D. M. Hadley, *The Northern Danelaw: Its Social Structure, c. 800–1100* (London, 2000), 298–341.

[38] *ASC* E 1064 [*recte* 1065], D 1065; other late references to Danes include *ASC* C 1054; Robertson, *Anglo-Saxon Charters*, 180, 208–10; F. E. Harmer, *Anglo-Saxon Writs* (Manchester, 1952; repr. Stamford, 1989), no. 58.

[39] Canute's law codes show his emphasis on institutional continuity and have the same emphasis on promoting Christianity as Æthelræd's: Robertson, *Laws*, 140–218; A. G. Kennedy, 'Cnut's Law Code of 1018', *Anglo-Saxon England*, 11 (1983): 72–81. For an overview of Canute's relations with the English church, see M. K. Lawson, *Cnut: The Danes in England in the Early Eleventh Century* (London, 1993), 117–60.

[40] Herman, 'De Miraculis Sancti Eadmundi', in *Memorials of St. Edmund's Abbey*, ed. Thomas Arnold, vol. 1 (London, 1890), 54; F. Kluge, 'Fragment eines angelsächsischen Briefes', *Englische Studien*, 8 (1885), 62; Kemble, *Codex Diplomaticus*, 4: 84.

which was then burnt around them.[41] Even after Canute, to quote a hopeful claim from an early version of his law code, 'fully made peace and friendship between English and Danes', there was tension and hostility between the two peoples, memory of which lingered to the Norman Conquest and beyond.[42] The *murdrum* fine, found in post-conquest sources and designed to protect Normans from assassination and ambush by laying a heavy fine on surrounding villages unless the murderers were brought to justice, may well have been created under Canute in order to protect Danes.[43] Edward the Confessor's biographer, recording how Edward had come to the throne after the death of Canute's son Harthacanute in 1042, speaks of the English as having been afflicted by barbaric servitude and describes the joy of everyone at 'native rule' (*dominatus nativus*).[44] Clearly the English were no slouches when it came to ethnic hostility and even violence.

Despite the hostility, a certain amount of assimilation, and probably a lot, had taken place between the English and the Scandinavians before 1066. A chronicler writing in the north about a decade after the Norman Conquest believed that Danes and English had become one people long before. Similarly, William of Malmesbury, writing in the early twelfth century, also believed that assimilation had occurred in the north and wrote, in a separate passage, about the merging of the customs of the two peoples (in other words, about acculturation) because the Danes had lived in England so long.[45] After the conquest any remaining separate Scandinavian identity rapidly disappeared. Reference to Danes can be found in post-conquest law books but these were simply drawn from pre-conquest law codes. Occasionally one comes across the surname *Dacus*, or Dane. Otherwise Danish identity seems to have vanished, though England's Scandinavian heritage was not forgotten.[46] I suspect that in large measure Danish identity disappeared so quickly after the conquest because assimilation and acculturation had proceeded sufficiently far that the remaining ethnic boundaries easily dissolved under the shock of the Norman Conquest and the common oppression at the hands of the Normans.

Only hints survive of the process of acculturation and assimilation before the

[41] ASC E 1002; Kemble, *Codex Diplomaticus*, 3: 327–30. It is likely that the targets were recent immigrants or merchants: Simon Keynes, *The Diplomas of King Æthelred 'the Unready' (978–1016): A Study in Their Use as Historical Evidence* (Cambridge, 1980), 203–5; Reynolds, 'What Do We Mean by "Anglo-Saxon"?', 411–12; Alfred P. Smyth, 'The Emergence of English Identity, 700–1000', in *Medieval Europeans: Studies in Ethnic Identity and National Perspectives in Medieval Europe*, ed. Alfred P. Smyth (New York, 1998), 36.

[42] Kennedy, 'Cnut's Law Code', 72.

[43] The most recent and convincing argument to this effect is Bruce R. O'Brien, 'From *Morðor* to *Murdrum*: The Preconquest Origin and Norman Revival of the Murder Fine', *Speculum*, 71 (1996), 321–57.

[44] Barlow, *Life of King Edward*, 14. See also W. Dunn MacRay, ed., *Chronicon Abbatiae Rameseiensis* (London, 1886), 129–43, and Geffrei Gaimar, *L'Estoire des Engleis*, ed. Alexander Bell (Oxford, 1960), 151, for later memories.

[45] H. H. E. Craster, 'The Red Book of Durham', *EHR* 40 (1925), 524; *WMGR* 196; José M. Canal, ed., *El libro "De laudibus et miraculis Sanctae Mariae" de Guillermo de Malmesbury*, 2nd edn. (Rome, 1968), 93. In the latter passage William was referring to the Danes of Denmark, but one assumes that the remarks held even truer for those who remained in England.

[46] Fuchs, *Domesday Book*, 105, 107, 128, 318–35.

Norman Conquest, and it is not my aim to explore this topic here.[47] The key point
is that, despite the bitter warfare and ethnic hatred aroused by both waves of Viking
invasions, the English were willing and able to work with, absorb, and integrate the
invaders, and to do so at even the highest levels. One of the most important churchmen of the tenth century, Archbishop Oda of Canterbury, paternal uncle to
Archbishop Oswald of York, was described as the son of a marginally Christian
Dane in Byhrtferth of Ramsey's *vita* of Oswald.[48] English nobles were willing and
able to work with Canute and his Scandinavian followers (and they, in turn, were
willing to work with the English).[49] Integration thus proceeded even at social
levels where the evidence for strong English identity is clearest. Neither the ethnic
hostility between English and Scandinavians, nor the cultural differences between
them, should be underestimated, but in the end the two peoples were willing and
able to overcome the ethnic divides.

In 1066 the French, as the English uniformly described them, formed the most
important recent immigrant group. Many but by no means all of these were
Norman. Emma, queen to both Æthelræd and Canute, was Norman, and Edward
the Confessor, her son by Æthelræd, was raised in exile in Normandy. Most French
members of the aristocracy undoubtedly came as courtiers or in the train of
courtiers, though C. P. Lewis, who has done important recent work on the group,
shows that by 1066 they had sunk roots into the countryside.[50] Attitudes toward
these and other Continental immigrants were mixed. The foreign monk Goscelin of
Saint-Bertin depicts the foreign-born bishop Herman extolling the hospitality of
the English to foreigners before Pope Leo in 1059.[51] But xenophobia could erupt
against the French as against the Scandinavians. Hostility between Earl Godwine
and some of the newer immigrants, in part over control of royal patronage, helped
spark the 1051–2 struggle between his family and the king, and in the end the French
were made scapegoats in order to achieve a peaceful resolution. The C and D
versions of the Anglo-Saxon Chronicle state that 'all the Frenchmen', except for
certain ones selected by the king, were outlawed in the peace settlement, because
'they promoted bad law and gave bad judgment and bad counsel in this land'.[52]
Clearly feelings about foreigners were muddled and lay somewhere in between the
openness depicted by Herman and the political bigotry expressed in the Chronicle.
Nonetheless, the xenophobia displayed toward the French is striking, because it was
not directed at a group like the Scandinavians with whom there was a long history

---

[47] For overviews on ethnic relations and assimilation, see Ann Williams, '"Cockles Amongst the
Wheat": Danes and English in the Western Midlands in the First Half of the Eleventh Century', *Midlands
History*, 11 (1986), 1–22; Hadley, 'Scandinavian Settlement', 69–96; id. *Northern Danelaw*, 298–341; Clark,
Words, Names and History, 20–36.

[48] *HCY* 1: 404. See also Eadmer, 'Vita Odonis', in *Anglia Sacra*, ed. Henry Wharton, vol. 2 (London,
1691), 78–87

[49] For Canute's English followers, see Lawson, *Cnut*, 176–7; Stafford, *Unification and Conquest*, 74.

[50] C. P. Lewis, 'The French in England before the Norman Conquest', *ANS* 17: 123–44. See also Fuchs,
Domesday Book, 107–26 for another overview.

[51] Goscelin of Saint-Bertin, 'Historia Translationis S. Augustini Episcopi', *PL* 155: 32. See also Barlow,
English Church, 1000–1066, 94.

[52] *ASC* CD 1051–2.

of war, and also because it was aimed at the very sort of people who would come to dominate England within decades.

Nonetheless, like the Scandinavians, the French who stayed in England for a long time (and a number did in fact survive the 1052 purge, or returned) underwent a process of assimilation into the English. This is attested by the number who gave their children English or Anglo-Scandinavian names such as Edmund, Wulfric, and Swein.[53] At the time of the Norman Conquest this group was partially but not fully integrated. As we shall see, they came to occupy an ambivalent position under the new regime, being legally treated and sometimes described as English, but for the most part politically treated as French or Norman.[54] As a result, they added a note-worthy element to the ethnic complexity of post-conquest England. They also provide another example of the English ability and willingness to assimilate outsiders, an important point to remember when exploring assimilation after the conquest.

English identity did not exist from the dawn of time but was forged during the Anglo-Saxon period by a combination of ideas, cultural traits, and historical events. By 1066 English identity, supported by a prestigious origin story and powerful institutions such as the royal government, the English church, and many saints' cults, was very strong indeed. If the surviving writing is any indication, a sense of Englishness permeated society, or at least its upper ranks, when the Normans invaded. After centuries of development Englishness had undoubtedly become an unconscious assumption rather than a conscious choice for most people. One may well question whether the development of strong English identity was altogether a good thing. The St Brice's Day massacres of the Danes and the anti-foreign prejudices that emerged show that medieval identities, like modern ones, had their dark sides. What is not in question is that English identity had become a powerful force. The Norman Conquest would prove both a shock and a challenge to that identity, and it should be noted that strong national or ethnic identities have disappeared frequently enough throughout history under the impact of conquest. Nevertheless, the fact that English identity was very strong before the conquest was one of the reasons why it eventually triumphed over the ethnic identity of the invaders.

[53] Lewis, 'French in England', 136–9.
[54] See below, pp. 110–11.

3

Normanitas

ACCORDING TO WILLIAM of Poitiers, when William the Conqueror addressed his troops just before battle, he reminded the Normans (ignoring the Breton, Flemish, and other non-Norman contingents under his command) of their *patria*, their noble deeds, and great name.[1] Whether or not William actually did so, his biographer's depiction of the speech reflects the fact that, in 1066, the Normans considered themselves a distinct and proud people with their own homeland and a glorious past. One of William's leading nobles, Roger de Montgomery, expressed his ethnic allegiance quite firmly in one of his charters, having the scribe call him 'Normannus ex Normannis'.[2] The Normans, as a people, have long captured the scholarly imagination. A quarter-century ago R. H. C. Davis set out to capture the nature of medieval Norman identity, or *Normanitas*, in *The Normans and Their Myth*, and others have explored the subject more recently.[3] These works leave no doubt that both before and after 1066 a strong sense of ethnic identity existed in Normandy, at least among the elites. To untangle the course of ethnic relations after the conquest, it is just as important to understand the basis of Norman identity, and its strengths and weaknesses, as it is to grasp the nature of pre-conquest English-ness.

Before turning to the nature of pre-conquest Norman identity, however, it is necessary to investigate whether this is the main way in which the conquerors of England viewed themselves. The formulaic phrase 'to his men, French and English', which appears in the opening lines of thousands of English charters, dating from shortly after the conquest to the early thirteenth century, raises the question of whether the invaders considered themselves Norman or French. Davis argued that in the late eleventh century the Normans were generally indifferent about whether they were called Norman or French.[4] I follow the more traditional view that the Normans considered themselves very distinct at this point. But the frequent use in England of terms for French such as *Franci* or *Francigenae* in documents, law codes, Domesday Book, and occasionally even narrative sources to designate the invaders, needs some explanation if one is to maintain that Norman rather than French iden-tity was most important among the invaders after the conquest.

---

[1] *GGWP* 124.

[2] David Bates, ed., *Regesta Regum Anglo-Normannorum: The Acta of William I (1066–1087)* (Oxford, 1998), no. 281.

[3] See the works listed in Chap. 1, n. 10.

[4] Davis, *Normans and their Myth*, 54.

Two important factors were involved. The first is the heterogeneity of the invaders. Rüdiger Fuchs, Marjorie Chibnall, and Katharine Keats-Rohan have shone a strong light on the extensive involvement of warriors from various peoples in the conquest.[5] Though the great majority of Continental landholders in Domesday Book were Norman, among the followers whom William the Conqueror established in England were many Flemings and Bretons.[6] These groups had their own ethnic identities and loyalties.[7] It would have been awkward to enumerate every possible group every time the invaders were described, so some umbrella term was needed.[8] At this time 'French' could refer simply to those of the Île de France; it was probably in this sense that William of Poitiers used the term in his description of the various Continental groups in William's army.[9] However, 'French' could also refer to all the people under the French king's nominal command or to any people, including some in the German empire, who associated themselves with the earlier Franks. The term could also have linguistic and cultural connotations. As a result, in the Crusades *Franci* could become a collective term, incorporating some who would not have considered themselves French in any other context. I would suggest that 'French' also served as an umbrella term after the Norman Conquest, for it already had a broad, inclusive sense which could be stretched to incorporate the Normans as French speakers and inhabitants of the French kingdom. The point that many of the invaders were not Norman is an important one to which I will return, but the fact that French could be used as an umbrella term did not nullify the Norman identity of the core of the conquering elite.

The second factor that promoted the use of the term 'French' versus 'Norman' was English usage. Sources written in Old English basically always referred to the Normans and others who immigrated in Edward the Confessor's reign and to the invaders themselves as French.[10] The Anglo-Saxon Chronicle does refer to Normans, or more specifically *normenn*, in 1066, but applies the term not to William's force but to the Norse army under Harald Hardrada.[11] The term 'Norman' came from 'north man', and was originally a collective term for the Vikings or Norse. It was clearly still used primarily in that fashion in Old English, where the etymology of the term would have been quite clear, and I would argue

[5] Fuchs, *Domesday Book*, 264–89, 310–18; Katherine Keats-Rohan, 'William I and the Breton Contingent in the Non-Norman Conquest, 1060–1087', *ANS* 13: 157–72; id., 'The Bretons and Normans of England 1066–1154: The Family, the Fief and the Feudal Monarchy', *Nottingham Medieval Studies* 36 (1992): 42–78; id., *Domesday People: A Prosopography of Persons Occurring in English Documents, 1066–1166* (Woodbridge, 1999), 7–8, 30–60; Chibnall, 'Racial Minorities', 49–61. See also David C. Douglas, *William the Conqueror: The Norman Impact upon England* (Berkeley, 1964), 266–70, and Judith Green, *The Aristocracy of Norman England* (Cambridge, 1997), 40–3.
[6] Keats-Rohan estimates that just over 21% of the foreign tenants-in-chief in Domesday Book were not Norman: 'Bretons and Normans', 75, n. 117.
[7] For the strength of Breton identity, for instance, see Keats-Rohan, 'Breton Contingent', 159; id., 'Bretons and Normans', 54–5. See, however, Fuchs, *Domesday Book*, 264–82.
[8] Davis, *Normans and their Myth*, 105; Short, '*Tam Angli quam Franci*', 163–4.
[9] *GGWP* 130.
[10] Davis, *Normans and their Myth*, 12; Lewis, 'French in England', 129–30.
[11] *ASC* CD 1066; Davis, *Normans and their Myth*, 12; Michael T. Clanchy, *England and its Rulers, 1066–1272*, 2nd edn. (Oxford, 1998), 21.

that English writers employed the term 'French' for the people of Normandy not only because they perceived them as culturally and linguistically French, but because 'Norman' was particularly ambiguous and confusing in their language. Many of William the Conqueror's early documents as king of England were in English, and even after the use of English dropped dramatically compared to Latin, he continued to use English or English-trained scribes.[12] The first appearances of the 'French and English' formula came early in William's reign, in an atmosphere in which English drafters and scribes still had an important role in his writing office. Once established, medieval formulae tended to be tenacious. English influence may also have been at work in Domesday Book, written out by an English or English-trained scribe, in the law codes, many of which were translations from English, and even in narrative sources. For instance, Henry of Huntingdon used the term 'Norman' more often than not, but occasionally employed *Franci* in passages relying heavily on the Anglo-Saxon Chronicle.[13] Strikingly, the English exile, Ælnoth of Kent, writing in Denmark in the early twelfth century, continued to use the term *Normanni* for the Norse, insistently referred to the invaders under William as French or Roman (*Francigeni* or *Romani*), and only grudgingly allowed William's title of duke of the Normans, qualifying it by calling him duke of the *south* Normans.[14] The frequent use of the term *Franci* for the invaders may ultimately say more about English perceptions than the self-identity of the invaders.

The common use of the term 'French' in English documents should not, therefore, obscure the predominance of a Norman identity among the invaders. 'Norman' is the term overwhelmingly used by William of Jumièges and William of Poitiers, the two earliest Norman chroniclers of the conquest.[15] In general, it appears much more frequently in later English or Norman narrative sources as well. On the rare occasions when a charter refers to the conquest in the body of its text, it normally describes the conquerors as Normans.[16] Moreover, when speakers and

---

[12] *RRAN* 1: p. xvi; Stenton, *Anglo-Saxon England*, 624–5, 642; Simon Keynes, 'Regenbald the Chancellor (sic)', *ANS* 10: 210–13, 217–21. For some early examples of the use of the phrase 'French and English' from English-language documents issued by William I, see Bates, *Acta of William I*, nos. 31, 38, 80, 107, 180, 189, 276, 338, 351.

[13] For the scribe of Domesday Book, see Pierre Chaplais, 'William of Saint-Calais and the Domesday Survey', in *Domesday Studies*, ed. J. C. Holt (Woodbridge, 1987), 69–70; Alexander R. Rumble, 'The Domesday Manuscripts: Scribes and Scriptoria', in Holt, *Domesday Studies*, 84; Alexander R. Rumble, 'The Palaeography of the Domesday Manuscripts', in *Domesday Book: A Reassessment*, ed. Peter Sawyer (London, 1985), 49. *HHHA* 376, 396, 398.

[14] Ælnoth of Canterbury, 'Gesta Swenomagni Regis et Filiorum eius et Passio Gloriosissimi Canuti Regis et Martyris', in *Vitae Sanctorum Danorum*, ed. M. Cl. Gertz, vol. 1 (Copenhagen, 1908), 82–4, 96–9.

[15] William of Jumièges refers to the invaders only as Normans; *GND* 2: 170, 178–84. William of Poitiers referred to some or all of the invaders twice as French and twice as Gauls. He refers to them as Normans well over twenty times, counting conservatively: *GGWP* 100–86. Guy of Amiens was more fluid in his terminology, using Norman, French, and Gaul almost interchangeably, but he was neither Norman nor a member of the invading force: *The Carmen de Hastingae Proelio of Guy Bishop of Amiens*, ed. Frank Barlow (Oxford, 1999), 2–48. Another writer Davis cites, Baudri de Bourgueil, was also not Norman, and the Bayeux Tapestry, yet another of Davis's examples, had heavy English influence in it; see below, p. 152.

[16] BL Add MS 47677, fol. 263[v]; *EEA* 11, no. 23; R. C. van Caenegem, *English Lawsuits from William I to Richard I*, vol. 1 (London, 1990), no. 163D.

writers of later generations referred back to the Continental background of the invaders, they focused not on the history and accomplishments of the Franks but on those of the Normans. French identity may have competed a little with Norman identity but, as we shall see, a streak of anti-French feeling in Normandy both before and after the conquest prevented it from being too much of a threat, and I suspect that most people saw French and Norman identity as two different levels of identity. Norman identity, in any case, lay at the core of how the majority of the invaders and their immediate descendants saw themselves. It is to the strength and development of Norman identity that I will therefore return.

As Viking invaders, the Normans were originally culturally quite distinct from their neighbours and subjects.[17] As time went on, however, they adopted the French language and a very similar culture to that of the surrounding people. The exact pace of the acculturation and the amount of Scandinavian influence that remained among the Normans are matters of some debate, but there is wide agreement that by 1066 French culture had come to dominate.[18] Nonetheless, the Normans managed to maintain a strong sense of their own identity. Partly they did so by developing a powerful origin myth and a pride in their history. The writer who laid down the written foundations for the Norman sense of the past, Dudo of Saint-Quentin, was not Norman, but presumably worked at the behest of his patrons, Duke Richard I and his sons Richard II and Count Rodulf.[19] He had, and has, little of Bede's prestige, but recorded an exciting past for the Normans. Other writers would build on this foundation. Shortly before the conquest William of Jumièges edited, adapted, and continued Dudo's work to his own time; William would then revise and extend his work once again after the Norman Conquest.[20] William of Poitiers's biography of William the Conqueror had a narrower focus than the earlier works, but it too contributed to the Norman myth. Elements of Norman history or myth can also be found in early Norman hagiographic works. Other works would continue the tradition long after the conquest, but for the moment I wish to discuss the Norman myth as it existed around the time of William's invasion.[21]

[17] For overviews of the early history of Normandy, see Bates, *Normandy Before 1066*; Musset, 'Naissance de la Normandie', 75–130; Searle, *Predatory Kinship*.

[18] For debate over this issue, see Bates, *Normandy Before 1066*; Searle, *Predatory Kinship*; Michel de Bouard, 'De la Neustrie carolingienne à la Normandie féodale: Continuité ou discontinuité?' *Bulletin of the Institute of Historical Research*, 28 (1955), 1–14; Lauren Wood Breese, 'The Persistence of Scandinavian Connections in Normandy in the Tenth and Early Eleventh Centuries', *Viator*, 8 (1977), 47–61; Elisabeth M. C. van Houts, 'Scandinavian Influence in Norman Literature of the Eleventh Century', *ANS* 6: 107–21; Jean Yver, 'Les Premières Institutions du duché de Normandie', in *I Normanni e la loro espansione in Europa nell'alto medioevo* (Spoleto, 1969), 299–366; Emily Albu Hanawalt, 'Scandinavians in Byzantium and Normandy', in *Peace and War in Byzantium*, ed. Timothy S. Miller and John Nesbitt (Washington, DC, 1995), 114–22.

[19] For Dudo, see Felice Lifshitz, 'Dudo's Historical Narrative and the Norman Succession of 996', *Journal of Medieval History*, 20 (1994), 101–20; Leah Shopkow, 'The Carolingian World of Dudo of Saint-Quentin', *Journal of Medieval History*, 15 (1989), 19–37; id., *History and Community: Norman Historical Writing in the Eleventh and Twelfth Centuries* (Washington, DC, 1997), 35–8; Emily Albu, *The Normans in their Histories: Propaganda, Myth and Subversion* (Woodbridge, 2001), 7–46.

[20] *GND* 1: pp. xxxii–xxxv.

[21] For general discussions of the Norman myth, see Davis, *Normans and their Myth*; Loud, 'Gens Normannorum'; Albu, *Normans in their Histories*.

Though obviously the different sources had different emphases, they share a number of broad themes that defined what made the Normans distinct. The first of these was an insistence on the Scandinavian heritage. Even when acculturation had progressed to the point where there was little to distinguish the Normans from their neighbours, they could always point to their Scandinavian heritage to set themselves apart, and as late as the 1160s Étienne of Rouen, in his *Draco Normannicus*, could casually refer to William the Conqueror's followers at Hastings as Danes.[22] A strong Scandinavian identity, of course, involved the Normans in a difficulty, namely that it connected them to pagan raiders, the destruction of monasteries, and other past atrocities. The neighbours of the Normans had a long memory of this disreputable past, and even William the Conqueror could be made defensive about his people's religious reputation; when the monks of Saumur insisted that certain gifts be made purely as alms, William is recorded as having said: 'Although we are Normans, we know that it ought to be done thus.'[23] Dudo and others responded to this historical problem in a similar way to Bede, by arguing that the Normans had been visited upon the French for their sins and that the migration was part of God's plan and designed to bring the possibility of salvation to the Normans. Dudo was explicit about this and even claimed that the Normans would renew the French once peace was made.[24] A similar theme was found even earlier, in a tenth-century life of the seventh-century saint Romanus, in which the saint is made to predict the coming and conversion of the Normans, and in other sources as well.[25] Like Bede's English, the Normans had become a chosen people.

One aspect of the Norman myth not found in its English counterpart is a claim to ancestry going back to the Greeks or Trojans. Such claims were very popular among medieval peoples and had their model in Virgil's *Aeneid*. The French, who were the Normans' chief rivals, had long boasted of Trojan ancestry.[26] Dudo, who was very familiar with the *Aeneid*, and clearly treated Rollo as a figure like Aeneas, provided a similar ancestry for the Normans by tracing their Danish forebears back to the Trojan Antenor. As Emily Albu has pointed out, Antenor had an evil reputation as a traitor in the Middle Ages, and if the Frenchman Dudo was aware of this reputation he may have been making a joke at the expense of his patrons and their preten-

---

[22] Dudo of St Quentin, *De Moribus et actis primorum Normanniae Ducum auctore Dudone Sancti Quintini Decano*, ed. Jules Lair (Caen, 1865), 141–3, 239–46, 276–87; *GND* 1: 32–4, 50–4, 88–90, 110, 126–8; Étienne of Rouen, *Draco Normannicus*, in *Chronicles of the Reigns of Stephen, Henry II, and Richard I*, ed. Richard Howlett, vol. 2 (London, 1885), 646–7.

[23] Marie Fauroux, ed., *Recueil des actes des ducs de Normandie de 911 à 1066* (Caen, 1961), no. 199. For the reactions of neighbours, see de Bouard, 'De la Neustrie', 7; Searle, *Predatory Kinship*, 43–4.

[24] Dudo, *De Moribus*, 124, 136, 141, 144, 146–7, 152–3, 170–1, 179–80, 193, 201–2, 207–8, 283–7. See also Shopkow, *History and Community*, 68–9, 148–9 for Bede's influence on Dudo.

[25] Felice Lifshitz, *The Norman Conquest of Pious Neustria: Historiographic Discourse and Saintly Relics, 684–1090* (Toronto, 1995), 250; see also 253. See John of St Ouen, 'Translationes Audoeni', *AASS* August, 4: 820–1, 823, and 'Libellus de Revelatione, Ædificatione et Auctoritate Fiscannensis Monasterii', *PL* 151: 713, for similar views. See, however, Shopkow, *History and Community*, 81–2, 87, for the relative unimportance of Dudo's theme of salvation history to William of Jumièges

[26] See Reynolds, 'Origines Gentium', 376–8, for these myths.

sions.[27] This story was probably not central to Norman identity but it may, despite Antenor, have given the Normans a certain cachet.

One very important aspect of the Norman myth, that they were a people destined for conquest, began developing in earnest only in the aftermath of William's successful invasion of England, in part because of that invasion.[28] Of course, the Normans had long pictured themselves as warlike; medieval peoples tended to. But even among the Normans there was probably no sense that they were significantly more warlike than others, at least if Dudo is any guide. Dudo could speak of the Normans as a 'warlike and savage people', but he could equally easily speak of the 'warlike Sicamber', and of 'the ferocity of such a great people', in reference to the French.[29] As warriors from Normandy began uniting South Italy, as William the Conqueror temporarily conquered Maine and permanently conquered England, and as Normans from Italy founded the principality of Antioch in the wake of the First Crusade, however, there developed a sense that the Normans were unusually successful in war and conquest. This belief would subsequently play a very important role in Norman identity.[30]

Norman identity, like English identity, was supported not only by beliefs but also by institutions such as ducal government and the Norman church. Though Normandy continued technically to be part of the French kingdom, the dukes headed what was basically an independent realm, often called a *regnum*, and held the prerogatives that had once belonged to the Frankish kings.[31] Though Norman government may have been somewhat less well developed than English government in 1066, it was still relatively sophisticated; William the Conqueror's very ability to stage the invasion of England is a tribute to its effectiveness. Ducal military and judicial power, Norman coinage, and the crystallization of Norman legal custom around the time of the conquest could all help support Norman identity.[32] It is no more possible to tell whether Norman government was powerful enough to influence peasant identity than it is in the English case, but here the question matters less, since relatively few Norman peasants migrated to England. Norman government did influence the warrior aristocracy and ecclesiastical elites, who made up the most important part of the Norman community in England. Thus, the

[27] Dudo, *De Moribus*, 130; Albu, *Normans in their Histories*, 13–15.

[28] Davis, *Normans and their Myth*, 62–7; Loud, 'Gens Normannorum', 104–7, 111–12; Bates, *Normandy Before 1066*, pp. xv–xvii, 241–6; John R. E. Bliese, 'The Courage of the Normans: A Comparative Study of Battle Rhetoric', *Nottingham Medieval Studies*, 35 (1991), 1–26.

[29] Dudo, *De Moribus*, 127, 236, 275.

[30] See, however, Campbell, *Encomium Emmae Reginae*, 32, for a pre-conquest view of the Normans as conquerors.

[31] For the Norman government before the conquest, see Bates, *Normandy Before 1066*, 147–88. For descriptions of it as a *regnum*, see Dudo, *De Moribus*, 180, 192, 229, 231, 243, 252–4, 263, 265, 273, 278, 281, 287; Fauroux, *Recueil des actes des ducs de Normandie*, nos. 62, 67, 122, 197; J. Laporte, ed., 'Inventio et Miracula Sancti Wulfranni', Société de l'histoire de Normandie, *Mélanges*, 14 (1938), 53; Warner of Rouen, *Moriuht: A Norman Latin Poem from the Early Eleventh Century*, ed. Christopher J. McDonough (Toronto, 1995), 88.

[32] For legal custom, see Emily Zack Tabuteau, *Transfers of Property in Eleventh-Century Norman Law* (Chapel Hill, 1988), 223–9.

Norman government was clearly in a position to support Norman identity among the people who matter for the purposes of this book.

The Norman church, as Cassandra Potts has argued, was another institutional focus of loyalty.[33] The boundaries of Normandy were broadly similar to the boundaries of the archdiocese of Rouen, and just as the see of Canterbury could serve as the apex of the English church, so William the Conqueror's father, Duke Robert, could speak of 'the holy church of Rouen, which is the head and chief city of our realm'.[34] According to one ducal charter, the dukes owed support to the church not only because they aided souls thereby, but also because such support 'advanced the state of the temporal realm and the health of the *patria*', thus showing a linkage between ruler, land, and church.[35] Saints' cults also played a role in reinforcing Norman identity, though in the absence of saints from their own people, the Normans appropriated earlier saints from the region.[36] Felice Lifshitz has shown in particular what an important role the cult of Romanus played in the Viking reconfiguration of themselves as Christian Normans and in the merging of conquerors and conquered as one people.[37] One collection of miracle stories speaks of the relics of those saints patronizing Normandy being taken to a meeting at Caen designed to promote the peace of God in the duchy, thus showing that Normandy, like England, was believed to have a body of saints who mediated between that realm and God, and protected the people as a whole.[38]

Warfare and rivalry with the French was also important in shaping and sustaining Norman identity in Normandy. In some ways, the struggle with the French played for the Normans the role that the struggle with the Vikings had played for the English. At first, as Viking interlopers in a late-Frankish or French world, the Normans had to fight to prevent themselves from being thrown out as other bands of Vikings had been. Later, as they became settled and acculturated, the Normans had to continue to fight for territory and their political autonomy against various neighbours, the most important of whom, over the long term, were the kings of France. Periodic wars helped solidify and maintain the ethnic as well as political loyalties of the Norman people, and particularly the warrior class. Norman attitudes toward the French and other neighbours were complex. To some degree they accepted that they had become part of their new world; hence their willingness to be described as French in English documents.[39] Nevertheless, there was a very strong

---

[33] Cassandra Potts, *Monastic Revival and Regional Identity in Early Normandy* (Woodbridge, 1997), 5–8, 133–7. See also Bates, *Normandy Before 1066*, 189–235.

[34] Fauroux, *Recueil des actes des ducs de Normandie*, no. 67.

[35] Ibid., no. 62.

[36] Cassandra Potts, 'When the Saints go Marching: Religious Connections and the Political Culture of Early Normandy', in *Anglo-Norman Political Culture and the Twelfth-Century Renaissance*, ed. C. Warren Hollister (Woodbridge, 1997), 17–31.

[37] Lifshitz, *Norman Conquest of Pious Neustria*, 137–219. See also John of St Ouen, 'Translationes Audoeni', 820–4.

[38] A. Poncelet, ed., 'Sanctae Catharinae Virginis et Martyris Translatio et Miracula Rotomagensia', *Analecta Bollandiana*, 22 (1903), 438.

[39] Bates, *Normandy Before 1066*, 46–93; Potts, 'Norman Identity', 139–52.

streak of hostility towards their neighbours, and particularly towards the French, expressed in their works.

Even Dudo, who was himself French and in some places extolled peace and even co-operation between the Normans and their neighbours, depicts the hostility between the Normans and the French throughout his work. Since he was working for Norman patrons, he put this in terms of French envy and plotting and of justified Norman fears.[40] Anti-French feeling can also be found in William of Jumièges and William of Poitiers. Indeed the former, though a monk, could celebrate the prowess of Duke Richard I's pagan allies in dispatching their French (and Christian) opponents to 'the underworld', thus placing ethnic over religious loyalties. Elsewhere, echoing Dudo, he could assert that: 'Ever since the Normans had begun to cultivate the lands of Neustria, the French had made it their custom to envy them; they incited their kings to turn against them.' He thereby depicted the hostility as perpetual, and naturally the fault of the French.[41] The anti-French sentiment found in these early sources would continue to be found long after the Norman Conquest.

Norman hostility can also be found towards other peoples.[42] Most important were slurs against the Bretons and Irish. In the twelfth century, as recent scholarship has shown, there would develop a very strong stereotype of the Celtic peoples as backward barbarians.[43] In contrast, anti-Celtic stereotypes do not seem to have been strong in late Anglo-Saxon England. But in pre-Conquest Normandy, Garnier of Rouen, in a poem directed against a rival poet, the Irishman Moriuht, who had ended up in Normandy thanks to Viking raids and the slave trade, unleashed a torrent of abuse against Moriuht and his people, attacking their agricultural backwardness, clothing, and sexual habits, and depicting them as pagans. It is not clear how seriously the poet meant his audience to take all this, but it does express variations of stereotypes that would later be very common.[44] Similarly, William of Poitiers would blast the Bretons for their supposedly barbarous marriage customs, pastoral economy, excessive violence, and 'for cultivating arms and horses more than fields or morals' ('as if', remarks R. R. Davies, 'arable farming and clean living went together').[45] Remarks about the failings of other peoples, whether French, Irish, or Breton, undoubtedly bolstered Norman pride and therefore Norman identity.

---

[40] For Dudo's hopes for peace and tranquillity, see *De Moribus*, 135–6, 144; for ethnic hostility, see ibid. 155–6, 187–9, 199, 202–3, 225, 229, 235, 238, 251–2; see also Searle, *Predatory Kinship*, 79–80, 84–5, 104, though I see more ambivalence in relations, as depicted by Dudo, than she does. See also Albu, *Normans in their Histories*, 24–6, for Dudo's attempts to limit hostilities.

[41] *GND* 1: 76, 82, 100–12; 2: 142–4; *GGWP* 42–50.

[42] For an attack against the Poitevins, see Dudo, *De Moribus*, 192.

[43] Bartlett, *Gerald of Wales*, 158–77; R. R. Davies, *Domination and Conquest: The Experience of Ireland, Scotland and Wales, 1100–1300* (Cambridge, 1990), 20–3; W. R. Jones, 'The Image of the Barbarian in Medieval Europe', *Comparative Studies in Society and History*, 13 (1971): 376–407; Gillingham, *English in the Twelfth Century*, 3–18, 41–58, 101–5.

[44] Warner of Rouen, *Moriuht*, 74.

[45] *GGWP* 74; Davies, *Domination and Conquest*, 22. See Shopkow, *History and Community*, 133, for some classical influences on this passage.

By 1066 Norman identity was well established and was supported by a powerful set of beliefs and a number of institutions; *Normanitas* was no flimsy construct ready to crumble under the slightest pressure. I have argued that English identity survived in large measure because it was so strong. But Norman identity too was very strong, which raises the question of why it eventually proved vulnerable in England. Most of the answer must wait for future chapters, but a study of two subjects, namely the interaction of the Normans with their allies in the conquest, and Norman identity in a comparative context after the conquest, can reveal some potential weaknesses of *Normanitas*, as well as shedding light on assimilation.

Given the conflicts and prejudices noted above, particularly towards French and Bretons, how did the Normans get along with their allies in England after 1066? The willingness of the Normans to incorporate powerful individuals from distinctly different ethnic groups into their new ruling elite for England provides an excellent example of an important theme of this book, namely the pragmatic tolerance of the Normans, and of their willingness to reach across ethnic lines when it suited their purposes. However, relations with their allies were not always smooth. William of Poitiers's insistence that William had maintained as harsh a discipline among his Norman soldiers as among his Breton and Aquitanian ones suggests charges of favouritism had been made.[46] When the partly Breton Earl Ralph rose in revolt in 1075, many Bretons joined him. William's (Lombard) archbishop Lanfranc referred, in a letter concerning that revolt, to the kingdom being purged of the 'filthiness' of the Bretons.[47] There is no sign of ethnic tensions among the invaders after 1075. Nonetheless, it is worth remembering that the Normans could express ethnic hostility even against their allies.

It is not clear how important a factor non-Norman Continental identities remained, nor how strong an ethnic cohesion the various minor groups maintained over the long term. The survival of ethnic bynames suggests that ethnicity was important to some individuals.[48] Katharine Keats-Rohan has traced the cohesiveness of groups of Bretons in England after the conquest, though since the groups could oppose each other, it is not at all clear that ethnicity, as opposed to ties of lordship, kinship, and political faction, served as the glue.[49] In Wales, the Flemish community in the south-west maintained a distinct identity until Gerald of Wales's time.[50] However, nothing like this last community appears in the surviving evidence for England. In general I suspect that, although ethnicity and ties to the region of origin might matter to individuals, any ethnic cohesion among the Flemings, Bretons, and other Continental groups in England quickly declined. Flemings, Bretons, Poitevins, and others certainly did not maintain themselves apart from the Normans in England, but seem to have been absorbed into a broad

---

[46] *GGWP* 160.

[47] *The Letters of Lanfranc Archbishop of Canterbury*, ed. Helen Clover and Margaret Gibson (Oxford, 1979), 124.

[48] See below, p. 100.

[49] Keats-Rohan, 'Bretons and Normans', 42–78. See, however, Fuchs, *Domesday Book*, 264–82.

[50] Gerald of Wales, *Speculum Duorum*, ed. Yves Lefèvre *et al.* (Cardiff, 1974), 36, 38; *GCO* 1: 24, 28; 6: 83.

Continental elite dominated by the Normans, in the same way that warriors from different groups could be absorbed into the Goths, Franks, Vandals and other successful peoples during the period of migrations. The topic of assimilation *within* the new Continental elite is beyond the scope of this work, but deserves further attention. In any case, there clearly was a good deal of ethnic heterogeneity among the conquerors at the beginning, and though this would have become less pronounced over time, it needs to be factored into the equation.

A number of important points emerge from this discussion, especially when combined with the earlier analysis of ethnic relations in England before the conquest. First, both the English and the Normans were capable of displaying hostility toward other groups and working with or even assimilating those groups *at the same time.* The ability of assimilation to occur simultaneously with at least a certain level of ethnic hostility is important to keep in mind when exploring relations between English and Normans. Second, though the maintenance of enduring ethnic boundaries may have been more common than assimilation in the central Middle Ages, the specific assimilation of the English and Normans was not an isolated event. The English were absorbing Scandinavians and Continental immigrants at the time of the conquest, and the Normans in England were integrating with their allies and with the English concurrently after the conquest. Whatever aspects of society made them more liable to assimilation than to building strong ethnic barriers apparently already existed. Third, one may speculate that the very heterogeneity of post-conquest society was important to easing assimilation and shifts in identity. The muddling and complicating of any simple division into English and Normans may have shifted a certain amount of focus away from that particular boundary. The somewhat easier assimilation between the Normans and their allies on the one hand, and the English and any remaining people who identified themselves as Scandinavians on the other, may have helped to pave the way for the integration of the two main groups. Some figures from outside the two main groups, like the Lombard Lanfranc and the Burgundian Anselm, may have been able to serve as bridges between the English and Normans precisely because they belonged to neither group.[51] Nonetheless, as we shall see, the conflict between English and Normans became paramount in the decades following the conquest.

As for a comparative study of Norman identity outside England after 1066, there is no need to devote much time to the strength of the Norman myth in the late eleventh and early twelfth centuries, for the phenomenon has been well and ably studied. As we have seen, there developed an image of them as great conquerors. The depiction of the Normans was not always wholly positive, as Albu has recently pointed out.[52] But in thinking about the triumph of Englishness, one should note how widespread and powerful the image of the conquering Norman was in the early twelfth century.[53] Nonetheless, a study of Norman identity in Normandy, southern

[51] See below, pp. 215–17, for the importance of these two figures in ethnic relations.
[52] Albu, *Normans in their Histories*, 13–15, 41–6, 62–4, 73–7, 88–105, 113–15, 119, 125–44, 150–64, 175–9, 185–6, 191–210, 222–3, 234–5, 239.
[53] Davis, *Normans and their Myth*, 62–7; Loud, 'Gens Normannorum', 104–16.

Italy, and the principality of Antioch will reveal not just strengths but also weaknesses of *Normanitas*.

In Normandy, Norman identity continued to flourish throughout the twelfth century. Robert of Torigni, a historian who early in his career had created yet another redaction of the *Gesta Normannorum Ducum*, could, in his universal chronicle, speak of the king of France, during the 1173–4 revolt, planning to enter Normandy and lay waste to the *patria*, and then depict Henry II reminding the barons how often their ancestors had driven the French shamefully from their borders.[54] The translations of Norman history into French by Wace and Benoît show the vitality of Norman tradition, and the eccentric *Draco Normannicus* of Étienne of Rouen, written in the late 1160s, is filled with a strong sense of Norman identity.[55] The French conquest completed in 1204 obviously affected the nature of *Normanitas*, but Norman identity did not go away. As late as the middle of the thirteenth century, the English chronicler Matthew Paris could speak of St Louis fortifying Normandy with Frenchmen and trying to encourage assimilation between the French and Normans, mistrusting the loyalties of the latter. The fact that Philip Augustus, Louis VIII, and St Louis all carefully avoided appointing Normans to the most powerful offices in Normandy indicates that this passage represented more than the wishful thinking of a notoriously xenophobic English writer.[56] These suspicions would slowly break down, but Philippe Contamine has argued that a separate Norman identity survived even in the late Middle Ages, though weakened by the lack of a dynasty to focus on, and unaccompanied by any interest in political independence from France.[57] *Normanitas* may have changed and weakened over time, but it did not disappear in Normandy.

In southern Italy it did, though only slowly. In the eleventh- and early twelfth-century chronicles of the regions Normans are everywhere, and in some writings *Normanitas* is a central theme.[58] Charters could sometimes distinguish Normans and Lombards up until the eve of Henry VI's conquest.[59] But the number of such

[54] *GND* 1: pp. lxxvii–xci; *Chronicle of Robert of Torigni*, in *Chronicles of the Reigns of Stephen, Henry II, and Richard I*, vol. 4, ed. Richard Howlett (London, 1889), 263–4. See also Shopkow, *History and Community*, 166.

[55] Benoît, *Chronique des Ducs de Normandie par Benoit*, ed. Carin Fahlin and Östen Södergård, 3 vols. (Uppsala, 1951–67); Wace, *Le Roman de Rou*, ed. A. J. Holden, 3 vols. (Paris, 1970–3); Étienne of Rouen, *Draco Normannicus*, 589–757.

[56] Matthew Paris, *Chronica Majora*, ed. Henry Richards Luard, vol. 5 (London, 1880), 626; Joseph Reese Strayer, *The Administration of Normandy under Saint Louis* (Cambridge, Mass., 1932), 91–2, 95.

[57] Philippe Contamine, 'The Norman "Nation" and the French "Nation" in the Fourteenth and Fifteenth Centuries', in *England and Normandy in the Middle Ages*, ed. David Bates and Anne Curry (London, 1994), 215–34. See also Marjorie Chibnall, *The Normans* (Oxford, 2000), 161–73.

[58] The works of William of Apulia, Amatus of Monte Cassino and Geoffrey of Malaterra centred around Norman rulers and are replete with references to the Normans: William of Apulia, *La Geste de Robert Guiscard*, ed. Marguerite Mathieu (Palermo, 1961); Amatus of Montecassino, *L'Ystoir de li Normant et la Chronique de Robert Viscart*, ed. M. Champollion-Figeac (Paris, 1835; repr. New York, 1965); Geoffrey of Malaterra, *De Rebus Gestis Rogerii Calabriae et Siciliae Comitis*, ed. Ernesto Pontieri (Bologna, 1927–8). Normans play a prominent role in the Chronicle of Monte Cassino from the second decade of the eleventh century well into the twelfth: Hartmut Hoffman, ed., *Chronica Monasterii Casinensis* (Hanover, 1980), 236–603.

[59] G. A. Loud, 'How "Norman" was the Norman Conquest of Southern Italy?', *Nottingham Medieval*

identifications had already tapered off by then, and in the chronicles of the late twelfth century, such as those of Romuald of Salerno, Alexander of Telese, and the pseudo-Hugo Falcandus, all intimately concerned with the doings of the 'Norman' kings of the period, the Normans as a distinct group disappear. There remains a memory that the kings are of Norman descent, but little sign that anyone thought of their own contemporaries as Normans.[60] In contrast to Britain and Ireland, where outside of Scotland the descendants of the invaders generally became English, there was no local ethnic identity strong enough to win Norman allegiance. Strong local identities, and also regional ones centred around Sicily, Apulia, and Calabria, seem to have emerged instead.[61] In some ways Norman identity proved even weaker in southern Italy than in England. As for Antioch, there is little local evidence for a strong Norman identity, though writers elsewhere stressed the Norman role in the foundation of that state. Instead, Alan Murray has argued, Antioch accepted the common Frankish or French identity that developed in the crusader states as a whole.[62]

What made Norman identity vulnerable away from Normandy? Davis argued that an attachment to the land of Normandy was one important aspect of the Norman myth, and it is noteworthy that Amatus of Montecassino and Geoffrey of Malaterra, both important chroniclers of the Normans in the south, had brief descriptions of Normandy near the beginnings of their works.[63] But obviously attachment to a land one rarely if ever visited was less likely as time went on. Orderic wrote of one Norman who went to Apulia and 'forgot Normandy'.[64] At the same time as people left the land itself behind, they also left behind the institutions of government and church that helped to create and reinforce Norman identity before the conquest. In Chapter 15 I will discuss how new loyalties of place aided the triumph of English identity in England, but it is worth noting here that these new loyalties often involved a loss of old ones. The evidence of Italy and Antioch at least

Studies, 25 (1981), 24; G. A. Loud, *Church and Society in the Norman Principality of Capua, 1058–1197* (Oxford, 1985), 88–9; Joanna H. Drell, 'Cultural Syncretism and Ethnic Identity: The Norman "Conquest" of Southern Italy and Sicily', *Journal of Medieval History*, 25 (1999), 199–200.

[60] Alexander of Telese mentions the early conquest of the Normans, but does not speak of Normans otherwise; *Alexandrini Telesini Abbatis Ystoria Rogerii Regis Sicilie, Calabrie, atque Apulie*, ed. Ludovica de Vava, (Rome, 1991), 3. The pseudo Hugo Falcandus notes the Norman/French origins of King Roger, but likewise ignores Norman identity thereafter: Graham A. Loud and Thomas Wiedemann, eds., *The History of the Tyrants of Sicily by "Hugo Falcandus" 1154–69* (Manchester, 1998), 58; Romuald of Salerno could write of Normans in the eleventh century, but also avoids describing contemporaries as Norman: *Romualdi Salernitani Chronicon*, ed. C. A. Garufi (Città di Castello, 1935), 173–87.

[61] e.g. *Romualdi Salernitani Chronicon*, 238, 239, 240, 245; Loud and Wiedemann, *History of the Tyrants of Sicily*, 252–63.

[62] Alan V. Murray, 'Ethnic Identity in the Crusader States: The Frankish Race and the Settlement of Outremer', in *Concepts of National Identity in the Middle Ages*, ed. Simon Forde *et al.* (Leeds, 1995), 59–73; id., 'How Norman was the Principality of Antioch? Prolegomena to a Study of the Origins of the Nobility of a Crusader State', in *Family Trees and the Roots of Politics: The Prosopography of Britain and France from the Tenth to the Twelfth Century*, ed. K. S. B. Keats-Rohan (Woodbridge, 1997), 349–59.

[63] Davis, *Normans and their Myth*, 57–8, 67–8; Amatus of Montecassino, *L'Ystoir de li Normant*, 9; Geoffrey of Malaterra, *De Rebus Gestis Rogerii*, 7–8.

[64] *EHOV* 2: 126.

suggests that *Normanitas* had a hard time surviving the loss of those loyalties over the long haul.

The Italian evidence also suggests that, in the short term, the sense of being an embattled minority surrounded by hostile and possibly inferior peoples, but also of belonging to a militarily gifted and extremely tough group that would ultimately prevail, made up for the loss of institutional and geographic ties.[65] I have discussed how closely tied Norman identity was with conquest and military success. Obviously this aspect of the Norman myth or construct derived from the need of the Normans both in England and in Italy to fight hard not just for victory but for survival, and their success in doing so. But this raises at least the possibility that the very success of the Normans undermined the need for their identity. As powerful kings in both England and southern Italy established an unusually strong internal peace (in the latter case, only after unification under Roger II), there was less need to keep hold of an identity that centred so much around success in war. One might take it out and dust it off occasionally, but it would not be as attractive for well-established landlords as for embattled warriors. This in turn would give other identities a chance to win out.

Another factor that emerges from looking at *Normanitas* in a larger context is that there was no strong ideological association with being a Norman *per se*. The identities of some conquering peoples have been closely bound up with a religious mission or a desire to spread their own civilization, motives which served in turn to justify their actions. There were certainly religious aspects to the conquests of Sicily and Antioch, but these motives helped underscore what the Normans had in common with other Western Christians, helping to create a kind of Latin identity in the former and a Frankish one in the latter.[66] In England, William had a cause, but it had nothing to do with *Normanitas*. Thus, the Normans had no ideological reasons for maintaining a Norman identity in their new land, merely pragmatic ones and ones of sentiment.

Finally, none of these Norman conquests were purely Norman affairs, and the divisions in the identities of the conquerors may have helped undermine those identities. Lanfranc was a Lombard and Orderic's father may have been from the region of Orleans rather than Normandy.[67] For such people, Norman identity may have been no more plausible than an identity centred around their new home, and they could therefore act as pioneers in the acceptance of new identities. Collective Norman identities obviously emerged for a time in England and Italy anyway, and could in theory have absorbed non-Normans as easily as the local identities did, but diversity among the invaders was one more factor weakening *Normanitas*.

Much of this discussion of the failure of Norman identity outside of Normandy

[65] William of Apulia, *Geste de Robert Guiscard*, 98, 102, 110, 122, 136, 140, 142, 146, 154, 168, 176–8; Amatus of Montecassino, *L'Ystoir de li Normant*, 24–5, 38, 48–50, 52, 83, 170; Geoffrey of Malaterra, *De Rebus Gestis Rogerii*, 8, 10, 12, 14–15, 22–3, 40, 64, 102.

[66] For Latin identity, see Amatus of Montecassino, *L'Ystoir de li Normant*, 241; Loud and Wiedemann, *History of the Tyrants of Sicily*, 201. For Frankish identity, see above, n. 62.

[67] For Orderic's father, see *EHOV* 3: 142.

is necessarily speculative; it is even harder to find evidence for why things did not happen than for why they did. And none of this is to argue that Norman identity was foredoomed to failure in England from the beginning. Some successful identities emerged in the Middle Ages in circumstances that seem much less propitious. Moreover, the strength of Norman identity in the generations immediately following the conquest should not be underestimated because of later changes. Nonetheless, Norman identity outside of Normandy was clearly vulnerable over the long term.

4

Ethnic Identity and Cultural Difference

ENGLISH SOCIETY IN the late eleventh century was permeated by an awareness of ethnic difference, and of the contrast between English and Normans. As one might expect, when contemporary chroniclers wrote about the wars and other events of the conquest, they spoke in terms of English opposing French or Normans. But they also used ethnic distinctions when discussing the coronation, peaceful interaction, and even campaigns in which Normans and English worked together.[1] Ethnic awareness penetrated to the most mundane levels. The *vita* of Wulfstan, the only native English bishop to survive the conquest for any length of time, reveals surviving English lords turning to him to consecrate churches, thereby avoiding the foreign bishops of their own diocese.[2] On the other side, Archbishop Lanfranc, in reading canon law, marked out for special attention a canon of an Iberian church council in which the Goths were urged to maintain unity in the face of a subject (Roman) population, and the clergy were called upon to be especially loyal to the king; clearly Lanfranc found this canon relevant to his own situation.[3]

Most strikingly, awareness of ethnic difference spread throughout bureaucratic systems and documents. As noted earlier, the phrase 'French and English' became a common formula in the address clause of charters, and individual charters contain references to 'French and English' in the context of juries and court attendance.[4] During the Domesday Book inquest, panels of eight men, four French and four English, were selected to give testimony in each hundred, and throughout the survey one periodically finds passages about the statements or assessments of 'the French' or 'the English' or both. In several counties in the survey, minor tenants-in-chief were clumped together into the category of king's thegns on the one hand and royal sergeants or artificers on the other, and despite occasional confusion, these were clearly ethnically based categories. Similarly, landholders with native names were sometimes lumped together in the holdings of major landholders while

---

[1] See e.g. *ASC* D 1066, D 1068 [*recte* 1069], D 1070, E 1073, D 1074 [*recte* 1073], E 1080, E 1083, E 1087 [*recte* 1088], E 1102; *GND* 2: 168, 170, 176, 180; *GGWP* 128–36, 150; Guy of Amiens, *Carmen*, 24–38, 48. Writers sometimes oppose French and Northumbrian forces in the north. For the latter identity, see below, pp. 270–3.

[2] *VW* 32, 45.

[3] Michael Richter, ed., *Canterbury Professions* (Torquay, 1973), p. lxvii.

[4] Bates, *Acta of William I*, nos. 69, 118, 225.

foreigners among the ordinary population might be distinguished as *francigenae*.[5] This was a world in which people took ethnic difference, and the distinctions between French and English, for granted.

This chapter provides the cultural background for the ethnic split described above. As one foreign cleric who settled in England not long after the conquest wrote, under William I French custom (*mos*) grew and English things (*res*) began to change.[6] An understanding of the level of the cultural divide between the two groups, and the nature of the precise differences, is an important prerequisite to understanding the interaction between them. Not all cultural differences are equally important in any given instance of ethnic division. Here I will concentrate on ones that contemporaries described, because those are the ones most likely to have served as markers of ethnic difference in post-conquest England. Other differences certainly existed, but I wish to view cultural differences as much through the prism of contemporary sources as possible. Fortunately for the development of ethnic harmony, the English and the conquerors had much in common, thus lessening the possibility of irreconcilable cultural clashes that could permanently divide them. Nonetheless, the cultural differences were by no means negligible, and this chapter will show that a fair amount of acculturation was necessary before the two peoples could hope to become one.

What characteristics distinguished the two peoples? At the most basic level, place of origin was a determining feature in the first generation, and in succeeding generations this was transformed into questions of ancestry. Another important mark of distinction in the early days was political allegiance. Ethnicity was no absolute determinant of political allegiance, particularly once many English began supporting William, at least temporarily, and the ethnic aspects of an affair like the 1075 revolt could be quite complex. Nonetheless, Hastings was a battle between English and Continental armies, most rebellions against William in England were distinctively English ones, and William himself soon came to rely primarily on the Normans and his other Continental followers to exercise power. Indeed, the interplay between ethnicity and political allegiance was at first the most important factor in ethnic relations. Yet another distinction, at least once the invaders had largely destroyed the existing elites, was that of class, a subject I will pursue later in the book. All three of these distinctions were powerful ones.

As in so many cases of ethnic division, language was also a key ethnic divider. The history attributed to Simeon of Durham, written early in the twelfth century, speaks of an English bishop deciding to flee not long after the conquest because he feared the rule of a foreign people 'whose language and customs he did not know'.[7]

---

[5] For the jurors, see Lewis, 'Domesday Jurors', 17–44. For instances of testimony by 'the French' or 'the English', see *DB* 1: 2b, 32a, 65a, 69b, 114a; 2: 18a, 23a, 38b. For the categories of thegn and sergeant, and some of the minor confusions, see Williams, *ENC* 109–15; Fuchs, *Domesday Book*, 251–3. For instances of clumping of native tenants of great landholders, see *DB* 1: 87b, 124a-b, 224a, 228a-b, 267b. In his foundation charter to Castle-Acre Priory, Earl William de Warenne listed gifts of tithes by natives separately from those of his *homines francigeni*; BL, Harley MSS 2110, fol. 1^{r-v}.

[6] Herman, 'De Miraculis', 58.

[7] *SMO* 2: 190.

Archbishop Lanfranc, in a letter of 1072–3 to Pope Alexander, stated that he had sought to avoid appointment to Canterbury partly because the local language was unknown to him.[8] Language barriers tend to be particularly important ethnic boundaries for the obvious reason that they create a communication gap that is difficult to bridge. In a famous miracle story recorded in the 1180s, recalling an earlier incident, an English priest protested when the saintly hermit Wulfric, to whom he devoted much attention, gave a deaf man the ability to speak French as well as English, but failed to give the priest the same miraculous ability to speak the former language. In the course of this story, the priest revealed his inability to communicate with his ecclesiastical superiors, the archdeacon and bishop.[9] For the educated, the shared use of Latin could bridge the gap, especially in the written sphere.[10] But even in the written sphere there was a cultural gap, for the English wrote a great deal in the vernacular, which denied access to these writings to the immigrants. The relationship between language, ethnicity, assimilation, and identity in England ended up being quite complex, but certainly the linguistic difference was an important barrier to integration that had to be overcome.[11]

Christianity should have acted as a bridge between the two peoples, and in the long run it did, but in the short term minor differences of custom and practice could lead to sharp tensions between the English and Normans. It was a Norman abbot's attempt to tinker with the liturgy at Glastonbury that provoked the bloody confrontation there.[12] Severe tensions are recorded at other monasteries in the decades following the conquest, most notably at St Augustine's in Canterbury. The sources do not describe these conflicts in ethnic terms, and scholars differ on whether or not they had an ethnic component, but it seems likely that ethnic and cultural differences played a role, even if there may have been other, more immediate causes of those disputes.[13] There was also division and even tension over allegiance to saints. Recent scholarship has shown that this tension has sometimes been exaggerated, and there is growing debate over the precise attitude of the Normans toward English saints.[14] Nonetheless, there can be no doubt that some cults were

---

[8] *Letters of Lanfranc*, 30.

[9] John of Ford, *Wulfric of Haselbury*, ed. Maurice Bell (Frome, 1933), 28–9. See also, Stubbs, *Memorials of St. Dunstan*, 236–7.

[10] Michael Richter, *Sprache und Gesellschaft im Mittelalter: Untersuchunger zur Mündlichen Kommunikation in England von der Mitte des elften bis zum Beginn des vierzehnten Jahrhunderts* (Stuttgart, 1979), discusses throughout the use of Latin as well as French and English in England from the eleventh through the fourteenth century.

[11] I will pursue the issue of language, ethnicity, and identity more fully in Chap. 23.

[12] For discussion of this incident, see David Hiley, 'Thurstan of Caen and Plainchant at Glastonbury: Musicological Reflections on the Norman Conquest', *Proceedings of the British Academy*, 72 (1986), 57–90.

[13] For St Augustine's, see Charles Plummer and John Earl, eds., 'Acta Lanfranci', in *Two Saxon Chronicles Parallel*, vol. 1 (1892; repr. Oxford, 1972), 290–2. For other monasteries, see Stubbs, *Memorials of St. Dunstan*, 144–51, 234–8; E. O. Blake, *Liber Eliensis* (London, 1962), 213; *WMGP* 172. For overviews of the subject, see David Knowles, *The Monastic Order in England: A History of its Development from the Times of St Dunstan to the Fourth Lateran Council 940–1216*, 2nd edn. (Cambridge, 1963), 114–17; Williams, *ENC* 133–5.

[14] See below, pp. 291–3.

influenced by political and ethnic concerns. Most strikingly, an informal cult grew up around the rather unsaintly Earl Waltheof after his execution, and another, less well-documented one, grew up around a former bishop of Durham whom William had imprisoned. Clearly these cults, particularly Waltheof's, served at least implicitly as a rebuke to the new regime.[15] Even pre-conquest saints could be problematic. The *Liber Eliensis* records that Hereward, during his rebellion, had his men swear loyalty at the tomb of St Etheldreda, though this may simply be legend.[16] One wonders if Lanfranc's initial doubts about the sanctity of Alfeah, one of his predecessors, stemmed partly from the fact that, judging by the life of him written by the English monk Osbeorn, he was chiefly seen as someone who stood up to a violent and rapacious army of invaders, a description that could just as easily apply to the Normans as to the Vikings who killed Alfeah.[17] I shall return to the question of saints, but clearly allegiance to individual saints could form another barrier between French and English, one that was sometimes politically charged. Though the religious differences between Normans and English were minor compared to the strength of their shared religious customs and values, even insignificant points of variation could serve as flashpoints in an atmosphere of mistrust and hostility.

Yet other cultural divides were found in the area of law.[18] On a general level, the English and Normans had to cope with the existence of two different legal systems. On a more specific level, and with more dangerous potential consequences, some laws and legal distinctions themselves divided the two peoples. Orderic Vitalis attributed the execution of Earl Waltheof and the perpetual imprisonment of Earl Roger after the revolt of 1075 to differences in English and Norman law, though one suspects that politics played as large a role here.[19] The *murdrum* fine, revived by William after the conquest, created different procedures and punishments for the murders of an immigrant and a native.[20] Laws that probably reflect real legislation by William I acknowledge procedural differences for English and Normans in the important arena of methods of legal proof. These issues are still found in the *Leges Henrici Primi* from the second decade of the twelfth century. That same legal compilation states in other instances that particular punishments or procedures *should* apply to both English and French, which implies that even where there were not *de*

---

[15] *EHOV* 2: 346–50; *WMGP* 271, 321–2; John A. Giles, ed., 'Vita et Passio Waldevi Comitis', in *Original Lives of Anglo-Saxons and Others Who Lived before the Conquest* (1854; repr. New York, 1967), 1–31.

[16] Blake, *Liber Eliensis*, 176.

[17] Osbeorn of Canterbury, 'Vita Sancti Elphegi', *PL* 149: 371–86; Eadmer, *The Life of St Anselm, Archbishop of Canterbury*, ed. Richard W. Southern (Oxford, 1972), 50–4. Lawson has argued that the cult earlier served as a focus of resistance to Canute: Lawson, *Cnut*, 140–2.

[18] For discussions of ethnic distinctions in law, see Frederick Pollock and Frederic William Maitland, *The History of English Law Before the Time of Edward I*, 2nd edn., vol. 1 (Cambridge, 1968), 88–92; George Garnett, 'Franci et Angli', 109–37. Garnett is more optimistic than I about the rapid disappearance of ethnic distinctions in law.

[19] *EHOV* 2: 314, 318–22; Pollock and Maitland, *History of English Law*, 1: 91; Garnett, 'Franci et Angli', 131.

[20] Robertson, *Laws*, 238, 264; L. J. Downer, ed., *Leges Henrici Primi* (Oxford, 1972), 234–6, 284–92. For modern work on the murdrum fine, see Frederick Coyle Hamil, 'Presentment of Englishry and the Murder Fine', *Speculum*, 12 (1937), 285–98; Garnett 'Franci et Angli', 116–28; O'Brien, 'From Morðor to Murdrum', 321–57.

jure distinctions, members of the two groups may have been treated differently and perhaps unequally in practice.[21] As late as Henry II's reign, a statute formally prohibited the English from claiming land unless they or their predecessors had possessed it at the death of Henry I. Presumably this was simply a practical measure to prevent them from claiming lands lost through the conquest, but once again it set the English apart from their conquerors.[22]

Both discrimination and simple difference were involved in these legal distinctions. Waltheof's punishment, the *murdrum* fine, and Henry II's statute can all be described as discriminatory in nature, even if the discrimination was made on practical grounds. The procedural differences are an example of a wider phenomenon in medieval law, namely the 'personality' of law, whereby laws and legal procedures could differ within the same geographic area or administrative unit according to ethnicity.[23] The 'personality' of law served to greatly reinforce ethnic boundaries, and thereby to impede assimilation. When combined with discriminatory practices, as in the Celtic regions controlled by the English, it could also be a source of great hostility. In England legal distinctions proved ephemeral, and the two legal systems merged.[24] But one should not dismiss the degree to which legal differences and formal or informal discrimination may have underscored ethnic divides in the period before assimilation was complete, nor their potential, fortunately unrealized, to create enduring barriers between the English and Normans.

Yet another initially important cultural boundary had to do with appearance, most notably with hair and clothes.[25] William of Poitiers described how the Normans and French marvelled at the long hair of the hostages that William the Conqueror took with him to Normandy in 1067, and made reference to their girlish beauty.[26] The Bayeux Tapestry vividly illustrates the differences in hair length and

---

[21] For questions of procedure, see F. Liebermann, ed., *Die Gesetze der Angelsachsen*, 3 vols. (Halle, 1903–16), 1: 483–4, 486–8; 3: 271–3, 277–81; Robertson, *Laws*, 240; Downer, *Leges Henrici Primi*, 120, 204. For statements that the English and French should be treated the same way, see Downer, *Leges Henrici Primi*, 182, 188, 254.

[22] R. C. van Caenegem, *Royal Writs in England from the Conquest to Glanvill: Studies in the Early History of the Common Law* (London, 1959), no. 169. See also nos. 165, 172. For discussion of the statute and related writs, see Doris M. Stenton, *English Justice Between the Norman Conquest and the Great Charter, 1066–1215* (Philadelphia, 1964), 31–2; van Caenegem, *Royal Writs*, 216–18; R. C. van Caenegem, *The Birth of the English Common Law* (Cambridge, 1973), 55–6.

[23] Some scholars of the early medieval world are beginning to doubt or downplay the old and widely held view about the personality of law in that period: Musset, *Germanic Invasions*, 210–11; Geary, *Aristocracy in Provence*, 110–11. However, the phenomenon is well attested for Ireland and Wales: R. R. Davies, *Lordship and Society in the March of Wales, 1282–1400* (Oxford, 1978), 154–5, 162–3, 310–12; id., *The Revolt of Owain Glyn Dŵr* (Oxford, 1995), 66; id., *The Age of Conquest: Wales, 1063–1415* (Oxford, 1991), 367–70, 432–3; Robin Frame, *Colonial Ireland, 1169–1369* (Dublin, 1981), 105–10; G. J. Hand, *English Law in Ireland, 1290–1324* (Cambridge, 1967), 198–205.

[24] See below, pp. 278–9.

[25] For the significance of hairstyles, see Robert Bartlett, 'Symbolic Meanings of Hair in the Middle Ages', *TRHS* 6th ser., 4 (1994), 43–60; Henri Platelle, 'Le Problème du scandale: les nouvelles modes masculines aux xie et xiie siècles', *Revue belge de philologie et d'histoire*, 53 (1975), 1071–96. See also, R. R. Davies, 'The Peoples of Britain and Ireland 1100–1400: III. Laws and Customs', *TRHS* 6th ser., 6 (1996), 13–15; Williams, *ENC* 188–90.

[26] *GGWP* 178–80.

the absence of facial hair on the Normans.[27] The latter characteristic fits in with an anecdote recorded by William of Malmesbury in which Harold's scouts reported that William's entire army looked like priests, because they kept their faces clean-shaven.[28] The tapestry does not show notable differences in clothing, but Orderic Vitalis wrote that the English seemed contemptible to the French in their native dress.[29] All in all, it must initially have been quite easy to distinguish between English and Normans simply by sight. Indeed, an English exile, Ælnoth of Canterbury, wrote that William the Conqueror, as he prepared for a planned invasion by King Canute of Denmark, fearing widespread English support for the invasion, ordered that the English 'shave their beards, change their arms and clothes to the style of the Romans, and, in order to delude the sight of the invaders, in everything imitate the French, whom we prefer to call Romans'. Ælnoth noted with satisfaction that few carried out the orders, which ultimately proved unnecessary because Canute was assassinated.[30] Clothes and hairstyles can form particularly important ethnic markers because they are so apparent.

Ælnoth's statement also points to another boundary, namely differences in military equipment, technology, and technique. Orderic Vitalis wrote that the English lacked castles, and though the use of fortifications was nothing new in England, the Normans certainly introduced motte-and-bailey castles and stone towers.[31] William of Malmesbury, Geoffrey of Malaterra, and the Bayeux tapestry all associated the English with the use of the battle-axe.[32] The author of the *Carmen de Hastingae Proelio* described, in scornful terms, the English preference for fighting on foot rather than horseback, and though there has been debate on this subject the likelihood is that his observation was accurate.[33] Recent work has rightly tended to downplay any large technological gap or dramatic difference in the arms and

[27] David M. Wilson, *The Bayeux Tapestry* (New York, 1985), plates 1–17, pp. 177, 185, 193, 208. The literature on the Bayeux Tapestry is vast. Important works include Frank Stenton *et al.*, eds., *The Bayeux Tapestry: A Comprehensive Survey*, 2nd edn. (London, 1965); N. P. Brooks and H. E. Walker, 'The Authority and Interpretation of the Bayeux Tapestry', *PBC* 1: 1–34; Daniel J. Bernstein, *The Mystery of the Bayeux Tapestry* (Chicago, 1987); Wolfgang Grape, *The Bayeux Tapestry: Monument to a Norman Triumph* (Munich, 1994); Richard Gameson, *The Study of the Bayeux Tapestry* (Woodbridge, 1997).

[28] *WMGR* 450. See also *VW* 23. William was not entirely consistent, however: *WMGR* 458.

[29] *EHOV* 2: 256. Williams argues that Orderic is contradicted by William of Poitiers's account of Continental admiration for English cloth and the clothes King William and his men brought back from England: Williams, *ENC* 188–9. But it is possible that the Normans admired some aspects of English clothing, particularly the embroidery and use of gold threads, while viewing other aspects as unfashionable.

[30] Ælnoth of Canterbury, 'Gesta Swenomagni Regis', 98–9. See also Thomas Walsingham, *Gesta Abbatum Sancti Albani*, ed. Henry Thomas Riley, vol. 1 (London, 1867), 42.

[31] *EHOV* 2: 218. See Matthew Strickland, 'Military Technology and Conquest: The Anomaly of England', *ANS* 19: 369–73, for a judicious overview of recent work on castles and the changes the Normans made.

[32] *WMGR* 440; Geoffrey of Malaterra, *De Rebus Gestis Rogerii*, 74; Wilson, *Bayeux Tapestry*, plates 10, 28, 31, 61–72; Fuchs, *Domesday Book*, 24.

[33] Guy of Amiens, *Carmen*, 22. The increasing acceptance of this source as an early one makes this evidence more telling. Wace later made the same observation: Wace, *Roman de Rou*, 2: 206. For an overview of the question of the English and cavalry, see Strickland, 'Military Technology', 359–60.

armour of the English and Normans.[34] But in a society dominated by warriors, even minor differences in arms could matter in ethnic relations, and differences in fighting styles must have been even more important. Not only did such differences serve as markers of ethnicity, but incompatible or at least different military styles probably made it harder for the two aristocracies to integrate in the short term (and for aristocratic relations after the conquest, the short term mattered a great deal). Even when English and Norman troops fought in alliance, they probably could not do so in an integrated style, thus reducing the likelihood for developing camaraderie. Different fighting techniques would have made it harder for English warriors to join the war bands and thus the households and patronage networks of the king and his Norman magnates. Though the Normans could and did fight dismounted, they would have preferred warriors who were experienced both as infantry and cavalry. They probably also would have preferred ones with experience in warfare involving castles. However effective English warriors may have been on their own terms, in a military setting dominated by Normans their skills would have been less useful. If, as has been argued, the Normans introduced new rules for warfare and the treatment of aristocratic prisoners to England, differences in military ethos may also have divided the two aristocracies.[35] In the long term, the few native aristocratic families that survived adapted to Norman military ways, but it is likely that, in the short term, military differences contributed to a breakdown in relations between the Normans and the English aristocrats, and to the nearly complete destruction of the latter group.

There were other types of cultural differences that distinguished the two peoples as well. William of Malmesbury wrote that the English consumed all their income in small and worthless houses while the French and Normans spent frugally but built ample and fine edifices, and though there was a moralizing edge to this statement, it may reflect a real difference in consumption patterns. Certainly the Norman taste for architecture on a grand scale is well known, and some of the resources devoted to building must earlier have been directed to other forms of consumption.[36] The ale/wine line, which later would be a stereotypical dividing-point between the English and the French, existed to some degree in England after the conquest. The Evesham Chronicle claimed that the first Norman abbot of that house planted the first vineyards in England, and the early immigrant poet Reginald of Canterbury jokingly said that *Francia*'s muse was stronger than England's because it was taught by wine rather than ale.[37] Even such small things as ways of

[34] Stephen Morillo, *Warfare Under the Anglo-Norman Kings, 1066–1154* (Woodbridge, 1994), 27–8; Strickland, 'Military Technology', 353–82.

[35] Matthew Strickland, 'Slaughter, Slavery or Ransom: The Impact of the Conquest on Conduct in Warfare', in *England in the Eleventh Century*, ed. Carola Hicks (Stamford, 1992), 41–59; Gillingham, *English in the Twelfth Century*, 56–7, 209–29.

[36] *WMGR* 458; Williams, *ENC* 187–8; C. R. Dodwell, *Anglo-Saxon Art: A New Perspective* (Manchester, 1987), 231–2. The topic of architecture and ethnicity is one I will pursue mainly in Chap. 22.

[37] William Dunn MacRay, ed., *Chronicon Abbatiae de Evesham* (London, 1863), 97; F. Liebermann, ed., 'Raginald von Canterbury', *Neues Archiv der Gesellschaft für ältere deutsche Geschichtskunde*, 13 (1888), 531. However, there are indications from the twelfth century that at least parts of Normandy were still predominantly ale-drinking, so the ale–wine divide may not have been as important as it later

counting could become ethnic markers; the use of the 'long hundred', namely 120, was introduced to England from Scandinavia, but at one point Domesday Book refers to a number calculated in this way as having been computed 'English style'.[38] This last example should remind us that there were probably many other minor differences that no one bothered to note, but that frequently served to remind people of ethnic distinctions.

How crucial were the various cultural differences described above? Placing them in a comparative context may provide some perspective. The Normans and English had cultural and intellectual differences, but these were minor compared to the vast cultural gaps experienced, for instance, by the Europeans and the peoples they encountered in the period of European expansion. The meeting between the Polynesians of Hawaii and Captain Cook's expedition can stand as an example of this. In that encounter the Hawaiians strove hard to figure out how these new-comers fitted into their cosmology, and to make sense of this in some ways impressive group that nevertheless had the shocking and obviously degenerate custom of allowing men and women to eat together. Meanwhile, the Europeans did not so much try to make sense as take advantage of the, to them, equally shocking but delightful sexual customs of the Polynesians. Compared to the radical differences between many cultures, those between the Normans and English, who shared the same cosmology and many other cultural attributes, pale to insignificance.[39]

What about comparison with other ethnic encounters and the cultural differences involved with them in the Middle Ages? In this context, the absence of any fundamentally important religious differences between Normans and English was particularly important. Had the Normans and English not shared the same religious allegiance, assimilation would have required conversion of one group or the other. In other respects, the cultural divisions between the two peoples *may* have been less marked than in some cases in which enduring ethnic divides emerged despite shared religious allegiance.[40] For instance, later English commentators on the Irish and Welsh often focused on what they viewed as the backward economies and political structures of their societies, on their failure to follow the rules of war now held by the English, and on marital and social customs the commentators portrayed as morally unsound.[41] There is good reason to believe that these English

---

became: Wace, *Roman de Rou*, 2: 64; 3: 229; *Les Œuvres poétiques de Baudri de Bourgueil*, ed. Phyllis Abrahams, (Paris, 1926), 350; Adrian Morey and C. N. L. Brooke, eds., *The Letters and Charters of Gilbert Foliot* (Cambridge, 1967), 279; Hans Walther, 'Scherz und Ernst in der Völker- und Stämme-Charakteristik mittellateinischer Verse', *Archiv für Kulturgeschichte*, 41 (1959), 271, 278, 294–5.

[38] *DB* 1: 336a.

[39] Discussion of the Hawaiian encounter is drawn from Marshall Sahlins, *Islands of History* (Chicago, 1985), 1–9, 104–35.

[40] See Brian Golding, *Conquest and Colonisation: The Normans in Britain, 1066–1100* (New York, 1994), 179, and Morillo, *Warfare under the Anglo-Norman Kings*, 22, for a broadly similar argument.

[41] Bartlett, *Gerald of Wales*, 159–71; Davies, *Domination and Conquest*, 9–10; id., *Age of Conquest*, 69–70, 139, 161–2, 177–8; Gillingham, *English in the Twelfth Century*, 3–18, 41–58; id., 'Killing and Mutilating Political Enemies in the British Isles from the Late Twelfth to the Early Fourteenth Century: A Comparative Study', in *Britain and Ireland, 900–1300: Insular Responses to Medieval European Change*, ed. Brendan Smith (Cambridge, 1999), 114–34.

prejudices stemmed to some degree from real economic, political, military, and social differences. That the English had well-developed political and economic institutions by the standards of the time may help explain why the Normans were more willing to accept them as potential equals.

Several important caveats need to be introduced here, however. Although one can certainly see a difference between the level of cultural difference, say, between the English and the Hawaiians in Captain Cook's time, and that between the Normans and English after 1066, levels of cultural difference are harder to measure when closer together. Were the differences between the English and Irish in the twelfth century dramatically greater than those between the English and Normans in the eleventh? Perhaps, but how and by what standards does one measure this, particularly given our scanty sources? What matters most are the cultural differences that people seized on, and a cultural difference that may seem minor in one ethnic encounter can be crucial in another. This means that the overall level of cultural difference may matter less than specific important differences. Moreover, how, as modern scholars, do we measure what were the key cultural differences, except through the sources of the time? But this raises the problem of the interaction between construct and culture. Some of the same scholars who have shown that the comments of English medieval writers on the Welsh and Irish were based to a certain degree on reality have also shown how the commentary included value judgements that will seem bigoted to most modern readers, and distortions and exaggerations that vitiate their value.[42] For instance, the Celtic peoples probably were less attuned to the developing canon law of the Church than other areas, but that hardly meant, as some of their critics argued, that they were barely Christian. In some cases commentators may exaggerate cultural gaps because of existing preconceptions. In other cases they might emphasize and moralize cultural differences to justify hostility generated through warfare, greed, or politics. This means that we must take the comments of contemporary writers on cultural differences with a grain of salt, and should at least query the impression they give that the gap between the English and the Irish or Welsh was vastly greater than that between them and the Normans. A final, and very important caveat is that tremendous ethnic hostility can exist even when cultural differences are slight. The most notable recent example of this was the conflict in Bosnia, where groups that were culturally very similar slaughtered each other in large numbers. In short, although there can be no doubt that the level of cultural difference has a strong potential effect on ethnic relations and the possibilities of assimilation, there is no precise correlation between the size of a cultural gap, assuming one could even measure it, and the friendliness or hostility between peoples.

Moreover, the level of cultural difference between the English and Normans was not negligible, even if it was smaller than in other instances of cultural contact. There was at least a limited tendency among Continental and immigrant writers to view the English as somewhat backward, even as barbarians, while writers who

[42] See particularly Bartlett, *Gerald of Wales*, 159–77, and Davies, *Domination and Conquest*, 9–10.

associated themselves with the English could be quite critical of the Normans.[43]
The potential for cultural prejudice and enduring ethnic barriers based on cultural
differences clearly existed. Obviously, some ethnic markers and distinctions
mattered more than others. On their own, different styles of counting hardly
mattered. Styles of clothing changed easily, and when Orderic Vitalis noted that
English clothing was contemptible to the conquerors, he also stated that the English
began adopting French styles almost immediately after the conquest.[44] Long hair
became all the rage for aristocrats, and then for townspeople and peasants, in the
reigns of William II and Henry I, and although no contemporary writer linked this
to traditional English fashions, it certainly removed the ethnic difference of hairstyles.[45] On the other hand, some of the ethnic boundaries and differences were
much more potentially dangerous. The most obvious of these was language, which
throughout history has been a frequent source of strife, but the military, legal, or
even religious differences could have provided fodder for enduring ethnic divides
as well.

More important was the whole bundle of ethnic differences, both crucial and
trivial. In Ireland in 1297 there was legislation against the English having Irish haircuts, not because people cared so deeply about hairstyling, but because it was one
particularly obvious marker of a whole range of ethnic differences that cumulatively created a deep and bitter ethnic divide, and, more practically, because an
Englishman with such a haircut could accidentally be killed as an Irishman.[46] In
the late eleventh century there was clearly a similar agglomeration of differences
between English and Normans that individually may sometimes have been minor,
but which taken together represented a major barrier to the assimilation that
eventually occurred. This could have proved disastrous for ethnic relations. One of
my aims in this book will be to see how, instead, the barriers were overcome
through interaction between individuals, debates over the cultures of the two
peoples, and cultural assimilation.

---

[43] This is an issue I pursue in Chap. 15.

[44] *EHOV* 2: 256.

[45] Ibid. 4: 268; *HN* 48, 214; *WMGR* 558; William of Malmesbury, *Historia Novella*, ed. Edmund King
and K. R. Potter (Oxford, 1998), 10–12.

[46] Philomena Connolly, 'The Enactments of the 1297 Parliament', in *Law and Disorder in Thirteenth-
century Ireland: The Dublin Parliament of 1297*, ed. James Lydon (Dublin, 1997), 158–60. For discussion of
this law, see Bartlett, 'Symbolic Meanings of Hair', 45–6; James F. Lydon, 'Nation and Race in Medieval
Ireland', in *Concepts of National Identity in the Middle Ages*, ed. Simon Forde *et al.* (Leeds, 1995), 103; Seán
Duffy, 'The Problem of Degeneracy', in *Law and Disorder in Thirteenth-century Ireland: The Dublin
Parliament of 1297*, ed. James Lydon (Dublin, 1997), 88–9.

5

A Chronology of Assimilation

SHORTLY BEFORE HIS death Edward the Confessor had a prophetic dream, according to his first biographer, writing not long after the conquest. In this dream two monks Edward had known during his exile in Normandy came to him to prophesy that God, because of the sins of the earls, bishops, abbots, and those in sacred orders, would deliver his kingdom into the hands of the devil and unleash war upon it, which the biographer implicitly linked to the Norman Conquest. When Edward asked how long God's anger would last, they said that England would suffer until a green tree, which had been cut in half, with half carried off for a distance of three furlongs, should be reunited without human aid and begin to grow anew.[1] A couple of generations later, in the 1120s, William of Malmesbury wrote: 'We have experienced the truth of this prophecy, for England has become the habitation of outsiders and dominion of foreigners. Today, no Englishman is earl, bishop, or abbot, and newcomers gnaw away at the riches and very innards of England; nor is there any hope for an end of the misery.' A slightly later contemporary of William of Malmesbury, Osbert of Clare, delivered a nearly identical interpretation of this 'green tree prophecy' in a work finished in 1138.[2] This prophecy, and the commentaries on it, vividly illustrate the enduring quality of the great ethnic and class divisions within English society that were created by the Norman Conquest.

Yet when Aelred of Rievaulx, an influential intellectual of native English descent, rewrote the *vita* of Edward the Confessor in 1162 or 1163, he developed an interpretation of the green tree prophecy that was radically different. For Aelred, the three furlongs in the prophecy signified the three reigns of Harold, William I, and William II. The tree was rejoined when Henry I married Edith-Matilda, a descendant of the English royal house and relative of Edward the Confessor. The tree flourished under their daughter, the Empress Matilda, and bore fruit with the birth of Henry II, who 'joined each people as if a cornerstone'. 'Now indeed,' Aelred went on, 'England has a king from the English people; it has bishops and abbots from that same people; it has also princes and excellent knights who were procreated by the joining of both seeds.'[3] I shall argue shortly that Aelred was something of an

---

[1] Barlow, *Life of King Edward*, 116–22.
[2] *WMGR* 414–16; Marc Bloch, ed., 'La Vie de S. Édouard le Confesseur par Osbert de Clare', *Analecta Bollandiana*, 41 (1923), 107–9; Barlow, *Life of King Edward*, 130–2.
[3] Aelred of Rievaulx, 'Vita S. Edwardi Regis et Confessoris', *PL* 195: 773–4.

optimist, but clearly ethnic relations and the position of the English had changed radically since the late eleventh century, and even since early in the reign of Stephen, when Osbert of Clare finished his work.

The aim of this chapter is to provide a chronological overview of relations between the English and the Normans through to the end of the twelfth century, by which time assimilation seems to have been complete. In it, I will emphasize the harshness and brutality of the conquest and therefore of the dealings between the two peoples in William the Conqueror's reign. I do so to explain and underscore the early hostility between English and Normans, which can too easily be minimized through the lens of hindsight, and to show thereby just how surprising is the speed with which assimilation took place. Thereafter, I will trace the changing relations of the two peoples over succeeding reigns and generations. In doing so, I hope to provide as good a chronology as possible from the little surviving evidence for the timing of the conciliation and assimilation between the English and Normans.

As far as the overall question of how long it took for assimilation to be complete, it is probably partly because of the difficulties involved that historians have tended to 'reply cautiously', in the words of John Gillingham, with a date around the end of the twelfth century. Gillingham was speaking of the speed with which the Normans came to think of themselves as English, but the two processes were closely intertwined, though not, as we shall see, identical. Gillingham himself, however, sees a much swifter shift, with the decades between the 1120s and 1140s as crucial.[4] The nineteenth-century historian Edward Freeman also saw a swift assimilation, though perhaps with a more ideological motive; as a nationalist, Freeman wanted to turn the Normans into Englishmen as quickly as possible.[5] I myself must confess to caution, and would see a date around the end of Henry II's reign, and certainly by the end of the twelfth century, for the completion of assimilation. I do agree with Gillingham that important shifts had taken place by the 1140s, but I view the process of harmonization and assimilation as a gradual one that began in 1066, and continued for more than a century. Even with a later and more cautious dating, however, one is speaking of a comparatively rapid process.

I would also argue that the processes of improving ethnic relations and of assimilation were not only gradual but extremely complex, and progressed in a lurching and uneven manner. This is true of such processes in general. Even the civil-rights movement, as important as it was, hardly brought complete harmony between whites and blacks in the United States, but was instead only an important step, and one that created its own tensions and backlash, on a road that will hopefully lead to such harmony. Moreover, at any one time attitudes and relations will vary according to generation, class, region, and individual temperament and experience. In Chapters 2 and 3 I argued that both the English and the Normans could simultaneously express hostility toward and work with or even absorb other peoples. The same was true in their relations with each other, which would make it hard even for contemporaries to accurately gauge the nature of ethnic relations at

---

[4] Gillingham, *English in the Twelfth Century*, 123–32, 140.
[5] Freeman, *History of the Norman Conquest*, 5: 825–39.

any given time. To give a parallel example, Paul Knoll, in his study of relations along the Polish–German frontier during the later Middle Ages, quotes two roughly contemporary sources, one speaking of natural enmity between Poles and Germans, the other stating 'that the Germans and Slavs live together in partnership and that there are no other groups in the world who are so friendly and courteous towards one another'.[6] These considerations have a number of implications for a chronology of assimilation between English and Normans. First, one should not expect any neat linear developments. Second, one should expect ambiguity and contradictions in the sources. Third, not only *must* any chronology be imprecise, but it probably *should* be. Thus the very roughness of the chronology outlined in this chapter, though it stems from problems of evidence, has the virtue of reflecting the blurry nature of the process of assimilation itself.

Relations between the English and Normans did not start on a promising footing. It is easy for modern historians to overlook the brutality involved in the Norman Conquest and for those of us who have not experienced the effects of war, but have been desensitized by media coverage of so many modern atrocities, to underestimate its emotional impact. The conquest was not *unusually* savage by medieval standards, but normal medieval warfare was savage indeed. Moreover, the fighting and violence involved in the conquest were unusual in their scale. There is a danger that the very knowledge that war tends to be a nasty affair can lull us into ignoring the emotional impact of killing, raping, and plundering on the people involved, particularly the victims. There is also a danger that our very familiarity with the events of the conquest will dull our sense of just how traumatic an experience it must have been, though recently Elisabeth van Houts has brought the trauma of the conquest back into focus by arguing that it had an impact on historical writing in the generations immediately following.[7] Because the violence generally pitted the Normans and their allies against the English, it is important to bear in mind the potential it had for creating tremendous ethnic hostility. Moreover, violence affected every one of the social groups to be discussed in this work. The military history of the Norman Conquest is well known, and I do not intend to reiterate it here in any detail.[8] But I do intend to emphasize the scale and nature of the violence and brutality involved, and to explore their influence on ethnic relations.

[6] Paul Knoll, 'Economic and Political Institutions on the Polish–German Frontier in the Middle Ages: Action, Reaction, Interaction', in *Medieval Frontier Societies*, ed. Robert Bartlett and Angus MacKay (Oxford, 1989), 152.
[7] Elisabeth van Houts, 'The Memory of 1066 in Written and Oral Tradition', *ANS* 19: 171–2; id., *Memory and Gender in Medieval Europe, 900–1200* (Toronto, 1999), 129–30.
[8] For some overviews of the campaigns involved in conquering and securing England, see Freeman, *History of the Norman Conquest*, 3: 378–562; 4: 101–318, 450–83, 564–605; Stenton, *Anglo-Saxon England*, 586–612; Douglas, *William the Conqueror*, 181–223, 231–3; Marjorie Chibnall, *Anglo-Norman England, 1066–1166* (Oxford, 1986), 9–19, 36–7, Golding, *Conquest and Colonisation*, 27–49. For the battle of Hastings, see Stephen Morillo, ed., *The Battle of Hastings: Sources and Interpretations* (Woodbridge, 1996); Barlow's introduction to Guy of Amiens, *Carmen*, pp. lxi–xc. For the revolts, see Williams, *ENC* 14–70. For fighting in the North, see William E. Kapelle, *The Norman Conquest of the North: The Region and Its Transformation, 1100–1135* (Chapel Hill, 1979), 106–41; William M. Aird, *St Cuthbert and the Normans: The Church of Durham, 1071–1153* (Woodbridge, 1998), 64–99.

William came to the throne after one of the biggest and bloodiest battles of the Middle Ages, and following a campaign of devastation in the south-east and around London. After he became king there was a period of peace and co-operation, but this proved short-lived. A series of rebellions and disturbances sprang up between 1067 and 1071 in different parts of England. In some cases the rebellions were on a large scale and were supported by fleets from Denmark. In others, nobles fled into the woods and began a type of guerilla warfare; such fighters were called *silvatici*, from a Latin word for forest.[9] Norman rule came under severe threat in these years, but fortunately for William his opposition was poorly co-ordinated and badly led. William himself campaigned brilliantly, and by the end of 1071 had largely secured his hold on England. Despite William's early victories, other rebellions and violent incidents that were at least partly (though generally not solely) acts of English resistance continued throughout his reign. In 1075 and 1080 revolts broke out which were not, strictly speaking, English revolts against the Normans, but the latter began to develop in that direction, and Earl Waltheof gave the former an English component. In the decade-and-a-half after William's arrival most parts of England experienced warfare, and some faced it several times.

Both sides in the conflict could be ruthless. In revenge for one major setback the Normans, according to the *Norman* writer William of Jumièges, slaughtered most of the population of York, one of the country's largest cities, 'from the youth to the aged'.[10] A fragment of a Skaldic poem in honour of Earl Waltheof, probably composed not long after his death by the Norse poet Þorkell Skallason, exults, with the appalling flair common to Old Norse (and Old English) poetic accounts of violence, that on one occasion: 'The warrior burned a hundred followers of the king in the hot fire. For men that was an evening of scorching . . . The ash-grey wolf got food from the corpses of Frenchmen.'[11] Sources sympathetic to Bishop Walcher provide a vivid description of how he and his followers were trapped in a church by their native enemies, who slaughtered them as they came out, ignoring the bishop's pleading for his life, mutilating his body, and burning down the church to force out the last survivors.[12] Though the *murdrum* fine was probably adapted from legislation by Canute, the fact that the Normans revived it suggests that they faced serious danger from ambush and the guerilla warfare of the *silvatici*.[13] On a larger scale, the northern English on two occasions ambushed or trapped and wiped out William's northern forces. Given the stakes involved, it is not surprising that both

[9] *EHOV* 2: 216–18; Susan Reynolds, 'Eadric Silvaticus and the English Resistance', *Bulletin of the Institute of Historical Research*, 54 (1989), 102–5.

[10] *GND* 2: 180.

[11] Alistair Campbell, *Skaldic Verse and Anglo-Saxon History* (London, 1971), 16. The translation is Campbell's.

[12] *CJW* 3: 34–6; *LDE* 212, 216–18. For the outrage produced by the murder, see Thomas Wright, *The Anglo-Latin Satirical Poets and Epigrammatists of the Twelfth Century*, vol. 2 (London, 1872), 150–2.

[13] For the *murdrum* fine, see above, p. 49. O'Brien argues that since *murdrum* was revived from a law issued by Canute, it cannot be used as evidence of ethnic hostility, though he certainly does see its revival as a measure to protect Continental troops from attacks by the men of English lords: 'From *Morðor* to *Murdrum*', 350, 354. It clearly does demonstrate the violence involved in the conquest, and it is hard for me to believe that this violence was not accompanied by hostility along ethnic lines.

sides could be ruthless, but that would not lessen the hostility that such ruthlessness created.

This hostility helps to explain the nearly complete destruction of the old English elites, which could in turn produce further hostility. Ælnoth of Canterbury, working in Denmark in the early twelfth century, wrote: 'Of their notable dukes, earls, lords, nobles, and individuals of diverse rank, some were slain by iron, others placed in prisons. Certain ones were deprived, both in honour and inheritance, of the ranks and treasures of their fathers; many were driven from their native land and the rest oppressed as if by public servitude.'[14] Medieval writers are notorious for their powers of exaggeration, but there is no doubt that the fate of the aristocracy was grim, and this was another source of bitterness to the English.

As the death of Walcher indicates, non-combatants were not spared the violence of the conquest, and even the religious were not immune. English laywomen were even more likely to be directly affected by the violence of conquest, for rape accompanied war, as it so often does. Rape was among the sins for which Norman soldiers were called upon to do penance in the penitential issued by the Norman bishops and confirmed by the papal legate Ermenfrid, not long after the conquest.[15] Orderic lamented the 'dishonouring' of noble girls, and no doubt ordinary women and girls suffered as much or more.[16] No record survives from the women affected, but I think it easy to imagine the trauma they experienced and the bitterness they must have felt toward the invading Normans.

Peasants, both male and female, also suffered from the plundering and devastation carried out by the Normans. From the beginning William frequently employed the common medieval military practice of devastating large areas of countryside in an effort both to inspire terror and to economically undermine the enemy.[17] The Bayeux tapestry provides a striking image of a woman and child fleeing a burning house.[18] Domesday Book is filled with entries concerning waste, and although there is debate about how many of these entries stemmed from the warfare of the conquest, clearly military operations were an important factor.[19] A number of chroniclers also wrote of widespread devastation, especially in the north.[20] Most

[14] Ælnoth of Canterbury, 'Gesta Swenomagni Regis', 97. See also Blake, *Liber Eliensis*, 172; *EHOV* 2: 266, 272; 3: 214.

[15] Whitelock *et al.*, *Councils and Synods*, 584.

[16] *EHOV* 2: 268. See also *Letters of Lanfranc*, 166; *HN* 124.

[17] John Gillingham, 'William the Bastard at War', in *Studies in Medieval History Presented to R. Allen Brown*, ed. C. Harper-Bill *et al.* (Woodbridge, 1989), 141–8. For the importance of deliberate devastation more generally, see John Gillingham, 'Richard I and the Science of War in the Middle Ages', in *War and Government in the Middle Ages*, ed. John Gillingham and J. C. Holt (Totowa, 1989), 83–5; Stephen Morillo, *Warfare Under the Anglo-Norman Kings*, 98–102; Matthew Strickland, *War and Chivalry: The Conduct and Perception of War in England and Normandy, 1066–1217* (Cambridge, 1996), 258–329.

[18] Wilson, *Bayeux Tapestry*, plate 50.

[19] In particular, there is much debate about precisely how much the massive drops in values and the many villages without population recorded in the Yorkshire section of Domesday Book reflect reality, but I think there is no denying that the region was hard-hit. For an overview of the debate, see Williams, *ENC* 41–4.

[20] *ASC* D 1066, D 1067, D 1068 [*recte* 1069], E 1069; *EHOV* 2: 230–2; *LDE* 218; *CJW* 3: 10, 36; *WMGP*, 208.

strikingly, the chronicle of the monastery of Evesham, in a section that was probably written within a few decades of the conquest, describes refugees, 'old and young, women with their little ones', flocking to that monastery as a result of William's campaigns. So ravaged were their bodies from hunger, according to the chronicler, that even though they received food there, 'almost daily, five or six men, sometimes more, died miserably and were buried by the prior'. Indeed, the chronicler's description reads eerily like that of a modern refugee camp.[21] Even after discounting the exaggerations of chroniclers and the misleading elements in Domesday Book, it is clear that the extensive campaigning of the conquest brought widespread suffering to ordinary English people. That such activities as pillaging and deliberate devastation were standard practice in war was hardly a consolation to the victims, nor was it likely to lessen their resentment against those who inflicted suffering on them. When assessing ethnic relations after the conquest, one must remember that the fighting itself gave English people of all classes plenty of reasons to hate the conquerors.

It would be a mistake to underestimate the hatred engendered on both sides by the violence of the conquest simply because the two peoples later achieved amity and assimilation. When Ælnoth of Canterbury wrote of 'the ferocity of their tyrant', namely William the Conqueror, he was expressing feelings that the English who remained in their homeland may have felt but could not express.[22] William of Poitiers wrote straightforwardly in one passage that the men of Kent, whom he describes shortly thereafter simply as English, hated the Normans.[23] Orderic Vitalis describes how one abbot was deposed around 1085, 'because he was an Englishman and hateful to the Normans'.[24] Relations between English and Normans started off in the worst possible way, which only makes the speed of assimilation that much more surprising.

In one respect, however, the brutality of the conquest furthered the cause of ethnic harmony and assimilation in the long term, even as it poisoned relations in the short term. Because William so thoroughly and successfully obliterated his opposition, and inspired such terror, the large-scale violence following the conquest was relatively limited in duration. Though the English in later generations remembered the killing, raping, and devastation that accompanied the Norman Conquest, there were no new rounds of massive violence after 1080 to exacerbate tensions. One could contrast this with many other ethnic conflicts; for instance, medieval Wales, where generations of warfare between Welsh and English leaders, and revolts long after Edward I's conquest, periodically reinforced ethnic hostility.[25] Ward-Perkins has argued, I believe rightly, that it was the successful resistance of the Britons to the Anglo-Saxons that made ethnic barriers so much stronger

[21] MacRay, *Chronicon Abbatiae de Evesham*, 90–3. The writer notes that some of the refugees were even noble, but by implication the bulk were ordinary peasants. For the date, see Antonia Gransden, *Historical Writing in England, c. 550 to c. 1307* (Ithaca, NY, 1974), 89, 112.

[22] Ælnoth of Canterbury, 'Gesta Swenomagni Regis', 97.

[23] *GGWP* 182–4.

[24] *EHOV* 2: 344.

[25] Davies, *Age of Conquest*, 100–1.

in Britain after the collapse of Roman political power than elsewhere. He also argues that the easy conquest of Gaul by the Franks may have made acculturation much more likely there than across the Channel.[26] In post-conquest England, after a generation had passed, the passions raised by violence could slowly start to cool, thus eventually removing a barrier to assimilation. Ironically, the very savageness of the Norman Conquest, though heightening tension considerably in its immediate aftermath, thereafter helped to facilitate assimilation by dramatically lessening the possibility of rebellion, thus preventing the sort of continuing violence that could have permanently turned English society into two hostile camps divided along ethnic lines. Not all the factors that contributed to assimilation are ones that modern readers would applaud.

Despite all the violence and hostility that characterized William I's accession and reign, those decades also saw elements of co-operation and the beginnings of the process of integration and assimilation. Even during the height of the rebellions, William had some English support.[27] Though high-level English participation in the government and church practically vanished because of the revolts, at lower levels, as Domesday Book and other sources make clear, the Normans continued to rely on English collaboration. Even in the military sphere, William received an important amount of support from the English.[28] Moreover, Orderic Vitalis believed that intermarriage and cultural assimilation began almost at once, though in his view it was quickly interrupted by rebellion.[29] As later chapters will show, intermarriage and other types of interaction clearly did begin during William's reign. Nor was the ethnic hostility described earlier unalloyed. The attitude of the anonymous writer of the Anglo-Saxon Chronicle towards William, critical but balanced and certainly not uncompromisingly hostile, probably epitomizes the best that could be hoped for between the two peoples at that stage. But it was a start.[30] Reconciliation and assimilation were hardly inevitable in 1087, but a beginning had been made in William's reign.

The nearly fifty years covered by the reigns of William II and Henry I saw continuing hostility and prejudice combined with progress toward harmony, integration, and assimilation. Both reigns started out in a promising fashion, with the kings gaining extensive English support, according to several chroniclers, in putting down predominantly Norman baronial revolts. Moreover, Henry I took the important step of quickly marrying Edith-Matilda, a descendant of the old line of kings.[31] But relations between English and Normans remained deeply strained.

---

[26] Ward-Perkins, 'Anglo-Saxons', 527–9.
[27] ASC D 1067 [recte 1068]; GGWP 184–6; EHOV 2: 206–8, 228; Letters of Lanfranc, 124.
[28] See below, p. 246.
[29] EHOV 2: 256.
[30] ASC E 1086 [recte 1087]. The passage was written after William's death, but the writer had once lived in the king's court.
[31] ASC E 1087 [recte 1088]; CJW 3: 50, 98; WMGR 546–8, 714–16; EHOV 4: 124–8, 134; 5: 310, 314, 318; HHHA 414. I will argue in Chap. 15 that several chroniclers had ideological reasons to exaggerate the level of English support, but there is no reason to doubt that the sons of William the Conqueror received help from their native subjects.

Orderic depicts William II sneering at the superstition of the English on the eve of his death, and Eadmer wrote that he seized fifty men 'from the old nobility of the English who still seemed to enjoy the vestiges of their wealth', on trumped-up charges of killing the royal deer.[32] William of Malmesbury's note that Henry I's opponents insulted him simply by referring to him and his wife by the (distinctively English) names Godric and Godgiva indicates that his marriage brought him a certain amount of ethnically based opprobrium.[33] One might also point to William of Malmesbury's pessimistic interpretation of the green tree prophecy noted earlier, or Eadmer's famous complaints about prejudice against the English in church appointments.[34] Henry of Huntingdon was so pessimistic about the situation of the English in the early versions of his work, written late in Henry's reign, that he stated that God had brought the Normans to wipe the English out and to destroy them as a people.[35] In the eyes of contemporaries, the position of the English and their relations with the Normans remained very bad even toward the end of Henry I's reign.

Moreover, there is evidence that minor outbreaks of violence could still assume ethnic overtones in Henry I's time. A passage in the Welsh chronicle *Brut y Tywysogion* records that in 1109 there was discord between a Welsh prince, Madog, and the French because certain Saxons (as the Welsh called the English) were plundering and committing various crimes against the king then fleeing to Madog. One is reminded of the *silvatici*, and though this is clearly not anything like a formal rebellion, the chronicler does make ethnic distinctions. Perhaps one can speak of banditry tinged by ethnic hostility or at least ethnic difference.[36] In the pipe roll of 1130 a number of men, some with English names, were recorded as owing fines for the killing of Tochi or Toki.[37] As O. J. Padel has shown, John of Cornwall, probably writing late in Stephen's reign, in his version of the prophecies of Merlin depicted this as part of a feud, but also as a killing by Cornishmen of a Frenchman about which Normandy should take note.[38] Again one cannot speak of rebellion, but at

---

[32] *EHOV* 5: 288; *HN* 102.

[33] *WMGR* 716; Cecily Clark, 'Onomastics', in *The Cambridge History of The English Language*: vol. 2, *1066 to 1476*, ed. Norman Blake (Cambridge, 1992), 560.

[34] *HN* 191–2, 224. The passage on church appointments was in a section of his work begun in 1119 and completed probably not long after Archbishop Ralph's death in 1122: R. W. Southern, *Saint Anselm and his Biographer: A Study in Monastic Life and Thought 1059–c. 1139* (Cambridge, 1966), 299, 307. Freeman, intent on seeing a very early reconciliation between peoples, argued that 'English' in this context incorporated second- and third-generation immigrants, but Fuchs ably rebuts this argument: Freeman, *History of the Norman Conquest*, 5: 151–2, 827–9; Fuchs, *Domesday Book*, 154–7.

[35] *HHHA* 14, 402, 412; Gillingham, *English in the Twelfth Century*, 128–9.

[36] Thomas Jones, ed., *Brut y Tywysogion or The Chronicle of the Princes: Red Book of Hergest Version*, 2nd edn. (Cardiff, 1973), 62–5.

[37] *Pipe Roll 31 Henry I*, 159–60. Toki's name, which can be found in pre-conquest England, is found in Normandy only in the family name Tocque and in place-names such as Tocqueville: Jean Adigard des Gautries, *Les Noms de personnes scandinaves en Normandie de 911 à 1066* (Lund, 1954), 149. This may cast some doubt on John of Cornwall's identification of Toki's sons as French, but in fact I am as interested, if not more so, in John's interpretation as the actual event.

[38] O. J. Padel, 'Geoffrey of Monmouth and Cornwall', *Cambridge Medieval Celtic Studies*, 8 (1984), 20–7; Michael J. Curley, 'A New Edition of John of Cornwall's *Prophetia Merlini*', *Speculum*, 57 (1982), 233, 238.

least of ethnically tinged violence. What these minor incidents suggest is that ethnic hostility was still high enough in Henry I's reign that acts of violence, which may well have had completely different origins, could be perceived through the lens of ethnic difference.

In contrast to the gloomy pronouncements and violent incidents noted so far, the late twelfth-century writer Walter Map wrote that Henry I, to overcome the continuing unrest found in the reigns of his father and brother, 'joined both peoples into a firm peace', through making marriages between them and by other unspecified means.[39] There is no evidence of any deliberate policy by Henry I to actively promote ethnic harmony, and Walter may have projected later developments back in time. Nonetheless, the kinds of personal relationships and intermarriage across ethnic lines that I will explore later in the book were continuing at a steady pace during the reigns of William II and Henry I. Even aside from Henry of Huntingdon's hyperbolic statements, it seems likely that commentators in Henry I's reign were overly pessimistic about relations between the Normans and English. Because the process of integration and assimilation was gradual, these commentators may not have realized how much had changed. Nonetheless, they were in a better position to judge relations than we are, and their gloomy picture of ethnic relations up through the 1120s must be treated seriously.

Osbert of Clare's version of the life of Edward the Confessor, finished in 1138, carried the pessimism into Stephen's reign. His gloomy interpretation of the green tree prophecy was noted earlier. He also stated that the consequences of England's downfall after Edward's death were still being felt 'today' by the native English (*innati Angli*).[40] More striking still, the *Liber Eliensis* records a short-lived plot led by an episcopal official in the Isle of Ely early in Stephen's reign to seize the English kingdom, and notes that the conspirators swore oaths 'to the ruin of the French'. It may have been some rumour of this incident that prompted Orderic Vitalis to speak of a plot, discovered by the bishop of Ely, to kill all the Normans on an appointed day and turn rule of the kingdom over to the Scots, whose kings had the best hereditary claim to follow the old West Saxon line.[41] On the face of it, there seems to be strong evidence of continuing hostility in Stephen's reign.

The whole episode of the English plot, however, is mysterious, and it is particularly hard to know what to make of an anti-French conspiracy in which one of the leaders, according to the *Liber Eliensis*, was called Ralph the Burgundian. The editor of that text, E. O. Blake, argued that in fact it was Bishop Nigel of Ely who was plotting against the king, and that the others were simply scapegoats.[42] Gillingham, building on Blake's theory, and linking this incident to a passage in Henry of Huntingdon's history about the treacheries of the Normans in Stephen's reign,

[39] Walter Map, *De Nugis Curialium: Courtiers' Trifles*, ed. M. R. James, rev. C. N. L. Brooke and R. A. B. Mynors (Oxford, 1983), 436.
[40] Osbert of Clare, 'Édouard le Confesseur', 103, 107–9.
[41] Blake, *Liber Eliensis*, 296–9; *EHOV* 6: 494.
[42] E. O. Blake, 'The *Historia Eliensis* as a Source for Twelfth-Century History', *Bulletin of the John Rylands Library*, 41 (1959), 318–26.

suggests that the terms 'Norman' and 'French' in these passages referred simply to a political faction at Stephen's court.[43] I remain unconvinced. Much of Gillingham's argument is based on connecting Henry's passage about the treacheries of the Normans, which appears at the beginning of Book 10 of his work, to Henry's own political connections and views. However, this statement seems to me to be much more obviously linked to Henry's general theme of the rise and fall of various peoples in Britain, including the Normans, which he addresses at the beginning of several books, and more specifically to his arguments that once the Normans had served as God's punishment for the English they began tearing themselves apart.[44] I agree with Gillingham that Henry was coming to see the Normans in England as more and more English by the time he wrote this passage, but would argue that this led Henry into a terminological muddle when it came to collective identities (see below, p. 75). In my view he was using 'Norman' in the traditional ethnic sense at the beginning of his last book, and I do not think one can dismiss the ethnic elements in references to the plot of the English against the Normans. The well-known speeches that Henry of Huntingdon and Aelred of Rievaulx placed before the battle of the Standard extolling past Norman victories show that Norman identity was still alive and well in Stephen's reign, and the obvious ethnic meaning of the terms 'French' and 'Norman' in accounts of the plot seems to me the correct one.[45] This in turn would indicate that ethnic tensions still existed in Stephen's reign. Even if Blake's theory of a cover-up is correct, that would at least show that ethnic tensions were high enough to make an ethnically inspired conspiracy seem sufficiently plausible to be used in concocting a fictional plot.

Nevertheless, there are reasons to think that relations between the English and Normans continued to improve in Stephen's reign. Gaimar's conciliatory history of the English in French was written early in that reign.[46] Moreover, as Gillingham and others have pointed out, accounts of the battle of the Standard link the two groups in the fighting.[47] Alfred of Beverley, describing the peoples of Britain, wrote of the Britons being in Wales, the Picts and Scots in Scotland, and the Normans and English throughout, *mixtim*, though unfortunately it is not clear if he means that the Normans and English were intermixed or, more likely, that they were mixed in

[43] Gillingham, *English in the Twelfth Century*, 135–7.

[44] *HHHA* 14, 272, 338–40, 402, 412, 700. See also Green's comments on Gillingham's argument in *Aristocracy*, 435. Gillingham also points to a passage in the *Liber Eliensis* stating that by Norman, the author meant someone whose parents were both Norman and who was raised in Normandy, and suggests that different definitions of Norman were possible. This may well be so, but the passage in question refers specifically to William the Conqueror being the first Norman king, and it seems to me the clear contrast is with Edward the Confessor, whose mother was Norman. How applicable this passage is to broader questions is debatable: Gillingham, *English in the Twelfth Century*, 137; Blake, *Liber Eliensis*, 171.

[45] *HHHA* 714–16; Aelred of Rievaulx, 'Relatio de Standardo', in *Chronicles of the Reigns of Stephen, Henry II, and Richard I*, ed. Richard Howlett, vol. 3 (London, 1886), 185–9.

[46] Gaimar, *L'Estoire des Engleis*. For its date, see Ian Short, 'Gaimar's Epilogue and Geoffrey of Monmouth's *Liber Vetustissimus*', *Speculum*, 69 (1994), 323–43. For its conciliatory nature, see below, pp. 85–6.

[47] *HHHA* 712–18; Aelred of Rievaulx, 'Relatio de Standardo', 181–99; Gillingham, *English in the Twelfth Century*, 129–30; Williams, *ENC* 179, 185–6; Green, *Aristocracy*, 435; Clanchy, *England and its Rulers*, 13–14.

among the other peoples of the island.[48] Finally, one might point to the silence of most sources on the subject of ethnic hostility. Though one always has to use such negative evidence cautiously, ethnic fissures often explode into violence and revolt in times of political turmoil and weak government such as Stephen's reign. But other than the pathetic Ely conspiracy, there is no hint of any ethnic violence in the many accounts of the troubles in the reign. It is hard to believe that ethnic tensions were at a constant boil between 1135 and 1154 but left hardly a trace. It is also hard to believe that the level of harmony that was apparently achieved in Henry II's reign emerged overnight. Thus, I suspect that relations in Stephen's reign were better than Osbert of Clare's comments and the accounts of plots would suggest.

Strong positive evidence that radical changes had occurred emerges from Henry II's reign. Aelred's optimistic interpretation of the green tree prophecy in the early 1160s stands in marked contrast to Osbert's pessimistic view. Walter Map may have been overly optimistic about the complete achievement of harmony in Henry I's reign, but his statement is clear evidence that he believed that harmony had been achieved well before the early 1180s, when he was writing.[49] Finally, there is the famous statement by Richard Fitz Nigel in the *Dialogue of the Exchequer*, probably written in the 1170s, that the Normans and English had become so intermingled through living together and intermarrying that among free people it was impossible to distinguish them.[50] Obviously, relations had improved dramatically since Henry I's reign, and assimilation had taken hold strongly.

However, there were also lingering traces of division and resentment in Henry's reign.[51] Aelred himself admitted that other people might disagree with his interpretation, and the nun of Barking who translated his work into French, probably not long after he wrote it, included a rare intrusion of her own authorial voice to disavow responsibility for the interpretation.[52] Perhaps Aelred and his translator anticipated objections from those who felt the interpretation was prematurely optimistic. Richard Fitz Nigel still believed that the unfree could be distinguished as purely English, and undermined his claim that the two peoples were indistinguishable by speaking, in a nearby passage, about what he had learned from the *indigeni*, a term he uses elsewhere for the native English, about the fate of English landholders after the conquest. This indicates at the very least that there were people in Richard Fitz Nigel's lifetime, and probably even in the 1170s, who could still be identified as native English.[53] Thus, even the classic expressions of ethnic harmony undercut themselves to some degree.

Moreover, the statute from early in Henry II's reign barring the English from claiming land unless they or their predecessors had possessed it at the death of

---

[48] Alfred of Beverley, *Annales sive Historia de Gestis Regum Britanniae*, ed. Thomas Hearne (Oxford, 1716), 10.

[49] Walter Map, *De Nugis Curialium*, 436.

[50] Richard Fitz Nigel, *Dialogus de Scaccario*, ed. Charles Johnson *et al.*, rev. edn. (Oxford, 1983), 53.

[51] See also Searle, *Predatory Kinship*, 243.

[52] Aelred of Rievaulx, 'Vita S. Edwardi Regis', 774; Östen Södergård, ed., *La Vie d'Edouard le Confesseur: poème anglo-normand du XIIe siècle* (Uppsala, 1948), 262.

[53] Richard Fitz Nigel, *Dialogus de Scaccario*, 53–5, 64.

Henry I only makes sense in an ethnic context, and demonstrates a continuing ethnic divide. As late as 1182, a pipe roll entry shows a member of the Yorkshire gentry, William of Leathley, invoking the statute against another prominent local landholder, John son of Essulf, though he apparently gained no benefit thereby.[54] It is worth noting that William was the descendant of an immigrant landholder who appears in Domesday Book, and that Essulf was clearly an insular name, but it is also worth noting that two years earlier William had married the daughter and heiress of another prominent local landholder of English descent. This would suggest that one could still sometimes distinguish native from immigrant ancestry, but that William's action was a legal ploy rather than an expression of deep-seated prejudice.[55] Nonetheless, the statute and the case belie an overly optimistic view of assimilation in Henry II's reign.

The clearest evidence for surviving divisions comes from the speeches attributed to Richard de Lucy in The *Chronicle of Battle Abbey*, in which he told the king that he and 'we Normans' ought to glorify the abbey; reminds him of the conquest of England by William with the help of 'our' (i.e. the Normans') relatives or ancestors; and warns against the plots of the English.[56] The chronicle contains events in the 1180s, and was probably written around that time, and the speech, if historical, was delivered in 1157. Gillingham argues that this too should be interpreted in a political and factional rather than ethnic context, but whatever political manoeuvers may have been involved, Richard was clearly speaking of Normans as the descendants of immigrants who had gained land in England directly or indirectly through William the Conqueror's victory, thus appealing to ethnic solidarity.[57] Since Battle Abbey was founded because of the Norman Conquest, and the speech was made in a lawsuit on its behalf, the passage may reflect rather narrow, or narrowly focused, sentiments. Nevertheless, it indicates that Richard, or the chronicler, felt there was still enough ethnic division early in Henry II's reign to make an appeal based on ethnicity worthwhile.

It should not be surprising that the end of ethnic hostility came gradually, and that traces remained even as writers like Aelred of Rievaulx were making rosy statements about ethnic relations and assimilation. The kind of hostility still found in Henry I's reign was not going to vanish without a trace in a generation or two. But clearly it was in the process of vanishing, and Henry II's reign seems to me to be the period in which ethnic boundaries fully broke down. After his reign one basically hears no trustworthy accounts of ethnic division or tension. Gerald of Wales, it is

---

[54] Stenton, *English Justice*, 32; *Pipe Roll 28 Henry II*, 45; *Pipe Roll 31 Henry II*, 66.

[55] For William of Leathley's family, marriage, and in-laws, see *EYC* 3: 478; 11: 137–9, 243–5; W. Paley Baildon, 'The Family of Leathley or Lelay', in Thoresby Society, no. 11, *Miscellanea* (Leeds, 1904), 2–36. For John son of Essulf's family, see Charles Clay, 'The Family of Thornhill', *Yorkshire Archaeological Journal*, 29 (1929), 286–321.

[56] Eleanor Searle, *The Chronicle of Battle Abbey* (Oxford, 1980), 178–82.

[57] Gillingham, *English in the Twelfth Century*, 137–9. See also Short, '*Tam Angli quam Franci*', 165. Richard cannot be traced back to any great beneficiary of the conquest, but he did inherit land in England from his mother: Emilie M. Amt, 'Richard de Lucy, Henry II's Justiciar', *Medieval Prosopography*, 9 (1988), 62–3.

true, on one occasion wrote as though the ethnic divide was still very much alive in his own time, when he insulted the English by saying that they were the vilest of slaves to the Normans in their own land, but outside this instance of invective, a genre in which Gerald was quite happy to distort the truth, there is no sense in his work of a continuing ethnic divide.[58] The *murdrum* fine, and with it the process of presentment of Englishry, did last into the fourteenth century, but the whole point of the passage on intermarriage in the Dialogue of the Exchequer was that one could only present Englishry by proving the victim was a serf, and thus (in theory) purely English.[59] The phrase 'French and English' continued to be used sporadically in royal charters up to the beginning of John's reign, though it looks as though it was dropped from chancery practice sometime in his first year.[60] A review of several hundred private charters with the formula suggests a continuing but declining use of the phrase in such charters in the last two decades of the twelfth century, with a marked drop-off around the same time as the change at the royal chancery. For instance, Earl Hugh II of Chester's charters made frequent use of the phrase in the 1150s, 1160s, and 1170s, while it appeared in a smaller but still significant number of Earl Ranulf III's charters from the 1180s and 1190s, and in only a handful of instances in his numerous charters after 1200.[61] Clearly this formula (variations of which con-

[58] *GCO* 3: 27. For a plausible alternative view, that Gerald was speaking specifically of oppression by the Norman kings, as he described the kings of his own day, see John Gillingham, '"Slaves of the Normans"? Gerald de Barri and Regnal Solidarity in Early Thirteenth-century England', in *Law, Laity and Solidarities: Essays in Honour of Susan Reynolds*, ed. Pauline Stafford *et al.* (Manchester, 2001), 160–71. Matthew Paris claimed that in Richard I's reign the rebel Londoner William 'cum barba' wore a beard because of the ancient indignation against Normans, but since there are no contemporary references to differences in hairstyle from after Henry I's reign (and those seem to be referring to an earlier period), it seems clear that this is an anachronism: Matthew Paris, *Chronica Majora*, 2: 418.

[59] Richard Fitz Nigel, *Dialogus de Scaccario*, 53. However, Hamil believed that if villeinage were sufficient grounds for presentment of Englishry, it would have been presented more often, and a comment by Doris Stenton on the Worcester eyre of 1221 indicates that she thought it was still possible to prove Englishness on the basis of descent at that date: Hamil, 'Presentment of Englishry', 294; Doris Mary Stenton, *Rolls of the Justices in Eyre for Lincolnshire 1218–19 and Worcestershire 1221* (London, 1924), p. lxviii. However, an addition to a treatise from the 1230s or 1240s linked villeinage and Englishry in the same way Richard Fitz Nigel did: Paul Hyams, *Kings, Lords, and Peasants in Medieval England: The Common Law of Villeinage in the Twelfth and Thirteenth Centuries* (Oxford, 1980), 253; H. G. Richardson and G. O. Sayles, eds., *Select Cases of Procedure without Writ under Henry III* (London, 1941), p. ccii. A Latin text, *De consuetudinibus comitatus Kancie*, from before 1278, attacking the application of *murdrum* in Kent, remarks that there was no longer any distinction between Normans and Englishman: F. R. H. Du Boulay, *The Lordship of Canterbury: An Essay on Medieval Society* (New York, 1966), 144. Other legal treatises and commentaries simply state the procedure for proving Englishry, without discussing what the basis of Englishness was, and a quick survey of the published eyre rolls has provided no additional information about what made someone English in the eyes of the law. Certainly by the fourteenth century it is inconceivable that the courts could have distinguished by descent, which means that there must have been some other means of determining Englishry.

[60] See BL Cotton Claudius D xiii, fol. 41^{r-v}; BL Cotton Titus C viii, fol. 17^{r-v}; *Mon. Ang.* 2: 231; Lionel Landon, ed., *Cartae Antiquae Rolls 1–10* (London, 1939), no. 37; Michael Gervers, ed., *The Cartulary of the Knights of St. John of Jerusalem in England: Secunda Camera* (Oxford, 1982), no. 9; Thomas Rymer, *Foedera*, vol. 1, pt. 1 (London, 1816), 78, for royal charters with the formula in John's reign, most from the early months of his reign. My review of John's charters is far from comprehensive, so my conclusion that the formula was abandoned in his first year must be viewed as tentative.

[61] Geoffrey Barraclough, *The Charters of the Anglo-Norman Earls of Chester c. 1071–1237* (Gloucester, 1988), nos. 123–437.

tinued to be used in areas such as Wales and Ireland where ethnic divides remained in force) was sufficiently far out of date after 1200 that it seemed ridiculous to all but the most conservative of scribes, and one would expect a certain lag of time between the ending of ethnic hostility and the disappearance of the by then venerable formula.

Otherwise there is silence, and while one cannot completely rule out that the occasional person of an older generation still harboured lingering resentments and prejudices even after 1189, it seems overwhelmingly likely that the process of reconciliation and assimilation was essentially complete by the end of Henry II's reign. A century-and-a-quarter is a long time, but given the depths of hostility between the English and Normans in William I's reign, the speed of assimilation between the two peoples is quite remarkable.

6

A Chronology of Identity

Some stood for Harold, and all for their *patria*, which they wished to defend
against foreigners even though their cause was unjust.

(William of Poitiers)[1]

The language of fighting for one's country in this passage takes us back to similar
ones in pre-conquest sources, where, as I argued in Chapter 2, they represented the
power of England and Englishness on people's imaginations. Did this language
and the sentiments it expressed become obsolete with the conquest, appearing in
later works only to describe a vanished past? Obviously, the creation of a new elite
drawn from the Continent was going to make the use of such expressions at least
temporarily inappropriate; no one was likely to describe the nobles and other
warriors who came with William I as fighting for the *patria* of England. But the idea
of devotion to England remained durable and eventually captured the imagination
of the descendants of the invaders, as the following set of quotations will suggest,
and as I hope to demonstrate throughout the work. Orderic wrote of the English (by
which in this case he clearly meant the native English) and the bishops of England
working for the 'serene peace of the *patria*' during the revolts against William II.[2]
During the civil war of Stephen's reign Lawrence of Durham, asked why he had
stopped composing poetry, wrote poetically about the 'many disasters of my
patria', referring immediately thereafter to *Anglia*.[3] Later in the twelfth century
Nigel Wireker could make fun of the whole concept in the *Speculum Stultorum*. The
anti-hero of the work, Brunellus the Ass, seeking to have his tail lengthened and
having received from a doctor a ridiculous list of ingredients, encounters in Salerno
a merchant (and conman) who just happens to have all that was necessary in ten
glass jars. The merchant, who says of himself, '*Anglia* bore me, born among the
citizens of London', kindly consents to sell the ingredients because he 'burn[s] with
love for the *patria*' (perhaps London, perhaps England, more likely both) and has
no money to return.[4] More sincerely, at the beginning of the thirteenth century
Stephen Langton could write from exile during the interdict, in a letter warning the

---

[1] *GGWP* 126.

[2] *EHOV* 4: 128.

[3] Lawrence of Durham, *Dialogi Laurentii Dunelmensis Monachi ac Prioris*, ed. James Raine (Durham,
1880), 2.

[4] Nigel de Longchamp, *Speculum Stultorum*, ed. John H. Mozley and Robert R. Raymo (Berkeley,
1960), 47–8.

English against opposing the church, that 'from tender years, I naturally (*naturali*) loved our kingdom, with a tender love'.[5] In the thirteenth century, as Michael Clanchy has remarked, the idea of England as a cause to fight for was one familiar to writers.[6]

A chronology of the triumph of Englishness will, not surprisingly, look similar to the chronology of assimilation described in the last chapter. However, though assimilation and the re-emergence of a dominant English identity were closely related, they were separate processes, with somewhat different dynamics. The shift in identity needs to be conceptualized in a different manner than in the past, and this requires treating its chronology independently of that for assimilation. Moreover, in the chronology of identity there was an additional phase, lasting into the thirteenth century, in which the descendants of Normans in the aristocracy moved from simply accepting English identity to embracing it and making it a part of their political agenda and propaganda.

Writers in the post-conquest period, and perhaps more generally in the Middle Ages, I would argue, tended to conceptualize the interplay of assimilation and identity, and the transition between identities, in a different way than we do. The major difference is that medieval intellectuals were less likely to think in terms of a *group* transitional identity, such as Anglo-Norman, and more likely to think in terms of individuals having more than one identity. The older model for the shift can be roughly summarized in the following terms: because of intermarriage, cultural change, and adaptation to England, the invaders and their descendants progressed, perhaps gradually, perhaps swiftly, from a unitary Norman identity to a unitary English one, possibly through a mediating Anglo-Norman phase. The model I would propose is one in which over a number of generations competing identities were available to a greater or lesser degree for individuals without any intermediate choice. Individuals might choose one, pick more than one as true for themselves, or simply avoid the issue. Ultimately the results would be the same: as fewer people picked the Norman option, and more came to see Englishness as their sole or at least primary identity, there would be an overall shift to English identity. Nevertheless, the nature of the process would be different, with important consequences.

The first basis for my argument stems from an observation already made by John Gillingham, that there was no common contemporary term equivalent to Anglo-Norman.[7] While it is perfectly reasonable for us to continue using Anglo-Norman as a convenient and useful category, we must remember that people of the time did not use it. Thus, there was no easy transitional catch-all for those who felt both English and Norman, or somewhere in between. Gillingham draws different

---

[5] William Stubbs, ed., *The Historical Works of Gervase of Canterbury*, vol. 2 (London, 1880), p. lxxxi.

[6] Clanchy, *England and its Rulers*, 175.

[7] Gillingham, *English in the Twelfth Century*, 124. The term *Normanglorum* in the Hyde Chronicle may serve that purpose, but that is not beyond doubt, and the term was used only in a single source: Edwards, *Liber Monasterii de Hyda*, 296–319. See Gillingham, *English in the Twelfth Century*, 142–4, C. Warren Hollister, *Monarchy, Magnates and Institutions in the Anglo-Norman World* (London, 1986), 46–7, and David Bates, 'Normandy and England After 1066', *EHR* 104 (1989), 877–80, for different views of the chronicler's use of the term.

conclusions from the absence of any transitional or mediating group identity than I do, for as noted in the last chapter, he sees a fairly quick shift in identity between the 1120s and 1140s.[8] So short a transitional period would make the absence of an Anglo-Norman collective identity less surprising. However, as I have argued, the transitional period was probably much longer. Ian Short, who in his important 1996 article on the shift in ethnic identity also argued for a slower transition in identity, attempted to revive a sort of Anglo-Norman identity, centred around language, that survived in a cultural sense even after its members had come to accept an English identity by the end of Henry II's reign.[9] But the fact that he can never point to a single name or phrase for such a group raises serious questions about whether such a group existed as a self-conscious entity. If one sees a long transitional period between English and Norman identity, the lack of an Anglo-Norman identity becomes perplexing.

The fact that English identity could be applied to immigrants both by others and themselves very soon after the conquest makes the problem even more vexing. There are several examples of this. The immigrant writer Goscelin wrote to his friend and former protégé Eva that, 'although you are known to have been a foreigner among the English people, from a Danish father and Lotharingian mother of honorable lineages you emerged an English daughter'.[10] Both Goscelin and Eva lived in England before the conquest, but this passage was written after, when other pre-conquest immigrants, including Normans, could also be treated in some way as English.[11] More important, post-conquest immigrants could also quickly become English on some level. Reginald of Canterbury, an immigrant monk of the late eleventh century, could write of *gens Anglica nostra*.[12] Most famously, Lanfranc could both be described and describe himself (and also Thomas, the first Norman archbishop of York) as English, albeit with some qualifying phrase such as *novus* or *rudis*.[13] Nobody forgot that Lanfranc was originally from Lombardy, or that Eva was of foreign birth, and Reginald of Canterbury remembered his birthplace fondly.[14] But on some level they all considered themselves, and were considered, English, and this in the first generation after the conquest. Englishness was a possible choice for immigrants from the very beginning, while a Norman identity was at least possible for their descendants even in Henry II's reign.

Clearly the period of transition from plain Norman (or Breton or Lombard) to more or less plain English (of Norman descent) was a long one, and there was ample

---

[8] Gillingham, *English in the Twelfth Century*, 123–42.

[9] Short, '*Tam Angli quam Franci*', 153–75.

[10] '... te quoque cum Anglica gente constat fuisse advenam: sed et patre Dano et matre Lotaringa a claris natalibus filiam emersisse Anglicam': 'The Liber Confortatorius of Goscelin of Saint Bertin', ed. C. H. Talbot, *Studia Anselmiana*, 37 (1955), 41.

[11] See below, p. 110.

[12] Liebermann, 'Raginald von Canterbury', 551; Williams, *ENC* 5, 135; A. G. Rigg, *A History of Anglo-Latin Literature, 1066–1422* (Cambridge, 1992), 12.

[13] Chibnall, *Anglo-Norman England*, 39; Williams, *ENC* 5; *HN* 16; *WMGR* 536; *Vita Lanfranci*, PL 150: 48; *Letters of Lanfranc*, 38, 40, 156.

[14] Rigg, *Anglo-Latin Literature*, 11; Wright, *Anglo-Latin Satirical Poets*, 2: 263–5.

scope for an 'in between' Anglo-Norman or Anglo-French identity, had con-temporaries generally thought in those terms. In this respect post-conquest writers seem to have been less able or willing to conceptualize the mixing of peoples than modern writers. We are quite happy to throw about Anglo-Norman, Anglo-Irish, African-American, and other hyphenations with abandon. All these terms are, of course, fudges, and perhaps medieval writers were generally less comfortable with fudging (though the occasional pre-conquest variants of Anglo-Saxon do form an exception). In any case, because writers of the time did not normally think in terms of Anglo-Norman identity, their conceptualization of the process was different from, and in a certain respect somewhat more limited than, ours.

In another respect, their conceptualization of the process was at least as flexible as ours, if not more so. Though we can consider a person both Irish and American or Pakistani and English, depending on the context or definition, it appears to me that they were more willing to view people as having more than one ethnic identity, in some cases changing over time, but in many cases operating concurrently. William of Malmesbury could, borrowing earlier language, describe Lanfranc as a *rudis Anglus* in one passage and Lombard by *gens* in another.[15] Robert, appointed bishop of Bath in 1134, could be described as Flemish by *genus* but born in England, and Robert Chesney, who became bishop of Lincoln in 1148, as 'natione quidem Anglicus, sed cognatione Normannus' (probably best translated as 'English by birth but Norman by ancestry').[16] The champion of multiple ethnicity was Gerald of Wales, whose identity has been studied by Robert Bartlett, and whose origins in one of the marcher families of South Wales gave him more options. Gerald mainly oscillated between being English and Welsh, depending on whom he wanted to please and whom he was angry at, but on one occasion he described his background as being British (i.e. Welsh) and Norman, and on another occasion complained that an enemy made him out as 'Welsh to the French' and 'French to the Welsh'. He objected to the subterfuge but seemed to take Frenchness in his stride. It is also worth noting that he could describe one nephew with benefices in Ireland as Irish, and in the same letter describe another nephew as 'Welsh, well, really Flemish'.[17] If post-conquest writers avoided speaking about mixed peoples, they had no hesita-tion in speaking about mixed people.

I would argue that a picture of the Normans becoming more intermixed and culturally assimilated with the English, and as a result subsequently shifting broadly to an English identity, oversimplifies matters. Instead, immigrants and their descendants, especially those of mixed birth, had a choice of identities, and of mixed identities, from the immediate aftermath of the conquest well into Henry II's reign. Some, such as Orderic, might choose an English identity enthusiastically. Others, such as William of Malmesbury, might have a more ambiguous or nuanced view of their identity and allegiances. Still others, such as Hervey de Glanvill and Richard de Lucy, judging by the staunchly Norman speeches attributed to them,

---

[15] *WMGR* 536; *WMGP* 37.
[16] *CJW* 3: 212; *GCO* 7: 34, 198.
[17] Bartlett, *Gerald of Wales*, 9–26, 50–7; *GCO* 1: 332; 3: 120; Gerald of Wales, *Speculum Duorum*, 190–2.

might choose to emphasize their own and others' Norman identity at fairly late dates.[18] Obviously, as time went on and the effects of intermarriage, acculturation, and other factors discussed below came to be felt, Norman identity became less attractive and English identity more so. But the period in which different choices were plausible was spread out, and different individuals made different choices throughout that period. This subtly different model of the shifting of identity has important implications for our understanding of the impact of identity on post-conquest society and the interaction of identity and assimilation in the period.

The first implication has to do with the relationship of identity and assimilation. If shifts of identity follow cultural and biological assimilation both temporally and causally, then the relation is simple and unidirectional. In the model I have described above, however, the influence could go both ways. Archbishop Lanfranc instituted a number of reforms aimed at improving Canterbury and the English church as a whole, which incidentally brought the English and Norman churches into closer alignment, thus promoting cultural assimilation. By identifying himself as English on some level, he signalled his willingness to respect at least some of the indigenous tradition, and by identifying himself at least partially with the con-quered, he almost certainly made his reforms more palatable, and more easily gained the support and loyalty of native monks.[19] Thus, the model I have suggested allows for a more complex picture of the interaction of assimilation and identity.

Another implication of the model is that, although most individuals may have had clear ideas about their own ethnic identities, however complex, group iden-tities, particularly at the elite levels, soon became extremely problematic and ambiguous, and remained so for some time. Here the absence of an 'in between' category was particularly important. The starting-point of this discussion will be words and language, but the stakes involved were not simply semantic. Ethnic constructs are unlikely to have much impact unless they can be conceived and articulated. With the breakdown of a clear demarcation between English and Normans, and with an increasingly blurred and blurry group identity at the top of society, not only did Norman identity have less impact, but so too, for a time, did English.

The problem for writers was how to describe group identity among the elites, once the relatively simple categories of 1066, with English on one side and French or Normans on the other, became ever less satisfying, and as individuals among the intellectual, social, and political elites began thinking of themselves in complex and often highly individual ways. One way of handling this was through what Short has called the polyvalence of individual terms such as English and Norman, namely the tendency to use them in different ways.[20] An excellent example of this comes from Orderic Vitalis's different uses of the word English. When Orderic writes about the English in the revolts in England against William II and Henry I, the context makes clear that he is speaking of the native English in contrast to the immigrants. In his

---

[18] For these speeches, see above, p. 65.
[19] See below, pp. 215–16.
[20] Short, '*Tam Angli quam Franci*', 165.

discussions of Henry I's wars in Normandy, however, though he sometimes speaks of Normans, or Normans and English, at other times he describes the king's forces simply as the English, though those forces contained both immigrants to England and at least some who resided in Normandy. Clearly here English has a much broader context, perhaps emphasizing the king's heavy reliance on fighters of whatever ethnicity coming from England, or perhaps simply designating followers of the king of the English.[21] All too rarely writers used some adjective or definition to clarify their meaning, as when Orderic spoke of *Angli naturales* in 1088, Osbert of Clare wrote of *Angli innati*, or the *Liber Eliensis* distinguished William I from Edward the Confessor as the first Norman king of England by describing him as Norman from both parents (though his mother was Flemish) and raised in Normandy.[22] Clearly Short and other scholars have been quite correct in stating that English and Norman could mean quite different things, and this of course helped circumvent the problem of how to describe group identities.[23] It is also clear that the exact shades of meanings, when undefined, would often have been more apparent to contemporaries than to us.

Nevertheless, I would also argue that sometimes writers were not merely confusing, but instead, because of the problems of group identity discussed above, quite simply confused. Perhaps there was some subtle plan to Orderic's ethnic terminology in Henry I's Norman wars, but to me he just looks inconsistent. Such confusion and inconsistency appears most strikingly in descriptions of the forces at the battle of the Standard in 1138. Henry of Huntingdon has the bishop of Orkney address the Norman nobles of England, but it is the English who say amen to his speech, and the *gens Normannorum et Anglorum* that fights. In King David's multi-ethnic army, however, he lists the English and Normans as separate peoples. Aelred has Walter Espec addressing a Norman audience, has Robert de Brus complain that David is opposing the English and Normans, and speaks of an army of the English. Other sources simply speak of the English or of the army of the English winning the battle.[24] This is a mess, but the sort of mess one might expect in a situation in which there were not only clear-cut Normans and clear-cut English, but many with a mixed identity, and in which the collective identity was therefore highly ambiguous, not to say muddled. Finally in this respect, it should be noted that the famous statement in *The Dialogue of the Exchequer* about the inability to know who was English and who was French above the level of peasant, whatever conclusions one may reasonably draw from it, is an expression not of unity but of uncertainty about elite identity.[25]

[21] *EHOV* 1: 161; 4: 124–8, 182; 5: 214, 216, 310, 314; 6: 88, 190, 206, 216, 236, 350.

[22] Ibid. 4: 124; Osbert of Clare, 'Vie de S. Édouard', 103; Blake, *Liber Eliensis*, 171.

[23] Short, '*Tam Angli quam Franci*', 165; Gillingham, *English in the Twelfth Century*, 137; Fuchs, *Domesday Book*, 363.

[24] *HHHA* 714–16; Aelred of Rievaulx, 'Relatio de Standardo', 182, 185–98; Richard of Hexham, *De Gestis Regis Stephani et de Bello Standardi*, in *Chronicles of the Reigns of Stephen, Henry II, and Richard I*, vol. 3, ed. Richard Howlett (London, 1886), 164–5; *HCY* 2: 529; *Dialogi Laurentii Dunelmensis*, 75. Aelred also speaks of William of Aumales's presence with *Morinis et Ponciis*, and Walter de Gant's band of *Flandrensibus et Normannis*, though judging by the former, these may refer to mercenaries.

[25] Richard Fitz Nigel, *Dialogus de Scaccario*, 53.

The most important symptom of the problem of group identity in post-conquest England is the widespread avoidance of ethnic terminology in histories from most of the twelfth century, when compared to the preceding and following periods, outside formulas such as *rex Anglorum*, and particularly in contexts involving the elites. This phenomenon has been noted by Short, who quite rightly points out how often writers avoided referring to the English (or for that matter the Normans) by tacking on a genitive to *Anglia*.[26] Thus one gets the nobles of England, not the English nobles. The avoidance of direct ethnic terminology is most obvious in discussions of civil wars in which political elites were naturally involved. Ethnicity or nationality *was* clearly to the fore in discussions of the 1051–2 revolt, and though it was not a direct issue in the revolts of William II's reign and at the beginning of Henry I's reign, ethnic terms were freely used. As we shall see, ethnic or national terminology and issues can also be found in abundance for the wars at the end of John's reign and the beginning of his son's reign. But outside the accounts of the battle of the Standard, direct references to combatants from England as either English or Norman are quite rare for the wars of Stephen's reign, or for the English segment of the 1173–4 revolt against Henry II.[27] I do not believe that this is simply a trick of language, but rather a sign of profound uncertainly and ambiguity about the collective identity of the elites.

The problems of constructing a collective ethnic identity for the elites stemmed from very real issues of descent and culture, but if constructs reflect reality, they also influence it. The lack of a clear-cut collective ethnic identity for the elites helped ensure that ethnicity would have little impact on politics in the twelfth century, no matter how strongly individuals might feel about their own identities. The lack of a collective 'in between' identity made it much harder for people to clearly distinguish themselves, as a group, both from the Normans of Normandy and from the native English, in the way that 'Creole' identities allowed immigrants to the New World to distinguish themselves both from Europeans and from their neighbours who were not of European descent.[28] The elites of England either had to put up with ambiguity or, as they eventually did, settle on one of the two identities as their primary allegiance.

Problems of evidence make it no more possible to chart out a precise chronology of the adoption of English identity by the Normans than to chart one of assimilation. Evidence is limited, partly because of the avoidance of ethnic terms, and

---

[26] Short, '*Tam Angli quam Franci*', 167.

[27] As Short notes in the passage cited above, William of Malmesbury, despite his own Englishness, carefully avoids the term *Angli* in his *Historia Novella*, which recorded Stephen's reign. I will take two more sources as examples here. In the *Gesta Stephani* I have found only two references to English, or *Anglenses*, both in very broad contexts: 4, 138. Jordan Fantosme's *Chronicle*, has a reference to the land of the *Engleis*, to the Scots plundering the *Engleis*, and some rude comments about *Engleis* by the Earl of Leicester's wife: *Jordan Fantosme's Chronicle*, ed. R. C. Johnston (Oxford, 1981), 8, 48, 72. These constitute very few instances in large works, and though they may well include the elites among the English, as Gillingham has argued in one case, none refers solely to the elites in the way that the formulations based on the genitive often do: Gillingham, *English in the Twelfth Century*, 123, n. 2.

[28] Anderson, *Imagined Communities*, 47–65; Peggy K. Liss, *Mexico Under Spain, 1521–1556: Society and the Origins of Nationality* (Chicago, 1975), 95–117.

writers sometimes projected anachronistic views of ethnicity backwards. What evidence survives is often hard for us, if not necessarily for contemporaries, to interpret. For instance, during the 1173–4 revolt the rebel earl of Leicester faced a royalist army under the earl of Arundel and Humphrey de Bohun, both descendants of immigrants. Jordan Fantosme has the countess of Leicester urge her husband not to delay on account of them, saying that the English are great boasters and drinkers but do not know how to fight. Does this indicate that the earl of Arundel and Humphrey were perceived as English, but the earl and countess of Leicester were not, and if so, what distinguished them?[29] Even with more and better evidence, I suspect the question would be extraordinarily complex, given the many possible shades of 'in between' identity, and therefore hard to pin down in any definitive chronology. The chronology given here is therefore not meant to supersede earlier ones, such as that in Short's 1996 article, but to provide a useful and provocative alternative that incorporates the model of shifting identity outlined above.[30]

My framework consists of three broad and overlapping phases. In the first, which lasted until late in Henry I's reign, strong distinctions remained between the conquerors and conquered, and Norman or other Continental identities remained strong, both at the collective and individual level. The continuing strength of Norman identity into Henry I's reign is uncontroversial, and important parts of the evidence have been set out earlier, namely the interpretations of the green tree prophecy and complaints of prejudice against the English. A striking story not mentioned previously comes in William of Malmesbury's account of Henry I's effort to promote an abbot of Italian origin, Faritius, to the see of Canterbury in 1114 at an assembly at Windsor. Those present objected, saying they had had enough foreigners (*alienae gentis homines*) as archbishops and wanted someone with the language of the *patria*. The person chosen was Ralph, bishop of Rochester, who had recently come from Normandy and was explicitly described in the passage as being from a Norman family. Obviously a strong sense of Norman identity was at play here.[31]

However, this was also a period in which some individuals of Continental descent were adopting at least partially English identities, and in which ambiguity was developing about collective identities. The adoption of English identity by the post-conquest immigrants Lanfranc and Reginald of Canterbury has already been noted, and the Englishness of Orderic Vitalis, William of Malmesbury, and Henry of Huntingdon, all children of immigrants, is well known and will be discussed more fully in the course of the work. Other scholars have noted the allegiance to Englishness, at least on some level, of Bishop Alexander of Lincoln, and the anonymous compiler of two key legal texts drawing heavily on pre-conquest law, the *Leges*

---

[29] *Jordan Fantosme's Chronicle*, 72. The countess was probably heiress to the honour of Grandmesnil and therefore Norman in geographic as well as ethnic background: G. E. Cockayne and Vicary Gibbs, *The Complete Peerage of England, Scotland, Ireland, and the United Kingdom*, rev. edn., vol. 7 (London, 1929), 532–3.

[30] Short, '*Tam Angli quam Franci*', 173–4.

[31] *WMGP* 126.

Henrici and *Quadripartitus*, who was Francophone and therefore probably Continental by origin.[32] To these may be added the author of a treatise on falconry, almost certainly the famous scholar Adelard of Bath, who states to his nephew that he is writing the treatise 'chiefly because we are English by *genus*, and their (*sic*) knowledge is well known among other peoples', but who later makes reference to the old English (*veteri Angli*). This looks like another case of the child of an immigrant adopting an English identity (albeit a hesitant one that recognized a different kind of Englishness) and taking pride in that identity.[33] Though English identity was available to immigrants at the beginning of this phase, no doubt it was more common and seemed more plausible and acceptable at its end, after decades of intermarriage and cultural assimilation, and as early as Henry I's reign the pull of Englishness was apparently strong, despite continuing prejudice and allegiance to *Normanitas*.

In the second phase, roughly consisting of the reigns of Stephen and Henry II, *Normanitas* remained a possible and in some ways attractive identity, but nobles whose interests centred on England turned increasingly to an English identity, although perhaps not a very intense one. Throughout this period ambiguity about collective identities remained strong. Much of the evidence for continuing Continental identity in the reigns of Stephen and Henry II has been discussed in the previous chapter. It should be noted that for Henry II's reign most of this concerns a continuing distinctiveness from the English. Given the polyvalence of the term English, this may be more indicative of a continuing distinctiveness of immigrants from the *native* English than a strong sense of Norman identity. The main positive evidence for such an identity was the speech attributed to Richard de Lucy in the *Chronicle of Battle Abbey*. To this should be added the fact that Roger of Howden, working late in the century, thought it reasonable to place in the mouth of the earl of Arundel, before a battle in Normandy in 1173, a speech largely lifted from the one Henry of Huntingdon ascribed to the bishop of Orkney at the battle of the Standard, extolling Norman identity.[34] But this, of course, was the same earl of Arundel whom Jordan Fantosme seems to have envisioned being berated as English that same year, thus showing the continuing ambiguity of identity.

It was also a period in which, as far as the scant evidence tells us, English identity increasingly became the norm for descendants of earlier immigrants, at least as individuals. Two neglected pieces of evidence are particularly important in this respect. The first is a list, compiled in the 1180s by Herbert of Bosham, of the learned members of Thomas Becket's household, each of whose *natio* is described. Several were described as Lombards and one as Welsh, but of the remainder only one is

---

[32] Gillingham, *English in the Twelfth Century*, 134–5; Williams, *ENC* 178; Downer, *Leges Henrici Primi*, 42–4; Wormald, *Making of English Law*, 473.

[33] The Latin is 'precipue cum et nos Angli sumus genere et eorum inde scientia pre ceteris ge(n)tibus sit probata . . .': Charles Burnett, ed., *Adelard of Bath, Conversations with his Nephew: On the Same and the Different, Questions on Natural Science, and On Birds* (Cambridge, 1998), 238, 264; Charles Burnett, *Adelard of Bath: An English Scientist and Arabist of the Early Twelfth Century* (London, 1987), 7–8, 25–7.

[34] [Roger of Howden], *Gesta Regis Henrici Secundi Benedicti Abbatis*, ed. William Stubbs, vol. 1 (London, 1867), 52–3.

described as *natione Normannus*, and this was Hugh Nonant, future bishop of Coventry, who was born in Normandy. Ten others, including Reginald Foliot, Reginald de Bohun, and Gilbert de Glanville, all members of powerful families of Continental ancestry, are described as *natione Anglus*. Reference to two others by the cities in which they were born indicates that *natio* primarily refers to birthplace here, and there is no guarantee that any of these men saw themselves only or primarily as English. Nevertheless, it is a sign of declining Norman identity that Herbert could define them in this way. It should be noted in this respect that a charter of 1186 of one of these very men, Reginald de Bohun, could employ the term *optimates Angli* rather than the more conventional form *optimates Angliae*.[35] The other important piece of evidence is a list of participants in a tournament of 1179, preserved decades later in the poem of William Marshal but probably based on a contemporary source, which lists men by ethnicity, including Normans, Flemings, and so on. Fourteen names appear under the English heading, and these include members of powerful families such as William himself, Robert Fitz Walter, and Earl David of Huntingdon, as well as lesser men whose surnames indicate a Continental background, such as Robert de Wancy, William Revel, John de St Michiel, and Robert le Breton. That Earl David was a brother of the king of Scotland suggests that this English category was something of a simplification, but it is nonetheless striking that such figures would appear in it.[36] If these sources are representative, it looks as though when people thought of members of Anglo-Norman elite families, they thought of them first, if not necessarily only, as English by the end of Henry II's reign. At the same time, collective references to groups of elites as English remain rare in the sources.

The final period was one in which ambiguity about collective elite identity was shed, and the elites as a whole became firmly identified as English. The true change came in collective terminology, but it is worth noting first that there is further evidence for the description of elite individuals as English, since group identity resulted from broadly consistent individual identities and, given the meagerness of evidence, examples provided here will help show that the earlier pieces of evidence were not flukes. Most notably, the anonymous chronicler of Bethune, writing in the 1220s but referring in the relevant passages to the fall of Normandy and the later civil wars associated with Magna Carta, described Robert Fitz Walter, Earl Saher de Quincy and his son Robert, Gilbert de Clare, William de Mowbray, William de Mandeville, John de Lacy, and the younger William the Marshal, all powerful lords of Norman descent, as *Englois*. Indeed, he wrote that the ignominious surrender by the first two of a castle in Normandy shamed the English.[37] Other examples may also be found.[38] This reinforces the argument that it had become normal to see

[35] *Becket Materials*, 3: 523–30; *EEA* 10, no. 98.
[36] Paul Meyer, ed., *L'Histoire de Guillaume le Maréchal*, vol. 1 (Paris, 1891), 167–8; David Crouch, 'The Hidden History of the Twelfth Century', *Haskins Society Journal*, 5, ed. Robert B. Patterson (1993), 116.
[37] Anonymous of Béthune, *Histoire des ducs de Normandie et des rois d'Angleterre*, ed. Francisque Michel (Paris, 1840), 97, 190, 194–5, 209.
[38] *GCO* 1: 94–5; 3: 219, 221, 298–9; William Stubbs, ed., *Chronica Magistri Rogeri de Hovedene*, vol. 3 (London, 1870), 73.

powerful individual Anglo-Normans primarily as English by the beginning of the thirteenth century.

As for collective terminology, the change was slower. The genitive construct based on *Anglia* was well established and continued to be used. References to collective Continental identity continued to be found both in the second and third phases in the context of the Welsh marches, suggesting a slower shift in that region.[39] But Englishness triumphed among the invaders of Wales by the early thirteenth century, and seems to have been dominant among the invaders of Ireland from the beginning, testifying to the growing allegiance to that construct.[40] Moreover, chroniclers were becoming more and more comfortable describing groups of elite or predominately elite figures (such as armies, which generally had elite landholders at their cores) as English during Richard's reign.[41] Particularly interesting are accounts concerning Richard I's decision to begin sanctioning tournaments in England. Richard's own charter refers to *comites et barones Angli.* Ralph of Diceto wrote that his decision was designed to prepare knights in case of attack by foreign peoples (*gentes exterae*), and spoke of the ones to be trained by tournaments as English. William of Newburgh stated that Richard instituted tournaments because the *Galli* were better trained in war, and he wished the knights of his own kingdom to train within their borders, so that they would learn to fight better and so that the *Galli* would not insult English knights (*Angli milites*) as inexperienced and less expert.[42] Clearly writers were coming to think of a distinct, straightforwardly English nobility in Richard's reign.

By the time of Magna Carta and the related wars this idea had become ingrained, for reasons that I will explore more fully in Chapter 20. King John made a practice of extracting hostages and charters of fealty from powerful men; clause 49 of Magna Carta simply and straightforwardly refers to these as being taken from the English.[43] As Michael Clanchy has noted, a royal document from 1217 looks forward to the English recovering their lands in Normandy.[44] Who could these English be but noble families descended from the conquerors who still had strong enough ties with Normandy to retain land there in 1204? Most striking of all is the constant reference to English combatants in the fighting that developed after John repudiated Magna Carta and his opponents called in Louis, son of King Philip of France. It is no surprise that a foreign invasion should bring out ethnic or national identity, but as noted earlier, invasions and civil war in 1173–4 had not done so nearly to the same degree. Significantly, English and French were not simply convenient terms to

[39] Henry Richard Luard, *Annales Monastici,* vol. 1 (London, 1864), 18; *The Historical Works of Master Ralph de Diceto,* ed. William Stubbs, 2 vols. (London, 1876), 1: 437; 2: 163; *GCO* 1: 28; 3: 128; 4: 147, 151; 6: 83, 169; Gerald of Wales, *Speculum Duorum,* 36–8; John Williams Ab Ithel, ed., *Annales Cambriae* (London, 1860), 57–62, 68–72; Jones, *Brut y Tywysogion,* 146, 148, 162, 164–6, 188, 198.

[40] For the Englishness of the invaders of Ireland, see Gillingham, *English in the Twelfth Century,* 145–60.

[41] Richard of Devizes, *The Chronicle of Richard of Devizes of the Time of King Richard the First,* ed. John T. Appleby (London, 1963), 19, 20, 22, 36, 38, 75–6; *Historical Works of Gervase of Canterbury,* 1: 529.

[42] *Historical Works of Ralph de Diceto,* 2: pp. lxxx–lxxxi, 120; *WNHA* 422–3.

[43] J. C. Holt, *Magna Carta* (Cambridge, 1965), 328.

[44] Clanchy, *England and its Rulers,* 181; *Rot. Litt. Claus.,* 1: 329.

describe the respective forces of John and Henry III on the one hand and Louis on the other. Chroniclers were careful to talk about the foreigners in the royalist party and consistently portrayed Louis's followers from England as English.[45] There is no doubt that to chroniclers in the aftermath of that war the elite families of England were quite simply English. It is true that there were powerful new immigrants who were not English. Moreover, as we shall see, pride in Continental and particularly Norman descent remained so common that it could be adopted even by elite families of English descent. Nonetheless, by the second decade of the thirteenth century the descendants of the conquerors had not only become English, but quite firmly and, as a group, unambiguously so. Englishness even became an aspect of their politics.

Before turning to the various factors that caused the collective shifts in identity, it is worth turning for a moment to the level of the individual for a reminder that people made conscious or unconscious decisions about their identities for various, often highly personal reasons. A good illustration of this comes from the case of Orderic Vitalis, the son of an immigrant priest, who spent most of his life in a Norman monastery but chose, and fiercely held on to, an English identity. Marjorie Chibnall has argued, and I agree, that his Englishness must have stemmed partly from a (probably) English mother, and that his first teacher, Siward, helped instill in him an identification with the conquered English.[46] Both of these factors could have been fairly common. But I would suggest a third major influence that was of a less ordinary nature, namely the trauma of being torn from home and family at the age of 10 and shipped off to a Norman monastery. This seems to have been an extremely painful experience for Orderic.[47] Years later he remembered feeling 'an exile in Normandy . . . unknown to all, knowing no one', describing himself as an outsider, 'an Englishman . . . a barbarous and unknown foreigner'. A particularly difficult aspect of the experience was parting from his father; for though he described both as weeping, he still felt as though his father was sending him off 'as if a stepson, hateful to him'. Psychohistory is a dangerous enterprise for a period so removed from our own, especially given the parlous state of our own knowledge

---

[45] Ralph of Coggeshall, *Radulphi de Coggeshall Chronicon Anglicanum*, ed. Joseph Stevenson (London, 1875), 175, 179–80, 182, 185; Luard, *Annales Monastici*, 3: 45, 47, 51; *The Barnwell Chronicle*, in *The Historical Collections of Walter of Coventry*, William Stubbs, ed. (London, 1873), 2: 230, 233; Anonymous of Béthune, *Histoire des ducs de Normandie*, 148–9, 170, 172, 174, 177, 184–7, 190, 193–6, 198, 201–2; Meyer, *L'Histoire de Guillaume le Maréchal*, 2: 180, 225, 243, 247, 275; Roger of Wendover, *The Flowers of History*, ed. Henry G. Hewlett, vol. 2 (London, 1887), 200, 216, 221–2; Thomas Wright, ed., *The Political Songs of England from the Reign of John to that of Edward II* (London, 1839), 19–23; *GCO* 4: 174–5; H. François Delaborde, ed., *Oeuvres de Rigord et de Guillaume le Breton*, vol. 1 (Paris, 1885), 313–14. See also Rymer, *Foedera*, 1: 148. Michael Clanchy (who otherwise notes the way the struggle is framed in terms of Englishness) has noted one passage in the poem of William the Marshall, in which the Normans in the royalist army demanded the first blow in the battle as their prerogative, as evidence of residual Norman pride, but since both the younger William Marshall, who was seen as an intermediary, and the earl of Chester, who was awarded the privilege instead, were implicitly seen as not belonging to this group, it is likely that it represents exiles or mercenaries rather than Anglo-Normans: Meyer, *L'Histoire de Guillaume le Maréchal*, 220–1; Clanchy, *England and its Rulers*, 181.

[46] *EHOV* 1: 2; Marjorie Chibnall, *The World of Orderic Vitalis* (Oxford, 1984), 9–11.

[47] *EHOV* 3: 6–8, 150; 6: 552–4.

of the human psyche, but surely it is not unreasonable to speculate that a strong ambivalence about his immigrant father and his father's action in sending him off to a strange land may have played a role in Orderic's steadfast clinging to (his mother's?) English identity. If I am right about this, a very important factor in Orderic's strongly felt Englishness was an individual response to an uncommon experience. In the discussion of the broad factors contributing to the triumph of English identity that follows, it is worth remembering that these factors were mediated through the lives and experiences, each unique, of individuals such as Orderic, and that the collective adoption of Englishness by the descendants of the invaders emerged from an accumulation of individual decisions and beliefs based on individual histories.

7

Ideology, Prejudice, and Assimilation

PART II OF this book is devoted to the first of my three levels of approach, personal interaction, but before turning to that I need to discuss attitudes towards ethnicity and assimilation, which, of course, also relate to the level of construct. The evidence is scanty, and one cannot speak of official or even organized ideology, but rather of outlooks and ways of thinking. To the degree that people thought about these issues, I will argue, there was a loose bias towards ethnic concord and assimilation. There were also several ideological factors that indirectly supported the trend toward amity and unification. None of these attitudes were strongly held, and the effects of some ideologies were limited precisely because they were indirect. Equally important, however, there was also no ideology of ethnic purity or exclusion, despite the strong pre-conquest identities of both peoples.[1]

Yet there can be no doubt that the Norman kings and the invaders practised what we would call discrimination along ethnic lines in their restructuring of the secular elites and in their ecclesiastical appointments. What were the roots of this obvious and established discrimination and how can it be reconciled with the apparent swiftness and ease of assimilation? I believe that they are reconcilable because the prejudice was pragmatic in nature rather than being ideologically based, or founded on deep-seated cultural biases, and that once the practical reasons for discrimination passed, so too did the discrimination. William of Malmesbury argued that the Normans normally treated foreigners with whom they lived well, but that William the Conqueror had dispossessed and killed English landholders and barred English monks and clerics from the highest positions in the church out of necessity.[2] That Normans practiced tolerance on pragmatic grounds, making use of the personnel and skills of their subject peoples, has nearly become a cliché. What I suggest here is that they could also practice intolerance on the same grounds. The Normans did have a certain ethnocentric feeling of cultural superiority to the English.[3] But this was nothing compared to the kinds of prejudices that existed

---

[1] See, however, Michelle R. Warren, *History on the Edge: Excalibur and the Borders of Britain, 1100–1300* (Minneapolis, 2000), 43–8, for an argument that incidents in Geoffrey of Monmouth express anxiety about ethnic intermingling.

[2] *WMGR* 470.

[3] See below, pp. 241–57.

against the Jews, or those that developed against Celtic and Slavic peoples, particularly in the twelfth century, and helped to create very strong ethnic barriers indeed.

Part of the reason why the Normans felt no apparent desire for ethnic purity stems from their origin myth. Though the Normans emphasized that the bulk of their ancestors were Danish, they nonetheless saw themselves explicitly as a heterogeneous and new people.[4] In a vision by Rollo in which the hero's destiny is revealed, a key moment in the Norman myth as expounded by Dudo, Rollo sees birds flocking together to bathe peacefully. Dudo has a Christian captive interpret this by saying that men of diverse provinces and kingdoms will come under Rollo's lordship. Later, once Rollo has gained territory in France, Dudo says that he offered safety to all peoples (*gentes*) and filled the land with his soldiers and foreigners. A hagiographic work on the relics and miracles of St Vulfrann, which Elisabeth van Houts dates to 1053–4, describes Rollo as instituting laws and rights to conciliate men of all types and arts and make one people (*populus*) out of diverse peoples (*gentes*). In a vividly imagined encounter between Saint Romanus and some demons, in the *vita* of that saint, in which the arrival of the Normans is prophesied, Romanus predicts that this group, once 'not a people' (*non populus*), would become a people of God (*populus dei*).[5] Even the term Norman, or north man, suggests a heterogeneous Scandinavian background. Thus, the idea that the Normans were a mixed people was implicit or explicit in several sources. Moreover, according to Dudo and William of Jumièges, some of Rollo's followers were English.[6] Thus, there were strong precedents within the Norman myth itself for assimilation, though generally involving the assimilation of other people to the Normans, rather than the reverse.

This willingness to assimilate did not disappear when the Normans began their series of conquests beyond Normandy. William of Apulia, in his biography of Robert Guiscard, written at the end of the eleventh century, stated that during an early part of the Norman conquests of southern Italy the Normans accepted any malefactors who fled to them, and taught them their own language and customs, 'so that one people would be made', and while this hardly suggests assimilation as an ideological end, it does indicate that William of Apulia's Norman patrons saw it as a useful tool.[7] Closer to home, William of Malmesbury wrote in his description of the Normans that they were accustomed to join in marriage with those they conquered, and linked this with calling them the most benign of peoples.[8] The evidence

[4] Bates, *Normandy Before 1066*, 56–7; Davis, *Normans and their Myth*, 36–7, 53; Searle, *Predatory Kinship*, 2, 244; Potts, 'Norman Identity', 139, 142; Marjorie Chibnall, *The Debate on the Norman Conquest* (Manchester, 1999), 126–7; Albu, *Normans in their Histories*, 17–18.

[5] Dudo, *De Moribus*, 146–7, 171; Laporte, 'Sancti Wulfranni', 27; Elisabeth M. C. van Houts, 'Historiography and Hagiography at Saint-Wandrille: the *Inventio et Miracula Sancti Vulfranni*', ANS 12: 237; Lifshitz, *Norman Conquest of Pious Neustria*, 250.

[6] Dudo, *De Moribus*, 148, 160; *GND* 1: 32, 58–60. This may have resulted from *Anglo-Scandinavian* immigration to Normandy (see Bates, *Normandy Before 1066*, 7), but the sources only speak of English.

[7] William of Apulia, *Geste de Robert Guiscard*, 108.

[8] WMGR 460. As William's comments on the Norman adaptation of English gluttony, drunkenness, and luxurious living show, however, he did not view all forms of acculturation in a positive light: WMGR 458, 472.

is limited, but what there is suggests an atmosphere among the Normans that was open to intermarriage and assimilation.

One might also note that Bede's origin legend of the English implicitly points to assimilation as well, a fact that scholars rarely note, partly because Bede's emphasis is on the unity of the English people. Any reader who went to Bede to find out the origins of the English (and where else would any medieval reader go but to Bede or sources derived from him?) would learn that there were not originally one but three peoples (*populi*), the Angles or English, Saxons, and Jutes. Another passage in Bede implies that some ancestors might come from other Continental peoples as well.[9] Bede saw his three main groups as being the ancestors of the inhabitants of various kingdoms or regions such as Northumbria, Kent, or the Isle of Wight, and 'English' for him was more an umbrella term than a description of one people created out of three. But once separate Saxon and Jutish identities had disappeared, anyone familiar with Bede would have had to see the English as a mixture of these three peoples. It is still easy to unconsciously read Bede through the prism of past 'Germanist' scholarship, as much as we may rebel against its racist basis, and to therefore treat the Angles, Saxons, and Jutes as 'really' being one people. There is no reason to believe that medieval readers would have had the same view, and thus they were more likely to see assimilation as part of the English myth. The importance of the assimilation of peoples implicit in Bede's model once the Jutes and Saxons had disappeared as separate groups in England should not be exaggerated, since it was never, to my knowledge, used as a precedent to encourage the assimilation of later immigrants. However, it would have made any attempt to base English identity purely on biological descent from time immemorial difficult.

There is little evidence of any conscious policy to promote assimilation in the post-conquest period, such as modern nation states have sometimes instituted, though it is interesting that Walter Map could envision Henry I purposefully working to promote unity.[10] Instead, what little evidence we have suggests that contemporaries favoured ethnic concord and that assimilation was accepted as a fact of life, and perhaps viewed in a slightly positive way. For instance, William of Malmesbury certainly favoured the Norman openness to intermarriage, as we have seen, though of course the fact that he was of mixed background may have played a role.

Less directly, as several scholars have noted, the writers Gaimar and Aelred of Rievaulx took, in their works, a very conciliatory approach that could support ethnic harmony. Gaimar, who was probably an immigrant or of immigrant stock, wrote an entertaining history of England in French drawing heavily on at least one version of the Anglo-Saxon Chronicle.[11] Though Gaimar's main interest was in telling a good story, the very act of conveying English history to a Francophone

---

[9] Bede, *Bede's Ecclesiastical History of the English People*, ed. Bertram Colgrave and R. A. B. Mynors (Oxford, 1969), 50, 476. For discussion of this passage, see Walter Pohl, 'Ethnic Names and Identities in the British Isles: A Comparative Perspective', in *The Anglo-Saxons from the Migration Period to the Eighth Century: An Ethnographic Perspective*, ed. John Hines (Woodbridge, 1997), 12, 14–15.

[10] Walter Map, *De Nugis Curialium*, 436.

[11] For Gaimar, see Williams, *ENC* 181–3; Gillingham, *English in the Twelfth Century*, 235.

audience was noteworthy. More important, he criticized William I for his treatment of the northern English nobility, and made the English rebel, Hereward, the hero of a substantial portion of his history.[12]

Aelred of Rievaulx was a more prominent advocate of ethnic concord and assimilation.[13] If one accepts his interpretation of the green tree prophecy at face value, there was no need for an advocate for conciliation by the 1160s, but we have already seen grounds for suspicion that affairs were more complex. I suspect that Aelred's statement had a touch of advocacy in it, and that he was not only describing a change that had taken place, but also suggesting how things ought to be. Hints of Aelred acting as an advocate for reconciliation can also be found elsewhere. Some years earlier he wrote a work called *Genealogia Regum Anglorum*, dedicated to the future Henry II.[14] Aelred undoubtedly designed this work to inspire the future king, descended through his grandmother, Edith-Matilda, from the West Saxon line, with pride in the English part of his ancestry. But Aelred was also holding up these kings as models for Henry, and one of the reasons he gives for praising Edgar was that 'he settled the kingdom of the English into a heavenly peace, and joined peoples of different tongues by the pact of one law'.[15] Whether this refers to Edgar's hegemonic dominance over surrounding peoples throughout the British Isles or the assimilation of the Vikings, it would suggest that Aelred saw the promotion of ethnic amity as an important lesson for Henry.

I would also point to the fact that in his various works Aelred gave a strikingly positive view of the Normans and the Norman Conquest. He accepted William's claims without question, savagely criticized King Harold and his family, and noted the reforms brought by the invaders.[16] As we shall see, other English writers accepted some or all of the Norman version of the conquest, but most at least criticized the Normans for their behaviour during that conquest. None of this appears in Aelred's works, and in his account of the battle of the Standard he placed a long speech depicting the glorious military successes of the Normans in the mouth of the nobleman Walter Espec.[17] In part, Aelred's charity toward the conquerors probably stemmed from the fact that the wounds in English society caused by the conquest had begun to heal, but he may also have desired to bring about reconciliation by abandoning the hostile debates between the two peoples and treating the rifts between them and the oppression of the English as things of the past. In addition, he avoided offence to the Normans while promoting the history of the English and celebrating the good qualities of both peoples. How Henry II and others reacted is unknown, but Aelred at least was one influential intellectual who both advocated and celebrated reconciliation and assimilation.

---

[12] Gaimar, *L'Estoire des Engleis*, 171, 173–81.
[13] Williams, *ENC*, 182–6; Short, '*Tam Angli quam Franci*', 169–72; Rosalind Ransford, 'A Kind of Noah's Ark: Aelred of Rievaulx and National Identity', in *Religion and National Identity*, ed. Stuart Mews (Oxford, 1982), 137–46.
[14] Aelred of Rievaulx, 'Genealogia Regum Anglorum', *PL* 195: 711–38.
[15] Ibid. 726.
[16] Ibid. 734; Aelred of Rievaulx, 'Vita S. Edwardi Regis', 747–8, 765–7, 772–3, 777–9.
[17] Aelred of Rievaulx, 'Relatio de Standardi', 185–9.

Moreover, though there was no official ideology of assimilation, there clearly was a theoretical policy, stemming from the king, that the conquered English had rights and should be treated justly. William claimed to be the rightful heir to King Edward, and a corollary to this claim was the expectation that he should act as a king ought to towards his new subjects.[18] The D version of the Anglo-Saxon Chronicle records that Archbishop Ealdred forced William to swear an oath, before he would crown him, 'that he would treat this people as well as any king before him did, if they were loyal to him'.[19] The Norman sources mention no such oath, but William of Poitiers in particular stressed the king's just treatment of the conquered English.[20] Steps were taken to ensure that the English were not mistreated beyond what was militarily necessary. One of the most striking documents to come out of the conquest was the ordinance detailing a series of penances imposed by Norman bishops and a papal legate on William's soldiers. Penances were imposed even for actions in the battle of Hastings, or against rebels after William's coronation, but greater penances were imposed for killing when plundering for gain rather than supplies, for offences against women, for violations of churches, and for ordinary killings.[21] In short, the English were not simply fair game, but instead sharp distinctions were drawn between proper and improper behaviour toward them, and even violence done in the proper circumstances required penance.

William's rulings concerning legal procedure noted in Chapter 4, even if they may have been slanted toward the conquerors as some scholars argue, clearly established that the English had rights and ought to be treated accordingly in courts of law.[22] The summoning of half-French and half-English juries for the Domesday inquest not only provided the survey's commissioners with a source of information from King Edward's time, but also theoretically provided the two communities with an equal voice in one of the most important endeavours of the new government. William was constrained by his own claims to the throne, his oaths, and his propaganda to create an 'official' policy of treating the English justly, perhaps even equally. Concern for amity between the English and Normans continued to be reflected in later legal compilations made in the Anglo-Norman period, as Bruce O'Brien has argued in relation to the *Leges Edwardi* and a collection from St Paul's Cathedral.[23] In particular, compilations attributed to William I have the king

---

[18] For a detailed discussion of William's early propaganda and its consequences, see George Garnett, 'Coronation and Propaganda: Some Implications of the Norman Claim to the Throne of England in 1066', *TRHS* 5th ser., 36 (1986), 91–116. For the difference that different rationales of conquest made between England and Ireland, see Robin Frame, ' "Les Engleys Nées in Irlande": The English Political Identity in Medieval Ireland', *TRHS* 6th ser., 3 (1993), 85–6.

[19] *ASC* D 1066. See also *WMGP* 252.

[20] *GGWP* 158–64, 174.

[21] Whitelock *et al.*, *Councils and Synods*, vol 1, part 2, pp. 583–4; H. E. J. Cowdrey, 'Bishop Ermenfrid of Sion and the Penitential Ordinance following the Battle of Hastings', *Journal of Ecclesiastical History*, 20 (1969), 225–42; Garnett, '*Franci et Angli*', 114–16; Garnett, 'Coronation and Propaganda', 95–9.

[22] Liebermann, *Die Gesetze der Angelsachsen*, 1: 483–4, 486–8; Downer, *Leges Henrici Primi*, 120, 158. For the argument that the rulings were slanted, see Fuchs, *Domesday Book*, 150–1; Garnett, '*Franci et Angli*', 133–4. See, however, Pollock and Maitland, *History of English Law*, 1: 89–90.

[23] Bruce O'Brien, *God's Peace and the King's Peace: The Laws of Edward the Confessor* (Philadelphia, 1999), 4, 14, 17–18, 26–7.

stating that 'peace and security' or 'peace, security, concord, and justice' should be kept between the English and Normans. Though these statements are probably drawn from one of Canute's codes, and may or may not record precise legislation by William, they do reflect a continuing ideal of amity and equity under the law.[24]

Given the actual treatment of the English described in Chapter 5, this 'official' policy obviously deserves to be treated with a fair degree of cynicism. It was little consolation to peasants suffering devastation, arson, and rape that their oppressors, assuming they paid any attention to the episcopal decrees, would have to do penance. But as Freeman pointed out, if in the short run legal fictions would have caused bitterness, in the long term they could have helped lead to fusion.[25] William's willingness to tolerate a major gap between theory and practice allowed him to practise *realpolitik* without creating overtly discriminatory policies or laws that could have survived to help maintain a long-term or even permanent gap between the English and the Normans. Once political and other tensions between the two peoples eased, and cross-ethnic ties began to form, a loose policy of 'equal rights', or perhaps, 'equal rights for people of equal ranks', could, for all the short-comings that probably continued to exist in practice, have helped the process along.[26]

On the English side there developed a belief that loyalty to the new ruling house was morally acceptable, even laudable. This emphatically did not occur simply because ethnic or national allegiance was foreign to people's thinking in this period. As late as the early twelfth century, Ælnoth of Canterbury was writing a hagiography of a king who, according to Ælnoth, sought to restore 'that most noble [English] people to its pristine liberty'.[27] But several factors paved the way for the relatively swift development of English loyalty to the new dynasty. First, though one can obviously speak of 'national' loyalties, there was no cult of nationalism similar to that found in many modern societies. Second, once the English leadership had sworn oaths to William at his coronation they faced a moral dilemma in rebelling, though one many obviously found themselves able to overcome. Third, in overthrowing Harold, William had destroyed a dynasty that was less than a year old, and Edgar Atheling, who represented the traditional dynasty and lived well into Henry I's reign, eventually accepted the new ruling house.[28] By marrying Edgar's niece, Henry I, in the eyes of some natives, gained added legitimacy for his dynasty.

Fourth, and most important, was the idea that William's victory represented divine judgement, an idea that appears in English writings as early as the entry for 1066 in the D version of the Anglo-Saxon Chronicle.[29] For serious historians in the Middle Ages, the belief that God interfered frequently in human affairs to give

[24] Robertson, *Laws*, 238, 244; Kennedy, 'Cnut's Law Code', 72.

[25] Freeman, *History of the Norman Conquest*, 5: 49–51.

[26] Susan Reynolds suggested the latter phrase in a conversation at a conference, and given medieval class biases, I think it is an appropriate one.

[27] Ælnoth of Canterbury, 'Gesta Swenomagni Regis', 97.

[28] See Nicholas Hooper, 'Edgar the Ætheling: Anglo-Saxon Prince, Rebel and Crusader', *Anglo-Saxon England*, 14 (1985), 197–214, for this figure's life and relations with the Normans.

[29] *ASC* D 1066.

individuals and peoples their just reward was not simply a cliché but an analytic framework, inherited from the Bible, and the most important model by which medieval intellectuals of all sorts could decode and understand history.[30] Therefore, the success and failure of individuals or peoples, and particularly those accompanied by apparent signs of divine favour or disfavour, could be used, in their eyes, as objective evidence of the rightness or wrongness of a cause. For example, William of Malmesbury clearly had doubts about the defence that the English made for Earl Waltheof, namely that he was forced into the 1075 conspiracy, but said that the miracles at the earl's tomb would seem to support the argument.[31] The Norman Conquest, preceded by a comet, largely determined by a single decisive battle, and wide-reaching in its effects, was an obvious candidate for interpretation involving divine intervention.

God, it could be argued, had clearly sanctioned William's claim, and acceptance of him as king and allegiance to the new regime was therefore not only expedient but an acceptable moral choice, perhaps even a duty. Not everyone agreed with this point of view, as the many rebellions show, but the very destruction of those uprisings would only have supported the idea that God was on William's side. Orderic Vitalis, despite harshly criticizing the oppression that led to the rebellions early in William's reign, nevertheless praised the English who remained loyal to the new king, saying of them that they 'kept their faith to God and revered the king established by him'.[32] Orderic, of course, had strong ties to the invaders, but it is striking that several laudatory sources record Bishop Wulfstan of Worcester's support for the new regime, including his military support during the rebellions of 1075 and 1088.[33] In the modern world a figure like Wulfstan could easily be reviled as a collaborator, and one may well wonder how he was viewed by exiles, but the sources that survive depict him as a saint. Even the writer of the *Gesta Herwardi*, one of the most anti-Norman pieces of the period, recorded Hereward (probably ahistorically) as making an honourable peace with King William and living out his days as a loyal subject.[34] Loyalty to the new regime was clearly not something that writers felt needed to be explained away, but was viewed as entirely compatible with upright, even heroic or saintly, behaviour.

In this context, it is worth noting the emphasis in many sources on the support provided by the English for William the Conqueror and his sons. This emphasis had more than one purpose, as I shall argue later, but one was to stress the specific loyalty of many English people to the new regime. The approbation of writers for this support only underscores the argument made above concerning loyalty to the

[30] See R. W. Southern, *Scholastic Humanism and the Unification of Europe*, vol. 1 (Oxford, 1995), 102–33, for the importance of the Bible in general for intellectuals. For discussion of the issue of divine will in early British historiography, see Hanning, *Vision of History in Early Britain*.

[31] *WMGR* 468–70; *WMGP* 321–2.

[32] *EHOV* 2: 206–7 (Chibnall's translation).

[33] *ASC* E 1088; *CJW* 3: 24, 52–6; *VW* 24, 26, 34. Mason, however, does suggest that Coleman downplayed Wulfstan's role in the Norman government, though he did not hide it completely: Emma Mason, *St Wulfstan of Worcester, c. 1008–1095* (Oxford, 1990), 131–2.

[34] Hugh M. Thomas, 'The *Gesta Herwardi*, the English, and their Conquerors', *ANS* 21: 229–31.

new dynasty. More important, it suggests that acceptance of loyalty to the new regime extended well beyond the handful of writers who discuss the issue. Of course, many people supported the new regime out of simple expedience, but the existence of arguments to justify collaboration would have made this psychologically much easier. Increasing loyalty to the new regime, the arguments that supported it, and the open emphasis put on it by writers were crucial to relations between the English and Normans. By decreasing the risk of violent English revolt, these factors helped prevent the continued stoking of ethnic hatreds. A strong loyalty to the king gave writers, and perhaps others, licence to criticize the conquerors in general, as we shall see, letting off dangerous steam on the one side, and perhaps prompting change on the other. Most important, the fact of, and equally, the advertisement of English loyalty helped bridge the political gap between the Normans and English, and it is noteworthy that the natives last appear as an independent political or military factor during their support for Henry I at the beginning of his reign. Kings and nobles who did not fear the English would be less likely to take measures to restrict English power and preserve ethnic boundaries. In the short run the English gained little apparent benefit from their loyalty, and indeed the Anglo-Saxon Chronicle records that William II kept the promises he made to the English in return for their support for only a short time.[35] But in the long run barriers to English advancement disappeared as ethnic boundaries broke down and able or lucky natives prospered through service to the king and other lords.

In Chapter 4 I noted that minor religious differences served to divide the English and Normans, but as one might expect, the theme of shared Christianity played a role in promoting reconciliation. For instance, it certainly helped undergird the theory that the English should be treated justly. William of Poitiers portrayed William the Conqueror, having told his chief men to be mindful of God, as stating that they should not excessively oppress the conquered, who were 'equals in Christian faith to the victors'.[36] On the other side, the theme of shared Christianity could be used to urge acceptance of foreign influence in the church. Goscelin of Saint-Bertin, who was a pre-conquest immigrant but sympathized with the conquered, recorded an interesting episode in his collection of the miracles of St Augustine of Canterbury, whom Goscelin frequently described by such terms as 'patron of England', 'guardian of the *patria*', or 'father of the English'. In this miracle, King Æthelstan, having collected a fleet at Sandwich to combat a foreign invasion, turns aside to pray at the saint's shrine. One of his chief men, complaining that the king is not with the host, sarcastically says, 'how beautiful that the king of so many peoples bows at the tomb of some dead foreigner'. In response the king describes how much is owed to the missionary for coming to settle, preach, and convert. The detractor ignores all this, rides off in a fury, and of course immediately suffers divine punishment in the form of a fatal accident. 'Rightly he inherited hell,' wrote Goscelin, 'who disinherited our patriarch from this, his *patria*, with brutish arrogance.' The obvious message of this story is to warn against denigrating St

---

[35] *ASCE* 1088.   [36] *GGWP* 158.

Augustine. But given that this story was written by an immigrant churchman, who may have been under the patronage of another immigrant churchman, Anselm, there may well be a secondary message, namely that the English owed their faith to immigrant missionaries and would be unwise to reject the guidance of later immigrants.[37] The role of figures such as Lanfranc and Anselm will be explored more fully later, but here it suffices to say that many pro-English writers did praise the reformers who came to England after the Norman Conquest.

The ideals of the church could also be used to attack discrimination, at least on a limited scale. Eadmer lashed out at Henry I's custom, abetted by bishops and magnates, of appointing as abbots only foreigners who hated the English and passing over the natives. He argued that those passed over were no less qualified than the foreigners, but that no amount of virtue could win an Englishman an appointment, whereas the mere appearance of goodness was sufficient for foreigners.[38] Obviously this is evidence of continuing bias against the English, but the point to note in this context is that Eadmer clearly believed that any such bias was self-evidently wrong. Here, the theoretically meritocratic values of the church were used to urge an end to discriminatory practice, at least with ecclesiastical appointments. As usual, it is nearly impossible to assess the direct impact of Eadmer's statement, or whether such arguments were frequently made, but discrimination within the church did eventually end, and it is possible that this and similar appeals may have played a role. Appeals to shared Christianity almost certainly formed a significant ideological component of the quest for reconciliation.

All in all, this is a pretty modest harvest of ideology and advocacy concerning ethnicity, ethnic relations, and assimilation, and much of it is derived from ideals of kingship and Christian behaviour only indirectly related to those subjects. This in itself reveals one of the major differences between the medieval and modern period. Modern nationalist movements have been accompanied by a tremendous amount of theorizing, which in multi-ethnic states has generally involved thinking about ethnic relations as well. As a result, ideologies of ethnic purity, racism, assimilation, and multiculturalism have spread widely. In the late eleventh and early twelfth centuries, the revival of complex systems of intellectual thought that formed an essential part of what scholars call the Twelfth Century Renaissance was only in its early stages, and the efforts of intellectuals were usually focused on theology. As the intellectual revival proceeded, scholars began thinking increasingly about politics, law, and other topics we would consider secular, but the fact remains that in this period thinking about ethnic relations, assimilation, and ethnic aspects of politics tended to remain in the sphere of common sense, custom, and unreasoned premise.[39] To give two examples of this, Orderic Vitalis spoke of Viking rulers

[37] Goscelin of Saint-Bertin, 'Libellus de Miraculis Sancti Augustini', *AASS* 1: 539. For Goscelin's connection to Anselm, see Goscelin of Canterbury, 'Historia Translationis S. Augustini Episcopi', 13.

[38] *HN* 224 (see also 191–2).

[39] This last phrase comes from Susan Reynolds, who has reconstructed much early medieval political theory in the absence of theoretical treatises and the like: Reynolds, *Kingdoms and Communities*, 250, 320.

supplanting English kings who ruled England 'naturally', and Osbert of Clare, describing the accession of Edward the Confessor after the reigns of Canute and his sons, wrote of the kingdom leaving 'Egyptian servitude', and receiving a king who was *innatus*, which could mean both native and natural.[40] Here, the assumption seems to be that England ought to be ruled by native English kings, but this idea remains a passing assumption and no more.

In short, the English and Normans did not have much of a theoretical framework for dealing with relations between ethnic groups. This made a difference in two ways. First, theories of ethnic relations, no matter how viciously irrational (one thinks of Nazi theorizing), when actively propagated by institutions or movements are far more likely to have a sustained and consistent impact than casual assumptions and attitudes. It is noteworthy that neither Orderic nor Osbert felt the need to apply the logic of the assumptions noted above to the Norman case. Obviously it is hard to assess the impact of an absence of theory, since various theories would have had very different consequences. But it is certainly true that as long as other factors were conducive to assimilation, the absence of theory meant that there were no strong ideological bars to it. Second, the absence of theory limited and concealed discussion of ethnic relations and assimilation in the sources. Ethnic relations and identity did matter a great deal to intellectuals, and undoubtedly to others, in the period, as shall become clear in the course of this work. But in the absence of the widespread body of theory about ethnic relations available even to ordinary modern people, there was no precedent, and perhaps no perceived need, for dealing with the subject in a systematic way. Moreover, writers lacked any models or sophisticated vocabulary to call upon, and were more likely to operate in the realm of assumption and stereotype. Thus the modern historian is left with little direct evidence either for what relations between the two people were like or how people thought they should be. It is worth reiterating, however, that what little evidence survives for the latter question does suggest that people were more likely than not to be in favour of ethnic harmony and assimilation.

One must, of course, ask why pragmatic prejudice did not develop into ideological prejudice, as it sometimes does when people want to justify their biases. One must also ask how the English overcame the mild ethnocentrism that did exist, as we shall see. The ideological factors that indirectly supported ethnic harmony and the casual attitudes that favoured assimilation were hardly strong enough on their own to ensure the unification of the two peoples, nor do they explain the absorption of the Normans by the English rather than the reverse. They did, of course, play their part, but the lack of any strong ideology concerning ethnicity in the period means that one must turn to other factors to understand the outcome of relations between the English and their conquerors.

---

[40] *EHOV* 2: 340; Osbert of Clare, 'Édouard le Confesseur', 73.

PART II

Personal Interaction, Assimilation, and Identity

8

The Interaction of English and Normans: Methodological Considerations

ASSIMILATION AND THE construction and maintenance of ethnic identities are social processes, and one must not lose sight of the fact that individual humans are the driving force behind them. Individual people, by developing new relationships across ethnic lines over the course of generations, cumulatively create assimilation. By exchanging beliefs, practices, and ideas between different groups, they bring about cultural assimilation. The collective impact of their personal decisions causes the loss, maintenance, or triumph of a particular ethnic identity. Part II is designed to look at the people behind the processes and to explore, to the extent possible, the interaction of Normans and English within different social groups. Before turning to the substance of this Part, however, I need to address important issues and problems of methodology, terminology, evidence, and definition, some of them quite thorny.

First, because the interaction occurred over several generations, I need to address the precise role of descent in ethnicity in this society.[1] Though modern scholarship has thoroughly discredited any belief in a biological basis for ethnicity, descent was still one tremendously important factor in the medieval period. It mattered mainly because families were normally the single most important conduit for the transmission of culture and identity, which is one reason why people, then as now, were inclined to link ethnicity and descent. Ethnicity is often culturally inherited, though it is not biologically based.

Descent also mattered because birth was one of the things that medieval people considered when they thought about ethnic identity. The speeches on behalf of Battle Abbey attributed to Richard de Lucy, in which Norman identity is clearly linked to familial descent, illustrate this best.[2] It should be noted that what matters in terms of identity is ancestry *as it was acknowledged and remembered*. In the short term, of course, most people would have been quite aware of the ethnic identities of their immediate forebears, and would have found it hard lie about such matters.

---

[1] The published debate contained in Pohl, 'Ethnic Names and Identities in the British Isles', 35–8, contains a good example of excellent scholars talking past each other on this subject.

[2] Searle, *Chronicle of Battle Abbey*, 178–82.

But over the long term the memory of inconvenient ancestors could be discarded, downplayed, or simply not preserved, and thus people could reshape their ancestry to suit their needs. In this respect, it was not the biological facts themselves that mattered so much as how they were preserved and presented. Nonetheless, ancestry affected ethnic identity, even if genetic inheritance did not.

By exploring the interaction and intermixing of two originally discrete (or largely discrete) groups over the course of several generations, I will be following in Part II a traditional approach to understanding assimilation and shifts in identity. By focusing largely on ethnicity by descent, I will also be ignoring, for the time being, individual shifts in ethnic identity that had nothing to do with ancestry. This, of course, is not because I reject current thinking about the culturally constructed and fluid nature of ethnicity. On the contrary, one of my arguments in Part II will be that intermixing and even intermarriage cannot fully explain why an aristocracy that retained many aspects of Continental culture, many ties to the Continent, and a strong belief in its Norman ancestry merged with the conquered people and adopted an English identity. But work on constructions of identity sometimes make them seem free-floating, almost random, barely connected to culture and not at all to the people who make up the groups involved. It is time to investigate how constructed identities were anchored not just to culture but also to individuals and the interaction between identity, culture, and people.

Because descent mattered in ethnicity, I will be focusing to some degree on intermarriage and sexual relations. The importance of intermarriage was recognized in the twelfth century, most notably in the famous statement in the *Dialogue of the Exchequer* that the French and English had become so intermingled through living together and intermarrying that among free people it was impossible to distinguish between them.[3] Intermarriage also mattered in terms of identity. When William of Malmesbury wrote that he could take a middle road between Norman praise and English criticism of William the Conqueror because he had the blood of both peoples in him, he was establishing a hereditary link to both ethnic groups.[4] But one of my key arguments is that study of a *variety* of social relationships is crucial to understanding assimilation and identity. All too often, assimilation is equated simply with intermarriage. What might be called biological assimilation may be crucial to broader assimilation, but marriages and sexual unions take place and therefore must be studied in the context of a broad range of social relationships.

Where two peoples are divided by mutual hatred, or by strong ideological barriers such as a deeply felt religious difference, marriage is very rare, which allows ethnic division to persist. Intermarriage promotes assimilation, but is only likely to take place in the context of a broader rapprochement. Moreover, in the class- and status-conscious societies of the Middle Ages, relatives and others who had a say in marriage generally expected at least broad social parity between spouses, something to keep in mind in light of the gap in power and wealth between English and Normans after the conquest. Casual sex and unsanctioned sexual partnerships can

---

[3] Richard Fitz Nigel, *Dialogus de Scaccario*, 53.
[4] WMGR 424.

cross entrenched ethnic, racial, or class boundaries more easily, but that does not necessarily lead to assimilation, because broader relations and social mores often determine how resulting children are treated. To take only the most obvious example, sexual relations between people of European, African, and Native American origins were common in the European colonies in the New World, but did not lead to assimilation. Children of such unions were generally lumped in with the subordinate group or formed new intermediate groups of mestizos and mulattos, and as a result the racial categories and constructs developed in the colonial period still remain strong. Obviously the experience of England after the conquest was quite different. To understand why, and to fully understand the transformation of ethnic relations and the destruction of ethnic boundaries, it is necessary to look not just at sex and marriage, but at a variety of relationships, including friendship, working relationships, and ties of lordship or obedience, neighbourhood, and profession.

In talking about English and Normans in terms of descent as well as in terms of constructed identity, however, I face a problem of terminology. This is a problem that also existed in the primary sources. As noted earlier, the term English can and could be used in quite different ways. First, it could describe people with that identity before the conquest and their descendants afterwards. Second, it could describe all those who saw themselves or were seen as English after the conquest, whatever their descent. Contemporaries only rarely distinguished the two. In Part II, when I refer to the English without qualification I will be referring to the former, whom I will also describe as the natives or native English in parallel with the Latin *indigeni*, which was used in the *Dialogue of the Exchequer*.[5] Similarly, I will describe the conquerors and their descendants as Normans or immigrants, even though the shift to an English identity was under way from the beginning. Though necessarily somewhat arbitrary, my usage will, I hope, at least be clear.

A temporary focus on those who were English and Norman by descent, however, raises an even greater methodological problem, namely how to trace the two groups over several generations. Genealogical information normally remains only for the very greatest families, and can be spotty even for them. As for lesser members of the landholding classes, little information exists between Domesday Book and the middle of the twelfth century for many families, and hardly any at all survives for townspeople, ordinary clerics, and peasants. Only rarely was an individual's ethnicity described, and even then we cannot always be certain that the identity in question was based on descent. Other indications of ethnicity can sometimes be found, especially in Domesday Book.[6] But the most important indicators of ethnic descent are names, especially forenames but also bynames. Unfortunately, they are also tricky and problematic indicators, and therefore their use requires a certain amount of explanation and justification.

Forenames can be used as ethnic indicators because the naming pools of the

[5] Richard Fitz Nigel, *Dialogus de Scaccario*, 53–5, 64.

[6] See Thomas, 'Significance and Fate', forthcoming, for discussion of ethnic identifiers in Domesday Book.

English and of the invaders were generally quite distinct—Edwards, Wulfstans, and Brictrics on one side, Williams, Ralphs, and Roberts on the other. A number of scholars have worked on the subject of onomastics in Domesday Book and other sources from the period, and the great majority of names, particularly the more popular ones, can easily be assigned to one of the pools.[7] A number of problems should be noted, however. First, there are some names that simply cannot be classified, but fortunately they were held by a tiny fraction of the population. More important, because of the common Scandinavian influence on nomenclature in England and Normandy, which gave both groups names such as Thorkel and Wimund, and because of a few anomalous cases such as the English name Alfred, which had gained popularity in Brittany before the conquest, there is a certain over-lap between the name pools. Naturally, I have avoided using any names common to both pools as ethnic indicators in the absence of other evidence about the ethnicity of their bearers. Such names were held by a larger number of people than the unclassifiable names, but still a small part of the population. These two problems are relatively minor ones.

A far greater problem was the tendency for people from one group to give their children names from the naming pool of the other group, if that group was politi-cally dominant. The shifts in naming practices began even before the conquest, when the children of French immigrants established in England in Edward the Confessor's time received English names.[8] Far more serious difficulties arise from the widespread adoption of Continental names, and of biblical, patristic, and non-English saints' names, by the English after the conquest.[9] This started with the more prosperous of the surviving English and spread down the social ranks until the Old English naming pool had almost completely vanished. This shifting of naming patterns, along with the other problems, naturally creates havoc with the use of names as ethnic indicators. Cecily Clark and more recently C. P. Lewis have written eloquently on some of the problems involved, and the dangers of assuming too much about descent from names, which may reveal more about cultural influences or 'socio-linguistic attitude' than ancestry. Obviously these dangers must be taken seriously.[10] Nonetheless, forenames can be used as reasonably reliable indicators of ethnic background in two ways.

[7] The chief authorities on which I have relied are Olof von Feilitzen, *The Pre-Conquest Personal Names of Domesday Book* (Uppsala, 1937); Adigard des Gautries, *Les Noms de personnes scandinaves*; Gillian Fellows Jensen, *Scandinavian Personal Names in Lincolnshire and Yorkshire* (Copenhagen, 1968); Thorvald Forssner, *Continental-Germanic Personal Names in England in Old and Middle English Times* (Uppsala, 1916). The works of Cecily Clark have also proved very useful. Many of her important articles have been collected in *Words, Names and History*. See also Cecily Clark, 'English Personal Names Ca. 650–1300: Some Prosopographical Bearings', *Medieval Prosopography*, 8 (1987), 31–60; id., 'Onomastics', 542–606.

[8] Lewis, 'French in England', 136.

[9] Cecily Clark provides an overview of this process in 'Onomastics', 552–62. See also David Postles, 'Cultures of Peasant Naming in Twelfth-Century England', *Medieval Prosopography*, 18 (1997), 25–54.

[10] Clark, 'English Personal Names', 31–2, 36–7; id., *Words, Names and History*, 222–7; C. P. Lewis, 'Joining the Dots: A Methodology for Identifying the English in Domesday Book', in *Family Trees and the Roots of Politics: The Prosopography of Britain and France from the Tenth to the Twelfth Century*, ed. K. S. B. Keats-Rohan (Woodbridge, 1997), 70–7. The term 'socio-linguistic attitude' comes from Lewis.

First, as Clark pointed out, names in documents from the first generation after the conquest, including the greatest source of all for the period, Domesday Book, can generally be safely used to distinguish English and Normans.[11] The children of some of Edward's Continental followers could have English names, but this was a fairly small group, whose Continental background can often be detected in other ways. A handful of identifiably English people had Norman forenames or a dual name and there may have been others like them.[12] But there are scores of instances of land passing from native landholders to their sons or other heirs between 1066 and 1086, and almost invariably the successors drew names from the pre-conquest naming pool. Thus, forenames can generally be used with confidence as ethnic indicators at least through William I's reign.

As Clark noted, names that are unambiguously from the pre-conquest English naming pool can also be used as fairly reliable indicators of at least partial English ancestry even in later generations.[13] The shift in naming patterns was one-sided, especially for men; immigrants and their male offspring almost never adopted English names in the eleventh and twelfth centuries. A good 'exception that proves the rule' is the chronicler Orderic, son of Odelarius, for even he was forced to adopt the Continental name Vitalis when he entered a Norman monastery.[14] When instances do occur of a father having a Continental name and the son an English one, it is generally because there is English or at least mixed ancestry anyway. For example, a Yorkshire knight named Torfin son of Robert turns out to be Torfin son of Robert son of Copsi, indicating an indigenous origin.[15] Thus male English names remain very good indicators of partial or, often enough, full English ancestry. Female English names are a little bit more problematic, given their slightly greater continuing popularity, but as Cecily Clark has argued, this popularity may partly be related to intermarriage and English descent on the maternal side.[16] Because there were some exceptions to the rule that no Normans adopted English names, no individual can be certainly identified as English solely because of such a name. Nonetheless, because the shifting in names was so one-sided, it is safe to assume that the overwhelming majority of people with traditional English names had partial or complete English ancestry. Fortunately none of my major arguments depend on individual people identified as English solely by name, but rather on collections of examples, in which one or two cases of mistaken identity will not invalidate the overall picture.

The real problem comes from the fact that Continental forenames alone are unreliable indicators of ethnicity after the first generation or so. Sometimes a patronym can help. A William son of Wulfstan is almost certainly English, at least in the male line. But even this becomes less useful as one moves on in time—a

---

[11] Clark, *Words, Names and History*, 128.
[12] N. E. S. A. Hamilton, *Inquisitio Comitatus Cantabrigiensis* (London, 1876), 97; Williams, *ENC* 11, 83–5; Tsurushima, 'Fraternity', 329–31; H. Tsurushima, 'Domesday Interpreters', *ANS* 18: 212–13.
[13] Clark, *Words, Names and History*, 128.
[14] *EHOV* 6: 554.
[15] *EYC* 5: 53–6.
[16] Clark, 'Women's Names in Post-Conquest England', in *Words, Names and History*, 117–43.

Robert son of William who appears in a document may in fact be a Robert son of
William son of Robert who was part of William the Conqueror's army, or he may be
a Robert son of William son of Wulfstan. This means that English people often
become hidden from view because they have Continental names and even
Continental patronyms. It also means that one can never assume that in the twelfth
century a William, Robert, or Ralph was of entirely or even partially Continental
ancestry unless there is corroborating evidence.

The difficulties of identifying people of Continental ancestry are mitigated somewhat by bynames. Bynames were just beginning to develop into family names
among the upper classes, and they can sometimes link individuals to prominent
Norman families even when genealogical sources are unavailable. Loconyms that
refer to places on the Continent are obviously fairly good indicators of Continental
background, though even here caution is needed, since sometimes people picked
up and even passed on to their descendants loconyms based, say, on a period of
study in a place.[17] The rarer bynames based on ethnic categories, such as Brito,
Peitevin, Francigena, or Franceis, some of which developed into family names, are
also useful indicators of ethnicity; for instance, Gilbert Foliot matter-of-factly
discussed one man with the byname Brito as specifically Breton.[18] As usual, such
bynames are not infallible guides. The appearance of an Edward Franceis in a
twelfth-century English document shows one case in which either the generalization about English forenames or the generalization about ethnic bynames is probably wrong.[19] But, again, it is groups of cases rather than individual ones that
support my arguments. Thus bynames, when combined with the larger amount
of genealogical information available for the Normans, can provide a partial but
reasonably good picture of the descendants of the invaders in the twelfth century.

Another important set of methodological and terminological issues concerns
class and social status. In previous work on interaction between English and
Normans class is a key variable that has received insufficient attention. Contemporaries noted that the invaders monopolized, or nearly monopolized, the positions
of greatest power after the conquest, and that the mass of ordinary people remained
overwhelmingly English.[20] Scholars have recognized this as well, but the implications of these facts for assimilation and ethnic identity have never been fully
explored. A story from the *Gesta Herwardi*, a highly romanticized account of the life
of the historical rebel Hereward, which was almost certainly written by a monk of
Ely named Richard between 1107 and 1174, can bring into focus the importance
of social status and its potential influence on ethnicity. When Hereward, a noble of
prominent ancestry (according to this account), wished to spy out William the
Conqueror's camp he trimmed his hair and beard, changed into filthy clothes, and

---

[17] Simon of Paris, who passed the loconym on to his daughter, had a father, Eadmund the physician,
and grandfather, Osmar, with English names and therefore probably a native background: Emma
Mason, *Westminster Abbey Charters, 1066–c. 1214* (London, 1998), nos. 196, 201–2, 372, 460–1.

[18] Morey and Brooke, *Letters and Charters of Gilbert Foliot*, 246.

[19] Stuart A. Moore, ed., *Cartularium Monasterii Sancti Johannis Baptiste de Colecestria*, vol. 1
(London, 1897), 180–1.

[20] WMGR 414–16; Osbert of Clare, 'Édouard le Confesseur', 109; HN 224.

adopted the guise of a common potter. In the fictionalized world of this work, his change of social class through disguise made all the difference. A witch called in by the Normans for assistance freely discussed her plans in his presence, because 'believing him to be a peasant (*rusticus*)' she assumed he spoke no French. An official and others noted the 'potter's' resemblance to Hereward, but only 'insofar as a poor man could resemble a noble, or a peasant, a knight'. Hereward's disguise therefore held. But it also got him into trouble, for the servants in the king's kitchen felt free to mock and insult him. Of course the noble hero could not endure such treatment, which drew him into a comic battle involving forks and logs; only a daring escape freed him from his predicament.[21]

At heart, this is simply an exciting and amusing story, but it nonetheless draws the reader or listener into the perspective of the commoner, or at least of the person treated as a commoner by the Normans. Little evidence survives of the actual relations between English peasants and Norman lords, but this story may give a hint of what they were like. The contemptuous dismissal of the very presence of an apparently monolingual peasant in discussions of sensitive matters, the stereotypes about class appearance that led William's officials to overlook the obvious similarity between the 'potter' and their dangerous foe, and the abuse that the disguised hero suffered at the hand of kitchen servants all reveal the sort of indignities common English people *might* have suffered. Evidence of this sort can only be taken so far, especially since humorous tales of spying in disguise were common in the Middle Ages, but the story serves as a forceful reminder that social status mattered tremendously in this society, and must be taken into account when considering ethnic relations, something that scholars fail to do when they simply assume that overall demographics were sufficient to ensure assimilation and the victory of Englishness. To put it bluntly, how attractive was assimilation and identification with English peasants likely to seem to aristocrats of Continental descent? An obvious answer is that the breakdown along class and ethnic lines was much more complex than a mere division into Norman lords and English peasants. Nonetheless, it is clearly crucial to factor class into any discussion of assimilation and identity after the Norman Conquest.

I have already noted three questions raised by the issue of social status: why did the Normans eventually accept the identity of the conquered; who formed the *Traditionskern* for English identity after the virtual destruction of the English aristocracy: and how did class affect sexual relations and intermarriage? One might also ask why ethnic lines did not become permanently linked to class or social status, as they have in so many societies. For ethnically distinct elites, linking ethnicity to class and even to specific privileges is an obvious way to monopolize and protect high social status. In such instances, class divisions can become strong barriers to ethnic assimilation, and become dangerous to social harmony as well, since those denied the power and status they might otherwise have had, simply

---

[21] T. D. Hardy and C. T. Martin, eds., *Gesta Herwardi*, in *Lestorie des Engleis*, vol. 1 (London, 1889), 384–8. For further discussion of this story, see Thomas, '*Gesta Herwardi*', 226–7.

because of their ethnicity, can become dangerous fomenters of rebellion. In general, class and ethnic boundaries can easily end up reinforcing each other.[22]

In England after the conquest a certain linkage did in fact develop in the minds of some contemporaries between Englishness and peasant status. R. C. van Caenegem argues that 'English' was considered basically interchangeable with terms for serfs and peasants. He bases this on the similarities between writs limiting the English from making legal claims to land and one forbidding rustics from doing the same, and also on the view of Richard Fitz Nigel in the *Dialogue of the Exchequer* that serfs were English whereas free people had become intermixed by his day.[23] In my view, his argument that the terms were interchangeable goes too far, but there are certainly passages from the time that seem to link Englishness with the lower classes, and with rusticity in general.[24] Why, then, did the de facto linkage between ethnicity and social status in the generations following the conquest never become, as it were, de jure?

Because of the importance of class in this society, it is necessary to explore as precisely as possible the presence of English and Normans at different social levels, and to investigate the effects of social status on different kinds of relationships that crossed ethnic lines, in order to understand how assimilation occurred despite the broad differences in class and power between the two groups. On what social levels did assimilation occur most readily? To what degree did assimilation proceed between individuals of different classes? How, in practical terms, did assimilation come about despite the constraints of social intercourse across class lines? To answer these questions, I have tried to reconstruct as much as possible the ethnic make-up of various classes and social groups, drawing upon the work of others, most notably Ann Williams, as well as my own research. Obviously, given the problems with identifying Normans and English discussed earlier, I will be able to give no precise figures, but I do believe it is possible to move beyond the existing picture of the participation of the two peoples in a variety of social levels.

However, the very idea of class in this society requires some consideration. I use the word 'class' in broad terms to denote the variations of status, wealth, and power that so obviously existed in medieval England, but I have no precise, technical definition, for two major reasons. First, the complexity of the social structure of the time hampers any attempt to neatly divide individuals into discrete classes. Domesday Book clearly reveals that the rural elites formed a spectrum of wealth and power, as in later periods, ranging from great magnates with scores of holdings in a number of counties to individuals with one moderately sized manor.[25] Peasants too

---

[22] For the dangers of the reinforcement of ethnicity by class lines, see Eriksen, *Ethnicity and Nationalism*, 50–2. For a specific medieval example, see Benedykt Zientara, 'Nationality Conflicts in the German-Slavic Borderland in the 13th–14th Centuries and Their Social Scope', *Acta Poloniae Historica*, 22 (1970), 217–19.

[23] Van Caenegem, *Royal Writs*, 216–18, nos. 165, 169, 172, 175; id., *Birth of the English Common Law*, 55, 96; Richard Fitz Nigel, *Dialogus de Scaccario*, 53. See also, Hyams, *King, Lords and Peasants*, 253.

[24] Guy of Amiens, *Carmen*, 26; *EHOV* 6: 350; *The Chronicle of Jocelin of Brakelond*, ed. H. E. Butler (London, 1949), 33; Joseph Stevenson, ed., *Chronicon Monasterii de Abingdon*, vol. 2 (London, 1858), 284.

[25] J. J. N. Palmer, 'The Wealth of the Secular Aristocracy in 1086', *ANS* 22: 287–8.

were divided: Domesday Book employs various terms to categorize them into different status groups, and the Middlesex portion reveals they had different-sized holdings.[26] Moreover, to distinguish between nobles and peasants is to ignore that there was no sharp break in the spectrum of land and wealth between the two groups, and it is not even obvious that there was any clear line of social demarcation. How does one describe those who held, say, a single hide with a couple of tenants, who were clearly not ordinary peasants but would not count as nobles by the definitions of most modern historians? How, moreover, does one fit in lessees or estate officials, townspeople of varying wealth, and members of different ranks within the church hierarchy? An additional factor to complicate the picture was social mobility. This was a society in which rags-to-riches tales were rare, but individuals did move up and down the social ladder, and over time families could move up or down quite far.[27] In short, there can obviously be no neat, simple, and easy division of Normans and English into individual classes or social groups.

The second major problem is that the terminology of contemporaries provides little guidance about class divisions. David Crouch has remarked that there were gentry and magnates in this period: 'But where categorization falls flat is that in the twelfth and thirteenth centuries the historian is dealing with a period when the idea of social categories was hardly in the forefront of the conscious contemporary mind.'[28] Later periods may have seen, for instance, the careful breakdown of landholding society into a series of ranks ranging from dukes down to gentlemen, but the Normans normally used only fairly general terms such as *rustici* or *nobiles* to distinguish social groups.[29] Thus, reliance on medieval social divisions is not a viable option.

Before turning to my solution to these problems, it is worth noting that the very nature of the social structure, and the way contemporaries conceptualized it, provides part of the answer to the question of why ethnic and class lines did not become joined. The existence of a spectrum of wealth and status in English society, and the very fluidity and imprecision of Norman ideas about class and status, made it harder for contemporaries to link class and ethnic boundaries. How could one draw a precise line between English and Normans on the basis of class if there were no well-defined social demarcations between the rank of earl or count, which was too high, and the old English divisions between peasants, which were too low? If the ranks (as opposed to the professions) of knight or squire had not been developed yet, how could they be denied to the English, and if there were no legal privileges reserved for nobles, how could they be withheld from the conquered? In other

---

[26] H. C. Darby, *Domesday England* (Cambridge, 1977), 61–74; *DB* 1: 127a–130b.

[27] Gillingham, *English in the Twelfth Century*, 259–76.

[28] David Crouch, 'From Stenton to McFarlane: Models of Societies of the Twelfth and Thirteenth Centuries', *TRHS* 6th ser., 5 (1995), 199.

[29] Even terms that later came to describe fairly well-defined ranks, such as *baro* or *miles*, were used in looser or different ways in the eleventh century. For the early stages of the process whereby various ranks were formed, see David Crouch, *The Image of Aristocracy in Britain, 1000–1300* (London, 1992), 106–73; Peter Coss, 'Knights, Esquires and the Origins of Social Gradation in England', *TRHS* 6th ser., 5 (1995), 155–78.

words, the Normans had no obvious mechanism by which to turn their early de facto prejudice into a de jure one. This explanation cannot provide the whole answer (for they could always have developed such a mechanism), but it undoubtedly forms a part of it.

In any case, in the absence of clear social breaks or contemporary guidelines, individuals can only be lumped into broad and to some degree anachronistically defined groups. I have broken down post-conquest society into five categories for the purposes of this book: the landed aristocracy; the peasants; the middling sorts; townspeople; and the religious, namely clerics, monks and nuns. These categories, which I define more closely in the respective chapters, are nonetheless broader and looser than is ideal for social analysis. But in the absence of evidence for sharper, more precise categories based either on eleventh- and twelfth-century social divisions or on detailed information about wealth and social standing, I proceed on the assumption that rough social categories are better for analysis than none.[30]

A final important point about social status in Anglo-Norman society, and its influence on the respective positions of the English and the Normans, is that power was relative and that magnates were not the only ones who mattered. A great magnate might sneer at a minor lord who held only one manor or at a wealthy burgess. These individuals might sneer in turn at a prosperous peasant. But the minor lord would have clout on his own land and in his own neighbourhood, the burgess could have a dominant role in his town, and the prosperous peasant might be a person of standing and influence in his own village. Despite the strongly patriarchal nature of this society, women of various classes also had power and influence. Therefore, in order to understand the relations of English and Normans, and for that matter the distribution of power, authority, and influence in society as a whole, it is worth looking beyond the people at the top. Nonetheless, it is with the elites that I shall start.

---

[30] For a discussion of social classification and the difficulties therein, see Hugh M. Thomas, *Vassals, Heiresses, Crusaders, and Thugs: The Gentry of Angevin Yorkshire, 1154–1216* (Philadelphia, 1993), 7–12; Crouch, *Image of Aristocracy*, 1–38; Peter R. Coss, *Lordship, Knighthood and Locality: A Study in English Society, c. 1180–c. 1280* (Cambridge, 1991), 11–19; Green, *Aristocracy*, 7–15.

9

The Aristocracy

IN STARTING MY discussion of personal interaction among English and Normans with the aristocrats, I am giving them no more than what they would have considered their due in the loose, informal, but powerful class structure of Anglo-Norman society. By the landed aristocracy, I mean those who in later periods would be described as the middle to upper gentry and the nobility; families that could live comfortably off the income of their lands, and aspire to both leisure and military pursuits. A landholder with five hides or carucates (nominally 600 acres, and the landholding requirement for a ceorl to become a thegn in one pre-conquest legal work) would certainly qualify, as long as the bulk of the land was in his or her own hand, or let out at a good rent.[1] Someone with three or four hides might, depending on how much income they could draw from them. This is a fairly broad definition of aristocracy, but I have deliberately made it so in order to include as many natives, who tended to cluster towards its lower end, as possible.

This society, like most in the Middle Ages, channelled a disproportionate amount of influence to the great rural landholders, who possessed extensive military, economic, and political power. As a result, it is important to study relations between the new immigrant nobles and surviving English nobles and rising families of native descent. To what degree did English aristocrats assimilate and absorb Norman ones? To what extent were native aristocrats responsible for the survival and triumph of English identity? Did English nobles provide a *Traditionskern* for Englishness? An important part of the story will be left for the next chapter, when I discuss arguments about the role of native aristocratic women in the first generation after the conquest, and their role in transferring land to the Normans and in anglicizing them through intermarriage. In this chapter I will be focusing on patrilineal native lineages that survived the Norman Conquest or rose into the aristocracy afterwards.

As is well known, the Normans destroyed most of the old aristocracy, but the potential influence of even a greatly weakened native aristocracy on ethnic relations may be seen by a comparison with medieval Wales, a society that never experienced the level of assimilation found in England after the Norman Conquest. There were many reasons for the difference, but some important ones are to be found at the aristocratic level. There, in the course of the long, slow conquest that culminated

---

[1] Liebermann, *Die Gesetze der Angelsachsen*, 1: 456–7.

in Edward I's victories, the native aristocracy suffered heavily.[2] By the fourteenth century the surviving Welsh squirearchy was impoverished and depressed in social stature and power. Yet they retained a leadership in native Welsh society that reflected but also promoted ethnic divisions between Welsh and English. As patrons, they also helped to preserve a distinctively Welsh culture that reinforced ethnic boundaries.[3] Most important, they had the power to foment revolts which themselves greatly increased ethnic hostility and therefore ethnic divides.[4] Anyone who values Welsh identity and culture would rightly applaud the cultural and political resistance of minor Welsh landholders, but there can be no doubt that they served as one important bar to ethnic harmony and assimilation in Wales. A crucial question for this work is why the surviving English aristocrats did not play a similar role.

My argument is that the Normans, wittingly or not, carried out a superb strategy for preventing the English aristocracy from serving as any kind of separatist ethnic leadership. On the one hand, they were intelligently ruthless in largely destroying this powerful group that had the most to lose from the conquest and was most capable of resisting or rebelling against Norman cultural and political dominance. Comparisons are complex, of course, but it appears to me that if one factors in the relative size and wealth of the two countries, and sets aside the northernmost counties of England, where English aristocratic survival was unusually extensive, English aristocrats had an even smaller share of wealth, power, and social influence in early twelfth-century England than Welsh squires had in fourteenth-century Wales. This in itself made ethnic relations less volatile.

On the other hand, the Normans provided opportunities for some natives from the beginning, and over the course of time they came to treat surviving aristocrats and successful new men as equals. Once again, a comparative contrast may be useful. One of the many reasons for the continuing strife in medieval Ireland is that the English were never willing to fully incorporate native elites into the new order.[5] A closer parallel to England is Wales after Edward I's thorough military conquest. There, as in England after the conquest, some native aristocrats and new men co-operated with the Normans and benefited from the change in power. The English continued to rely heavily on the Welsh squirearchy for the local exercise of power. There was even a certain degree of integration within the upper classes. For example, the great rebel Owain Glyn Dŵr had an ethnically English wife and served the English government as a soldier. But the English continued to discriminate against Welsh landholders through the fourteenth century and beyond, barring them from the highest positions and limiting their possibilities for advancement. By leaving the Welsh squires substantial power but discriminating against them the English

    [2] A. D. Carr, 'An Aristocracy in Decline: The Native Welsh Lords after the Edwardian Conquest', *Welsh History Review*, 5 (1970–1), 103–29; Davies, *Age of Conquest*, 360–1.
    [3] Davies, *Lordship and Society*, 417–18; id., *Age of Conquest*, 415–19; id., *Revolt of Owain Glyn Dŵr*, 49–57; Frame, *Political Development*, 206–12; Ralph A. Griffiths, *Conquerors and Conquered in Medieval Wales* (New York, 1994), 53–63.
    [4] Davies, *Age of Conquest*, 385–6, 458–9; id., *Revolt of Owain Glyn Dŵr*, 277, 284–7, 322.
    [5] Frame, *Political Development*, 213–14.

were playing with fire, as they discovered to their cost with Owain's rebellion.[6] In contrast, in England the Normans integrated the surviving patrilineages into their own ranks within a few generations. This reduced the motivation not only for potentially divisive revolts, but also for any kind of separatist ethnic or cultural leadership by native aristocratic survivors. One should probably not speak of a conscious Norman policy, at least for the overarching strategy outlined above, but the pragmatism of the Normans, reflected both in their pragmatic prejudice and their pragmatic tolerance, helped prevent the English aristocracy from becoming a hindrance to ethnic harmony and assimilation. This leaves open, however, the question of just how much the native patrilineages, in their reduced state, could or would do to further assimilation or preserve and promote English identity.

I begin with a summary of findings I have published elsewhere concerning English landholders in Domesday Book, their position within the new regime, and their fate after 1086.[7] There were, in fact, a fair number of them, somewhere between 800 and 1,300 by my calculations, though the true number was probably toward the lower end of the spectrum. But collectively, and, for the most part individually, they were much poorer than their Norman counterparts. As a group, those recorded landlords who can be identified with a fair degree of certainty as native English held approximately 6 per cent of the land in England by fiscal measurements and 4 per cent by value, though both of those figures should be bumped up slightly to account for any native landholders excluded from my study because they held names common to English and Normans. However, only four native landholders, Edward of Salisbury, Colswein of Lincoln, Thorkel of Warwick, and Gospatric, could be considered magnates.[8] Another twenty-odd held twenty fiscal units or income of £20 or more. Including the above individuals, about 200, with a wide margin of error on either side, held five fiscal units or £5 income or more. As these figures suggest, English landholders, though surprisingly numerous, were more likely to be members of the middling levels of society than to be aristocrats by my definition.

Recently, several scholars have rightly argued that Domesday Book does not fully record English landholding, but some of the groups and many of the individuals they point to would have fallen into my middling category. As for the aristocracy, a continuing transfer of land from natives to immigrants after 1086 would have more than counterbalanced any additions we might make to Domesday Book. The families of the magnates did comparatively well, though Gospatric's descendants lost most of his land and were far reduced in status. More striking, the lands of almost all of those in the next rank (holding twenty fiscal units or £20 income or more), and of many lesser figures, passed to Norman patrilineages. Given the lack

[6] Davies, *Revolt of Owain Glyn Dŵr*, 43–4, 68, 134, 136–41, 145–9, 203, 322–3; Frame, *Political Development*, 209–10; James Given, *State and Society in Medieval Europe: Gwynedd and Languedoc Under Outside Rule* (Ithaca, NY, 1990), 158–66, 219.

[7] Thomas, 'Significance and Fate', forthcoming.

[8] For convincing evidence that Edward was native, which was long disputed, see Williams, *ENC* 105–6. Gospatric's lands produced little income in 1086, according to Domesday Book, but were extensive, and could have produced a baronial income once economic recovery had occurred in Yorkshire: *DB* 1: 330a.

of evidence for minor aristocratic families between Domesday Book and the mid-twelfth century, it is difficult to measure how extensive the shift of lands was after 1086, but it looks to have been widespread.[9] Thus, even if one factors in gaps in Domesday Book, it almost certainly leaves an *inflated* picture of long-term English aristocratic survival after the conquest.

This picture of fragmentary survival by the English conforms to that provided by witness lists, which reveal the leading figures at the royal court and in the households of magnates. Though natives make up about a quarter of attesters to genuine English documents of William I that can be securely dated to between 1066 and 1071, and also form the majority of addressees, the only native layman to appear in writs and charters that can be securely dated to after 1071, with one or two possible exceptions, is Edward of Salisbury, the sheriff of Wiltshire, though some native churchmen also continue to appear.[10] Moving to the twelfth century, the approximately 1,500 charters calendared for Henry I (many of them admittedly involving Normandy, where English natives were far less likely to appear) include hundreds of figures making thousands of appearances; I have found about a dozen laymen, making less than seventy-five appearances, whom I am confident were English in the male line.[11] One can hardly find any at all for Stephen's reign.[12] Though the collected charters for Henry II and Richard I have not been published, the many charters and other sources I have seen certainly reveal no native rush into government, though, as we shall see, individual instances can be found. There is, of course, the issue of changing names to bedevil us, and some later new men may well have been of native ancestry. But we tend to know far more about great royal favourites and officials than about most people, and the evidence is clear that immigrants and their descendants maintained an overwhelming dominance in the innermost royal circles right through the period of concern to us.

There are relatively few charters of magnates surviving from the late eleventh century, but those that do exist suggest that baronial affinities, like the royal court, were dominated by foreigners.[13] An extensive survey of surviving baronial charters

<hr/>

[9] Thomas, 'Significance and Fate', forthcoming.

[10] See Bates, *Acta of William I*, nos. 11, 32, 35–8, 81, 138, 180, 216, 223, 254, 286, 291–2, 295–7, 299, 345, for the charters between 1066 and 1071. For appearances after 1071 of Edward, see Bates, *Acta of William I*, nos. 39, 60, 154, 176, 193, 195, 323, 341. The possible exceptions, who attest once each, are Leuret and R. son of Alwart (nos. 146, 195). There are also some individuals with ambiguous names. Natives attest seven documents that cannot be securely dated to either before or after 1071 but in some cases there are independent reasons to suggest an early date: Bates, *Acta of William I*, nos. 1, 33, 82, 276, 287, 339–40.

[11] *RRAN* 2: 1–389. Stephanie Christelow has shown how Danegeld exemptions and other privileges in Henry I's only remaining pipe roll can also help reconstruct royal favour and patronage: Stephanie L. Mooers [Christelow], 'Patronage in the Pipe Roll of 1130', *Speculum*, 59 (1984), 282–307. Some non-clerical natives did receive such favour, but they were mainly minor figures, and the paucity of instances simply reinforces the picture of the charters: *Pipe Roll 31 Henry I*, 6, 108 (Siward of Arden), 11 (Robert son of Toli), 15, 22 (Walter son of Edward of Salisbury), 22 (Swein Arcarius), 34 (Bertram de Bulmer), 41, 56 (Robert son of Siward), 62 (Harding, *serviens* of the queen), 152 (Hugh son of Ulger and Tovi the Engineer).

[12] *RRAN* 3: 1–374.

[13] For some examples of eleventh-century magnate charters with extensive witness lists and few or no natives, see *Mon. Ang.* 5: 165–6 (William, Count of Mortain, 0 of 18 native witnesses); R. T. Timson, *The Cartulary of Blyth Priory*, vol. 1 (London, 1973), no. 325 (Roger de Builli, 0 of 13); Mason, *Westminster*

of the twelfth century reveals that English names can be found only rarely, whereas men who not only had Continental forenames but also surnames that indicate Continental origin can be found quite easily, which tends to militate against any possibility that natives were flooding into immigrant service and thereby gaining a foothold in the aristocracy.[14] It is admittedly somewhat easier to trace natives in affinities in the latter part of the century, a point to which I will return, but even then their numbers were limited. One of the best-documented affinities of the middle and later parts of the century is that of Roger de Mowbray, active from 1138 to 1188, for whom a huge number of charters survive. Mowbray did have English tenants holding manors from him, and men with native names do attest his charters. But even though much of Roger's honour was in Yorkshire, where native gentry were more common than further south, none of the men who appear most frequently in his charters, a sign of their importance in his affinity, can be proven to be native. The majority, including many of his new men, had surnames names such as Daiville, Flamville, Buscy, Bellun, and Malebisse that indicate a Continental origin.[15] Not all affinities in the second half of the twelfth century remained an immigrant preserve to the degree that Mowbray's did, and as usual the problem of identifying natives after the shift to Continental nomenclature remains, but one should probably think of a trickle or perhaps a slow stream rather than a flood of natives into the house-holds and affinities of magnates in the second half of the century.

In general, it is very hard to find aristocratic families of English descent, even by the broad definition of aristocrat that I have given. One of my priorities in the research for this project was to find as many such families as possible, but an extensive search through the surviving materials produced very little result, uncovering only a few families beyond those already known to scholars. The paucity of results may best be illustrated by reference to the number of native families I have found in the *Cartae Baronum*, an incomplete but massive survey of the holders of knight's fees throughout England, both tenants-in-chief and their immediate vassals, in 1166. Of the approximately 5,600 fees recorded there, Earl Patrick, grandson of

Abbey Charters, nos. 436 (Geoffrey de Mandeville, 1 or 2 of 9), 462 (Geoffrey de Mandeville, 1 possibility out of 10), 488 (Robert Dispenser, 0 of 19); David C. Douglas, *Feudal Documents from the Abbey of Bury St. Edmunds* (London, 1932), no. 170 (Gilbert de Clare, 0 of 11 of Gilbert's men, 1 of 8 of abbot's men); *EYC* 4, nos. 1 (Count Alan, 0 of 7), 4 (Count Stephen, 0 of 8); *EYC* 8, no. 2 (William de Warenne, 0 of 12); Diana Greenway, 'Conquest and Colonization: The Foundation of an Alien Priory, 1077', in *The Cloister and the World: Essays in Medieval History in Honour of Barbara Harvey*, ed. John Blair and Brian Golding (Oxford, 1996), 55–6 (Geoffrey de la Guerche, 1 possibility out of 10 men of Geoffrey and 22 total witnesses). An exception is a charter from 1072 of Robert of Stafford, but since a number of the natives involved were members of one of the four most powerful surviving families it is likely to be anomalous: R. W. Eyton, 'The Staffordshire Chartulary, Series I–II', *William Salt Archaeological Society Collections for a History of Staffordshire*, 2: 178–276 (Birmingham, 1881), no. 1.

[14] This statement is based on reading through practically all the published collections of charters and a representative sample of unpublished ones. I should note that many early charters are published even when the cartulary or collection in which they were preserved is not, and though I have not read every single relevant charter, I have read the majority.

[15] D. E. Greenway, ed., *Charters of the Honour of Mowbray 1107–1191*, (London, 1972), 20–259. A lineage of chamberlains who served the family were descended from one Alfred, whose English name was also found on the Continent: p. lxv.

Edward of Salisbury, held in the neighbourhood of sixty fees, and men with English names or patronyms, or with an English ancestry that I have been able to trace, held less than 100, generally as subtenants (I have listed the figures involved in Appendix 1).[16] This survey ignores tenants who held further down the feudal chain and landholders who held by sergeanty or fee farm, as many natives did. In Appendix 2 I have therefore fleshed out the list with other aristocratic families from outside the northernmost counties. The number is not large.

Obviously the lists of families I have compiled are incomplete. I have no doubt that future prosopographical studies, especially ones conducted by scholars with an intimate command of local areas, will track down and reconstruct additional native aristocratic families. I have no doubt that even more aristocratic native patri-lineages survived into the twelfth century, but simply cannot be traced in the surviving sources because of the problem of names. Nonetheless, the evidence that does survive leads me to argue for an even more pessimistic picture of English aristocratic survival than that found in the traditional historiography.

To these small numbers of survivors, who form the main subject of this chapter, Lewis has argued that the pre-conquest French landholders and their descendants should be appended. In political terms, however, they clearly were normally treated far better than native English landholders. Three out of the five leading pre-conquest immigrants, or their sons, benefited from the conquest, and the son of a fourth, Ralph the Staller, held the rank of earl when he made the mistake of joining the revolt of 1075.[17] Lesser pre-conquest immigrants had varying fortunes, but in aggregate they obviously did better than the native English. Clearly, the pre-conquest immigrants and their children were considered more politically reliable than the English, and perhaps their command of the French language and know-ledge of Continental culture made them socially more amenable to the conquerors. Nonetheless, Lewis is surely right to note their incorporation into English society before 1066, and as he and others have pointed out, one legal compilation that probably reflects actual legislation by William treats these immigrants as English in regards to the *murdrum* fine.[18]

As at least partially assimilated immigrants, some of them undoubtedly with English mothers or wives, they could have served as bridges between the two groups, acting to help start the process of assimilation and also helping to preserve English culture. Regenbald, an immigrant who served Edward and then probably became William the Conqueror's first chancellor, no doubt helped maintain con-tinuity in the government.[19] William of Malmesbury wrote that William the Conqueror's first bishop of Exeter, Osbern, who came from one of the greatest

---

[16] The figure for the total number of fees comes from Thomas K. Keefe, *Feudal Assessments and the Political Community Under Henry II and His Sons* (Berkeley, 1983), 218, n. 8. There are contradictory reports on the number of fees Earl Patrick inherited from his mother: Hubert Hall, ed., *The Red Book of the Exchequer*, vol. 1 (London, 1896), 213, 236, 239–41, 298.

[17] For gains by Ralph the Staller and his son, Ralph, see *DB* 2: 119b-135b, 136a, 137a, 269a, 284b–86b, 287a, 292b, 294a, 301b, 333a, 335b, 373a, 381a, 397a, 446a, 448b.

[18] Lewis, 'French in England', 136; Robertson, *Laws*, 238. See also, *DB* 1: 66a.

[19] Keynes, 'Regenbald the Chancellor', 210–11, 217–21.

Norman families but served King Edward in England before the conquest, was 'more inclined to English customs in dress and other things, and undertook little Norman pomp'.[20] Regenbald and Osbern were clerics rather than secular figures, but their examples are suggestive of the ways pre-conquest Continental immigrants could have served the process of acculturation and helped span the gap between the two peoples. They would have been particularly important in the early period of highest tension, but some families could have had influence over several generations. The descendants of Harold, son of Earl Ralph the Timid, continued to be prominent figures on the Welsh marches.[21] Henry of Essex, great-grandson of Edward the Confessor's favourite, Robert son of Wymarch, was one of the leading magnates and a royal favourite in the reigns of Stephen and Henry II, at least until he lost the latter king's favour.[22] Such high-level families may have been particularly useful in promoting assimilation and acculturation at the upper levels of society. Nonetheless, their numbers were very limited, and their identities and cultural allegiances were likely to have been muddied, and thus less of a force for anglicization.

Even if one includes pre-conquest immigrants and their descendants, the destruction of the native aristocracy in southern England is striking, particularly when compared to Norman practices in southern Italy and Sicily. Little systematic work has been done on elite survival after the 'other' Norman Conquest, which makes comparisons tricky, but it looks as though in some Lombard regions, and perhaps in some Greek regions as well, native landlords had a greater chance of survival than their counterparts in England. For instance, several cadet lines of the princely house of Salerno survived the Norman takeover of that region, and Errico Cuozzo has argued that enough powerful Lombard families survived in that principality to play an important role in a revolt as late as the early 1160s.[23] Moreover, Lombards, Greeks, and even converted Muslims often held powerful and important positions at the royal court, such as that of admiral, throughout the period of Norman rule.[24] Further work may modify this picture, but it seems that the

---

[20] *WMGP* 201–2.

[21] For their baronies, see I. J. Sanders, *English Baronies: A Study of Their Origin and Descent, 1086–1327* (Oxford, 1960), 43, 85–6. For the activities of one of Harold's sons, a 'vir stemmatis ingenuissimi', during the reign of Stephen, see K. R. Potter and R. H. C. Davis, eds., *Gesta Stephani* (Oxford, 1976), 20.

[22] For the family and its barony, see Sanders, *English Baronies*, 139; Emilie Amt, *The Accession of Henry II in England: Royal Government Restored, 1149–59* (Woodbridge, 1993), 66, 73–4, 114–15; Lewis, 'French in England', 123, 128–9, 136–7; Freeman, *History of the Norman Conquest*, 4: 734–6.

[23] Errico Cuozzo, 'À propos de la coexistence entre Normands et Lombards dans le Royaume de Sicile: la révolte féodale de 1160–1162', in *Peuples du Moyen Âge: Problèmes d'identification*, ed. Claude Carozzi and Huguette Taviani-Carozzi (Aix-en-Provence, 1996), 45–56; G. A. Loud, 'How "Norman" was the Norman Conquest of Southern Italy', 27; 'Byzantine Italy and the Normans', 223; 'Continuity and Change in Norman Italy: The Campania during the Eleventh and Twelfth Centuries', 324–6, 329–33; 'The Abbey of Cava, Its Property and Benefactors in the Norman Era', 161–3; all in *Conquerors and Churchmen in Norman Italy* (Aldershot, 1999); Drell, 'Cultural Syncretism and Ethnic Identity', 193–5, 201. It should be noted that Drell disagrees with Cuozzo on the Lombard nature of the revolt: Drell, 'Cultural Syncretism and Ethnic Identity', 198.

[24] The best recent discussion of the government of Norman Sicily and Italy is in Hiroshi Takayama, *The Administration of the Norman Kingdom of Sicily* (Leiden, 1993). He concentrates on administrative

Normans in southern England went far beyond their counterparts along the Mediterranean in eliminating natives from the power structure.

The Norman treatment of native aristocrats in most of England may also be compared to those areas that ended up as northernmost England, many of which were only brought firmly under Norman control after 1086, and therefore form a different stage of the Norman Conquest.[25] Here I am referring to what Helen M. Jewell, in her book on the north–south divide, has called the middle north and far north, namely Cumberland, Westmorland, Northumberland, Durham, Lancashire, and Yorkshire.[26] Scholars have long recognized that there was a greater concentration of prominent native families in the north.[27] But I do not think it has been properly appreciated how great the contrast is, particularly if one focuses on the twelfth century, after many of the families found in the south in Domesday Book had disappeared. It is worth dwelling a little on the difference in the level of native aristocratic survival in the south and north because it can tell us much about Norman approaches to the conquered aristocrats.

Within the north, Yorkshire probably had the smallest percentage of native patrilineages, but even there many could be found. Charles Clay, in his introduction to *Early Yorkshire Families*, a collection of brief histories of aristocratic families, noted twenty-two with male English ancestors, though four of these were immigrant families in the male line who inherited through marriage in the twelfth century.[28] In other parts of the north native survival was even more pronounced. Early thirteenth-century surveys record a number of grants by Henry I to natives in Northumberland, Cumberland, Westmorland, and Lancashire, and the particularly detailed surveys for the last county also reveal many grants by immigrant barons to natives.[29] Many of these latter grants were tied to marriages. Warin Buscell, Richard Buscell, Robert de Mulinas, Hervey Walter, Albert Gresley, Adam de Montbegon, and Michael of Furness (also known as Michael the Fleming), who together represented almost all of the immigrant baronial families in Lancashire, all married off daughters or sisters to men with indigenous names.[30] Some of these grants and marriages may have reflected the creation of new elite native families in the north, but in many cases I suspect that these grants were in fact confirmations of

---

structures, but reveals much in passing about administrative personnel, and a comparison of his book and Judith A. Green's *Government of England Under Henry I* (Cambridge, 1986) can show how great was the disparity in native office-holding at higher levels.

[25] Kapelle, *Norman Conquest of the North*, 105–230; Paul Dalton, *Conquest, Anarchy and Lordship: Yorkshire, 1066–1154* (Cambridge, 1994), 19–78.

[26] Helen M. Jewell, *The North–South Divide: The Origins of Northern Consciousness in England* (Manchester, 1994), 24.

[27] See e.g. Stenton, 'English Families', 10; W. Percy Hedley, *Northumberland Families*, vol. 1 (Gateshead, 1968), 16; Williams, *ENC* 97.

[28] Charles Clay and Diana A. Greenway, *Early Yorkshire Families* (Wakefield, 1973), pp. vii–viii, 1, 6, 24–5, 28–9, 38–40, 42–4, 46–7, 57–8, 59–61, 67–8, 76–8, 87–92, 97–9. See also *EYC* 3: 352; 4: 121–3, 142–4; 11: 243–5, for families not included in that collection, and Margaret L. Faull and S. A. Moorhouse, *West Yorkshire: An Archaeological Survey to A. D. 1500*, vol. 2 (Wakefield, 1981), 251–4 for the West Yorkshire area.

[29] *The Book of Fees, Commonly Called Testa de Nevill*, vol. 1 (London, 1920), 197–221.

[30] Ibid. 1: 208, 210–11, 214–15, 219.

the rights of existing landholding families, and that the marriages were designed to tie the old and new aristocracies together. In any case, powerful native northerners can be found far more easily than their southern counterparts in the pipe rolls, in saints' lives, and in chronicles.[31] Above all, they can be found in charters, both as donors and, earlier than elsewhere in England, attesters to the charters of important men.[32] Overall, the evidence is so rich that the native northerners probably deserve their own study, and genealogists and historians have already gathered information on a large number of native families.[33]

Though most aristocratic native families in the north would have been equivalent to later gentry (with a large middling group underneath them), at least some of the leading figures and families in northern society were native. Several were wealthy enough to found religious houses.[34] Two of Henry I's sheriffs in Northumberland were native, and one—possibly both—founded moderately prosperous lineages.[35] Ansketil of Bulmer, sheriff of Yorkshire under Henry I, had

[31] For a sampling of passages in the pipe rolls revealing a number of powerful northerners with native names or backgrounds, see *Pipe Roll 31 Henry I*, 33; *Pipe Roll 4 Henry II*, 120; *Pipe Roll 7 Henry II*, 23–4; *Pipe Roll 9 Henry II*, 10–11, 43; *Pipe Roll 15 Henry II*, 133. For saints' lives, see Reginald of Durham, *Libellus Beati Cuthberti*, 275; id., *Libellus de Vita et Miraculis Sancti Godrici, Heremitæ de Finchale*, ed. Joseph Stevenson (London, 1847), 220, 226–8, 441; *Becket Materials*, 1: 160–2; 2: 229–34. For chronicles, see *Jordan Fantosme's Chronicle*, 108; Richard of Hexham, *De Gestis Regis Stephani*, 166; *LDE* 306; *SMO* 2: 261, 298.

[32] The number of charters are too vast to list, but any northern cartulary with material from the period will yield examples.

[33] For discussion of some of the native aristocrats, see Green, *Aristocracy*, 117–20; Kapelle, *Norman Conquest of the North*, 200–2; Charles Phythian-Adams, *Land of the Cumbrians: A Study in British Provincial Origins, A.D. 400–1120* (Aldershot, 1996), 30–1, 136–8, 141–2, 148–51, 155–9, 176–81; Aird, *St Cuthbert and the Normans*, 320–4. It is impossible to list all the articles on individual families, but collections of notes on families can be found in Hedley, *Northumberland Families*, 1: 10–12, 16, 37, 39, 54, 143–5, 204, 209, 217, 233, 235–41, 244–8, 258–62, 264–8; 2: 89, 239–41; Richard Lomas, *North-East England in the Middle Ages* (Edinburgh, 1992), 25–6; William Farrer, ed., *The Lancashire Pipe Rolls and Early Lancashire Charters* (Liverpool, 1902), 347–9, 351–2, 361, 404–6, 407–8, 409–11, 430–1; William Farrer, ed., *The Chartulary of Cockersand Abbey*, 7 vols (Manchester, 1898–1909), 1.2: 234–5, 263, 306–8; 2.1: 337–8, 392–3, 472, 488, 491, 501, 507, 514; 2.2: 531, 546, 673; 3.1: 883, 904; 3.2: 930–1, 1000, 1004–5; *VCH Lancaster*, 3: 23, 32, 46, 53, 76, 95, 158, 167, 169, 172, 175, 177, 209, 230, 237, 248–9, 265, 276; 4: 92, 97, 102, 106, 118, 137, 252, 340–1, 364–5; 5: 39, 94, 116, 182, 192, 211, 213, 263, 273, 294; 6: 25, 37, 67, 103, 108, 169, 193, 197, 252–3, 258, 264, 266, 303–4, 326, 335, 336, 411, 417, 424, 479; 7: 108, 117, 153, 159, 179, 185, 191–2, 214, 228, 232, 273, 276, 285, 320; 8: 2, 66, 67, 70, 72–3, 139, 141, 143, 210, 242, 266, 330, 331, 338–9, 364, 365, 392–3, 402, 407; Northumberland County History Committee, *History of Northumberland*, 15 vols. (Newcastle-upon-Tyne, 1893–1935), 1: 322, 408–9; 2: 10–14; 4: 303–4; 7: 14–106, 163; 9: 32, 73–7; 10: 37–41, 52, 57–8, 235–6, 389; 11: 91–2; 12: 199–201, 529; 13: 107, 158, 345–6; 14: 267–9, 281, 292, 399–400, 401, 419, 422–3, 426, 441, 508; 15: 203–4, 236, 239, 242–3, 382, 390–1, 396, 397, 438; *VCH* Durham, 3: 217–18, 286, 290, 294, 325–6. For Yorkshire, see above, n. 28.

[34] Francis Grainger and W. G. Collingwood, *The Register and Records of Holm Cultram* (Kendal, 1929), 91–2 (Holm Cultram); A. N. Webb, ed., *An Edition of the Cartulary of Burscough Priory* (Manchester, 1970), 6 (Burscough); Farrer, *Lancashire Pipe Rolls and Early Lancashire Charters*, 357–8 (hospital of Conishead); *EYC* 2, no. 787; *EYC* 3, nos. 1665, 1669–71 (Monkbretton); *Mon. Ang.*, 6: 869 (Shapp); Sally Thompson, *Women Religious: The Founding of English Nunneries after the Norman Conquest* (Oxford, 1991), 174 (Neasham).

[35] C. H. Hunter Blair, 'The Sheriffs of Northumberland 1076–1602', *Archæologia Æliana*, 4th ser., 20 (1942), 25–6; John Horace Round, 'Odard the Sheriff', *The Genealogist*, NS 5 (1889), 25–8. Hedley has disputed Round's argument that Odard the sheriff, father of Adam the sheriff and ancestor of the Vescount family, was son of the native Ligulf of Bamburgh: Hedley, *Northumberland Families*, 142–3. For Aluric's family, see *History of Northumberland*, 10: 37–41, 52, 57, 235–6; Hedley, *Northumberland Families*, 1: 143–5.

a Scandinavian name common to England and Normandy, but the fact that he had
served as a translator in 1106, before many immigrants were likely to have bothered
to learn English fluently, tips the balance of probabilities towards a native background. His son, Bertram of Bulmer, was also sheriff of Yorkshire, and between
them they built up a large estate in Yorkshire and Durham.[36] Other important
native patrilineages in the north included the ancestors in the male line of the
Nevilles of Raby, the descendants of the Yorkshire thegn Ailric, the FitzWilliams,
descended from William son of Godric son of Ketelbern, and the Greystokes,
descended from Forne son of Sigulf.[37] The respective lords of Gilsland in Cumberland and of Kendal in Westmorland were native early in the twelfth century.[38]
Finally, Waltheof and Gospatric, sons of Earl Gospatric of Northumbria, who
flirted with service to William I but was eventually driven into Scotland, were
granted extensive areas in Cumberland and Northumberland by Henry I, in which
they created a predominantly native gentry made up of the descendants of younger
sons, sons-in-law, and followers.[39] In short, far more of the top men in the north
remained native than elsewhere in England.

The degree of native survival in the north should not be taken too far. Most of the
greatest tenants-in-chief and magnates in the north were immigrants, for many of
the families noted in the previous paragraph might be described at best as minor
barons in the twelfth century. Richard Lomas, in his work on Northumberland,
estimates that natives held approximately forty townships in chief from the king
and Normans 400. Since the majority of these manors were subinfeudated, this
figure tells us little about landholding itself, but it says a lot about the top of the
landholding structure.[40] In addition, a number of the native lordships discussed
in the last paragraph passed through marriage or forfeiture to families that were
Continental in the male line in the twelfth century. It should also be noted that

---

[36] Van Caenegem, *English Lawsuits* 1: 138; Dalton, *Conquest, Anarchy, and Lordship*, 104; see, however,
Tsurushima, 'Domesday Interpreters', 219–20. For the family's early history, see *EYC* 2: 122, 126–31; 7:
153–5; 11: 180–1; Clay and Greenway, *Early Yorkshire Families*, 8–9; Green, *Government of England*, 200,
238–9. For appearances in royal charters, see *RRAN* 2, nos. 995, 1072, 1124, 1181, 1237, 1272, 1287, 1336, 1357,
1382, 1459, 1532, 1541, 1621, 1627, 1679.
[37] For Ailric and his family, see Hugh M. Thomas, 'A Yorkshire Thegn and his Descendants after the
Conquest', *Medieval Prosopography*, 8 (1987), 1–22. To the property discussed there may be added ½
knight's fee granted to Ailric's grandson, Adam, by the Ferrers: Hall, *Red Book of the Exchequer*, 338. See
also, Dalton, *Conquest, Anarchy, and Lordship*, 189–91, for a good discussion of this family's role in the
politics of Stephen's reign. For the FitzWilliams, see Cokayne and Gibbs, *Complete Peerage* 5: 518–27;
EYC 3: 335–6; Clay and Greenway, *Early Yorkshire Families*, 28–9; Timson, *Cartulary of Blyth Priory* 1: pp.
xxxv–xxxvi. For the Greystokes, see *EYC* 2: 505–9; Clay and Greenway, *Early Yorkshire Families*, 38–9;
Hedley, *Northumberland Families*, 233; Phythian-Adams, *Land of the Cumbrians*, 30, 141, 179.
[38] Phythian-Adams, *Land of the Cumbrians*, 155; George Washington, 'The Parentage of William de
Lancaster, Lord of Kendal', *Transactions of the Cumberland and Westmorland Antiquarian and
Archaeological Society*, NS 62 (1962), 95–100.
[39] The best accounts of the family may be found in *History of Northumberland*, 7: 14–106, and Hedley,
Northumberland Families, 10–11, 235–41, 244–8. A document describing the distribution of land by
Waltheof and his son Alan may be found in James Wilson, ed., *The Register of St. Bees* (Durham, 1915),
no. 498.
[40] However, Lomas also thinks most enfeoffments by Normans went to Normans; *North-East
England*, 26, 28.

native survival varied within this region. Though there were some prominent native families in the eastern parts of Yorkshire, survival was far more pronounced in the Pennine uplands and dales in the western part of the county, where the pattern seems to resemble that of neighbouring Lancashire and Westmorland. In general, north-western England seems to have had a greater survival rate than north-eastern England. Nonetheless, particularly at the gentry level, there remained a vibrant native aristocratic community, interconnected by marriage and landholding, throughout the North.

The varying level of native aristocratic survival in the various lands and regions conquered by the Normans strongly suggests that the level of dispossession in most of England was prompted by pragmatic concerns, rather than any deeply ingrained ethnic bias. I argue elsewhere that the massive dispossession in the areas brought firmly under Norman control by 1086 was not simply a reaction to rebellions or a matter of grabbing land, though certainly those factors were involved. I believe that William and his followers developed, probably sometime during the early rebellions, a proactive if loose policy to reduce the power of the native aristocracy. Richard Fitz Nigel wrote, in his late twelfth-century *Dialogue of the Exchequer*, that English survivors could only hope to gain (or recover) lands by grant from the conquerors in return for active service, and that all right to land had to have a post-conquest basis, and I believe his claims had a basic core of truth. Richard claimed to have learned this from natives, and I have shown that there were not only possible contacts in royal government who could have been his informants, but also that he was closely related by marriage to the descendants of Harding son of Eadnoth the Staller. There are also many individual pieces of evidence for his argument, none of them individually decisive, but collectively convincing in my view.[41] Such a policy would have allowed William and his nobles to dispossess or disinherit anyone they feared or did not trust, and would have easily allowed them to rip the heart out of potential aristocratic opposition and to leave only a token handful of native aristocrats in possession of land.

There were good pragmatic reasons for the Normans to decimate the native aristocracy. The Normans had to fear rebellion as long as English elites retained sufficient power to seriously hope a revolt might succeed. This was partly because the English nobility was tightly linked together by networks of kinship, lordship, and friendship. Such ties meant that it was dangerous to replace only a portion of the existing aristocrats, for the rest would be likely to feel honour-bound by their personal ties to avenge the slain or help those dispossessed recover their lands.[42] If Cuozzo is right about the role of Lombard aristocrats in the Salernitan revolt of the 1160s, one could argue that the Normans in Italy would have been wise to emulate the ruthlessness of their cousins in England.[43] Given the importance of English identity to this book, it is also worth noting that, according to contemporary

[41] Richard Fitz Nigel, *Dialogus de Scaccario*, 53–4; Thomas, 'Significance and Fate', forthcoming.

[42] Family claims to confiscated land also complicated matters: Robin Fleming, *Kings and Lords in Conquest England* (Cambridge, 1991), 143.

[43] Cuozzo, 'Normands et Lombards', 45–56.

writers, part of the pragmatic concerns of the Normans had to do not just with personal ties among the nobility, but also with ethnic or national solidarity. Orderic Vitalis, who grew up in the aftermath of the conquest, wrote that the English rebelled because they saw the Normans mistreating their associates and friends, and because they were angry 'at the loss of their patrimonies and the killing of relatives (*parentes*) and countrymen (*compatriotae*)'.[44] Norman fears of the combined effects of ethnic or national feeling and ties of kinship and lordship are illustrated in a passage from William of Poitiers concerning Copsi, an English nobleman whom William had appointed to control northern England early in his reign. According to this passage, Copsi's followers urged him 'that for his own honour he defend the ancestral liberty. First they begged, then implored, as if for the sake of the commonwealth (*gratia rerum publicarum*), that he desert the foreigners and follow the will of the best men of his people and kin group (*natio et consanguinitas*).'[45] In the event, Copsi was murdered by another native, probably as much because of earlier feuds and local politics as any loyalty to William, but what matters is the way in which this passage reveals Norman concerns.[46] William and his followers came to believe, perhaps rightly, that to a very large degree ethnic identity and networks of existing ties would determine loyalty, and they reacted accordingly. By reducing the English elites to insignificance they could hope to effectively lay the dangers of ethnic and kinship ties to rest, thereby incidentally helping set the stage for the cessation of violence that I argued earlier was so vital to assimilation.

The greater survival of natives in the north resulted equally from Norman pragmatism. Given the strains placed on aristocratic Norman manpower by the conquest, it was probably harder to get large numbers of Normans to participate in the conquest and consolidation of power in those areas. William Kapelle has argued that the limits of wheat production heavily influenced the limits of the first wave of Norman expansion (as represented in Domesday Book), arguing that the invaders were uninterested in places that could not produce the finer types of white bread aristocrats preferred.[47] One need not accept Kapelle's arguments on the specific desire for white bread to suggest that large parts of northern England, with its many upland regions, relatively harsh climate, and poverty, would have been much less attractive to immigrants than other parts of England.[48] A parallel might be found in Wales and Ireland, where Anglo-Norman invaders sometimes left less attractive pieces of territory, particularly in the uplands, to indigenous aristocrats and to the natives in general, partly because they were often harder to conquer, but also, one suspects, because they were not as desirable.[49]

[44] *EHOV* 2: 222.

[45] *GGWP* 184–6.

[46] Kapelle, *Norman Conquest of the North*, 106–8; Williams, *ENC* 16–17.

[47] Kapelle, *Norman Conquest of the North*, 214–25.

[48] See Green, *Aristocracy*, 101, 120.

[49] Davies, *Lordship and Society*, 302–6; Seán Duffy, *Ireland in the Middle Ages* (New York, 1997), 115, 169; Frame, *Colonial Ireland*, 44; Lynn H. Nelson, *The Normans in South Wales, 1070–1171* (Austin, Tex., 1966), 108–9. Some of these references concern peasant settlement, which is not the issue here, but clearly Irish and Welsh aristocrats tended to be left with less attractive regions.

A more important factor is that the native aristocracy in the north represented a kind of Goldilocks level of threat; not too much, but not too little. In the years immediately following 1066 the Normans had their backs to the wall, or rather to the English Channel. Any revolt had the potential to sweep across the country and drive them into the sea. Many Yorkshire and, after 1080, Durham thegns and magnates got caught up in William's programme to prevent this from happening by destroying the native elites. But by the time the Normans had consolidated their control over more distant counties in the reigns of William Rufus and Henry I, the situation was different. A revolt by native northern aristocrats *might* sweep the Normans out of large parts of the North, but they could not easily hope to go further, since their southern counterparts had been destroyed, and they would clearly be vulnerable to a massive counterstroke from the south. Having seen what happened to their southern counterparts, moreover, northern natives had good reason not to risk such a revolt, and both sides knew it. Natives would have been more likely to accept what they could get than in the 1060s and 1070s. For their part, northern immigrant magnates in Henry I's reign would have been less nervous about revolt than their counterparts a generation earlier. Thus, the survival of substantial numbers of native aristocrats in the northern counties represented an acceptable risk to the invaders in the twelfth century, whereas a comparable level of aristocratic survival throughout England did not in the eleventh century.

Conversely, native aristocrats probably could not have survived to such a degree had they not represented something of a threat, at least as individuals. Much of the terrain in the north was suitable to guerilla warfare, and many native aristocrats already had or subsequently developed ties across the fluid Scottish border, which would have made them harder to root out.[50] References to raiding and fighting by native aristocrats in Stephen's reign reveal that they remained military leaders to be reckoned with.[51] William son of Godric son of Ketelbern was at best a fairly minor landholder when he made his family's fortune by marrying the wealthy heiress and widow Aubrey de Lisours. Yet he was well enough connected, quite likely among the interwoven houses of native aristocrats, that both Henry II and the pope stepped in to remove canon-law impediments to the marriage when discord

[50] For cross-border ties of natives, see *History of Northumberland*, 7: 14–106; Keith J. Stringer, *Earl David of Huntingdon 1152–1219: A Study in Anglo-Scottish History* (Edinburgh, 1985), 199; George Washington, 'The Anglo-Scottish Lords of Leitholme and Great Strickland', *Transactions of the Cumberland and Westmorland Antiquarian and Archaeological Society*, NS 60 (1960), 46–51; Clay and Greenway, *Early Yorkshire Families*, 40; Richard D. Oram, 'A Family Business? Colonisation and Settlement in Twelfth- and Thirteenth-century Galloway', *Scottish Historical Review*, 72 (1993), 117–18, 124–5, 130. For English–Scottish relations in the period, which include discussions of the ties of many natives in what became England to the kings of Scotland, see G. W. S. Barrow, 'The Kings of Scotland and Durham', in *Anglo-Norman Durham, 1093–1193*, ed. David Rollason et al. (Woodbridge, 1994), 311–23; Barrow, 'Scots and the North of England', in *The Anarchy of King Stephen's Reign*, ed. Edmund King (Oxford, 1994), 231–53; Dalton, *Conquest, Anarchy, and Lordship*, 196–230; Paul Dalton, 'Scottish Influence on Durham, 1066–1214', in *Anglo-Norman Durham, 1093–1193*, ed. David Rollason et al. (Woodbridge, 1994), 339–52.
[51] Reginald of Durham, *Vita Sancti Godrici*, 220; Richard of Hexham, *De Gestis Regis Stephani*, 166; *LDE* 306; *SMO* 2: 298.

threatened to erupt between the prospective couple's kin groups.[52] This is a late example, but it is likely that at an earlier date immigrant families, while continuing to hold the upper hand collectively, may often have found it expedient to come to terms with local aristocratic families. Thus, because they posed no overwhelming threat but could be bothersome as enemies (and useful as allies), native northern nobles had a better chance of survival than their southern peers.

The amply attested survival of greater numbers of natives in the northern aristocracy only underscores how feeble survival was in the south, and indicates that the lack of evidence for aristocratic families there is not simply a trick of the sources. But aristocratic survival in the north also demonstrates the flipside of pragmatic prejudice, namely pragmatic tolerance. Where the benefits outweighed the costs, the Normans were apparently quite happy to coexist with a fairly large number of native aristocrats, and indeed to intermarry with them extensively, as in Lancashire.

This brings us to the second important theme of the chapter. Though the Norman conquerors in England almost obliterated the native aristocracy in most areas of the country, they subsequently incorporated survivors and rising natives into their ranks with few signs of lingering prejudice. Indeed, on some level the process began in 1066, though with a dozen steps backward for every step forward in the first years after the conquest. There is general agreement that William made a genuine effort to rule in conjunction with the native elites in the first years of his reign, and I concur, though I also suspect that he always considered massive destruction of the English aristocracy as an option in case co-operation proved a failure. My study of native landholders in Domesday Book shows that some, and perhaps many, held new lands granted by the conquerors. Some undoubtedly received these in recompense for lands lost elsewhere, but others, including the magnates Edward of Salisbury and Colswein of Lincoln, clearly prospered as a result of the Norman Conquest. If I am right about William's policy on native land-holding and inheritance after the conquest, moreover, even the survivors who retained or inherited land did so because they actively served the Normans.[53]

Indeed, William the Conqueror and his sons received much English military help, long after the bulk of the dispossession is likely to have taken place.[54] Domesday Book also reveals many Englishmen (and at least one Englishwoman) acting in various capacities for the king or for Norman magnates.[55] Scholars have

---

[52] See above, n. 37, for the marriage and for William's family, the FitzWilliams. For the papal ruling, see C. R. Cheney, *From Becket to Langton* (Manchester, 1956), 58–9; Charles Duggan, 'English Secular Magnates in the Decretal Collections', in *Decretals and the Creation of 'New Law' in the Twelfth Century* (Aldershot, 1998), art. IV, 606–8; Emil Friedberg, ed., *Corpus Iuris Canonici*, vol. 2 (Leipzig, 1881), 673–4.

[53] Thomas, 'Fate and Significance', forthcoming.

[54] *ASC* E 1073, D 1074 [*recte* 1073], E 1075, D 1076 [*recte* 1075], D1079, E1088; *CJW* 3: 22, 24, 50, 72, 98; Gaimar, *L'Estoire des Engleis*, 174, 175; *HHHA* 398, 414; *WMGR* 476, 546–8, 714–16; *EHOV* 2: 206–8, 212, 228, 306–8; 3: 110; 4: 124–8, 134; 5: 310, 314, 318; *Letters of Lanfranc*, 124.

[55] *DB* 1: 31b, 42a, 100a, 112b, 136b, 148b, 154b, 155a, 164a, 218b, 230b; 2: 38b, 98a, 99a, 103a, 133b, 149a, 176b–177a, 217b, 272a, 282a, 282b, 283a, 284b, 287a–287b, 299b, 371a, 446a, 448b. See also Robin Fleming's discussion of lordship and jurors, many of them English, in Domesday Book: *Domesday Book and the Law: Society and Legal Custom in Early Medieval England* (Cambridge, 1998), 20–8.

often argued, on the basis of various types of evidence, that a large portion of the English survivors had ministerial positions, and I believe this is correct.[56] Many of the people who cooperated with the Normans would have come from the middling level of society, but some, such as the sheriff, Edward of Salisbury, were clearly of aristocratic status. Thus, throughout the darkest period of ethnic relations there was co-operation between some English aristocrats and the new regime.

No doubt relations between the English and Norman aristocrats were generally businesslike at best and often heavily strained. This may be illustrated by the fate of Bishop Walcher, whom William appointed to Durham. Exceptionally, Walcher went out of his way to build relations with the natives, and had English advisors and followers, most notably an aristocrat named Liulf. However, some of the bishop's Continental followers and kin murdered Liulf out of jealousy and resentment because he had gained the bishop's favour. When Liulf's relatives slaughtered the bishop and his men in turn, they spared two of the bishop's native followers, specifically described as English, because they were kin to the attackers, and then staged an abortive rebellion. New bonds of lordship proved fragile in the tense circumstances of William I's reign, and in the end were generally no match for old ties of kinship and ethnicity.[57] This is no doubt one reason why the English aristocracy continued to decline even after 1086.

However, even in the first generation closer ties of lordship may have begun to form in some instances, and not just short-lived ones such as that between Walcher and Liulf. This is suggested by a document from Glastonbury Abbey that describes how the immigrant baron Walter of Douai, thinking he was on his deathbed, summoned his brother, his steward, and others and sent them to promise that he would return land to the monastery, where he also decided to become a monk. However, Walter began to get better and his followers, fearing they would not find a better lord, threw the monks out of Walter's sickroom and reclothed him in secular garb, showing their devotion to him. The witness list to this document reveals that the steward was a man named Uluric, who in 1086 held three estates from Walter.[58] Normally in English documents Uluric represented the Old English name Wulfric, and though Keats-Rohan has recently pointed to the Flemish name Ulric, which can be found in the milieu from which Walter of Douai came, there is at least a reasonable chance that Uluric was English.[59]

Even if Uluric was not English, other natives in the late eleventh century were forming the kinds of bonds that would help their families survive into the twelfth

[56] *VCH* Wiltshire, 2: 76–8; W. E. Wightman, *The Lacy Family in England and Normandy, 1066–1194* (Oxford, 1966), 247–8; James Campbell, 'Some Agents and Agencies of the Late Anglo-Saxon State', in *Domesday Studies*, ed. J. C. Holt (Woodbridge, 1987), 210–12; Golding, *Conquest and Colonisation*, 109–10, 181–2; Judith Green, 'The Sheriffs of William the Conqueror', ANS 5: 131–2; Williams, *ENC* 71–125, esp. 78–9, 86–7, 96, 113, 115–17; Fleming, *Domesday Book and the Law*, 45–6.

[57] *CJW* 3: 32–6; *LDE* 212, 216–20; *ASC* E 1080.

[58] Aelred Watkins, ed., *The Great Chartulary of Glastonbury*, vol. 1 (Frome, 1947), 126–8; *DB* 1: 95a, 111b. For a discussion of Walter and this case, see N. E. Stacy, 'Henry of Blois and the Lordship of Glastonbury', *EHR* 114 (1999), 14–15.

[59] Keats-Rohan, *Domesday People*, 438.

century and beyond. Two of the native families most successful at building their fortunes in post-conquest society and at integrating into the new, predominantly Continental aristocracy were the Ardens and the Ingoldsbys.[60] Members of the Arden family, including Thorkel of Warwick, its leading Domesday Book representative, attested a 1072 charter by Robert of Stafford, thus indicating their early willingness to build contacts with the Normans.[61] Colgrim, ancestor of the Ingoldsbys, was described as a 'man' of Count Alan of Richmond in Domesday Book, and seems to have been some sort of royal official in Lincolnshire during William II's reign.[62] Co-operation and service by natives early on could sometimes plant the seeds for both the survival and integration of their families in later periods.

Though the families descended from natives in the male line were few in number throughout most of England in the twelfth century, those who did survive were able to play an active role in the new aristocratic order, and came to operate on a level playing-field with their Norman peers. Though up to 1086, and probably for some time thereafter, the position of English aristocratic patrilineages was very precarious, and most found themselves marginalized even if they co-operated with the new regime, in the course of the early twelfth century this changed. At some point native families obviously gained as much tenurial security as other families, for those that can be traced into the second third of the twelfth century tended to continue on as long as they could produce male heirs. Those that served kings and magnates were naturally rewarded, and unlike the rewards for service before 1086, which were often limited or precarious, later rewards to members of native patrilineages were no different than those for immigrants. The number of natives serving as important followers of the king and magnates would continue to remain small, partly because the number of potential native aristocratic recruits was restricted. Nonetheless, after a certain—hard to identify—point, natives were treated no differently than immigrants within the aristocracy, and had the same opportunities for prosperity and participation in aristocratic rule as their immigrant counterparts. Obviously this shift was part of the overall process of assimilation, but the shift also allowed native aristocrats to help the process of integration forward.

The centre of the new order, and the greatest source of potential patronage, was the royal government and particularly the royal court. Those few native aristocrats who did break the nearly complete immigrant monopoly on royal favour and the holding of important offices were therefore very important. Their presence in the highest court circles helped prevent the potentially disastrous linkage between class and ethnicity. Moreover, the royal court attracted many of the most powerful people in the realm and was thus an ideal place to create horizontal bonds of various sorts across ethnic lines which could further promote the process of assimilation.

---

[60] See below, pp. 123–4, 133–4.
[61] Eyton, 'Staffordshire Chartulary, Series I–II', no. 1; Ann Williams, 'A Vice-Comital Family in Pre-Conquest Warwickshire', *ANS* 11: 279, 290–2; Williams, *ENC* 104.
[62] *DB* 1: 348b; *RRAN* 1, no. 408; Williams, *ENC* 108.

Edward of Salisbury and his descendants were the most important natives at royal court, and their history best illustrates the ability of some English to gain royal favour, rise in society, and integrate themselves into the new aristocracy.[63] Edward himself had been sheriff of Wiltshire under William I and thereby built up a solid basis of wealth through the estates he had acquired in the years leading up to 1086. Edward's son and heir, Walter, occasionally appeared as attester or addressee in charters of Henry I, Queen Edith-Matilda, and Stephen, and may have served for a time as sheriff of Wiltshire.[64] Another Edward of Salisbury, who was probably a younger son of the first Edward, appeared more frequently in Henry's charters, and was the king's standard-bearer at the battle of Brémule in Normandy.[65] Walter's son and heir, Patrick, served the Empress Matilda during the civil war, and she made him a royal constable and then earl of Salisbury. He subsequently served her son, acting as sheriff of Wiltshire for a few years, and attesting Henry's charters both before and after he became king.[66] In 1168 Patrick accompanied the king to Poitou, where Henry assigned him to protect his queen, Eleanor of Aquitaine, in which duty he was killed by Poitevin nobles.[67] Patrick's son and heir, William, had a lower profile during the remainder of Henry II's reign, but seems to have risen in prominence during Richard's, serving as sheriff of Wiltshire among other tasks. When he died, his daughter and heiress Ela was married to Henry II's illegitimate son, William Longsword.[68] Thus, a century or more of service to kings was capped by marriage to the royal house.

Naturally the family prospered as a result of royal favour and the good connections they no doubt built up. Besides his acquisitions before 1086, the elder Edward may have gained, with an immigrant wife, lands that were passed on to the younger Edward. The second Edward married a wealthy heiress, Adeliz de Rames, with lands in Normandy as well as England, while Walter received three valuable manors and a number of knights' fees in marriage with his wife Sybil.[69] After his appointment as earl, Patrick received the third penny from the Wiltshire county court, and he also received part of a valuable royal manor from Matilda or her son during the civil

---

[63] For histories of Edward's family, see *VCH* Wiltshire, 2: 99, 107–10; Cokayne and Gibbs, *Complete Peerage* 11: 373–82; Williams, *ENC* 105–7

[64] *RRAN* 2, nos. 544, 971, 1715; 3, nos. 189, 684, 944.

[65] *RRAN* 2: p. xiv, nos. 684, 1012, 1062, 1183, 1222, 1246, 1255, 1284, 1363, 1446, 1466, 1648; *EHOV* 6: 236.

[66] Meyer, *L'Histoire de Guillaume le Maréchal*, 1: 6–7, 13–15; Potter and Davis, *Gesta Stephani*, 214; *RRAN* 3, nos. 180, 272, 704, 795, 796, 839; Léopold Delisle, ed., *Recueil des actes de Henri II roi d'Angleterre et duc de Normandie*, vol. 1 (Paris, 1916), nos. 6, 43; W. H. Rich Jones, *Register of S. Osmund*, vol. 1 (1883), 238–9; *EYC* 1, no. 76; 2, no. 1120; *Mon. Ang.*, 6: 1105, 1296; Hall, *Red Book of the Exchequer*, 2: 649; *Pipe Roll 2 Henry II*, 56; *Pipe Roll 6 Henry II*, 16; R. H. C. Davis, *King Stephen*, 3rd edn. (London, 1990), 137.

[67] Meyer, *L'Histoire de Guillaume le Maréchal*, 1: 58–61; *Chronicle of Robert of Torigni*, 236; *Chronica Magistri Rogeri de Hovedene* 1: 273–4; *Historical Works of Ralph de Diceto*, 1: 331; *Historical Works of Gervase of Canterbury*, 1: 205; *The Letters of John of Salisbury*, ed. W. J. Millor et al., vol. 2 (Oxford, 1986), 566; M. P. Boissonnade, 'Administrateurs laïques et ecclésiastiques Anglo-Normands en Poitou à l'époque d'Henri II Plantagenet (1152–1189)', *Bulletin de la Société des Antiquaires de L'Ouest*, 3rd ser., 5 (1922), 159–65.

[68] *Chronica Rogeri de Hovedene*, 3: 14, 137, 153, 241, 247–8, 268; 4: 13; Cokayne and Gibbs, *Complete Peerage*, 11: 377–82.

[69] *EYC* 9: 49–53; Hall, *Red Book of the Exchequer*, 1: 239–41, 298.

war.[70] Both he and his son married wealthy widows.[71] In the late twelfth century the family were poor as earls went, but then, that is a little like being a poor billionaire, and though a number of magnates were closer to their respective kings than the younger Edward and Earl Patrick, these two were nevertheless in the inner royal circle.[72]

Several points stand out from this account, the first being that a family that was native in the male line could receive honour, wealth, and the highest possible title from the royal house. Second, here was a powerful family acting in ways quite similar to other noble families; only this one was native. Other important points, to which I will return later in the chapter, are the integration to Continental fighting styles by the younger Edward and Earl Patrick, and extensive intermarriage by the family with immigrant families, which include not only the marriages noted above, but ones of daughters to the Bohuns, Marshals, and counts of Perche.[73] No native family was more successful in the generations immediately following the conquest than the descendants of Edward of Salisbury.

Edward of Salisbury and his descendants were distinctly atypical of native patri-lineages in terms of their wealth and power, but their path to higher standing and integration into the new aristocracy through royal service was not unique. Another good, and hitherto overlooked, example of a native in royal service was one Ailward, whose ancestry I have not been able to trace but whose name was clearly English. Henry II appointed him as butler or chamberlain to the households of several of his sons, most prominently that of Henry, the Young King.[74] Henry wanted trusted people to keep an eye on his sons, and when the younger Henry went into revolt in 1173, Ailward was one of several of the Young King's officials who remained loyal to the father.[75] Ailward was duly rewarded for his service. By 1166 he already held a manor, perhaps temporarily, from the king, and after he proved his loyalty in the revolt Henry II made the permanent grant of a manor in Essex worth £18 or £20 a year.[76] Ailward also made a good marriage, to Rohesia de Helion, member of an important local family, and descendant of a Breton tenant-in-chief

---

[70] *Pipe Roll 2 Henry II*, 57; *Pipe Roll 27 Henry II*, 94.

[71] Cokayne and Gibbs, *Complete Peerage*, 11: 377–8.

[72] Brock W. Holden, 'The Balance of Patronage: King John and the Earl of Salisbury', in *Haskins Society Journal*, 8, ed. C. P. Lewis and Emma Cownie (Woodbridge, 1996), 80; D. A. Carpenter, *The Minority of Henry III* (Berkeley, 1990), 30.

[73] Cokayne and Gibbs, *Complete Peerage*, 11: 374, n. e, 375 n. f; *Chronicle of Robert of Torigni*, 236.

[74] Ailward appears periodically in the pipe rolls in his official capacities: *Pipe Roll 11 Henry II*, 56; *Pipe Roll 12 Henry II*, 100–1; *Pipe Roll 13 Henry II*, 1; *Pipe Roll 16 Henry II*, 61, 111, 112, 118, 128, 162; *Pipe Roll 18 Henry II*, 79, 84; *Pipe Roll 25 Henry II*, 43, 101. He can also be found attesting royal charters: J. C. Holt and Richard Mortimer, eds., *Acta of Henry II and Richard I*, (Richmond, 1986), nos. 115, 119; Landon, *Cartae Antiquae Rolls 1–10*, no. 79; Rosalind Ransford, *Early Charters of the Augustinian Canons of Waltham Abbey, Essex, 1062–1320* (Woodbridge, 1989), no. 26.

[75] *Chronica Rogeri de Hovedene*, 2: 46; [Roger of Howden], *Gesta Regis Henrici Secundi Benedicti Abbatis*, 1: 43.

[76] Hall, *Red Book of the Exchequer* 1: 408–9; *Pipe Roll 23 Henry II*, 145; *Book of Fees*, 1: 276; Moore, *Cartularium Monasterii de Colecestria*, 1: 143; 2: 547. He also picked up some property on his own: *CRR* 4: 34–5.

of Domesday Book.[77] Ailward's story reveals that even natives of obscure origin could rise into important positions and could help integrate the elites, not just through service, but also through marriage.

Throughout the twelfth century a handful of other natives can be found holding high places in the royal government or at the royal court. Native sheriffs in the north have already been noted. To these may be added an undersheriff of Essex in Henry I's reign, a sheriff or undersheriff of Sussex with the native name Ailwin in Stephen's reign, and a couple of sheriffs of urban origin from Henry II's time.[78] Picot son of Colswein seems to have been an important royal representative in Lincolnshire under Henry I, for he was the addressee of a number of writs concerning that county, and late in Henry II's reign Nigel of Ingoldsby, great-grandson of the Lincolnshire king's thegn Colgrim, had a short-lived but active career in royal service.[79] Two men of probable native background in the next generation, Stephen of Segrave, grandson of a Hereward, and Roger Huscarl, whose family name suggests descent from an Anglo-Danish warrior, had very successful careers indeed.[80] As we shall see in Chapter 13, there were also prominent native clerics at royal court. Thus, though one certainly cannot speak of the upper reaches of the royal court and government as well integrated, they were never completely segregated either, and this helped ease the path to assimilation.

The presence of at least some natives in the households and affinities of magnates throughout the period, and their increasing participation as time went on, was also important. Noble households and affinities were among the most important, if informal, political and social institutions in medieval society, and the patronage of powerful lords was an important asset for any individual or family. For one native, indeed, the patronage of a magnate was literally life-saving. A document from Sibton Abbey describes how a man with the English name of Ailwy (who changed it to Geoffrey) had two sons. The younger son, Robert Malet, entered the service of Earl Hugh Bigod and became a knight. Robert's nephew, the son of his elder brother, killed a man he found kissing his mistress, and was in danger of execution,

---

[77] Gervers, *Cartulary of the Knights of St. John*, no. 322; Christopher Harper-Bill and Richard Mortimer, eds., *Stoke by Clare Cartulary*, vol. 2 (Woodbridge, 1983), no. 281. For her family, see J. H. Round, 'Helion of Helions Bumpstead', *Transactions of the Essex Archeological Society*, NS 8, pt. 2 (1901), 187–91. Ailward lived on into Richard's reign, and left five children behind him: *Pipe Roll 6 Richard I*, 24; *Pipe Roll 7 Richard I*, 52.

[78] The undersheriff was Alfred, whom Keats-Rohan has suggested may be identical with the Domesday Book landholder Alfred of Attleborough; Keats-Rohan, *Domesday People*, 28–9, 140. For Ailwin, see Mason, *Westminster Abbey Charters*, no. 272. For the sheriffs in Henry II's reign, see below, pp. 193–4. Two sheriffs with ambiguous names in Henry I's reign, who have been noted as possible natives, were Wigot and William son of Hacon, both sheriffs of Lincolnshire: Green, *Government of England*, 155.

[79] For Picot, see *RRAN* 2, nos. 531, 536, 964, 1116, 1118. For Nigel, see CUL, Peterborough D&C MS 1, fol. 132ʳ; *Pipe Roll 28 Henry II*, 61; *Pipe Roll 29 Henry II*, 72; *Pipe Roll 30 Henry II*, 23; *Pipe Roll 31 Henry II*, 10–11, 91–2, 117; *Pipe Roll 32 Henry II*, 70, 81, 92, 94, 124, 144; *Pipe Roll 33 Henry II*, 23–4, 52, 67, 95; *Pipe Roll 34 Henry II*, 55, 66. For accounts of his family's history, see *EYC* 5: 255–7; Clay and Greenway, *Early Yorkshire Families*, 46–7.

[80] Ralph Turner, *Men Raised from the Dust: Administrative Service and Upward Mobility in Angevin England* (Philadelphia, 1988), 120–42; Ralph Turner, 'Roger Huscarl, Professional Lawyer in England and Royal Justice in Ireland, c. 1199–1230', in *Judges, Administrators and the Common Law in Angevin England* (London, 1994), 215–23.

but Robert, through the intercession of his lord, obtained a pardon from Henry II for his nephew.[81] Patronage not only proved of great benefit to individual natives, as in this case, but also forwarded the integration of the two peoples. Any Englishman who entered the following of an immigrant magnate automatically worked closely with Normans, and became part of the network of powerful relationships that dominated English society after the conquest. Thus, even a limited English presence could have an impact in breaking down ethnic barriers within the aristocracy.

The story of one successful native can illustrate both the rewards and the level of integration such service might bring. Conan, lord of Richmond and duke of Brittany, recruited as his chamberlain Ralph son of Meldred of Middleton, a younger son of a family that was clearly native and probably descended from a minor Yorkshire thegn of 1086. Ralph, who frequently accompanied Conan to Britanny, thus rose from relative obscurity to an important position in one of the leading households of Europe, and he then passed into the service of Conan's daughter Constance and son-in-law Geoffrey, son of Henry II. He also married the widow of one of the richest immigrant tenants of the honour of Richmond.[82] As a result of his service to Duke Conan, this native Englishman from the fringes of the aristocracy was absorbed into the heart of a cross-channel, largely immigrant aristocracy.

Ralph son of Meldred was not alone. Colgrim of Ingoldsby's son Osbert maintained his father's connections with the earls of Richmond and probably gained a knight's fee in Yorkshire from the honour.[83] Thorkel of Warwick was made an under-tenant of the first earl of Warwick and, judging by attestations to charters, his son and grandsons preserved their positions by entering the affinity of the earls of Warwick. Thorkel's great-grandson William was Earl Waleran's steward at the end of the twelfth century.[84] The Audley family, certainly native and probably descended from a minor king's thegn of Staffordshire named Gamel, accumulated status and lands throughout the period in question through service and connections to the Staffords, the Clintons, the Verdons, and eventually the earls of Chester.

[81] P. Brown, ed., *Sibton Abbey Cartularies*, 4 vols. (Woodbridge, 1985–8), 1: 70–3; 3, no. 817. See also *CRR* 11: 173 for the way in which the patronage of Bishop Hugh de Puiset helped one native named Uctred or Vincent son of Gamel gain land in Northumberland.

[82] *EYC* 4: 51, nos. 47, 50–6, 58–9, 64, 66, 70, 80; 5: 356, no. 400; Judith Everard and Michael Jones, *The Charters of Duchess Constance of Brittany and her Family, 1171–1221* (Woodbridge, 1999), nos. Ge8, Ge9, C19, M3; J. A. Everard, *Britanny and the Angevins: Province and Empire, 1158–1203* (Cambridge, 2000), 101, n. 28, 135, n. 51; *Pipe Roll 29 Henry II*, 27.

[83] *Pipe Roll 31 Henry I*, 27; *EYC* 5: 255–8.

[84] For the holdings of Thorkel's descendants, see *Book of Fees*, 1: 507–14; 2: 956–7. For attestations to charters, see BL Harley 3650, fols. 10ᵛ, 12ʳ, 18ᵛ, 21ᵛ–22ʳ; BL Cotton Caligula A xiii, fol. 67ᵛ; Bodleian Library MS Dugdale 13, fols. 449, 522; Bodleian Library MS Dugdale 15, fol. 290; Lewis C. Loyd and Doris Mary Stenton, eds., *Sir Christopher Hatton's Book of Seals* (Oxford, 1950), no. 510; Emma Mason, ed., *The Beauchamp Cartulary Charters 1100–1268* (London, 1983), nos. 281, 285; B. R. Kemp, *Reading Abbey Cartularies*, vol. 1 (London, 1986), nos. 579, 580; *Mon. Ang.*, 4: 106; 6: 1326–7. For William as seneschal or steward, see *Report on the Manuscripts of Lord Middleton*, Historical Manuscripts Commission (London, 1911), 24–5. For an overview of the Arden family, see Coss, *Lordship, Knighthood, and Locality*, 186–209, 280–4.

At the end of Henry II's reign, Adam of Audley married a wife, Emma, who was the daughter of another largely native family but had a Norman sheriff, Nicholas Beauchamp, for a great-grandfather.[85] Eventually the Audleys would join the parliamentary nobility.

All of these families began building ties of lordship to the Normans well before the midpoint of the twelfth century. As one passes that date it becomes still easier to find natives in the affinities of magnates. This is best illustrated by the number of men with the titles of important household officials and insular names or known native ancestry, who can be found in the *Cartae Baronum*, charters, and other sources.[86] One great magnate, Earl Ranulf III of Chester, had several men of native descent in his affinity, including his sheriff Liulf, Stephen of Segrave, and Henry of Audley.[87] Some native officials became fairly powerful men, such as William of Ridware, who was great-grandson of a minor landholder, 'Atsor the Englishman', and became steward of the Earl Ferrers. William obtained a valuable heiress of Norman ancestry for his younger son and a manor for himself from the earl, accumulated a number of other estates, and gained sufficient power to bully a local prior.[88] The numbers of aristocrats of native descent in the affinities of magnates

[85] For the early history of the Audleys, see J. H. Round, *Peerage and Pedigree: Studies in Peerage Law and Family History*, vol. 2 (London, 1910), 28–33. For their connections to magnate families, see Eyton, 'Staffordshire Chartulary, Series I–II', nos. 4–5, 14, 26–8; George Wrottesley, ed., 'The Staffordshire Chartulary, Series III', in *William Salt Archaeological Society Collections for a History of Staffordshire*, vol. 3 (Birmingham, 1882), 225; Isaac Herbert Jeayes, ed., 'Descriptive Catalogue of the Charters and Muniments Belonging to the Marquis of Anglesey', *William Salt Archaeological Society Collections for a History of Staffordshire*, vol. 61 (Kendal, 1937), nos. 34–5, 41; BL Harley 3650, fols. 8^{r-v}, 14^v–15^r, 62r, 65^{r-v}, 66^r, 71^v; BL Cotton Charters xi 7; *Pipe Roll 27 Henry II*, 73; *Pipe Roll 32 Henry II*, 150; *Pipe Roll 33 Henry II*, 20–1; Carpenter, *Minority of Henry III*, 288, 346–7, 349, 351; Barraclough, *Charters of the Earls of Chester*, nos. 211, 214, 229, 231, 282, 283, 310, 315, 349, 355, 356, 359, 360, 373, 374, 378, 379, 381, 384, 393–6, 402, 408, 409, 411, 440, 441, 445, 448, 451, 452, 454, 461, 462. For the marriage, see George Wrottesley, 'An Abstract of the Contents of the Burton Chartulary', *William Salt Archaeological Society Collections for a History of Staffordshire*, vol. 5 (London, 1884), 13, 35–6.

[86] The sources do not always expressly identify whose officials they were, but it seems likely they were officials of the nobles from whom they held land or who issued the charters in question. Besides those discussed below, see Beatrice A. Lees, *Records of the Templars in England in the Twelfth Century* (London, 1935; repr. Munich, 1981), 168–9 (Eadmund seneschal of Walter Fitz Robert); Eyton, 'The Staffordshire Chartulary, series II', no. 17 (Wluriz or Wulfric, chamberlain of Robert of Stafford); *EYC* 8, no. 31 (William son of Raven, sheriff of William III, Earl Warenne); Hall, *Red Book of the Exchequer*, 1: 270 (Godwin, steward of Gervase Painel), 351 (Edmund the Chamberlain on the Montefichet fee), 432 (Edward, chamberlain of the honour of Skipton, for whom see also *EYC* 7, nos. 7, 9, 17). From a somewhat later period, one can point to Thomas of Horbury, steward of the Earl de Warenne in the first decade of the thirteenth century and grandson of a man with the insular name of Saxi, or Robert son of Edolf, steward of the Northumberland baron, Robert Bertram, in 1206; *EYC* 8: 212–13; *CRR* 4: 223.

[87] For Henry of Audley, see above. For attestations of Liulf, generally as sheriff, to Ranulf III's charters, see Barraclough, *Charters of the Earls of Chester*, nos. 213, 245, 256, 257, 261, 283, 284, 300, 321, 340, 348–9, 356, 372, 379, 394–5. For his family, see James Tait, ed., *The Chartulary or Register of the Abbey of St. Werburgh Chester*, vol. 2 (Manchester, 1920–3), 315–17; George Ormerod, *History of the County Palatine and City of Chester*, 3 vols., 2nd edn. (London, 1882), 2: 200–5; 3: 135, 210–11. For connections between Stephen of Segrave and Ranulf, see Barraclough, *Charters of the Earls of Chester*, nos. 248, 310, 322, 328, 336, 351, 355, 365–7, 393, 402, 417–21.

[88] George Wrottesley, 'The Rydware Chartulary', *William Salt Archaeological Society Collections for a History of Staffordshire*, vol. 16 (London, 1895), 232–40, 243, 260–1, 264–7, 270–1, 273–5, 277, 279, 280, 295–6, 299.

was never likely to be huge, because there were so few of them in the first place, but it looks as though their numbers increased as time went on, which was partly a result of the integration of the two peoples and the decline of ethnic hostility, but was also a contributory factor toward those processes.[89]

Though the families I have discussed so far mainly came from at least the fringes of the aristocracy, the patronage of kings and magnates gave them a certain degree of upward mobility, and the possibility for such upward mobility was crucial for ethnic harmony. The example of Wales, where native leaders such as Owain Glyn Dŵr could only advance so far, clearly demonstrates how the barring of advancement or social mobility on ethnic lines was bound to exacerbate ethnic tensions. In contrast, the hope for advancement could cause powerful or able and ambitious natives to downplay ethnic tensions and their own sense of ethnic separateness. Social mobility was also important because it could increase the numbers of native families in the aristocracy, and help push existing families to further heights within the spectrum of aristocratic landholding and power, where the English presence was smallest.

A family whose remarkable rise can illustrate social mobility in the period, and also show more fully how upwardly mobile English families integrated themselves into the predominantly immigrant aristocracy, was the Cockfields. The Cockfields did not appear in Domesday Book, and clearly emerged from among the more prosperous sokemen of Bury St Edmund's. The earliest known member of the family, Wulfric of Groton, had lands producing less than five shillings rent a year. His son or son-in-law Lemmer (OE Leofmær) held more substantial lands in Cockfield and nearby Lindsey by socage tenure at the beginning of the twelfth century. Lemmer may also have held the whole of Cockfield at farm from the monks.[90] After Lemmer's death, his widow Sagiva married a man with a Continental name, which at this early date may still point to a Continental origin; if so, the existence of Norman connections may help to explain the further rise of Lemmer and Sagiva's son, Adam.[91]

More certainly, Adam's rise came through patronage, in this case monastic patronage. Adam attested many charters of Anselm, abbot of Bury St Edmund's from 1121 to 1148, and may have served as his steward. Anselm in turn converted the lands Adam inherited to tenure by knight's service (which substituted more aristocratic forms of service for rent), confirmed Adam in various acquisitions, and granted him new lands.[92] Adam himself made valuable connections through

---

[89] It may be easier to find more natives in the affinities of magnates as time went on simply because of increased evidence. Against this factor, however, one should weigh the fact that it is harder to detect men of native descent in later periods because of changing naming patterns.

[90] *DB* 2: 359a–b, 369a. For Wulfric's land, see Douglas, *Feudal Documents*, no. 122. For Lemmer's land, see Douglas, *Feudal Documents*, nos. 120, 122; *Chronicle of Jocelin of Brakelond*, 138–9. I am unconvinced by Blake's suggestion that the Lemmer of Barningham who appears as a knight in one Ely miracle story was the same as Lemmer of Cockfield: Blake, *Liber Eliensis*, 274, n. 3.

[91] Cyril Hart, 'An Early Charter of Adam of Cockfield, 1100–1118', *EHR* 72 (1957), 466–9.

[92] Adam also attested a couple of charters of Anselm's predecessor, Albold. I am basing the suggestion that Adam may have been steward on the fact that both Adam of Cockfield and Adam the seneschal

marrying Athelice Criquetot, member of an important local immigrant family.[93] Less typically, Adam was one of those enterprising fellows who saw not anarchy but opportunity in Stephen's reign. He built a motte-and-bailey castle in his holding of Lindsey and thereby gained the lease of two nearby Bury manors, which the monks could not otherwise defend, at good rents. He also picked up land from the monks of Ely during the war, and his son Robert can be found holding a knight's fee from that house in 1166.[94] To what degree Adam was involved in the kind of raiding, extortion, and devastation attributed to other castle men of the time cannot be known, but he certainly benefited from building up local military power. It is no surprise that Abbot Anselm could speak about him holding his lands in the same fashion as 'his peers, namely the knights of the abbey'.[95]

Adam's descendants continued to be powerful local figures. His son Robert retained the family's important patronage ties with the abbey, attesting charters of Abbots Hugh and Samson, gaining land from the former, and serving as custodian of the abbey during a vacancy. When Abbot Samson became embroiled with the monks of Canterbury in a jurisdictional dispute over the right to try certain accused murderers, he sent Robert with a gang of about eighty men on a successful raid to seize the prisoners, a sign of Robert's importance among the abbey's tenants and men.[96] Robert's son Adam was less closely tied to the house, although he played an important role in the abbey's court.[97] The abbey's ties with the family were strained by Abbot Samson's efforts to recover control of the two manors that the first Adam gained during the civil war, the parts of Cockfield that the monks claimed were held only at farm, and a hundred court which the family claimed to hold for rent hereditarily. Unfortunately for Bury, the family had by this time built up other ties of patronage, kinship, and friendship.

Even in Adam I's time there is a document in which Adam appears among Abbot Ording of Bury's men, but his son Robert appears among those of Earl Aubrey de Ver; in 1166 Robert held three knights' fees from the Vers.[98] Robert also held one new fee from the greatest East Anglian magnate, Earl Hugh Bigod. When Robert died, Adam II came to see Abbot Samson 'with his kinsmen, Earl Roger Bigod, and many other powerful men', to resist the abbot's demands. The abbot tried to hold firm, pointing to his face and saying: 'May I lose these eyes on that day and hour in

attested a number of charters, but never the same ones: Douglas, *Feudal Documents*, nos. 108–9, 112–14, 119, 121, 123–4, 126, 133. For Anselm's benefactions and the conversion of tenure, see nos. 120, 122, 129–30; *Chronicle of Jocelin of Brakelond*, 138–9.

[93] BM Harley MS 2110, fol. 93ᵛ.

[94] *Chronicle of Jocelin of Brakelond*, 138–9; Blake, *Liber Eliensis*, 383; Hall, *Red Book of the Exchequer*, 1: 364. For what was probably Adam's castle, see Adrian Pettifer, *English Castles: A Guide by Counties* (Woodbridge, 1995), 239.

[95] Douglas, *Feudal Documents*, no. 122.

[96] Ibid., nos. 144, 147, 148, 162, 165; R. H. C. Davis, *Kalendar of Abbot Samson of Bury St. Edmunds and Related Documents* (London, 1954), nos. 56–7, 72, 102, 138; *Pipe Roll 27 Henry II*, 93; *Pipe Roll 28 Henry II*, 73; RCR 2: 10; *Chronicle of Jocelin of Brakelond*, 8, 10, 50–1.

[97] RCR 1: 16–17; Davis, *Kalendar of Abbot Samson*, no. 109.

[98] George F. Warner and Henry J. Ellis, eds., *Facsimiles of Royal and Other Charters in the British Museum* (Oxford, 1903), no. 18; Hall, *Red Book of the Exchequer*, 1: 352.

which I let a hundred be held hereditarily', but faced with this powerful display of connections and support the abbot had to come to a generous compromise, raising the rent slightly on one manor, and giving Adam well over one hundred acres of land in return for control of the court.[99] When Adam II died in or before 1198, the family died out in the male line, though the descendants of his daughters and of cadet lines of the family remained prominent. Local knights estimated that Adam's lands had been worth £104 12s., which may be compared to Sidney Painter's calculation of £115 as the median income of a baron at that time.[100] Through marriage, service, the acquisition of powerful patronage, the construction of local networks of power, and a capacity for violence which they had adapted to Norman military innovations such as the castle, the Cockfields rose out of the middling ranks of society, established themselves as important figures in the county of Suffolk, and gained an estate equivalent to that of many lesser barons, in the process thoroughly integrating themselves into the new order that had been created after the Norman Conquest.

The evidence discussed so far clearly indicates that lineages descended from natives in the male line could survive and indeed prosper over time, but that they did so by adapting to the new realities. Rather than keeping themselves apart and maintaining positions as leaders in some sort of separatist English community, as many modern people would think the honourable thing to do, they embraced the new networks of patronage and kinship that the immigrants had established, and joined themselves to the new order. In the process they placed themselves in a position to interact with aristocratic Normans regularly and thus to influence both the identity and the culture of the aristocracy as a whole, as well as to have their own identity and culture affected by that of the immigrants.

Native aristocrats could interact with Normans in a number of contexts. I have already made clear the importance of the royal court and the affinities of magnates. Integration into neighbourhood aristocratic networks was also important, though somewhat harder to trace. Native aristocrats sometimes appear as witnesses in the charters of neighbours of similar status, including ones of clearly Continental background, and minor immigrant aristocrats attested theirs as well. It is likely that this sometimes resulted from ties of neighbourhood.[101] It is also likely that Adam II of Cockfield assembled his imposing group of powerful allies through such ties as well as through lordship when he confronted Abbot Samson. Courts of law formed another important, and closely related, set of venues for interaction. I will discuss these more fully in Chapter 17, but it is worth noting that native aristocrats func-

---

[99] Hall, *Red Book of the Exchequer* 1: 397; Davis, *Kalendar of Abbot Samson*, 71–2, no. 90; *Feet of Fines of the Reign of Henry II and Richard I* (London, 1894), 9–11; *Chronicle of Jocelin of Brakelond*, 29, 58–9, 138–9.

[100] *CRR* 1: 36; Sidney Painter, *Studies in the History of the English Feudal Barony* (Baltimore, 1943), 170.

[101] For some early examples involving the Ardens, see BM Harley 3650, fols. 15^{r-v}, 16^v–17^r, 31^{r-v}, 37^{r-v}; Bodleian Dugdale MS 13, fols. 139, 449, 469; Dugdale MS 15, fol. 142; Loyd and Stenton, *Sir Christopher Hatton's Book of Seals*, no. 46. See also Thomas, 'Yorkshire Thegn', 12, for the attestations of immigrants to charters of Adam son of Swain.

tioned alongside their counterparts in royal, regional, and even honorial courts. For instance, Harding son of Eadnoth the Staller was one of several men dispatched by William Rufus to hear pleas in Devonshire and Cornwall, and Simeon of Durham included Forne son of Sigulf and Odard the Sheriff among the leading men at the Durham county court in 1121.[102] Others can be found in scattered documents relating to various types of courts.[103] Thus, native aristocratic families interacted with immigrants in a number of contexts, all of which could aid assimilation within the aristocracy.

The most important form of interaction between natives and immigrants, however, came through intermarriage. I have already noted cases of intermarriage involving the Salisburys, Ailward, the Audleys, the Ridwares, and the Cockfields, not to mention the extensive intermarriage in Lancashire. The marriage network involving the Salisburys was particularly impressive, and they were not unique. Peter of Birkin, eldest son of Essulf, who founded several important Yorkshire families, married Emma de Lascelles in the middle of the twelfth century; their son Adam may have married first a sister of Adam son of Swain, a native baron, but then married the wealthy heiress Emma de Caux; and their son John married a daughter of Jordan Lenveise, and then Agnes de Flamville, another wealthy heiress. Four out of five of these marriages were to immigrant families.[104] Late in the twelfth century Henry son of Hervey, great-grandson of Bardulf, illegitimate brother and important tenant of the first lords of Richmond, married Alice of Greystoke, who was descended from Sigulf son of Forne. At around the same time Adam of Staveley, descendant of the Yorkshire tenant-in-chief Gospatric, married Alice de Percy, member of a cadet branch of that important immigrant family. In the next generation the son and heir of the first couple married the daughter and heiress of the second.[105] For most native families marriage patterns are hard to reconstruct, and the earlier one goes the harder it is, for often the names of wives, much less their ancestry, remain unknown. Nevertheless, given the paucity of evidence, the number of marriages across ethnic lines that can be traced indicates that surviving

---

[102] Van Caenegem, *English Lawsuits*, 1: 117; *SMO* 2: 261. For the question of whether Odard was of native background, see above, n. 35. See *WMGR* 470, for a comment that may refer to Harding's skill in courts.

[103] For an early account of the involvement of some English aristocrats in a case, see van Caenegem, *English Lawsuits*, 1: 38. For some appearances of native aristocrats in wapentake or county courts, see *EYC* 6, no. 139; William Henry Hart and Ponsonby A. Lyons, *Cartularium Monasterii de Rameseia*, vol. 1 (London, 1884), no. 81; J. R. West, *St. Benet of Holme, 1020–1210*, vol. 1 (1932), no. 178 (Walter Hautein); William T. Lancaster, ed., *Abstracts of the Charters and Other Documents Contained in the Chartulary of the Cistercian Abbey of Fountains*, vol. 1 (Leeds, 1915), 313, 355. For the appearance of native aristocrats in honorial courts, see *EYC* 3, no. 1526; *EYC* 8, nos. 110, 153 (Henry and Hugh of Eland, William and Thomas of Horbury), 158 (Thomas and William of Horbury). For native knights serving in the royal courts in the reigns of Henry II, Richard I, and John, see *EYC* 1, no. 610; *RCR* 2: 79, 165; *CRR* 1: 287, 429; 3: 127, 320; 5: 176; 6: 194, 222, 277 (Theobald Hautein), 362; 7: 261.

[104] *EYC* 3: 358–9; Clay and Greenway, *Early Yorkshire Families*, 6; C. W. Foster and Kathleen Major, eds., *The Registrum Antiquissimum of the Cathedral Church of Lincoln*, vol. 7 (Hereford, 1953), 209–19. John's brother Roger married a daughter of Roger son of Richard Touche: *EYC* 3: 359, no. 1748.

[105] *EYC* 2: 507; Clay and Greenway, *Early Yorkshire Families*, 89–90; Bodleian Library, Dodsworth MS 129, fol. 110ʳ.

native patrilineages must have married with immigrant families on a regular basis, certainly from the middle of the twelfth century on and perhaps earlier.[106]

One of the striking things about aristocratic marriages across ethnic lines is that men of English descent were as likely to marry Norman women as Norman men were to marry English women, at least once native patrilineages had been firmly established in the new order. Since land could sometimes be passed through marriage, Normandy was increasingly a society that focused on dynastic patrilineages, and the Normans may originally have been short of women in England, one could imagine a pattern in which immigrant men would marry women from the subordinate ethnic group but not marry their own women to English men.[107] There probably was a certain marriage imbalance in the first generation, but even then William the Conqueror married one of his relatives, Judith, to Earl Waltheof.[108] By the second third of the twelfth century, if not earlier, this imbalance had disappeared and English men were as likely to benefit from marriages to Norman women, including heiresses, as Norman men were from marriage to the few available English aristocratic women and heiresses. The FitzWilliams and Birkins in particular benefited spectacularly from such marriages, and they were not alone. The ability of English patrilineages to gain land through marriage to immigrant heiresses is an indication of the way in which English aristocrats were, or at least came to be, perceived as equals, and the way in which they eventually operated on a level playing-field. Marriage may, in the generation or two after the conquest, have served to transfer land from the English to the Normans (though see my doubts in the next chapter), but thereafter it simply knitted the two groups within the aristocracy together, and favoured the well connected and fortunate rather than the 'ethnically correct'.

Though few in number, the aristocratic English patrilineages were thus a dynamic group whose contribution to the integration of the two peoples was more important than numbers alone would suggest. Nonetheless, given the limited size and power of this group, one should not overestimate their impact. First of all, much of the evidence for the success of native families and their integration into the immigrant aristocracy concerns the reign of Henry II and after, which corresponds

[106] For marriages not noted elsewhere in the chapter, see BL Add MS 35296, fols. 360ʳ–361ʳ; Edmund King, ed., 'Estate Records of the Hotot Family', in *A Northamptonshire Miscellany* (Northampton, 1983), 17; *VCH Cambridgeshire*, 5: 38, Keats-Rohan, *Domesday People*, 125; Ormerod, *History*, 3: 61, 187; R. W. Eyton, *Antiquities of Shropshire*, 12 vols. (London, 1854–60), 10: 185; G. R. Elvey, ed., *Luffield Priory Charters*, vol. 1 (Welwyn Garden City, 1968), pp. xlvii–xlix (though it must be noted that none of the families Elvey describes as Saxon were English beyond a shadow of a doubt): R. H. Hilton, ed., *Stoneleigh Leger Book* (Oxford, 1960; repr. Nendeln, 1968), 8; J. H. Round, ed., *Rotuli de Dominabus et Pueris et Puellis de XII Comitatibus [1185]* (London, 1913, repr. Vaduz, 1966), pp. xlvi, 45, n. 3, 47, n. 4, 55, 57–8; *EYC* 2: 122, 127, 129; 3: 106, 256–7, 285, 478, 507; 5: 56, 238; 6: 220; 8: 141, 144; 9: 140–1; 11: 180–1, 244–5; Clay and Greenway, *Early Yorkshire Families*, pp. viii, 43–4, 57–8, 59–60, 76–7, 97–9; Joseph McNulty, ed., *The Chartulary of the Cistercian Abbey of St Mary of Sallay in Craven*, vol. 2 (Wakefield, 1934), 678; *CRR* 11, no. 868; Hedley, *Northumberland Families*, 192, 197, 236–7, 246, 261; *EEA* 14, no. 3; H. S. Offler, 'Fitz Meldred, Neville and Hansard', in *North of the Tees*, ed. A. J. Piper and A. I. Doyle (Aldershot, 1996), 6–9, 12.

[107] For shifts in Norman aristocratic family structure, see J. C. Holt, 'Feudal Society and the Family in Early Medieval England: I. The Revolution of 1066', *TRHS* 5th ser., 32 (1982), 193–212.

[108] For discussion of intermarriage in the generation after the conquest, see below, pp. 146–51.

chronologically to the final stages of assimilation and its aftermath. Though some figures like the early Salisburys and Ardens clearly were pioneers in breaking down ethnic barriers, the issue of cause and effect becomes much more blurred for many of the figures discussed here. To what degree did the successful native aristocrats foster assimilation and to what degree did they simply benefit from a broader process?

Second, the limited numbers of native aristocratic patrilineages outside the north meant that the shift in relations between English and Normans did not come because the English recovered sufficient power to demand better treatment. In the north, as I have argued, the immigrants probably had to come to some kind of accommodation with the native elites, but in most of England English families prospered because the new elites let them. What power such families as the Salisburys and Cockfields did gain was exercised to their own benefit, not that of the English as a whole or even of groups of aristocratic survivors. Thus, assimilation took place in the context of a continuing and pronounced asymmetry of status, wealth, and power between the two peoples, and to explain it one must look elsewhere than to any profound shift in the relative social positions of the English and Normans.

A final, and crucial, point stemming from the imbalance of power between Norman and English patrilineages is that, at the upper reaches of society, it was not so much the Normans who were absorbed by the English as the English by the Normans. In the north it may have been slightly different. One can find the earliest known member of the Buscells, one of the leading Norman families in Lancashire, issuing a charter attested only by immigrants, and then observe more and more natives attesting the charters of his successors at the same time as the Buscells inter-married with native families over the course of the twelfth century.[109] In the north-western counties one can probably speak of native and immigrant aristocracies merging, rather than one group being absorbed by the other. In the south, however, native patrilineages must often have found themselves isolated, at the aristocratic level, within a sea of immigrants. Frequent intermarriage meant that, as time went on, families like the Birkins and Salisburys found themselves in kinship networks dominated by immigrant patrilineages, and had more and more Continental ancestry through maternal lines. For all native patrilineages, functioning within the aristocracy must surely have required adaptation to immigrant ways. Their small numbers would therefore have limited the ability of aristocrats from native patrilineages to anglicize the immigrants, and in fact would have left them open to Normanization.

Indeed, what little evidence survives suggests that native patrilineages *were* Normanized. Obviously, cultural influence to some degree went both ways, and the existence of native patrilineages no doubt contributed to the growth of bilingualism

---

[109] W. A. Hulton, ed., *Documents Relating to the Priory of Penwortham* (Manchester, 1853), pp. xviii–xix, nos. 3–6, 10, 35; Farrer, *Lancashire Pipe Rolls and Early Lancashire Charters*, nos. 14.1, 14.3, 14.5; *Book of Fees*, 1: 210–11. It is also worth noting the large numbers of natives who were attesting charters of the Rumillys and their husbands in the middle of the twelfth century: *EYC* 7, nos. 7, 9, 12–18.

among the aristocracy as a whole.[110] But, in what might broadly be termed the 'shift to knighthood', it was very definitely the natives who made the adjustment throughout. By this phrase I do not simply mean the specific adoption of the title knight or *miles*, which in the post-conquest period was still a very flexible term, but the adoption of new styles of fighting, the integration of native landholders into the system of knights' fees, and the embrace of chivalry.[111] On the military side, it is clear that those native patrilineages who had sufficient wealth and connections adapted to the new world of castles and fighting on horseback; for instance, Earl Patrick was mounting his charger in preparation to fight when he was killed, and as Henry I's standard-bearer at Brémule, the younger Edward of Salisbury must have learned Continental styles of warfare.[112] Early in the twelfth century a Lewin, possibly a Domesday Book landholder, served as armiger or squire to Ralph de Buceio.[113] Late in that century one of Forne son of Sigulf's descendants can be found fighting for Richard I in Normandy.[114] As for castles, Adam of Cockfield made good use of one in Stephen's reign, and one of the many sons of Essulf, Jordan, served as constable of Wakefield, a castle of the Earl Warenne.[115] During the 1173–4 revolt, according to Jordan Fantosme, 'Gospatric the son of Orm, an old white-headed Englishman', whose maternal grandfather was the magnate Waltheof of Allerdale, served as constable of Appleby Castle. He surrendered ignominiously, and was fined for it, but so too were members of the Morville and Engaine families, both of immigrant stock, who had apparently been placed under him.[116] In the aftermath of the revolt, Torfin son of Robert, a native landowner in Westmorland and Yorkshire, served with sergeants in another royal castle.[117] In short, the few English aristocrats who remained were drawn into the new ways of warfare, and learned how to fight side by side with their immigrant counterparts.

Learning new military techniques does not necessarily require broader acculturation, but the shift to knighthood had social elements as well. Obviously the adoption of new methods of fighting and the use of castles were closely connected to the slow incorporation of natives into immigrant patronage networks; according to one Canterbury miracle story, Jordan son of Essulf delayed a promised pilgrimage in order to attend upon his lord, the Earl Warenne.[118] This shift also involved

---

[110] Short, '*Tam Angli quam Franci*', 155–9.

[111] However, for the designation of Englishmen as knights, see *DB* 1: 16b, 18a, 62a, 77a, 77b, 130a, 138a, 241b, 270a; 2: 372; BM Harley MS 662, fols. 8ʳ, 104ᵛ; CUL Add. MS 3020, fol. 168ʳ; J. Conway Davies, ed., *Cartae Antiquae Rolls 11–20* (London, 1960), no. 497; Loyd and Stenton, *Sir Christopher Hatton's Book of Seals*, no. 138; M. J. Franklin, *The Cartulary of Daventry Priory* (Northampton, 1988), nos. 797–8; Spencer Robert Wigram, ed., *The Cartulary of the Monastery of St. Frideswide at Oxford*, vol. 2 (Oxford, 1896), no. 1123; Douglas, *Feudal Documents*, no. 111, *EYC* 1, no. 37.

[112] Meyer, *L'Histoire de Guillaume le Maréchal*, 1: 60–1; *EHOV* 6: 236.

[113] Keats-Rohan, *Domesday People*, 290; J. Horace Round, *Calendar of Documents Preserved in France Illustrative of the History of Great Britain and Ireland* (London, 1899), no. 1132. See also Swein, *scutiger* of Henry I; *Pipe Roll 31 Henry I*, 12.

[114] *EYC* 2: 507.

[115] *EYC* 8, no. 71.

[116] *Jordan Fantosme's Chronicle*, 108; *Pipe Roll 22 Henry II*, 119–20.

[117] *Pipe Roll 21 Henry II*, 165.

[118] *Becket Materials* 1: 160–2.

the switch to tenure by knight's fees, which occurred not only for the Cockfields but other families as well.[119] Shifts in tenure may seem a minor cultural change, but mattered for a couple of reasons. First, tenure by knight's service exposed one's family to control of the guardianship and marriage of minors by the lord of the fief, which had the possible effect of drawing the family very tightly into the lord's orbit. Second, it involved a shift to primogeniture, which was obviously an important social change from traditional English practices. Even though its effects could be diminished or even entirely circumvented through grants to children other than the heir, families that made the change found themselves operating under entirely new inheritance rules.[120] Indeed, Holt has remarked how the Cockfields, though English in origin, used Norman ideas about inheritance to help establish hereditary title to lands which they did not hold by knight's service.[121] This shift also helped prevent the kind of link between ethnicity and tenure that marked medieval Wales under the English, where tenure became yet another important legal and social barrier between the two peoples. In England tenure remained a matter of class rather than ethnicity.[122]

Finally, military transformation also brought the English into the world of chivalry, which had originated on the Continent.[123] Earl Patrick appears in the life of his nephew, William Marshal, who was present at his death, as a chivalric figure, even something of a hero.[124] Native aristocrats sometimes adopted seals which depicted them as equestrian figures, no doubt wishing to project the attendant social as well as military associations of that imagery.[125] Most striking of all, one of the earliest references in England to tournaments comes from a charter of Osbert of Arden, either the son or more likely the grandson of Thorkel of Warwick. In this charter Osbert gave land to a certain Thorkel Fundu in return for carrying his lances from London or Northampton to his home, and for accompanying the donor when he went overseas to tournaments.[126] In crossing the Channel to participate in these mock wars on horseback, Osbert was tightly embracing the culture of the conquerors. Interestingly, in the thirteenth-century romance *Gui de Warewic*, which has been linked to the earls of Warwick, the father of the hero, who was seneschal of

[119] Faull and Moorhouse, *West Yorkshire*, 2: 254.
[120] See Pollock and Maitland, *History of English Law*, 1: 252–356, for different sorts of free tenure. See Holt, 'Revolution of 1066', 193–212, for the importance of the shift brought by the Normans. See Thomas, *Vassals, Heiresses, Crusaders, and Thugs*, 117–24, for the general tendency to practice modified primogeniture. See Williams, *ENC* 207–9, for a related point about the influence of the conquest on English aristocratic tenure.
[121] J. C. Holt, 'Feudal Society and the Family in Early Medieval England: II. Notions of Patrimony', *TRHS* 5th ser., 33 (1983), 193–8, 218.
[122] Davies, *Age of Conquest*, 420; id., *Lordship and Society*, 313–14, 407–8.
[123] There were, admittedly, parallels in the aristocratic society of Anglo-Saxon England, but I still think it safe to describe chivalry as an import. For the similarities and differences, see Gillingham, *English in the Twelfth Century*, 168–85.
[124] Meyer, *L'Histoire de Guillaume le Maréchal*, 1: 6–7, 13–15, 57–61.
[125] e.g. BL Additional Charters 20580 (Ingoldsbys); *EYC* 7: 71 and n. 2 (Henry son of Swain); Stenton, *Danelaw Documents*, no. 493 (Keals); Loyd and Stenton, *Sir Christopher Hatton's Book of Seals*, nos. 138, 159 (Ardens).
[126] Warner and Ellis, *Facsimiles of Charters in the British Museum*, no. 12. For Osbert's relation to Thorkel, see *CRR* 5: 241–2; Williams, *ENC* 104, n. 34, Coss, *Lordship, Knighthood and Locality*, 280.

the fictional earl, was one Sequart, a name not far off from that of Osbert's uncle or brother, Siward of Arden, who served in the affinity of the earls and was grandfather to an actual steward of an earl of Warwick. Another important figure in the story was Gui's mentor as a knight, Heralt of Arden. It is at least possible that this romance was indirectly celebrating the chivalric prowess of one of the great native patrilineages.[127] If so, it is an indication that the natives not only sought out the chivalric world introduced by their conquerors, but were welcomed into it with open arms. This can stand as a symbol for the way in which native patrilineages were socially and culturally absorbed into the new immigrant aristocracy.

The greater cultural impact of the Normans on English aristocrats than of the reverse also raises questions about the ability of the latter to influence the identity of the former. On some level, native patrilineages could not help but support English identity and status. Their very existence as wealthy and high-status families could help refute the stereotypes about the English as peasants that I will pursue more fully later in this work. The presence of English aristocrats in county courts, aristocratic gatherings, and kin groups may also have helped temper any open Norman prejudice against the English. More positively, interaction between the English and the immigrants on the aristocratic level, as equals or near equals, no doubt helped reshape how the Normans thought about their native counterparts, and about the English in general. Thus, though evidence for these assertions is lacking, it seems likely that, intentionally or not, English aristocrats advanced the cause of Englishness. Nonetheless, there were a couple of factors limiting their influence and their contribution to the triumph of English identity. Their small numbers outside the north and their limited collective power would have diminished their ability to foster Englishness. More important, however, is that what evidence survives, most of it admittedly late or indirect, suggests that native aristocrats, far from consciously championing Englishness, downplayed it, and may even have tended to stress maternal Norman roots or sometimes to invent Norman ancestry.

In 1157, when Richard de Lucy made his speech before Henry II invoking the history of the Normans and the Norman Conquest and warning against the plots of the English, among his supporters in the audience, apparently raising no objection to his arguments, were Earl Patrick and Henry of Essex.[128] No fiery defenders of the English these, and it may well be that Henry and even Patrick considered themselves more Norman than English. When Maurice, a descendant of Eadnoth the Staller, adopted his mother's surname of Gant, or when Geoffrey son of Robert son of Meldred of Raby took on the surname Neville, they were probably mainly concerned with emphasizing their descent from a more prestigious maternal line, but they may also have wished to stress Continental at the expense of English ancestry.[129] The descendants of a native Yorkshire landowner, Gospatric, adopted a

[127] Alfred Ewert, ed., *Gui de Warewic*, vol. 1 (Paris, 1933), 3–6. For a possible link of the work with the earls of Warwick, see Emma Mason, 'Legends of the Beauchamps' Ancestors: The Use of Baronial Propaganda in Medieval England', *Journal of Medieval History*, 10 (1984), 30–2.

[128] Searle, *Chronicle of Battle Abbey*, 178–82, 190–2, 196, 208.

[129] For Maurice and his family, see below, pp. 196–8.

surname that appeared as the Latin de Monte Alto and the French Mohaut; one might say 'Highmount' in modern English. It is hard to say in what language, French or English, the name first appeared in conversation, but it is striking that it was the French version that stuck, perhaps because it gave the false cachet of Continental ancestry.[130]

More concretely, French ancestry was attributed to families of native ancestry. A clearly spurious ancestry among the Norman nobility for Edward of Salisbury was developed in the thirteenth century, though this admittedly was largely designed to justify a claim to land in Normandy given to William Longsword, who married Earl Patrick's granddaughter, Ela.[131] The *Meaux Chronicle*, which is from around 1400 but used earlier materials, traces the Meaux family of Yorkshire back to a certain Gamel son of Ketel, who came from Meaux with the army of William the Conqueror, despite the fact that his name was clearly insular. In the same passage the chronicle implies a similar Continental origin for Siward of Sutton, whose forename was certainly English, and Basing of Wawne, whose name probably was.[132] A charter in the Sibton cartulary spoke of an Edric son of Wlric who came over with the conqueror, and cases in the thirteenth-century royal courts speak of an Olaf father of Swane who came to England during the conquest, and an Edgar who acquired a knight's fee at the conquest.[133] For all the families involved, Continental ancestry was being substituted for native origins and, to some degree, a Norman identity was being created.

It must be stressed again that the evidence for an emphasis on matrilineal Norman lines and for fictitious claims of Norman ancestry is late and hard to interpret. We do not know how early fictitious claims began; clearly, it would have taken at least a generation or two and perhaps some intermarriage and acculturation before they would have been believable. Moreover, we do not know if they were consciously invented, or if families simply forgot the ethnic identities of their ancestors at some point, and assumed that, since they were aristocratic, they must have come with the conqueror. It is very difficult to say, from the surviving evidence, what aristocrats in the twelfth century itself thought about their ancestry, although it should be noted that the fact that Richard Fitz Nigel could report on what the natives told him about landholding after the conquest suggests that consciously native English memories and identity were alive in his own day among aristocrats whose ancestors would have grappled with the policies of the new regime at first hand.[134] Despite the problems of evidence, and the caveat I have just raised, two points may be made. First, a downplaying or even denial of English ancestry would fit neatly into the picture drawn in this chapter of native aristocrats

---

[130] *EYC* 7: 253 and n. 8.

[131] Williams, *ENC* 105; Freeman, *History of the Norman Conquest*, 4: 801.

[132] Edward A. Bond, ed., *Chronica Monasterii de Melsa*, vol. 1 (London, 1866; repr. 1967), 78 (discussion of the date of the chronicle and its use of earlier sources may be found on pp. xliv, lxx–lxxiv).

[133] Brown, *Sibton Abbey Cartularies*, 3, no. 700; *CRR* 10: 137–38; Paul Brand, ' "Time out of Mind"; The Knowledge and Use of the Eleventh- and Twelfth-Century Past in Thirteenth Century Legislation', *ANS* 16: 47. See also *CRR* 5: 60–1.

[134] Richard Fitz Nigel, *Dialogus de Scaccario*, 53–4.

being absorbed by the Continental aristocracy. Second, the surviving English aristocrats clearly did not tenaciously cling to memories of their lineage and of their English ancestry in the way that, for instance, Welsh landholders and freemen memorialized their Welsh ancestry long after the final English conquest of Wales.[135]

The fictitious Norman ancestry raises a broader point, namely that the immigrant patrilineages maintained a very strong tradition that they were descended from invaders into the thirteenth century and beyond; this is precisely why false ancestries were created for English patrilineages. When Wace described the actions of many Norman aristocrats at Hastings he may have been writing for their descendants in Normandy, but some of these were also English landholders.[136] The famous 'rusty sword' story, in which the Earl Warenne faced Edward I's *quo warranto* hearings by tracing his ancestry, and claims to property, to a participant in the conquest whose sword he showed the justices, was based on the fact that aristocrats still considered Norman ancestry important.[137] The adoption of an English identity by immigrant aristocrats did not come about because intermarriage or interaction with native patrilineages made them forget or ignore their Norman roots and emphasize English ones. If anyone forgot their ancestry it was the English aristocrats, and their survival alone cannot explain the ultimate triumph of English identity.

The native patrilineages that survived the Norman Conquest or rose into the aristocracy during the period of assimilation were a surprisingly successful group in the long term. The Audleys were not the only family descended from the English in the male line who eventually joined the parliamentary nobility. The Greystokes and FitzWilliams became part of that narrow elite. So too did the first line of Cromwells, descended from a moderately prosperous king's thegn of Nottinghamshire in 1086, Alden or Haldane; the Lumleys, descended from a Durham figure with the insular name of Uchtred; and possibly the Stanleys, who may have shared the same origins as the Audleys.[138] Most notably, the Nevilles of Raby, who counted Warwick the Kingmaker among their number, were descended from a major native tenant of Durham Priory named Dolfin son of Uchtred, who lived in Henry I's reign and who some scholars have suggested was connected to the lineage of Earl Gospatric.[139] After a generation or so of pragmatic prejudice against natives in the aristocracy, any bar to their advancement clearly disappeared sometime in the early twelfth

---

[135] Davies, *Lordship and Society*, 358–64; id., *Revolt of Owain Glyn Dŵr*, 49–50, 129–31, 197, 200, 201, 204; id., 'The Peoples of Britain and Ireland 1100–1400: IV. Language and Historical Mythology', *TRHS* 6th ser., 7 (1997), 21–3.

[136] Wace, *Le Roman de Rou*, 2: 193–210.

[137] For a discussion of the story, see Michael T. Clanchy, *From Memory to Written Record: England, 1066–1307*, 2nd edn. (Oxford, 1993), 35–43.

[138] Cokayne and Gibbs, *Complete Peerage*, 1: 337–46; 3: 551–3; 5: 518–27; 6: 188–201; 8: 266–79; 12: 243–52; Round, *Peerage and Pedigree* 2: 31–6; Clay and Greenway, *Early Yorkshire Families*, 38–9; M. W. Barley, *Documents Relating to the Manor and Soke of Newark-on-Trent* (Nottingham, 1956), pp. xxix–xxx.

[139] For the early history of the family, see J. H. Round, *Feudal England* (London, 1909), 488–90; id., *Family Origins and Other Studies* (New York, 1930), 54–9; Offler, 'Fitz Meldred, Neville and Hansard', 1–17; Charles R. Young, *The Making of the Neville Family in England, 1166–1400* (Woodbridge, 1996), 49, 54–7, 82–7, 95–6, 99–149.

century. This not only allowed a few families to rise to great heights but, more importantly, allowed surviving and rising families to have some impact on assimilation and identity in the twelfth century.

Nonetheless, the surviving and rising native patrilineages were in no position to absorb the Normans on their own, and to bring about either assimilation or the triumph of English identity. They were certainly not the *Traditionskern* for the survival of Englishness. One could easily imagine from the evidence of this chapter a scenario of Norman identity spreading to the English, starting at the top of society and moving downwards. One could also imagine an alternative scenario, in which the population became ethnically divided, with members of the upper classes identifying themselves as Normans, whatever their actual origins, and labelling everyone else English and therefore inferior, thus justifying and reinforcing their domination on somewhat fictive lines of ancestry. To some degree the latter scenario did come about, with aristocrats down to the present day taking pride in their (sometimes invented) Norman ancestry. But obviously the aristocracy did become English, without forgetting its Norman roots, and Norman ancestry became a matter of antiquarian interest rather than a fundamentally important source of loyalty separating the population partly on class lines, in the way that Englishness functioned for so many centuries in Wales and Ireland. I have stressed that assimilation was a complicated affair, involving many groups and factors. It is time to look beyond male aristocrats, as influential as they were, to other groups, starting with three groups of women who interacted with Norman men basically on their own in a highly patriarchal society.

10

English Women and Norman Men

WOMEN OF BOTH peoples and of all social levels played a crucial part in the process of assimilation. Their role in the integration of the public sphere was of course limited by the sexism of the society in which they lived, but to the extent that women acted in that sphere, they could, like their male counterparts, contribute to ethnic rapprochement. Far more important was their part in the integration of families. Any English woman who married a Norman man, and any Norman woman who married an English man, helped to break down ethnic barriers and to create families of mixed heritage in which cultural interchange was bound to happen. Therefore, although the sources do not allow us to see their role as fully as that of men, women appear throughout this book, and particularly in the chapters in Part II on personal interaction. This chapter, however, will focus on three specific groups: two queens of partially English royal background; English women, particularly aristocratic ones, who married Normans in the first generation or so after the conquest; and native women, mainly from outside the aristocracy, who became mistresses of powerful Norman men in later generations.

What justifies this strange grouping (as one reader rightly put it) of queens, one generation of wives, and mistresses? The factor unifying these three groups is that they were all made up of *English* women who helped integrate the two peoples more or less independently from family ties within England. For obvious reasons, there were no Norman queens marrying native kings after the conquest, and no large groups of Norman women marrying English aristocrats in the first generation or acting as mistresses of native nobles in later generations. What sets these groups apart from other English women who helped integrate the two societies, especially through intermarriage, is that the other women generally did so as members of established families within England interacting with social equals. As the previous chapter showed, such interaction was as likely to involve English men marrying Norman women as the reverse, and thus women had no special role in that area of integration, except insofar as the role of mothers differed from that of fathers (a point I will pursue further in this chapter). Later marriages can be seen as family alliances and part and parcel of the integration between English and Norman patrilineages. In contrast, the women in the groups listed above did not have powerful families in England to back them up. The family power of the queens lay outside of England. The dispossession of male English aristocrats meant that even aristocratic English women who married in the first generation generally lost whatever family backing they once had, and mistresses normally came from less powerful families than their lovers. Thus, instead of dealing with interaction between English and Norman families, as was so often the case in the creation of marriages, we are dealing with interaction between women of the defeated ethnic group and men of the dominant group. These three groups will therefore allow us to study the interaction of ethnicity and gender, and the third group allows a focus on the interaction of class with gender and ethnicity as well.

Each of these groups had a role in the integration and assimilation of the Normans, and particularly the Norman aristocracy. Given the decimation of the male English aristocrats through death, dispossession, and exile, the interaction between English women and aristocratic Norman men can help explain how the elites became integrated and anglicized. However, it is necessary to raise questions about the number of marriages or relationships between English women and Norman men, and about the effect of gender roles on matters of culture and identity, before assessing the role of the English wives and mistresses of Normans in these processes. Once again, a comparative approach can be useful. There is scattered anecdotal evidence for intermarriage between elite Irish women and English invaders in Ireland after the English invasion, just as there is for English women after the Norman Conquest. Strongbow's marriage to Aífe, daughter of Diarmit Mac Murchada, Hugh de Lacy's marriage to Rose, daughter of Ruaidrí Ó Conchobair, William de Burgh's marriage to a daughter of Domnall Mór Ó Briain, and other similar marriages all must have brought some acculturation, but failed either to bring assimilation between the two peoples or to Gaelicize the invaders sufficiently to cause them to adopt a new identity.[1] Aífe and her daughter Isabel, who married William Marshal, were clearly absorbed into English culture rather than absorbing their husbands into Irish culture.[2] The situation in Ireland was of course radically different from the one in England, but that merely serves as a reminder that marriages and liaisons of indigenous women to invaders were only one set of factors that must be evaluated in conjunction with others. The comparison with Ireland also spotlights the question of evidence. Given the anecdotal nature of the evidence among each group, is there reason to assume that England saw a much higher rate of marriage between immigrant aristocrats and native women than Ireland? Finally, the failure of Irish women to assimilate and fully Gaelicize English men underscores the importance of questions about how gender, status, power, and ethnicity all intersected.

The potential of English wives and mistresses to help absorb and anglicize the Norman invaders will be obvious, but one must be careful about simply assuming that women would have more influence on culture and identity than men, even within the family sphere. English wives and mistresses of Norman men faced a twofold or even threefold imbalance in power in their relationships. Because they were women, society generally gave them less influence, independence, and power

---

[1] For the marriages, see Duffy, 'The Problem of Degeneracy', 89–95; Frame, 'Les Engleys nées in Irlande', 84–5.

[2] Duffy, 'The Problem of Degeneracy', 89–90.

than men of equal status, and made them to some degree dependent on male relatives or husbands. The Normans may not have radically worsened the position of women, as scholars once thought, but that is largely because the Anglo-Saxon period was never the golden age for women that some considered it.[3] Because they were English, moreover, these women were members of an ethnic group that had been subjugated to that of their husbands and lovers. As for women who were not of aristocratic background, they suffered from inferior social status, which is why they were often mistresses rather than wives. To what degree would these imbalances have limited their ability to affect ethnic relations and identity? To what degree could wives and mistresses influence and acculturate the new immigrant circles in which they found themselves, and to what degree could they pass on their culture to their children? Whose identity mattered for children, their father's, their mother's, or both? To what degree was English ancestry through women remembered over the long term? While the possibility for English women to absorb and anglicize the immigrant aristocracy remains clear, possible countervailing factors should also be investigated.

When Aelred of Rievaulx proclaimed that the green tree prophecy had been fulfilled, a key element in his interpretation was the marriage of Edith-Matilda to Henry I, which in his view joined together the tree that had been split apart in Edward the Confessor's vision, and united 'the seed of the kings of the Normans and English'. Thus, Aelred saw this partially English woman as crucial to reconciliation between the two peoples on both a prophetic and practical level.[4] Modern scholars also note that Henry I, when he married Edith-Matilda, was not only marrying the daughter of the king of Scotland, but a scion through her mother of the old English ruling house, and most agree that the marriage was a factor in assimilation.[5] When the future King Stephen married another Matilda, the daughter of Edith-Matilda's sister, he was doing the same thing, though this was generally ignored in the twelfth century and is widely forgotten now. These facts raise two important and related questions, the latter of which can also help further our understanding of ethnicity in the period. Just how much of a role did each of these queens play in assimilation and anglicization of the Normans; and why, as we shall see, did their roles differ?

One might have expected the marriage of Henry I to a descendant of the old ruling house to bring a dramatic increase in the presence of the English at the royal court, or a general rise in the influence and authority of natives, but this did not occur. Edith-Matilda can be found supporting men with English names in various

---

[3] Pauline Stafford, 'Women and the Norman Conquest', *TRHS* 6th ser. 4 (1994), 221–49.

[4] Aelred of Rievaulx, 'Vita S. Edwardi Regis', 774.

[5] For recent discussions of Edith-Matilda, see Lois L. Huneycutt, 'The Idea of the Perfect Princess: The *Life of St Margaret* in the Reign of Matilda II (1100–1118)', *ANS* 12: 81–97; id., ' "Proclaiming her Dignity Abroad": The Literary and Artistic Network of Matilda of Scotland, Queen of England 1100–1118', in *The Cultural Patronage of Medieval Women*, ed. June Hall McCash (Athens, Ga., 1996), 155–74.

ways, and almost certainly had more native connections than a queen of Continental background would have had, but the effects of her patronage were limited. She supported the candidacy of one Eadwulf to become abbot of Malmesbury, which was under her patronage.[6] She founded Aldgate Priory with help from the English Cnihtengild, a powerful group of native Londoners, and the man she appointed as its first prior, Norman, was probably native, though he studied overseas and had a name that was in both naming pools.[7] Within her own household she had at least two important followers with English names.[8] Thus, at least in a limited way, she acted as a patroness of individual English and perhaps of the English in general.[9] Nonetheless, Edith-Matilda's tenure as queen had very little effect on the composition of the royal court or the relative political power of the two peoples.

Indeed, more evidence survives of Edith-Matilda's patronage of Continental people and of immigrants than of the English. As the gibing description about the royal couple as Godric and Godgiva by their aristocratic opponents suggests, her Englishness had its political drawbacks, given the (admittedly mild and largely pragmatic) prejudices of the Normans.[10] It was therefore important for her to gain support among immigrants and to build up her reputation on the Continent itself. William of Malmesbury wrote explicitly that she tended to favour foreigners (*extranei*) in her patronage, and confirmation for this statement comes from letters of Ivo of Chartres and Hildebert of Lavardin asking or thanking her for gifts.[11] Closer to home, her letters to Anselm reveal an acute anxiety to win his favour, while another immigrant churchman, Herbert Losinga, sought her support in one letter and elsewhere expressed his confidence that he had it.[12] An account concerning Gilbert, the founder of Merton Priory, who was born in Normandy but became the sheriff of three counties in England, recounts that Edith-Matilda supported his pious foundations and describes in detail how she adopted him as a foster-son when

[6] David Knowles, C. N. L. Brooke, and Vera C. M. London, *The Heads of Religious Houses in England and Wales 940–1216* (Cambridge, 1972), 55.

[7] 'Norman' was a more common name among the English than the Normans, and Anselm described Norman as being 'nacione Anglicus nomine Normannus'. For Anselm's statement, and an account of Norman and the foundation of Aldgate, see G. A. J. Hodgett, ed., *Cartulary of Holy Trinity Aldgate* (London, 1971), 223–7, no. 871.

[8] *RRAN* 2: p. xiv, nos. 675, 887, 971, 1090, 1108, 1143; 3, nos. 37–8; Martin Biddle, ed., *Winchester in the Early Middle Ages: An Edition and Discussion of the Winton Domesday* (Oxford, 1976), 81, 391; Mason, *Westminster Abbey Charters*, nos. 99–100, 102–4; *Pipe Roll 31 Henry I*, 150.

[9] She was also said to have supported a moneylender with the English name Bricstan, who wished to become a monk but was persecuted by royal officials and imprisoned, though only after Bricstan was blessed by a miracle; *EHOV* 3: 346–58; Blake, *Liber Eliensis*, 266–9.

[10] *WMGR* 716.

[11] Ibid. 756; Ivo of Chartres, 'Letters', *PL* 162: 125–6, 148–9; Hildebert of Lavardin, *Opera*, *PL* 171: 153–5, 160–2. For Edith-Matilda's patronage in general, see Huneycutt, 'Proclaiming her Dignity Abroad', 155–74

[12] *S. Anselmi Cantuariensis Archiepiscopi Opera Omnia*, ed. Francis Schmitt, 6 vols. (London, 1946–61), 4: 150–2; 5: 244–6, 248–9, 327, 339, 344; *Epistolae Herberti de Losinga*, ed. Robert Anstruther (London, 1846), 48–51. For Anselm and Edith-Matilda, see Southern, *Saint Anselm and His Biographer*, 183–5, 188–93; id., *Saint Anselm: A Portrait in a Landscape* (Cambridge, 1990), 260–2; Sally N. Vaughn, *Anselm of Bec and Robert of Meulan: The Innocence of the Dove and the Wisdom of the Serpent* (Berkeley, 1987), 223–5, 276–9, 357–8.

his own mother died.[13] In short, Edith-Matilda did at least as much to support foreigners and immigrants as she did for the native English.

Overall, Edith-Matilda did little to alter the status quo established after the conquest, or to improve the general standing of the English. Given the political situation, the degree to which the new order had become fixed by 1100, and the queen's need to defer to Henry I, it may be unrealistic to expect that she would have been able to radically alter the position of the English, even assuming that it was a high priority for her. As a woman, even as the most powerful woman in the realm, there was only so much she could do to anglicize the royal court, and she herself was drawn into a network of immigrant and Continental patronage ties.

Edith-Matilda, however, did act as a bearer and promoter of English culture. She showed an interest in pre-conquest history, and encouraged William of Malmesbury to write his *Gesta Regum Anglorum*, one of the key texts in the preservation and defence of English history and identity. William also reveals that she had a special interest in Saint Aldhelm, who was believed to be one of her relatives through the West Saxon royal house. It may be no accident that Abbot Faritius of Abingdon, one of the doctors appointed to care for her during her pregnancy, wrote a life of the saint.[14] Her patronage of Continental scholars demonstrates that Edith-Matilda was a cosmopolitan figure, and she is noteworthy as the probable patron of one of the earliest surviving works in French, the Anglo-Norman *Voyage of St Brendan*.[15] But English history was clearly one of her interests, and she may have brought back a bit of English culture to the royal court.

Edith-Matilda's most important contribution was as a peace weaver, to use the phrase from Old English heroic poetry. Her ties to both natives and immigrants allowed her to build bridges between the two peoples. The prologue of the *vita* of her mother Margaret, composed at her request, extols both the Norman and the English ancestors of Edward the Confessor, though the former more fully, which is suggestive of the ways in which she might have tried to promote amity between the two peoples.[16] Edith-Matilda's mere presence at Henry I's side undoubtedly made a difference in ethnic relations, and she was a very important symbol. Her marriage signalled the new king's willingness to seek the loyalty of his ethnically English subjects and, as the reports of English support for the new king indicate, the marriage was a political success in this respect. Her marriage also helped reconcile natives to the new royal line, as noted earlier, thus lowering tensions and reducing the possibility of revolt, which in turn helped preserve the peaceful atmosphere that paved the way for assimilation.

Moreover, the marriage would have made it hard for Henry I or his immediate

---

[13] Marvin L. Colker, 'Latin Texts Concerning Gilbert, Founder of Merton Priory', *Studia Monastica*, 12 (1970), 249, 252, 257, 259. For Gilbert's career, see Green, *Government of England*, 197–8, 199–200.

[14] *WMGR* 2–8; Stevenson, *Chronicon Monasterii de Abingdon*, 2: 50; Faritius, 'Vita S. Aldhelmi', *PL* 89: 63–84.

[15] R. L. G. Ritchie, 'The Date of the *Voyage of St. Brendan*', *Medium Ævum*, 19 (1950), 64–6; Huneycutt, 'Proclaiming her Dignity Abroad', 164–5.

[16] Hodgson Hinde, ed., 'Vita S. Margaretae Scotorum Reginae', in *Symeonis Dunelmensis Opera*, vol. 1 (Durham, 1868), 237–8. For discussion of this work, see Huneycutt, 'Idea of the Perfect Princess', 81–97.

descendants to admit to, regularize, or codify the de facto discrimination against the English in church appointments and other spheres that was found in the generations immediately following the conquest. This effectively closed the door to any development of the sort of legal, formal, institutional bias that so bedevilled relations between the English and their Celtic subjects in later periods, and for which many other parallels can be found throughout history. In addition, the very presence of a powerful, sophisticated, and cultured queen of partially English ancestry may have helped combat stereotypes about the English as backward and rustic. The marriage must also have muted open expressions of disdain for the English at the highest ranks. William of Malmesbury described how Henry I laughed off the Godric-Godgiva gibes, silently biding his time.[17] Given the way in which the king broke the power of his chief opponents in England, there were probably few such gibes thereafter, at least in public, and in general, courtiers must have paid attention to the queen's sensibilities. Thus, the mere existence of a queen with English ancestry must have improved ethnic relations, and the ultimate descent of the royal line from her only served to solidify the results of her marriage.

In contrast, King Stephen's queen, Matilda, was far less important for ethnic relations than her aunt. There is no sign that she supported ethnically English people, or that she helped promote English culture. Her marriage to Stephen did guarantee that throughout the twelfth century there was always an English element 'by blood' in the royal house. Her ancestry also meant that ethnicity was not likely to be a factor in the civil war of her husband's reign, a development that could have greatly exacerbated ethnic tensions had it occurred. Though Robert of Torigni wrote that Edith-Matilda's ancestry strengthened the claims of her descendants to the throne, and William of Malmesbury put the same claim into the mouth of Henry I, the fact that Stephen's wife shared that ancestry meant that the Empress Matilda was less likely (assuming she wished to) to try to use her English ancestry to attract specifically native support in the same way that her father did at his accession.[18] Thus, Matilda III, like her aunt Edith-Matilda, did help the cause of ethnic harmony, but only in a small way.

Moreover, the Englishness of both queens was something that could be emphasized or ignored; this brings us back to the question of memory and also to the way in which the Irish princesses who married English invaders failed to bring about the absorption into Irish society of the new conquering elite, including their own descendants. Edith-Matilda normally appears in the sources simply as Matilda, but her ownership of a pair of names is fitting, for, as far as her English ancestry is concerned, she has something of a dual image in the sources.[19] Much was written about her, and she is praised in glowing terms in the sources for her piety, goodness, and generous patronage. But only to some writers was her English ancestry important. For chroniclers with a primarily Continental or Norman perspective, such as the Hyde Chronicler or Wace, and for Continental intellectuals such as Ivo of Chartres,

---

[17] *WMGR* 716.
[18] *GND* 2: 240–2; William of Malmesbury, *Historia Novella*, 6–8.
[19] Only Orderic mentions that Edith was her baptismal name: *EHOV* 4: 272; 6: 188.

Marbod of Rennes, and Hildebert of Lavardin, who wrote letters to her or, more significantly, poems in her honour, her connection to the old royal house was not worth mentioning; at most there might be a general comment on her mother as well as her father being of unspecified royal birth. From the Norman side, apart from Robert of Torigni's reference to claims to the throne passing through her, the only references to her Englishness were the references by immigrant nobles to Henry and Edith-Matilda as Godric and Godgiva.[20]

In contrast, Eadmer, William of Malmesbury, Henry of Huntingdon, Orderic Vitalis, Aelred of Rievaulx, and the writer of the Anglo-Saxon Chronicle entry for 1100, all pro-English writers on some level, uniformly noted and in some cases stressed her descent from the pre-conquest line. In a couple of cases their discussion seems to have an ideological bent. In the Anglo-Saxon Chronicle she is described as a member of 'the rightful royal line of England'. William of Malmesbury recorded the hope that her son William would fulfill Edward the Confessor's prophecy about the green tree, though this was dashed by the prince's death in the wreck of the White Ship. In sending a copy of his *Gesta Regum Anglorum* to the queen's daughter, the Empress Matilda, William of Malmesbury also made a point of the queen's own interest in her ancestry. As we have seen, for Aelred of Rievaulx the eventual accession of the empress's son, Henry II, did fulfill the green tree prophecy, and the new king's descent through Edith-Matilda formed the entire basis of his *Genealogia Regum Anglorum*.[21] To some her English ancestry was not particularly noteworthy, but to others it was one of the most important facts about her, and had profound political and ethnic implications.

As for Matilda III, Stephen's queen, even Robert of Torigni and William of Malmesbury seem to have forgotten her English ancestry in their comments about the claims of Edith-Matilda's descendants. Her English royal ancestry was not entirely ignored, for Aelred of Rievaulx placed her son, William, among the prominent figures of his own time descended from the old royal line, as did some writers who drew on him.[22] Nonetheless, her English ancestry was not something most commentators emphasized.

Why the difference between the perceived ethnicity of the two queens, given that they shared the same ties to the old English line and were both multi-ethnic by descent?[23] Why was Edith-Matilda's Englishness sometimes stressed and some-

[20] Edwards, *Liber Monasterii de Hyda*, 305; Wace, *Le Roman de Rou*, 2: 261; Ivo of Chartres, *PL* 162: 125–6, 148–9, 177; Hildebert of Lavardin, *Hildeberti Cenomannensis Episcopi Carmina Minora*, ed. A. Brian Scott (Leipzig, 1969), 21–2, 25; Hildebert of Lavardin, *PL* 171: 153–5, 160–2, 289–90, 1443–5; Marbod of Rennes, 'Opera', *PL* 171: 1660; *WMGR* 716.

[21] *ASC* E 1100; *WMGR* 8, 416, 714–16, 758; *HN* 121; *HHHA* 380; *EHOV* 4: 272; 5: 298–300; Aelred of Rievaulx, 'Vita S. Edwardi Regis', 773–4; Aelred of Rievaulx, 'Genealogia Regum Anglorum', 711–38.

[22] Aelred of Rievaulx, 'Genealogia Regum Anglorum', 736–7; Henry of Huntingdon, *The History of the English*, ed. Thomas Arnold (London, 1879), 295–7; Adam of Dryburgh, *De Tripartito Tabernaculo*, *PL* 198: 722–3. See also *EHOV* 4: 274.

[23] Besides the non-English strains of their immediate ancestry, their descent from an exile branch of the English royal house involved a multi-ethnic background. For recent discussion of possible Continental antecedents from the family's period of Continental exile, see Norman W. Ingham, David Faris, and Douglas Richardson, 'The Origin of Agatha—The Debate Continues', *The New England*

times ignored? The difference between the two queens probably stemmed from cultural affinities and possibly from how they perceived themselves. Edith-Matilda, though the daughter of a Scottish king, was raised at least partly in traditional English nunneries, whereas Matilda, the daughter of the count of Boulogne, was raised in Continental circles, and must have been in cultural terms much less English. Matilda III may not have thought of herself as English at all. This can serve as a reminder of the importance of both personal circumstances and cultural affinities to ethnicity.

But in the case of Edith-Matilda much clearly depended on the interests and concerns of the writers, and in the long term, the way the ancestry and identity of the two queens were recorded and remembered mattered as much as their actual ancestry or cultural connections. In other words, had the Normans in England maintained a separate, staunchly Norman identity, it is easy to see how the English ancestry of the queens and their offspring could have been basically ignored, as in fact it was already being ignored in contemporary sources with a Norman or Continental perspective. In that case, the ancestry of these queens would have mattered no more in the long run than the fact that some of the great Anglo-Irish houses were descended from Irish princesses. In England, however, the insistence of influential historians on the English background of Edith-Matilda meant that her Englishness was firmly embedded in the historical consciousness. In the case of William of Malmesbury's history, Edith-Matilda herself had a hand in preserving and disseminating the memory of her English ancestry. Nonetheless, it was the fact that there were writers willing to emphasize her Englishness, and that there was apparently a constituency for the celebration of her Englishness, that meant that the memory was preserved in the long term.

There were strong limits to what even as powerful and able a woman as Edith-Matilda could do, partly because of the limitations placed upon women in this society. When her husband was actively discriminating against the English in ecclesiastical appointments, Edith-Matilda could hardly hope to improve the lot of the English in any meaningful way, or to extensively integrate the royal court.[24] Though Edith-Matilda did actively promote memory of her own English heritage, it might have mattered little in the long run had not a group of influential writers taken up that theme, and had there not been a general move to assimilation and the revival of English identity across a broad social spectrum. Moreover, when it came to patronage, culture, and even her very name, Edith-Matilda adapted to the new, immigrant order more than she changed or anglicized it. The marriage between Edith-Matilda and Henry did not dispel the sense of continuing ethnic hostility that one finds in chroniclers in his reign, and indeed, one would hardly expect one marriage, no matter how important, to overcome the legacy of hostility created by the conquest. Thus, the royal marriages, although very important, were no guarantee of the

Historical and Genealogical Register, 152 (1998), 215–35; Norman W. Ingham, 'Has a Missing Daughter of Iaroslav Mudyri Been Found?', *Russian History/Histoire Russe*, 25 (1998), 231–70.

[24] HN 224.

triumph of English identity and assimilation, or even of ethnic harmony, but were merely one contributing factor among many. Nonetheless, Edith-Matilda in particular was an important figure in the history of ethnic relations after the conquest. If the story of assimilation and identity is made up of the stories of countless individuals, Edith-Matilda's was clearly one of the most noteworthy.

Edith-Matilda and her niece Matilda III were, of course, not the only women of English descent to marry Normans. William of Malmesbury listed among the characteristics of the Normans their willingness to intermarry with their subjects (*subditi*), a term that, in its context, clearly referred to the English and other conquered peoples.[25] Orderic Vitalis claimed that after the conquest intermarriage began almost immediately in towns, castles, and cities, though he saw this as ending with the rebellions.[26] Could the marriage of powerful immigrants to aristocratic and other English women have absorbed and anglicized the new aristocracy? Neither William of Malmesbury nor Orderic Vitalis specified that Norman men tended to marry English women, but it is certainly possible that the men in an invading army, including those who became part of the new landed aristocracy, might well look locally for marriage partners. If so, such marriages may have been very numerous and could have played a pivotal role in anglicizing and acculturating the aristocracy. Investigation of this possibility demands a study of how numerous such marriages were, particularly at the aristocratic level, and how the wives influenced the cultural milieu of their husbands and, more important, their offspring.

    Recorded instances of intermarriage at the level of manorial landholders are hard to come by in the decades following the conquest, but there certainly are some.[27] In the conquest generation, the wealthy noble William Malet, who may have been part English through a pre-conquest marriage, may himself have married an Englishwoman.[28] Among tenants-in-chief, Geoffrey de la Guerche, Walter of Douai, and Robert d'Oilly married Englishwomen.[29] On the level of less important manorial lords, William Peche, Jocelin, father of the saint Gilbert of Sempringham, Richard Juvenis, and a knight named Odo all had English wives.[30] There are also a handful

---

[25] *WMGR* 460.

[26] *EHOV* 2: 256.

[27] Clark, *Words, Names, and History*, 121–2; Williams, *ENC* 12, 101, 198–200.

[28] The author of the *Carmen de Hastingae Proelio* wrote that William had Harold buried by someone who was part Norman and part English, while William of Poitiers named William Malet as the man in charge of Harold's burial: Guy of Amiens, *Carmen*, 34; *GGWP* 140. Domesday Book records that Archbishop Stigand gave land to William Malet's wife, who may therefore have been English, but it cannot be ruled out that Stigand, who remained a powerful figure for a few years after the conquest, might have hoped to build contacts with a powerful follower of the new king by giving land to a Norman wife: *DB* 2: 450a.

[29] Greenway, 'The Foundation of an Alien Priory', 55–6; Watkins, *Great Chartulary of Glastonbury*, 1: 126–8; *Book of Fees*, 1: 116; *ASC* D 1079. See also *DB* 1: 149a, where a holding of Robert d'Oilly is described as the fee of his wife.

[30] For Peche, see Hart and Lyons, *Cartularium Monasterii de Rameseia*, 1, no. 30; *RRAN* 2: 1629. For Jocelin, see Raymonde Foreville and Gillian Keir, *The Book of St Gilbert* (Oxford, 1987), 10. For Richard Juvenis, see *DB* 1: 167a. For Odo, see G. J. Turner and H. E. Salter, *The Register of St. Augustine's Abbey*

of passages in Domesday Book recording marriages to unnamed heiresses, though by 1086 it is at least possible that these heiresses were the daughters of Normans rather than English.[31] To these may be added some early couples from the first or second generation, of whom the husband had a Continental and the women an English name, revealed by the *libri vitae* of Hyde Abbey and Thorney Abbey, and recently studied by John Moore.[32] Clearly, at least some Normans, including prominent figures, married English women in the immediate aftermath of the conquest.

The question remains how common this intermarriage was, and whether it was extensive enough to radically affect ethnic relations, particularly at the aristocratic level. Unfortunately, in most cases we simply do not know the identity of the wives of immigrant landholders in the first or second generation, especially for the numerous minor lords. But it is worth remembering that a high level of ethnic hostility existed during the first two generations, and that ethnic tensions lingered even longer, which raises a priori questions either about how much intermarriage there was in the first generation, or how successful it was in bringing ethnic unity and harmony. John Le Patourel doubted that there was much early intermarriage, especially involving the upper reaches of the aristocracy. Similarly, Katherine Keats-Rohan has recently noted that intermarriage cannot be found among the greatest tenants-in-chief and warns against any tendency to exaggerate the amount of early intermarriage.[33]

It would certainly be a mistake to automatically assume that the immigrants could not have brought wives, daughters, and marriageable women across from the Continent once they had established their control in England. The anecdotal evidence for Norman women in the upper ranks of the aristocracy is much greater than that for English women, and in the *libri vitae*, which mainly recorded figures of lesser stature, there were far more men with Continental names whose wives had Continental names than ones whose wives had insular names.[34] Presumably, most men who were already married would have wanted to bring over their wives and children. As for the unmarried, it would likely have been no easier to take marriageable women from England to Ireland than from Normandy to England, but the English in Ireland either brought enough women to sustain their identity,

---

Canterbury Commonly Called the Black Book, vol. 2 (London, 1924), 433; Ann Williams, 'The Anglo-Norman Abbey', in *St Augustine's Abbey*, ed. Richard Gem (London, 1997), 60.

[31] e.g. *DB* 1: 48b. See *DB* 1: 48a for a case in which land clearly changed hands with the daughter of a Norman.

[32] W. de Gray Birch, ed., *Liber Vitae: Register and Martyrology of New Minster and Hyde Abbey, Winchester* (London, 1892), 30, 66–7, 72–4, 123, 125, 136; BM Add Ms 40,000 Thorney Liber Vitae 2ʳ–3ᵛ, 9ᵛ–10ᵛ; John S. Moore, 'Prosopographical Problems of English *libri vitae*', in *Family Trees and the Roots of Politics: The Prosopography of Britain and France from the Tenth to the Twelfth Century*, ed. K. S. B. Keats-Rohan (Woodbridge, 1997), 183–7.

[33] John Le Patourel, *The Norman Empire* (Oxford, 1976), 254–5; Keats-Rohan, *Domesday People*, 28.

[34] This is particularly true in the Thorney *liber vitae*, which provides more examples. However, even if one takes a fairly early cut-off date of 1113, to take a convenient date from Moore's dating schema, many of these marriages were in the second generation, by which time the process of name changing was under way: Moore, 'Prosopographical Problems', 183–6.

or absorbed the Irish women without losing their own identity and many aspects of their culture.[35] Obviously, there would have been inconveniences for settlers in trying to bring over women to marry, but there also would have been inconveniences in marrying women who spoke a different language, and who might hate their husbands for the violence they or their families had faced. Even minor manorial lords must have been able to afford to bring women from Normandy, though the same may not necessarily be true for the less important immigrants to be discussed in the next chapter. All in all, there is no reason to merely *assume* widespread early intermarriage between aristocratic Norman men and English women.

The chief reasons for thinking that early intermarriage between Norman men and English women at the aristocratic level might have been widespread come from theories developed by Cecily Clark and Eleanor Searle.[36] Clark, in an article on women's names after the conquest, showed that in a variety of estate and urban surveys spread over the late eleventh and twelfth centuries English women's names tended to disappear from circulation more slowly than English men's names. Clark hypothesized that this might be because of a shortage of immigrant women and a tendency for the Normans to take English wives. Though the great bulk of her evidence comes from social levels other than the aristocracy, she argues that upper-class people set the fashion for names, and that the survival of women's names at lower levels of society occurred because of early intermarriage between English women and Norman men at the aristocratic level after the conquest.[37]

Though there can be no doubt about the discrepancy in naming patterns Clark describes, I remain unconvinced that her hypothesis about intermarriage can be extended to the aristocracy, even by the broad definition I have used here. Because immigrants outside the aristocracy had fewer resources, I think it quite possible, indeed probable, that there was a gender imbalance at that level and therefore much early intermarriage. But when it comes to the upper classes, there is only limited evidence for survival of English women's names. My impression from scattered references in charters and other sources is that English women's names were somewhat more common, on a proportional basis, than English men's names in the lower reaches of the aristocracy, which would of course be indicative of a certain amount of intermarriage. But the fact remains that it is hard to find aristocratic women, even from the lesser aristocracy, with native names. Of course, the predominance of Continental names may be indicative of an early shift in nomenclature among women, though this would weaken Clark's argument that their survival influenced women's names among peasants and townspeople. It may also, however, indicate widespread immigration by women at that level. Alternative explanations could be put forward for a lag in the shift in naming patterns for

---

[35] There was probably, it should be noted, more settlement of English peasants in Ireland, which could have made a difference; see below, p. 162.

[36] Searle, 'Women and the Legitimization of Succession', 159–70, 226–9; Clark, 'Women's Names in Post-Conquest England: Observations and Speculations', in *Words, Names, and History*, 117–43.

[37] Clark, *Words, Names, and History*, 128–43.

women. For instance, the swifter shift in men's names may have to do with the greater public role of men in this society. Families might have found it more urgent to flatter aristocratic men by naming their sons after them, and been more concerned that their sons' names should reflect patterns common among the new elites. In short, Clark's argument that the discrepancy between male and female naming patterns reflected in part extensive aristocratic intermarriage must remain a hypothesis.

Searle, in her important article 'Women and the Legitimization of Succession at the Norman Conquest', put forward two important arguments with implications for intermarriage between Norman men and English women. The first was that several marriages proposed or arranged by William the Conqueror, including those between Harold and his own daughter, Waltheof and one of his kinswoman, and Earl Edwin and one of his daughters, were designed to integrate the two aristocracies and arrange for a peaceful takeover. Though the marriages and proposed marriages she discusses were all between English men and Norman women, the reverse could also have been true. The second was that Normans frequently channelled land and inheritance through women and marriage, and that, after the Norman Conquest, they married women from the families whose land they had acquired in order to gain some sort of hereditary claim to the land and to achieve an understanding with the dispossessed. She limits this latter argument to 'those who would hold only in England', and to 'the knightly level'. If this theory is correct, it would mean that the rate of intermarriage between women of the old aristocracy and lesser Norman landholders was quite high, for it would indicate that such lesser Norman aristocrats often, perhaps regularly, married English women.[38]

Of these arguments, I find the first utterly convincing, and would suggest that at least some of the early marriages between English women and Norman men should be seen in an early context in which William was trying to gain the co-operation of his new English subjects. Robert d'Oilly's marriage to Edith, daughter of the English magnate Wigot, must have occurred soon after the conquest, judging by the marriage of their daughter to Miles Crispin before 1086. While it is possible that, despite the survival of Wigot's son Toki until 1079 (when he was killed in battle bringing a horse to William I), the marriage was intended all along to bring Wigot's land to Robert, as Searle suggests, it seems more likely that the marriage was originally designed instead to create a marriage tie between an English magnate and a Norman follower of the king.[39] Other marriages could have been made for the same reason. Orderic places his statement about intermarriage *before* some of the early revolts, when the hope for co-operation between English and Norman nobles might have led to intermarriage for political reasons.[40] At least some of the

---

[38] Searle, 'Women and the Legitimization of Succession', 159–70, 226–9.

[39] See Williams, *ENC* 101, for the date of the marriage. The fact that Earl Edwin transferred one of his followers to Robert suggests that the latter did develop cordial relations with the English in the years immediately following Hastings: *DB* 1: 154b.

[40] *EHOV* 2: 256.

marriages between English women and Norman men should probably be seen in the context of early attempts to knit together the Normans and English.

The scenario outlined above suggests the possibility of a fair amount of inter-marriage, involving both English men and English women, in the first couple of years after the conquest. However, the striking thing about the marriages and pro-posed marriages Searle discussed was their utter failure to bring peace; two did not even take place. Given the suspicions from the beginning, the number of people willing to enter such marriages may have been limited. Moreover, once William decided to destroy rather than conciliate the old elites, this important motive for intermarriage would have vanished abruptly, at least outside the far north.[41] Existing marriages would have come under great strain; according to later family tradition, Waltheof's wife was involved in his downfall and death.[42] Because English noblewomen who had contracted such marriages posed no military threat, marriages between them and Norman men were more likely to survive, thus ensuring at least a certain English presence among the new elites. Nonetheless, the formation of marriages to create bonds between the English and Norman aristocracies would have been a precarious and short-lived strategy, and was not likely to lead to an overwhelming predominance of English over Continental women.

Searle's second argument is the principal one for believing there could have been widespread intermarriage between English women and Normans in the lower ranks of the aristocracy, but about this argument I have fundamental doubts. If I am correct that the Normans discounted pre-conquest claims to land, and required that even surviving landholders get some sort of new grant of their land, then marriage to women from pre-conquest families would not give any additional legal security, and any claims to that effect would be risky, because they would open the door to all English claims from before the conquest. Indeed, reliance by some Normans on marriage to claim English lands would be dangerous for other Normans, since at least some must have been married on the Continent before they gained English lands, and others acquired the land of many different English land-holders, with all of whose families they could not hope to create marriage ties. Such figures would surely have resisted the idea that marriage was necessary to solidify claims to English lands. Moreover, to my knowledge, no lands in surviving legal disputes were claimed by right of marriage to a woman from a dispossessed family. Strikingly, in a case involving land that may have come to William Peche through his wife, his descendants never derived their claim through her and the land con-tinued to be claimed by William's son by another marriage.[43] All in all, it seems highly unlikely that marriage to an English woman provided any tenurial security to Normans.

[41] It is worth noting that Walter of Douai, who originally married an English widow, later had a wife with the Continental name of Emma: Watkins, *Great Chartulary of Glastonbury*, 1, no. 172.

[42] Giles, 'Vita et Passio Waldevi Comitis', 2, 13.

[43] John Hudson, 'Life Grants of Land and the Development of Inheritance in Anglo-Norman England', *ANS* 12: 68–9. That William and Alfwen held the land as a life grant may make a difference, although obviously the heirs were trying to convert the grant to hereditary tenure.

The other part of the second argument Searle makes for Norman intermarriage with English women was the need to conciliate survivors from the English aristocracy. Given the destruction of the pre-conquest elite that I have described in the previous chapter, I doubt that the Normans had any need for or interest in such conciliation, except in the case of the few patrilineages that survived. It is true, as Searle says, that the Normans could not kill all the English thegns, but they did kill many, exiled others, and reduced the rest to impotence, at least insofar as the possibilities of active revolt were concerned. Nor am I sure that it would have been all that much consolation for an English thegn, who was deprived of his lands and relegated to a lesser status, to know that a female relative was going to marry one of the men responsible. In the tightly knit world of the Norman aristocracy, channelling marriage through land may have been an effective way of getting land into competent hands without angering families, whose males lost out, to the point of rebellion, but I think it unlikely that the same methods could have overcome deep political and ethnic barriers and hostility.[44] Moreover, would it not have made more practical sense for individual Norman landlords to try to create marriage ties within the new elite rather than to reach out to members of a hostile and now impotent group? Norman lords with daughters must have been looking for wealthy husbands for them and, after the crushing of the English aristocracy, such women would have provided more useful political ties for ambitious Norman men, including minor ones, than English brides. Thus, there are good reasons to doubt a scenario in which marriages were used to conciliate the old elite once it had been destroyed. In general, I think Searle's arguments for widespread marriage between lesser Norman aristocrats and aristocratic English women are much weaker than they first appear.

The question of how much intermarriage occurred between Norman men and English women at the aristocratic level in the immediate aftermath of the Norman Conquest must remain an open one. Clearly there was some, but I am sceptical about how widespread it was even for the lesser nobility. However, even the amount of intermarriage indicated by a minimalist interpretation of the sources is significant. That some Norman men viewed English women as worthy of marriage indicates at least a certain level of respect for the English, and is another indication of the pragmatic nature of Norman prejudice (though the early intermarriage in Ireland did not prevent the English there from holding or developing strong prejudices against the Irish). Early marriages, and the children they produced, might not have guaranteed assimilation and anglicization, if they were few in number, but they could certainly contribute to it. How much of a role aristocratic English women played in assimilation, however, must remain a question, simply because it is hard to say how many gained a place in the new order.

There is also the problem of the relative power of men and women to shape and influence the society around them, and of the relative ability of fathers and mothers

---

[44] See Searle, *Predatory Kinship*, 159–77, for her model of how kinship and marriage functioned in Norman society. It should be noted that she argues that it was used there to incorporate Frankish enemies.

to mould the culture and identity of their children. Though it is merely common sense to assume that English wives must have had some effect in acculturating the Norman upper classes, and that English mothers could shape their children in important ways, getting at hard evidence is very difficult, and so, therefore, is understanding their precise role. Moreover, there are many important factors about which we know little, such as the respective roles of mothers and fathers in raising children; the impact of the training of young aristocrats outside the home, perhaps in the households of great lords where wives were very unlikely to be English; and the degree to which English wives might have been isolated in the new immigrant aristocratic milieu. Van Houts has discussed the ways in which English women helped to preserve memories of the conquest and the English past, but even here the evidence is scanty.[45] To try to answer these questions I will draw on some evidence that is fairly indirect or from beyond the strictly aristocratic level.

I will start at an oblique angle, with embroidery, a widespread skill among aristocratic English women (and their female servants or slaves), and specifically with the Bayeux Tapestry. It is widely though not universally agreed that native women embroidered the Bayeux Tapestry, though it was almost certainly Odo of Bayeux who commissioned it, and may have been a native monk who designed it.[46] Gameson has rightly described this as an Anglo-Norman work, incorporating artistic and other elements from both cultures.[47] If the general presumption that English women were involved is correct, their skills and knowledge clearly contributed some of the Englishness of the work. This provides one example of the way in which English women could help to preserve English culture and contribute to the acculturation of the two peoples. More speculatively, a number of scholars have argued that the Bayeux Tapestry had a complex message that might have been read in different ways by the English and the Normans, though this has been hotly contested.[48] This phenomenon is often attributed to the designer, perhaps a monk, but surely it is possible that English embroiderers could have had a role or at least been accomplices in any intended double reading. There are many uncertainties here, but the Bayeux Tapestry raises interesting questions about the possible ability of women, as embroiderers and in other capacities, to subvert the dominant, pro-Norman narrative of the conquest. One can easily envision English mothers pro-

---

[45] Van Houts, *Memory and Gender*, 71, 74, 137–42.

[46] For the English origins and Odo's patronage of the tapestry, see Wilson, *Bayeux Tapestry*, 201–212; Stenton, *Bayeux Tapestry*, 29–34; Brooks and Walker, 'Authority and Interpretation of the Bayeux Tapestry', 1–34; Bernstein, *Mystery of the Bayeux Tapestry*, 26, 29–30, 37–50, 60–88; René Lepelly, 'A Contribution to the Study of the Inscriptions in the Bayeux Tapestry: *Bagias* and *Wilgelm*', in *Study of the Bayeux Tapestry*, ed. Richard Gameson, 39–45; Richard Gameson, 'The Origin, Art, and Message of the Bayeux Tapestry', in ibid. 163–74. Bernstein has suggested the designer was a monk: *Mystery of the Bayeux Tapestry*, 59, as has Richard David Wissolik, in 'The Saxon Statement: Code in the Bayeux Tapestry', *Annuale Mediaevale*, 19 (1979), 77. For a recent dissenting view on the tapestry's English origins, see Grape, *Bayeux Tapestry*, 44–54. See van Houts, *Memory and Gender*, 102–3, for a discussion of tapestries, women, and historical memory.

[47] Gameson, 'Origin, Art, and Message', 173–4.

[48] Bernstein, *Mystery of the Bayeux Tapestry*, esp. 192–5; Wissolik, 'Saxon Statement', 69–97; Suzanne Lewis, *The Rhetoric of Power in the Bayeux Tapestry* (Cambridge, 1999); Albu, *Normans in their Histories*, 88–105.

viding similarly subversive accounts of the conquest to half-Norman children. Nonetheless, it is also important that the main and most straightforward point of the Bayeux Tapestry was to hammer home that dominant narrative. As a result, English women found their artistic skills being enlisted in the service of Norman propaganda, a clear example of the limits of their ability to influence, rather than be influenced by, the new aristocratic milieu in which they found themselves.

Two individual examples also suggest the possibilities for aristocratic wives to influence their husbands' milieu, and the limits on those possibilities. In Chapter 9 I described the loyalty between Walter of Douai and his followers, including a steward, Uluric, who was possibly English. Walter was also one of the few immigrant aristocrats who can be shown to have married an English woman, and it seems quite likely that, if Uluric was English, the two facts, and perhaps the two natives, were related.[49] On the other hand, the charter of Geoffrey de la Guerche that reveals his marriage to the English woman, Alveva (by that time deceased), has a witness list that includes twenty-three names, only one of which might have been English, indicating that Geoffrey continued to operate in a predominantly Continental circle despite his marriage.[50] Even if marriage of aristocratic English women to Norman men was widespread, the small number of even minor English male aristocrats who can be found in the sources suggests that the ability of wives to help their male kinsmen and integrate their husbands' followings was limited. How much influence they were able to have on their husbands and the circle of their husbands in such circumstances must remain debatable.

One would presume that the English wives of Normans were able to have an important role in shaping the culture and identities of their children, for instance by teaching them English, or by passing on some sense of the English as a people. Unfortunately, evidence for this is almost wholly lacking. Some possibilities emerge, however, in the cases of certain writers. Marjorie Chibnall and Diana Greenway, in their editions of the works of Orderic Vitalis and Henry of Huntingdon, have suggested, on the basis of these authors' knowledge of English, their pro-English sentiments, and in the former case, Orderic's description of himself as *angligena*, that these two writers, both the sons of immigrant clerics, had English mothers. This seems quite plausible, though it cannot be proved since neither ever mentioned his mother.[51] William of Malmesbury described himself as being of mixed heritage, and though he does not describe which parent came from which people, van Houts has suggested that it was probably his mother who was

---

[49] Watkins, *Great Chartulary of Glastonbury* 1: 126–8.

[50] Greenway, 'Foundation of an Alien Priory', 55–6.

[51] *HHHA*, p. xxvi; *EHOV* 1: 2; Chibnall, *World of Orderic Vitalis*, 8–10. Chibnall's argument, that Orderic's description of himself as *angligena* indicates that his mother must have been English, is a strong one, but not absolute proof, since although such terms with the root *gens* more often referred to ancestry than to birth, they did not invariably do so, and Orderic himself referred in one passage to William I as *angligena*: *EHOV* 4: 78. If Orderic's statement that when he arrived in Normandy he heard a language, like Joseph in Egypt, that he did not know, is taken to mean that he did not know French, then the likelihood that his mother was English rather than French is even stronger: *EHOV* 6: 554.

English.[52] All of these suggestions are based on sensible presumptions about the role of mothers, but of course that means that any attempt to use these examples to *prove* that mothers could influence their children would be to engage in circular reasoning. What we are left with are plausible scenarios or hypotheses about the role of putatively English mothers on these important and, in two cases, highly influential writers. If these hypotheses are correct, they would indicate that women might play a very important role indeed in identity and culture.

However, the fathers of all three of these men were also important to their sons, and this serves to remind us that the influence of mothers had to compete with that of fathers. Though Orderic and Henry never mentioned their mothers, they memorialized their fathers. Though William credited his *parentes*, meaning relatives or parents, with encouraging his love of reading and study, he singled out his father on this score.[53] Obviously, both parents would normally have influenced children, and no doubt many children of mixed marriages felt ties of culture and identity to both peoples, as William of Malmesbury did.[54] The importance of this for assimilation and acculturation needs no emphasis. There was nevertheless always the possibility that the children could be absorbed largely into the culture and identity of their fathers, as were the descendants of the Irish princesses noted earlier. In this context it is worth noting that, according to the *Leges Henrici*, when it came to determining whether or not a *murdrum* fine should be levied when the victim was of mixed parentage, the ethnicity of the father was what mattered.[55] Obviously, the way people thought about the ethnicity of children of mixed marriages was more complex than this, but it does show how, in this patrilineal society, fathers may have had more influence than mothers in shaping the identity of their children, and the same may well have been true of culture as well.

For aristocratic women who married after the conquest, the problem of memory must also be considered, even more so than for queens. Were female English ancestors remembered in such a way as to give their descendants a sense of being English 'by blood', to borrow William of Malmesbury's terminology? Certainly some English women were remembered down through the generations. The author of the *vita* of Gilbert of Sempringham, writing shortly after 1200, noted that Gilbert's mother was English.[56] In 1212 it was remembered that the lords of Wallingford had been descended from Wigot of Wallingford's daughter.[57] Knowledge of the marriages of Earl Waltheof's half-native, half-immigrant daughters, and of the descent of powerful families, including the royal house of Scotland, from them was widespread.[58] This suggests that memories of English female

[52] *WMGR* 424; van Houts, *Memory and Gender*, 138.

[53] *EHOV* 3: 142–50; 6: 552; *HHHA* 458; *WMGR* 150.

[54] *WMGR* 424.

[55] Downer, *Leges Henrici Primi*, 236.

[56] Foreville and Keir, *Book of St Gilbert*, 10.

[57] *Book of Fees*, 1: 116.

[58] *EHOV* 6: 54; Giles, 'Vita et Passio Waldevi Comitis', 18–22; Aelred of Rievaulx, 'Genealogia Regum Anglorum', 736; Jocelin of Furness, 'Vita Sancti Waltheni', in *Acta Sanctorum: Augusti Tomus Primus* (Paris, 1867), 252; Adam of Dryburgh, *De Tripartito Tabernaculo*, 723.

ancestry could be maintained over a long period, particularly when the women brought property to Norman patrilineages. Nonetheless, the question remains of how these memories influenced their descendants' sense of identity. It is worth reiterating here the emphasis that later aristocrats placed on Norman ancestry. In individual cases, memories of female ancestors may have given nuance to this continuing view of the aristocracy as Continental in origin. But there is absolutely no indication that when the aristocratic descendants of the invaders began to adopt an English identity, they based their newfound Englishness on a widespread knowledge of descent from English women. In the collective memory of the aristocracy, the influence of female English ancestry was clearly quite limited, either because early intermarriage was not that common, or because the patrilineal Norman ancestry mattered more and the English women had been forgotten as a group, even if not necessarily as individuals.

Undoubtedly, the English women who married Norman aristocrats in the first generation or two after the conquest were a factor in the assimilation of the two peoples and the triumph of English identity, but I do not think they can be seen as decisive. Their numbers may have been limited, and their influence somewhat constricted. They certainly brought no immediate end to hostility, and their influence on identity was clearly indirect and at most very partial, since it was the Norman ancestry of the aristocracy that continued to be emphasized. Had other factors not been at work, it is quite possible that they would have been simply absorbed by the Normans, just as the elite Irish wives were by the English. But if the role of English wives from the immediate post-conquest period was not decisive, neither should it be ignored. Relations between peoples turned out differently in England than in Ireland, and for this the English women who married into the Norman aristocracy must be given their share of credit.

Aristocrats with a Continental origin also formed less formal attachments to English women. In theory, sexual attraction can be a powerful force for assimilation, but its effectiveness is heavily influenced by the nature of the relationships created around sexual activity, which can be influenced in turn by the respective social status of the participants. Potential native marriage partners would have been limited for Norman aristocrats after the first generation, and in any case marriages must normally have been used to create connections between families, rather than being based on sexual attraction. But liaisons between Norman men and English women must have continued to be common. As one might expect, the ability of English mistresses to influence the aristocratic milieu was even more limited than that of English wives. Nonetheless, English mistresses did serve to create connections between the English and the Normans that made a modest contribution to assimilation.

The most interesting and best-documented account of a liaison across ethnic lines (as well as of another, attempted liaison) comes from the *vita* of the English hermit and abbess Christina of Markyate, and involves the notorious Ranulf

Flambard.[59] As one of William II's most important officials, and later as bishop of
Durham, Flambard provides a good example of a powerful Norman man on the
prowl. Before he became bishop Ranulf had taken Christina's aunt, Alveva, as a
concubine and had children by her. He later set her aside and married her off to a
prominent citizen of Huntingdon, her family's town, but continued to visit her
periodically when travelling, as bishop, between London and Durham. On one
occasion, when he was visiting and Christina's family went to Alveva's house to pay
their respects, Ranulf tried to seduce Christina herself, who feared to be raped if
she refused. She asked for permission to get up to bolt the door, which Ranulf
permitted only when she swore that she did not deceive him in claiming that that
was her intent. She then fulfilled her oath by bolting the door *from the outside*, thus
making her escape. Shortly afterwards, according to the *vita*, Ranulf got revenge by
arranging Christina's betrothal to another native citizen, Burthred, thus creating a
major stumbling-block to Christina's desire to enter the religious life. The *vita*'s
account of Ranulf's motives in arranging the betrothal seems far-fetched, and Ruth
Morse has cast doubts on the story of Christina's escape from Ranulf's clutches and
other aspects of the *vita*. Nonetheless, Christina herself was the most important
source for the *vita*, and the core account appears quite plausible.[60]

Christina's *vita* shows the potential dangers facing women from powerful men in
this society, but it also shows how Ranulf's relationship with Alveva narrowed the
social distance between him and her English family. Ranulf maintained some sort
of friendship with her and her family, whom, according to the author of the *vita*, he
honoured for her sake. Whatever his motives, he involved himself in their affairs to
the extent of helping arrange a marriage for Christina, which Christina's parents
wanted even if she did not. H. S. Offler and William Aird have suggested that a
Richard of Huntingdon, who attested a charter in which Ranulf enfeoffed his own
nephew with land, was a relative of Alveva.[61] Thus, Ranulf's relationship with
Alveva brought close interaction between one of the most powerful Normans of
the day and a well-to-do but much less powerful English family. But the most
important fact is that the union produced children, who thereafter had contacts 'by
blood' with both Normans and English. There is no way to be certain that Alveva
was Ranulf's only mistress, but it is possible that the sons whom Ranulf raised to
positions of moderate power were her children.[62] Thus liaisons, like marriages, may
occasionally have brought children of mixed background into the lower ranks of
the new elites.

Another example also shows how liaisons could create ties between families of
differing social levels. A dispute over the status and patronage of St Andrew's,
Plymouth, reveals that Reginald de Vautortes, a powerful lord in the south-west,

[59] C. H. Talbot, *The Life of Christina of Markyate: A Twelfth Century Recluse* (1959; repr. Oxford, 1987),
40–4. For Ranulf and his career, see R. W. Southern, *Medieval Humanism and Other Studies* (Oxford,
1970), 183–205.
[60] Ruth Morse, *Truth and Convention in the Middle Ages* (Cambridge, 1991), 149–52.
[61] H. S. Offler, *Durham Episcopal Charters 1071–1152* (Gateshead, 1968), 105; Aird, *St Cuthbert and the
Normans*, 203–4.
[62] Southern, *Medieval Humanism*, 201; Aird, *St Cuthbert and the Normans*, 204.

had an illegitimate son named Thomas by the daughter of Dunpriest, the hereditary and English priest of that church. There is no way to be certain about the precise nature of the relationship between Reginald and Dunpriest's daughter. However, the fact that Reginald asked the patron of St Andrew's to appoint Thomas in succession to Dunpriest's own son and successor, William, shows that he acknowledged his son, and points to continuing relations between the families.[63]

An English woman who achieved far more for herself and her family, and who also helped to integrate aristocratic Norman society, was Edith, daughter of Forne, one of Henry I's many mistresses and clearly a redoubtable woman in her own right. Her father, Forne son of Sigulf, appears in Domesday Book as a newly established king's thegn in a single Yorkshire manor, though he may have had older roots in Cumbria. Edith bore Henry a son named Robert, and the king then married her off, with the gift of a valuable manor, to the baron Robert d'Oilly, sheriff of Oxford, and heir of the Robert d'Oilly who had married the daughter of Wigot. *Domina* Edith, as she was called in one charter, asserted herself more than most aristocratic wives, at least judging by the evidence, for she persuaded her husband to found Oseney Abbey, and he recorded her consent to several other grants. As a widow she continued to be a dominant figure within the family, a generous donor to religious houses, and apparently a perfectly respectable and pious figure.[64] Her descendants in the d'Oilly family prospered, and her son by the king, Robert Fitz Regis, became a leading baron as a supporter of the Empress Matilda during Stephen's reign. In 1166 he held approximately ninety knight's fees.[65] Her natal family also prospered. Forne himself attested a number of royal charters, and Henry I either granted to him or allowed him to keep the Cumberland barony of Greystoke, whence his descendants took their name. Forne also picked up significant new lands in Yorkshire and Durham. It is hard to say whether or not Forne's rise to such heights began before his daughter came to the king's attention, but it seems likely that having a daughter in the king's bed did not hurt his position.[66] While one would not want to call Edith a woman raised from the dust, to paraphrase Orderic Vitalis, she certainly did well by herself and her family through her affair with Henry I.

Obviously Edith's case was an exceptional one, in that her liaison was with a king. Even Henry I could only have so many mistresses, and most of his mistresses were

[63] Bodleian Library MS James 23, fols. 164–5; *EEA* 11, no. 23.

[64] H. E. Salter, ed., *Eynsham Cartulary*, vol. 1 (Oxford, 1907), nos. 66–7; Wigram, *Cartulary of St. Frideswide*, vol. 2, no. 951; H. E. Salter, ed., *The Cartulary of Oseney Abbey*, 6 vols. (Oxford, 1929–36), 1, no. 1; 4: 11, nos. 19, 20, 65A, 71; 5: 206, nos. 572A, 690–1; Agnes M. Leys, ed., *The Sandford Cartulary*, vol. 1 (Oxford, 1938), nos. 62, 127; H. E. Salter, ed., *The Thame Cartulary*, vol. 1 (Oxford, 1947), no. 2; *VCH Buckinghamshire*, 4: 227; David Postles, 'The Foundation of Oseney Abbey', *Bulletin of the Institute of Historical Research*, 53 (1980), 242–4; David Postles, '"Patronus et Advocatus Noster": Oseney Abbey and the Oilly Family', *Historical Research*, 60 (1987), 100–2.

[65] For Robert Fitz Regis's career and holdings, see *RRAN* 3, nos. 274, 632, 634, 699; *SMO* 2: 310; Hall, *Red Book of the Exchequer*, 1: 251–4.

[66] For Forne and the early history of the Greystokes, see *DB* 1: 330b; *RRAN* 2, nos. 1264, 1279, 1326, 1357, 1494, 1541, 1557; *EYC* 2: 505–9. For the suggestion that Forne's father Sigulf was established in Cumberland before the Norman conquest of that region, see Phythian-Adams, *Land of the Cumbrians*, 30, 141, 179.

not English, although he apparently slept with a second Edith, whose daughter by him married the count of Perche.[67] In some respects, however, this example follows the patterns noted in the other liaisons. The affair created connections between a powerful Norman and the family of his mistress, and bridged but did not eliminate the social and ethnic gaps between them. A late, but probably far more typical, example of a liaison involves a minor aristocrat and a peasant woman. Around 1180 or 1190 Thomas of Cuckney, great-grandson of one Joceus the Fleming, who, according to family tradition preserved by the family's monastic foundation, came to England at the conquest, was preparing for a pilgrimage to the Holy Sepulchre in Jerusalem, and made a grant to his mistress, Aileva, and to their younger daughter. The grant consisted of her father's holding of one bovate of land, along with Aileva's brother and his land. The bovate originally held by Aileva's father was a more or less typical peasant holding, and the gift of Aileva's brother, which must have made for some interesting family dynamics, indicates that they were of servile background. In other words, the descendant of an immigrant landholder apparently had an established relationship with the daughter of one of his serfs. That Thomas provided for his mistress and daughter in a document witnessed by several churchmen, including a minor abbot, shows that the relationship was acknowledged by Thomas and accepted by local society. But it was not a marriage, and it did not bring Thomas's illegitimate younger daughter into Thomas's own social class. With a bovate and overlordship over her uncle, this daughter could probably hope to marry a member of the middling sort, but she was highly unlikely to marry into a family of her father's rank, and thereby influence the ethnic make-up and identity of the upper classes. Once again, Thomas and Aileva's affair shortened, but did not eliminate, the social distance between their respective families.[68]

It is worth turning, for a moment, to the story of an attempted liaison between an aristocratic Norman woman and an English man, since it can shed additional light on the roles of gender and power in liaisons across ethnic lines. The story in question is that of the mother of Hugh de Morville (probably Beatrice de Beauchamp), and a hapless follower of her husband with the insular name of Lithulf.[69] According to this story, which appears in a life of Becket and was used to discredit the family of one of his murderers, Beatrice made sexual advances that were rebuffed by Lithulf. To gain revenge, she persuaded him to draw his sword in front of her husband, to whom she then called out a warning (in English) which prompted him to execute Lithulf for treachery and attempted murder. For all the doubts one may have about this incident, it is revealing of social attitudes. Here the issue of a high-status Norman pursuing an English person who was of at least somewhat lower status once again comes into play, and in this case the lower status person supposedly lost his life as a result. Status mattered. But gender mattered as well. Aristocratic

---

[67] *Pipe Roll 31 Henry I*, 155; *EHOV* 6: 41, n. 11.

[68] Bodleian Library, Nottinghamshire charters, no. 2; *Mon. Ang.*, 6: 872–3.

[69] *Becket Materials*, 1: 128. For recent commentary on this story, see Roger Dahood, 'Hugh de Morville, William of Canterbury, and Anecdotal Evidence for English Language History', *Speculum*, 69 (1994), 40–56.

Norman women, given the double standard of the period, could only hope to pursue a clandestine affair, whereas all the powerful males discussed earlier were quite open about their liaisons, even though some were married. Moreover, Beatrice could only exercise her power, and punish Lithulf, through a ruse. Liaisons between Norman men and English women at least had the possibility for reducing ethnic barriers, for all the latent potential for violence and the abuse of power within them, but liaisons between Norman women and English men of lower status would have been socially explosive. Lithulf was not killed in this story because Beatrice's husband discovered an affair, but had that happened, it is unlikely that his fate would have been much happier. Social constraints would have severely limited high-status Norman women and English men of lower status from acting on their sexual desires, or made any actions clandestine, and this would have greatly lessened the potential for sexual attractions between these two specific groups to promote assimilation.

Even when one focuses on English women and Norman men, the fact that sexual attraction often led to liaisons rather than marriage had an important impact, which underscores the importance of the broad class divisions between English and Normans. There were clearly limits on how much such liaisons could do to help the English absorb the immigrant aristocracy. Indeed, it is likely that sexual aggression by Norman aristocrats could sometimes increase ethnic tensions. Even where liaisons were amicable, English mistresses would have been in an even more limited position than wives to influence the aristocratic milieu of their lovers. Such liaisons produced children of mixed ancestry, but most would have been of lower status than their fathers, and generally outside the aristocracy, thus limiting their effect on the identity and integration of the elites. That said, such liaisons form yet one more contributing factor to assimilation and the absorption of the Norman aristocracy. A few children of such marriages did end up in the aristocracy, and more important, such liaisons helped to integrate the middling level of society, where many of the offspring surely ended up. Moreover, such liaisons helped to create ties between aristocratic immigrants and their ethnically English social inferiors, including not just the mistresses but the families of those mistresses. Liaisons between the Normans and English were certainly not a decisive nor invariably positive factor in ethnic relations, but amicable liaisons did play at least a small role in furthering the integration of the two peoples.

Throughout this chapter I have raised questions about the degree to which the absorption of the Norman aristocracy by the English can be explained by marriages and liaisons with English women. More specifically, I have raised questions about arguments for extensive early intermarriage. Though there is no way to definitively settle the question, my own view is that, at least for the aristocracy, intermarriage in the first generation was probably limited. I have also suggested that there were limits to the ability of mistresses, wives, and even queens to affect the culture and identity of the new, predominantly Continental elites. Given the efforts of many women's historians to correct the traditional disregard for the historical importance of women, this may seem a retrograde position. It is not intended to be, but is rather an acknowledgment of the many imbalances in power and authority between genders that women's historians have also shed so much light on. In addressing this issue, I have tried to view ethnicity, gender, and social status as interlocking factors, in which gender and class influenced the precise nature of relations across ethnic lines between individuals, and to show that gender and class biases could limit the influence of such relations. Nonetheless, it would be misleading to end the chapter on too negative a note about the role of women in assimilation and the absorption of the Normans by the English. On the English side, it is probably fair to say that Edith-Matilda was the individual who made the most important contribution to ethnic harmony and assimilation, both by what she did and by who she was. The spouses and lovers of immigrant aristocrats may have found their influence limited in many ways, but they had influence nonetheless, and furthered the integration of the two peoples. The English wives and mistresses discussed in this chapter may not have been able to guarantee the absorption of the invaders on their own, any more than Irish women could, but their contribution to the process is certainly one worth stressing.

11

The Peasants and the Middling Sort

No work on assimilation can ignore the role of common people, most of whom lived in the countryside in the medieval period. This chapter begins with the immigrant presence in rural areas, outside of the aristocracy. But most of it concerns the relations of the ordinary English people of the countryside with the immigrants, and explores their influence on identity and culture in England after the conquest. It also further explores the interaction of class and ethnicity, particularly through a discussion of relations between native country people and Norman aristocrats. I do not intend to argue that class divisions prevented English peasants, still less the natives who were among the middling ranks, from playing any role at all in assimilation, acculturation, or questions of identity. But I do wish to provide a nuanced picture of their role and the way in which class divisions limited it.

The term 'peasant' and the phrase 'middling sort' have broad meanings, and some definition is needed here. By peasants, I mean the ordinary people of rural society, including landless labourers, cottagers with a few acres, serfs and free people with up to 60 acres, and even rural craftsmen and craftswomen. Among the middling sorts I would include unusually rich villagers, who held 60 acres or more, or who held minor administrative positions. I would also include moderately important household officials such as cooks in wealthy households, and also the lords of what might be termed manors if those manors were only a hide or two in size. The middling category is admittedly somewhat artificial, designed specifically for this study because it was the single segment of the rural secular social spectrum where there was a large representation of both groups, who could easily interact among themselves, and could also act as a hinge between the predominantly Continental aristocracy and the predominantly native peasantry.[1]

Immigration after the conquest was not limited to the elites but included lesser people as well. The potential importance of migration by people outside the elites, or the lack thereof, may best be seen through a comparison with the historiography of other early conquests and migrations in Britain and Ireland. Scholars once posited that the replacement of the British by the English, and the later influence of the Vikings on place-names, language, and other attributes of certain regions of

---

[1] I have a somewhat less powerful group in mind than did Crouch, when he used the term 'middle ground', in *Image of Aristocracy*, 23–7. The sorts of people Ann Williams discusses in 'The Abbey Tenants and Servants in the 12th Century', in *Studies in the Early History of Shaftesbury Abbey*, ed. Laurence Keen (Dorchester, 1999), 131–60, more closely fit my definition of the middling category.

England, must have been the result of massive immigration from the Continent. In some cases these hypotheses were made on the basis of racial beliefs about ethnicity, but in other cases cultural theories of ethnicity, and assumptions about the level of immigration needed to transform cultures, lay at their heart. More recently, however, many scholars have begun to shed doubt on theories of mass migration in both cases, and to argue that cultural and, in the former case, ethnic change came primarily through elite influence.[2] Ironically, while Germanic and Viking immigration to England has been shrinking in the historiography, scholars have been arguing for greater English migration to Wales and Ireland than was once thought likely. Moreover, leading scholars have argued that this immigration was important to the long maintenance of English identity and ethnic boundaries in those countries.[3] Both historiographic shifts may, of course, be correct. But the shifts both indicate the importance of studying the size of Norman migration outside the aristocracy, and bring us back to the question of how much the relative size of ethnic populations mattered in the outcome of ethnic encounters. There is no question of massive peasant immigration from the Continent into England, but some immigrants or their descendants did end up among the peasantry. Moreover, there is good evidence for fairly large numbers of immigrants who ended up in the middle ranks of society. Both groups were in a position, had ethnic relations evolved differently, to shore up a distinctively Norman identity and culture. But they were also in a position to interact and assimilate with the large numbers of natives among whom they lived.

  There are a variety of immigrant groups that would have ended up in the middling or even the peasant levels of society. Some of the minor named immigrant tenants of Domesday Book would have fallen into the middling category. In addition, Sally Harvey has revealed that over 300 of the nameless *milites* in Domesday Book had less than two hides, and others were simply lumped in with the peasant populations of individual manors.[4] Other immigrants of lesser status do not even appear in the main text of Domesday Book. In his study of the jurors of the Domesday inquest, Lewis found that forty-three of the seventy-eight French jurors did not appear in the survey. Though a few of these may have been manorial lords who were ignored because they were subtenants of tenants, most probably came from the part of the English social spectrum between well-to-do manorial lords and peasants.[5]

  Another, perhaps overlapping, group consisted of the unnamed *francigenae*

---

[2] For the debate over Viking settlement, see above, p. 28. For critiques of theories of massive Germanic migration to Roman Britain, see Nicholas Higham, *Rome, Britain and the Anglo-Saxons* (London, 1992), 1–16, 108–208, 224–36; Ward-Perkins, 'Anglo-Saxons', 513–33.

[3] Davies, *Age of Conquest*, 97–100, 158–60; id., *Lordship and Society*, 337–53; id., *Domination and Conquest*, 11–15; Duffy, *Ireland in the Middle Ages*, 83–4, 111–12; C. A. Empey, 'Conquest and Settlement: Patterns of Anglo-Norman Settlement in North Munster and South Leinster', *Irish Economic and Social History*, 13 (1986), 5–31; Frame, *Colonial Ireland*, 69, 77–84; Brendan Smith, *Colonisation and Conquest in Medieval Ireland: The English in Louth, 1170–1330* (Cambridge, 1999), 51–2, 127. For an early reference to bringing English settlers to Ireland, see *Rot. Litt. Claus.*, 394b.

[4] Sally Harvey, 'The Knight and the Knight's Fee in England', *Past and Present*, 49 (1970), 15–18.

[5] Lewis, 'Domesday Jurors', 24.

recorded in Domesday Book within the general population of manors. These were recorded in large numbers only in Hertfordshire, where fifty-six appear, and a number of West Midlands counties where, for instance, forty-one appeared in Cheshire and thirty-six in Staffordshire. *Francigenae* simply meant French, and Domesday Book uses the term in various ways, but generally they seem to have been very minor figures. One from Worcestershire had the holding of a villein, and in Herefordshire, the one county in which Domesday Book provides much information about their holdings, they usually seem to have had one plough or ploughland, more than the average peasant but hardly a wealthy holding.[6] It is striking that the Domesday commissioners in the West Midlands and in Hertfordshire saw them as part of the general population, admittedly, in the former case, along with priests and *radmen*, native free tenants who held land for services such as carrying messages and serving as escorts. This suggests that these *francigenae*, like priests and *radmen*, would have been part of village life, and would have rubbed shoulders with ordinary English peasants on a day-to-day basis even if they, like prosperous villagers in later times, probably consciously maintained their superiority to the poorer villagers. Scholars have not generally associated them with the peasantry, arguing that they were mercenaries or sergeants with ministerial functions.[7] But it looks as though they were being settled into local society. What, after all, could be more likely than lords rewarding loyal archers, footsoldiers, or servants with large peasant or middling holdings in return for participation in the conquest or years of loyal service? In sum, I would argue that Domesday Book and the lists of jurors indicate French penetration into that part of the English social spectrum between lords and ordinary peasants, and into the upper ranks of village society in some settlements.

The numbers of French settlers at this level were probably larger than generally realized. If Lewis's figure of forty-three French jurors omitted in the main survey was more or less typical for one county and three out of ten hundreds in a second county, this would add up to around 1,000 throughout England, still a fairly small number. However, it is likely that not all settlers became jurors. Moreover, Domesday Book is clearly not consistent about recording *francigenae* among village populations and there were undoubtedly many more than the approximately 250 recorded there. In Hertfordshire, the county with the largest recorded number, twenty out of fifty-three come from the lands of St Alban's and nine of the twenty manors of the abbey in that county include *francigenae*. It is quite possible that St Alban's simply had an unusual number of settlers, but it is also possible that what was unusual was the care that went into recording immigrant tenants in this particular case. If that were so, there might have been thousands throughout England. Another reason for thinking that there may have been larger numbers of immigrants outside the aristocracy than those recorded in the records is the likelihood that immigrant landholders brought household officials and personal servants who

---

[6] *DB* 1: 175a, 181a-187a.

[7] Fuchs *Domesday Book*, 256–63, 340–52; Golding, *Conquest and Colonization*, 77; Williams, *ENC* 196–7, with works referred to there.

spoke their own language with them from the Continent. That very low-ranking but useful people could be drawn to England is shown by a miracle story that records the immigration of a French gardener to England.[8] Lesser manorial land-lords would surely have brought male relatives with them as well, whom they could not hope to establish in the aristocracy but might set up among the middling sorts or reward with the land of a peasant. Even if one assumes only two or three such figures for each Continental aristocrat, the number would still run well into the thousands.

As time went on, moreover, downward mobility, particularly of younger sons and daughters, would have added to the number of immigrants and their descen-dants at the middling levels of society, and even among the peasantry. It is well known that landholders after the conquest, though generally practising primo-geniture, often gave land to younger sons and to daughters.[9] Such gifts ensured that younger children had the economic wherewithal to settle down and produce their own offspring, but did not guarantee that they would stay in the same social class as their parents. Inevitably many descendants, even of prosperous landholders in Domesday Book, must have sunk into the middling class, and where two or three generations of younger children were involved some may have sunk lower. Du Boulay has shown how cadet lines from some Kentish knightly families merged into the local peasantry.[10]

That the descendants of immigrants could be minor figures indeed by Henry II's reign is suggested by the survey of Templar estates in 1185, in which several men with surnames like Francigena or Peitevin held small peasant holdings.[11] Some late charters even reveal serfs with surnames such as Franceis or Francigena that are strongly suggestive of Continental origin.[12] There are not likely to have been many serfs of Continental descent, but the initial influx of less powerful immigrants, combined with the downward mobility of younger children, meant that there must have been a fairly large number of immigrants and their descendants at the middling levels of society, and a sprinkling even further down, during the period of assimilation. Most of these lesser immigrant figures remain invisible in the records, but it is important to remember their existence.

In sum, I would argue that there was a greater immigrant presence in the rural population of England than scholars have generally recognized, though most of it would have been among the middling ranks rather than the ordinary peasantry. I do not want to exaggerate the numbers I am suggesting. Even on the Hertfordshire estates of St Albans, where the concentration of *francigenae* was greatest in Domes-day Book, they still made up little more than 6 per cent of the recorded population, and I would argue for a much smaller percentage than this overall. The problems of evidence make comparisons difficult, but I would not see immigration outside the

---

[8] 'Goscelini Miracula S. Ivonis', in MacRay, *Chronicon Abbatiae Rameseiensis*, pp. lxxx–lxxxi.

[9] Thomas, *Vassals, Heiresses, Crusaders, and Thugs*, 119–25, and works cited there in 121, n. 64.

[10] Du Boulay, *Lordship of Canterbury*, 60, 68. See also, Chibnall, *Anglo-Norman England*, 209–10.

[11] Lees, *Records of the Templars*, 28, 32, 35, 118.

[12] BL Harley MS 662, fol. 25ᵛ; Foster and Major, *Registrum Antiquissimum*, 6, no. 1938 (dated 1215–25); BL Cotton MS Titus C viii, fol. 91ʳ.

aristocracy as being on the same level as was found in parts of Wales and Ireland, let alone parts of central Europe, to which perhaps 200,000 people immigrated in the twelfth century.[13] Even so, the presence of thousands of immigrants at the middling level of society could, in other circumstances, have bolstered Norman identity over the long term. Immigrant families of middling rank could have provided marriage partners, especially for younger sons and daughters, had the Normans chosen to remain endogamous. Such figures could have provided a cultural buffer between the aristocracy and the peasantry, and supported the survival of a culturally distinct upper class. Alternatively, they could have served as a conduit for the spread of *Normanitas* into the countryside. These possibilities are, of course, counterfactual, but they raise the question of why these lesser Normans had such a limited impact on culture and identity in England.

One obvious answer is that numbers did matter, at least when it came to migration outside the aristocracy. It seems likely that such immigration had to reach a certain critical mass before it could really affect ethnic relations, and before ordinary immigrants could seriously shore up the cultural distinctiveness or dominance of an immigrant elite. In this respect, I believe that the traditional view of the importance of the small number of Normans is correct. Another important factor was the settlement pattern of these minor immigrants and, for that matter, of the minor members of the aristocracy, who were basically scattered across the countryside. In the more alien, and in the long term more threatening, regions of the Holy Land, Western settlers tended to clump together in cities or Frankish villages.[14] In Wales, English settlers tended to congregate in lowland areas, and sometimes Welsh were expelled from an area to create English settlements. Moreover, English boroughs were created, from which the Welsh were theoretically excluded and in which the English generally remained dominant. Though the level of ethnic segregation varied from region to region, Englishries and Welshries became part of the human geography of Wales.[15] In both of these cases the immigrants could more easily retain their solidarity and separateness. The Norman settlement pattern in England was, in part, another legacy of their overwhelming early victory; so thoroughly had they defeated the opposition that even in 1086 there was little danger in being spread throughout the countryside. In any case, the settlement pattern had important consequences. The greater landlords would undoubtedly

---

[13] For central Europe, see Charles Higounet, *Les Allemands en Europe centrale et orientale au moyen âge* (Paris, 1989), 105.

[14] Joshua Prawer, *The Latin Kingdom of Jerusalem: European Colonialism in the Middle Ages* (London, 1972), 60–93; id., *Crusader Institutions* (Oxford, 1980), 102–42; Powell, *Muslims Under Latin Rule*, 171–2. Ronnie Ellenblum has challenged this picture insofar as the local Christian population goes, but she also argues that the crusaders generally settled apart from non-Christians: *Frankish Rural Settlement in the Latin Kingdom of Jerusalem* (Cambridge, 1998), 3–38, 282–5.

[15] Davies, *Lordship and Society*, 304–10, 319–20, 325–8, 341–2, 345–7; id., *Age of Conquest*, 97–100, 371–3, 421; id., *Domination and Conquest*, 88–9; Given, *State and Society in Medieval Europe*, 99–101, 112; A. D. M. Barell and M. H. Brown, 'A Settler Community in Post-conquest Rural Wales: The English of Dyffryn Clwyd, 1294–1399', *Welsh History Review*, 17 (1995): 332–55. For the importance and experience of English burgesses and settlers in resisting Owain Glyn Dŵr's rebellion, see Davies, *Revolt of Owain Glyn Dŵr*, 221–2, 269–77.

have continued to socialize and intermarry among themselves, and therefore would have remained in a predominantly Norman world. But for lesser immigrants, scattered across the country and tied to one or two villages, remaining in a separate world from the English would have been much more difficult. Geographically scattered peoples can and sometimes do maintain their closest ties with each other across long distances, but it is hard over the long term, and requires strong reasons for doing so, such as religious difference, which did not exist in this case.

In fact, it is likely that the lesser Normans and their descendants helped to integrate the two groups rather than aiding any potential segregation. Unfortunately, this must remain speculative. The social connections and marriage patterns of immigrants in the middling level of society and among the peasantry basically remain invisible in the evidence, because the increasing use of Continental names by natives makes such figures hard to distinguish. Nonetheless, the likelihood is that they quickly integrated themselves with their English neighbours, at least once the initial hostility of the conquest had passed. This group was the least likely to bring in brides, and therefore the most likely to intermarry at an early stage. They would have found it expedient to incorporate themselves into village life and regional networks, where many, perhaps most, of their peers were English. For them, the picture of small numbers of Normans being absorbed into the mass of English population is surely correct. No doubt they would have maintained ties with local Norman aristocrats, but that simply meant that they could act to some degree as intermediaries between the two groups and even help bring them together. They could also act as conduits for cultural exchange between the two peoples. Moreover, the existence of many immigrants and their descendants outside the aristocracy, and particularly the fact that some would have been peasants, helped prevent any tendency to treat ethnic and class lines as identical. Thus, it seems likely that the Normans within the middling ranks and peasantry in England played a moderately important role in assimilation and acculturation.

What of relations between the English masses and the Norman elites? It seems likely that these relations were more difficult and less conducive to assimilation, partly because this was a difficult time in relations between lords and peasants. There is no question that the Norman Conquest generally worsened the position of the English peasantry, though it is less easy to discern how great the damage was. Though not all English peasants felt the effects of plundering and deliberate devastation by Norman armies, the impact on those affected must have been terrible. Moreover, new landlords, bound less by customs and local ties than their predecessors, and visibly backed by force, often tightened the financial screws on peasants. The Anglo-Saxon Chronicle describes how King William demanded higher payments from his estate managers, not caring how they oppressed the peasants to get the money, and Domesday Book makes reference to extortionate rents.[16] The rise in manorial values between 1066 and 1086 found on many manors must often represent greater extraction by landlords rather than greater produc-

---

[16] *ASC* E 1086 [*recte* 1087]; *DB* 1: 2b, 38a; 2: 38b, 291a.

tion.[17] Another change that Domesday Book reveals was the reduction in status of many free peasants, for large numbers seem to have disappeared between 1066 and 1086.[18] Clearly, some peasants suffered gravely as a result of the conquest, both in war and peace, though the question remains how general the suffering was, and whether the increased exploitation was a temporary or enduring affair.

In a recent book Rosamond Faith has argued that the effects of the Norman Conquest on the peasantry were in fact very widespread, and that they greatly strengthened two trends that had already begun, namely the intensification of lordship, and the consequent subjection of peasants to more burdens and restrictions. In part, her argument depends on her view that Anglo-Saxon society was less manorialized than previously thought, and that there were large numbers of peasants only loosely linked to the seigneurial economy, but much of her attention focuses on the actions and attitudes of the conquerors. Relying on recent work on manorialization after the conquest, studies on village structures by historical geographers, and reinterpretation of well-known sources, she depicts the period between 1066 and 1200 as one of much greater change for the peasantry, almost all of it bad, than previously believed. She sees three main causes at work: the ability of the conquerors to reorganize peasant society; their introduction of Continental ideas and practices that many scholars have argued had already led to a widespread depression of peasant status across the Channel; and population pressures, which strengthened the hands of lords against their peasants. Together, she sees these factors as leading to a reduction in the autonomy and status of large numbers of peasants, which was eventually codified by the creation of common law villeinage.[19] Faith's arguments will doubtlessly be carefully scrutinized and hotly debated in the years to come. Nonetheless, she has made a case for significant and widespread suffering of the peasantry at the hands of the new elites that will need to be addressed by anyone who would downplay the effects of the conquest on the rural population.

It seems likely that mistreatment of and increased demands on the peasantry by the Normans would have raised the level of both ethnic and class frictions. Bruce O'Brien has argued against seeing the *murdrum* fine as evidence for violent opposition to the Normans, at least by the peasantry.[20] But Faith's arguments and the known sufferings of some peasants add plausibility to the traditional assumption that the fine was designed to stop the rural population from attacking immigrants, or at least from collaborating with aristocratic natives who were doing so. More generally, class tensions that resulted from the conquest and the changes it brought must have made the development of ethnic harmony and any kind of integration between the vast majority of the English peasantry and the predominantly Norman aristocracy much more difficult to accomplish.

[17] Reginald Lennard, *Rural England 1086–1135: A Study of Social and Agrarian Conditions* (Oxford, 1959), 155–7.
[18] R. Welldon Finn, *An Introduction to Domesday Book* (New York, 1963), 145–6; Darby, *Domesday England*, 62–3.
[19] Rosamond Faith, *The English Peasantry and the Growth of Lordship* (London, 1997), 178–265.
[20] O'Brien, 'From *Morðor* to *Murdrum*', 354.

Relations between Norman lords and English peasants were self evidently not so bad as to make ethnic harmony impossible. More specifically, though Faith argues that the intensification of peasant subjection in Normandy led to the peasant revolt there earlier in the eleventh century, the Normans suffered no such outbreak in England, which could have had disastrous consequences for ethnic and class relations.[21] No doubt this is partly a testament to the terror the Normans inspired, but there were also factors that ameliorated relations between Norman lords and English peasants. Over time there would have been a slow if grudging acceptance of the impositions made after the conquest and a decline of tensions to the regular level of resentment towards landlords. Moreover, one group benefited from the conquest, namely slaves. David Pelteret argues that, although the decline of slavery in England had begun well before the conquest, the Normans accelerated and completed the process.[22] Strikingly, one of the few documents involving an English manorial lord in the decades after the conquest concerns the sale of a slave by Harding son of Eadnoth, and this serves as a reminder that the oppressiveness of Norman lords was a matter of degree, not a new phenomenon.[23] Moreover, most scholars have seen the twelfth century in particular as an economically prosperous period, which may have made the position of the peasantry less grim than in Faith's picture, and eased the kind of class tensions that could supplement ethnic ones.[24] Nonetheless, the sources of tension between lords and peasants discussed earlier probably made any kind of integration that crossed both class and ethnic lines much more difficult, and thereby reduced the importance of the English peasantry to the absorption of the Normans.

Moreover, the fact that English peasants and Norman lords never tried to kill each other in large numbers, at least after the completion of the conquest, did not in itself reduce the social distance between the two groups. Unfortunately, there is very little evidence of the precise nature of relations between Norman lords and their English peasants. Obviously, peasants must have had at least limited contact with resident or visiting Norman lords, though probably much interaction was carried out through estate officials, and presumably through translators at first. Even limited contact between villagers and landlords was likely to lead to sexual attraction and therefore to relations between peasant women and immigrant lords, as I discussed in the last chapter. But, given class prejudices and what we know of the

[21] Faith, *English Peasantry*, 252–3.

[22] David A. E. Pelteret, *Slavery in Early Mediaeval England: From the Reign of Alfred until the Twelfth Century* (Woodbridge, 1995), 205, 233–4, 247, 253–4.

[23] Benjamin Thorpe, *Diplomatarium Anglicum Aevi Saxonici* (London, 1865), 648–9; David A. E. Pelteret, *Catalogue of English Post-Conquest Vernacular Documents* (Woodbridge, 1990), no. 107.

[24] For some important works on the economy in this period, see Lennard, *Rural England*; Edward Miller, 'England in the Twelfth and Thirteenth Centuries: An Economic Contrast?', *Economic History Review*, 2nd ser., 24 (1971), 1–14; Edward Miller and John Hatcher, *Medieval England: Rural Society and Economic Change, 1086–1348* (London, 1978), 27–164; Richard H. Britnell and Bruce M. S. Campbell, *A Commercialising Economy: England, 1086 to c. 1300* (Manchester, 1996); Edmund King, 'Economic Development in the Early Twelfth Century', in *Progress and Problems in Medieval England: Essays in Honour of Edward Miller*, ed. Richard Britnell and John Hatcher (Cambridge, 1996), 1–22; Richard H. Britnell, *The Commercialisation of English Society, 1000–1500*, 2nd edn. (Manchester, 1996), 5–75.

English social hierarchy in later periods, as well as the specific sources of possible class tensions discussed earlier, there must be an a priori assumption that powerful lords and ordinary peasants were not generally likely to develop bonds of friendship and marriage.

That such an assumption is correct is suggested by two pieces of evidence I have already discussed, namely the treatment of Hereward when disguised as a potter, as described in the *Gesta Herwardi*, and the relationship between Thomas of Cuckney and his mistress Aileva. A third important piece of evidence is the exclusion of serfs in the famous statement about intermarriage and living together in the *Dialogue of the Exchequer*. This exclusion was something of an oversimplification since there were likely instances of unfree peasants with Continental ancestry, but it shows that Richard Fitz Nigel thought that assimilation and intermarriage extended only so far down the social ladder. One may well wonder whether he thought poor free peasants were involved, but in any case, his statement indicates that a significant portion of the English population played a very limited role in the process of assimilation.[25] In general, relations between English peasants and Norman lords, even of the sexual sort, were normally likely to remain too distant to create much assimilation. As a result, the overwhelming predominance of the English among the common people mattered less than one might expect. The native rural population did, however, play some role in assimilation for two reasons: the existence of many vertical ties of lordship, and the presence of both English and immigrants at the middling level of society.

Vertical bonds of service and patronage were extremely important in post-conquest England, as in all medieval societies. Such bonds naturally depended on differences of wealth and power, but also bridged those divides and created sometimes intensive interaction across social ranks, especially above the ranks of ordinary villagers. Given the loose, de facto, links between ethnicity and social status in England after the conquest, vertical ties also bridged ethnic divides. Not all these bonds were equal; a noble's relationship with one of his knights was quite different from that with one of his estate managers, which was quite different in turn from that with an ordinary servant. As a result, different types of vertical bonds had different effects on ethnic relations. The most common sort of vertical tie, between a lord and a peasant who paid rents and performed services, but had little personal contact, was unlikely to matter much. But closer vertical ties created the sort of interaction that could aid the process of assimilation over the long term, and the rewards and power many received for their service also helped maintain a strong English presence in the middling levels of society.

Lords needed intermediaries between them and their peasants, and often enough these intermediaries were English. As one might expect, reeves with English names

---

[25] Given that freedom and unfreedom were fluid concepts in this period, only slowly being defined by the common law, and given that Fitz Nigel elsewhere seems to have seen free men as a fairly exalted group, he may indeed have meant to exclude much of what later would have been the free peasantry: Richard Fitz Nigel, *Dialogus de Scaccario*, 53, 109. For the development of common law villeinage, see Hyams, *Kings, Lords, and Peasants*, 221–65.

can frequently be found. Such figures were generally minor, but they did interact even with powerful lords, and they occasionally got the kind of rewards that raised them into the middling level of society.[26] More important were the many English who continued to serve as local royal officials and as lessees or *firmarii* of estates, long after the time of Domesday Book. It is well known that the English remained active in the lowest ranks of the royal administration, serving as minor officials and particularly as estate managers, not only in 1086 but into the reign of Henry I.[27] The widespread pattern of name-changing makes such figures harder to trace in later periods, and indeed W. L. Warren, in his article on Norman administrative incompetence, argued that such native officials died out, leaving the conquerors to make a bureaucratic mess of things.[28] But in fact some officials and *firmarii* with English names can be found even in Henry II's reign, which suggests that many more were concealed under Continental names, and that the native presence in the lower ranks of the royal government was never interrupted.[29] *Firmarii* with English names also continued to be found in the employ of nobles, abbots, and bishops as well. The unusually full evidence of two monasteries with early to mid-twelfth-century records, Burton and St Mary's, York, show how the Continental abbots of those houses relied extensively, though certainly not exclusively, on natives to manage their lands.[30] Lease agreements and charters from other houses, and very occasionally from magnates, suggest that these abbots were not anomalous.[31] In general, it seems likely that natives remained important as local administrators and managers throughout the period in question.

The survival of English in such positions is important for two reasons. First, it increased the number of natives at the middling level of society. Some, like the Cockfields, even used their positions as *firmarii* as a springboard into the aristoc-

---

[26] For some documents in which reeves with English names can be found taking orders from immigrant magnates or attesting their charters, see J. Armitage Robinson, *Gilbert Crispin, Abbot of Westminster: A Study of the Abbey under Norman Rule* (Cambridge, 1911), no. 7; *EEA* 8, no. 68; Robert B. Patterson, ed., *Earldom of Gloucester Charters: The Charters and Scribes of the Earls and Countesses of Gloucester to A.D. 1217* (Oxford, 1973), no. 2; C. D. Ross and Mary Devine, eds., *The Cartulary of Cirencester Abbey*, vol. 2 (London, 1964), nos. 673, 707. I have also found several dozen reeves with English names in the charters of lesser lords. For a relatively large gift to native reeve, see *EEA* 1, no. 176

[27] Williams, *ENC* 109–19; Green, *Government of England*, 156; Golding, *Conquest and Colonisation*, 182; *Pipe Roll 31 Henry I*, 7, 12, 22, 38, 41, 53, 62, 78, 124.

[28] W. L. Warren, 'The Myth of Norman Administrative Efficiency', *TRHS* 5th ser., 34 (1984), 117–18.

[29] *EYC* 1, nos. 402, 484–5; Round, *Rotuli de Dominabus*, 6, 9, 14; *Pipe Roll 7 Henry II*, 30; *Pipe Roll 13 Henry II*, 128; *Pipe Roll 14 Henry II*, 174; *Pipe Roll 15 Henry II*, 8; *Pipe Roll 17 Henry II*, 23; *Pipe Roll 18 Henry II*, 45; *Pipe Roll 24 Henry II*, 124; *Pipe Roll 27 Henry II*, 106, 108; *Pipe Roll 33 Henry II*, 18; *Calendar of Charter Rolls Preserved in the Public Record Office*, vol. 4 (London, 1912), 442–3. This does not include royal officials in towns, whom I will discuss in the next chapter.

[30] Wrottesley, 'Staffordshire Chartulary, Series III', 227–8; Wrottesley, 'Burton Chartulary', 30–7; Charles G. O. Bridgeman, 'The Burton Abbey Twelfth Century Surveys', in *William Salt Archaeological Society Collections for a History of Staffordshire*, 3rd ser., 41 (1916), 216–17, 223–9; *EYC* 1, no. 629; 2, nos. 1063, 1242; 3, no. 1303; 4, nos. 87–8; 9, nos. 134–5; BL Harley MS 236, fols. 40ᵛ–41ʳ.

[31] For some particularly full examples of leases to natives, see William Hale, ed., *The Domesday of St. Paul's* (London, 1858), 122–4; Mason, *Westminster Abbey Charters*, no. 247; id., *Beauchamp Cartulary*, no. 356.

racy.[32] Equally important, officials and *firmarii* had to interact with their lords and with the Norman followers of their lords. For instance, leases from Burton Abbey reveal that English leaseholders acted as hosts for the Norman abbots when they travelled, a duty that would have had English and Normans socializing as well as working together.[33] Though natives in these positions would obviously have been socially inferior to their lords, they may well have interacted with their Norman peers as equals. Thus, though positions such as minor royal official and *firmarius* created working relationships first and foremost, they also had the potential to create more personal relationships.

The most important vertical ties came because secular and ecclesiastical landholders of Continental origin sometimes appointed natives to moderately important positions in their households and followings. Examples can be found of bakers, cooks, marshals, foresters, huntsmen, goldsmiths, nurses, and individuals described as *servientes*, all with English names, in the service of powerful immigrants, including earls, bishops, and abbots.[34] These would not have been among the highest household officials, such as stewards, who in the greatest households were generally moderately wealthy landholders themselves, nor were they necessarily within the inner circles of the affinities of their lords, but neither were they insignificant servants such as maids or grooms. Positions as household officials by their very nature brought natives into close association and interaction with immigrants. Gifts of land to household members or their kin suggest that powerful Normans sometimes developed feelings of gratitude and warmth toward their native household officers and even servants, as when Alice de Berkeley gave a half-virgate and a mill to the son of her nurse, Toka, or Bishop Jocelin of Salisbury granted a half hide to 'my faithful *serviens*, Segar'.[35] More striking still is the record in the pipe rolls of a payment in Henry II's reign of £6. 13s. 4d. for doctors and care during the illness of an otherwise unknown Godman, *serviens* of the king. The disbursement of so large a sum for an obscure figure suggests that the king himself took a personal interest in Godman's recovery.[36] Thus, personal service seems to have created genuine ties of affection across both social and ethnic divides.

It is difficult to assess the overall impact on ethnic relations of vertical ties between Norman lords and ordinary natives. Such ties could self evidently coexist

---

[32] For another family that did so, see George Wrottesley, 'An Account of the Family of Okeover of Okeover, co. Stafford, with Transcripts of Ancient Deeds at Okeover', *William Salt Archaeological Society Collections for a History of Staffordshire*, NS 7 (London, 1904), 3–187.

[33] Wrottesley, 'Burton Chartulary', 35–6.

[34] For minor household officials explicitly tied to immigrant lords, see *EEA* 11, no. 64; C. J. Holdsworth, ed., *Rufford Charters*, vol. 2 (Nottingham, 1974), no. 793; Greenway, *Charters of the Honour of Mowbray*, no. 112; *EEA* 18, nos. 61, 132; *EYC* 11, no 66; Bridgeman, 'Burton Abbey Surveys', 239; *Pipe Roll 34 Henry II*, 14; Isaac Herbert Jeayes, ed., *Descriptive Catalogue of the Charters and Muniments in the Possession of the Rt. Hon. Lord Fitzhardinge at Berkeley Castle* (Bristol, 1892), no. 55; *S. Anselmi Opera Omnia*, 5: 263. For natives with the titles of officials attesting charters of immigrant lords, see BL Cotton Vespasian B xxiv, fol. 41r; CUL, Peterborough D&C MS 1, fol. 131r; Moore, *Cartularium Monasterii de Colecestria*, 1: 154, 156–7, 177–8, 241, 258; Mason, *Westminster Abbey Charters*, no. 234; Elvey, *Luffield Priory Charters* 1, no. 1; West, *St. Benet of Holme 1020–1210*, 1, no. 147.

[35] Jeayes, *Charters and Muniments at Berkeley Castle*, no. 55; *EEA* 18, no. 132.

[36] *Pipe Roll 32 Henry II*, 199.

with continuing social divides and in other societies they have coexisted with ethnic or racial ones as well. One thinks of Southern elite figures in the United States who formed genuine attachments to African American slaves or servants while staunchly defending slavery or segregation. Chivalric literature and other sources indicate that ties of lordship within the elites were expected to be important and influential bonds, but it is not at all clear that the same holds true for most vertical ties beyond the elites, and resentment or distrust may have been as common in such relationships as affection. Overall, vertical ties between members of the elite and ordinary natives were unlikely to have been a major force for assimilation, once again underscoring the limited influence of the majority of English on the integration of the two peoples. Nonetheless, assimilation was a multifaceted affair and, in a society moving toward integration anyway, patronage, affectionate vertical ties, and working relationships across both ethnic and class lines could help the process along.

More important than vertical ties was the existence of a middling level of society in which the English, as well as Normans, were present in large numbers. The middling ranks were important not only because English people and Normans at that social level could interact as equals, but also because the former could create ties upwards to the predominantly Norman aristocracy. Indeed, because of the collective power of the middling sort and the relatively high position of individuals in it, at least compared to most peasants, the Norman elites had to interact with and gain a certain level of co-operation from the English members of this social rank.

There is plentiful evidence for an extensive English as well as Norman presence among the middling social ranks. Since the average size of holdings controlled by the English in Domesday Book was less than 2 hides or carucates, many of the named individuals who held only one holding would have fallen into the category, as did many English jurors, farmers, and minor officials.[37] A number of scholars have also noted the existence of native freemen who were wealthier than most peasants but still only modest landholders in other records, and in fact the evidence for large numbers of English in this category is widespread.[38] Such native landholders, whether lords or tenants, can be found scattered throughout the charters, and surprising numbers can also be found in later records of the royal courts, many of which referred back to earlier generations.[39] They can also be found in estate and regional surveys. In the first Burton Abbey survey, dating to 1114–18, besides the

---

[37] Thomas, 'Significance and Fate', forthcoming.

[38] F. M. Stenton, *Documents Illustrative of the Social and Economic History of the Danelaw* (London, 1920), pp. xcviii–ci; Greenway, *Charters of the Honour of Mowbray*, p. xxxix; Lees, *Records of the Templars*, pp. clxxxiii–clxxxiv, ccv.

[39] For some examples from charters, chosen more or less at random, see BL Additional Charter 20415; Stenton, *Documents Illustrative of the Danelaw*, nos. 60, 61, 427; Avrom Saltman, *Theobald, Archbishop of Canterbury* (London, 1936), nos. 124–5; F. M. Stenton, ed., *Facsimiles of Early Charters from Northamptonshire Collections* (Northampton, 1930), no. 18. For evidence form the royal courts, see *RCR* 1: 192, 213; 2: 51, 75, 135, 235; *CRR* 1: 4, 8, 9, 61, 158, 227–8, 249, 250–1, 270, 312, 350, 387; 2: 2, 24, 84, 85, 126, 184; 3: 18, 53, 93, 201, 213, 239; 4: 2, 62, 121, 218, 301; 5: 160, 165–6; 6: 313, 379; 7: 19–20, 102, 188, 197–8, 293–4; 8: 351; 9: 318–19; 11, nos. 1530, 2103, 2224, 2349; 12, nos. 331, 582, 1347, 1608, 1983, 2036, 2274, 2545; 13, nos. 1036, 1511; 14, nos.1584, 2399; 16, no. 422; 17, no. 210; 18, no. 259.

lessees of estates noted earlier, there are thirty-eight tenants with a half-carucate or more, of whom about two-thirds had English names, and at this date, about a half-century after the conquest, some with Continental names were undoubtedly English.[40] Most surveys do not include so many prosperous tenants with English names, but such figures can be found in almost every twelfth-century survey.[41] Finally, the pipe roll of 1166 lists around 125 named individuals from royal manors who owed payments for the marriage of Henry II's daughter, and of these between 42 and 52 per cent had English elements in their names, despite the fact that the shift to Continental names had been in progress for a century. Their individual payments indicate that they were important manorial tenants.[42] Though the Normans pushed many English families at the middling rank into the mass of peasantry, many others obviously survived at or rose into that level.

There is much evidence for interaction between the English in the middling levels of society and the Norman elites. Indeed, to some degree the two groups co-operated in the domination and governance of local society, though with the latter clearly as senior partners. In this context, the power and importance of the farmers and others in the middling rank, whatever their ethnicity, should be underscored. I have argued that power was dispersed in this society, and the members of the middling rank provide a good illustration of this. Obviously farmers and the holders of a half-hide or even 1 or 2 hides were minor figures in comparison to those with 5 or 6 hides, and insignificant compared to barons. But anyone controlling half a hide or carucate was likely to be a leading figure in his or her village, and anyone with even 2 hides could be a figure of standing in the neighbourhood. The co-operation of such figures would have been valuable even to the most powerful aristocrats. As for officials and managers, the power they wielded, though it derived from delegated authority, could be considerable. Royal officials might be particularly powerful, even if minor and far from the inner circle of the king. The *Liber*

---

[40] Bridgeman, 'Burton Abbey Surveys', 209–300. About half the twenty-eight tenants with a half-carucate or more in the second survey had English names.

[41] BL Cotton MS Vespasian B xxiv (Evesham Abbey), 12^r, 53^r, 53^v, 67^r; BL Harley MS 61 (Shaftesbury Cartulary), 37^v–39^r, 41^r–42^r, 43^{r-v}, 44^v–45^r, 51^v, 52^v–53^v, 54^v, 56^{r-v}, 58^r, 59^r, 67^r, 68^v–69^r, 71^{r-v}, 74^v, 77^v, 79^v–81^r; J. H. Round, 'The Northamptonshire Survey', in *VCH Northamptonshire*, 1: 367, 377, 378–9, 385, 387; Douglas, *Feudal Documents*, 26, 34, 35, 43, 44; David C. Douglas, *The Domesday Monachorum of Christ Church Canterbury* (London, 1944), 82, 87, 95, 104; Marjorie Chibnall, ed., *Charters and Custumals of the Abbey of Holy Trinity Caen* (London, 1982), 37, 46, 68; C. W. Foster and Thomas Longley, eds., *The Lincolnshire Domesday and the Lindsey Survey* (Gainsborough, 1924; repr. 1976), 244; Thomas Stapleton, ed., *Chronicon Petroburgense* (London, 1849), 162, 164–5; Stevenson, *Chronicon Monasterii de Abingdon*, 2: 302–5; Hart and Lyons, *Cartularium Monasterii de Rameseia*, 3: 257, 278, 301, 305, 309, 312; Lees, *Records of the Templars*, 54, 84, 85, 119; David Austin, ed., *Boldon Book* (Chichester, 1982), 14, 22, 24, 32, 36, 42, 44, 54, 56, 66; Marjorie Hollings, ed., *The Red Book of Worcester*, 4 pts. (London, 1934–40), 1: 109; 2: 146, 205–6; 3: 315; N. E. Stacy, ed., *The Surveys of the Estates of Glastonbury Abbey, c. 1135–1201* (Oxford, 2001), 136, 195, 199, 201, 205, 209.

[42] *Pipe Roll 14 Henry II*, 23, 40–2, 47–8, 53–4, 65–6, 103–5, 129–32, 145–7, 161–3, 195. There were nearly 250 people named, but just under half of the individuals came from places that were at some point in the medieval period considered boroughs according to M. W. Beresford and H. P. R. Finberg, *English Medieval Boroughs: A Hand-List* (Totowa, 1973). Whether all these places were boroughs in 1166 is questionable, but fortunately the question is moot, for the percentage of those with English elements in their names is virtually identical for the two groups.

Eliensis records that when Abbot Simeon of Ely made the mistake of calling in royal support against a recalcitrant tenant, a royal official with the English name Aeilwinus and nickname Cattlebelly (*Reðeresgut*) took the opportunity to oppress and rob the abbey by making Ranulf Flambard angry at the monks.[43] When the first Norman abbot of Abingdon intimidated the English reeve of a royal manor by striking him and by forcing him to take a humiliating plunge into a river on another occasion, the reeve was able to have the abbot fined by complaining to the queen.[44] More prosaically, the Tosnys turned over management of the soke of Necton, a complex of manors in Norfolk, to one Estangrin, and later to his son William, in return for a large annual rent of £80. Estangrin and his son, though only minor landholders in their own right, had by this arrangement responsibility over large amounts of land and money and over large numbers of people (the soke had a recorded population of over 250 in Domesday Book).[45] It is likely that estate managers, whether great or small, had as much influence over the daily lives of tenants as their immigrant lords, if not more.[46] In short, these were figures to be reckoned with on the local level.

The relative power and importance of the English among the middling ranks, along with their individual talents and skills, made them useful to the Normans, and this in turn led to extensive interaction across ethnic and class divides. Hirokazu Tsurushima has analysed a set of documents in which William d'Aubigny and eleven officials and tenants of his large manor of Elham, six of them with English names, acted together in granting tithes to and gaining confraternity with Rochester Cathedral Priory, in an interesting instance of religious co-operation between Normans and English. In this context Tsurushima wrote: 'The names of the more important inhabitants [of Elham] are supplied by the Textus Roffensis, and they are very significant. But for them, Norman settlers could not have exploited the manors in England. William of Aubigny needed them, and they needed a protector under the unstable social conditions after the Norman Conquest.'[47] The importance of the mutual dependence described here cannot be emphasized enough. Indeed, the frequent address of charters, 'to my men, French and English', formulaic as it quickly became, recognizes the fact and necessity of co-operation across ethnic lines long after most of the English among the aristocracy had been wiped out.

Much of this co-operation came through the ties of lordship I discussed earlier in the chapter, but the middling sorts as a group, and thus the English among them, were also allowed a certain share in the business of governing society. An early example of the latter can be found with the co-operation of English jurors in the

---

[43] Blake, *Liber Eliensis*, 219. For another example of a powerful native royal reeve, see Geoffrey of Burton, *Life and Miracles of St Modwenna*, ed. Robert Bartlett (Oxford, 2002), 190–2.

[44] Stevenson, *Chronicon Monasterii de Abingdon*, 2: 10–11.

[45] Mason, *The Beauchamp Cartulary*, nos. 356–8; *DB* 2: 235a–236b. Estangrim was a Scandinavian name, and may possibly have been Norman, but it was more likely to be native.

[46] See Lennard, *Rural England*, 196–200, for the control of farmers over the tenants of lands they leased.

[47] Tsurushima, 'Fraternity', 320–2. See also Williams, *ENC* 85.

Domesday inquest. Similarly, the English can be found in inquests throughout the period of assimilation. For instance, in a long list of men swearing to the bounds of a Yorkshire royal forest early in Henry II's reign, natives of the middling ranks can be found alongside men with Continental bynames.[48] Most important was the activity of many English in various law courts. I have discussed the participation of native aristocrats in the courts, but the bulk of the English participation would have come from the middling levels. Many people at this level (and sometimes below) owed suit of court, which theoretically required their attendance at periodic judicial sessions, and Williams has shown the continuing participation of the English in county and hundred courts.[49] Indeed, some early witness lists associated with hundred courts suggest that natives dominated them in numerical terms. English participation in courts, including the expanding royal courts, continued in Henry II's reign and beyond.[50] Natives must often have been the least important figures in these courts. Nevertheless, they *were* actively participating in courts and in royal governance in general. This participation was important to ethnic relations partly because it undoubtedly helped to alleviate ethnic tensions and feelings of exclusion on the part of the English, and also because it helped to create networks of power and influence that crossed ethnic and class divides.

Because of their power and connections, derived from landholding, participation in courts and government, and often from offices, the English in the middling level of society were even in a good position to intermarry with Norman families.[51] This would have been especially easy with those Normans in the middling ranks, but it also occurred with those in the bottom of the aristocracy. The Red Book of Worcester recounts how a *radman* named Osbert son of Aldide, who already held one half-hide of the bishopric, married the niece of an archdeacon, Gervase, through whom he received 1¼ hide, and the conversion of his tenure of both holdings to knight's service.[52] A thirteenth-century law case reveals a kinship tie in the mid-twelfth century between a minor Lincolnshire landholder with the Anglo-Scandinavian name of Bondi and a member of the knightly Benniworth family.[53] Another case reveals a marriage late in the twelfth century between the sister of the constable of Kenilworth, Hugh Bardolf, and Peter son of Ketelbern of Canley, whose father had established himself as the intermediary between the tenants in a

[48] *EYC*1, no. 402.
[49] Bridgeman, 'Burton Abbey Surveys', 216–17, 224; Hart and Lyons, *Cartularium Monasterii de Rameseia*, 3: 257–8, 261, 301; Davis, *Kalendar of Abbot Samson*, 4–5, 25, 35, 36, 58; BL Harley MS 61, fols. 41ᵛ–42ʳ, 56ʳ, 58ʳ, 67ʳ, 69ʳ, 71ʳ, 74ᵛ, 78ᵛ, 79ᵛ; Williams, *ENC*159–62.
[50] Scattered throughout the pipe rolls of Henry II's reign are amercements for mistakes in court, and among those amerced are people with English names; see e.g. *Pipe Roll 12 Henry II*, 10, 46–9, 57, 76, 108; *Pipe Roll 14 Henry II*, 70–1.
[51] See Clark, *Words, Names and History*, 132–3, for a similar point about the likelihood of intermarriage at these levels. Williams also discusses marriage in the middling ranks, although many of the examples she uses are ones I would place at the lower end of the aristocracy in my own scheme of class divisions: Williams, *ENC*198.
[52] In an interesting twist, Osbert's brother Thomas had received the 1¼ hide earlier from bishop Simon, who then sold it to the archdeacon after Thomas's death: Hollings, *Red Book of Worcester*, 4: 431, 440.
[53] *CRR*12, no. 1608.

royal holding and the royal government.[54] It is difficult to know how common marriage involving immigrants and natives from middling ranks was, but it clearly played some role, and possibly a large one, in integrating the Normans into English society.

Strikingly, all of these examples seem to show men from English families marrying upward, in several cases gaining land as a result. This in itself shows the decline of ethnic biases, and the growing willingness of the Norman elites to treat the English equally, at least in comparison to immigrants of the same class. It also suggests that horizontal marriages between Normans and English in the middling levels of society were even more likely, though the invisibility of most of these figures in the sources makes such a contention impossible to prove. More important, these examples show how social mobility and the existence of a middling range of society with upward ties created possibilities for intermarriage and assimilation that would have been rare between ordinary peasants and powerful lords, though a couple of *possible* examples of the latter exist.[55]

The meeting-point at the middling levels of the landholding spectrum, along with the vertical ties created through service, helped to ameliorate the effects of the broad class division between the English and the Normans. Vertical ties helped to break down ethnic barriers. The importance of the English among the middling sorts, and the downward mobility of some Normans, blurred class lines. The middling level of society also provided a platform from which some native families could rise into the elite, thus further obscuring any link between ethnicity and class, and helping to integrate the aristocracy. Native families of middling rank could even provide reasonably attractive marriage partners for immigrant families. All in all, the middling range of society in particular, with its ethnic mix and its ability to interact upwards with the Norman elites, must have been an important arena for interaction and assimilation.

What effect did the dominance of the English among the peasantry and the survival of large numbers among the middling levels of society have on questions of culture and acculturation? Since this is a very large topic for which little evidence survives, I will limit myself to some observations and suggestions. First of all, the fact that the bulk of the population remained English meant that many distinctively English aspects of culture, including the English language, would continue to dominate the countryside. Undoubtedly many Normans outside the aristocracy found this dominance hard to resist. However, to some degree culture in the Middle Ages divided along class as well as ethnic lines. English peasants were unlikely to be soaking up the chivalric ethos from their new Norman lords, and immi-

---

[54] R. H. Hilton, ed., *The Stoneleigh Leger Book* (Oxford, 1960; repr. Nendeln, 1968), 30–4; Hyams, *Kings, Lords, and Peasants*, 259–60; Coss, *Lordship, Knighthood and Locality*, 134. An entry in the book of fees reveals the marriage of the widow of Walter Tusard, a tenant by sergeanty, to a reeve named Godwin: *Book of Fees*, 2: 1325–6. The Tusards were descended from Tosard, a Norman from the time of Domesday Book; Keats-Rohan, *Domesday People*, 540–1.

[55] Stenton, *Facsimiles from Northamptonshire Collections*, no. 34; Foster and Major, *Registrum Antiquissimum* 4, no. 1233.

grant aristocrats did not go out to learn the subtleties of farm work from their serfs and servants. Moreover, the Normans in general were not likely to be eager to emulate the ways of peasants. These considerations must have limited the degree to which acculturation occurred between Norman aristocrats and English peasants, and to which the English culture of the vast majority of people would have anglicized the immigrant elite.

That said, some suggestions can be made for ways in which the natives in the rural population may have influenced the culture of their new lords. English law in this period saw a fusion of English and Continental practices (as well as a great deal of innovation).[56] No doubt the continuing presence in courts of English, most of them not aristocrats, had something to do with this aspect of acculturation. When it came to art and music, English people of humble rural backgrounds may also have had influence. Though many craftsmen and craftswomen would have been based in towns, surviving records mention men with English forenames and craft-related bynames like *aurifaber* (goldsmith), *pictor* (painter), and *citharista* or *cithareda* (harper) in a rural context.[57] This serves as a reminder that Norman lords, particularly minor ones, must sometimes have relied on local English artists and entertainers. This must surely have influenced their artistic and musical sensibilities, though equally, the English may have tried to adapt to Norman tastes. In either case, a certain amount of acculturation would have been the result.

In general, the English masses and Norman elites must have accommodated each other on some practical aspects of culture, most notably language, working together as they did in a variety of contexts, from individual aristocratic households to the courts. The *Chronicle of Battle Abbey* reveals that Abbot Odo, who could preach in Latin and French, did so in English, when addressing the 'unlearned masses'.[58] A family chronicle from the thirteenth century refers to a twelfth-century ancestor as 'William de Grauntkort who was called William of Clopton by the lesser sort, since an English surname was easier in their language than a Norman one'.[59] Any immigrant aristocrat or churchman who wanted to communicate with ordinary people had to use English. Not all did so. Peter of Blois, a late immigrant in the time of Henry II, confessed in a somewhat shamefaced way that he did not often preach because he did not speak English well.[60] Nonetheless, even powerful Normans had a certain incentive to learn some English, and for the immigrants in the middling ranks acquisition of English must have been a necessity. English nursemaids and servants probably also promoted bilingualism, particularly among

---

[56] See below, pp. 277–9.

[57] Bridgeman, 'Burton Abbey Surveys', 239; Doris Mary Stenton, ed., *Pleas Before the King or His Justices, 1198–1212*, vol. 4 (London, 1967), no. 4292; Tait, *Chartulary of St. Werburgh, Chester*, 1: 235; G. Herbert Fowler, ed., *Cartulary of the Abbey of Old Wardon* (Aspley Guise, 1930), no. 37; Chibnall, *Charters and Custumals*, 71.

[58] See also Jocelin of Brakelond's passage on Abbot Samson preaching in English, in a Norfolk dialect, 'to the people': *Chronicle of Jocelin of Brakelond*, 40. Neither Odo's nor Samson's ancestry is known, but the point remains that preaching to ordinary people required the use of English.

[59] King, 'Estate Records of the Hotot Family', 44.

[60] *The Later Letters of Peter of Blois*, ed. Elizabeth Revell (Oxford, 1993), 195.

the children of immigrants, though evidence for this is limited.[61] At the same time, ambitious English had an even stronger incentive to learn French. The fact that the vast majority of ordinary people were Anglophone did not lead aristocrats to abandon French, at least as a second language, but it may well have led to increased bilingualism and caused some decline in quality in the French spoken in England because even the elites came to speak it as a second language.[62] In general, the English among the peasantry and middling sorts must have helped acculturate and anglicize the Norman nobility a little, even though their influence should not be exaggerated.

What effect did the dominance of the English among the peasantry, and the survival of large numbers among the middling levels of society, have on the question of ethnic identity? Here we must ask again the question of whether ordinary people in the countryside even had a strong English identity.[63] The evidence after the conquest, as before, is largely indirect. Certainly writers could think of common people as English. The link between rusticity and Englishness that I have noted before worked both ways; writers may have thought of the English as rustics, but equally they thought of peasants, and probably the middling sorts as well, as English. When Jocelin of Brakelond could speak of an estate manager as a serf, 'English by *natio*', he explicitly identified a person of low rank as English.[64] Such passages show what educated writers, not peasants or even landholders of middling rank, thought, but peasants who found themselves described as English might think of themselves as English.

The Norman Conquest itself, and the ethnic divide it created, may have increased English identity among the peasants and the members of the middling range of society. The very intrusion of a new people who spoke a different language and had different customs may have emphasized to such figures what they had in common with the surviving English of other classes and with peasants from other regions, whereas before the differences might have seemed more important. Labels were needed to distinguish natives from the new groups introduced to England by the conquest, and it is likely that native peasants accepted the same label of Englishness that elite writers assigned to them. Because the Norman Conquest was an event with such widespread consequences, moreover, it may also have helped individuals think of local history in national terms. In testimony about very local affairs, twelfth-century village jurors, some of them with English names, can be found referring to 'the Conquest of England' or the period before 'the Normans con-

---

[61] The best discussion of this may be found in Clark, *Words, Names and History*, 123–4. To the evidence there may be added the fact, noted earlier, that Alice de Berkeley, a descendant of Normans, had a nurse with the insular name, Toka: Jeayes, *Charters and Muniments at Berkeley Castle*, no. 55.

[62] W. Rothwell, 'The Teaching of French in Medieval England', *Modern Language Review*, 63 (1968), 37–46; W. Rothwell, 'The Role of French in Thirteenth-Century England', *Bulletin of the John Rylands Society*, 58 (1976), 445–66; Ian Short, 'On Bilingualism in Anglo-Norman England', *Romance Philology*, 33 (1980), 467–79; Short, '*Tam Angli quam Franci*', 155–9; R. M. Wilson, 'English and French in England, 1100–1300', *History*, 28 (1943): 37–60.

[63] See also Davies, 'Language and Historical Mythology', 21–3, for a discussion of peasants, historical memory, and ethnic identity.

[64] *Chronicle of Jocelin of Brakelond*, 33.

quered England'.[65] Jurors who could talk about the history of England, however sketchily, could probably think of themselves as English.

That peasants and people from the middling ranks probably thought of themselves as English does not mean that Englishness was necessarily all that important to them. Among a group of humorous stories recorded in the twelfth-century chronicle of Ramsey Abbey about the discomfiture of Danish landholders in Canute's reign is one that may shed some light on peasant patriotism, or the lack thereof. It concerns a Dane who fears the English because he thinks they will hate him since the Danes had invaded their *patria*. To protect himself, he forces the peasants on his English estate to keep watch at night. His plan backfires when they get fed up with this imposition and ask why they should suffer to protect the life of 'alienigena iste' who grows rich at their expense. They decide to do him in themselves, whereupon he flees.[66] Unfortunately, the term *alienigena* could mean foreigner, as in 'not English', but could also mean something like 'not from around here'. Moreover, this rare expression of a peasant voice in a medieval chronicle is not found in a very straightforward source. Though Antonia Gransden has argued that this set of stories may have been written before the conquest and only copied later, they look to me like oral tradition, in which case we probably have a much later writer imagining what peasants might have thought and said.[67] There is also probably an element of class-based humour, with the Danish warrior ignominiously taking refuge behind and then fleeing from his own peasants. But if I am right that this is a twelfth-century recasting of oral tradition, it provides interesting insights into one writer's assumptions about peasant identity. On the one hand, by referring to the Dane with a term that often meant foreigner, the peasant may be speaking of himself as English. But on the other hand, the peasants are implicitly separated from the English who would hate the Danes for conquering the *patria*, and when they do take action it is because of their own grievances. One should not make too much of one humorous story set in an earlier period, but this account should warn us about the dangers of assuming a strong English identity among the peasants, or exaggerating the degree to which any Englishness might affect their actions.

Even if English identity among the peasantry and the middling classes was quite strong, it was not likely to have much effect on the Norman elites. It is hardly probable that powerful immigrant barons and knights would have adopted English identity so that they could please English peasants, or so that they could go down to the local alehouse and fit in more comfortably—quite the contrary! One of the stereotypes about the English, which would have made English identity distasteful, concerned their supposed rusticity, and the fact that Normans could see English

[65] Hart and Lyons, *Cartularium Monasterii de Rameseia*, 1, no. 100; *EEA* 11, no. 23; CUL, Peterborough D&C MS 1, fols. 133ʳ⁻ᵛ. See also *CRR* 1: 264.

[66] MacRay, *Chronicon Abbatiae Rameseiensis*, 140–3.

[67] Antonia Gransden, 'Tradition and Continuity During the Last Century of Anglo-Saxon Monasticism', *Journal of Ecclesiastical History*, 40 (1989), 194–5. In my view, the stories have too many improbable and literary or folkloric elements to be likely candidates for contemporary or near-contemporary historical records.

peasants all around them was what made this charge such a powerful one. To the extent that serfs and the poor in general identified themselves or were identified as English, this was as likely as not to make immigrants spurn such an identity. Thus, once again, the numerical superiority of the English probably mattered less than one might think.

Overall, I would argue that the probable English identity of peasants and of the middling sorts *did* matter, but only to a limited degree. It mattered in a negative way in that any triumph of Norman identity would have had to overcome the existing Englishness of large numbers of people. It also mattered because the middling range of society was a recruiting ground for monks and priests, many of whom, as we shall see, did take Englishness quite seriously, and who collectively played an important role in defending English honour and pride. In addition, the survival of many natives at the middling level meant that, as moderately respectable people who interacted extensively with Normans, they were in a position to influence the immigrants' attitudes about Englishness, and perhaps even to influence their sense of ethnic identity. But the last should serve as a reminder that influence could have gone both ways. Surely it would have been less surprising for natives of the middling ranks, as they became more intertwined with the Normans, to have adopted the ethnic identity of their social superiors, and for the least important immigrants, especially the downwardly mobile ones, to retain their Continental identity as a mark of prestige. Surely, as intermarriage proceeded, it would have made more sense for children to pick the more aristocratic ethnic identity. Presumably, in the long run, even the peasantry could have changed identities, in the same way that they adopted Continental personal names. In the event, the numerical superiority of the English in the lower classes did make a difference, but as my questions suggest, it was no guarantee of the eventual triumph of English identity, any more than it was a guarantee that the Norman elites would be absorbed by the mass of the peasantry.

12

Townspeople

TOWNSPEOPLE WERE FAR less numerous than peasants, but more important to assimilation, and perhaps to the survival of Englishness. Towns were important centres of ethnic interaction, for there was a fair amount of immigration from the Continent to urban centres, and natives also remained an important presence at all levels of urban society. Towns and cities were therefore obvious places in which Normans and English could intermingle and cultural influences could be interchanged. More important, the native elites in towns remained a powerful group, who not only helped to assimilate the immigrant urbanites, but also interacted with the rural elites. Though other scholars have noted the presence of English among the elites of various towns, I do not think that the strength of that presence throughout England, in both large cities and small towns, has been sufficiently explored.[1] Moreover, I would argue that scholars have not always fully appreciated the power, wealth, and status of the richest burgesses, whatever their ethnicity. Although the urban elite was collectively smaller and less powerful than the rural aristocracy, individually the wealthiest burgesses had power, wealth, and status to match all but the great barons and earls. Because a relatively small social distance divided rural landholders and powerful townspeople, many of whom were rural landholders themselves, wealthy native townspeople could interact and intermarry not only with their immigrant counterparts in towns, but also with immigrant aristocrats. All townspeople, French and English, poor and rich, played a role in assimilation and the question of identity, but the native urban elites were particularly important.

The evidence for Continental immigration into English towns and cities is extensive.[2] Orderic Vitalis referred to English and French living together (and intermarrying) in towns, castles, and cities soon after the Norman Conquest.[3] Domesday Book reveals French settlement in a number of urban centres. In Southampton, for instance, there were sixty-five French settlers, making up nearly 40 per cent of the recorded population, and in Shrewsbury, there were forty-three French burgesses, holding a sizable portion of the inhabited dwellings there in

---

[1] It should be noted, however, that Williams has already gathered evidence for London, Winchester, and Lincoln: Williams, *ENC* 205–6.

[2] See also Le Patourel, *Norman Empire*, 38–40, 315–18; Golding, *Conquest and Colonization*, 77–9; Williams, *ENC* 201–4.

[3] *EHOV* 2: 256.

1086.[4] A biography of Thomas Becket, whose parents were immigrants to London, states that many from Rouen and Caen crossed the Channel and 'made themselves inhabitants of the city', and Eilert Ekwall, who has studied naming patterns in London, suggests a strong Norman presence there, especially in the upper reaches of society.[5] Twelfth-century surveys for Winchester, Battle, and Canterbury also provide useful evidence for immigration, and Searle, Clark, and the contributors to *Winchester in the Early Middle Ages* have studied them for information about the ethnic composition of those towns.[6] For instance, in Winchester a survey of *c*.1110 indicates that around one-fifth of those paying tax in the town were clearly Norman (though some of these were non-resident landlords), while only one-quarter had English names. As usual the problem of names looms large, but clearly there was a large immigrant presence there.[7] Not surprisingly, immigrants soon moved into positions of power in towns; in Domesday Book two of the twelve lawmen of Lincoln, leading town officials, were immigrants, as was an important official of Canterbury during the episcopacy of Archbishop Anselm.[8] Many prominent London officials were also Norman.[9] In short, the evidence indicates an immigrant presence, sometimes quite large, in a wide number of urban centres, both big and small, and it is likely that there were Continental settlers in most towns and cities.

Nonetheless, the English almost certainly remained the majority in most urban centres, and many survived in positions of prominence. Since medieval towns could not generally maintain their populations without immigration from the surrounding countryside, the immigrant presence in English urban centres probably started declining within a generation or two of the conquest (though continuing Continental settlement may have offset this to some degree). Moreover, wherever good evidence survives for towns, powerful and wealthy natives with leading roles in urban government can be found. London, for instance, had a large number of powerful native lineages among its elite families.[10] Natives continued to dominate the Cnihtengild, an important pre-conquest institution that lasted until 1125. It drew on the wealthy ranks of goldsmiths, moneyers, and cathedral

[4] *DB* 1: 52a, 56a, 179a, 189a, 252a, 298a; 2: 116a, 311a. An Evesham survey, based on Domesday Book, mentions French burgesses in Gloucester: BL Cotton MS. Vespasian B xxiv, fol. 57ʳ; calendared in the Appendix to the Phillimore edition of *Domesday Book: Gloucestershire*, ed. John S. Moore (Chichester, 1982).

[5] *Becket Materials*, 4: 81; Eilert Ekwall, *Early London Personal Names* (Lund, 1947), 100.

[6] Biddle, *Winchester in the Early Middle Ages*, 32–228, 474–6; Searle, *Chronicle of Battle Abbey*, 52–8; William Urry, *Canterbury under the Angevin Kings* (London, 1967), 221–382; Eleanor Searle, *Lordship and Community: Battle Abbey and Its Banlieu, 1066–1538* (Toronto, 1974), 71–7, 465–6; Clark, *Words, Names, and History*, 179–206, 221–40. See also ibid. 84–91, 133–42, 271–8.

[7] Biddle, *Winchester in the Early Middle Ages*, 475.

[8] *DB* 1: 336a; Clark, *Words, Names and History*, 186.

[9] Ekwall, *Early London Personal Names*, 100–1.

[10] Christopher N. L. Brooke and Gillian Keir, *London, 800–1216: The Shaping of a City* (Berkeley, 1975), 29, 31–2, 219–20, 246–8; Pamela Nightingale, 'Some London Moneyers and Reflections on the Organization of English Mints in the Eleventh and Twelfth Centuries', *Numismatic Chronicle*, 142 (1982), 35–42, 47–8; id., *A Medieval Mercantile Community: The Grocers' Company and the Politics and Trade of London, 1000–1485* (New Haven, 1995), 21–34, 54–5; Susan Reynolds, 'The Rulers of London in the Twelfth Century', *History*, NS 57 (1972), 337, 346, 354–7; Williams, *ENC* 205–6.

canons.[11] Men with English names led other guilds as well in the twelfth century, including the weavers' guild in Henry I's reign and the pepperers' guild in Henry II's.[12] More important, a survey of the property of St Paul's in London reveals that as late as 1127, over sixty years after the conquest, the vast majority of aldermen still had English names.[13] When one reaches the greatest offices of city reeve, sheriff, or justiciar, the preponderance of natives thins out, but one could point to Leofstan, a reeve or sheriff in Henry I's reign; Theodoric son of Derman, a justiciar in Stephen's reign; or Brichtmar of Haverhill, a sheriff in Henry II's reign.[14] Most strikingly, the first mayor of London, Henry, who served probably from 1190 or 1191 to his death in 1212, had a father and grandfather with the English names Ailwin and Leofstan.[15] Immigrant families such as the Beckets may have played leading roles in London society, but they had plenty of English company.[16]

Prominent natives can be traced in most provincial towns and cities as well, from the late eleventh century on. Some of the best evidence survives for Oxford in the late twelfth century. In the reigns of Henry II and Richard I many of the important town officials whose names survive, including Leofwin the Glover, Lambert son of Thovi, Laurence Harding, Henry son of Segrim, and William son of Sueting, have English elements in their names.[17] Another indication that natives were important in Oxford society was their frequent appearance as witnesses to charters, which showed that they were heavily involved in public business and that their word carried weight. One leading citizen, Thomas son of Eilrich, was witness to over eighty surviving charters.[18] Particularly important was the frequent appearance of such men in documents connected with the town's court, or portmoot. In one concord made in the portmoot in the 1180s, one of the two aldermen, both bailiffs, and eleven of the twenty-four other witnesses had names indicating indigenous origins.[19] Since the shift to Continental names had been under way for over a century, the number of leading citizens of Oxford with English elements in their names is remarkable, and shows the strength of the natives in that town's elite.

[11] Hodgett, *Cartulary of Holy Trinity Aldgate*, 229, no. 871; *RRAN* 2, nos. 663, 1467, 1793; 3, no. 505; Brooke and Keir, *London, 800–1216*, 96–9; J. H. Round, *The Commune of London and Other Studies* (Westminster, 1899), 102–6.

[12] *Pipe Roll 31 Henry I*, 144; *Pipe Roll 26 Henry II*, 153–4.

[13] H. W. C. Davis, 'London Lands and Liberties of St. Paul's, 1066–1135', in *Essays in Medieval History Presented to Thomas Frederick Tout*, ed. A. G. Little and F. M. Powicke (Manchester, 1925), 56–9.

[14] Reynolds, 'Rulers of London', 354–5.

[15] Brooke and Keir, *London, 800–1216*, 246–8; Reynolds, 'Rulers of London', 346, 349.

[16] See Frank Barlow, *Thomas Becket* (London, 1986), 13–15, for the place of Thomas's father in London society.

[17] Salter, *Cartulary of Oseney Abbey*, 1, nos. 68, 83; 2, nos. 513, 983, 1097, 1099; 3: pp. x–xi.

[18] Wigram, *Cartulary of St. Frideswide*, 1, no. 613; Salter, *Eynsham Cartulary*, 1, no. 172; 2, nos. 775, 786; Salter, *Cartulary of Oseney Abbey*, 1, nos. 27, 42, 52, 55, 58, 79, 83–4, 108, 112, 132, 133, 140, 175, 176, 208, 230, 252, 257, 352–4, 381, 382, 384, 385, 386, 404, 456; 2, nos. 512–13, 518, 535, 536, 538, 543A, 549, 606–8, 655–6, 745A, 837, 842–3, 902–3, 905, 907, 964, 983, 1097, 1101, 1110; 4, nos. 14, 21, 42B, 44A, 48, 48B; 6, no. 962C; H. E. Salter, ed., *Cartulary of the Hospital of St. John the Baptist*, 3 vols. (Oxford, 1914–16), 1, nos. 70, 159, 275, 403, 419, 449, 487; 2, nos. 556, 561, 564, 614, 784, 786, 794, 917.

[19] Salter, *Cartulary of Oseney Abbey*, 1, nos. 68, 83 (the concord mentioned in the text), 85; 2, nos. 513, 983, 1097.

In York, natives can be traced in the elites from the conquest through the twelfth century. A document contemporary to Domesday Book suggests that a powerful native oligarchy, which provided a number of witnesses to the rights of the Archbishopric, existed in 1086.[20] In 1106 the hereditary, native lawmen still served as a functioning body at York.[21] In 1130 Thomas son of Ulviet, probably a son of one of the lawmen of 1106, became head of the guild of merchants there, and as late as 1175 he and his son got into trouble for trying to create a commune in York. Three other leading Yorkshire citizens at that time were the brothers Gerard and Hugh son of Lewin (or Leofwin), and Thomas son of Richard, whose mother had the English name of Alveva.[22]

The elites of London, Oxford, and York were by no means unusual in having natives among their members. Hervey, an early alderman of the guild of merchants in Cambridge, and probably first mayor there, was the grandson of a man with the distinctively English name of Dunning.[23] Other important individuals or lineages with English names can be found at Lincoln, Bristol, Winchester, Northampton, Huntingdon, Coventry, Canterbury, Nottingham, Norwich, Gloucester, West-minster, and Carlisle.[24] The pipe rolls reveal that a number of royal officials in towns (who were normally drawn from the urban elites) had English names.[25] Less information survives for smaller market towns, but the lists of prominent local individuals paying sometimes quite large sums for the marriage of Henry II's daughter in 1166 included nearly 125 people from small urban centres, and between 42 and 52 per cent had names suggesting English ancestry, even a century after the shift in names had begun.[26] In short, natives remained a very strong presence among urban elites across England, in towns large and small, up to and beyond the time ethnic boundaries ceased to matter.

Many of these townspeople became very rich through such activities as minting,

[20] F. Liebermann, 'An Early English Document of About 1080', *Yorkshire Archaeological Journal*, 18 (1905), 412–16. See D. M. Palliser, *Domesday York* (York, 1990), 6–9, 25, for the date. Williams suggests these were the lawmen of York: Williams, *ENC* 160.

[21] van Caenegem, *English Lawsuits*, 1: 39.

[22] C. T. Clay, 'A Holderness Charter of William Count of Aumale', *Yorkshire Archaeological Journal*, 39 (1957), 339–42; *RRAN* 2, no. 1621; *EYC* 1: 175, 443; 2, nos. 841–4; *Pipe Roll 31 Henry I*, 34; *Pipe Roll 21 Henry II*, 180, 182.

[23] Helen M. Cam, *Liberties and Communities in Medieval England* (London, 1963), 23–4; J. M. Gray, *The School of Pythagoras (Merton Hall), Cambridge* (Cambridge, 1932), 1–11.

[24] J. W. F. Hill, *Medieval Lincoln* (Cambridge, 1948; repr., Stamford, 1990), 385–93; Robert B. Patterson, 'Robert Fitz Harding of Bristol: Profile of an Early Angevin Burgess-Baron Patrician and His Family's Urban Involvement', *Haskins Society Journal*, 1, ed. Robert B. Patterson (London, 1989), 109–22; Biddle, *Winchester in the Early Middle Ages*, 424, 447; Amt, *Accession of Henry II*, 37–42, 99–100; William Farrer, *Honors and Knights' Fees*, vol. 1 (London, 1923), 41–4; Talbot, *Life of Christina of Markyate*, 10–11; Coss, *Lordship, Knighthood and Locality*, 72–6; Urry, *Canterbury Under the Angevin Kings*, 70, 98–9, 171–2; Holdsworth, *Rufford Charters* 1, no. 28; West, *St. Benet of Holme*, 1, no. 121; Thomas of Monmouth, *The Life and Miracles of William of Norwich*, ed. Augustus Jessopp and Montague Rhodes James (Cambridge, 1986), 27; Mason, *Westminster Abbey Charters*, nos. 289, 303, 322, 406–11, 441, 446, 448; J. E. Prescott, *The Register of the Priory of Wetherhal* (London, 1897), nos. 73–4

[25] *Pipe Roll 11 Henry II*, 14; *Pipe Roll 16 Henry II*, 79; *Pipe Roll 31 Henry I*, 118; *Pipe Roll 10 Henry II*, 23; *Pipe Roll 14 Henry II*, 75; *Pipe Roll 17 Henry II*, 23; *Pipe Roll 20 Henry II*, 104; *Pipe Roll 24 Henry II*, 90, 99; *Pipe Roll 25 Henry II*, 47; *Pipe Roll 26 Henry II*, 58; *Pipe Roll 31 Henry II*, 46.

[26] See above, p. 173.

money-changing, trading, building, leasing property, and moneylending, which did not become a monopoly of the Jews until the late twelfth century.[27] One miracle story, probably set in the 1120s or early 1130s, speaks of one Deorman, almost certainly a member of an important family of moneyers traced by Pamela Nightingale, as 'an extremely rich, splendid, and distinguished merchant of the city of London, who outshone all the other dealers in expensive spices, silks, and robes'.[28] The pipe rolls of Henry II's reign show the king repaying approximately £3,800 in loans from the Northampton native Robert son of Sawin over the course of nineteen years; this does not include payments that may not have shown up in the pipe rolls. This is roughly £200 a year, but it reached over £500 in one year, and nearly as much in another.[29] Comparisons with aristocratic incomes are tricky, because the sums listed above represented capital as much as income, and because this capital was probably recycled in fresh loans to the king. But, given that Sidney Painter calculates that the average income of fifty-four baronial estates between 1160 and 1220 was £202, and their median income only £115, and given that Henry II's government deemed that an income of 16 marks, or £10. 13s. 4d., was sufficient to demand that its possessor purchase the arms of a knight, Robert son of Sawin was a wealthy man indeed.[30] During the last twenty-five years of Henry II's reign Lewin of York and his sons Hugh and Gerard paid the staggering sum of £830 to the king for a variety of transgressions, in addition to which Hugh paid a share of £100 for the goods and land of his father-in-law, another prominent York merchant. Few *barons* could easily have survived such a drain of capital, and one suspects that the family fortunes were much reduced, but Hugh can be found leasing land during the Third Crusade, and attending a judicial eyre at York in 1202, indicating his continued standing in the city.[31] The amount this family paid to the Crown was unparalleled among native city-dwellers, but other large payments to the king by such figures can be found.[32] In short, English merchants and moneylenders could have huge sums of money at their disposal and, in terms of liquid capital, their wealth might rival or exceed that of most members of the rural elites.

[27] Robert C. Stacey, 'Jewish Lending and the Medieval English Economy', in *A Commercialising Economy: England, 1086 to c. 1300*, ed. Richard H. Britnell and Bruce M. S. Campbell (Manchester, 1995), 87–93.

[28] Thomas Arnold, ed., *Memorials of St. Edmund's Abbey*, vol. 1 (London, 1890), 183; Nightingale, *Medieval Mercantile Community*, 29–30.

[29] See Amt, *Accession of Henry II*, 99, n. 42, for sums paid from 1156 to 1170. Her totals add up to just under £2,800. To these may be added sums of £40 in 1162 and £8. 6s. 8d. in 1167 that she did not include in her figures: *Pipe Roll 8 Henry II*, 6; *Pipe Roll 13 Henry II*, 115. The following payments were made in the succeeding years: £223 in 1171; £484 in 1172; £72 in 1173; £170 in 1154.

[30] Painter, *English Feudal Barony*, 170; William Stubbs, ed., *Select Charters and Other Illustrations of English Constitutional History*, 8th edn. (Oxford, 1900), 154.

[31] *Pipe Roll 11 Henry II*, 49; *Pipe Roll 12 Henry II*, 39, 49; *Pipe Roll 13 Henry II*, 93; *Pipe Roll 18 Henry II*, 60; *Pipe Roll 21 Henry II*, 182; *Pipe Roll 22 Henry II*, 106; *Pipe Roll 23 Henry II*, 72; *Pipe Roll 28 Henry II*, 38, 46; *Pipe Roll 31 Henry II*, 76; *Pipe Roll 32 Henry II*, 95; *Pipe Roll 33 Henry II*, 88, *Pipe Roll 34 Henry II*, 86; *Pipe Roll 3 Richard I*, 76; York Minster Library MS XVI.A.1, fol. 129ʳ. It should be emphasized that the £830 was paid in full by the end of the reign.

[32] For instance, £100 from Liulf of Coventry, Ailmund de Hereford, and William son of Warner son of Turgar at different points. Liulf and Ailmund, at least, paid off their debts: *Pipe Roll 4 Henry II*, 184, *Pipe Roll 6 Henry II*, 35; *Pipe Roll 33 Henry II*, 132; *Pipe Roll 3 Richard I*, 16; *Pipe Roll 5 Richard I*, 88–9.

Many native townspeople also built up considerable landed properties. Much of this was urban property. In Henry II's reign, one Richard son of Outi held in Lincoln property worth over £22 annually, which alone would have given him an income greater than that of many knights.[33] More important, in terms of the inter-action between urban and rural elites, is the fact that many native townspeople had substantial rural interests. A number of English landholders in 1086 were based in towns, and in the Bedfordshire section of Domesday Book there was a separate heading for burgesses of Bedford who possessed rural estates.[34] Native Londoners appear in a late eleventh-century list of tenants by knights' service of the arch-bishopric of Canterbury.[35] Important townspeople in the twelfth century con-tinued to hold or gain rural as well as urban interests. Robert son of Sawin inherited one half-hide in one village from his brother, acquired 140 acres elsewhere in Northamptonshire, held one or two knight's fees of the honour of Chokes, and acquired several holdings from the king, including a manor worth £14 yearly. Robert was a generous donor to monasteries, and only part of his land passed to his heirs, but when his son died, late in Henry II's reign, he had urban and rural property potentially worth more than £27 yearly.[36] Robert was no ordinary town-dweller, but many others had rural interests, sometimes only a hide or two, but sometimes including one or more substantial manors.[37] Indeed, the descendants of some, including the first mayor of London, passed into the rural elites.[38] In general, rural landholding by native members of the urban elites gave them both additional wealth and a likely motive and framework for interacting with immigrant knights and nobles. It also placed them closer to equality with the rural elites.

Members of the urban elites gained influence and power not only through civic office-holding and wealth, but also through the exercise of violence, both individu-ally and as leaders in their communities. This could involve both strong-arm tactics on a local level and formal military service. Hervey, grandson of Dunning, alder-man of Cambridge and a local landowner, provided a good example of the former when he led a band against the family of an opponent in land litigation, breaking the arm of his opponent's mother, and beating the opponent's brother.[39] Urban

[33] *Pipe Roll 22 Henry II*, 88; *Pipe Roll 26 Henry II*, 49.

[34] *DB* 1: 218a. Other urban figures who were also landowners include the Lincoln lawman, Sortbrand son of Ulf, Deorman of London, and Sawold of Oxford: *DB* 1: 130b, 142a, 154a, 160b, 336a, 370b. See also Williams, *ENC* 160–1.

[35] Douglas, *Domesday Monachorum*, 58–63, 105.

[36] Farrer, *Honors and Knights' Fees*, 1: 41–4; Amt, *Accession of Henry II*, 99–100; Delisle, *Recueil des actes de Henri II*, 2, no. 512; W. O. Hassall, ed., *The Cartulary of St Mary Clerkenwell* (London, 1949), nos. 14–15, 18; Round, *Rotuli de Dominabus*, 21–2.

[37] Coss, *Lordship, Knighthood, and Locality*, 72–6; Brooke and Keir, *London, 800–1216*, 220, 246–7; Nightingale, 'Some London Moneyers', 38–9; Cam, *Liberties and Communities*, 23–5; Gray, *School of Pythagoras*, 2–4; Hill, *Medieval Lincoln*, 39, 386, 390, 393; Searle, *Chronicle of Battle Abbey*, 212; L. F. Salzman, ed., *The Chartulary of the Priory of St. Pancras of Lewes*, vol. 1 (Lewes, 1932), 14; Audrey M. Woodcock, *Cartulary of the Priory of St. Gregory, Canterbury* (London, 1956), p. xiv, no. 34; *CRR* 12, no. 420; Clay, 'A Holderness Charter', 339–42; *EYC* 1, no. 547 and note; 2, nos. 841–4, 971, 1242; 5, no. 143; Charles Clay, ed., *Yorkshire Deeds*, vol. 4 (Leeds, 1924), nos. 92–4.

[38] Reynolds, 'Rulers of London', 346. See also K. S. B. Keats-Rohan, 'The Making of Henry of Oxford: Englishmen in a Norman World', *Oxoniensia*, 54 (1989), 292–3.

[39] *RCR* 2: 97, 143–4; Cam, *Liberties and Communities*, 24.

contributions to medieval warfare should not be forgotten. Domesday Book's occasional discussion of urban centres reveals that many of them were expected to provide the king with fighters for his armies or navies, and that burgesses could sometimes have heriots consisting partly of arms.[40] Orderic Vitalis reports that the men of Winchester, London, and Salisbury, led by the Norman bishop Geoffrey of Coutances, put down one West Country revolt very early in William's reign, and that the citizens of Exeter defended his interests against another branch of the rebellion.[41] The military support the English were able to provide William II and Henry I, early in their reigns, after native rural elites had largely been destroyed, may well have come partly from towns. Collectively, the Londoners turned the tide for King Stephen and against the Empress Matilda in 1141 by driving the latter out of their city before her coronation.[42] Native urban leaders, either as individuals or as community leaders, could not hope to challenge Norman military power on their own, and thus were not a dangerous threat, but their military potential gave them power and influence in society.

The combination of money, estates, military potential, and civic leadership was a potent one, and historians should not underestimate the power and influence of urban leaders, including the many who were native. Someone like Henry son of Ailwin was an actor on the national scene. As mayor of the country's greatest city, he was a prominent figure who must have interacted with the king and great magnates on a periodic basis. He expressed and advertised his connections to King Henry II by giving gifts to a number of monasteries for the monarch's soul, and he played a role in suppressing John's revolt against Richard in 1193–4 by arresting one of his messengers.[43] Henry son of Ailwin was a powerful man.

Even native leaders in very small urban centres could be big frogs in small ponds, and have important roles regionally. One native regular canon, Peter of Cornwall, who became prior of Holy Trinity, Aldgate, compiled a collection of miracle stories that included several accounts involving his relatives. Peter described his grand-father Ailsi as 'an inhabitant and citizen' of Launceston who, like so many other important townspeople, also had land outside the town. At one point, when a local priest felt aggrieved with Ailsi over payment of tithes, the priest did not dare to complain to anyone but Ailsi, because of 'the great authority . . . in which he was held in that *provincia*'. Peter's own father, Jordan of Trecarrel, was an even greater figure, who was reeve or provost of the town of Launceston at one point, but also held half a knight's fee from the bishop of Exeter, and was considered an important legal expert. Peter describes Jordan as having 'a great name in that region', depicts him as supporting Launceston Priory in the county court, and records that at his funeral his body was carried to the priory 'on the shoulders of magnates and honourable

---

[40] *DB* 1: 1a, 64b, 100a, 154a, 179a, 189a, 230a, 238a, 252a.

[41] *EHOV* 2: 228. Williams, however, suggests that this may refer to the castle garrisons: *ENC* 37.

[42] For a recent overview of this incident, see Jean A. Truax, 'Winning over the Londoners: King Stephen, the Empress Matilda, and the Politics of Personality', in *Haskins Society Journal*, 8, ed. C. P. Lewis and Emma Cownie (Woodbridge, 1996), 43–61.

[43] *Chronica Rogeri de Hovedene*, 3: 236; Mason, *Westminster Abbey Charters*, no. 351; Hassall, *Cartulary of St Mary Clerkenwell*, no. 279; Hodgett, *Cartulary of Holy Trinity Aldgate*, nos. 426, 866.

men'.[44] Powerful townspeople, even from small boroughs like Launceston, were influential figures, especially when they were also rural landholders.

As wealthy and powerful figures, moreover, leading townspeople, including natives, made claims to a surprisingly high status. Christina of Markyate came from a prominent native family in the town of Huntingdon that also had some rural interests.[45] Her hagiographer firmly placed her and her family in an urban setting, for instance, describing her parents as leaders in the local guild of merchants, but he or she also insistently referred to Christina, her family, her fiancé, the members of the guild, and the leaders of the town as nobles. The term 'noble' was not a technical one at this point, but it certainly implied a high status. The hagiographer's view of Christina's family may have come from the saint herself. She was obviously the writer's main source, and in one passage, when the servant of a hermit offered to smuggle her out of town to escape her unwanted marriage and pursue the life of religion she desired, the *vita* states that she was embarrassed, even ashamed, partly because 'it would be disgraceful for a daughter of Auti to be found in the fields with such a boy'. Despite her struggles with her family over their desire to marry her off, she was keenly aware of and concerned about its status and honour.[46] This claim of high status was not unique. Henry son of Ailwin and Hervey, grandson of Dunning, both had equestrian seals, and the latter, at least, claimed the status of knight. Henry son of Ailwin was listed among the 'nobles' of London in one charter, and the alderman Peter Blund, son of an important merchant Edward Blund, was given the title *dominus*, normally reserved for knights, in another.[47] Still earlier, a Ramsey charter from the reign of Henry I was addressed to four men, including two with the English names of Leofstan and Ordgar, and to 'the barons of London'. The citizens of London continued to claim the title baron, even as that title rose greatly in the status it signified.[48] In short, members of the urban elite were not shy about pressing claims to a dignified position in society equal to that of aristocratic rural landholders.

Power and status were relative and debatable things, and the discussion in the above paragraphs needs to be put in some perspective. While a number of native townspeople probably had wealth and status comparable to knights, few could compete with even moderately wealthy barons when landholding and power are

---

[44] 'Peter of Cornwall: The Visions of Ailsi and his Sons', ed. Robert Easting and Richard Sharpe, *Mediaevistik*, 1 (1988), 225, 228, 243–4, 247–8.

[45] Apart from the evidence of Christina's *vita*, the Ramsey Cartulary puts her father, Auti, in a prominent place in the witness list of an early twelfth-century agreement between the abbot and the royal steward, Ranulf son of Ilger. For this document and for the family's rural landholdings, see Hart and Lyons, *Cartularium Monasterii de Rameseia*, 1, nos. 59–60; 2, no. 390; MacRay, *Chronicon Abbatiae Rameseiensis*, 257; Talbot, *Life of Christina of Markyate*, 11.

[46] Talbot, *Life of Christina of Markyate*, 34, 44, 48, 58, 64, 82, 86, 94.

[47] Reynolds, 'Rulers of London', 346; Cam, *Liberties and Communities*, 23; Hodgett, *Cartulary of Holy Trinity Aldgate*, no. 270; Kemp, *Reading Abbey Cartularies* 2, no. 838. For Peter's position as alderman, and relationship to Edward Blund, see Moore, *Cartularium Monasterii de Colecestria*, 2: 299, 592; Ransford, *Early Charters of Waltham Abbey*, 565.

[48] Hart and Lyons, *Cartularium Monasterii de Rameseia*, 1, no. 50. For the fairly broad but still prestigious use of the term 'baron' in the twelfth century, and its later rise, see Crouch, *Image of Aristocracy*, 107–13.

factored in, and none could hope to match the greatest rural magnates. That prominent townspeople made claims to high status may not mean that those claims were always accepted outside towns. The slighting references in the *Dialogue of the Exchequer* to knights or other freemen lapsing from the dignity of their rank by acquiring wealth through trade, or even worse, moneylending, provides an alternative perspective.[49] Thus, one should be careful not to inflate the power and influence of townspeople, or to necessarily take their claims about social status at face value, given that rural nobles may have taken a different view. That said, there was clearly much less social distance between Norman aristocrats and prominent native townspeople than between the former and most of the surviving English. This fact is crucial to an understanding of the full role native townspeople played in assimilation after the conquest.

It is time now to turn to ethnic interaction, first between native townspeople and the new order, then among the urban inhabitants of both ethnicities, and finally between the native members of the urban elites, the royal government, and immigrant landholders. At first, relations between English townspeople and the invaders must have ranged from tense at best to hostile at worst. London resisted William before he was crowned, and Exeter and York were involved in early rebellions.[50] The massacre at York described by William of Jumièges was probably only the worst example of violence suffered by English urbanites at Norman hands.[51] Though Domesday Book was unsystematic and incomplete in its treatment of towns, it amply reveals the disastrous impact of the Norman Conquest on many urban centres. Dover was burned, and over a dozen towns saw a sometimes massive loss of dwellings or inhabitants, whether through violence and oppression, or perhaps because of disruption of trade routes and temporary local economic dislocations. Many towns also saw houses destroyed to build castles.[52] There was probably no love lost between the Normans and many English townspeople in the years immediately following the conquest, which might, if it had festered over time, have proven a serious obstacle to ethnic harmony and assimilation.

Yet aside from devastation that was closely linked to war and military necessity, the Normans treated English townspeople much better than they treated the native aristocracy and the peasantry. They recognized and maintained urban rights; one of William's earliest surviving English writs confirmed the rights of the Londoners.[53] The native urban elites remained strong, perhaps because they posed less of a threat than their rural counterparts, but mainly because most of William's military followers would probably have been far more interested in becoming landholders than merchants, and because the natives could be useful to the new regime. Once again, Norman pragmatism ruled when it came to ethnic relations, in this case to

[49] Richard Fitz Nigel, *Dialogus de Scaccario*, 109.

[50] *GGWP* 146; *GND* 2: 170, 178–80; *ASC* D 1066, D 1067, E 1068; *WMGR* 462; *EHOV* 2: 180–2, 210–12, 216, 222, 226.

[51] *GND* 2: 180.

[52] *DB* 1: 1a, 2a, 56a, 75a, 154a, 162a, 189a, 203a, 238a, 252a, 262b, 280a, 298a, 336a–b; 2: 116a–b, 117b, 118b–119a, 290a.

[53] Bates, *Acta of William I*, no. 180.

the benefit of the English. From the English point of view the new regime, after it became established, provided the strong and peaceful rule that was essential to trade and urban prosperity. Once the violence of the conquest had passed, there was nothing to prevent the development of cordial relationships between native townspeople and the new regime, which could help pave the way for ethnic harmony.

Within towns, relations between natives and immigrants may also initially have been tense. Even those Continental settlers who had not been involved in the conquest itself probably faced the resentment of English townspeople who had suffered in the fighting. Moreover, native urban elites would have faced new competition from immigrants who could profit from their ties to the new aristocracy. Some passages in Domesday Book also suggest that French settlers were exempted from certain dues and taxes, or at least avoided them, which could also produce resentment.[54] Early ethnic hostility within towns may be indicated by a certain amount of residential segregation. One early twelfth-century charter refers to the English borough of Nottingham and later sources reveal that the town was divided into French and English sections.[55] Southampton had its French quarter as well, and in Norwich at the time of Domesday Book, the French seem to have dominated a newly created suburb.[56] In addition, studies of the surveys of Winchester and Battle show a certain clumping of English and French in particular neighbourhoods, though this probably had to do at least partly with class, since it is likely there would have been few immigrants in the poorest districts and more in the wealthier ones.[57] Robert Bartlett has described how medieval towns could be sites of ethnic exclusion and hostility in the Middle Ages, and at least initially there may have been the danger of towns becoming centres of ethnic confrontation in England after the conquest.[58]

Fortunately, the early hostility and segregation was limited and never took firm hold. The division of Nottingham, which survived long after assimilation because there were differences in legal practice between the two districts, seems to have been quite unusual, and the clumping tendencies in Winchester and Battle did not prevent English and Normans from frequently living next door to each other in those cities and others as well. Outside, perhaps, of Nottingham, ethnic segregation was not sufficient to impede assimilation. Rather, the small, densely settled space of English towns and cities must have been conducive to interaction across ethnic lines.

As a result, towns soon became centres of ethnic integration rather than division. The sort of interaction that could lead to assimilation is most obvious in London,

---

[54] Susan Reynolds, 'Towns in Domesday Book', in *Domesday Studies*, ed. J. C. Holt (Woodbridge, 1987), 308–9.

[55] *Mon. Ang.*, 5: 111; W. Henry Stevenson, *Records of the Borough of Nottingham*, vol. 1 (London, 1882), 124–6, 168–74, 188.

[56] For Southampton, see Colin Platt, *Medieval Southampton: The Port and Trading Community, A. D. 1000–1600* (London, 1973), 6–7. For Norwich, see *DB* 2: 118a.

[57] Biddle, *Winchester in the Early Middle Ages*, 475–6; Searle, *Lordship and Community*, 74–6. The tendency of the elite among the English to adopt Continental names more quickly may muddle the picture to some degree: Clark, *Words, Names and History*, 227.

[58] Bartlett, *Making of Europe*, 233–5.

from which many early charters survive. These charters show that by the early twelfth century, if not earlier, immigrants and natives were regularly doing business together, selling property to each other, witnessing the same documents, and sitting in the same courts.[59] The existence of English as well as Norman city officials shows that they must have co-operated in town government. In addition, professional affiliations helped to link Normans and English. An early twelfth-century charter of Bernard son of Ralph the goldsmith, whose father's name at this date strongly suggests a Continental origin, is attested by eight goldsmiths, the majority of them with English names.[60] It is possible even in urban settings for different ethnic groups to keep very much to their own spheres, but the London evidence overwhelmingly indicates that this was not the case after the Norman Conquest. Other cities and towns also provide evidence of co-operation and interaction. For instance, English and Normans appear together in a number of early documents from Exeter.[61] Much later, in Lincoln, one William de Paris can be found accounting for the farm of the city with Ailwin Net, supervising the repair of the local jail with Reginald son of Eilsi, and attesting a charter of Godwin the Rich.[62] Only glimpses survive of interaction in towns, but they suggest that co-operation and integration between Normans and English started early and continued strong in urban settings.

Not surprisingly, this interaction could lead to intermarriage between towns-people. As noted before, Orderic Vitalis spoke of intermarriage in urban settings immediately after the conquest.[63] The lack of documentation for towns in the eleventh century makes it impossible to verify Orderic's story, but marriages can certainly be traced in the twelfth century. The most famous group of examples centres around a powerful Londoner, Gervase of Cornhill, who was a moneylender, rural landholder, prominent city official, and royal servant in the reigns of Stephen and Henry II. Gervase himself was of Norman descent, but, as J. H. Round showed, his wife Agnes was the daughter and granddaughter of two important native Londoners, Edward of Cornhill and Edward of Southwark. Gervase's brother, William Blemond, married a member of the family of native moneyers studied by Nightingale, and Robert son of Ralph son of Herlwin, probably a cousin of Gervase, married a woman whose maternal grandfather was English.[64] This level of inter-marriage in a single family is hard to match (though mainly, I suspect, because of a paucity of relevant evidence for most families), but Ekwall and Clark have noted

[59] The best cache of early London documents is that found in the Appendix to the *Ninth Report of the Royal Commission of Historical Manuscripts* (London, 1883; repr., Nendeln, 1979), 18–21, 24–6, 28, 30–1, 61–8. Early London charters can also be found in Marion Gibbs, *Early Charters of the Cathedral Church of St. Paul, London* (London, 1939); Hodgett, *Cartulary of Holy Trinity Aldgate*; Hassall, *The Cartulary of St Mary Clerkenwell*; and Mason, *Westminster Abbey Charters*, among other places.

[60] *Ninth Report*, 61.

[61] Thorpe, *Diplomatarium Anglicum*, 622, 633–4, 636, 639–40, 646–7; Pelteret, *Catalogue of English Documents*, nos. 99, 102–3, 113, 140.

[62] Hill, *Medieval Lincoln*, 385, 392–3; *Pipe Roll 10 Henry II*, 23; *Pipe Roll 34 Henry II*, 67.

[63] *EHOV* 2: 256.

[64] J. H. Round, *Geoffrey de Mandeville: A Study of the Anarchy* (London, 1892), 304–11; id., *Commune of London*, 106–8; Brooke and Keir, *London, 800–1216*, 210–11; Clark, *Words, Names and History*, 240–1; Williams, *ENC* 206; Nightingale, 'Some London Moneyers', 36.

several other probable or certain London marriages across ethnic lines, some of them quite early.[65] Such marriages can also be found in other towns. A Robert Russell, whose byname was of French origin, gave away property in Winchcombe that had belonged to his mother's grandfather, a man with the Anglo-Scandinavian name Toki, suggesting intermarriage in at least one of the previous generations.[66] In two late examples, Matilda, granddaughter of Eilsi of Lincoln and sister of the first mayor there, was married in the late twelfth century to a prominent Lincoln man named James Fleming, and around 1200 Roger son of Haldane of Scarborough was married to Beatrice, daughter of Matilda Francigena.[67] As usual, the paucity of evidence and the difficulties raised by naming patterns make it hard to compile more than anecdotal evidence, but it seems likely that towns were important and early centres of intermarriage and assimilation.

More surprising was the level of interaction and intermarriage between native urban elites and the immigrant aristocracy of the countryside. This came not only from the relatively small social distance between the two groups, but also from their differences and complementarity. Wealthy urbanites could provide skills and services rarely found among the rural elite, and this led to the creation of bonds of lordship and patronage between the two groups, which could lead to other, closer forms of interaction as well. The unusually full records of the royal government and household, especially the pipe rolls, can best illustrate certain aspects of the relationship between urban and rural elites. The royal government was, of course, by its nature exceptional, but evidence from that sphere can be suggestive about more general forms of interaction involving the rural nobility. Moreover, the royal government was itself an important site of intermingling.

One area of complementarity was with moneyers, who were an important group for continuity within urban elites. Because of the skill of English moneyers, the Norman kings found it prudent to retain them in service for several generations after the conquest.[68] Towns also produced the richest moneylenders, such as Robert son of Sawin, whose services the king sometimes needed. In addition, urban areas could provide men skilled in building. Beginning in his fourth year, Henry II paid one Ailnoth *Ingeniator* just over £10 a year, an income equivalent to that of a modest knight, to supervise a variety of building tasks, including the building of a quay, chapel, and fishpond at Westminster, the repair of a bridge and glass windows there, and the demolition of castles of nobles held suspect by the king.[69] He was obviously a specialist, but in other cases prominent townspeople who were prob-

---

[65] Ekwall, *Early London Personal Names*, 102–4; Clark, *Words, Names and History*, 140–2.

[66] David Royce, ed., *Landboc sive Registrum Monasterii Beatae Mariae Virginis et Sancti Cenhelmi de Winchelcumba in Comitatu Gloucestrensi Ordinis Sancti Benedicti*, vol. 1 (Exeter, 1892), 235–6. For the name Toki, see above, p. 63, n. 37.

[67] Hill, *Medieval Lincoln*, 386–7; *EYC* 1: 287.

[68] Michael Dolley, *The Norman Conquest and the English Coinage* (London, 1966), 11–15; Biddle, *Winchester in the Early Middle Ages*, 409–22, 444, 447, 463, 476; Hill, *Medieval Lincoln*, 53; Nightingale, 'Some London Moneyers', 34–50.

[69] Ailnoth appears in the London section of every pipe roll of the reign from the fourth on. For his activities, see Colvin, *The History of the King's Works*, 1: 34–5, 58, 493. It cannot be proved that Ailnoth was a Londoner by origin, but he certainly held property there: BL Harley MS 662, 74ᵛ–75ᵛ.

ably not specialists served as organizers or managers of building projects for the king and others.[70] Indeed, the pipe rolls show that Henry II relied quite a bit on English townspeople for the construction and maintenance of his castles, as well as other buildings.[71] Towns also, of course, housed merchants, who provided luxury goods and performed other useful services as well. Henry II's favourite merchant in England was the Londoner Edward Blund. Edward can be found selling goods for the king, overseeing building, transporting goods, and above all purchasing a wide variety of items for the king and his family, ranging from mundane items such as wagons and wax to luxury items, including a gilded saddle worked with scarlet, and many pieces of the richest and most ornate clothing imaginable. Edward seems to have purchased most of the clothing for the Young King's coronation, extending to the king a large amount of credit for the purpose.[72] All this work by native moneyers, builders, and merchants must have entailed a fair amount of contact with royal officials, many of them immigrant, and sometimes with the kings themselves. To view such interaction as largely impersonal and businesslike may be anachronistic. A grant by the king of a rectorship to one of Edward Blund's sons suggests that their relationship, at least, was not simply commercial but one of service and patronage as well.[73]

Moreover, kings occasionally pulled urban natives into important positions beyond the towns, thus mixing them in with powerful immigrant figures. It is noteworthy that many of the native new men in Domesday Book, among them Edward of Salisbury, Colswein of Lincoln, and Odo of Winchester, were associated with towns.[74] As for later periods, some of the most important urban figures who entered royal service were clerics, and will be discussed in the next chapter. But Robert son of Sawin became sheriff of Northamptonshire.[75] More important was Henry of Oxford, son of an Eilwi and grandson of a Godwine. An Angevin supporter during the civil war of Stephen's reign, Henry held office in Wallingford and served as sheriff of Berkshire and Oxfordshire. He even accompanied a royal army to the great Angevin stronghold of Chinon, where Henry II confirmed to him property

---

[70] An earlier *ingeniator* with the insular name Tovi may be found in *Pipe Roll 31 Henry I*, 152. Peter of Cornwall provides an interesting description of how his father served as a building manager for the local priory: Easting and Sharpe, 'Peter of Cornwall', 222–4, 239.

[71] *Pipe Roll 18 Henry II*, 5, 55, 79, 100, 130; *Pipe Roll 19 Henry II*, 2, 13, 146, 157, 167; *Pipe Roll 20 Henry II*, 37, 49, 77; *Pipe Roll 23 Henry II*, 144; *Pipe Roll 25 Henry II*, 39, 43; *Pipe Roll 26 Henry II*, 8, 25, 75, 82, 131, 143; *Pipe Roll 27 Henry II*, 110, 145, 147; *Pipe Roll 28 Henry II*, 21, 91, 148; *Pipe Roll 29 Henry II*, 57, 107, 155; *Pipe Roll 30 Henry II*, 128; *Pipe Roll 31 Henry II*, 224; *Pipe Roll 32 Henry II*, 86, 135; *Pipe Roll 33 Henry II*, 147–8, 158, 181; *Pipe Roll 34 Henry II*, 67. Not all the natives with native names listed here were town-dwellers, but most probably were.

[72] Edward appears in every pipe roll but one between Henry II's ninth and thirty-first years, usually under the London section. For his purchases for the young king's coronation, see *Pipe Roll 16 Henry II*, 14–15, 20, 61, 62, 79, 93, 105, 115, 135, 141, 154, 157; *Pipe Roll 17 Henry II*, 80–1, 147–8; *Pipe Roll 18 Henry II*, 144–5. Nightingale argues that he may have been head of the pepperers' guild and held the powerful office of king's chamberlain of London: *Medieval Mercantile Community*, 54–5.

[73] *Book of Fees*, 1: 269.

[74] Campbell, 'Some Agents and Agencies', 210.

[75] Robert was sheriff from Henry's sixteenth year to his own death in Henry's twentieth year. He had also farmed the town Northampton from Henry II's second year on: *Pipe Roll 2 Henry II*, 42; *Pipe Roll 16 Henry II*, 19–20; Robert; *Pipe Roll 20 Henry II*, 50–5.

inherited from his father, his grandfather, and his uncles, Robert and William Peitevin, as well as estates given by Geoffrey de Clinton, Brian Fitz Count, Empress Matilda, and the king himself, and all of Henry's property in the towns of Oxford and Wallingford.[76] Neither the number of native urbanites in royal service, nor the heights to which most of them reached, should be exaggerated. But sheriffs were important people, and the duties of all these men would have caused them and their families to interact intensively with Normans, sometimes in ways that could extend beyond the performance of duties. For instance, Robert son of Sawin's son Hugh served as one of the pledges for the powerful royal official Geoffrey Ridel on one occasion, an indication of friendship or some other tie between them.[77] Moreover, the rewards of land they received from the king placed them on equal or even superior footing to all but the greatest landlords. Henry of Oxford's extensive properties included two manors worth £20 and £10 a year respectively.[78] His total landed income is impossible to calculate, but may have approached that of a minor baron. In sum, the royal records show how the various skills common among prominent townspeople could bring them at least into the fringes of the predominantly immigrant court, and also how some were able to use their more general administrative skills to move more fully into that world, and into the rural aristocracy.

Presumably, immigrant aristocrats, like the king, called upon the services of urban merchants and builders, including native ones; they certainly resorted to native moneylenders.[79] Immigrant aristocrats can also be found interacting with native urbanites through hosting arrangements. Rural aristocrats sometimes owned townhouses, but often found it more convenient to stay with wealthy townspeople, sometimes setting up arrangements to do so. As early as William the Conqueror's reign, Gundulf, the Norman bishop of Rochester, stayed with an important Londoner named Eadmer the One Handed while overseeing the construction of the White Tower. Similarly, two twelfth-century charters show moderately important Yorkshire landholders making agreements for periodically staying with York citizens with English names.[80] Such arrangements had their effects on personal relations. For instance, Eadmer the One Handed subsequently gave land to Rochester Cathedral and arranged for burial and confraternity there. P. R. Coss has found evidence that an upwardly mobile native inhabitant of

---

[76] Landon, *Cartae Antiquae Rolls 1–10*, no. 141; Stevenson, *Chronicon Monasterii de Abingdon*, 2: 184–5; *RRAN* 3, no. 88; Hall, *Red Book of the Exchequer*, 2: 657–8; *Pipe Roll 2 Henry II*, 35–6; *Pipe Roll 6 Henry II*, 8; *Pipe Roll 9 Henry II*, 48; *Book of Fees*, 1: 114–15; John Blair, 'Frewin Hall, Oxford: A Norman Mansion and a Monastic College', *Oxoniensia*, 43 (1978), 54–7; Amt, *Accession of Henry II*, 50, 57, 62–3. An excellent account of Henry's career and background may be found in Keats-Rohan, 'The Making of Henry of Oxford', 287–309.

[77] Admittedly, he was one of many: *Pipe Roll 24 Henry II*, 52.

[78] Keats-Rohan, 'The Making of Henry of Oxford', 287–309; Landon, *Cartae Antiquae Rolls 1–10*, no. 141; H. E. Salter, ed., *Facsimiles of Early Charters in Oxford Muniment Rooms* (Oxford, 1929), no. 42.

[79] Davies, *Cartae Antiquae Rolls 11–20*, no. 479. See below for Robert Fitz Harding.

[80] Thomas Hearne, *Textus Roffensis* (Oxford, 1720), 212; *EYC* 1, nos. 267–8. See also Cotton MS Vespasian B xxiv, fol. 56ʳ, for a hospitality agreement between Abbot Reginald Foliot and Sperling the priest, whose name Ekwall, at least, believes is English: Ekwall, *Early London Personal Names*, 62.

Coventry, Liulf of Brinklow, served as host for the powerful noble, Eustace Fitz John. One can only surmise that Liulf found the connection useful.[81] Like the king, great nobles could also sometimes call on the administrative skills of townspeople. For instance, Earl Simon of Northampton relied on Robert son of Sawin, the moneylender and sheriff, to serve as *firmarius* on at least one manor.[82] William, earl of Gloucester from 1147 to 1183, appointed one Lewin (or Leofwin) son of Ailric of Bristol to the important household office of chamberlain, in which position Lewin built up a comfortable estate in Bristol, its suburbs, and surrounding villages.[83] Thus, this urban native passed into a predominantly immigrant affinity, and thence into the rural landholding class.

The attestations of other townsmen to noble charters show that they were at least occasional presences in aristocratic settings, and of course the widespread practice of rich urbanites gaining rural holdings would have involved them in networks of feudal or honorial lordship.[84] Thus, Norman nobles and native townspeople intersected in a number of ways: through the royal court, through hosting, through the need of nobles for urban services and the recruitment of able townspeople, and through lordship of land. Though individual instances of contact must often have been fleeting or impersonal, cumulative ties could be important. Diana Greenway has noted Roger de Mowbray's various ties to several leading citizens of York (most of them at least partly native), and has linked them to the dominance Jordan Fantosme says he temporarily achieved in the city during the 1173–4 revolt.[85] Thus, extensive ties existed between the urban elites and the aristocracy and, because so many prominent townspeople were native, this helped to promote the integration of the two peoples in the upper reaches of society.

All of this helps to explain the surprising number of marriages that can be found between the families of immigrant aristocrats and native urban lineages. A group of charters from late in Henry I's reign show that a sister of Hugh son of Wulfgar, a member of the London Cnihtengild, married the son of a minor immigrant landlord who held land of the counts of Boulogne.[86] It must have been in the same reign that Henry of Oxford's father, Eilwi, married a member of a knightly family called the Peitevins, who judging by their name had a Continental background.[87] Around the middle of the twelfth century a sister of Richard Rollos, a leading knightly

---

[81] Coss, *Lordship, Knighthood, and Locality*, 73–4.

[82] *Mon. Ang.*, 5: 208.

[83] Patterson, *Earldom of Gloucester Charters*, nos. 7, 36–7, 182; Watkins, *Great Chartulary of Glastonbury*, 2: 551, 562, no. 1028; Ross and Devine, *Cartulary of Cirencester Abbey*, 2, no. 630.

[84] For some examples of townspeople attesting aristocratic charters, see *EYC* 8, no. 16; 11, nos. 10, 37; Hill, *Medieval Lincoln*, 390; Holdsworth, *Rufford Charters*, 3, nos. 721, 751; van Caenegem, *English Lawsuits*, 1: 295; Gervers, *Cartulary of the Knights of St. John*, no. 291; *Mon. Ang.*, 4: 150. For comments on urban natives and feudal or honorial ties, see Douglas, *Domesday Monachorum*, 58, 63. However, in the absence of frequent attestations by honorial tenants of urban origin, I am not inclined to see honorial lordship as necessarily creating close bonds.

[85] Greenway, *Charters of the Honour of Mowbray*, p. xxx.

[86] Round, *Commune of London*, 119–21.

[87] Keats-Rohan, 'The Making of Henry of Oxford', 288–90, 292, 305, 308; Landon, *Cartae Antiquae Rolls 1–10*, no. 141.

tenant of the honour of Richmond with extensive lands in Normandy as well, married a burgess of Richmond with the English name Aldred.[88] Basilia, a descendant of a minor Domesday Book tenant-in-chief, Maino the Breton, married Turbern of Northampton, by 1171 at the latest.[89] These marriages between urban English families and members of moderately important immigrant lineages are noteworthy and, given the difficulties of evidence for these groups, the examples listed here probably represent a larger number for which evidence has not survived.[90]

Still more interesting are marriages connecting native town-dwellers to the families of some of the greatest immigrant magnates. Peter of Cornwall casually mentions that he was related by marriage to Henry I's illegitimate son Reginald, who became earl of Cornwall during Stephen's reign and remained one of England's leading nobles during Henry II's early years as king.[91] Another instance was the marriage between a kinswoman of Gilbert de Clare, earl of Pembroke from 1138 to 1147, and the prominent Londoner Theoderic son of Deorman of London.[92] A final example is the marriage, perhaps in the 1140s, of a kinswoman of Earl Roger of Hereford to a burgess of Gloucester named Wlfric Mortdefreit, whose forename, at least, was probably English (bynames could sometimes be translated into various languages).[93] That rich native townspeople could form marriage links not only with minor immigrant landlords but also with the greatest magnates is a striking testament to the power and influence of this group. It is also indicative of their ability to help integrate the immigrant aristocracy.

Before ending discussion of interaction between native urbanites and immigrant aristocrats, it would be useful to discuss one last set of marriages and the English family involved, for, though this family was unusual, its history serves to sum up many of the factors discussed in this chapter, particularly the potential wealth and power of native urbanites, their usefulness to the Normans, and their ability to assimilate with the immigrant rural elites. The family was that of Robert Fitz Harding.[94] What made Robert unusual is that he came from a noble family: his grandfather was the Eadnoth the Staller who died fighting for William the Conqueror, and his father Harding, though not nearly as wealthy as Eadnoth, was a

---

[88] *EYC* 5: 97, nos. 197–8, 264–5.

[89] Elvey, *Luffield Priory Charters*, 2: pp. xxxix–xlii, no. 555.

[90] In addition to the instances noted above, a twelfth-century cleric named Godfrey de Mandeville had a concubine named Ragenild, whose name could be Continental or Anglo-Scandinavian, but who was probably related to a woman with the thoroughly English name of Elveva: BL Cotton Vitellius D ix, fols. 72ᵛ–73ʳ. Godfrey almost certainly came from the Mandeville family established in the south-west by Richard de Redvers: Robert Bearman, *Charters of the Redvers Family and the Earldom of Devon, 1090–1217* (Exeter, 1994), 38.

[91] Easting and Sharpe, 'Peter of Cornwall', 225.

[92] Nightingale, 'Some London Moneyers', 38–9; Douglas, *Domesday Monachorum*, 62–3; *Calendar of Charter Rolls Preserved in the Public Record Office*, vol. 2 (London, 1906), 71–2.

[93] David Walker, ed., 'Charters of the Earldom of Hereford, 1095–1201', in *Camden Miscellany*, 22 (London, 1964), no. 39.

[94] For much of what follows, I draw on Amt, *Accession of Henry II*, 37–42, and above all on Patterson, 'Robert Fitz Harding of Bristol', 109–22. Many of the most important documents may be found calendared in Jeayes, *Charters and Muniments at Berkeley Castle*.

landowner with clout.[95] But Harding's rural estates went to another son, Nicholas, whose family, the Meriets, lapsed into moderately prosperous obscurity. Robert, meanwhile, became a prominent citizen in Bristol, where he held much property, and had the good fortune to be the financier of some of the future Henry II's early campaigns. Robert ended up both with enormous wealth and royal favour. In Henry II's reign he remained a powerful figure in Bristol and kept there a home large enough to house in style the infamous King of Leinster, Diarmit Mac Murchada, when he came to seek help from Henry II in 1166 or 1167.[96] But Robert, like many other wealthy townspeople, also used his wealth and connections to gain rural holdings, though on a scale that dwarfed the efforts of any of the figures discussed so far. He acquired a number of estates from a variety of nobles, in some cases through purchase or foreclosure on mortgages. His greatest acquisition, however, came in 1153 when Henry II granted him land theoretically worth £100 yearly in the large manor of Berkeley. This acquisition involved Robert's family in its first known marriages with immigrants, for Henry had seized the land from Roger of Berkeley, and to make peace between the two families arranged for Robert's eldest son, Maurice, to marry Alice, daughter of Roger, and for Roger's eldest son to marry one of Robert's daughters.

Robert accumulated enough wealth to found a fairly wealthy monastery, St Augustine's, Bristol, emulating many a great noble in the process, but he still had plenty of wealth (and influence) left over to provide for his children.[97] One son, Henry, entered both the church and the royal service. Henry was treasurer to Henry II when the latter was still duke of Normandy, and continued to hold the post for a short time early in his reign as king of England. Later on, Robert provided his son with good livings from his own estates, and his influence may have helped Henry gain the posts of dean of Mortain in Normandy and archdeacon in the see of Exeter.[98] His other younger sons, his daughters, and at least one brother received land from him, and undoubtedly money as well. In 1182 one of the sons, also named Robert, offered the large sum of 540 marks to marry Avice de Gant, a wealthy noble heiress of Continental origin. The younger Robert's son, Maurice, inherited, taking on the Gant family name as noted in Chapter 9.[99] It was, however, Robert Fitz Harding's eldest son, Maurice of Berkeley, who did best of all out of the family, inhabiting an estate worth some £114 yearly, for which he was able to pay the king 1,000 marks as a relief.[100] His descendants still hold Berkeley.

In many ways Robert, despite his wealth and power, remained a peripheral figure

[95] Keats-Rohan has argued that Henry of Oxford was also descended from pre-conquest thegns: Keats-Rohan, 'The Making of Henry of Oxford', 292, 298–306.

[96] Goddard Henry Orpen, *The Song of Dermot and the Earl* (Oxford, 1892), 18–20, 24; Marie Therese Flanagan, *Irish Society, Anglo-Norman Settlers, Angevin Kingship: Interactions in Ireland in the Late Twelfth Century* (Oxford, 1989), 76, 116–17.

[97] David Walker, ed., *The Cartulary of St Augustine's Abbey, Bristol* (Bristol, 1998), pp. xi–xxii, nos. 66–71, 73. His wife Eva founded a nunnery and hospital: Thompson, *Women Religious*, 45–7.

[98] *EEA* 11: pp. xxxix, xli.

[99] *EYC* 6: 34–5. He paid off the 540 marks in less than three years: *Pipe Roll 28 Henry II*, 113–14; *Pipe Roll 30 Henry II*, 125

[100] Patterson, 'Robert Fitz Harding of Bristol', 118; *Pipe Roll 6 Richard I*, 3; *Pipe Roll 7 Richard I*, 176, 179.

within the nobility. Though he certainly had local influence, as well as the king's favour, he was not a central figure at court and only occasionally appeared in the company of magnates.[101] Nonetheless, his descendants quickly merged into the predominantly Norman aristocracy through their marriages and landholding. For instance, late in Henry II's reign Robert's son Maurice was in charge of the key Welsh lordship of Glamorgan, perhaps under the earls of Gloucester and certainly under the king. A generation later Robert's grandson, Maurice de Gant, was one of the barons participating in the Magna Carta revolt against King John.[102] The degree of this family's success and of its integration into the nobility is unparalleled among urban native families, and probably owes something to Robert's own aristocratic background. But in other respects they were fairly typical of such families, parlaying their wealth into landed estates, offering their skills to the king or nobles, and interacting and intermarrying with elite immigrant lineages.

The fact that townspeople were involved in a great deal of interaction across ethnic lines, both within towns and with rural elites, makes it likely that they could have promoted acculturation as well, though of the sort in which cultural influence went in both directions. As with peasants and the middling sorts, only a few general observations can be made on this subject. Clark, in her study of language use in Canterbury, suggests that the level of lexical borrowing found there probably indicates a large degree of bilingualism stemming from friendly relations between the two populations.[103] Native urban craftsmen and craftswomen, like their rural counterparts, must have preserved many aspects of English material culture. Native urban moneyers, for instance, helped to preserve the English system of coinage intact through the immediate post-conquest period.[104] At the same time, immigrants could have introduced new styles and techniques, and professional interaction in towns and cities in guilds like that of the goldsmiths in London probably produced a fruitful cultural and artistic interchange. Immigrants conformed to English institutions of town government in the short term, but over the long term their Continental ties may have helped to promote Continental ideas such as communes, or the title and office of mayor, again suggesting an influence that went both ways.[105] Native townspeople with aspirations to aristocratic bearing, like their counterparts in the countryside, even adopted such chivalric trappings as equestrian seals, as we have seen. All in all, townspeople were probably particularly actively involved in cultural interchange, and therefore acculturation. However, since cultural influences went both ways, native townspeople cannot be said to have simply absorbed and anglicized the immigrants in cultural terms.

What, therefore, of the role of native townspeople in the preservation and triumph of English identity? As with peasants and the middling sorts, evidence is limited, but two very intriguing and important pieces survive. The first concerns

---

[101] For an instance of his local influence, see *EEA* 10, no. 15.

[102] *Pipe Roll 30 Henry II*, 110–11; *Pipe Roll 31 Henry II*, 5–7; *EYC* 6: 35.

[103] Clark, *Words, Names and History*, 197–8.

[104] See above, n. 68.

[105] Round, *Feudal England*, 552–62; Round, *Commune of London*, 219–60.

the family of Christina of Markyate. In one of many passages about the nobility of the saint and her connections, her hagiographer described her origins as coming from *antiqui angli nobiles atque potentes*. Whether by this the writer meant that her family could trace itself back to the pre-conquest nobility or simply that it was well established is not clear. What *is* clear is that the hagiographer certainly saw it as an English family, and since Christina was the main source, as I suggested earlier, it seems likely that this represents the family's own identity. One has to be cautious about interpreting a single passing reference, but it seems possible, even likely, that powerful native families like Christina's held onto and thus helped preserve English identity.[106] The second anecdote is even more noteworthy. In an early thirteenth-century paean to the city of Chester, the cleric Lucian scolded the inhabitants for being diverted from the glorious saints of their town by worldly spectacles, and described how on one occasion, which can probably be dated to 1185, they had rushed out of the town to see a duel or joust before the future King John, in which 'the Englishman [*Anglus*] prevailed, as you wished'. This tantalizing passage, all the more interesting because it is tossed out so casually, suggests that the inhabitants of Chester supported one unnamed combatant against another because of a shared English identity, and that there was nothing surprising about this. The date is late, and the inhabitants of Chester, close to the Welsh marches and involved in trade across the Irish Sea, may have had more occasion to think about their Englishness than most townspeople, but the story is at least suggestive of widespread English identity in towns, and not just among the urban elites.[107] If so, townspeople in general could have been mainstays of English identity in the period in which it was under threat.

Obviously, such scanty detail can only be taken so far. It suggests, though it does not prove, that urban natives played something of a role in the triumph of English identity, and probably a greater one than the peasantry. But some of the same questions may be asked about townspeople as about the peasants and middling sorts in the countryside. Why did Continental identity not spread from powerful rural and urban immigrants to English townspeople, rather than vice versa? Descendants of marriages across ethnic lines, such as that between Gervase and Agnes of Cornhill, could just as well have stressed their Continental rather than their English heritage; why did they eventually end up as primarily English? Surely it is at least somewhat surprising that interaction and intermarriage between immigrant nobles and English townspeople would have promoted English rather than Continental identity, and it is noteworthy in this respect that Robert Fitz Harding's grandson adopted the Continental surname of Gant. Thus, even in towns, where the English remained powerful as well as numerous, demographic factors alone cannot fully explain the triumph of Englishness. The Englishness of native townspeople was at best only part of the explanation.

---

[106] Talbot, *Life of Christina of Markyate*, 10, 82.
[107] *Liber Luciani de Laude Cestrie*, ed. M. V. Taylor ([Edinburgh], 1912), 9–10, 61–2.

13

The Religious

THE CLERGY, REGULAR and secular, native and immigrant, were central to assimilation and the triumph of English identity on all three of the levels outlined in Chapter 1. On the level of the personal, the church provided an existing set of institutions and relationships that drew English and Normans together and forced them to interact, ultimately with very positive results for ethnic harmony. Religious difference in the Middle Ages was one of the greatest sources of ethnic hostility, and in Christian Europe, including England, religious minorities suffered terribly.[1] But in the case of the English and Normans, religion ultimately helped to unite the two peoples. Far greater evidence survives of close co-operation and of affective relationships at an early stage involving Norman and English monks, nuns, and clerics than the laity. Undoubtedly this owes much to the bias of the sources toward the religious, but I would also argue that many within the church were pioneers in creating harmonious relationships across ethnic lines.

The potential importance of monks, nuns, and clerics to cultural assimilation will be obvious. Simply because of their position as religious leaders, they were guardians of some of the most highly valued aspects of Continental and English culture. They had a near monopoly on written culture and dominated the intellectual life of the time. Their position as patrons and producers of music and art also gave them great cultural influence. Both by medieval lights, and in terms of what modern people would call high culture, the religious were important cultural figures. Because English and Norman clergy shared the same broad cultural values and world-view, shaped as both were by Christianity, there was plenty of scope for the interchange and melding of distinctive cultural attributes. Influence went both ways, and the religious did much to create a unified Anglo-Norman culture.

If any group can be described as the *Traditionskern* of English identity in the post-conquest period, it was the English clergy. They were not the only preservers of English identity, but a variety of factors limited the impact of other groups on the survival and revival of Englishness. In contrast, the religious can be shown to be deeply involved in the maintenance of English identity. Walter Pohl has suggested that the success of barbarian kingdoms depended heavily on their 'ability to control and channel ethnic and political discourse'.[2] In this chapter I will set the stage for a

---

[1] For discussion of the Jews in England as a religious Other, see below, pp. 308–10.

[2] Walter Pohl, 'Social Language, Identities and the Control of Discourse', in *East and West: Modes of Communication: Proceedings of the First Plenary Conference at Merida*, ed. Evangelos Chrysos and Ian Wood (Leiden, 1999), 140.

later argument that a number of clerical and monastic writers seized control of the ethnic discourse by preserving English traditions and defending English honour. Many of these writers were demonstrably of at least partial English ancestry, and the survival of many natives in the church gave them a favourable environment in which to work. Naturally, the religious monopoly on the written word may exaggerate the role of the clergy in the triumph of Englishness. But both Anthony Smith and Adrian Hastings have argued that priests and other clergy were crucial to the creation and maintenance of ethnic or national identity in the pre-modern world.[3] I would argue that the English religious, working as prestigious insiders within the church, were likewise crucial to the survival and spread of English identity.

Shared Christianity was certainly not automatically a decisive factor for integration and assimilation in the Middle Ages. Apart from the issue of sectarian difference, strong ethnic divides could coexist even with theological harmony. Robert Bartlett has shown how the church could simply become another battleground in ethnic struggles.[4] Though ecclesiastical relations in Ireland and Wales were complex, the churches there certainly became important venues for confrontation and competition.[5] That the church acted as a unifying factor in England after the conquest was partly due to the generally pragmatic nature of Norman prejudice and partly to the choices of some prominent early individuals. More broadly, relations within the church formed only one factor among many, and in the long run integration among the clergy proceeded smoothly only because ethnic harmony developed throughout society. Overall, however, I would argue that in the case of England, the church and relations involving the religious greatly furthered ethnic harmony.

I

I begin by tracing the presence of both immigrants and natives in various positions within the church. As is well known, there was decisive change at the top of the ecclesiastical hierarchy following the conquest. What needs to be emphasized more fully than in the past, however, is the surviving presence of large numbers of English people in religious houses, as hermits, and among the secular clergy long after the generation of English priests and monks already in place in 1066 would have died out. The strong native presence meant at the most basic level that the church *could* be an institution through which many relationships across ethnic lines were created. Moreover, many of the natives did hold important positions and offices, though generally not the very highest ones. One of the problems raised in the

---

[3] Anthony Smith, *Ethnic Origins of Nations*, 119–24; Hastings, *Construction of Nationhood*, 191–3.
[4] Bartlett, *Making of Europe*, 221–30.
[5] Nelson, *Normans in South Wales*, 160–5; Davies, *Age of Conquest*, 439–41; Davies, *Revolt of Owain Glyn Dŵr*, 58–61; Lydon, *Lordship of Ireland*, 285–7; Duffy, *Ireland in the Middle Ages*, 107–10; Smith, *Colonisation and Conquest*, 73, 90, 92; John A. Watt, *The Church and the Two Nations in Medieval Ireland* (Cambridge, 1970), 57, 71–6, 92–8, 174–6, 181–97, 205–8, 214–16.

Introduction was the interaction of class and ethnic boundaries. Even parish priests and ordinary monks and nuns had more than average influence in medieval society, and some English people obtained positions of surprising importance and power through the church, even in the reign of Henry I, when Eadmer complained about discrimination. Thus relationships involving English and Norman churchmen or nuns were more likely to be between equals or near equals than those among the laity, and this could influence the exact nature of relationships—two fellow cathedral canons were much more likely to have a close friendship than a powerful bishop and a minor parish priest. Prestige and status also mattered when it came to maintaining and defending English customs, honour, and identity. For obvious reasons, scholars have tended to focus on the dramatic change in the leadership of the church hierarchy. What this section seeks to do is demonstrate the strong survival of natives at the lower and even middle ranks of the church hierarchy, to emphasize their collective power and influence, and to show that they were therefore in a position to influence ethnic relations and identity.

There is no need to devote much time to the dramatic displacement of natives at the top of the ecclesiastical hierarchy, since it is well known. At the rank of bishop, William created a new, immigrant hierarchy with remarkable speed; by 1073 there were only two English bishops, though a few of the others were foreigners left over from Edward the Confessor's reign.[6] One of Edward the Confessor's English appointees, Wulfstan of Worcester, was able to play a role in the formation of ethnic relations under the new order because he survived until 1095, but neither William I nor his sons appointed any native bishops to established English sees.[7] In 1133 Henry I did make his confessor, whose name appears in the sources in a variety of forms which may represent the Old English Æðelwold or Æðelwulf, or the German Adelulf, a bishop. But he appointed him to the new see of Carlisle, in a region that was only incorporated into England in the reigns of William II and Henry himself. To find a bishop of an established see who was clearly of English descent one has to wait until 1175, when John of Oxford, son of Henry of Oxford, was appointed to the see of Norwich.[8]

Pragmatic prejudice was the primary motivation for this shift rather than any belief that the English were unworthy to be bishops. John of Worcester was surely right that King William's main motive in depriving many English of their offices and appointing men 'of his own people' was to consolidate his hold on his new realm.[9] Norman Kings were quite happy to support the appointment of English monks such as Turgot, prior of Durham, and the historian Eadmer, to Scottish sees, but the monarchs avoided such selections in England.[10] More striking still was

   [6] Frank Barlow, *The English Church, 1066–1154* (New York, 1979), 57.

   [7] For Wulfstan's life and career, see *VW*, and Mason, *St Wulfstan of Worcester*.

   [8] For John's family, see above, pp. 193–5. For John and his career, see Christopher Harper-Bill, 'John of Oxford, Diplomat and Bishop', in *Medieval Ecclesiastical Studies in Honour of Dorothy M. Owen*, ed. M. J. Franklin and Christopher Harper-Bill (Woodbridge, 1995), 83–105.

   [9] *CJW* 3: 12.

   [10] R. H. Forster, 'Turgot, Prior of Durham', *Journal of the British Archaeological Association*, 63 (1907), 32–40; *HN* 279–86.

Henry I's appointment of Algar to Coutances in 1132. Nothing is known of Algar's family background, but his name was a typically English one, representing the Old English Ælfgar, and he went to Coutances from England. Thus there is a strong probability that he was of native English descent. Algar had a distinguished career before he became bishop. He was a *magister*, having studied in Laon (and later, in south-west England, protected some visiting canons of Laon from a mob outraged by a dispute over the historicity of King Arthur[11]). He was also an Augustinian canon who played an important role in founding the Cornish house of Bodmin. Algar was a pious, educated, and cosmopolitan figure, and obviously good episcopal material.[12] If Algar was of native English stock, the fact that he was appointed to a Norman rather than an English see, despite the fact that nothing connects him to Normandy before his appointment, may indicate that as late as 1132 Henry I was following a policy of barring natives from established English sees. However, this appointment to a Norman see surely indicates that Henry's policies emerged from practical (and probably outdated) concerns about giving the natives power in England rather than from personal prejudice or from any concern about strong Norman prejudices against the English. Algar's appointment, I believe, represents a marvellous example of the limits to Norman prejudice, and of the Norman pragmatism I have described earlier, but it also underscores the absence of English bishops in England itself.

When it came to abbacies, the situation for the English was only slightly better than for bishoprics. The evidence largely bears out the complaints of Eadmer and others about prejudice in appointments, for the abbots appointed to the great Benedictine houses were overwhelmingly Continental in origin, and generally immigrants themselves until Henry I's death.[13] As Williams has shown, however, there was a lingering presence of native abbots in the late eleventh century.[14] Even in Henry I's reign Abbot Aldwin of Ramsey, who was deposed in 1102, was reappointed in 1107, and there continued to be a sprinkling of men and women with English names or English ancestry (such as Abbot Lawrence of Westminster) appointed in his reign and thereafter to Benedictine houses and priories.[15] Moreover, from Henry I's reign the foundation of houses in the new monastic orders that blossomed during the twelfth century gave natives opportunities that were rarely available to them in the traditional, wealthy Benedictine houses.[16] Though the

[11] Hermann, 'De Miraculis S. Mariae Laudunensis', *PL* 156: 983.

[12] 'The Life of Guy of Merton by Rainald of Merton', ed. Marvin L. Colker, *Mediaeval Studies*, 31 (1969), 259–61; Freeman, *History of the Norman Conquest*, 5: 362–3. I would like to thank David Spear for sharing his knowledge of Algar's history with me.

[13] Knowles, *Monastic Order in England*, 112, 704. See above, p. 63, for the complaints of prejudice.

[14] Williams, *ENC* 131–2. Williams also notes some early twelfth-century abbots.

[15] Lawrence was a kinsman of the indubitably English Aelred of Rievaulx: Walter Daniel, *The Life of Ailred of Rievaulx*, ed. Maurice Powicke (London, 1950; repr. Oxford, 1978), 41–2. For others, see Knowles *et al.*, *Heads of Religious Houses*, 32, 42, 50, 55, 57, 62, 63, 85, 92–4, 96, 211–12. Another abbot of probable English ancestry in the middle of the twelfth century was William II of St Benet of Holme, who had a brother named Asgar and a nephew named Edward: West, *St. Benet of Holme*, 1, nos. 177, 181; 2: 240–1.

[16] Knowles *et al.*, *Heads of Religious Houses*, 116, 129, 140–1, 158, 163–4, 168, 171, 177, 179, 180, 182–3, 189, 194, 201, 202–4. For Norman, at Aldgate, see above, p. 141, n. 7.

new houses generally could not compete in wealth and power with the greatest
Benedictine ones, at least early in their existence, their leaders could be quite
influential. For instance, Aelred of Rievaulx was one of the best-known monks in
England.

The exceptions described above have their importance, not least in showing that
the discrimination against the English in the church, though pervasive, was never
complete or rigidly applied. Nonetheless, immigrants and their descendants did
dominate the ranks of abbots, particularly of the great Benedictine houses. By comparison, the Normans of Sicily, though they introduced immigrant prelates, seem
to have been more willing to allow a strong Lombard presence both among abbots
and bishops.[17] Even in the areas of Ireland controlled by the English, and in Wales
after the Edwardian conquest, natives initially seem to have had greater access
to high ecclesiastical position than in England after the conquest.[18] Despite the
exceptions noted earlier, the degree to which the Normans in England controlled
the highest positions in the church was remarkable. This only underscores the complaints of Eadmer and others, and it also makes my claims about the importance of
the church in ethnic integration seem surprising at first glance. The church was able
to further ethnic harmony despite deliberate prejudice in church appointments
only because of the extensive survival of the English at lower ranks in the hierarchy
and because of the good relations created between them and their immigrant
superiors and peers.

The question of the ethnic make-up of the membership of religious houses after
the conquest has not received much attention. English monks and nuns were not
normally expelled from their houses. But immigrant abbots must generally have
brought at least some monks with them and they often appointed them to high
positions within their monasteries.[19] New foundations with Continental connections continued to receive monks from the Continent; as late as 1378 there were
more than 140 French monks in England.[20] At least as early as Domesday Book, the
sons and daughters of Norman landowners and clerics began to enter religious
houses, supplementing the numbers of immigrants therein.[21] One source, the *Gesta
Abbatum Sancti Albani*, paints a picture of a slow ethnic shift in the monastery of St
Alban's as the English monks grew old and died, to be replaced by Normans, though
it should be emphasized that this source is late in its present form and owes much to
Matthew Paris, who had an axe to grind when it came to foreigners.[22] But Knowles

[17] Loud, 'Churches and Churchmen in an Age of Conquest: Southern Italy 1030–1130', 41–2, 45–6;
Loud, 'The Abbey of Cava, its Property and Benefactors in the Norman Era', 159, both in Loud,
Conquerors and Churchmen in Norman Italy.
[18] Davies, *Age of Conquest*, 375; Duffy, *Ireland in the Middle Ages*, 107; Watt, *Church and the Two
Nations*, 52–4, 56–7.
[19] See e.g. Margaret Gibson, *Lanfranc of Bec* (Oxford, 1978), 175–6, for Christ Church, Canterbury.
[20] Donald Matthew, *The Norman Monasteries and their English Possessions* (London, 1962; repr.
Westport, Conn., 1979), 110.
[21] *DB* 1: 98a.
[22] *Gesta Abbatum*, 1: 66. For Paris's attitudes toward the Norman Conquest and the effect of contemporary politics on these, see Rebecca Reader, 'Matthew Paris and the Norman Conquest', in *The
Cloister and the World: Essays in Medieval History in Honour of Barbara Harvey*, ed. John Blair and Brian
Golding (Oxford, 1996), 118–47.

thought that a large proportion of the monks came from Anglo-Norman land-holding families in the fifty years after the conquest, and Williams has suggested that as monasteries grew in size the English may have come to be outnumbered, since, she argues, the Benedictines recruited from the aristocracy, which quickly came to be overwhelmingly Continental.[23]

Though the increased French presence in monasteries is undeniable, there is also evidence of a continuing and strong English presence throughout the period of greatest ethnic discord, and my own sense is that the English remained a majority, or at least a very sizeable minority, even in Benedictine houses. Pre-conquest monks and nuns would have had a powerful presence in the decades following 1066, and child oblates like Eadmer, shaped by the defining events of the conquest, could survive well into Henry I's reign. More important, even the Benedictines recruited from urban areas, clerical families, and the middling sort, all groups in which the English had a strong presence.[24] The new orders, with their increased demands for members, must surely have relied even more heavily on such groups, and therefore on the English. Thus, it would be a mistake to discount the English presence in religious houses.

The evidence for this presence is varied, though much of it comes from prominent Benedictine houses. Emma Mason has analysed the names in a list of Worcester monks dating from 1104, and states that half of the brethren were English, while many others had the sort of biblical, patristic, or classical names that became popular after 1066 among the English who adopted new names upon entering religion.[25] In a list, probably from the early twelfth century, of the first seventy-three monks to enter Durham Cathedral Priory, established in 1083 after the expulsion of the secular clerics there, approximately half have English names, another 10 per cent have names common to both pools, and 16 per cent have biblical, patristic, or classical names. The English were clearly a majority. A later addition to this list, from about fifty years later, adds the names of the next 156 monks to join, and presents a different picture. Only about 11 per cent of the names are English and another 10 per cent are ambiguous; however, the biblical, patristic, and classical names, popular among the native religious, rise to just over one-third of the total. At the least one can speak of a strong continuing English presence.[26] Table 13.1, which summarizes a list of monks of Hyde Abbey in the *liber vitae* of that house, demonstrates a continuing presence there as well, especially since the brothers are probably listed with the name of the abbot under whom they *entered* the monastery, and a number were specifically described as boys.[27] At other Benedictine houses,

[23] Knowles, *Monastic Order in England*, 424; Williams, *ENC* 132–3.

[24] For the recruitment of several men with English names from a single urban centre, Wallingford, in at least two cases from after the conquest, see *Book of Fees*, 1: 110–12. The *Textus Roffensis* reveals the continuing recruitment from very minor English landholding families at Rochester: Hearne, *Textus Roffensis*, 161, 162, 183–4.

[25] Mason, *St. Wulfstan of Worcester*, 222; J. Stevenson, ed., *Liber Vitae Ecclesiae Dunelmensis* (London, 1841), 14. My own tally of the names gives slightly different figures than hers, but supports her overall picture.

[26] *LDE* 6–15. See also the *Durham Liber Vitae*, 44–5; Aird, *St Cuthbert and the Normans*, 137.

[27] Birch, *Liber Vitae*, 35–44.

such as St Benet of Holme, Ramsey, and Bury St Edmund's, a number of monks with English elements in their names can be found attesting charters issued by their abbots.[28]

TABLE 13.1 *'Brothers of Newminster' according to type of name*

Abbot	English		Continental		Uncertain[1]		Biblical, etc.		TOTAL
Wulfric (?1069–72)	25	(96%)			1	(4%)			26
Riwallon (1072–88)	18	(46%)	11	(28%)	5	(13%)	5	(13%)	39
Robert Losinga (–1098)[2]	6	(25%)	14	(58%)	1	(4%)	3	(13%)	24
Geoffrey I (1106?–24)	4	(11%)	16	(44%)	4	(11%)	12	(33%)	36
Osbert (1125–35?)[3]	12	(26%)	25	(53%)	1	(2%)	9	(19%)	47
Salidus (1151?–71)	2	(5%)	29	(71%)	2	(5%)	8	(20%)	41

Notes: [1] Includes ambiguous names, and names that cannot be easily assigned to any category; [2] No listings under Abbot Hugh, 1100–?; [3] No listing under Abbot Hugh, 1142?–49?

But the most useful sources for the existence of a strong English presence in religious houses are two sets of mortuary rolls. In these rolls, participating English houses sometimes listed by name individuals for whom they requested prayers. These might include long-dead bishops, abbots, and patrons, but when ordinary monks and nuns were listed, they must normally have been, as one English nunnery put it, 'the recent dead'. In a roll of *c.*1113 for Matilda, daughter of William the Conqueror and abbess of Caen, sixteen English monasteries and four nunneries of a variety of orders listed a total of 143 monks and thirty-five nuns, of whom about 40 per cent in each category had English names, though within the individual houses percentages varied widely, from places like St Alban's and Blyth, where there were no English names, to Hyde Abbey and Nunminster in Winchester, where English names dominated. In Abbot Vitalis of Savigny's roll of *c.*1122, sixteen monasteries listed seventy-two monks, of whom about a quarter had English names, and three nunneries listed ten nuns, of whom three had English names.[29] As all these figures show, there remained a powerful English presence in the monasteries even at the nadir of English fortunes in the early twelfth century.

[28] West, *St. Benet of Holme*, 1, nos. 119, 126, 130, 131, 141, 168, 307; Hart and Lyons, *Cartularium Monasterii de Rameseia*, 1, nos. 46, 89; MacRay, *Chronicon Abbatiae Rameseiensis*, nos. 299, 307; Douglas, *Feudal Documents*, nos. 106, 110, 115, 117, 119, 120, 122, 123, 135, 136, 142, 144, 172; Rodney Thomson, 'Twelfth-Century Documents from Bury St Edmunds Abbey', *EHR* 92 (1977), 806–19, no. 2. See also Clark, *Words, Names and History*, 182–3, for continuing English influence at Canterbury Cathedral Priory.

[29] Léopold Delisle, ed., *Rouleaux des morts du IXe au XVe siècle* (Paris, 1866), 186, 188–90, 193–5, 198–204, 312–16, 326–7, 329–31, 336–9, 341. I have listed only ordinary monks and nuns, on the premiss that some of the monastic officials listed, almost all of them priors, may have been pre-conquest, as some of the abbots and abbesses were. It should be noted that in Vitalis's roll the status of named individuals is sometimes unclear, so the figures for monks and nuns may be slightly distorted.

As the Durham lists indicate, it becomes much harder to find English names of monks and nuns as time passes. The shift in names *may* reflect a continuing change in ethnic membership, as more and more descendants of Continental settlers entered religious houses. But one begins to find monks with Norman names but English or mixed ancestry, such as a Ralph son of Colswain at Ely, or the historian William of Malmesbury, at various monasteries at a fairly early date, and it is likely that much of the change in monastic nomenclature simply reflects naming fashions.[30] It is striking that there are nearly as many biblical, patristic, and classical names as Norman ones in the later Durham list, a much higher ratio than was common in Anglo-Norman society, and it is likely that many monks with these 'ethnically neutral' names, as well as some with Norman ones, were English. Thus there is reason to believe that the English presence remained important in religious houses beyond Henry I's reign.

The English not only remained important among the rank and file, but a surprising number rose to high office in wealthy monasteries throughout the twelfth century, long after the Norman takeover of the church had been completed. Monks with English names, as well as one nun (the evidence for nunneries is very slim), can be found in the twelfth century as sub-priors, cellarers or sub-cellarers, sacrists or sub-sacrists, chamberlains, and precentors or cantors at a variety of mainly powerful and wealthy monasteries.[31] At Battle, the very monastery founded to celebrate the Norman Conquest, control over the abbey's property was given to a monk of the house with the English name of Eilward in 1124 during a vacancy, thus indicating that he had high standing within the house.[32] Most striking, however, was the number of eleventh- and twelfth-century native priors at large Benedictine houses, since priors were effectively the second-in-command at their monasteries, and at cathedral priories basically ran the place. Priors with English names or a known English identity can be found at Bury St Edmund's, Durham, Burton Abbey, Crowland, Norwich, Rochester, Peterborough, Westminster, Thorney, Worcester, and Christ Church, Canterbury.[33] Though the majority of monastic officials

---

[30] For Ralph son of Colswain, see Blake, *Liber Eliensis*, 265. See Clark, *Words, Names and History*, 338–47, for an argument for continuity at Thorney despite a major shift in naming patterns there.

[31] For sub-priors, see West, *St. Benet of Holme*, 1, no. 141; J. G. Jenkins, ed., *Charters of Missenden Abbey*, vol. 1 (Twichells End and London, 1938), no. 71; BL Add MS 35296 fol. 37ᵛ. For cellarers or sub-cellarers, see West, *St. Benet of Holme*, 1, no. 307; Douglas, *Feudal Documents*, nos. 106, 136; Reginald of Durham, *Libellus Beati Cuthberti*, 237. For sacrists or subsacrists, see Blake, *Liber Eliensis*, 289; S. *Anselmi Opera Omnia*, 5: 326–7; Reginald of Durham, *Libellus Beati Cuthberti*, 61; Arnold, *Memorials of St. Edmund's Abbey*, 2: 297. For chamberlains, see West, *St. Benet of Holme*, 1, no. 141; *Letters of John of Salisbury*, 1: 100; Saltman, *Theobald, Archbishop of Canterbury*, 268; Kemp, *Reading Abbey Cartularies*, 2, no. 1133. For precentors and cantors, in addition to Osbeorn and Eadmer at Christ Church, see Blake, *Liber Eliensis*, 289; BL Add MS 9822, fol. 61ᵛ; *CJV* 3: 206–8; *EEA* 8, no 17; Delisle, *Rouleaux des Morts*, 337.

[32] Searle, *Chronicle of Battle Abbey*, 132.

[33] *Fasti*, 2: 9, 33, 59, 78–9; S. *Anselmi Opera Omnia*, 4: 182; 5: 325; Douglas, *Feudal Documents*, nos. 135, 136, 186; Wrottesley, 'Burton Chartulary', 31–6; *EHOV* 2: 322; Mason, *Westminster Abbey Charters*, nos. 245, 248a; Cyril Hart, *The Thorney Annals 963–1412 A. D.* (Lewiston, NY, 1997), 12; BL Add MS 40,000, fol. 10ᵛ; *VW* 56–7. I have not included some priors listed in the mortuary rolls, since some may have been pre-conquest. See Emma Mason, *Westminster Abbey and its People, c. 1050–c. 1216* (Woodbridge, 1996), 89, for the argument that the appointment of an English prior suggests an ongoing presence of a substantial body of ethnic Englishmen at Westminster.

208 The Religious

were probably of Continental origin, nonetheless the number of natives holding important monastic posts is evidence both for the limits of Norman prejudice and for the continuing importance of natives in the monastic setting.

The collective power and influence of English monks and nuns should not be underestimated, particularly when one includes those few who served as heads of houses. Even abbots and abbesses of new or minor houses were locally influential, while the exceptional English abbot of a rich Benedictine house, such as Aldwin of Ramsey or Ording of Bury St Edmund's, had a position equivalent to a wealthy or powerful baron. But I have argued that power was relative in this society, and a 'mere' prior such as Elmer, head of Christ Church, Canterbury, though he may not have been equivalent to an archbishop, bishop, or major noble, must have been of equal influence to many abbots and even minor barons. William of Malmesbury wrote that Turgot, prior of Durham, was so powerful that Bishop Ranulf Flambard did not want to replace him when he left to become bishop of Saint Andrew's.[34] Lesser figures, such as cellarers and sacristans, had positions of importance within some of the most powerful corporate bodies in the land, and as such could have dealt on terms of social equality or even superiority with most of the immigrants and their descendants. Moreover, some of these officials, and particularly precentors, would have had cultural influence that far exceeded whatever economic or political power their positions would have supplied. Even ordinary monks, at least in powerful monasteries, must have had more than average influence and standing in this society. For all their personal poverty, they were members and had some say in the governance of extremely wealthy bodies. More important, their positions gave them religious and cultural influence that outweighed their political and economic clout. Despite the immigrant seizure of almost all the abbacies, the survival of many English in religious houses, in many cases as officials, placed a surprising amount of influence and authority in native hands.

If the English had a strong presence among the regular clergy, they dominated the ranks of anchorites and hermits, a group that has received much recent attention.[35] Several scholars have noted the fact that so many solitaries were English, and indeed it would be a challenge to find one who was clearly of Norman descent.[36] The predominance of English among the solitaries is not surprising, since the bulk of the population was English and there were no legal bars to any free person becoming a hermit or anchorite. Nonetheless, the importance and social influence of English

---

[34] WMGP 273–4. See Aird, St Cuthbert and the Normans, 151–5, 171–2, for Turgot's position, influence, and authority.

[35] H. Mayr-Harting, 'Functions of a Twelfth-Century Recluse', History, NS 60 (1975), 337–52; Ann K. Warren, Anchorites and their Patrons in Medieval England (Berkeley, 1985); Christopher Holdsworth, 'Hermits and the Powers of the Frontier', Reading Medieval Studies, 16 (1990), 55–76; Brian Golding, 'The Hermit and the Hunter', in The Cloister and the World: Essays in Medieval History in Honour of Barbara Harvey, ed. John Blair and Brian Golding (Oxford, 1996), 95–117.

[36] Holdsworth, 'Hermits and the Powers of the Frontier', 58–9; Talbot, Life of Christina of Markyate, 12–13; Mayr-Harting, 'Functions of a Twelfth-Century Recluse', 337–8. Published lives of native hermits include Life of Christina of Markyate; John of Ford, Wulfric of Haselbury; Reginald of Durham, Vita Sancti Godrici; Paul Grosjean, ed., 'Vitae S. Roberti Knaresburgensis', Analecta Bollandiana, 57 (1939), 364–400; Geoffrey of Coldingham, 'Vita Bartholomaei Farnensis', SMO 1: 295–325.

solitaries should not be forgotten. They had, by definition, little or no wealth or conventional secular power, but as Mayr-Harting and Holdsworth have argued, drawing on the work of Peter Brown on holy men in late antiquity, the spiritual authority and supernatural power attributed to these figures made them very influential.[37] Once again, religion placed power into the hands of natives despite the overall imbalance of power between the two ethnic groups.

Immigrants and their descendants came to occupy a strong place among the secular clergy, as among the regular. Indeed, England developed a reputation as a land of promise for ambitious clerics. Baudri de Bourgueil wrote in his epitaph for an Angevin scholar, Frodo, drawing upon Virgil, that the 'accursed hunger for gold' had led him to England, where he perished.[38] Orderic Vitalis recorded that his father, Odelarius, one of three leading clerics in the household of Roger of Montgomery, gave to a monastery £200, the yearly income of a prosperous baron, thus revealing the kind of fortune that even a churchman who did not become a bishop might accumulate.[39] It would, of course, be simplistic to treat all the immigrant ecclesiasts as only being ambitious for wealth and power; Odelarius, after all, gave his accumulated fortune away. But the fact remains that England was attractive to clerical immigrants.

Foreigners not only monopolized appointments to bishoprics but also began moving into the secondary ranks of ecclesiastical office, although they had much less of a monopoly at this level. About half of the canons of St Paul's, London, were foreigners in the earliest lists dating to the late eleventh century.[40] Domesday Book reveals that a number of prebendaries of the rich church of St Martin's, Dover, were also foreigners, and though the survey reveals little about the identities of most priests, it does show at least some foreigners holding wealthy parish churches, though more English than foreign priests are named there.[41] Clerics such as Odelarius also served in the households of secular and ecclesiastical magnates. Though immigration was most prevalent in the first generation, Henry I continued to rely heavily on immigrant churchmen in his appointments, and even in Henry II's reign foreigners such as Peter of Blois could receive preferment. Moreover, the descendants of immigrants, both landlords and non-celibate clergy, were in a good position to attain lucrative church office, and many clearly did so. Thus, men of Continental origins or ancestry became common among the secular clergy, though the question of how common remains.

Immigrants may have been restricted largely to the upper and middle reaches of the secular clergy. The general view is that the English dominated the lowest rank of the secular clergy, namely at the parish level, and this is almost certainly true.[42] In

[37] Mayr-Harting, 'Functions of a Twelfth-Century Recluse', 337–52; Holdsworth, 'Hermits and the Powers of the Frontier', 55–76. See also Golding, 'The Hermit and the Hunter', 95–117.

[38] *Oeuvres poétiques de Baudri de Bourgueil*, 83. The phrase 'auri sacra fames' appears in Virgil's *Aeneid*, 3: 57.   [39] *EHOV* 3: 148.

[40] C. N. L. Brooke, 'The Composition of the Chapter of St. Pauls 1086–1163', *Cambridge Historical Journal*, 10 (1951), 121–2.

[41] *DB* 1: 1b, 20a, 39a, 40a, 57b, 58a, 62a, 65b, 143b; Williams, *ENC* 127.

[42] Barlow, *English Church, 1066–1154*, 58, 133, 311; Lennard, *Rural England*, 332; Williams, *ENC* 130.

my own research I have encountered hundreds of local priests and clerics with English names, both as members of the older-style collegiate minsters and more frequently as local parish priests, in documents ranging from the late eleventh to the late twelfth century and beyond.[43] An unusually large witness list to a charter which Peter de Valognes issued to the new Benedictine cell at Binham, from between 1101 and 1107, is particularly suggestive of the continuing importance of the English at the local level. Though all three of Peter's chaplains and one of the two chaplains of the two abbots on hand had Norman names, nine of the fourteen other clerics, many of them clearly parish priests, had English names, and one other had a name common to both English and Normans.[44] These were rural priests, but towns and cities had plenty of native priests and clerics as well—the unusually full records of St Paul's, London, reveal around three-dozen London clerics with English names.[45] In both town and country, English clergy clearly remained common.

We are accustomed to think of the parish clergy as very minor figures, and so they were in comparison to wealthy landholders and those in the upper ranks of the church hierarchy, but the wealth and social position of parish clergy, including the natives among them, varied widely, and even the poorer parish priests must often have been influential figures in a village context.[46] One tends to get only glimpses of their influence, such as a royal writ addressed to a local English priest, or the settlement of an important legal case at the house of another English priest in Oxford. Most striking of all is a scene in the *vita* of Wulfric of Haselbury, one of the most important of the native hermits, in which the parish priest, also English, organizes successful resistance to an attempt by the monks of Montacute to forcibly move the hermit's body to their monastery.[47] Parish priests could sometimes be fairly wealthy by local standards. Indeed, a knightly family in Yorkshire could trace itself back to a priest named Edwin.[48] Moreover, their position as religious and ceremonial leaders gave priests the potential for influence and power beyond what their wealth could provide them. A list of property demised by Edward, priest of St Augustine's, London, which included rich silk vestments and a silver cup with gold inlay among other treasures, gives a glimpse of how wealth and religious authority might converge. Not only was Edward surrounded by wealth in a poor society, but the wealth was used to underscore his ceremonial position, and even this 'ordinary' parish

[43] For examples of English figures in minsters, see William Henry Hart, *Historia et Cartularium Monasterii Sancti Petri Gloucestriæ*, vol. 2 (London, 1865), no. 777; Denis Bethell, 'The Lives of St. Osyth of Essex and St. Osyth of Aylesbury', *Analecta Bollandiana*, 88 (1970), 120; *EEA* 8, no. 108; *Mon. Ang.*, 6: 303. As late as Archbishop Theobald's time, one of these churches, South Malling, had a dean with the Anglo-Scandinavian name of Ælav: Saltman, *Theobald, Archbishop of Canterbury*, 80–1, nos. 177–8, 180. As for parish priests, the references are too numerous to list.

[44] BL Cotton Claudius D xiii, fols. 2ʳ–3ʳ. Printed in *Mon. Ang.*, 3: 345–6.

[45] *Ninth Report*, 61–8; Gibbs, *Early Charters of the Cathedral Church of St. Paul*, nos. 217, 220.

[46] For the position and status of parish clergy in this period, see Barlow, *English Church 1000–1066*, 131–4; Martin Brett, *The English Church Under Henry I* (London, 1975), 218–22; Lennard, *Rural England*, 327–32.

[47] *RRAN* 2, no. 1469; Stevenson, *Chronicon Monasterii de Abingdon*, 2: 119; John of Ford, *Wulfric of Haselbury*, 127–9.

[48] *EYC* 6: 219–21; Clay and Greenway, *Early Yorkshire Families*, 43–4.

priest must have cut a very impressive figure during masses and other rituals.[49] Yet again, the church provided significant numbers of natives with positions of at least modest power and influence.

Moreover, even if natives were long barred from becoming bishops, they could still gain important intermediate positions among the secular clergy. After the Norman Conquest, in line with ecclesiastical developments elsewhere, the offices of rural dean and archdeacon were created to provide regional oversight and jurisdiction over the church.[50] I have found around fifty men with English elements in their names called deans in the post-conquest period, and though the term 'dean' was a flexible one, it is likely that the great majority were rural deans. There were fewer native archdeacons, but the first known archdeacon of London was a man named Edward, and I have found at least ten other native archdeacons ranging in date from the late eleventh century through Henry II's reign.[51] Archdeacons were powerful, and the natives among them were no exception.[52] *Magister* Steingrim, archdeacon of Norfolk, was prominent enough to serve as a papal judge-delegate, and *Magister* Edmund, archdeacon of Coventry, had the resources and influence to found a hospital in that town.[53] Rural deans were lesser figures, but still locally significant.[54] Rural deans were also more likely than ordinary parish priests to be well off. One such native figure, Thurstin the dean, held the church of Thornham in Norfolk along with 230½ acres from Norwich Cathedral Priory at a small rent; another, named Swain, was able to build a mill, which must have represented a large capital investment.[55] Rural deans were in a position to participate in the local and regional circles where many minor Norman landowners must have operated, and archdeacons were among society's elite, and thus on an equal footing to many Normans, both within the church and without.

Another very prominent group were cathedral canons. The exceptionally good early records of St Paul's, London, and Exeter Cathedral show that natives

---

[49] *Ninth Report*, 64.

[50] For the office of archdeacon, see Christopher Brooke, 'The Archdeacon and the Norman Conquest', *Tradition and Change: Essays in Honour of Marjorie Chibnall*, ed. Diana Greenway *et al.* (Cambridge, 1985), 1–19. For rural deans and the conquest, see Brett, *English Church Under Henry I*, 213.

[51] For Edward, see *Fasti*, 1: 8; Stubbs, *Memorials of Saint Dunstan*, 155–6, 241–4. Other archdeacons included Ailward, archdeacon of Colchester (*Fasti*, 1: 18, 45); Aelfric, archdeacon of Worcester (*Fasti*, 2: 104); *Magister* Steingrim, archdeacon of Norfolk (*EEA* 6: p. xli; *Fasti*, 2: 65); Harold, Archdeacon of Bath (*EEA* 10, no. 7; 11, no. 18); Alnoth and Henry son of Harding, archdeacons of Exeter (*EEA* 12: 306–7); William son of Toli, a relative of abbot Aelred of Rievaulx (*Fasti*, 6: 36); Wulmar, an archdeacon in the diocese of Chester (*EEA* 14: 127); *Magister* Edmund, archdeacon of Coventry (*EEA* 16: pp. xxxv–vi, 113). Turgot, prior of Durham, also served as archdeacon, and two archdeacons in the diocese of Lincoln were named Alfred, and thus could have been English (*Fasti*, 2: 33, 37; 3: 35, 39).

[52] See Brett, *English Church Under Henry I*, 179–211, for an overview of archdeacons in the period.

[53] *EEA* 6: p. xli; *Mon. Ang.*, 6: 658–9.

[54] For the duties and position of rural deans, see Barlow, *English Church, 1066–1154*, 49–50, 137, 155–6, 227; Brett, *English Church Under Henry I*, 212–15.

[55] *CRR* 16: 327–30; *Pipe Roll 12 Henry II*, 47. Thurstin had a name common to both naming pools, but his son, Elveric (OE Ælfric) had an English one, which would indicate that Thurstin himself was English. For another important dean, Hugh, dean of Derby, who had a brother with the Anglo-Scandinavian name of Aghemund, and for his family, see Reginald R. Darlington, *The Cartulary of Darley Abbey*, vol. 1 (Kendal, 1945), pp. xxxv–xl.

remained a strong presence in those cathedrals into the early twelfth century. Indeed, the first recorded dean and cantor at St Paul's, both of whom held office around 1100, had English names.[56] Less information survives for other secular cathedrals, but there were English deans at Hereford and Salisbury after the conquest, and as late as c.1122 the treasurer and precentor of Salisbury, and at least one other canon, had English names.[57] The records of London and Exeter cathedrals, however, also reveal a sharp shift from indigenous names to Continental ones. To a larger degree than in less important church offices, this surely reflects a shift in ethnicity, as well-connected immigrant clerics, and the clerical sons of powerful immigrant families, entered important and lucrative posts. But the presence of canons with English patronyms such as Osbert son of Algar at Exeter, and Ralph son of Algot and Geoffrey and Robert sons of Wulfred at St Paul's, shows that as usual part of the shift was simply in nomenclature rather than ethnicity.[58] In any case, there continued to be at least some cathedral clergy with indigenous names throughout the twelfth century.[59] Natives could also be found holding prebends at other wealthy collegiate churches such as St Martin's, Dover, Beverley Minster, and Waltham, among others.[60] Cathedral and collegiate clergy were comparatively wealthy and powerful men, members of the clerical elite, and able to operate on terms of social equality with many a Norman, not least their immigrant peers in their own institutions.

A final clerical group, among whom the English were well represented, which was of growing importance in the twelfth-century church were the masters, or *magistri*, who were clerics with more than the usual education. References to *magistri* with English names or patronyms are scattered throughout the sources, and though *magister*, like dean, was a flexible title, it is likely that most were educated clerics.[61] *Magistri* were not necessarily wealthier or more powerful than other

---

[56] *EEA* 15, no. 7; *Fasti*, 1: 4, 23, 27, 29, 36, 40–1, 45, 49, 57, 65, 71, 73, 74, 77, 78, 79, 83, 85, 87, 89; Brooke, 'Chapter of St. Pauls', 121–2; Brooke and Keir, *London, 800–1216*, 342–3; *EEA* 12: 312–13.

[57] *EEA* 7: p. li, 3; 'The Life of Saint Wulsin of Sherborne by Goscelin', ed. C. H. Talbot, *Revue Bénédictine*, 69 (1969), 84 (the title given is provost, which was undoubtedly equivalent to dean); *Fasti*, 4: 13, 17, 20; Edward J. Kealey, *Roger of Salisbury Viceroy of England* (Berkeley, 1972), 238–9.

[58] *EEA* 12: 315; *Fasti*, 1: 71, 74, 83; Brooke and Keir, *London, 800–1216*, 343.

[59] *Fasti*, 3: 144–5; 4: 121; 5: 57; 6: 36, 118, 119, 130, 132; Delisle, *Rouleaux de Morts*, 199; *EEA* 10: p. xliv.

[60] *DB* 1: 1b; BL Harley MS 491, fol. 47ᵛ; Leslie Watkiss and Marjorie Chibnall, eds., *The Waltham Chronicle* (Oxford, 1994), 82, 84; Ransford, *Early Charters of Waltham Abbey*, no. 14; Richard T. W. McDermid, *Beverley Minster Fasti* (Huddersfield, 1993), 13; *EEA* 5, no. 117; Harper-Bill and Mortimer, *Stoke by Clare Cartulary*, 1, no. 70; H. E. Salter, ed., *The Boarstall Cartulary* (Oxford, 1930), no. 1; *Mon. Ang.*, 6: 1326; Williams, *ENC* 127–30.

[61] It should be noted that some *magistri* were monks, though I have tried to focus on ones among the secular clergy here. BL MS Harley 3650, fols. 20ʳ⁻ᵛ, 25ᵛ⁻26ʳ; *EEA* 1, no. 160; 5, no. 117; 6, nos. 84–5, 121, 335; 7, nos. 125, 150, 204; 11, no. 98; 18, no. 163; P. L. Hull, *The Cartulary of Launceston Priory* (Torquay, 1987), nos. 62, 241–2; Darlington, *Cartulary of Darley Abbey*, 1: pp. xxxix–xl; Gervers, *Cartulary of the Knights of St. John*, no. 582; Loyd and Stenton, *Sir Christopher Hatton's Book of Seals*, no. 105; Stenton, *Documents Illustrative of the Danelaw*, nos. 334–5, 375; Ross and Devine, *Cartulary of Cirencester Abbey*, 2, no. 669; Woodcock, *Cartulary of St. Gregory, Canterbury*, nos. 33, 131; Walker, 'Charters of the Earldom of Hereford', no. 65; Una Rees, ed., *The Cartulary of Haughmond Abbey* (Cardiff, 1985), no. 280; Kemp, *Reading Abbey Cartularies*, 1, no. 546; Salter, *Eynsham Cartulary*, 1, no. 166; H. Mayr-Harting, *The Acta of the Bishops of Chichester, 1075–1207* (Torquay, 1964), 10–12; *Mon. Ang.*, 5: 482; 6: 468; 6: 1326; Becket

clerics, but education was a route to upward mobility in the church, and by their very training masters formed an influential intellectual elite.

This overview of the ethnic composition of the religious in England shows that, though the complaint made by Eadmer and others that English churchmen were barred from such offices as abbot and bishop was basically true, there were a few exceptions, and, more important, it was *only* true of these highest of offices. English monks and clerics could rise quite high in the hierarchy. Undoubtedly this only made it all the more frustrating to be denied the very highest offices, but that should not obscure the fact that many of these officials were important figures. I do not want to give an overly optimistic picture of English power within the church. Though the problem of names and the inadequacy of the sources make it impossible to accurately guage the proportions of English and Normans at any level but the very highest, the evidence does suggest what one might expect, namely that the proportion of English narrowed the further one went up the ecclesiastical hierarchy, particularly among the secular clergy. Nonetheless, the bar of prejudice in the English church was placed quite high, was never made formal, and, as John of Oxford's appointment shows, eventually disappeared. In broad terms, the church, though dominated by immigrants, provided natives with greater access to wealth, power, status, and influence than did the secular landholding structure. As a result, it formed a very important setting for the survival of English influence, and therefore for social interaction and the defence of English identity, which will be the subject of later sections of this chapter.

Before turning to these subjects, however, it is worth briefly pausing to consider why the Normans left so much power in the hands of the English and did not monopolize lesser positions in the church, as they monopolized the highest ones. In ideological terms it was hard for the Normans, claiming to come not as conquerors but as Christian upholders of William's rightful claims, to simply push out existing monks and priests. Even at the highest reaches, William and his followers found reasons, or at least pretexts, to depose abbots and bishops, and sometimes they simply waited until the incumbents died. At a more practical level, it would have been difficult for the Normans to find enough clerics, nuns, and monks to fill all the offices, even with Continental recruiting stretching far beyond the boundaries of Normandy. As the years passed, the children of settlers increased the pool of possible recruits, but with the new magnate families continuing to give out land well into the twelfth century, and with the frequent granting of land to younger sons and daughters, there was less economic motive for aristocrats to place children in the church. Obviously some children of immigrants had genuine vocations, but there existed no compelling worldly reason for the immigrants to monopolize all religious positions for themselves.

In general, pragmatic prejudice once again came into play. Where English power represented a threat (and that of English abbots and bishops, like that of the English

Materials, 1: 134; 2: pp. xlv, 353–450; 3: 141, 498; 4: 75; Anne J. Duggan, ed., *The Correspondence of Thomas Becket, Archbishop of Canterbury, 1162–1170* (Oxford, 2000), 1: 588.

nobility, might potentially do so), it was eliminated. Where English talents could be utilized without serious risk, both for practical and for religious ends, natives were given positions of responsibility, at least so long as they did not compete too much with the Normans. The appointment of English churchmen to Scottish sees also fits this pattern—such figures could hardly rally English opposition to the Norman kings in England, but they could further Canterbury's hegemonic claims. Similarly, Algar's appointment to Coutances posed no threat, but enabled the king to make use of a worthy churchman. Because pragmatic Norman prejudice allowed room for pragmatic Norman tolerance, natives continued to have an important role within the church, and this allowed the church to be an important venue for ethnic integration, cultural interaction, and the maintenance of English identity.

II

If the survival of many English religious within the church in the generations after the conquest shows the potential for interaction, the aim of this section is to show its existence. The very number of natives in positions of ecclesiastical authority well into the twelfth century in itself provides an a priori argument for the existence of at least working relationships between conquerors and conquered. Fortunately our evidence allows us to go further, and to show the development of strong affective relationships that crossed and helped dissolve ethnic boundaries. This interaction involving the religious was particularly important for several reasons: the institutional church was itself an important social sector; harmony within the church improved the atmosphere for cultural exchange and acculturation; and the religious could serve as role models for the rest of the society and therefore as influential pioneers in ethnic integration.

I will begin with interaction in religious houses. Monasteries and nunneries by their very nature forced individuals to interact constantly and closely with others. As a result, such houses could become emotional pressure-cookers in the wrong circumstances, and it is easy to imagine how ethnic and cultural differences could blow the lid off. One spectacular example of this was the confrontation and massacre at Glastonbury. But under the right leadership religious houses could provide an environment conducive to co-operation and the breakdown of ethnic division. The emphasis on obedience and strict discipline in Benedictine monasticism provided able abbots with the tools to keep ethnically based disputes under control and to maintain order in spite of any tensions that might exist, thus creating working relationships that could, in the absence of open divisiveness, slowly transform into deeper ones. More important still, the common purpose of worship and prayer to which all monks and nuns were directed, at least in theory, provided a strong ideological bridge across ethnic divisions. This was particularly so given the growing emphasis in this period on monastic friendship, a type of relationship that often involved more passionate emotions than we envision when thinking of friendship.[62] Thus, it is not surprising that some of the earliest affective relationships between individual English and immigrants can be found in the monasteries.

Some of the best evidence survives from the cathedral monastery at Canterbury. Harmony there may have owed much to the first two archbishops under the new regime, Lanfranc and Anselm. As I suggested in Chapter 3, the fact that neither was Norman may well have helped them reach out to the English. But their characters also mattered. Individual relationships obviously depend on individual personalities, and both Canterbury and the whole English Church were fortunate to have these men at the helm, particularly when it came to ethnic relations. This is not to paint an overly rosy picture of the two, and particularly of the former. Lanfranc was a key figure in the Norman seizure of the English Church, and cannot be separated or exonerated from the injustices involved, particularly the deliberate and prejudicial exclusion of natives from the highest offices, in which Anselm too acquiesced. Lanfranc was also extremely harsh in disciplining monks of Canterbury's other major house, St Augustine's, in a dispute that may well have involved ethnic tensions.[63] Nonetheless, though neither archbishop was particularly concerned with improving ethnic relations per se, both took their religious ideals and duties seriously, and for both shared ties of religion were more important than ethnic barriers. Had ethnic divisions been accompanied by deep religious ones in post-conquest England, both men would probably have proved intolerant, but in the event they ultimately helped to pave the way to ethnic harmony.

Lanfranc took the first steps. From shortly after his appointment he sent English monks to Bec, in Normandy, in some cases to discipline them but also to train them intellectually and give them experience in a recently reformed house, so that they could help reform the church at Canterbury.[64] He commissioned the life of the important Canterbury saint Alfeah from the native Osbeorn, and may have appointed a cleric and teacher with the English name of Lefwin to his own new foundation of St Gregory's, Canterbury.[65] As we shall see, he also developed a good relationship with Bishop Wulfstan of Worcester, who shared his monastic background and concerns. As a result, although he was closely associated with the hated

---

[62] For a discussion of the passions involved in monastic friendship, which has the advantage of focusing on two natives, Christina of Markyate and Aelred of Rievaulx, see Ruth Mazo Karras, 'Friendship and Love in the Lives of Two Twelfth-Century English Saints', *Journal of Medieval History*, 14 (1988), 305–20. See also below, n. 68.

[63] Plummer and Earl, 'Acta Lanfranci', 290–2.

[64] For English monks at Bec, see *S. Anselmi Opera Omnia*, 3: 141, 149–51, 186–7; 4: 104–5. See also, A. A. Porée, *Histoire de l'abbaye du Bec*, vol. 1 (Evreux, 1901), 629–34, for a list of monks at Bec, in which Olric, Farman, Harward, and Chetellus, all with names which may be insular in origin, appear under Herluin, who died in 1078, and Alestannus, Levinus, Britric, Alveric, Osulf, Leufredus, Olric, and Alvin appear under subsequent abbots. Orderic Vitalis describes the training of English monks in French houses as a general phenomenon: *EHOV* 2: 248.

[65] For Lanfranc's commission, see Osbeorn of Canterbury, *Vita Sancti Elphegi*, 376; Eadmer, *Life of St Anselm*, 53–4. For Lefwin, see Gibson, *Lanfranc of Bec*, 186; Woodcock, *Cartulary of St. Gregory, Canterbury*, no. 1. However, see Tim Tatton-Brown, 'The Beginnings of St Gregory's Priory and St John's Hospital in Canterbury', in *Canterbury and the Norman Conquest: Churches, Saints and Scholars, 1066–1109*, ed. Richard Eales and Richard Sharpe (London, 1995), 42, for doubts about the authenticity of the donation charter by Lanfranc which mentions Lefwin.

new regime, Lanfranc earned the deep respect of English monks such as Osbeorn, Eadmer, and the anonymous writer of the Anglo-Saxon Chronicle who called him the 'father and solace of monks'.[66]

Anselm went still further and gained the love of his English monks. Among his preoccupations, as Southern has shown, was a concern with friendship and its spiritual usefulness, particularly in the context of the monastic life.[67] In his letters he expressed or described friendship in extraordinarily passionate, even at times homoerotic, terms.[68] Anselm's ideas about friendship had a theological and cerebral aspect to them, but his emphasis on deep, passionate, and intensive friendship, and the vivid language he used to express his relationships, allowed him to reach across the divisions of ethnicity and create close relations with individual English monks. Best-known is Anselm's complex but strong relationship with Eadmer, whom he once described as his dearest son and the support of his old age. Eadmer followed Anselm into exile during his disputes with William II and Henry I, and wrote his *vita*, as well as the *Historia Novorum*, dedicated to defending Anselm's opposition to the two kings over various matters.[69] Anselm was also close to the hagiographer and precentor Osbeorn. While abbot of Bec, Anselm wrote to Lanfranc: 'Dom Osbeorn, whom your authority ordered to be sent back to you, has, I admit, attached himself to my soul with the attachment of such affection that my heart could not endure separation from him without considerable rending.'[70] Osbeorn himself later wrote Anselm letters beseeching him to accept the post of archbishop. Anselm also seems to have developed friendships with several other Canterbury monks, including Osbeorn's cousin Hulvard (probably OE Wulfward); a monk named Ordwy; Elmer, one of his students and later prior of Christ Church; and Alexander, whose classical name conceals an English identity.[71] Because he was archbishop, Anselm's ties with English monks and nuns, some casual, some more intense, stretched beyond Canterbury. He can be found supporting the English prior of Bury St Edmund's in his demands that a canonical election be held for abbot, and advising an informal community of English nuns.[72]

---

[66] *HN* 10–16; Stubbs, *Memorials of Saint Dunstan*, 142, 232; Osbeorn of Canterbury, *Vita Sancti Elphegi*, 376; Eadmer, *Life of St Anselm*, 50; Eadmer, 'Vita S. Bregwini', in *Anglia Sacra*, ed. Henry Wharton, vol. 2 (London, 1691), 188; 'Edmeri Cantuariensis Cantoris Nova Opuscula de Sanctorum Veneratione Obsecratione', ed. A. Wilmart, *Revue des Sciences Religieuse*, 15 (1935), 366–7; *ASC* E 1089.

[67] Southern, *Saint Anselm: A Portrait in a Landscape*, 138–65.

[68] For debate over the question of Anselm's sexual orientation, see Brian Patrick McGuire, 'Love, Friendship, and Sex in the Eleventh Century: The Experience of Anselm', *Studia Theologica*, 28 (1974), 146–50; John Boswell, *Christianity, Social Tolerance, and Homosexuality: Gay People in Western Europe from the Beginnings of the Christian Era to the Fourteenth Century* (Chicago, 1980), 215, 218–20; Southern, *Saint Anselm: A Portrait in a Landscape*, 148–53.

[69] *S. Anselmi Opera Omnia*, 4: 104–5; *HN* 27–220; Eadmer, *Life of St Anselm*; Southern, *Saint Anselm and His Biographer*, 198–201; id., *Saint Anselm: A Portrait in a Landscape*, 404–36.

[70] *S. Anselmi Opera Omnia*, 3: 186–7. Translation from Walter Fröhlich, ed., *The Letters of Saint Anselm of Canterbury*, vol. 1 (Kalamazoo, 1990), 187–8. For Osbeorn, see Jay Rubinstein, 'The Life and Writings of Osbern of Canterbury', in *Canterbury and the Norman Conquest: Churches, Saints and Scholars, 1066–1109*, ed. Richard Eales and Richard Sharpe (London, 1995), 27–40.

[71] *S. Anselmi Opera Omnia*, 3: 141, 149–51, 186–7, 195–6; 4: 6–10, 13–14; 5: 256–7, 258–9, 295–7; R. W. Southern and F. S. Schmitt, *Memorials of St. Anselm* (Oxford, 1969), 245.

[72] *S. Anselmi Opera Omnia*, 4: 134–5, 182; 5: 325, 359–62.

He even wrote to Gunhilda, a daughter of Harold Godwineson, of his love and friendship for her, though both religious ideals and (probably) political loyalty caused him to condemn her sharply for leaving Wilton for liaisons with Alan the Red and Alan the Black, successive lords of Richmond.[73] Anselm's passionate personality and his deep devotion to Christian, and particularly to monastic ideals, caused him to ignore or perhaps rather to break through ethnic boundaries and hostility in creating the kinds of relationships and in following the sorts of practices he believed his religion required of him.

Anselm was an unusual figure, and something of an outsider among the Normans, but as the head of the English church, and one of the leading religious thinkers and writers of the day, he was an extremely influential person, and his example of creating both casual and intense ties with a number of natives was an important one. The effects of his example can clearly be seen in his immediate sphere of influence. Anselm's successor at Canterbury, Ralph, spoke in warm terms of Eadmer in two letters. Eadmer himself may have had strong opinions about the Norman Conquest, but that did not prevent him from befriending other immigrants besides Anselm. Anselm conveyed Eadmer's greetings to a Norman archdeacon in one letter, and in a letter to his own nephew, also named Anselm, wrote, 'Eadmer, who loves you with sincere love, sends his greetings'. Eadmer in turn wrote of the younger Anselm, who became abbot of Bury St Edmund's, that after he lived in England for a long time he was loved by the natives (*indigeni*) 'as if one of them'. It is worth noting that the witness lists of charters Anselm issued as abbot from 1121 to 1148 indicate that a small group of English monks were prominent at Bury during his reign, and also that he was a patron of the upwardly mobile native, Adam of Cockfield.[74] The works of the immigrant monk Reginald of Canterbury reveal a network of friendships between learned native and immigrant monks at the two Canterbury monasteries and Rochester that overlapped with Anselm's circle.[75] Anselm's example of creating strong relationships across ethnic lines affected those around him, native and immigrant alike.

Though Anselm's example was obviously important, he was not the only immigrant prelate to reach out to English monks, nor was his circle the only one in which friendship and co-operation developed between native and Continental monks. According to William of Malmesbury, Walkelin, the first Norman bishop of

[73] Ibid. 4: 43–50. See Searle 'Women and the Legitimization of Succession', 167–9, for a discussion of the political dangers involved in the marriage. I would emphasize more strongly than she the danger presented by a marriage between a powerful lord of Breton background and a daughter of King Harold, particularly in light of Breton participation in the 1075 revolt. For a different view of the political implications of the marriage, see Keats-Rohan, *Domesday People*, 49–50. See Southern, *Saint Anselm: A Portrait in a Landscape*, 262–4, for Anselm's spiritual concerns.

[74] HN 228, 250, 281–2; S. *Anselmi Opera Omnia*, 4: 103, 232; Douglas, *Feudal Documents*, nos. 110, 113, 114–15, 117, 119–24, 126, 129–30; Thomson, 'Twelfth-Century Documents', no. 2. See also the friendship circle revealed by Elmer of Christ Church's letters: 'Écrits spirituels d'Elmer de Cantorbéry', ed. Jean Leclercq, *Studia Anselmiana*, 31 (1953), 62–109.

[75] Reginald of Canterbury, *The Vita Sancti Malchi of Reginald of Canterbury*, ed. Levi Robert Lind (Urbana, Ill., 1942), 38; Liebermann, 'Raginald von Canterbury', 539–40; Wright, *Anglo-Latin Satirical Poets*, 2: 265–7.

Winchester and a more typical Norman prelate than the Burgundian Anselm, was
at first hateful to the cathedral monks there as a newly arrived foreigner, but won
them over.[76] Another source notes that he took a monk named Blackman into his
service, and in the Durham *Liber Vitae* the bishop can be found arranging for
prayers for his English monks.[77] Under Walkelin, a Continental monk and noted
poet named Godfrey of Cambrai served as prior. Among Godfrey's laudatory epi-
taphs was one for an ordinary monk with the English name of Aithelric or Agelric
and another for Wulfnoth, brother of King Harold Godwineson, who was a hostage
in Normandy before the conquest and spent most of his life in captivity.[78] Like
Anselm, Godfrey apparently felt that even members of Harold's house could be
worthy of praise and friendship, and by implication that religious loyalties could
and should overcome political and ethnic divisions. Another member of Walkelin's
circle who developed good ties with at least one English monk was his brother,
Simeon. After Simeon became abbot of Ely in 1082 he brought a group of Winchester monks to shape things up there, at least as he saw it, and solidify his control.
Among them was a monk with the English name of Godric, who was remembered
as a holy man and a visionary in the *Liber Eliensis*. Strikingly, that work praised him
for 'striving in all things for the divine will, not for savagery and power, as is the
custom of foreigners'.[79] This statement, and William of Malmesbury's note that
the Winchester monks initially hated Walkelin as a foreigner, serve as reminders
that monastic co-operation and friendship across ethnic lines first developed in an
atmosphere of extreme hostility. Yet here we have a Norman bishop winning over
English monks, an immigrant prior praising a brother of Harold, and an English
monk supporting a Norman abbot, underscoring the potency of religious and
monastic ties in breaking through ethnic barriers.

The desire for monastic reform could work even more effectively to bring
English and Normans together. The best-known instance of co-operation is the
revival of monasticism in northern England, a movement begun by an English
monk named Aldwin and a Norman monk (formerly a knight) named Reinfrid.[80]
Co-operation and friendship can also be found among the reforming Augustinian
canons. Norman, prior of Aldgate, who was probably English, sent William Cor-
beil, a Norman and future archbishop of Canterbury, to found a daughter house,
and with him went a monk named Siward.[81] Algar, the future bishop of Coutances

[76] *WMGP* 172.
[77] A. W. Goodman, *Chartulary of Winchester Cathedral* (Winchester, 1927), no. 41; Raine, *Liber Vitae
Ecclesiae Dunelmensis*, 72.
[78] Wright, *Anglo-Latin Satirical Poets*, 2: 152–3; Frank Barlow, *William Rufus* (Berkeley, 1983), 65–6.
[79] *Liber Eliensis*, 208–9, 213.
[80] Important discussions of the Northern Revival include Knowles, *Monastic Order in England*,
159–71; Janet Burton, *Monastic and Religious Orders in Britain, 1000–1300* (Cambridge, 1994), 31–3; Anne
Dawtry, 'The Benedictine Revival in the North: The Last Bulwark of Anglo-Saxon Monasticism?', in
Religion and National Identity, ed. Stuart Mews (Oxford, 1982), 87–98; R. B. Dobson, 'A Minority
Ascendant: The Benedictine Conquest of the North of England, 1066–1100', in *Minorities and Barbarians
in Medieval Life and Thought*, ed. Susan J. Ridyard and Robert G. Benson (Sewanee, 1996), 5–26; Aird, *St
Cuthbert and the Normans*, 131–6; Williams, *ENC* 150–3.
[81] Hodgett, *Cartulary of Holy Trinity Aldgate*, 228.

who helped found the Augustinian house of Bodmin, formed a deep friendship with the Italian immigrant cleric Guy of Merton, whose biographer describes how Algar was overcome with grief at Guy's death.[82] Clearly, the excitement of monastic reform and revival helped make ethnic divides more permeable.

Given the paucity of sources for this period, there is thus a surprising amount of evidence for co-operation and close emotional bonds between native and Continental monks, beginning at a very early date after the conquest. As a result, English monks were brought into the influential monastic and intellectual circles headed by the immigrants that now dominated the leading English houses. From the Norman point of view this undoubtedly eased control over monasteries with large numbers of English monks—someone like Godric at Ely could serve as a bridge between English monks and a Norman abbot. But the flip-side of this was that ties with powerful immigrant churchmen helped bring native churchmen into positions of power in the monastic world. For instance, it seems clear that the patronage and support of Lanfranc and Anselm brought Osbeorn, Eadmer, and Elmer into prominence at Christ Church, Canterbury. Power and position within monasteries allowed some English to interact with most immigrants as equals, but it was clearly friendship that put them in such positions. On a broader scale, the formation of personal relationships within monasteries may have eased the grudging acceptance of the new regime by English churchmen, which in the long term helped eliminate political and therefore ethnic tensions. Thus, the early development of monastic friendship across ethnic boundaries had several important implications for relations between English and Normans.

Perhaps most important in this respect, however, was the fact that monks were intended to serve on some level as moral leaders and models of behaviour in medieval society, and that the creation of close relationships across ethnic lines within monasteries therefore sent strong signals to society as a whole. If figures like Lanfranc, Anselm, Walkelin, and Simeon were befriending and working with English monks, it would have been hard for lay people to argue that the overwhelming de facto exclusion of the English from the circles of power at the end of the eleventh century should become de jure. Moreover, the formation of monastic friendships could suggest that the development of bonds of lordship and friendship between English and Normans in the secular world was acceptable and even desirable.

To some degree these signals would have been muted by the theoretical isolation of monks from society, but that isolation should not be exaggerated. Though almost all of the relations I have described so far developed between members of religious orders, English and Norman monks also developed ties across ethnic lines outside of religious houses, thus bringing the sorts of boundary-breaking friendships I have described into society in general. For obvious reasons monks who became bishops were best able to influence society at large. From the Norman side, the best example once again is Anselm. Eadmer's *vita* speaks of Englishmen in Italy

---

[82] Colker, 'Life of Guy of Merton by Rainald of Merton', 259–61.

during Anselm's exile there paying him honour, and later records a miracle in which a certain 'rich and noble Englishman' who was sick asked Anselm to bless some bread and send it to him.[83] Anselm exchanged many letters with Henry I's queen, Edith-Matilda, and though their relationship was complicated, it seems to have been at least a cordial one, with the queen acting as intermediary between archbishop and king.[84] Thus, Anselm's influence in breaking down ethnic barriers extended beyond monastic walls.

From the English side comes an even better example, namely Wulfstan of Worcester, who may have preserved his position during the Norman drive to take over the church only because of a strong reputation for piety and the shared religious values of conquered and conquerors.[85] Over the course of his long episcopacy Wulfstan developed personal relationships not only with Norman churchmen, but also with nobles and kings. Emma Mason has argued that in a confraternity agreement of 1077 Wulfstan was trying to preserve English values in the face of the Norman Conquest, but he tried to do so by drawing in the Normans. Two of the abbots involved in that agreement were Norman, and in it Wulfstan and all the abbots declare their allegiance to King William and Queen Matilda, continuing an Anglo-Saxon monastic tradition of loyalty to monarchs but extending it to the new regime, and implicitly calling for the same royal support that some earlier kings had provided monasteries. Wulfstan kept his end of the bargain by supporting both William I and William II, providing help in the face of baronial revolts.[86] Wulfstan also worked loyally with Lanfranc and Anselm in a mutual struggle against the archbishops of York, and William of Malmesbury recorded that Wulfstan and Lanfranc also worked together to ban the export of slaves from England.[87] Wulfstan had a joking relationship with the warlike Norman bishop Geoffrey of Coutances, friendships with Norman abbots of nearby monasteries, and a particularly close bond with Robert, the Continental bishop of Hereford whom he had earlier ordained as priest.

Indeed, Wulfstan seems to have gained both the admiration and devotion of the Normans. Geoffrey of Cambrai wrote yet another epitaph in praise of him.[88] According to the Worcester monk Hemming, William I came to love him. More striking still, John of Worcester describes a scene from the 1088 baronial rebellion in

---

[83] One cannot be absolutely certain that Eadmer is referring to native English here, but at this early date it seems likely: Eadmer, *Life of St Anselm*, 114, 138.

[84] *S. Anselmi Opera Omnia*, 4: 150–2, 153–4, 156, 216, 228; 5: 244–6, 248–9, 250–1, 253–4, 261–2, 284–6, 326–8, 339, 344, 351. For Anselm and Edith-Matilda, see Southern, *Saint Anselm and his Biographer*, 183–5, 188–93; id., *Saint Anselm: A Portrait in a Landscape*, 260–2, and 262, n. 8; Vaughn, *Anselm of Bec and Robert of Meulan*, 223–5, 276–9, 357–8.

[85] See Emma Mason, 'St Wulfstan's Staff: A Legend and Its Uses', *Medium Ævum*, 53 (1984), 164–5, for a discussion of later stories of Wulfstan's near deposition, which are problematic but may contain a kernel of truth.

[86] Thorpe, *Diplomatarium Anglicum*, 615; *CJW* 3: 24, 52–6; *ASC* E 1087 [*recte* 1088]; *HHHA* 412–14; *EHOV* 4: 124; *WMGR* 544–6; Mason, *Wulfstan of Worcester*, 131–5, 139–45, 197–200.

[87] *VW* 24–6, 57; *WMGR* 496–8, 536; *HN* 45–6; *S. Anselmi Opera Omnia*, 4: 51–3; Mason, *Wulfstan of Worcester*, 110–17, 120, 184–6, 230.

[88] *VW* 46, 60–3; *CJW* 3: 32; Wright, *Anglo-Latin Satirical Poets*, 2: 153; Mason, *Wulfstan of Worcester*, 121–2, 128–9, 197–200.

which Norman loyalists, co-operating with Wulfstan in defence of the marches, urged him to leave the cathedral and take refuge in the castle, 'because they loved him greatly'.[89] Wulfstan operated in the world of high politics, and one must be wary of possible political posturing in professions of love and respect. There is more than a whiff of tokenism about the respect and co-operation offered to Wulfstan, since admiration for his qualities did not prevent William I and his successors from barring other worthy Englishmen from traditional English sees. Nonetheless, the admiration was probably not entirely feigned, and Wulfstan does seem to have created genuine bonds of respect and friendship with at least some immigrants. Even where posturing was involved, Wulfstan's relationships were important, for they reveal a belief that Christian bonds and shared service to the king *should* overcome ethnic divisions, and they also set an example to that effect.

Wulfstan was the last important survivor of the pre-conquest church, and thus something of an anachronism by the 1090s, but his ties with powerful immigrants foreshadow those of the few native monks who achieved important appointments in the twelfth century. The one possibly native bishop in Henry I's reign, Æðelwold of Carlisle, was prior of an Augustinian house, and often served as the king's own confessor, according to Robert of Torigni. Æðelwold's position as confessor strongly suggests a certain intimacy between the two men, and if Æðelwold was native, Henry, intentionally or not, was sending an important message about relations between immigrants and natives by establishing this relationship. More prosaically, Æðelwold's attestations to royal charters, and those of Algar of Coutances, show a modest importance at the royal court that lasted into Stephen's reign, and this would have meant that both were rubbing shoulders with powerful immigrants on a regular basis.[90] Abbot Aldwin of Ramsey and Abbot Ording of Bury can also be found operating in powerful circles, just as one might expect of abbots of prominent and wealthy houses, and so too can Aelred of Rievaulx.[91]

Evidence for co-operation and interaction between English monks and immigrants outside the monastery can be found somewhat further down the social scale as well, among the lower elites and middling sorts. Eadmer's *vita* of Anselm contains a miracle story in which Eadmer's nephew, the monk Haimo, used the archbishop's belt to cure a powerful knight named Humphrey, with whom he was friendly; at this early date it is likely that someone who was a knight and had a Continental name was in fact Norman. The *Liber Eliensis* records another miracle when an Ely monk with the English name of Brithmar was visiting a certain Walter the Fleming. The history of Fountains Abbey reveals the friendship between Ralph Haget, member of a local gentry family that was probably of Norman descent, and

[89] Hemming, *Chartularium Ecclesiae Wigorniensis*, ed. Thomas Hearne (Oxford, 1723), 407; *CJW* 3: 52–6.

[90] *Chronicle of Robert of Torigni*, 123. For Æðelwold at court, see *RRAN* 2, nos. 1334, 1459, 1463, 1701, 1764, 1900, 1902, 1908, 1910–11, 1913, 1915; 3, nos. 46, 99, 114, 271, 280–2, 335, 399, 452, 598, 608, 620–5, 627, 652, 655, 717, 718, 818, 919, 936, 942, 947, 975, 980. For Algar, see *RRAN* 2, nos. 1740, 1764, 1902, 1908; 3, nos. 46, 506, 718, 818, 944

[91] *RRAN* 1, nos. 295, 329–31, 373, 461, 462; 2, nos. 528a, 544, 547–8, 574, 579, 580–3, 966, 999; van Caenegem, *English Lawsuits*, 1: 288–9; *EEA* 2, no. 13; Walter Daniel, *The Life of Ailred of Rievaulx*, 42.

a lay brother of Fountains with the Anglo-Scandinavian name of Sunulph, who persuaded him to become a monk.[92] Despite the supposed isolation of monks, not just abbots but quite ordinary brothers did interact with lay people, including people of a different ethnic background. As a result, the continuing and strong English presence in religious houses created an avenue by which immigrant lay people as well as monks could be drawn into relationships crossing ethnic lines, thereby slowly breaking down ethnic boundaries, friendship by friendship.

Indeed, the whole network of patronage surrounding monastic houses meant that inevitably monks and lay people of different ethnicities would interact. Emma Cownie has shown that although many immigrant nobles favoured Continental houses in the generation immediately following the conquest, from the beginning some also supported English ones, and immigrant support for English monasteries and nunneries increased as time went by.[93] Often this patronage went from Norman magnates to Norman abbots, but in the eleventh or early twelfth century Abbots Ailsi and Aldwin of Ramsey can be found making confraternity agreements with the Norman lords Nigel Fossard and Ranulf son of Ilger.[94] More generally, Tsurushima has shown how the monastic confraternity at Rochester tied together Norman and English landowners, ranging from magnates to very minor figures indeed, with the monks of those houses, many of whom were English.[95] Unfortunately, we know little of how confraternities functioned in this period, but they may have served as an important vehicle for breaking down ethnic boundaries. Overall, the inmates of religious houses, both natives and immigrants, played a very important role in preparing the way for assimilation throughout society, despite their vows of celibacy and their theoretical isolation from the world.

Hermits and solitaries were another group able to form friendships across ethnic lines and thus help reshape ethnic relations. They were also able to cut across the divisions of wealth and power that so often divided English and Normans. Mayr-Harting has written how the English hermit Wulfric of Haselbury acted as a 'hinge-man' between the predominantly English world of the village and the predominantly Continental one of the aristocracy.[96] It is with Wulfric's aristocratic connections that we are primarily concerned here. John of Ford's *vita* explicitly states that Wulfric came from a lowly English background, but also shows that he had a strong friendship with his patron, William son of Walter, lord of Haselbury. Through William and through his own growing fame, Wulfric established contacts with prominent churchmen, including Henry of Blois, and with powerful nobles, including Agnes, a sister-in-law of the earl of Gloucester, whom the *vita* claims he

[92] Eadmer, *Life of Anselm*, 158–9; Blake, *Liber Eliensis*, 306; *Mon. Ang.*, 5: 304.

[93] Emma Cownie, 'The Normans As Patrons of English Religious Houses, 1066–1135', *ANS* 18: 47–62; Emma Cownie, *Religious Patronage in Anglo-Norman England, 1066–1135* (Woodbridge, 1998), 128, 133–7, 185–201.

[94] Hart and Lyons, *Cartularium Monasterii de Rameseia*, 1, no. 35; 2, no. 369.

[95] Tsurushima, 'Fraternity', 313–37. See also id., 'Forging Unity Between Monks and Laity in Anglo-Norman England: The Fraternity of Ramsey Abbey', in *Negotiating Secular and Ecclesiastical Power*, ed. Arnoud-Jan A. Bijsterveld *et al.* (Turnhout, 1999), 142.

[96] Mayr-Harting, 'Functions of a Twelfth-Century Recluse', 344–5, 350.

once rebuked. Muriel, wife of Robert de Beauchamp, seems to have been particularly close, visiting him yearly and travelling from Kent to Somerset after his death to see his tomb. Even Henry I and Stephen visited him, and apparently Wulfric did not hesitate to urge Stephen to a better life on one occasion, mixing criticisms with pious exhortations; on another occasion he criticized Stephen's queen, Matilda, for snubbing the wife of his patron. Given Wulfric's humble English background, he was remarkably free about handing out criticism and advice to extremely powerful people, if the *vita* is to be believed.[97] Wulfric's life shows the way religious bonds could bridge the linked divisions of ethnicity and class that developed after the conquest.

Wulfric was not the only solitary to form bonds with powerful immigrants. Christina of Markyate developed an extraordinarily close and passionate relationship with Abbot Geoffrey of St Alban's. Her *vita*, which devoted considerable space to the relationship, described him as her beloved, and depicted a vision in which they embraced; not surprisingly, there were rumours that they were lovers in the physical as well as spiritual sense. More to the point, this powerful abbot, like many of Wulfric's contacts, paid careful attention to Christina's advice.[98] Like Wulfric, a hermit named Sigar is said to have received royal visits, and Godric of Finchale and other English hermits received royal or noble patronage.[99] All this suggests that although Wulfric may have been an unusually prominent and famous English hermit, he was not unique in creating links with immigrants, including quite powerful ones. There were many hermits scattered throughout England, about whom we know little, but if Wulfric, Christina, Sigar, and Godric were at all typical, English solitaries, like monks and nuns, helped greatly to tear down the social barriers between English and Normans.

As for secular clerics, the best evidence for interaction between English and Normans comes through a study of native clerical membership in important immigrant households. Prelates and nobles of Continental origin or descent tended to prefer other immigrants as chaplains and clerics, but a surprising number can be found who had natives in those positions. As early as 1085 Bishop Robert Lotharingus of Hereford had several clerics with English names in his following, though given the loose distinctions between episcopal household and chapter at that time, these may have been cathedral clergy as well.[100] In the middle of the twelfth century one of Archbishop Theobald's household clerics, Wulfric of Wrotham, had an English name, and later still Archbishop Hubert Walter relied heavily on the services of one *Magister* Edmund.[101] Clerics with English names can

[97] John of Ford, *Wulfric of Haselbury*, 18, 21, 25, 56–8, 63–5, 88–9, 94, 105, 108–9, 111–12, 115–18, 125, 131–2.
[98] Talbot, *The Life of Christina of Markyate*, 134–56, 160–70, 172–82, 192; *Gesta Abbatum*, 1: 72–3, 101–5, 127; Karras, 'Friendship and Love', 316–18.
[99] Walsingham, *Gesta Abbatum*, 1: 105; Reginald of Durham, *Vita Sancti Godrici*, 302, 317; Patterson, *Earldom of Gloucester Charters*, no. 170; Grosjean, 'Vitae S. Roberti Knaresburgensis', 393–4; Golding, 'The Hermit and the Hunter', 100–1; Warren, *Anchorites and their Patrons*, 140, 153.
[100] *EEA* 7, no. 2.
[101] Saltman, *Theobald, Archbishop of Canterbury*, 216, nos. 59, 61, 151, 161, 252; *EEA* 2: pp. xxiv–xxv; 3, nos. 348–50, 527, 530, 639–40, 606, 648.

also be found in the households of a dozen other bishops and of abbots of several wealthy monasteries.[102] Though it is harder to find clerics with English names in the households of secular magnates, they did exist from a surprisingly early period. In the very generation of the conquest, the Norman baron Hubert de Ryes, father of William I's steward Eudo, had an English notary and chaplain named Ailward, and in a document of 1106 a chaplain named Bricius, which may represent OE Beohrtsige, can be found among the followers of Count Eustace III of Boulogne.[103] In Henry I's reign Henry, earl of Warwick, had a *Magister* Siward as a chaplain, and in the middle of the twelfth century William son of Alan, a baron in the Welsh marches, had a priest named Hemming in his following.[104] When one factors in the likelihood that many more clerics of native ancestry with Continental names could probably be added to these lists in later periods, English clerics clearly played an important role in integrating the households of magnates, particularly ecclesiastical ones.

I have emphasized in earlier chapters the importance for ethnic interaction of native service in important households, and the same points hold true for clerics as for the laity. The households of prelates and magnates served as one route for upward mobility. Native household clerics can be found gaining churches and property through the gifts or support of their patrons, and two, *Magister* Steingrim and *Magister* Edmund, rose to the position of archdeacon through their service in the households of bishops.[105] Household service for clerks, as for other natives, must have been conducive to the formation of close relationships with immigrants. The most important household, of course, was the king's, and here we are fortunate enough to have more information about English clerics. After the native element found in William I's court at the beginning of his reign faded away, native clerics were of course rare in the royal household, but some clear examples can be found.[106]

[102] Royce, *Landboc sive Registrum de Winchelcumba*, 1: 212; BL MS Harley 3650. fols. 46ʳ⁻ᵛ, 48ʳ; Mary Cheney, *Roger, Bishop of Worcester, 1164–79* (Oxford, 1980), 104; *Becket Materials*, 3: 82; Morey and Brooke, *Letters and Charters of Gilbert Foliot*, 426, 433, n. 391; *EEA* 6: pp. xliv; 11, nos. 42, 49, 50, 98; Hull, *Cartulary of Launceston*, no. 71; Lees, *Records of the Templars*, Hampshire documents, no. 1, Cambridge documents, no. 1; BM Cotton Claudius D xiii, fols. 137ᵛ, 140ʳ; *EEA* 10: p. xl; 16: pp. xxxv–xxxvi; 20, no. 48; *Correspondence of Thomas Becket*, 1: 588; Wrottesley, 'Burton Chartulary', 16, 32, 39, 43; Jeayes, 'Charters and Muniments Belonging to the Marquis of Anglesey', nos. 7, 23–5, 27–8, 30; Douglas, *Feudal Documents*, nos. 108–9, 113–14, 120–3, 125; Rodney Thomson, 'Twelfth-Century Documents', no. 4; *Mon. Ang.*, 3: 346; Hart and Lyons, *Cartularium Monasterii de Rameseia*, 1, nos. 53, 54, 58, 72, 79; 2, nos. 370, 374; MacRay, *Chronicon Abbatiae Rameseiensis*, 260, 262–3; Mason, *Westminster Abbey Charters*, no. 258. See also Brett, *English Church Under Henry I*, 181. I have included people in the households of powerful men only if they are explicitly said to be among their chaplains or clerics, or if they attest an unusually large number of charters.
[103] Crouch, *Image of Aristocracy*, 292; Moore, *Cartularium de Colecestria*, 1: 3, 82–3; *EEA* 15, no. 10; *RRAN* 2, no. 749.
[104] *Mon. Ang.*, 6: 1326; Una Rees, ed., *The Cartulary of Shrewsbury Abbey*, 2 vols. (Aberystwyth, 1975), 1, no. 83; 2, nos. 308, 310; Rees, *Cartulary of Haughmond Abbey*, no. 583.
[105] *EEA* 6: pp. xli, xliv; 16: pp. xxxv–xxxvi; 15, no. 10; Moore, *Cartularium de Colecestria* 1: 3, 82–3; BL Add. MS 47677, fols. 240ᵛ–241ʳ; Lees, *Records of the Templars in England*, Hampshire documents, no. 1; Wrottesley, 'Burton Chartulary', 32, 43; Jeayes, 'Charters and Muniments Belonging to the Marquis of Anglesey', no. 7; Mason, *Westminster Abbey Charters*, no. 258.
[106] Orderic Vitalis does write that a former royal cleric of English birth, Ingulph, became abbot of Thorney late in William I's reign: *EHOV* 2: 344–6.

Henry I not only had Æðelwold, the future bishop of Carlisle, as a confessor, but also a scribe named Leving (OE Leofing), and two brothers, Bernard the Scribe and Nicholas, sons of Ailsi of Launceston and uncles of Peter of Cornwall, in his following. Leving remains little more than a name.[107] But for Bernard, and to a lesser extent his brother, we have unusually good sources.[108] A summary of charters for land and churches Bernard acquired in various parts of England and even in Normandy shows how service at the royal court allowed this upwardly mobile native of urban origin to accumulate a respectable amount of wealth, which is also reflected in the gifts he and his brother made to Launceston, including a banner worked with gold, a hanging, and an ivory box with silver-work.[109] They show how Bernard acquired powerful benefactors and patrons, including not only the king but also figures such as Bishop William of Winchester, Robert de Ferrers, and Hugh Laval. Finally, they show how he was able to move with apparent ease between settings dominated by natives, such as a local court in Cornwall, to those dominated by Normans, such as the royal court and the Norman exchequer. Peter, in his reminiscences, exaggerates the brothers' closeness to the king, but even so these natives had achieved a respectable position at the royal court, the heart of elite, immigrant-dominated society. Peter's anecdotes and other works also suggest that Bernard's and Nicholas's connections benefited their family as well. Peter's circle, judging by dedications and letters, included such notable figures of Continental background as Godfrey de Lucy, bishop of Winchester, Gilbert de Glanvill, bishop of Rochester, and Peter of Blois, archdeacon of Bath, and one suspects the contacts of his uncles started him out on the road to success.[110] More important, the family's marriage-tie to Earl Reginald, noted in the last chapter, surely owed something to the connections Bernard and Nicholas had gained at royal court.

An even more successful native cleric at Henry II's court was John of Oxford, the one certain native to obtain episcopal rank in England during the twelfth century.[111] The son of the native Angevin supporter Henry of Oxford, John served the king with what many considered excessive loyalty during the Becket controversy. In return he gained great favour from Henry, who described him in one letter as his 'familiar cleric' and appointed him to distribute alms for his soul in his will.[112] John, described in some documents as a *magister*, was something of an intellectual, a patron of learning, and a conscientious bishop.[113] But it was royal service, not piety, that made him a leading figure in English society, who could interact with Norman prelates and magnates on terms, more or less, of equality. No doubt his rise to a

---

[107] Leving may have been the Living son of Leured who was a canon at St Paul's, London: *RRAN* 2, no 1032; Green, *Government of England*, 175, n. 166; *Fasti*, 1: 77.

[108] For these sources, see J. H. Round, 'Bernard, the King's Scribe', *EHR* 14 (1899): 417–30, and Easting and Sharpe, 'Peter of Cornwall', 207–62. See also Southern, *Medieval Humanism*, 225–8.

[109] For the gifts, see Easting and Sharpe, 'Peter of Cornwall', 227–8.

[110] Ibid. 209–14.

[111] What follows draws heavily from Harper-Bill, 'John of Oxford, Diplomat and Bishop', 83–105.

[112] *Correspondence of Thomas Becket*, 2: 1338; *GCO* 8: 191–3.

[113] For his patronage of learning and intellectual curiosity, see Daniel of Morley, 'Philosophia', ed. Gregor Maurach, *Mittellateinisches Jahrbuch*, 14 (1979), 212, 227–8.

bishopric was a result of the degree to which relations between the two peoples had
already improved by Henry II's reign, but his career nonetheless serves as an illustration of how interaction through loyal service by English clerics, and patronage by
kings and others, corroded and slowly destroyed the ethnic and class boundaries
that divided English and Normans.

A final glimpse of English clerics at the royal court is provided by Walter Map, in
a story concerning Adam of Yarmouth (whose paternal uncle had the English name
Edward), another royal official, and Henry II. Adam was not a particularly prominent royal official, but he did serve as a justice in eyre and worked in the king's
writing office.[114] A dispute arose when Thurstan son of Simon, a dispenser, refused
to give him two royal cakes when he had requested them for a guest, after which
Adam refused to turn over a writ free of charge, as was customary for court officials.
The king was called in to adjudicate, sided with Adam, and settled the case by
having him sit down with the writ next to him, ordering Thurstan to serve Adam
with the cakes on bended knee, and only then having Adam hand over the writ.
Afterwards the king spoke of the need for royal officials to help each other. This is a
fairly inconsequential story, but the king's speech shows the way that household ties
were expected to build close bonds that could include natives. More important, the
story shows how well integrated into the royal court Adam already was, with his
ability to engage successfully in petty bureaucratic warfare and to win the king's
support.[115] It was in Henry II's reign that ethnic divisions fully collapsed, and
Walter Map's story of a cleric of native descent, comfortably ensconced at court,
provides a minor example of the kind of integration, even at the highest levels of
society, that helped bring that about.

What about the role of native secular clerics in integration beyond households
and the royal court? The sources provide several glimpses of such clerics working
and interacting with immigrants, forming friendships, and thereby helping to integrate the two peoples. Late in Henry I's reign the bishop of Worcester acted as a
pledge for a debt for a canon named Sabricht.[116] At Exeter a native canon named
Leowin gave generous gifts for the soul of the immigrant bishop Osbern.[117]
Interaction also came at the lower levels of the hierarchy of secular clergy, where
natives were much more common. The life of William of Norwich shows how
William's uncle by marriage, the priest Godwin, was able to get episcopal support
for accusations against the Jews in a local synod; in this case it is unfortunate that
the barrier between English and Norman was not greater.[118] A more important
example of interaction involving parish priests comes from very early, when the
wealthy immigrant cleric Odelarius had one English parish priest baptize his son
Orderic, and turned him over for five years to another for his early education.[119]

[114] West, *St. Benet of Holme*, 1, nos. 44, 219, 243; 2: 238; *Pipe Roll 5 Henry II*, 10; *Pipe Roll 19 Henry II*, 19, 127, 159.
[115] Walter Map, *De Nugis Curialium*, 486.
[116] *Pipe Roll 31 Henry I*, 78.
[117] *EEA* 11: 15.
[118] Thomas of Monmouth, *Life and Miracles of William of Norwich*, 43–9. See also *EEA* 15, no. 26.
[119] *EHOV* 3: 6–8; 6: 552.

English priests not only associated with immigrant clerics but also with lay-people, especially local patrons. A charter concerning the Augustinian house of Walsingham shows the immigrant landowner, Geoffrey de Favarches, helping his English cleric Edwy set up the house, and the cartulary of Dunmow shows the participation of the Baynards and of Bricti, a priest who became the first prior there, in the establishment of that house.[120] Another charter was issued by a Norman nobleman at the house of an English priest, suggesting at least limited social concourse.[121] Wulfric of Haselbury's story provides an example of quite close social intercourse. Wulfric had been a parish priest before becoming a solitary, and was first appointed to a church by his faithful patron, William son of Walter. Long before Wulfric became famous, and while he was still a simple priest, according to his *vita*, he had 'familiarly adhered to that venerable man, William, and together they often ate bread at his table'.[122] In later periods there was a common pattern of interaction, socializing, and friendship between well-to-do parish priests and local landholders. The above examples seem to fit into that same pattern, and relations between the more prosperous English priests and immigrant landholders may have played yet another role in drawing the two peoples together. Presumably any immigrant clerics who served among the parish clergy (instead of simply using deputies), had to interact with their native parishioners as well. Thus, interaction involving parish as well as higher levels of clergy probably played an important role in the integration of the two peoples.

This is true even when it came to intermarriage and sexual relations, for there is evidence of marriages and liaisons involving the relatives of English and Norman clerics, and ones involving clerics themselves.[123] In the first category I have already noted the liaison between Reginald de Vautortes and the daughter of Dunpriest, the marriage connection between Bernard the scribe's family and Earl Reginald of Cornwall, and the marriage of a minor *radman* to the niece of an archdeacon.[124] Several London examples may also be noted.[125] In addition, Nicholas of Meriet, grandson of Eadnoth the Staller and brother of Robert son of Harding, married a niece of one of Henry I's most important followers, Bishop Roger of Salisbury, thus creating a tie between one of the few aristocratic English families to survive the conquest and one of the great immigrant clerical dynasties of the twelfth century.[126] In the second category I have already noted Ranulf Flambard's affair with Alveva of Huntingdon, and also the arguments of Chibnall and Greenway that the fathers of Orderic Vitalis and Henry of Huntingdon, both immigrant clerics, had English wives or concubines.[127] A William the Clerk, whose father Edulf had an English

---

[120] *Mon. Ang.*, 6: 73; *EEA* 15, no. 6; BL Harley MS 662, fol. 6ʳ.
[121] BL Harley 3650, fol. 14ᵛ.
[122] John of Ford, *Wulfric of Haselbury*, 14.
[123] See also Williams, *ENC* 199.
[124] See above, pp. 156–7, 175, 196.
[125] Round, *Geoffrey de Mandeville*, 309–10; Gibbs, *Early Charters of the Cathedral Church of St. Paul*, nos. 143, 180, 315; *Ninth Report*, 63. In some cases, more than one charter must be read to uncover the marriage.
[126] Hall, *Red Book of the Exchequer*, 1: 211.
[127] See above, pp. 153, 155–6.

name, married a relative of John de Sancta Elena, a prominent Abingdon tenant in Henry II's reign.[128] There are also good grounds for thinking that Hugh, 'rural' dean of Derby early in the reign of Henry II, who had a brother with the Anglo-Scandinavian name of Aghemund, was married to a member of the Tuschet family.[129] Despite the best efforts of religious reformers to promote celibacy, clerics, as well as their relatives, made a significant contribution, through marriages and affairs, to the assimilation of the English and Normans. But marriages and affairs were only the most spectacular ways in which the religious on both sides of the ethnic divide helped to integrate the two peoples.

III

The strong presence of both immigrants and natives within the church, described in the first section, was also crucial to cultural assimilation and to the triumph of English identity. Many of the contributions of the religious will be discussed in later chapters, but here I want to discuss how and why they could be so important. Immigrant religious were in a strong position to bring important cultural and intellectual changes to England. Writers often credited prelates with the impetus for rebuilding churches, and given the near monopoly of immigrants on the highest positions in the church, the dramatic shift in architectural styles after the conquest is hardly surprising.[130] More generally, as wealthy patrons they could bring their artistic taste and sometimes their artists with them. The use of French as a language in the cloister, documented by Dominica Legge, resulted from clerical immigration and the entry of aristocratic offspring into religious houses.[131] Most important, some of the great thinkers of the period, notably Lanfranc and Anselm, came to England because of the conquest. The conquest also brought many lesser writers, and scribes, who served as the footsoldiers of literate activity, and this placed the conquerors in an excellent position to reshape the intellectual landscape of England.[132] The conquest brought cultural change to many sectors of English society, but the church was one of the most important portals for Continental influence.

Nonetheless, the fact that many English religious survived, not just in the first generation after the conquest but in later years too, prevented anything like a clean sweep of English culture from the church. Many of the native religious had important cultural skills to offer their new overlords. The monk Blackman whom Bishop

---

[128] van Caenegem, *English Lawsuits*, 2: 608.

[129] Darlington, *Cartulary of Darley Abbey*, 1: pp. xxxv–xl.

[130] For some examples of building attributed to abbots or bishops, see *The Chronicle of Hugh Candidus a Monk of Peterborough*, ed. W. T. Mellows (London, 1949), 90; MacRay, *Chronicon Abbatiae de Evesham*, 55, 97–9; WMGP 69–70, 195–6; EHOV 2: 348, 6: 152; Stubbs, *Memorials of Saint Dunstan*, 142. For an overview of the changes in architecture, see below, pp. 369–70.

[131] M. Dominica Legge, *Anglo-Norman in the Cloisters: The Influence of the Orders Upon Anglo-Norman Literature* (Edinburgh, 1950), 1–136.

[132] For this reshaping, see below, p. 368.

Walkelin brought into his personal service was a goldsmith, as well as a forger of documents, and both skills no doubt made him useful.[133] According to William of Malmesbury, Anselm's friend Osbeorn was the foremost musician of his time.[134] Occasionally native religious even had a role in architecture, such as two sacrists of Bury St Edmund's, Toli, and Elias nephew of Abbot Ording.[135] Ordinary English priests, monks, and nuns could serve as artists, illuminators, and craftsmen and craftswomen, and could thus preserve aspects of traditional culture.

Most important, because it profoundly influenced identity as well as culture, was the role of native survival in the intellectual milieu, and in the culture of writing generally. Native English figures continued to be active as writers long after the conquest. The most significant of these writers for our purposes were a group of English or part English monks and clerics concerned with preserving English traditions and history.[136] In addition there were noteworthy native writers who were less concerned with English traditions per se, including Anselm's student Elmer, and Godwin, precentor of Salisbury Cathedral, author of a work arguing that the monastic life was not the only true Christian life.[137] Late in the twelfth or early in the thirteenth century an Augustinian canon called Orm wrote the *Ormulum*, a large collection of religious material and one of the earliest works in Middle English, and a parish priest who called himself Laȝamon (or Lawman), and whose father, according to one manuscript, was named Leovenað (a version of OE Leofnoth), translated into early Middle English Wace's French translation of Geoffrey of Monmouth.[138] Figures such as Elmer, Godwin, Orm, and Lawman, though open to Continental influence, probably did preserve some English traditions; certainly the last two were important for the English language. More generally, natives clearly remained active as writers, with obvious implications both for culture and identity.

Beyond these notable writers, one can also point to other figures with influence in the culture of writing and in the intellectual life of the period. I have already noted a number of cantors or precentors who were English. They were ideally expected to be learned men like Osbeorn and Eadmer, and two otherwise obscure natives holding that position appear in charters conveying land or income to their office for the express purpose of funding the copying of books.[139] There are also a number of references to *secretarii* and scribes with English names.[140] The importance, respect,

---

[133] Goodman, *Chartulary of Winchester Cathedral*, no. 41.

[134] *WMGR* 240, 592.

[135] Arnold, *Memorials of St. Edmund's Abbey*, 2: 289–90.

[136] See below, pp. 241–60.

[137] Southern, *Saint Anselm and His Biographer*, 202–3, 271–3; Teresa Webber, *Scribes and Scholars at Salisbury Cathedral, c. 1075–c. 1125* (Oxford, 1992), 123–9.

[138] Orm, *The Ormulum*, ed. Robert Holt (Oxford, 1878; repr., New York, 1974); Lawman, *Laȝamon: Brut*, ed. G. L. Brook and R. F. Leslie, vol. 1 (London, 1963–78), 2.

[139] For cantors, see above, n. 31. For praise of Osbeorn and Eadmer as writers, see *WMGR* 14, 240, 560, 572; *EHOV* 5: 206, 6: 168. For the charters noted above, see *EEA* 8, no. 17; BL Add MS 9822, fol. 61ᵛ.

[140] For *secretarii*, see 'Edmeri Cantuariensis Cantoris Nova Opuscula', 369; Richard of Hexham, 'History of the Church of Hexham', in *The Priory of Hexham*, ed. James Raine, vol. 1 (Durham, 1864), 55; *Chronicle of Hugh Candidus*, 83, 91; Delisle, *Rouleaux des Morts*, 339; Urry, *Canterbury under the Angevin Kings*, 223, 233, no. 8; Searle, *Lordship and Community*, 74–5; CUL, Peterborough D&C MS 1, fols. 130ʳ,

and cultural influence that such figures could command should not be under-estimated. Perhaps the most striking tribute to a native cleric or monk of this period is the famous portrait of Eadwine the scribe in the Eadwine psalter. Eadwine, who has been identified with the Eadwine who was a *secretarius* at Christ Church, Canterbury, is depicted in a magnificent full-page illustration, with an inscription around the border declaring, in the first person, that he was the 'scriptorum princeps', noting his genius, and stating that his fame would never die. This portrait and inscription may represent a remarkable piece of effrontery on Eadwine's part, though if so the fact that he got away with it indicates a high status at Canterbury. More likely, despite the first person of the inscription, this is a tribute to an impor-tant, though to us obscure, native intellectual by his contemporaries.[141] In addition, there were the numerous natives among the *magistri* who, as I noted, formed an intellectual elite. Finally, there were at least some moderately learned parish priests. Besides Lawman, one can point to a Yorkshire priest with the native name of Sigar, who recorded a vision by a local youth and sent it to the historian Simeon of Durham.[142] The list of possessions of the London priest Edward included four liturgical books, and the hermit Benedict of Farne, who had been a parish priest, was described reading and writing, among other activities.[143]

The demise of Old English can give the misleading impression of a rapid decline of intellectual life among native English. In fact, there continued to be a surprising amount of material written or copied in Old English and, as the examples of Orm and Lawman indicate, native religious also contributed to the later rise of written Middle English, once the old form of the language fell out of usage.[144] Much more was written and read in Latin by natives. When one looks not just at surviving authors, but at all those involved in reading and writing, the number of native par-ticipants in the intellectual culture of post-conquest England, and therefore their potential to influence that culture, was quite large. All of these figures could help to preserve English intellectual and religious traditions.

131[r-v]. For scribes, see BL Harley MS 2110, fol. 40[r]; Hodgett, *Cartulary of Holy Trinity Aldgate*, no. 967; *Ninth Report*, 63, 67–8; *Book of Fees*, 1: 111.

[141] There is much controversy about Eadwine's identity but it seems most likely that he was a con-temporary who was involved in the creation of the work. The fullest recent discussion of the work and Eadwine is in Margaret Gibson, T. A. Heslop, and Richard W. Pfaff, eds., *The Eadwine Psalter: Text, Image, and Monastic Culture in Twelfth-Century Canterbury* (London, 1992), esp. 85–7, 178–85. Pfaff's suggestion, included in that work (pp. 85–7), that Eadwine may refer to the pre-conquest scribe Eadui Basan would of course put the respect for Eadwine in a different light, though it would still demonstrate continuing respect for the work of native scribes. Interestingly, another scribal or authorial portrait may have been of Anselm's friend Osbeorn: Mildred Budny and Timothy Graham, 'Dunstan As Hagiographical Subject or Osbern as Author? The Scribal Portrait in an Early Copy of Osbern's *Vita Sancti Dunstani*', *Gesta*, 32 (1993), 83–96.

[142] Hugh Farmer, ed., 'The Vision of Orm', *Analecta Bollandiana*, 75 (1957), 76.

[143] *Ninth Report*, 64; Geoffrey of Coldingham, 'Vita Bartholomaei Farnensis', 301.

[144] N. R. Ker, *Catalogue of Manuscripts Containing Anglo-Saxon* (Oxford, 1957), pp. xviii–xix, xlviii; R. M. Wilson, *Early Middle English Literature*, 3rd edn. (London, 1968), 17–18, 94–102, 106–15; Derek Pearsall, *Old English and Middle English Poetry* (London, 1977), 75–6; Christine Franzen, *The Tremulous Hand of Worcester: A Study of Old English in the Thirteenth Century* (Oxford, 1991), 103–10; Pelteret, *Catalogue of English Documents*, 1–122; Richard Gameson, *The Manuscripts of Norman England (c. 1066–1130)* (Oxford, 1999), 25.

The church thus served as a vehicle both for the introduction of Continental culture and also for the survival of English traditions, but most of all it provided a key setting for cultural assimilation. The same common goals and discipline that made monasteries, nunneries, cathedrals, and the institutional church in general an important site for the development of relationships across ethnic lines also made it useful to cultural assimilation. The evidence of scribal hands suggests that English and Norman scribes worked side by side, sometimes co-operating on the same manuscript, to produce new books for monastic or cathedral libraries.[145] The kind of working relationships and friendships described in the previous section, some of which were formed around intellectual as well as religious interests, would only make fruitful cultural interchange more likely. Writers like Elmer, who elaborated on the ideas Anselm brought to England, Henry of Huntingdon and William of Malmesbury, who translated information from the Anglo-Saxon Chronicle into Latin, and the immigrant cleric Gaimar, who did the same into French, served as crucial figures in cultural and intellectual fusion.

Turning to the question of identity, the survival of many English monks, nuns, and clerics, and the continuing native intellectual activity, provides a crucial context for understanding the eventual triumph of Englishness. Only a limited number of writers whose works survive can be shown preserving English traditions, and an even smaller number were defending English pride and honour, but the survival of many native religious helps explain the milieu in which the writers were working and also has a number of implications for their endeavours. A first, straightforward point is that there remained sufficient monks and clerics with skills in the formal and increasingly archaic written form of Old English in the generation or two after the conquest to translate the sources into Latin and to train such important writers as William of Malmesbury and Henry of Huntingdon in the language. This did not prevent Old English from declining, but allowed English culture to survive in a Latin or even French medium, which was very important to the survival and triumph of English identity.

Equally important, writers preserving English tradition and defending English honour would not have been working in an isolated setting, overwhelmingly dominated by foreigners, but could have drawn support from ethnically English fellows. A closely related point is that they had a large potential audience of readers and listeners whose own ethnic background would have made them sympathetic, whatever the reactions of immigrants. Not much can be learned about specific readers of individual works in the eleventh and twelfth centuries, but at least one receptive reader can be found. A late twelfth-century copy of Henry of Huntingdon, who was one of the most successful preservers and translators of English history, contains an insertion by a chaplain with the English name of Edmund, who was 64 in 1197, and whose lifetime therefore spanned the period when assimilation became more or less complete. Edmund also copied a series of insertions drawn from Aelred of Rievaulx, describing the history of Edmund Ironside and his descendants,

[145] Anne Lawrence, 'Manuscripts of Early Anglo-Norman Canterbury', in *Medieval Art and Architecture at Canterbury Before 1220* (Leeds, 1982), 102–5; Gameson, *Manuscripts of Norman England*, 8.

and tracing both King Stephen's family and the Angevin royal house to that line through the marriages of Edith-Matilda to Henry I, and of Edith-Matilda's sister Mary to the count of Boulogne. With Edmund we may well have one native cleric who read and copied with a distinctively English point of view, and he was probably not alone.[146]

In addition, those few English monks and clerics who attained high position could act as patrons of works designed to preserve knowledge of the English past and to promote (sometimes fictitious) English traditions. Wulfstan of Worcester instigated the work that eventually resulted in the chronicle of John of Worcester, and appointed the monk Hemming to gather and copy diocesan records.[147] Geoffrey of Wells dedicated his largely spurious account of St Edmund's childhood to Abbot Ording of Bury St Edmund's and spoke of Prior Sihtric's encouragement.[148] Aelred of Rievaulx not only wrote himself but also urged others to do so; in particular he persuaded Reginald of Durham to collect miracles of the great English saint Cuthbert and to write the *vita* of the hermit Godric.[149] Immigrant prelates could also be concerned with preserving the past, but natives were more likely to show such interests.

Aelred of Rievaulx also served as one of Reginald of Durham's sources, which raises the point that the native religious could serve as oral sources of English traditions.[150] Elisabeth van Houts has recently reasserted the importance of oral history in medieval society, and the survival of many English religious helped to keep English tradition alive through that medium.[151] Obviously we only see this through writing today, but in the twelfth century oral traditions would have been crucial in their own right. Among the lineages of hereditary priests, family memory probably played an important role here. Aelred of Rievaulx could trace his family history from before the conquest, and with it the events that affected them directly or indirectly, such as the harrying of the region after Bishop Walcher's murder, or the replacement of clerics at Durham by monks. Aelred could also recount the great interest of some of his ancestors in English saints and particularly their involvement in the cult of Cuthbert. Aelred lays no particular emphasis on his family's Englishness, but it is likely that he gained his own sense of Englishness and his interest in English history, which he tried to pass on to Henry II in the *Genealogia Regum*, at the knees of his older relatives.[152] Older monks, nuns, and clerics in religious houses

[146] HHHA, pp. cxxxii–cxxxiii. For these passages, see the old Rolls Series edition of Henry's work (*The History of the English*, ed. Thomas Arnold), 295–7.

[147] EHOV 2: 186–8; Hemming, *Chartularium Ecclesiae Wigorniensis*, 282, 391.

[148] 'Geoffrey of Wells, De Infantia Sancti Edmundi', ed. R. M. Thomson, *Analecta Bollandiana*, 95 (1977), 34. Similarly, Orderic Vitalis wrote that he had included a history of St Guthlac in his work partly at the urging of Prior Vulfuin of Crowland: *EHOV* 2: 322.

[149] Reginald of Durham, *Libellus Beati Cuthberti*, 1, 4; *Vita Sancti Godrici*, 19, 269.

[150] Reginald of Durham, *Libellus Beati Cuthberti*, 4; *Vita Sancti Godrici*, 173, 176.

[151] Van Houts *Memory and Gender*.

[152] Aelred of Rievaulx, 'De Sanctis Ecclesiae Haugustaldensis et eorum Miraculis Libellus', in *The Priory of Hexham*, ed. James Raine, vol. 1 (Durham, 1864), 190–3; Reginald of Durham, *Libellus Beati Cuthberti*, 57–60. See also Richard of Hexham, 'History of the Church of Hexham', 49–50, 54–6. For modern accounts of Aelred's family, see Walter Daniel, *Life of Ailred of Rievaulx*, pp. xxxiv–vi; Hedley, *Northumberland Families*, 1: 12–14.

were also important oral sources. Reference to such sources are most common in the late eleventh century, but even in the late twelfth century the Waltham Chronicler, working between 1177 and 1189, called on information he had gained in his youth from a cleric who had been alive in 1066.[153] Some of the oral tradition that was recorded in the twelfth century was of dubious quality, but we have come to learn that 'invented traditions' can sometimes be as important as 'real' ones, particularly when it comes to questions of identity. Obviously laypeople as well as monks, nuns, and clerics, preserved oral traditions, but the latter were particularly important because of their prestige within medieval culture and because their memories were far more likely to eventually be preserved in writing.

Native religious who were teachers could play a particularly important role in the transmission of traditions and even identity, which also has implications for cultural assimilation. Record survives of several English clerics who worked as teachers in cathedrals, towns, and villages.[154] Little is known about teaching in this period, but Barlow suggests that parish clergy handled much of it, and if so, it was often done by natives.[155] Obviously, the main subjects of teaching would be basic skills of reading and writing, or religious in nature, but it is likely that teachers might in the process teach about the English saints and other aspects of English culture, and in doing so pass on some of their views. Orderic Vitalis's staunch Englishness may have stemmed partly, as Chibnall has suggested, from the fact that he studied from the age of 5 to 10 under the English priest Siward. Siward taught him psalms, hymns, how to read, and probably how to write, since Orderic later was able to copy Old English letters such as ð with ease. While Siward was teaching Orderic English letters, he may also have been consciously or unconsciously imparting the English perspective that later showed up in Orderic's historical works.[156]

A final important factor is that the interaction between English and immigrant clergy placed the former in a good position to influence Norman views about English culture or about specific points related to that culture. Siward's tutelage of the at least partly immigrant Orderic Vitalis is a case in point. Another likely example comes with Lanfranc's and Anselm's discussion of whether Archbishop Alfeah should be honored as a saint, which Eadmer put in the context of changes Lanfranc made 'in England' and of the new archbishop's doubts about certain saints established by 'the English', thus showing that Eadmer at least was thinking about the issue in ethnic terms.[157] As Lanfranc put the case, according to Eadmer, Alfeah had been a good man, but since he had died because he refused to pay off the Danes, rather than for religious reasons, he could not be considered a martyr. I have

[153] Watkiss and Chibnall, *Waltham Chronicle*, pp. xxxiii, 44. It is worth noting the number of natives, many of them religious, whom the immigrant writer, Symeon of Durham, was able to call upon in composing the history of his church: *LDE*, p. lxxvi.

[154] *VW*, 57; Kealey, *Roger of Salisbury*, 92; *Epistolae Herberti de Losinga*, 73; Herman, 'De Miraculis', 81.

[155] Barlow, *English Church, 1066–1154*, 226–8.

[156] *EHOV* 1: 4–5; 3: 6–8; 6: 552; Chibnall, *World of Orderic Vitalis*, 10–11.

[157] Eadmer, *Life of St Anselm*, 50–4. See Jay Rubinstein, 'Liturgy Against History: The Competing Visions of Lanfranc and Eadmer of Canterbury', *Speculum*, 74 (1999), 298–307, for Eadmer's reaction to Lanfranc's doubts.

noted earlier that Lanfranc may have had political reasons for worrying about the cult, and Eadmer argued that the reasons for Alfeah's death were more complex. Nevertheless, given the facts as he stated them, Lanfranc's case for doubt about Alfeah's status as a martyr was perfectly legitimate. Anselm, however, did not accept Lanfranc's argument, but instead made an ingenious reply that Alfeah gave his life for justice and therefore for truth, and could therefore be considered a martyr like John the Baptist. Southern has shown how this argument fitted neatly into Anselm's and Lanfranc's intellectual framework, but it is nonetheless hard to avoid the feeling that Anselm was engaged in special pleading.[158] An unstated but clear backdrop to this conversation must have been that 'the English', and particularly the English monks of the cathedral monastery, would have objected strongly to the elimination of Alfeah's cult; indeed, if Lanfranc openly bruited the possibility, he and Anselm may already have been the subject of lobbying. There is no reason to doubt that Anselm's argument was a genuine one, but one may ask whether he would have bothered to consider the issue had he not already formed close bonds with English monks such as Osbeorn, who subsequently wrote Alfeah's *vita*. Would Lanfranc have accepted Anselm's arguments, possibly against his better political as well as religious judgement, had he not established a relationship of mutual respect with English monks? It is impossible to know, but it certainly seems likely that the relationships discussed earlier between individual English monks and these two Continental intellectuals and archbishops helped to ensure the survival of that piece of English history and culture represented by the cult of Alfeah.

I hope to have set the stage here for my argument that if any group in post-conquest England can be described as the *Traditionskern* for English identity, it was the clergy. Native clergy, and particularly the intellectuals among them, through both the spoken and the written word, could preserve, maintain, and propagate English culture and identity without posing the sort of practical military and political threat to Norman power that aristocratic promoters of Englishness might have done. Integration within the church allowed them to influence their immigrant peers and superiors in matters of culture and identity. This contributed greatly to cultural fusion, as I suggested, but it contributed even more to the survival and triumph of English identity.

However, the large influx of immigrants into the English church, and their near monopoly of its most important positions in the generations following the conquest, raise important questions about the role even of the clergy in the eventual dominance of English identity. In theory, immigrant control of the English church could have made it a vehicle for Normanization, and Norman intellectuals could have helped the 'Norman myth' to triumph over English identity. We have seen that surviving English aristocratic families sometimes adopted a false Norman identity, at least insofar as ancestry went. Why did more monks, nuns, and clerics, particularly partly immigrant ones such as William of Malmesbury, not end up firmly identifying themselves with the socially and politically dominant ethnic group

---

[158] Southern, *Saint Anselm: A Portrait in a Landscape*, 42, 316–17.

rather than the conquered majority? The integration of the church could allow influence in matters of identity to flow both ways. After all, one of the key writers in the development of the Norman myth was Orderic Vitalis, despite his strong identity as English. Some of the best examples of the expression of Norman identity in England come from speeches placed before the battle of the Standard by Aelred of Rievaulx and Henry of Huntingdon, the former of whom was certainly of native ancestry, and both of whom considered themselves English. Why, despite the influence of the construct of *Normanitas* on these writers, did the tide of influence in matters of ethnic identity flow so strongly in the other direction? The native clergy were crucial to the survival and triumph of English identity, more so than any other group, but their importance only raises more questions about the interrelationships between ancestry, power, influence, and identity in England after the Norman Conquest.

Epilogue to Part II

A DISCUSSION OF the interaction of natives and immigrants goes far to explain assimilation, but raises as many questions as it answers about the triumph of English identity. Questions of ancestry can generally go only so far in explaining ethnic identity. The very process of assimilation complicates the effects of ancestry on identity. What determined whether the child of mixed parentage picked an English or Norman identity? After a few generations of mixing, one might argue that whichever 'blood' predominated would determine the identity, but that is clearly a vast oversimplification of what actually happened. By Henry II's reign many aristocratic Norman patrilineages must have absorbed some English ancestry through intermarriage, but it is hard to believe that they had been so fully absorbed into English lineages that a separate, Norman identity simply became untenable, especially since ancestry *as remembered* is what counts, and they saw themselves as being basically Norman by descent. More important, ethnicity could be dis-associated from ancestry throughout the period. For instance, Lanfranc and Reginald of Canterbury, who had no English ancestry, could describe themselves as English on some level quite soon after the conquest.[1]

There were, in fact, limits to the extent to which medieval thinkers connected descent and identity. We have seen that they did sometimes make the link. They could even think in quasi-biological or quasi-racial terms, as when writers linked the characteristics of an individual to ethnic ancestry.[2] But just as with thinking about assimilation, we are in the realm of casual assumptions and ideas, where there was no interest in developing consistent theory and where little distinction was made between cultural and genetic inheritance. The kind of thinking found in medieval sources may be contrasted with the body of 'scientific' racist theory, which sought systematically to define peoples as narrowly as possible along the lines of biological descent, and to describe biological inheritance as an overwhelming cause of cultural difference, with 'superior' cultures linked to 'superior' races. For medi-eval people, descent was only one factor to be considered when they thought about ethnicity and culture.

Indeed, in the few discussions of distinctions between peoples written in the period after the conquest, ancestry was rarely noted as a factor. This is probably

---

[1] *Letters of Lanfranc*, 36–8, 156; Liebermann, 'Raginald von Canterbury', 551.

[2] *WMGR*, 798; *GCO* 1: 360–1; 4: 161. See also R. R. Davies, 'The Peoples of Britain and Ireland 1100–1400: I. Identities', *TRHS* 6th ser., 4 (1994), 6–7, and Lydon, 'Nation and Race', 106.

because descent was simply taken for granted as a conduit by which ethnicity was passed on, but it is still noteworthy that it did not form the centrepiece of conscious commentary on ethnicity.[3] When Goscelin of Saint-Bertin wrote of an English daughter coming from a Danish father and a Lotharingian mother, he was pretty clearly implying that in the normal course of events children would take on the ethnicity of their parents, but there is nothing in the passage to indicate that there was anything especially bizarre or unnatural in the girl's ethnic shift. Some of the qualifications to Lanfranc's Englishness may have stemmed from the fact that he was not of English parentage, and references to 'innate' or 'natural' English probably had to do with ancestry, but again, none of the writers seems to have been unduly disturbed by the existence of people who were English in some other manner than birth.[4] On a common-sense level, medieval writers accepted what almost all modern scholars now believe, namely that there was more to ethnicity than ancestry. Indeed, my feeling (and it can be described only as a feeling) is that despite the widespread and generally heartfelt rejection of racist theory, modern people as a result of it are conditioned to link ethnicity and descent more closely than medieval people did. Whether or not this is true, the links between the two were loose enough in post-conquest thought to make ancestry only one factor in how people thought about their own identity and the identities of others. As a result, intermarriage and assimilation alone cannot explain the triumph of English identity.

[3] *GCO* 1: 113; 3: 122–3, 230, 244; David, *De Expugnatione Lyxbonensi*, 52; *Historical Works of Ralph de Diceto* 2: 17.
[4] See above, p. 75.

PART III

The Reconstruction of English Identity

14

The Defence of English Honour

IN AN ARTICLE published in 1973 R. W. Southern argued that a key inspiration for the burst of historical writing in England in the aftermath of the conquest was the desire to cope with the changes brought by it and to preserve as much as possible of the pre-conquest past. This is by now a well-established point in the historiography.[1] Here, I wish to go further and argue that much history, as well as other writing, was animated by a desire to protect English pride and honour against the accusations, negative stereotypes, and casual scorn of the Normans. To some degree I am modelling this argument on John Gillingham's contention that one of Geoffrey of Monmouth's main objectives in his *Historia Regum Britanniae* was 'to secure cultural respectability for his own nation'.[2] In my view, many writers who identified with the English had a similar objective as one purpose of their works.

William of Malmesbury wrote around 1125 that there were vociferous disputes between the English and the Normans about the characters and actions of key figures in the conquest such as William the Conqueror, Harold, and Earl Waltheof; clearly the conquest was still a topic for heated debate over a half-century after it occurred.[3] I would argue that these disputes about individuals spilled over into a broader debate about the two peoples. I should stress here that I am not talking about any sort of formal debate; indeed, the Norman side of the debate was fairly casual. After the conquest, pro-Norman writers sought to justify William the Conqueror's actions, and they sometimes did so by slighting the character not only of Harold but also of the English as a whole. Such writers also sometimes simply denigrated the losers, as victors often will, or let loose demeaning assumptions and stereotypes about the English in an offhand way. However, the Normans, pragmatic rather than ideological in their prejudices, and secure in their power and superiority, felt no need to systematically heap scorn on the English. To the English the whole debate was rather more important, as much because of circumstances as because of the mild biases of the Normans. For a conquered people who continued to face prejudice into the twelfth century, even casual insults and stereotypes could be humiliating, and it should be no surprise that many native English and part-English writers strongly defended the honour of their ethnic group and

---

[1] R. W. Southern, 'Aspects of the European Tradition of Historical Writing. 4. The Sense of the Past', *TRHS*, 5th ser. 23 (1973), 245–56. See also id., *Medieval Humanism*, 160–2.

[2] Gillingham, *English in the Twelfth Century*, 19–39.

[3] *WMGR* 354, 424, 468–70; *WMGP* 322.

counter-attacked against the Normans. Not every English writer engaged in this loose debate about the Normans and English, and not all of those who did treated it as a priority in their works, but participation among writers whose works have survived was nonetheless widespread. At the core of this debate was history, and not only the history of the conquest and the post-conquest period. Gabrielle Spiegel, in her book *Romancing the Past*, has shown how even histories of antiquity could be transformed in translation to address issues of concern for thirteenth-century patrons, and similarly eleventh- and twelfth-century historians reached back deep into the past, particularly the English past, to discuss the issues of their own day.[4]

The debate over Norman and English character was crucial for the eventual triumph of English identity. With the occasional exception, people will adopt a new ethnic identity voluntarily only if that identity is an honourable and respectable one. Rarely do people choose to belong to a low-status group, and thus any movement across ethnic lines tends to go toward the more prestigious group. But after the conquest the defeated English could face abuse from triumphalist Normans. I have already noted that Henry I's enemies could insult him and his wife simply by calling them Godric and Godgiva, and that Henry of Huntingdon wrote that the Normans had reduced the English to such a state that it was shameful to be called English. Henry also spoke of them losing their honour.[5] On a more personal note, Orderic Vitalis identified himself in one passage, albeit ironically, as a barbarous and ignorant English foreigner in Normandy.[6] An English monk, Alexander, who accompanied Archbishop Anselm into exile and kept a careful guard over him, replied to Anselm's request for privacy on one occasion by saying that if anything bad happened to the archbishop, people would say it was because 'you had worthless English servants'.[7] Clearly, to be English was to face the possibility of scorn. Yet eventually the descendants of those who scorned the English would embrace English identity for themselves. This came about only because pro-English writers and others successfully defended English pride, respectability, and honour, and deflated any claims of Norman superiority.

Before turning to the debate itself, it is important to note several factors that complicated and blurred the debate, preventing any simple demarcation between pro-English and pro-Norman propaganda. First, some key writers, notably William of Malmesbury, Orderic Vitalis, and Henry of Huntingdon, had divided allegiances. All identified themselves as English on some level, and in their works showed a strong attachment to the country, but all had Continental ancestors, and Orderic from the age of 10 lived in Normandy. Their divided allegiance meant that their judgements of the two peoples could be quite complex and nuanced, or sometimes simply confused. This can best be seen in the case of William of Malmesbury, who faulted both English and Normans for their biased discussions of William the

---

[4] Gabrielle M. Spiegel, *Romancing the Past: The Rise of Vernacular Prose Historiography in Thirteenth-Century France* (Berkeley, 1993).

[5] *WMGR* 716; *HHHA* 338–40, 402.

[6] *EHOV* 3: 6.

[7] Southern and Schmitt, *Memorials of St. Anselm*, 245.

Conqueror, and wrote that he would take a middle road in discussing the king.[8] Still other factors, I think, affected William's judgements: acceptance of some Norman stereotypes, a defensiveness about his English sympathies which led him to over-compensate by harshly criticizing English shortcomings, and a tendency to judge pre-conquest England by twelfth-century standards.[9] As a result, William would end up on both sides of the debate, sometimes contradicting himself. In many ways, William and the others can be described as both pro-English and pro-Norman, given their concern for both peoples.

Another factor, as I suggested with William of Malmesbury, is the tendency for conquered peoples to internalize the accusations and negative stereotypes of their conquerors.[10] Yet another was the political constraints faced by pro-English writers in England. Ælnoth of Canterbury, safe in exile in Denmark, could freely eulogize an enemy of the Norman regime, but writers in England undoubtedly had to be cautious about challenging the legitimacy of the new dynasty, though they could be surprisingly free in their criticisms of the Normans in general. Yet another constraint was the commitment to truth practiced by the best historians, then as now. Modern historians are often, and rightly, urged not to presume that medieval historians had the same values as we do. But William of Malmesbury's discussion about the historical treatment of William the Conqueror is a reminder that medieval people had at least a common-sense notion of objective truth similar to that held by modern, though perhaps not post-modern, historians.[11] No historian, then or now, ever fully lived up to the ideal of being completely objective, and some of William's contemporaries showed very little concern indeed for it, but for those writers who did take it seriously, the facts, as they understood them, could some-times counteract their desire to defend or promote their own people.[12]

A final factor stems from one way in which medieval historians did differ from modern ones, namely their strong belief, discussed earlier, in God's role in history. History could be used not only to judge causes, but also people or peoples. For instance, Henry of Huntingdon organized his whole history around the theme of successive peoples coming to Britain, earning God's wrath, and being crushed.[13] This made even pro-English writers susceptible to arguments that not only Harold Godwineson and his family but also the entire English nation must have done *something* wrong to deserve such severe divine punishment. Coupled with this was a tradition, also inherited from the Bible, and well established within the insular

---

[8] WMGR 424.

[9] For something very like an idea of progress held by William, See John Gillingham, 'Civilizing the English? The English Histories of William of Malmesbury and David Hume', *Historical Research*, 74 (2001), 17–43.

[10] For the psychological difficulties of a colonized people dealing with conquerors who look down on them, see Ashis Nandy, *The Intimate Enemy: Loss and Recovery of Self Under Colonialism* (New Delhi, 1983).

[11] See also *EHOV* 2: 188

[12] See James Campbell, 'Some Twelfth-Century Views of the Anglo-Saxon Past', *Peritia*, 3 (1984), 131–50, repr. in *Essays in Anglo-Saxon History* (London, 1986), 209–28, for the varying quality and com-mitment to accuracy of twelfth-century English historians.

[13] HHHA 4, 14.

tradition of historiography by writers such as Gildas and Archbishop Wulfstan of York, that the historian's job was to warn his or her people about the consequences of God's anger, and to berate them for their sins. Thus, pro-English historians were not necessarily less inclined to chastise the English than pro-Norman ones, though for different reasons.

The debate over English character by writers after the conquest encompassed several subjects. The first of these concerned loyalty and treachery. Accusations of disloyalty were common in the Middle Ages but took on special significance here because of the circumstances of the conquest. Pro-Norman historians obviously depicted those who opposed William I as traitors; this followed automatically from their claim that William was the legitimate heir and later legitimate king, and from their desire to justify Norman actions. Harold was the chief target, but since he had so much support, and since resistance continued long after he was dead, Norman animus sometimes spread to the whole English people or large sections of it. William of Poitiers wrote that at Hastings William 'cast down the enemy people who, rebelling against him, their king, deserved death'. The *Carmen de Hastingae Proelio* condemns that 'wicked people' (*improba gens*) which gathered in London after Hastings to resist the king, while Hugh the Chanter, in his history of the church of York, probably composed in the 1120s, wrote that the French were forced to ravage the region around York because the city and area around it remained 'unfaithful, hostile, and wickedly and violently pernicious'.[14]

The image in Norman historiography of the English as treacherous extended beyond the conquest itself, and indeed had earlier roots. Among the adventures Dudo provided Rollo in his chronicle was an expedition in support of an English king against rebels, during which Dudo refers casually to the 'perfidious English'.[15] Dudo, of course, was writing before relations between the Normans and English became an important issue, but his work continued to be influential, and as late as the 1170s or 1180s Benoît, in translating Norman history into the vernacular, could have the king in this episode, and his representative to Rollo, describe the 'Engleis' as being variously treacherous, perjured, and false.[16] Earlier, William of Jumièges had described King Æthelræd's massacre of the Danes in 1002 as a 'nefarious crime of treachery', and, unlike the pre-conquest English sources, which noted the slaughter rather matter-of-factly, treated it as an atrocity story. The translators Benoît and Wace, working in the reign of Henry II, both included the incident, and the former depicted King William as referring to it in his speech to his troops before Hastings.[17] Most important to the Norman picture was Earl Godwine's betrayal of Edward the Confessor's brother Alfred and his Norman followers, when Alfred

---

[14] *GGWP* 130 (see also 68, 142, 156, 182); Guy of Amiens, *Carmen*, 38; Hugh the Chanter, *The History of the Church of York, 1066–1127*, ed. Charles Johnson, rev. M. Brett, C. N. L. Brooke, and M. Winterbottom (Oxford, 1990), 2 (for the date, see p. xvii). See also *GND* 2: 178.

[15] Dudo, *De Moribus*, 158–60 (see also 148).

[16] Benoît, *Chronique* 1: 189, 197. For the date, see Jean Blacker, *The Faces of Time: Portrayal of the Past in Old French and Latin Historical Narrative of the Anglo-Norman Regnum* (Austin, Tex. 1994), 45.

[17] *GND* 2: 14–16; Wace, *Roman de Rou*, 1: 205–9, 2: 159–60 (see 3: 12–14 for the date); Benoît, *Chronique*, 2: 220–2. See also the Anonymous of Béthune, *Histoire des ducs de Normandie*, 47–8.

entered England to challenge Canute's illegitimate son, Harold I. This crime appeared in every Norman account of the conquest, and though normally it was used to attack Godwine's son, Harold II, William of Jumièges stated that the thousands of English deaths at Hastings represented God's judgement for the death of Alfred.[18] Though Norman writers did not consistently or constantly portray the English as innately treacherous, the image of English treachery *was* common in Norman sources.

The specific charges were difficult to refute. There was no English version of Rollo's adventure in England. With the fading of the Viking threat, the massacre of the Danes must have looked less justifiable, and the best anyone could try to do with the death of Alfred was shift the blame to the Danes, or focus it on Earl Godwine alone. Opposition to William the Conqueror was in theory easier to justify, but also more dangerous. The exile Ælnoth of Canterbury could present the conquest as a seizure by force, but that would have been trickier in England.[19] Some writers subtly challenged Norman claims. John of Worcester wrote that Edward chose Harold as successor, praised Harold as king, and otherwise ignored the whole question of legitimacy.[20] An anonymous chronicler of the archbishops of York, probably working in the 1140s, also wrote that Harold was chosen as heir, and added that he was elected by the leaders of England, but similarly avoided the question of William's claim. When he copied Hugh the Chanter's passage about the devastation of York and its region, he silently dropped Hugh's comment on the area's disloyalty.[21] One of three accounts of the revolt at Ely, all with different perspectives, included in the *Liber Eliensis*, written before 1174, seems to associate Hereward with Judas Maccabeus, his followers with the Israelites, and the Normans with their enemies through a series of allusions to the First Book of Maccabees.[22] For other staunchly pro-English writers, however, the evidence of divine judgement at Hastings was too powerful to ignore. For instance, Eadmer gave an account of Harold's actions that was fairly sympathetic, but ultimately accepted that God sided with the invaders in battle and punished Harold for his perjury. He placed the Norman Conquest in the context of a series of disasters that went back to God's anger at a particularly notorious act of treachery, namely the murder of the young English king Edward the Martyr in 978.[23] William of Malmesbury, Henry of Huntingdon, Orderic Vitalis, and Osbert of Clare all accepted William's claim to the throne as just, and all condemned the murder of Alfred (though William was not sure of the truth of stories about Alfred); William and Henry also criticized the massacre of the Danes. In addition, William of Malmesbury excused William's harshness to the English on the grounds that the king had found hardly any of them

[18] *GND* 1: 130, 2: 106, 170; *GGWP* 4–6; Edwards, *Liber Monasterii de Hyda*, 287; Wace, *Roman de Rou*, 2: 59–62, 160; Benoît, *Chronique*, 2: 406–8; Anonymous of Béthune, *Histoire des ducs de Normandie*, 60–1.

[19] Ælnoth of Canterbury, 'Gesta Swenomagni Regis', 96–7.

[20] *CJW* 2: 600.

[21] This writer probably worked not long after the death of Archbishop Thurstan in 1140: *HCY* 2: 348, 361.

[22] Blake, *Liber Eliensis*, pp. liv–lvii, 173–6.

[23] *HN* 1–10; Stubbs, *Memorials of St. Dunstan*, 215, 222.

faithful, and Henry of Huntingdon stated that God planned the destruction of the English for, among other things, their devotion to treachery.[24] Thus, even writers who identified wholly or partly with the English partially accepted and perpetuated the image of the treacherous English.

Many of these same writers, however, also worked to counteract or ameliorate that image, as did others. In general, they did so not by countering the charges head on, though Orderic did seek to exonerate Earl Waltheof, whose cult he supported, from charges of treason.[25] The most common strategy, which was more subtle but nonetheless very effective, was to emphasize and quite likely to exaggerate the role of the English in supporting both William II and Henry I against baronial, and therefore Norman-dominated, revolts early in their reigns. The anonymous author of the E version of the Anglo-Saxon Chronicle recorded that many French men betrayed William II, whereupon the king summoned the English and many of them flocked to him. John of Worcester gave basically the same picture of the revolt in 1088, and wrote that in 1101 the bishops, rural knights, and English stood by Henry I 'with a constant spirit'. William of Malmesbury claimed that William II, seeing almost all the Normans conspiring, wrote to request support from those proven and powerful English who were still left. The same themes run through Orderic's accounts of the two revolts; most strikingly, Orderic wrote that after William II had summoned the support of the bishops, earls, and native English (*Angli naturales*), 30,000 gathered to him, urging the punishment of traitors and pledging to fight to the death for him. Orderic depicts these 30,000 'eternally faithful' English as saying to the king: 'It is a detestable people that betrays its prince' and, 'study the histories of the English and you will find that the English are always faithful to their rulers'.[26]

This strategy for counteracting the image of English treachery, which the writers clearly adopted from one another, was extremely clever, for it allowed them to support rather than challenge the claims and legitimacy of the ruling kings, and it avoided the awkward possibility of questioning God's apparent judgement at Hastings. It permitted pro-English writers to admit that the English, or at least some English, had committed acts of treachery, but to present them as a basically loyal and trustworthy people. Finally, it let at least some of the writers turn the tables on the Normans when it came to the charge of treachery, and to undermine any moral superiority they might claim in that respect. Some also criticized the Normans more generally for treachery; for instance, William of Malmesbury says of the Normans that, with ill fortune, they consider treachery.[27]

A second attack on the English sometimes found in pro-Norman sources was that they were militarily deficient. Some of the technological differences have been noted earlier, but I wish to focus here on the question of reputation. William of

---

[24] *WMGR* 276, 336–8, 418–20, 446, 470; *HHHA* 338, 340, 370–2, 380–6, 392 (see also 274); *EHOV* 2: 134–8, 170–2, 176; Osbert of Clare, 'Édouard le Confesseur', 71, 108–9, 114–15.

[25] *EHOV* 2: 312–14, 320–2.

[26] *ASC* E 1088; *CJW* 3: 48–56, 96–8; *WMGR* 546–8; *EHOV* 4: 120–34; 5: 306–20. See also *HHHA* 412–14; Van Houts, *Memory and Gender*, 129–30.

[27] *WMGR* 460.

Poitiers has William the Conqueror refer to a history of defeats for the English in his pre-battle speech, and though battlefield speeches, real or imagined, were not meant to convey objective reality but to motivate troops, the speech does show that an image of the English as poor fighters existed.[28] The *Carmen de Hastingae Proelio* spoke of the English as a people unknowledgeable in war (*nescia gens belli*), and the *Gesta Herwardi* has a member of William's army state that he had often heard that his opponents were less accomplished or skilled in warfare compared to other peoples.[29] Moreover, the vigorous Norman triumphalism that made up an important part of the Norman myth ignored and implicitly devalued English military prowess. This is most apparent in the battlefield speeches that Henry of Huntingdon, Aelred of Rievaulx, and the anonymous author of the *De Expugnatione Lyxbonensi* placed in the mouths of leaders before the battle of the Standard or during the siege of Lisbon. In each of these speeches the speaker addresses a mixed force of English and Normans, but only refers to Norman prowess and a history of Norman success, ignoring the English.[30] Attached to the low opinion of English military prowess was the occasional depiction of the conquered people as effeminate. William of Poitiers's description of the girlish beauty of William the Conqueror's hostages may have been a hint in this direction. More concretely, the *Carmen de Hastingae Proelio* has one of William's envoys describe Harold's soldiers as 'effeminate youths, with combed and anointed hair', and Baudri of Bourgueil, in a poetic account of the conquest written for William the Conqueror's daughter Adela between 1099 and 1102, has William in his battlefield speech describe his opponents as 'a very unwarlike people (*gens*) and a womanly type (*genus*)'.[31]

It should be stressed that pro-Norman historians were inconsistent in their portrayals of the military prowess of the English. William of Poitiers could describe the English as timid in one place and prompt to take up iron (i.e. weapons) in another.[32] Pro-Norman writers had to proceed with some caution, since if the English were terrible fighters it was hard to explain how it had taken the warlike Normans some extremely hard fighting to defeat them, a point that William of Malmesbury made forcefully.[33] Nevertheless, the English were a defeated people, who had been conquered twice in less than a century; thus, in the sort of slanging-match over toughness and valour that was inevitable between two hostile peoples in a warlike period, pro-English writers would undoubtedly have felt the English to be vulnerable. Not only Henry of Huntingdon, who was partly Norman, but also Aelred of Rievaulx internalized the 'Norman myth' in relationship to battlefield speeches, and it should be noted that the former, like William of Poitiers, has

[28] GGWP 126.
[29] Guy of Amiens, *Carmen*, 22; Hardy and Martin, *Gesta Herwardi*, 378. See also Wace, *Roman de Rou*, 2: 206.
[30] HHHA 714–16; Aelred of Rievaulx, 'Relatio de Standardi', 185–9, 197; David, *De Expugnatione Lyxbonensi*, 104–10.
[31] GGWP 178–80; Guy of Amiens, *Carmen*, 20 (Barlow's translation); Baudri de Bourgueil, *Oeuvres Poétiques*, 205 (see 232 for the date).
[32] GGWP 138, 170.
[33] WMGR 422.

William I denigrate the English as fighters before the battle of Hastings. William of Malmesbury wrote that the English fought the Normans at Hastings more with rashness and fury than military knowledge, and in his translation of the life of St Wulfstan, Wulfstan is made to say that those sinful men who refused to cut their effeminately long hair would be of no more use than women in defending the *patria*, a prophecy that would (naturally) be subsequently borne out by the Norman Conquest.[34] Even those who identified at least partly with the English might not be overly impressed with English military prowess.

On the whole, however, pro-English writers were no more willing to leave unanswered the Norman image of English warriors as unskilled and effeminate than they were to ignore the image of the treacherous English. It is possible that one reason for the great interest during this period in the history of pre-conquest England may have been the desire to look back to a time of military glory and victory for the English in their wars with the Britons and early waves of Vikings, though here one may only infer. More certain responses can also be found. Orderic Vitalis followed William of Poitiers closely in long sections of his work, and included the passage about the French marvelling at the long-haired English hostages, but he quietly dropped the comment on their girlish beauty. More important, he argued that although the English were warlike and brave, they were handicapped by the Norman use of castles. William of Malmesbury, never one to be excessively consistent on the subject of the English, criticized those who exaggerated the numbers and underestimated the fortitude of the English who fought at Hastings, describing them as 'few and ready of hand'. When he described English support for William in Maine, he said that they 'who can easily be oppressed on their own soil, always seem victorious in foreign territory'. Both William and Eadmer, emphasizing the hard fighting at Hastings, attributed the Norman victory to God's will rather than Norman military skill, with the latter writer putting this belief in the mouths of the victors to enhance its credibility.[35]

The most striking response to the image of Norman superiority in war comes from the *Gesta Herwardi*. I have written elsewhere in detail about how this work sought to defend English pride and honour, particularly in the military sphere, so I will only summarize here. Hereward is depicted from the beginning as an *English* hero, and at a couple of points explicitly fights to avenge slights against *English* honour. The author seems to have been reacting not only to a view of the English as poor warriors, but also as unchivalric and poorly versed in the rules of war. No such image appears in the surviving Norman sources, but John Gillingham and Matthew Strickland have argued that the Normans brought chivalry and the new rules of war to England in the aftermath of the conquest, and it is quite possible that in lost written sources, or in conversation, the Normans accused the English of being backward in this respect.[36] The fact that most nobles were immigrants and most

---

[34] *HHHA* 390–2; *WMGR* 458; *VW* 23.

[35] *EHOV* 2: 198, 218; *WMGR* 422, 476; *HN* 9.

[36] Gillingham, *English in the Twelfth Century*, 209–29; Strickland, 'Slaughter, Slavery or Ransom', 41–59.

lower-class people were native could also have led to a view of the English as unchivalric. In any case, Richard invents exploits that allow Hereward to prove himself a chivalric and heroic warrior, able to fight on horseback, both in adventures in the Celtic never-never land that was coming to be the site for so many romances and in battles and tournaments on the Continent.

Most interesting, of course, is Hereward's struggle against the Normans. In reality, Hereward was the leader of a rebellion centred on Ely which William the Conqueror crushed without great difficulty. In the *Gesta Herwardi*, Hereward, who is something of a trickster, constantly outsmarts and outfights the Normans, defeating prominent Norman leaders and killing a man who should probably be identified with the new owner of Hereward's own estates in Domesday Book. The Normans, including the ancestors of powerful men in the writer's own time, are not at all chivalric, and their efforts to capture Ely and to catch Hereward verge on slapstick. At one point the invaders are reduced, in their effort to take Ely, to summoning an old witch. She performs a magic ritual against the defenders, which apparently mainly involves turning her back to the English and uncovering her rear end, not once but three times. Given the author's propensity for humorous moments, this episode is clearly an effort to ridicule the Normans, whose own writers cultivated an image of unstoppable military prowess, by depicting them as having no recourse but to rely on the comic antics of a ridiculous witch. Needless to say, even this magically assisted assault fails. In the end Ely only falls because of the capitulation of the monks, but Hereward escapes and eventually the mighty William the Conqueror is forced to make terms with him. In this work it is not the Normans who are great, chivalric warriors, and the English who are second-rate fighters, but rather the reverse.[37]

In yet another lively area of debate, Continental writers and speakers sometimes described the English as barbaric or rustic, or some related term. William of Poitiers on several occasions referred to the English as barbarians, or wild (*feri*). The *Carmen de Hastingae Proelio* at one point contrasted the French, 'skilled in fighting', with the 'rustica gens', they faced at Hastings.[38] Lanfranc, Anselm, and Ivo of Chartres all referred to the English as barbarians or barbaric at some point.[39] As with the charges discussed earlier, the frequency with which such terms appeared in pro-Norman and Continental sources should not be exaggerated, but they are sufficient to suggest at least nascent stereotypes.

Words such as barbarian or rustic, beyond simply being terms of abuse, had a variety of connotations. The reference to the *rustica gens* in the *Carmen de Hastingae Proelio* must be set within the debate over English military prowess discussed earlier, and so too must be a passage in Orderic Vitalis's history in which rebels in Normandy describe Henry I's troops as English, and a short while later as *pagenses*,

---

[37] Thomas, '*Gesta Herwardi*', 213–32.

[38] *GGWP* 128, 132, 162, 164, 166, 182; Guy of Amiens, *Carmen*, 26.

[39] *Letters of Lanfranc*, 30; *S. Anselmi Opera Omnia*, 3: 203; Ivo of Chartres, 'Letters', *PL* 162: 219. See also Searle, *Chronicle of Battle Abbey*, 92; Stevenson, *Chronicon Monasterii de Abingdon*, 2: 284, for examples involving other prelates, but see Susan Ridyard, *Condigna Veneratio*: Post-Conquest Attitudes to the Saints of the Anglo-Saxons', *ANS* 9: 190–2, for a discussion of the last passage.

or country bumpkins.[40] The latter passage may also have connotations of class, and, as I noted earlier, van Caenegem argues that 'English' was considered basically interchangeable with terms for serfs and peasants.[41] There was clearly a certain association of Englishness with the lower classes. Jocelin of Brakelond, writing about how Samson, who became abbot of Bury St Edmund's in 1182, deprived most leaseholders of manors to protect the abbey's interests, stated that he did leave one serf who could not speak French in place, implying that such a figure was too powerless to threaten those interests. Jocelin almost never identified the ethnicity of individuals, but he did describe this one person as English.[42] Given the broad class distinctions between natives and immigrants described earlier, it would be surprising if there had not been some association between the English and the lower classes. In a class-conscious society, such an association would have been demeaning.[43]

From the English point of view, the various laments on the destruction of the English nobility would suggest that if the Normans found the English excessively lower class they had only themselves to blame, while Aelred's interpretation of the green tree prophecy would argue that the upper classes were once more at least partly English.[44] Once again, however, the most interesting response comes from the *Gesta Herwardi*. In this work Hereward and many of his companions are explicitly depicted as noble, but in two passages, one discussed earlier, Hereward is able to thwart the Normans by disguising himself as a common person. The joke is on the invaders, who suffer because they cannot spot an English nobleman when they see one, and the author cleverly turns the tables by using an anti-English stereotype to allow his hero to outfox and humiliate the conquerors.[45] Such arguments and literary devices could not undo the disinheritance of the English nobility, but they could alleviate some of the resulting stigma to the English.

The most frequent connotation of terms relating to barbarity and rusticity, however, had to do with a broad view of the English and particularly the English church as both morally and intellectually backward, the two spheres of intellect and morality being more closely connected in the Middle Ages than today because learning centred to such a degree on religion and religious institutions. This connotation is most obvious in an account, written in the early twelfth century by Gilbert Crispin, of Archbishop Lanfranc's endeavours to improve the English church, in which Lanfranc is said to have reformed the monasteries, forced clerics to follow canonical rule, and 'forbidden the vanity of barbarous rites and taught the people the proper form of believing and living'.[46] This view of the English as backward may

[40] *EHOV* 6: 350.

[41] See above, p. 102.

[42] *Chronicle of Jocelin of Brakelond*, 33. See also Short, '*Tam Angli quam Franci*', 159–60. The figure was described as *ascripto glebe*. For the use of the word *ascriptus* for serf, see Hyams, *King, Lords and Peasants*, 26–7, 90, 109–10, 244–5, 253, 269–72.

[43] See Crouch, *Image of Aristocracy*, 17–20, for abuse against those labelled peasants.

[44] See above, pp. 56, 60.

[45] Thomas, '*Gesta Herwardi*', 225–7; Hardy and Martin, *Gesta Herwardi*, 340, 372–3, 376, 379, 384–90.

[46] Gilbert Crispin, *The Works of Gilbert Crispin Abbot of Westminster*, ed. Anna Sapir Abulafia and G. R. Evans (Oxford, 1986), 201.

include a stereotype of them as superstitious. According to Orderic Vitalis, when a Norman abbot sent a letter to William II warning him (on the basis of a dream) to reform and repent, the king replied by saying, among other things: 'Does [the abbot] think I act after the fashion of the English, who put off their journeys and business on account of the snores and dreams of little old women?'[47] The issue of the lack of formal learning is more obvious in the pro-English than the pro-Norman sources, but a late source, the *Gesta Abbatum Sancti Albani*, attributes to Abbot Paul of St Alban's the opinion that his English predecessors were uncouth and unlearned.[48] Barbarism was also sometimes related specifically to the widespread English use of the vernacular rather than Latin. The Italian immigrant Faritius, abbot of Abingdon 1100–17, wrote of finding information on the early English scholar and saint Aldhelm, whose life he was writing, in 'many pages, Latin and barbarian'.[49] Finally, in the moral sphere, William of Poitiers accused the English of excessive luxuriousness, a theme that would reappear among the pro-English writers.[50]

In many ways pro-English writers seem to have felt most vulnerable to this image of English intellectual and moral backwardness. There were several reasons why. First, the Normans did bring some measure of reinvigoration and reform to the English church. I agree with Antonia Gransden and Mary Frances Smith that the great divide between the English and Norman churches on the eve of the conquest, and the post-conquest reform, may have been something of a literary construct in post-conquest sources. But William did appoint the vigorous reformer Lanfranc to the key position of archbishop of Canterbury, and elsewhere Norman prelates did try to make changes and improvements, though as the Glastonbury riots indicate, the Normans and the English did not always agree on what constituted an improvement.[51] There was, however, enough reform to make the construct of English backwardness potentially believable. In the intellectual sphere, modern scholars have long associated the Norman Conquest with a reinvigoration of intellectual life, an expansion of libraries, and a new emphasis on patristic studies.[52]

[47] *EHOV* 5: 288–9 (Chibnall's translation). The story in the *Gesta Herwardi* of Norman reliance on a witch may have been designed partly to counter such a stereotype.

[48] *Gesta Abbatum*, 1: 62.

[49] Faritius, *Vita S. Aldhelmi*, 64.

[50] *GGWP* 152.

[51] Gransden, 'Tradition and Continuity', 159–64, 181–207; Mary Frances Smith, 'Archbishop Stigand and the Eye of the Needle', *ANS* 16: 215–18. For the Glastonbury riot, see above, p. 3. For discussion of church reform after the conquest, see Barlow, *The English Church 1066–1154*, 54–75, 122–9, 177–93; Brett, *English Church Under Henry I*, 90; R. Allen Brown, *The Normans and the Norman Conquest* (New York, 1968), 101–6, 253–60; Burton, *Monastic and Religious Orders in Britain*, 7–42; Douglas, *William the Conqueror*, 317–45; Golding, *Conquest and Colonisation*, 146–76, esp. 146; Knowles, *Monastic Order*, 78–81, 121.

[52] David C. Douglas, *The Norman Achievement 1050–1100* (Berkeley, 1969), 207–9; Knowles, *Monastic Order*, 94–9, 124–6, 495–6, 523; N. R. Ker, *English Manuscripts in the Century After the Norman Conquest* (Oxford, 1960), 7–8; Barlow, *English Church 1066–1154*, 236–7; Rodney M. Thomson, 'The Norman Conquest and English Libraries', in *The Role of the Book in Medieval Culture*, vol. 2, ed. Peter Ganz (Turnhout, 1986), 27–40; Katherine M. Waller, 'Rochester Cathedral Library. An English Book Collection Based on Norman Models', in *Les Mutations socio-culturelles au tournant des XIe–XIIe siècles: Études Anselmiennes* (Paris, 1984), 237–50; Webber, *Scribes and Scholars*, 31–75; Teresa Webber, 'The

Teresa Webber has pointed out that English religious houses were not that far behind many Norman ones in terms of patristic scholarship, and argues that the increased emphasis on the church fathers should be seen in the context of a widespread European intellectual shift, as well as in terms of the Norman Conquest.[53] A similar argument could probably be made for intellectual life in general; much of Normandy's intellectual life came from the importation of scholars, books, and ideas, and the same would have happened sooner or later in England without the conquest. But in fact it was Continental prelates, some of them leading European intellectuals, who brought the changes to England, and this could make the native English vulnerable to charges of backwardness. As for the use of the vernacular, it is true that the description of any vernacular as automatically barbarian because it was not Latin was frequent in the Middle Ages, even after its use became common in many societies.[54] But in 1066 the importance of the vernacular in English society was extremely unusual by Western European (though not insular) standards, and while modern people might view this as a sign of progress, even such a promoter of the use of English in writing as Alfred the Great had seen its use as simply a necessary step resulting from the lack of widespread knowledge of Latin.[55] It is not surprising that pro-English writers might feel vulnerable on this score. The most important factor in making pro-English writers feel susceptible to charges of moral and intellectual backwardness, however, was the intellectual framework that emphasized God's role in history. One way to explain the extraordinary catastrophe of the conquest was to focus on widespread moral decay, within which medieval writers included intellectual decay. As good Christians *and* as good Englishmen, it was their duty to demonstrate how sin led their people to disaster, in order to call individuals and the whole people to repentance.

The connection between English sin and the conquest was already made in the D version of the Anglo-Saxon Chronicle, which stated that God gave victory at Hastings to the French because of the sins of the people.[56] A more detailed account of English sins, also from shortly after the conquest, comes in the anonymous biography of Edward the Confessor in the context of the green tree prophecy. Subsequent versions of the prophecy by William of Malmesbury, Osbert of Clare, and Aelred of Rievaulx echoed and elaborated on this.[57] Osbert of Clare's statement elsewhere in his version of Edward's life, that the king's brother Alfred was killed by 'the cruelty of barbarians', indicates the link between sin and barbarity in the minds

Diffusion of Augustine's Confessions in England During the Eleventh and Twelfth Centuries', in *The Cloister and the World: Essays in Medieval History in Honour of Barbara Harvey*, ed. John Blair and Brian Golding (Oxford, 1996), 29–45.

[53] Webber, 'Diffusion', 40–1. See also, Peter Jackson, 'The *Vitas Patrum* in Eleventh-Century Worcester', in *England in the Eleventh Century*, ed. Carola Hicks (Stamford, 1992), 119–34.

[54] See e.g. Gerald of Wales, *Expugnatio Hibernica: The Conquest of Ireland*, ed. A. B. Scott and F. X. Martin (Dublin, 1978), 216.

[55] Henry Sweet, ed., *King Alfred's West-Saxon Version of Gregory's Pastoral Care*, vol. 1 (London, 1871), 2–8.

[56] *ASC* D 1066.

[57] Barlow, *Life of King Edward*, 116–22, 131–2; *WMGR* 414–16; Osbert of Clare, 'Édouard le Confesseur', 107–9; Aelred of Rievaulx, 'Vita S. Edwardi Regis', 772–3.

of pro-English as well as pro-Norman writers.[58] The acceptance by some pro-English writers of this and other accounts of English treachery obviously fits closely into a picture of moral backwardness. For writers who identified wholly or partly with the conquered people, however, English sinfulness and barbarity was only part of the story. By reaching back deep into English history, they were able to present a picture of the English people that was more complex and more complimentary to the English than a simple focus on the sins that supposedly led to the conquest would provide.

William of Malmesbury treated the subject most fully, in various works ranging in date from the 1120s to the 1140s.[59] The core of his argument may be found in his concise comparison of the English and Normans in the context of the conquest. In that comparison he is far harsher to the English, or more specifically the English in the period immediately preceding the conquest, than any surviving Norman source. In this passage William criticized the clergy for a decline in religion and particularly learning; the monks for their luxurious clothing and eating; the nobility for their oppression of the poor, luxurious lifestyles, drinking, lust, inattention to religion, and their practice of impregnating their female slaves and then selling them abroad. He also criticized their poor fighting skills, which he linked to their life of vice. In his following portrait of the Normans he credited them with a revival of religion, accepting that such a reform was needed.[60] Elsewhere William raised similar criticisms of the English, and attacked them for their innate credulity, echoing the charge that Orderic Vitalis put in the mouth of William II.[61] In places, he painted a damning portrait of the English.

His criticisms, however, formed only a part of William's overall picture of the English, and both in his main discussion and elsewhere he placed their character and level of civilization in a historical context. In William's view, the English were indeed barbaric when they first arrived in England as pagans, but he removed any possible claim that the Normans were inherently superior by anachronistically including them, along with the Vandals, Goths, and Lombards, among the migrating Germanic tribes.[62] With the conversion and development of Christianity, in William's view, things changed radically. In his comparison of the English and Normans, he depicted a vaguely defined golden age, when even kings gave up their thrones to become monks, and multitudes of religious figures and saints existed. In his account of the Anglo-Saxon period earlier in the *Gesta Regum* he discussed a number of exemplary intellectuals and religious figures, including Bede, Aldhelm,

---

[58] Osbert of Clare, 'Édouard le Confesseur', 71.

[59] See John Scott's introduction to his edition of William of Malmesbury's History of Glastonbury Abbey for a similar argument to the one made below, though one that does not set it in the context of a debate over the worth of the two peoples: *The Early History of Glastonbury: An Edition, Translation and Study of William of Malmesbury's De Antiquitate Glastonie Ecclesie* (Woodbridge, 1981), 15–18. See also Gransden, 'Tradition and Continuity', 202–3. For dating of the works involved, see Gransden, *Historical Writing in England*, 167–8; Rodney Thomson, *William of Malmesbury* (Woodbridge, 1987), 3–5.

[60] *WMGR* 458–60.

[61] Ibid. 60, 94, 102–4, 196, 452; *WMGP* 36, 70–1, 118–19, 179; *VW* 23.

[62] *WMGR* 20–2, 28, 456; *WMGP* 336.

Alcuin, Alfred, and the reformers of the late tenth century. He also devoted a long section to English saints.[63] Even more markedly, large sections of his *Gesta Pontificum* were devoted to these subjects, and at one point he contrasted, if only in passing, Englishness and barbarity.[64] Of his minor works, one was devoted to the history of the greatest English monastery, Glastonbury, and another was devoted to the figure of Dunstan who, as a reformer and therefore in some sense a predecessor of Lanfranc, could help counteract any picture of the English as inherently less religious than their conquerors.[65] In his historic contextualization of English character and morals, William showed both a certain deference to, and in one passage, a defensiveness against the French. As Gillingham has pointed out, William saw French influence civilizing England through a number of routes long before the conquest, starting with Bertha, the Frankish wife of Æthelbert of Kent.[66] In emphasizing this French influence as crucial, William was embroidering on his sources, perhaps influenced by the cultural pre-eminence of France in his own day and by the reforms brought after the conquest. The defensiveness shows up in a passage on Bede, in which William, after noting the letter of a pope to the great scholar, wrote: 'Thus, his fame was now so celebrated, that in unraveling questions Roman sublimity itself needed him, nor did even Gallic pride find anything in the Englishman which it could justly accuse.'[67] William was apparently working in an atmosphere of scepticism about English intellectual prowess and religiosity, but laboured mightily to show that whatever recent shortcomings might have existed, his people nonetheless had a glorious intellectual and moral past.

William argued, in his comparison of the English and Normans, that even in the immediate post-conquest period some English led worthy lives. A prime example of this would have been bishop Wulfstan, whose life William translated from English into Latin, and about whom he also wrote at length in the *Gesta Pontificum*. Among Wulfstan's many virtues, according to William, he was abstemious in food and drink, although in his hall others drank for hours 'according to the custom of the English'. In one episode William depicted Wulfstan as resisting the suggestion of a Norman bishop that he dress more richly, thus turning the stereotype of English luxuriousness and Norman restraint on its head.[68] In addition to Wulfstan, William praised other post-Conquest Englishmen, including Eadmer, Nicholas, prior of Worcester, and, above all, Stephen Harding, whose achievements William said were glorious for England.[69] William of Malmesbury's view of the English and the relationship of their culture to that of the Continent was clearly complex, even contradictory and confusing at times, but although he had much respect for the

---

[63] *WMGR* 44–6, 50, 82–98, 190–4, 240–2, 456–8.

[64] *WMGP* 3–443 (contrast of Englishness and barbarism on p. 230).

[65] William of Malmesbury, *Early History of Glastonbury*, 40–166; 'Vita Sancti Dunstani', in Stubbs, *Memorials of St. Dunstan*, 250–324.

[66] *WMGR* 28, 142, 152; *WMGP* 147; Gillingham, *English in the Twelfth Century*, 5–6, 28–9; Gillingham, 'Civilizing the English', 21–2, 37–8.

[67] *WMGR* 88.

[68] *WMGP* 281; *VW* 46.

[69] Harding was an English rather than Continental name: *WMGR* 14, 560, 576–84; *VW* 56–7.

latter, and a certain inferiority complex about the former, he nevertheless assembled an impressive amount of evidence for English religiosity and intellectual endeavour, past and present. In so doing, he prevented his criticisms from creating any picture of innate inferiority or barbarity among the English and protected English dignity by preserving a history of great accomplishments.

Orderic Vitalis followed a very similar strategy of admitting English short-comings at the time of the conquest but emphasizing a glorious past, though he focused almost solely on monasticism. In a long interruption to his praise of King William and Archbishop Lanfranc as reformers, Orderic provided a tendentious history of monasticism and monastic learning in England, describing high points after the initial conversion and under Alfred's descendants, and attributing the decline from both peaks to Viking invasions. Orderic digressed on this subject, he wrote, so that the reader might learn why the Normans found the English, who had been so well instructed under Roman guidance, rustic and almost completely unlearned.[70] Eadmer also admitted the decline of monasticism after the second set of Viking invasions, particularly at his own monastery, but he too depicted past reforms and golden ages of learning and religiosity, in his case in a series of saints' lives of the reformers Wilfrid, Oda, Oswald, and Dunstan, and of the early bishop Bregwin.[71] As R. W. Southern has shown, Eadmer changed details from the earlier versions of the lives he relied on to suit contemporary Canterbury ideals and interests, and in some ways he remodelled the saints in the image of Lanfranc and Anselm.[72] By altering earlier lives to fit current ideals, Eadmer reconfigured the pre-Conquest church to look up-to-date and thus eliminate any picture of the English church as always having been backward.

Other writers took up similar themes. Henry of Huntingdon devoted an entire book of his history to English saints, overwhelmingly from the pre-conquest period, and also briefly described a decline of English morals that led first to the Danish and then the Norman invasions.[73] Simeon of Durham, explaining how Bede could have been so learned (which was obviously considered surprising), depicted a golden age of learning established throughout England by Archbishop Theodore and Abbot Hadrian. The anonymous chronicler of the archbishops of York praised the education that an early archbishop, John of Beverley, whom he specifically described as being English, gained from Theodore and Hadrian, and described Bede as the 'teacher of the English, whose writings all Europe admires'.[74] It is worth noting that the Anglo-Norman period was one in which Bede, the best exemplar of pre-conquest learning, was extremely prestigious, and in which a large percentage of the surviving medieval copies of his *History of the English Church and People* were

---

[70] *EHOV* 2: 238–54.

[71] *HN* 5; 'Vita Odonis', 78–9; 'Vita S. Bregwini', 185; 'Vita Wilfridi Episcopi' and 'Vita Sancti Oswaldi', *HCY* 1: 161–226, esp. 182; 2: 1–59; 'Vita Sancti Dunstani', in Stubbs, *Memorials of St. Dunstan*, 162–249, esp. 236.

[72] Southern, *Saint Anselm and his Biographer*, 277–87.

[73] *HHHA* 274, 338–40, 620–96. The only contemporary saint Henry discussed was Wulfric of Haselbury, a native, though Henry did not remark on this.

[74] *SMO* 1: 227–8; *HCY* 2: 326–8. Similar praise of Bede is found in *LDE* 40–2, 64–76, and *SMO* 2: 23.

made.[75] Finally, there was an outpouring of hagiography after the conquest, which may have been motivated partly by a desire not just to preserve English traditions, but also to underscore England's great religious heritage.[76] In some senses, the whole burst of historical writing that Southern described served not only to preserve tradition but also to protect English pride.

As for the association between the vernacular and barbarity, many writers who identified with the English accepted it, just as they had accepted the general picture of English backwardness on the eve of the conquest. William of Malmesbury, Osbert of Clare, Osbeorn of Canterbury, and the anonymous historian of the archbishops of York all referred to English, or to English personal or place-names, as barbarous and William even expressed concerns about wounding the delicate ears of his listeners by including such barbarous appellations.[77] The perception of English, or any vernacular, as barbarous, is one of the many reasons for the decline of the use of written English. But by the very act of writing in Latin, and sometimes very good Latin by contemporary standards, English writers showed that they were fully capable of meeting 'civilized' expectations. More important, one of the great achievements of English writers in the century after the conquest was to translate what they considered the most valuable information in earlier vernacular writings into Latin. In so doing, they preserved English history and other aspects of English culture in the 'civilized' medium, thereby implying that the content of the writings, and thus of English culture in general, was worthy of civilized attention. The strategy of pointing to past glories may also have been used in the context of language. In Orderic Vitalis's section explaining why the Normans found the English rustic, he noted, drawing from Bede, that English students learned both Latin and Greek from Archbishop Theodore and Abbot Hadrian, and other writers also noted this as well, sometimes quoting Bede directly. Eadmer even claimed, anachronistically, that the study of Greek was common in the tenth century and that Archbishop Oda learned it.[78] The overall implication was probably that although Norman Latinity may have been greater in 1066, there had been a time when English intellectuals had command of not one but two sacred and learned languages, thus giving English pride a boost.

One writer, the anonymous author of a short piece in English known as the first Worcester fragment or St Bede Lament, took a different approach and counterattacked on the subject of the vernacular.[79] This piece, which survives only in a

---

[75] Gransden, 'Bede's Reputation as a Historian', 397, 403–19.

[76] Paul Antony Hayward, 'Translation-Narratives in Post-Conquest Hagiography and English Resistance to the Norman Conquest', *ANS* 21: 89–90.

[77] *WMGR* 14, 174–6, 272; *WMGP* 327; *VW* 23; Osbert of Clare, 'Édouard le Confesseur', 79; Osbeorn of Canterbury *Vita Sancti Elphegi*, 376; *HCY* 2: 330. See also MacRay, *Chronicon Abbatiae Rameseiensis*, 176. Ian Short argues that William of Malmesbury was pandering to snobbery among Francophone listeners and speakers, and this is possible, but I think the chief contrast was between English and Latin: '*Tam Angli quam Franci*', 161.

[78] *EHOV* 2: 246; Eadmer, 'Vita Odonis', 79; Southern, *Saint Anselm and his Biographer*, 281. See also *WMGP* 136, 333, 334; *LDE* 42; *SMO* 1: 228; *HCY* 2: 332; *CJW* 2: 168, 178.

[79] Bruce Dickens and R. M. Wilson, *Early Middle English Texts* (New York, 1951), 1–2.

copy made by the thirteenth-century scholar called by modern paleographers 'The Tremulous Hand', is very hard to date. For instance, Derek Pearsall dated it to *c.*1100, whereas J. P. Oakden dated it to *c.*1170.[80] In any case it is likely to have been written while the debate about the two peoples was still hot. The fragment begins by stating (probably erroneously) that 'Saint' Bede had translated works so that the English people (*Englise leoden*) could be taught. It then goes on to praise Ælfric for his biblical translations and to list thirteen Anglo-Saxon bishops and abbots, many of them, including John of Beverley, Dunstan, and Alfeah, the subjects of con-temporary post-conquest lives, whom it claimed taught 'our people' in English. But, it laments,

> The teaching is forsaken   and that folk is lost
> Now there is another people   who teach our folk
> And many of the teachers are damned   and that folk with them

It is hard to imagine a more forceful defence of the vernacular and the English who used it.

It is also hard to imagine a harsher condemnation of the new, foreign leadership of the church, and this brings me to a final and important aspect of the debate between the two peoples, namely English criticism of the morals and conduct of their conquerors. Writers may have hesitated to openly question the legitimacy of William the Conqueror's line, but the biblical tradition of condemning sin through the study of history gave them licence to harshly castigate the invaders and, in the process, to shoot down any idea of overarching Norman moral superiority. Orderic copied from William of Jumièges the idea that thousands of English had died at Hastings because of the murder of Alfred, but added that God avenged the English by the deaths of many Normans, punished for their greed and eagerness to shed blood.[81] Not surprisingly, much of the criticism of the Normans centred around the conquest itself. A number of clerical and especially monastic writers recorded and lamented the loss of lands, treasures, and even books belonging to their churches.[82] More generally, many authors chronicled and often harshly condemned the deliberate devastation of many regions, the destruction of the old elites, and the slaughter, plundering, and rape that accompanied William's victory over Harold and subsequently over rebels. Orderic Vitalis went so far as to depict William the Conqueror as repenting, in a deathbed speech, the violence with which the

---

[80] Franzen, *Tremulous Hand of Worcester*, 81, 84–5; Pearsall, *Old English and Middle English Poetry*, 76; J. P. Oakden, *Alliterative Poetry in Middle English: The Dialectical and Metrical Survey*, vol. 2 (Manchester, 1935; repr., 1968), 169.

[81] *EHOV* 2: 176–8. See also William of Malmesbury's suggestion, referring to the battle of Tinchebrai, that perhaps it was the judgement of God that Normandy was subjected to England on the same day of the year in which Norman troops had subdued it: *WMGR* 722–4.

[82] Stevenson, *Chronicon Monasterii de Abingdon*, 1: 345, 481; 2: 278; *Chronicle of Hugh Candidus*, 69, 84–5; *HCY* 2: 343–4; MacRay, *Chronicon Abbatiae Rameseiensis*, 144–5, 152–3, 175–6; *HN* 12; *Gesta Abbatum*, 1: 40, 53; Blake, *Liber Eliensis*, 103, 132, 152, 167–8, 188–90, 194–6, 202, 204–5, 210–12, 216–17; William of Malmesbury, *Early History of Glastonbury*, 152; Hemming, *Chartularium Ecclesiae Wigorniensis*, 253–7, 261, 263, 266–73, 281–2, 391; Herman, 'De Miraculis', 58–9. For a discussion of the de-spoliation of the monasteries, see Williams, *ENC* 140–5.

conquest was carried out.[83] More striking still, the anonymous historian of the archbishops of York described a dramatic scene in which Archbishop Ealdred visited William's court and boldly stated 'I crowned you though you were a foreigner and, God punishing the pride of my people, obtained the kingdom of Britain with much blood', whereupon Ealdred cursed the king to his face for wrongs to his church. At this point, according to the chronicler, the king threw himself to the archbishop's feet and begged forgiveness. Such a scene, whether true or not, would of course have been pleasing to clerics fed up with masterful kings, but it would also have been pleasing to English people fed up with masterful Normans. More important, it sharply undermined any sense of Norman moral superiority.[84]

Some writers also condemned the conquerors for subsequent actions. The writer of the 1087 annal in the E version of the Anglo-Saxon Chronicle praised William the Conqueror for many things, but condemned him for his greed, his fiscal oppression of his tenants and people, and the actions he took to improve hunting, including the setting aside of much arable land and the penalties imposed for poaching.[85] The anonymous historian of the archbishops of York, in introducing the great dispute over the relationship between the archbishops of York and Canterbury, blamed it on the Normans, saying, with some accuracy, that in 'Norman times' the Norman archbishops disturbed the peace, which had been preserved among the English archbishops.[86] Eadmer, probably with somewhat less accuracy, blamed the Normans for introducing the practices that led to the extension of the investiture controversy to England.[87] Thus, further damage was inflicted on any image of Norman moral superiority.

Even more important were negative characterizations about the Normans as a people. One possible attack came from Eadmer. As noted earlier, Eadmer placed the Norman Conquest in the context of a series of misfortunes going back to the murder of Edward the Martyr, and in both the Historia Novorum and his life of St Dunstan, Eadmer depicted Dunstan predicting disasters after the murder, including incursions of barbarians. Most obviously this referred to the Viking invasions in Æthelræd's time, but given that Eadmer linked the prophecy to the troubles of his

[83] EHOV 4: 94–6. See also ASC DE 1067–71; Hardy and Martin, Gesta Herwardi, 365; HCY 2: 356–57, 361; HN 124; MacRay, Chronicon Abbatiae de Evesham, 88–93; CJW 3: 10, 36; LDE 218–20; SMO 1: 246, 2: 188–90; Ælnoth of Canterbury, 'Gesta Swenomagni Regis', 96–7; WMGR 462–4; WMGP 208; EHOV 2: 196, 202, 214–16, 230–2, 256–8, 264–80, 350; 3: 256; 4: 42, 114; Osbert of Clare, 'Édouard le Confesseur', 103, 109.

[84] HCY 2: 350–3. This scene is obviously related to a less dramatic episode in WMGP 352–3. The anonymous chronicler had good sources on Ealdred, and I have argued in an unpublished paper that the incident should not be dismissed out of hand, but whether real or fictional, the writer's purpose would have been the same.

[85] ASC E 1086 [recte 1087]. See also HHHA 402–4; WMGR 504.

[86] HCY 2: 354. For the dispute between the archiepiscopal sees, see Barlow, English Church 1066–1154, 39–44; Gibson, Lanfranc of Bec, 116–21; Southern, Saint Anselm and His Biographer, 135–42; id., Saint Anselm: A Portrait in a Landscape, 340–7.

[87] HN 1–2. It is true that William the Conqueror could have introduced certain new ceremonial practices, and such practices were often the flashpoints for the conflict, but the pre-conquest kings had controlled the church quite strongly. For a discussion of this issue, see Chibnall, Anglo-Norman England, 60–2.

own time, it is possible that in a subtle (and deniable) way, he was lumping the Normans, who were originally Vikings themselves, in with the barbarians, thus reversing the stereotype directed against the English.[88] More concretely, William of Malmesbury, in his comparison of the two peoples, painted a generally favourable portrait of the Normans, but described their tendency to change allegiances, their ambition, their fleecing of their subjects, and their willingness to change opinions for money. Elsewhere he referred to Norman parsimony, and claimed that the Normans picked up luxuriousness, gluttony, and heavy drinking from the English.[89] Orderic Vitalis depicted the Normans as unruly and prone to sedition and crime when not kept under a firm hand, and dangerously ambitious.[90] Henry of Huntingdon wrote that God chose the Normans as the instrument of his wrath because of their savagery, and then went on to describe their tendency to oppress the people they conquered in England and elsewhere, and to bring themselves down, presumably through their own savagery.[91] Though these works also contain condemnations of the English, no one would have come away from them with a picture of the Normans as morally superior to the people they had conquered.

It is a cliché, and in this case a false one, that history is written (solely) by the winners. In some ways pro-Norman writers did frame the debate early on, and many pro-English writers certainly reveal the insecurities of a conquered and despised people. Yet the vigour with which many writers presented the perspective of the conquered, defended the English, and denigrated the Normans in turn, is remarkable. In part, this pro-English defence attests to the continuing strength of English identity. But it also helped to support that identity. Judging by the surviving written material, the English were able to argue the Normans at the very least to a draw. Some of the negative stereotypes of the English did survive, as we shall see in Chapter 18, but overall, English honour was successfully defended and any claim of Norman superiority refuted. To what degree the surviving writing reflects broader social concerns and beliefs is hard to say. However, the fact that the debate emerges from so many different written sources suggests that it was important at the very least among the intellectual elite, which played a crucial role in shaping identity. Moreover, the writings themselves could influence those with access to literacy, and Jean Blacker, who has studied some twelfth-century English writers, argues that audiences could be varied, and might include the laity in some cases.[92] The pro-English works I have described above were no doubt one important factor in destroying any nascent stereotypes about the innate inferiority of the English.

The importance of their success can be illustrated by reference to the dire effects

---

[88] *HN* 3–5; Eadmer, 'Vita Dunstani', in Stubbs, *Memorials of St. Dunstan*, 215. See Sally Vaughn, 'Eadmer's *Historia Novorum*: A Reinterpretation', *ANS* 10: 259–89, for a general characterization of Eadmer as a subtle and complex author.

[89] *WMGR* 458–60, 472; William of Malmesbury, *Early History of Glastonbury*, 158.

[90] *EHOV* 1: 158; 4: 14–16, 82; 5: 24–6.

[91] *HHHA* 402. See also 384. Even one non-Norman immigrant churchman, Herman, wrote of the customary greed of the Normans: Herman, 'De Miraculis', 58–9.

[92] Blacker, *Faces of Time*, 135–95. For a more pessimistic view of the impact of historical works on contemporaries, see Shopkow, *History and Community*, 212–47.

of the stereotype of the Irish and Welsh as barbarians, which I have suggested had roots in pre-conquest Normandy, and which became entrenched in the twelfth century.[93] This widely accepted stereotype was one of the factors that sustained ethnic divides in Ireland and Wales, and prevented the conquering elites in those two lands from merging with their subjects. Obviously there were differences in the two situations. The concept of the barbarian was a shifting one, and it may have been a less damning term in the late eleventh and very early twelfth centuries than it later became.[94] Gilbert Crispin, who referred to the barbarous rites of the English, also wrote that the customs in Normandy were still barbarous in the early part of the eleventh century, which would indicate that, like William of Malmesbury, he saw barbarism as a historical phenomenon that a people could pass beyond, rather than as some kind of innate and unalterable characteristic.[95] I have argued that one should be careful about drawing too close a link between the strength of stereotypes and degrees of cultural difference, but some of the differences in Irish and Welsh economies and social practices that led outsiders to dub them barbarians may not have existed with the English. Nevertheless, there was clearly at least a nascent image of the English as barbarians, and had the English not combated it so vigorously, in writings accessible to the conquerors, it is possible that it might have developed into a powerful and shameful stereotype. Instead, an image of the English as an imperfect people but one with a glorious past and much to take pride in, emerged. Thus, Englishness became an identity worthy of adoption. That it was an honourable identity, however, only explains why it became acceptable for Normans to adopt it. It does not explain why they came to choose Englishness, and it is to that question that the following chapters are devoted.

---

[93] See above, pp. 53–4, for the appearance of this stereotype in Norman sources. See below, pp. 310–11, for the development of these stereotypes.

[94] For the shifting nature of the term in the Middle Ages, see Jones, 'The Image of the Barbarian in Medieval Europe', 376–407; Bartlett, *Gerald of Wales*, 176–7.

[95] *Works of Gilbert Crispin*, 191, 201.

15

The Image of England and a Sense of Place

AN IMPORTANT SUPPORT for the construct of Englishness after the conquest was the construct of England. This is a blindingly obvious point, but it raises important questions about the relations between place and identity and about how a large and highly abstract geographic designation could command loyalty and therefore influence questions of ethnicity. As seen in Chapter 2, the concept of England was well established before the conquest.[1] In the Anglo-Saxon period, an ethnic construct, the English, had led eventually to a geographic one, England. This was typical of a process which Anthony Smith has called the territorialization of memory, by which ethnic identity can lead to a new conceptualization of landscape through linking a place to a people and their historical memory.[2] This chapter discusses a similar process going in the opposite direction, by looking at how a conceptualization of the landscape influenced ethnicity. More specifically, this chapter discusses the survival of the concept of England after the conquest, and its contribution to the triumph of English identity. It argues that in contrast to Englishness, which became problematic because of the introduction of ethnic divisions and the creation of a non-English ruling elite, the concept of England remained largely unaffected by the conquest. The two concepts could be uncoupled; invaders who still thought of themselves as Norman could easily think of themselves as living in England. Over time, however, the strength of the construct of England served to reinforce the strength of English identity.

It was not surprising that those who settled in a new place might adopt new geographic loyalties, but it was by no means inevitable that this would influence ethnicity.[3] Ethnic groups often reshaped geography in their own image in the Middle Ages: just as the English created *Engla Lond*, the Franks created *Francia*, the Lombards, Lombardy, and the Normans, Normandy. Even when immigrants adopt new identities, they often shun the identity of the locals. Geographic shifts played an important role in making the descendants of English and other settlers come to think of themselves as American or Australian, but did not make them

---

[1] See above, pp. 20–6.

[2] Anthony D. Smith, 'Culture, Community and Territory: The Politics of Ethnicity and Nationalism', *International Affairs*, 72 (1996), 453–5.

[3] See Werner, 'Les Nations et le sentiment national', 302–3, for the frequency of links between place and identity in the Middle Ages.

come to associate themselves with the existing inhabitants, whom they despised and slaughtered or evicted from much of their land. Closer in time and place to our subject, the English of Ireland, though they formed a strong attachment to their new homeland, and saw themselves as somewhat different from the English in England, nonetheless kept their original ethnic identity and their separateness from the Irish.[4]

The English in Ireland remained English partly because of continuing links with England. Many immigrants after the Norman Conquest, particularly among the most powerful, retained land in Normandy, and until 1204 (albeit with several breaks) there remained strong political connections with the homeland of the majority of the invaders. This consideration may be less serious than it first seems. In an age when travel was expensive and difficult, only the wealthiest would have found moving between holdings in Normandy and England very practical. Probably even in the first generation many, perhaps most, minor lords, not to mention *francigenae*, maintained homes only in England. As time went on more and more families divided their holdings. David Crouch has described the growing divide of the English and Norman aristocracies by concentrating on the elites of Warwickshire and Leicestershire, and showing how few leading local families retained land in Normandy, and how regionally focused most had become well before 1204.[5] Cross-channel holdings existed up to and indeed well after 1204, but only at the very highest social level of magnates did they remain common. Nonetheless, for those who did continue to have interests in Normandy its pull of place could be just as strong as England's. Moreover, some families centred on England might send their sons to Normandy for military or linguistic training, which could add a sense of attachment to place to a sense of attachment by ancestry.[6] The attraction to Normandy could thus potentially counteract the attraction of England for some.

Moreover, even if a geographic shift led to a shift in identity, it was not inevitable that Englishness would be the new identity. It is important to ask how important was the construct of England, and to what degree were new loyalties of place centred on it. We are so accustomed to taking England for granted that it is easy to overlook the importance of this question. To a modern person it seems perfectly obvious that settling in village *x* in county *y* in region *z* of England would lead to an attachment to England as a whole, as well as more local attachments, but in fact there is nothing natural about this. It does seem to me on some level normal for people to become attached to the place in which they live, to their house and village, to the woods in which they hunt or gather wood, to the fields that they plough or have their tenants plough. For members of the elite, one might automatically expect an attachment to the local region in which they were active, through which they would often travel,

[4] James Lydon, 'The Middle Nation', in *The English in Medieval Ireland* (Dublin, 1984), 23–6; Frame, 'Les Engleys Nées in Irlande', 83–103.

[5] David Crouch, 'Normans and Anglo-Normans: A Divided Aristocracy?', in *England and Normandy in the Middle Ages*, ed. David Bates and Anne Curry (London, 1994), 51–67.

[6] For military training, see Reginald of Durham, *Vita Sancti Godrici*, 427. For linguistic training, see below, p. 384.

and of which they would have vivid experience. But England was a larger and there-fore rather more abstract place. Few if any could personally visit and experience even a fraction of it. I have spoken before of Benedict Anderson's concept of imagined communities in which one feels a connection to large numbers of people one has never met.[7] In the same way, England was and still is an imagined place, to which people can feel attachment even when they have visited only a small piece of it, or even, in the case of some armchair Anglophiles, none of it at all.

In the modern world the construct of England has become so well established that it is hard to think of it as a construct rather than simply another natural phenomenon, even if outsiders, and some insiders, tend to confuse it with Britain or the United Kingdom. One can point to England, carefully delineated and colour-coded, on a map, read a guidebook to England, or frequently hear England dis-cussed as an entity. Not only in England itself but also elsewhere there are constant reminders that a place called England exists, and therefore it is second nature to think of Northumbria as being in the same place as Cornwall, and in a different place than Lothian or the Borders in Scotland. But to what degree would the immi-grants after the conquest have encountered such frequent reminders that they were now in England? To what degree did this abstract geographic concept impinge on their thinking, particularly in comparison to the more concrete villages and regions in which they lived and worked? Because England was every bit as much a construct as Englishness, and like all historical constructs could vary in nature and strength over time, one must be very wary about anachronistic assumptions concerning the power and influence of the concept of England in the post-conquest period, and therefore of its ability to reshape ethnic identity. There is no question that the idea of England existed then, but one must measure how strong it was, particularly in relation to other geographic constructs and identities, such as Britain. Only if we can establish that the construct of England was an influential one can we be sure that our assumption that settling in village x in county y in region z of England would promote Englishness is not simply anachronistic. Only through a study of the construct of England, and the institutions supporting it, can we understand precisely how it did contribute to the triumph of English identity.

Two considerations add further weight to the problems outlined here. First, when it came to grabbing land, the Normans who had conquered Edward the Confessor's realm certainly saw nothing sacred about England's boundary with Wales, but almost immediately began moving across it. Throughout the period in which the Normans were becoming English, many of them were also seeking their fortunes in Wales, Scotland, and Ireland. How could the abstract concept of England influence a group of people who cared little for England's boundaries in building up their own estates? The second consideration has to do with recent work on northern England and particularly the borderlands with Scotland.[8] As is well

---

[7] Anderson, *Imagined Communities*, 6–7.

[8] Paul Dalton, 'The Governmental Integration of the Far North, 1066–1199', in *Government, Religion and Society in Northern England, 1000–1700*, ed. John C. Appleby and Paul Dalton (Stroud, 1997), 14–26; W. M. Aird, 'Northern England or Southern Scotland? The Anglo-Scottish Border in the Eleventh and

known, the boundary between the two kingdoms was still shifting in this period. Increasingly, scholars have questioned the ties of northern to southern England, rightly seeing the existing north–south divide as having deep historical roots. They also point out that there were, and would continue to be, strong ties of kinship, language, and culture across what would eventually become the fixed border of the two countries. Building on this, they have questioned how much a part of England the northern counties were in that period. If England is a construct, it was still under construction in the twelfth century in the north, and one must be wary of teleological assumptions that the eventual fate of geographic and ethnic identity in the region can tell us much about what was going on there in the post-conquest period.

To further illustrate the dangers of assuming any simple correlation between geographic and ethnic identity, and the potential problem of making teleological assumptions, it is worth stressing that England was not the only large geographic construct popular at the time. Britain appeared again and again in the sources, and could in theory have provided a foundation for a new immigrant identity in the same way that England actually did. Henry of Huntingdon, Alfred of Beverley, an anonymous writer in French, Alexander Neckam, Gervase of Canterbury, and Gervase of Tilbury all wrote descriptions of Britain, drawing heavily (sometimes through the medium of Henry of Huntingdon) from Bede. Writers referred commonly and casually to Britain.[9] Moreover, the concept had much to offer; as an island, Britain could seem a less artificial construct than England. It had a fine classical heritage, always a source of snob appeal during the Twelfth Century Renaissance. On a practical level, it made a good vehicle for the hegemonic concerns of William and his successors, and of their archbishops of Canterbury. The corresponding ethnic term 'Britons' could in theory have been used in the same unifying way that it was from the eighteenth century on.[10] In the middle of the twelfth century, moreover, the concept of Britain received a tremendous shot in the arm from Geoffrey of Monmouth's wonderful, inventive, and extremely popular history.[11] Yet, unlike the concept of England, it had very little effect on ethnic identity in the period under discussion. As a group, immigrants came to think of themselves as English, even in other parts of Britain and in Ireland. There were reasons why the new inhabitants of Britain did not become British, which I will discuss later. Here, suffice it to say that geographic concepts alone, however popular, were not enough on their own to create or change ethnicity, and that the case of

Twelfth Centuries and the Problem of Perspective', in ibid. 27–39; Keith J. Stringer, 'State-building in Twelfth-century Britain: David I, King of Scots, and Northern England', in ibid. 40–62; Stringer, *Earl David of Huntingdon*, 207–11; Jewell, *The North–South Divide*, 1–213. See also Campbell, 'United Kingdom of England', 43–7, for some interesting commentary on this subject.

[9] *Bede's Ecclesiastical History*, 14–18; HHHA 10–24; Alfred of Beverley, *Annales de Gestis Regum Britanniae*, 4–10; A. Bell, ed., 'The Anglo-Norman *Description of England*: An Edition', in *Anglo-Norman Anniversary Studies*, ed. Ian Short (London, 1993), 31–47; Alexander of Neckam, *De Naturis Rerum with the Poem of the Same Author, De Laudibus Divinae Sapientiae*, ed. Thomas Wright (London, 1863), 456–61; *Historical Works of Gervase of Canterbury*, 2: 414–44; Gervase of Tilbury, *Otia Imperialia: Recreation for an Emperor*, ed. S. E. Banks and J.W. Binns (Oxford, 2002), 304–6.

[10] Linda Colley, *Britons: Forging the Nation, 1707–1837* (New Haven, 1992).

[11] See below, pp. 252–3.

Britain is further evidence that relations between identities of places and peoples were complex.

I hope to have shown sufficient reason for not simply taking it for granted that settling in the existing kingdom of England would automatically make immigrants English. That said, I would argue that traditional assumptions to this effect are correct, in part because, then as now, England was a powerful construct that had a powerful hold on people's imaginations, at least for those social groups, to which most Normans belonged, with access to literacy. Curiously enough, one of the best places to gain an understanding of the image of England and its power is in some of the descriptions of Britain, for, in the twelfth century, there was a tendency for these to slide into descriptions of England. Henry of Huntingdon's description of Britain was not restricted to England, yet he stated that the island was once called Albion, then Britannia, and now Anglia, devoted most of one section to an enumeration of the counties 'called shires in English', an enumeration that made sense only in an English context, and wrote another section about the wonders to be seen in England.[12] Alexander of Neckam felt his description of Britain, part of a broader geographic overview, was a logical place to comment favourably on the character of the English.[13] Gervase of Canterbury began a geographic work called the *Mappa Mundi* with a reference to the 'English isle', and gave a guided tour of England, list-ing religious houses, sees, hospitals, castles, islands, and bodies of water, county by county, after which he moved on far more briefly to Scotland, Wales, and overseas countries.[14] Several things seem to be going on here: an arrogant tendency of the English to confuse Britain with England; a recognition of England as a distinct unit within Britain; and, perhaps, a sense that England was as important a geographic concept as Britain. The tendency of England to butt into and even supersede descriptions of Britain is thus a tribute to its continuing power as a construct, and at the same time another minor factor in promoting that construct. Indeed, with Gervase of Canterbury, readers were provided with a detailed and useful mental map that could help them visualize the country in its particulars and in its whole.

At the same time, a strong and very positive literary image arose of England as a land of wealth, fertility, and abundance. This image too had its roots in descriptions of Britain, particularly Bede's, but was transferred in many different texts to England. Even before the conquest, Byrhtferth of Ramsey described England as 'a broad and fertile *patria*'.[15] Gervase of Canterbury began his *Mappa Mundi* by saying 'the situation, mildness, abundance, and wealth [that characterize] the region of the English isle have been described in splendid style by many men of great

---

[12] *HHHA* 12, 16–18, 22.

[13] Alexander of Neckam, *De Naturis Rerum*, 456–7.

[14] *Historical Works of Gervase of Canterbury*, 2: 414–49.

[15] [Byrhtferth], *Vita Sancti Egwini*, in *Vita quorundum Anglo-Saxonum*, ed. J. A. Giles (London, 1854), 361. The life of Ecgwin is set before the unification of England, but a nearby reference to the *Angligenam patriam*, and one to several kings of the *patria* in the statement itself, shows that England as a whole is meant. For Byrhtferth's authorship of this work, see Michael Lapidge, 'Byrhtferth and the *Vita s. Ecgwini*', *Medieval Studies*, 41 (1979), 331–53.

authority . . .'[16] Richard of Devizes had a fictional Continental Jew refer to England as a land of milk and honey.[17] Several Continental poets—Baudri of Bourgueil, Hildebert of Lavardin, and Hugh of Montacute—built on the image of England as a *terra ferax*, a 'fertile land', in works dealing with that country or figures associated with it.[18] More important, the image of England as an abundant land could apparently influence immigrants quite early on. An immigrant monk writing an account of the miracles of St Edmund not long after the conquest could speak of 'England, very happy, rich, and extremely sweet'.[19] Like Shakespeare's famous speech in *Richard II* on 'This blessed plot, this earth, this realm, this England', if to a lesser extent, these passages create a memorable and positive image of the country. Of course the image of fertile, abundant England in these works is rather literary. But for immigrants with access to literacy, it could help fix a strong and favourable picture of England in their minds, thus underpinning the construct of England, and increasing its influence on its conquerors.

More important than descriptions and images is the fact that England simply seems to have been taken for granted in the twelfth century, as today, for a construct is most successful when it simply appears to be part of the existing landscape rather than an artificial, historically contingent idea. Of course, the constructed image of England was not identical to the one existing today, and was probably somewhat less powerful, particularly among ordinary people. But it was similar enough to today's image to make its constructed nature nearly invisible to modern scholars, and it was powerful enough to exert an influence on ethnic identity. The degree to which England was an automatic frame of reference can be illustrated from discussion in the chronicle of Walden Abbey about Geoffrey de Mandeville the younger, whose family had founded the monastery. The chronicler wrote: 'He spent less time among his own (*sui*) in England than was good', and in a later passage: 'He was a strong man, and powerful in arms, great in the eyes of all, so that he spent little time in England among his own people (*sui*), and guarded fortifications and castles in Normandy which king Henry had entrusted to him.'[20] Geoffrey apparently saw the Continent as a natural sphere of activities, showing the continuing pull of Continental ties, but a monk at the family monastery, who may well have represented local opinion, obviously disagreed. The term *sui* here almost certainly referred to ties of lordship and perhaps of neighbourhood rather than ethnicity. But England was clearly seen as Geoffrey's proper sphere by the Walden writer. The land and power of the Mandevilles, like that of most magnates, was concentrated in particular regions and counties, not spread across the country as a whole, but it

---

[16] *Historical Works of Gervase of Canterbury*, 2: 414.

[17] *Chronicle of Richard of Devizes*, 64.

[18] Baudri de Bourgueil, *Itinerarium*, PL 166: 1173–4; *Hildeberti Cenomannensis Episcopi Carmina Minora*, 24–5; A. B. Scott, 'Some Poems Attributed to Richard of Cluny', in *Medieval Learning and Literature: Essays Presented to Richard William Hunt*, ed. J. J. G. Alexander and M. T. Gibson (Oxford, 1976), 196–7.

[19] Herman, 'De Miraculis', 33.

[20] Diana Greenway and Leslie Watkiss, eds., *The Book of the Foundation of Walden Monastery* (Oxford, 1999), 44, 60.

seemed perfectly natural to the writer of the Walden chronicle (and to us) to auto-matically think of Geoffrey de Mandeville's proper sphere of influence not as a region or town, but as the country. Similarly, when the poem of William the Marshal described his desire to visit the land of his birth, the land in question was not the village or region in which he was born and his family had influence, but *Engletere*.[21] Wrote one lovesick poet: 'All England sighs when my Phillis is sad.'[22] In fact, anyone who is familiar with the sources of the period will know that references to England were frequent and widespread, among not only native but also immi-grant writers. That immigrant writers should frequently use the term is hardly sur-prising when the invaders crossed the Channel with the construct of England firmly in mind; to take only one example, William of Poitiers made a rhetorical address to England at one point in his work.[23] Nevertheless, familiarity with and adoption of the construct is especially important in terms of its ability to influence immigrants.

Precisely because the construct of England is so powerful and pervasive, now as then, and because it seems so natural for writers to refer matter-of-factly to it, to describe it, or create an image of the land, it is easy either to overlook its significance in the period or to treat it simply as a given, almost a natural feature of the histori-cal landscape. We should do neither. On the one hand, it is important to study why it was such a powerful construct. On the other hand, the fact that the idea of England was an important and pervasive construct made it capable of affecting ethnicity, and this helps to explain why the traditional assumption that settling in England could in the long run lead to anglicization is correct. But it is important to move beyond assumption, and study how the construct of place affected the con-struct of identity.

Part of the answer will come in later chapters, but some preliminary points can be made here. First, medieval writers themselves recognized links between place and identity in the same common-sense way that they saw connections between descent and identity. The best illustration of this thinking, a famous passage from Fulcher of Chartres, comes from the context of the Crusades rather than Anglo-Norman England, but it can shed light on contemporary attitudes:

Consider, I ask, how in our time God turned West into East. For we who were westerners have become easterners. He who was Roman or French, in this land has become Galilean or Palestinian. He who was [a citizen] of Rheims or Chartres is now made [a citizen of] Tyre or Antioch. We have now forgotten the places of our birth ... He who was a foreigner is now like a native.[24]

Similarly, Eadmer could write that Anselm's father Gundulf was born in Lombardy, but was turned from a foreigner in his new home of Aosta into a citizen.[25] That

---

[21] Meyer, *L'Histoire de Guillaume le Maréchal*, 1: 56.

[22] J. H. Mozley, 'The Collection of Mediaeval Latin Verse in MS. Cotton Titus D. XXIV', *Medium Ævum*, 11 (1942), 22.

[23] *GGWP* 156

[24] *Recueil des Historiens des Croisades: Historiens Occidentaux*, vol. 3 (Paris, 1866, repr., Farnborough, 1967), 468.

[25] Eadmer, *Life of St Anselm*, 3.

medieval people could casually assume a link between changing place and shifting identity in no way ensured that immigration would affect identity, but it was far more likely to happen than if they had linked identity to descent alone.

Second, a powerful construct of place could attract the affection and even loyalty of people.[26] We have already seen that England, as a *patria*, could attract loyalty both before and after the conquest. When Goscelin of Saint-Bertin wrote the *Liber Confortatorius* to console the recluse Eva, the daughter of a Lotharingian and a Dane who had become English, and who was deeply homesick in her cell in Angers, he depicted a heaven in which Wilton existed, from which the nuns could look out on 'their England'.[27] The epilogue of a supposed letter from Prester John speaks of how it was obtained by Gilbert the Butler, who accompanied his lord, William de Ver, to the Holy Land, and of how William longed to return to his native land of England. The William in question is hard to identify, and it is hard to take seriously the epilogue to a letter from Prester John, but this passage does show the expectation that a member of a prominent Anglo-Norman family might feel homesick for England.[28] Such loyalty to a construct of place could easily be shifted to a construct of ethnicity; in other words, loyalty to England could become loyalty to the English, and in fact the two could reinforce each other. It is probably no accident that when Henry of Huntingdon, for whom English identity was important, sat down to write a description of Britain, England kept popping up.

Third, the idea of England could help create a sense of collective identity for the inhabitants of England even at a time when the concept of Englishness was still controversial, particularly as a collective identity. A study of one important historical work from the middle of the twelfth century, the *Gesta Stephani*, shows how this could work, and in particular how an identity linked to England could serve as a transition to Englishness. The author of the work, quite possibly the bishop Robert of Bath described in another source as Flemish but born in England, was one of many writers chary of referring to the English outside of genitive expressions, and clearly the construct of Englishness was uncomfortable for him. But England was everywhere in the work, serving not only as a strong geographic construct, but also sometimes as a collective identity. He speaks of England being troubled, of England suffering for the sins of its rulers, and of all England being at the siege of Winchester. England, the place, could stand in for its inhabitants, including elite warriors whom one might still hesitate to identify simply as English, and a collective identity focused around England could be expressed in non-ethnic terms.[29] Similarly, a later poet who wrote of England being chastised by God was of course referring to its

[26] David Rollo, *Historical Fabrication, Ethnic Fable and French Romance in Twelfth-Century England* (Lexington, 1998), 88–9.

[27] Goscelin of Saint-Bertin, 'Liber Confortatorius', 37–8, 41, 115. The text (and the MS on which it is based) refers to looking out at 'tota Anglica sua', but there is no obvious noun for Anglica to modify, and I believe it must be an error for 'tota Anglia sua'.

[28] M. Dominica Legge, *Anglo-Norman Literature and its Background* (Oxford, 1963), 201–4; Julia Barrow, 'A Twelfth-Century Bishop and Literary Patron: William de Vere', *Viator*, 18 (1987), 180–2.

[29] Potter and Davis, *Gesta Stephani*, 86, 130, 152, 154. See above, p. 76, n. 27, for this work's avoidance of the term English outside of genitive constructions.

inhabitants.[30] As time went on, after the ethnic divides that were so prominent after the conquest dwindled away, a collective identity centred around the idea of England could easily become a collective English identity

But what of local identities, which, I suggested earlier, need less construction than a large, abstract entity such as England?[31] To what degree did people form strong local attachments; did such attachment create local identities; and, if so, how did this affect shifts in ethnic identity and the triumph of English identity? The answer to the first two parts of the question is that people certainly did form local attachments and that these could create regional identities.[32] This was true not only in the north but also in the south, where I will start. First of all, the emotionally laden term *patria*, as noted before, was by no means restricted to England. Adam of Balsham, a scholar born in England who taught in Paris in the middle of the twelfth century, described himself as 'nascione Anglicus, patria Balsamiensis et genere Bellvacensis, mansione . . . Parisiensis'.[33] Adam was pointing to a series of geographic and ethnic loyalties, but it was the village from which he came for which he reserved the term *patria*. The many immigrant families that took surnames from villages and other places in England may not simply have been adopting convenient designations but also signalling new-found local loyalties of place. Cities and regions could also inspire great loyalty. One of Becket's hagiographers, William Fitz Stephen, devoted a long passage in his work to praise of London, and early in the thirteenth century Lucian, a cleric of Chester, wrote an entire work extolling and preaching to that town.[34] Around the same time, after an anonymous monk of Peterborough wrote a vitriolic and puerile attack on Norfolk and its inhabitants, one John of St Omer rose to the defense of his *patria*, as he described it, and of its people, the *gens Nortfohlchiæ* or *Nortfolchienses*, with comic earnestness.[35] Along with local identities could come parochialism of the worst sort. A miracle story by the hagiographer Goscelin describes how three inhabitants of Canterbury made a living travelling to various English cities and extracting silver from tailings left by moneyers, silversmiths, and so forth. At Bath, where they were perceived as foreigners (*advenae*), they were badly mistreated after removing a paving stone from a royal road, in a way that one suspects locals would have avoided.[36] Our sources are not overflowing with evidence of local attachments, narrow-minded or otherwise, but clearly they were a presence in the period, probably a strong one.

[30] BL Arundel MS 201 pt. 2, fol. 54ʳ. For discussion of the MS, see Rodney M. Thomson, 'Some Collections of Latin Verse from St. Albans Abbey and the Provenance of MSS. Rawl. C. 562, 568–9', in *England and the 12th-Century Renaissance*, ed. Rodney M. Thomson (Aldershot, 1998), 151–3.

[31] See also Thorlac Turville-Petre, *England the Nation: Language, Literature, and National Identity, 1290–1340* (Oxford, 1996), 142–55.

[32] Mercian, East Anglian, and West Saxon regional identities, which may have had lingering influence into the late Anglo-Saxon period, had little or no impact after 1066.

[33] 'Adam of Petit Pont's *De Utensilibus*', in *Teaching and Learning Latin in Thirteenth-Century England*, vol. 1, ed. Tony Hunt (Cambridge, 1992), 175.

[34] *Becket Materials*, 3: 2–13; *Liber Luciani de Laude Cestrie*.

[35] Thomas Wright, *Early Mysteries and other Latin Poems of the Twelfth and Thirteenth Centuries* (London, 1838), 93–106.

[36] Goscelin of Saint-Bertin, 'Libellus de Miraculis Sancti Augustini', 549–50.

Such regional loyalties and identities, however, seem to have posed no great threat to the construct of England or its influence on identities. Before and after 1066 local identities could easily coexist with broader ones. While Ealdorman Byrhtnoth is made to speak of defending the *eard* of England in the poem 'The Battle of Maldon', other characters refer to local or regional loyalties.[37] Lawrence of Durham, who could weep for the *patria* of England, could also lavish praise on his birthplace of Waltham in Essex, and on the wealth of his adopted county, Durham.[38] Henry of Huntingdon, so concerned with England and the English, also seems to have been devoted to Huntingdon and the surrounding regions.[39] Indeed, local patriots seem often to have thought of their own city or region within an English context. John of St Omer wrote that just as the knights of Normandy were the best knights across the sea, so those of Norfolk were the best in England.[40] Lucian compared the morals of the men of Chester to those of 'the rest of the English'.[41] London was often described as the chief city of England or some variant thereof, not least by William Fitz Stephen, indicating that its importance stemmed not just from its size and wealth but from its place in the kingdom as a whole.[42] Thus, far from competing with or detracting from the strength of attachment to England, and thereby undermining Englishness, local feeling may well have fed into and strengthened the constructs of England and Englishness. It is possible, for instance, that Henry of Huntingdon's love of a part of England helped to inspire his love of the more abstract whole, and that in this respect he was not alone. In any case, throughout the south, with one exception, regional and local attachments did not create or sustain identities that clashed with Englishness in any direct fashion; rather, they created and sustained separate levels of identity. The one exception, and it is a telling one, was Cornwall. Inhabitants of that county were sometimes, like the Welsh, identified as Britons, which clearly was an ethnic rather than simply a regional identity, and must surely have been meant as a contrast to the English.[43] But the Cornish were a special case. They had traditions and a history of their own, as well as their own language. This can serve as a reminder that although the relationship between constructs and culture is complex, it certainly existed. Nevertheless, within the south Cornwall was *sui generis*.

What of the north? Most of the work that has been done on this subject has focused not on how northerners and others defined the region and its inhabitants, but on political and cultural factors. Such factors lay behind identity, but as I have emphasized before, there is no precise way to predict the relationship between

---

[37] Dobbie, *Anglo-Saxon Minor Poems*, 8, 13–14.

[38] *Dialogi Laurentii Dunelmensis*, 2, 19–22, 40–1.

[39] *HHHA* pp. xl–xli.

[40] Wright, *Early Mysteries*, 106.

[41] *Liber Luciani de Laude Cestrie*, 65.

[42] *Becket Materials*, 3: 2; 4: 148; Potter and Davis, *Gesta Stephani*, 12; Reginald of Durham, *Vita Sancti Godrici*, 38; Södergård, *La Vie d'Edouard le Confesseur*, 181; 'The Life of Saint Wulsin of Sherborne by Goscelin', 75.

[43] *WWGP* 204; Robertson, *Laws*, 244. See also below, pp. 353–4.

culture and identity. Therefore, I think that more attention needs to be paid to how people of the time saw the situation, without, of course, ignoring previous findings. And in fact writers before and after 1066 did see northerners as different. A charter of Edward the Confessor describes him as king of the English and of the Northumbrians, treating the two peoples as distinct, and Wulfstan of Winchester stereotyped the latter as drinkers.[44] William of Malmesbury emphasized the 'harshness' of the language of the Northumbrians, and especially those of Yorkshire, which meant that 'we southerners', could not understand them. He spoke of the 'innate heat in the minds of the Northumbrians', and of the 'Northumbrian people (*populus*), always inclined to rebellion', describing them elsewhere as a savage *gens*.[45] The line between a regional and ethnic identity can be a thin one, and the Northumbrians do sometimes seem to have been viewed as a separate people with very distinctive attributes.

Nevertheless, there is ample evidence that contemporaries saw all the northern counties as part of England, and their inhabitants as English, albeit English with a difference. Significantly, this evidence comes partly from the north, though the caveat needs to be made here that no relevant material survives from the far north-west, which was firmly incorporated into the kingdom of England only under William II, and was probably the most distinctive area in cultural and linguistic terms. A number of passages, including ones written by such northern figures as Aelred of Rievaulx, Richard of Hexham, Reginald of Durham, the anonymous chronicler of the archbishops of York, and William of Newburgh, implicitly or explicitly treated the northern regions, including Northumberland and Carlisle (for the county of Cumberland was slow in developing), as part of England.[46] There never seems to have been any doubt, at least within England, that the northern regions formed part of that country. If anything, there was a tendency to view areas that then and now were politically part of the Scottish kingdom as parts of England; William of Malmesbury could describe the see of Whithern as being in the extreme borders of England, next to Scotland, and one writer of the Anglo-Saxon Chronicle referred to Lothian as being in England.[47]

Similarly, for all the talk of Northumbrians found in many sources, English identity was clearly widespread in the north. It is worth remembering that the army facing King David at the battle of the Standard, drawn largely from the north, was generally described as being Norman and English or simply as English.[48] Some northerners may have decided to support David, but that speaks only to their politi-

---

[44] Matthew, *Norman Monasteries and their English Possessions*, 143; Wulfstan of Winchester, *Life of St Aethelwold*, 22–4.

[45] *WWGR* 300, 498; *WWGP* 209, 271–2; *VW* 22–3.

[46] Aelred of Rievaulx, 'Relatio de Standardo', 181, 184; 'De Sanctis Ecclesiae Haugustaldensis', 190; Richard of Hexham, *De Gestis Regis Stephani*, 150–1, 159; Reginald of Durham, *Libellus Beati Cuthberti*, 16, 23, 65, 67; *Vita Sancti Godrici*, 41; *HCY* 2: 528; *SMO* 1: 140; *ASC* E 1017; E 1079; *CJW* 3: 10, 256; Potter and Davis, *Gesta Stephani*, 50; *WNHA* 105.

[47] *WMGP* 256; *ASC* E 1091.

[48] See above, p. 75.

cal loyalties, not to their ethnic identity, for Richard of Hexham could speak of one portion of the invading army being 'English from the Northumbrians and Cumbrians, from Teviotdale and Lothian'.[49] Not only did Englishness stand above local identities in the northern counties, as in the south, but it still did so even in parts of Scotland, as in the above quote, or when Adam of Dryburgh in Berwickshire stated that he was working in the land of the English and the kingdom of the Scots.[50] But the Englishness of the north in the twelfth century was still very much Englishness with a difference. A host of references, particularly in northern writers, to the northern English and the southern English, to Southanglia and to the southern or northern regions or provinces, shows that people were very much aware of a north–south divide, even if they thought of themselves as part of one unified English people.[51]

An exploration of contemporary attitudes therefore strongly reinforces the culturally and politically based arguments about the distinctiveness of the north and the artificiality of the boundary between the two countries in the period. There is no reason to think that the inhabitants of Northumberland or Cumbria would have been any less likely than those of Lothian to adopt a Scottish identity had King David's descendants held on to his acquisitions sufficiently long. Nevertheless, given that the aim of recent work has been to emphasize what set the north apart from the rest of England, it is worth stressing the strength of English identity in the region in the twelfth century, and though I have described it as Englishness with a difference, from the point of view of northerners of the period it may well have been southerners who were English with a difference.

In any case, the strength of Englishness in the borderlands revealed by the sources has two important consequences from a scholarly point of view. First, from a twelfth-century perspective it is more surprising that Lothian became ethnically Scottish than that Northumberland remained ethnically English; in other words, it is the change that needs to be explained rather than the lack of change, and the greater teleological danger is underestimating the Englishness of Lothian than overestimating that of the northern counties. Second, and far more important for our purposes here, it is crucial that even the strong regional identity of the north did not seriously undermine English identity in the area. This meant that the construct of England could exert its influence on ethnic identity there as elsewhere, and it also meant that native northerners could support that process. It is worth noting that one of the writers explicitly promoting English identity, Aelred of Rievaulx, was a quintessential northerner who was born at Hexham, spent part of his youth at the

---

[49] Richard of Hexham, *De Gestis Regis Stephani*, 152.

[50] Adam of Dryburgh, *De Tripartito Tabernaculo*, 723. For another example of a native of Scotland as English, see Reginald of Durham, *Libellus Beati Cuthberti*, 67–8. See also Jocelin of Furness, *Vita Sancti Waltheni*, 277, where the younger Waltheof's body at Melrose is listed as one of seven uncorrupted bodies in England, but Waltheof is also described as a patron of Scotland.

[51] Barlow, *Life of King Edward*, 74–6, 80; Aelred of Rievaulx, 'De Sanctis Ecclesiae Haugustaldensis', 182–3, 190; Richard of Hexham, *De Gestis Regis Stephani*, 155, 156, 160, 165, 171, 177, 178; James Raine, ed., *Miscellanea Biographica* (London, 1838), 42; Reginald of Durham, *Libellus Beati Cuthberti*, 38, 54, 212, 272; *Becket Materials*, 2: 447; EHOV 4: 94.

court of the king of Scotland, and then passed the majority of his adult years at the Yorkshire monastery from which he drew his name.[52]

It is worth pausing for a moment to look again at identity in the Norman kingdom of Sicily. There, as Norman identity faded, what took its place were local and regional identities rather than one that was related to the whole kingdom. In England, a writ from Henry I to Bishop Ranulf Flambard referred to French and English Northumbrians.[53] That shows that local identity could exert its influence on immigrants as well as natives. But ultimately the Normans who settled in the north became English, not just Northumbrians, in the way that some of their relatives became Apulians or Sicilians. Regional identities persisted, particularly in the north, and it is worth remembering that chroniclers could speak of a group of nobles from the area who were instrumental in the events leading to Magna Carta simply as the northerners.[54] But it is also worth remembering that places like Northumberland, Durham, Yorkshire, Cumberland, and Westmorland were northern only in relation to England, not to Scotland or to the island as a whole. In other words, when the northern barons of Continental ancestry adopted a regional identity, it was only within an English context, unlike the situation in the other great Norman kingdom, where no such overarching identity developed. This only underscores the importance of the construct of England and its strength even in the furthest reaches of the kingdom.

In summary, the idea of England, which had been developed before the conquest, remained a powerful one afterwards, despite its abstract nature and despite cultural differences between north and south. So strong was the idea of England that it suffered no real threat from powerful local allegiances and identities. So matter-of-factly was it accepted, then as now, that its existence as a contingent, historical development becomes almost invisible. Because it was such an important feature of the mental landscape of the time, in the long run it could exert influence on ethnic identity. But it is worth exploring further why the construct of England was so strong, and trying to understand how precisely it might affect immigrants. In the following chapters, therefore, study of the constructs of England and Englishness will go hand in hand.

---

[52] For Aelred's life and background, see Walter Daniel's *The Life of Ailred of Rievaulx*, and its introduction by Maurice Powicke.

[53] *RRAN* 2, no. LXIV; van Caenegem, *English Lawsuits*, no. 181.

[54] J. C. Holt, *The Northerners: A Study in the Reign of King John* (Cambridge, 1961, repr., 1992), 8–16.

16

Royal Government, England, and Englishness

THE ENGLISH GOVERNMENT, simply by its very existence, helped to maintain and propagate the constructs of England and Englishness, and played a role in the adoption of a new identity by the political elites. This is not a new idea. Susan Reynolds has been a notably strong advocate of the idea that governments created peoples rather than vice versa.[1] A number of scholars have argued that government was a factor behind the creation of England and English identity before the conquest.[2] Both Reynolds and Davies have noted government as a factor in the unification of English and Normans after the conquest.[3] But how and why did the royal government strengthen the ideas of England and Englishness? Modern rulers and politicians have often sought consciously to foster national identity, but there were no comparable attempts in post-conquest England. Indeed, even if it had occurred to the kings of England to foster Englishness, they probably would have preferred to foster ties of personal loyalty, since they were generally also rulers of other lands, and any promotion of a single identity in the face of other strong identities could drive their subjects apart. Given these questions, it is worth exploring in greater detail the government's influence on constructs of place and identity after the Norman Conquest and to try to lay bare some of the mechanics of how it worked.

Before turning to this subject, it is necessary to address briefly the scholarly debate over whether one can speak of an Anglo-Norman *Regnum* in which England and Normandy essentially formed a single political entity. John le Patourel was the chief proponent of this argument, a more modest version of which was put forward by C. Warren Hollister.[4] More recently, this view has come under attack by David Bates and Judith Green.[5] Clearly there was an interchange of ideas and personnel between the two lands, and the importance of the fact that they often had the same

---

[1] Reynolds, *Kingdoms and Communities*, 250–331, esp. 253; Reynolds, '*Origines Gentium*', 380–90.
[2] See above, pp. 22–4.
[3] Reynolds, '*Origines Gentium*', 385; R. R. Davies, 'The Peoples of Britain and Ireland 1100–1400: II. Names, Boundaries and Regnal Solidarities', *TRHS* 6th ser., 5 (1995), 13–14.
[4] Le Patourel, *The Norman Empire*; id., 'The Norman Conquest, 1066, 1106, 1154?', *PBC* 1: 103–20, 216–20; Hollister, *Monarchy, Magnates and Institutions*, 17–57.
[5] Bates, 'Normandy and England after 1066', 851–80; Judith A. Green, 'Unity and Disunity in the Anglo-Norman State', *Historical Research*, 62 (1989), 115–34.

ruler cannot be ignored, but the critics are right that at a fundamental level the governments were quite distinct, with their own rules and organization. The same was also true of the Angevin lands after 1154. Had there been a single, unified and integrated government linking England and Normandy or the Angevin territories, the effects on identity might have been quite different, but as it was there remained a distinct English government which could promote the dual constructs of England and Englishness.

In exploring how the government played a role in fostering the idea of England and the triumph of English identity, I wish to look first at two revealing episodes in post-conquest history, and then turn to a discussion of the ways in which the government could have a systematic impact. The first is revealed by a writ, almost certainly one of a series sent to all the counties, issued by Henry I in 1101 to one native and three immigrant leaders of Lincolnshire society, Picot son of Colswein, Bishop Robert of Lincoln, Osbert the Sheriff, and Ranulf Meschin.[6] In this writ, the king affirmed the promises made at his coronation, and then told the recipients to bind themselves with oaths to defend 'my land of England' against all men, and especially Duke Robert of Normandy, until Christmas Day. The persons addressed were expected to take the same oath from all the king's demesne tenants, French and English, and barons were expected to take the same oaths from their own tenants. Henry, of course, was motivated by a desperate desire to shore up his own position, not any abstract love of the *patria* of England, but the language and the means by which he attempts to do so here are remarkable. In essence, Henry was demanding that the immigrant elite join with natives in defence of their new country against other Normans. Though Henry's appeals had far less success among the immigrants than among the natives, it is remarkable that in a time of crisis the king or his bureaucrats hoped that they could shape loyalties by reference to the land of England. Despite their limited success, this writ is illustrative of assumptions about the links between government, place, and loyalty, and indicative of the way in which the idea of the realm of England was providing a new potential framework, only a few decades after the conquest, for the way immigrants could think about loyalty and allegiance.

The second episode is an embassy of Thomas Becket, while still chancellor, to King Louis of France, as recorded by one of his hagiographers, William Fitz Stephen.[7] In this account Thomas successfully used the embassy 'to show and demonstrate the opulence of English luxury'. He was accompanied by large numbers of retainers, including 250 footmen singing 'according to the custom of their *patria*', presumably England by the context. He also had a rich supply of goods, including two cartloads of ale, a beverage which we shall see was associated with the English and was described here as 'that clear, salubrious drink, better in taste and colour than wine'. It was to be given to the French, presumably to set them straight about the relative merits of the two drinks. Supposedly the French who saw this large retinue, upon discovering that it followed the chancellor of the king of the

---

[6] *RRAN* 2, no. 531; Foster and Major, eds., *Registrum Antiquissimum*, 1, no. 73.
[7] *Becket Materials*, 3: 29–32.

English, remarked that the king himself was a marvel, whose chancellor proceeded in that manner. Later, it is noted, Becket made a point of honouring the English scholars at Paris. Even if the strongly and self-consciously English slant of the embassy was nothing more than an invention by Fitz Stephen, it is a good example of the power of England in the mental landscape and of the way it could be linked to government. But Becket himself could describe the English as 'our people', and Henry II may well have thought it in his interest to stress his position as king of England rather than duke of Normandy or Aquitaine, in order to stress that he was an equal of the king of France, and to provide a not-so-subtle reminder of the resources he could draw on from his insular realm.[8] If so, this expression of royal and governmental power and, for all we know, others like it, could have served to promote the image of England as an abundant, delightful place, in a way that written texts could not.

In fact, in all its acts, great and small, the royal government maintained the strength of England as a construct and spread its influence to the wealthy and powerful immigrants, who after all were most likely to be affected by and involved in the bureaucracy of the time. Constructs remain powerful and continue to be treated as givens only through constant reinforcement. England as a political entity had been created by the West Saxon kings, and it could have disappeared as an independent political entity had William I chosen, just as Mercia, Kent, and other kingdoms had disappeared in the past. For good practical and propagandistic reasons William did not end the English kingdom, and that meant that the machinery of government continued to reinforce the idea of England after the conquest as before. Every time William held one of his ceremonial crown-wearings at Winchester, Westminster, and Gloucester, he was reminding his followers that they were now in a kingdom called England. When he ordered all important land-holders from 'ofer eall Engle land' to swear allegiance to him, he was driving home the point that the immigrants as well as the natives owed allegiance to him as members of an English polity. Not the least important fact about Domesday Book was that it was explicitly considered a description of England in contemporary sources. The massive effort, involving thousands of people, to describe the king-dom would have served as a powerful reinforcement in the minds of native and immigrant alike of the existence of the kingdom of England.[9]

When Henry I tried to demand that powerful lords swear to defend England, he was simply building on his father's foundation. When he referred in his 'corona-tion' charter to promises made with the council of the barons of the whole kingdom of England, and when Stephen at the beginning of his reign made promises to all his barons and men of England, they were speaking in platitudes, but they were also reinforcing the idea that England formed a polity to which the barons, largely of

---

[8] For Becket's Englishness, see *Correspondence of Thomas Becket*, 2: 1264.

[9] *ASC* E 1085–6 [*recte* 1085–7]; *CJW* 3: 44; Hemming, *Chartularium Ecclesiae Wigorniensis*, 288; W. H. Stevenson, 'A Contemporary Description of the Domesday Survey', *EHR* 22 (1907): 74, 77. That Domesday Book was missing northern regions that were considered English, and contained Welsh ones that were not, did not detract from its affect on the bulk of England.

immigrant descent, firmly belonged.[10] The post-conquest kings as a group, by maintaining English coinage, retained one of the most widespread means by which government reinforced the construct of England. Anytime someone changed or even handled money, it served as a reminder of the government and kingdom of England. This is revealed most strikingly in an incidental episode in a miracle story set during the Scottish invasions linked to the 1173–4 revolt against Henry II. In it, a Cumbrian alewife refused to accept a coin of the Scottish king, because he was an enemy to 'King Henry of the English, in whose kingdom she lived'.[11] The oaths taken by freemen that Wormald saw as important before the conquest could continue in importance afterwards.[12] Immigrants were not exempted from these influences; Normans had to use English money and change Norman money when shuttling back and forth between countries, and there is no evidence to indicate that minor or downwardly mobile immigrant landholders, including peasants, were exempted from oaths. New measures, such as Henry II's prohibition against selling arms or ships outside of England, and Richard's command for uniform measurements throughout England, only served to further reinforce the idea of England for the descendants of natives and nobles alike.[13] Even the constant use of the title 'king of the English', and the phrase 'kingdom of the English', subtly reinforced the idea that the English existed as a people. In short, the royal government, rudimentary as its bureaucracy was by modern standards, was more than adequate to make sure that the idea of England remained fixed in the minds of its inhabitants, particularly those of its elites.

The actions of government, imposed on immigrants and natives alike, also helped to create the sense of community, of shared experience and interests, that is so fundamental to ethnic unity. Nowhere was this truer than in the area of law, especially since a shared law was seen as an important marker of ethnicity by medieval thinkers. Specialists on Wales and Ireland have shown how administrative distinctions and discrimination between the English and Celts in the Middle Ages, and above all divisions between English law and Welsh or Irish law, often exploited to the advantage of the conquerors, helped to perpetuate ethnic divides and hostility.[14] Williams and van Caenegem have also emphasized how important it was that law served as a unifying factor in England after the conquest rather than a dividing one.[15] As we saw in Chapter 4, there were some legal differences between English and Normans, and therefore at least the possibility of the kind of dual legal

[10] Stubbs, *Select Charters*, 100, 119.
[11] Reginald of Durham, *Libellus Beati Cuthberti*, 277.
[12] See above, pp. 23–4.
[13] *Chronica Magistri Rogeri de Hovedene*, 2: 261; 4: 33–4.
[14] Davies, *Lordship and Society*, 309–17; Davies, 'Law and National Identity', 51–69; R. R. Davies, 'Lordship or Colony', in *The English in Medieval Ireland*, ed. James Lydon (Dublin, 1984), 151–3, 159–60; Davies, *Age of Conquest*, 432–4; id., 'Laws and Customs', 5–6, 9–12; Robin Frame, *The Political Development of the British Isles, 1100–1400* (Oxford, 1990), 213–15; id., 'Les Engleys Nées in Irlande', 85–90; Hand, *English Law in Ireland*, 198–205.
[15] Williams, *ENC* 164; van Caenegem, *Royal Writs*, 401; id., *Birth of the English Common Law*, 18, 25, 96–8.

system that emerged in the Celtic lands.[16] Two key factors allowed England to avoid that divisive possibility.

First, up to at least the middle of the twelfth century Norman kings and others professed an ideological commitment to maintain the laws of Edward, in other words, the laws in effect at the end of the Anglo-Saxon period. William I's early charter to London, Henry I's coronation charter, and Stephen's charter of promises to his barons and men all expressed a commitment to the laws of Edward, and a number of post-conquest legal treatises show Francophone and therefore probably immigrant intellectuals trying to grapple, not always successfully, with pre-conquest law codes.[17] That immigrants often called on natives for legal advice indicates that more than rhetoric was involved in the commitment to Edward's law.[18] But in practice traditional English law was mixed in with Continental customs and with innovations to create what would become the unified common law, and this is the second key point.[19] Obviously practice diverged from theory, but this was probably a good thing, since elite immigrants were unlikely to abandon all their own customs and legal expectations, and if the laws of Edward remained intact, the only alternative would have been to create a dual legal system, as William I did on the issue of judicial proof. Practice could diverge from theory without creating too much cognitive dissonance partly because the theory held open the possibility of emending the law, but mainly because law remained to a large degree oral and therefore flexible. Norman law was not written, and Wormald has argued that both pre- and post-conquest codes were largely ideological rather than practical.[20] While a few Norman intellectuals were wrestling with written English law, a new, unified law that made no ethnic distinctions was being hammered out in various courts, where, as we have seen, native and immigrants worked together. The class divide created by the destruction of the old aristocracy may have facilitated this; Continental influence could come to dominate land law affecting the predominantly immigrant elites, while traditional law could have a large role in issues affecting the largely native peasantry, with little disruption to the practices of

[16] See above, pp. 49–51.

[17] Stubbs, *Select Charters*, 83, 101, 119. For recent work on the Normans and old English law, see O'Brien, *God's Peace and King's Peace*; Mary P. Richards, 'The Manuscript Contexts of the Old English Laws: Tradition and Innovation', in *Studies in Earlier Old English Prose*, ed. Paul E. Szarmach (Albany, 1986), 181–7; Mary P. Richards, *Texts and Their Traditions in the Medieval Library of Rochester Cathedral Priory*, Transactions of the American Philosophical Society, NS 78, pt. 3 (1988), 10–11, 43–60; Wormald, *The Making of English Law*, 228, 402–15, 465–76; Williams, *ENC* 156–64. For the identity of one important legal writer as Norman, see above, pp. 77–8. For the argument that most post-conquest treatises were written by Normans, see O'Brien, *God's Peace and King's Peace*, 133–4.

[18] Stevenson, *Chronicon Monasterii de Abingdon*, 2: 2; MacRay, *Chronicon Abbatiae de Evesham*, 89; van Caenegem, *English Lawsuits*, 1, no. 5; Williams, *ENC* 144.

[19] For a recent overview of English law in the period, which deals extensively with the question of continuity and innovation, see John Hudson, *The Formation of the English Common Law: Law and Society in England from the Norman Conquest to Magna Carta* (London, 1996). See also Pollock and Maitland, *History of English Law*, 1: 79–110, 136–73; Stenton, *English Justice*; van Caenegem, *Birth of the English Common Law*; Fleming, *Domesday Book and the Law*, 1–85. For the issue of Continental influence on English law, see Paul Hyams, 'The Common Law and the French Connection', *PBC* 4: 77–92.

[20] Wormald, *Making of English Law*, 416–83.

both groups.[21] Work on traditional oral legal practice has shown that it can often accommodate change while maintaining an appearance and even a genuine sense of continuity. Thus, for instance, the immigrant Gilbert Foliot, writing in support of the canonization of Edward in 1161, could state that his laws still had a beneficial effect on justice and the poor.[22]

Both the theoretical and the practical facets discussed here were profoundly important. The ideological commitment to Edward's laws gave tremendous prestige to one aspect of native English culture at a time when many aspects of that culture, as we saw earlier, were coming under attack. The unity of law could help foster a general sense of unity, and because the law was described as Edward's law, immigrants could not ignore that this was a unity that crossed ethnic lines. The commitment to the law of Edward faded with time, but it was strongest at the time of greatest hostility, and the idea of a unified, *English* law continued; thus, the author of *Glanville* could speak of the laws he was recording in Henry II's reign as *leges Anglicanas*.[23] Of all the spheres of royal government, none was more important than law in fostering the sense of England as a community of people.

Government, in the persons of kings and queens, also provided a focus of loyalty that was linked, in the minds of contemporaries, to kingdom and people (often enough in the passages in question, England stands for its inhabitants, as it did in the *Gesta Stephani*). The effect of this was blunted to some degree by the foreign origins of England's kings, by their roles as rulers of other lands, and by the resulting complexity and ambivalence of their ethnic identities. The Englishness of the rulers remained problematic throughout the period of assimilation and anglicization, and beyond. Adam of Eynsham, the biographer of Bishop Hugh of Lincoln, could have the bishop lump King Richard in with the English, but then have the king refer to 'those English' as if he were not one.[24] Matthew Paris could describe the offspring of the Emperor Frederick II and Henry III's sister as 'English by blood', but then have Henry III asking if 'you English' planned to depose him during the baronial rebellions.[25] Southern has argued that the English kings were far less successful than the French ones at becoming symbols of their nation and winning the affection of their people, and their ethnic ambivalence may be one reason why.[26] Nevertheless, the vision of king, kingdom, and people as closely intertwined foci of loyalty remained a powerful ideology that not only generated attachment to kings but also to England and, eventually, the English.

Passages linking kings, England, and sometimes the English people appear throughout the period in question. When William of Poitiers chastised *Anglia* for not treating William I as it should a king, and when a poet wrote, in a panegyric to

---

[21] Hudson, *Formation of the English Common Law*, 17–18.

[22] Morey and Brooke, *Letters and Charters of Gilbert Foliot*, 177.

[23] G. D. G. Hall, ed., *The Treatise on the Laws and Customs of the Realm of England Commonly Called Glanvill*, 2nd edn. (Oxford, 1993), 2.

[24] Adam of Eynsham, *Magna Vita Sancti Hugonis: The Life of St Hugh of Lincoln*, ed. Decima L. Douie and David Hugh Farmer, 2nd edn., vol. 2 (Oxford, 1985), 105–6, 114.

[25] Matthew Paris, *Chronica Majora*, 4: 313; 5: 339.

[26] Southern, *Medieval Humanism*, 147–51.

that king, 'let festive *Anglia* sound with joyful approbation', they were expressing this ideology, albeit in rather strained circumstances.[27] Instances relating to Henry I and Edith-Matilda abound. Both, in letters trying to arrange Archbishop Anselm's return from exile, linked themselves to the people of England in making the request.[28] The immigrant bishop Herbert Losinga addressed the queen as the common mother of all England, and a poem describes her as the 'honour of the English, the glory of the realm'.[29] Henry was linked with England and its people time and time again in laments for his death. For instance, Gilbert Foliot, writing to Brian Fitz Count, stated that with his death 'the people was deprived of its father', and that since his death 'the face of England is devastated'.[30] Similar language was used for later rulers. Étienne of Rouen could say in praise of the Empress Matilda that 'England shines in the rising of this star', Henry of Huntingdon could write a poem in which Henry II is addressed as the saviour of England, and Geoffrey of Vinsauf could address a poem on the death of Richard I to England.[31] That rulers were linked to their land and people was a commonplace.

The fact that all these passages are conventional is in itself a sign of how widespread and influential a world-view they expressed. Generally, the purpose of the writers was to praise or support rulers, and their desire was to express how much the land and its inhabitants owed the ruler, and how much honour the rulers derived from their position. Nonetheless, such passages both expressed, and fostered, attachment and loyalty to the English realm, and sometimes to the English people. Not only did they reinforce the construct of England, and sometimes of the English, at a basic level, but they also presented them as objects worthy of concern. Edith-Matilda and the Empress Matilda derived honour from their association with England and the English, but that in itself implied that those concepts had honourable associations. In the laments for Henry I, one of the reasons for lamentation is that England and its people (not the writer, not a particular town or region, and only rarely England *and* Normandy) suffer. This implies that the fate of England and its inhabitants matters to the author and his audience. Moreover, they show how concern for and even loyalty to the ruler might easily become linked to concern for and loyalty to the realm. Such links are even more clearly revealed in a couple of charters issued by lords of immigrant ancestry in Henry II's reign. It was common for charters to state that donors were making gifts for the souls of various people, sometimes including the king. What is interesting about these is that after listing the king, one nobleman, Bernard de Saint-Valery, said that the gift was for 'the state of

[27] *GGWP* 156; André Boutemy, 'Notice sur le recueil poétique du manuscrit Cotton Vitellius A xii du British Museum', *Latomus*, 1 (1937), 304.

[28] S. *Anselmi Opera Omnia*, 4: 109; 5: 253–4.

[29] *Epistolae Herberti de Losinga*, 48; Boutemy, 'Notice sur le recueil poétique', 305.

[30] Morey and Brooke, *Letters and Charters of Gilbert Foliot*, 61. For similar passages, see Potter and Davis, *Gesta Stephani*, 2; *HHHA* 492; *EHOV* 6: 452; *Chronicle of Robert of Torigni*, 126; William H. Cornog, 'The Poems of Robert Parte', *Speculum*, 12 (1937), 243; Walter Map, *De Nugis Curialium*, 440; Thomas Wright, *Bibliographia Britannica Literaria* (London, 1846), 181.

[31] Étienne of Rouen, *Draco Normannicus*, 596; *HHHA* 776; Edmond Faral, *Les Arts poétiques du XIIe et du XIIIe siècle* (Paris, 1924; repr., 1962), 207–10. In a second poem Geoffrey links Richard to Neustria.

the whole kingdom of England', and the other, Robert of Stafford, that it was for 'the health and stability of the whole kingdom of England'.[32] This was important because, in the first generation after the conquest, immigrant loyalties might have been directed to the king but probably not to England. Over time, the close link seen between ruler, kingdom, and people could help engender within immigrants a sense of loyalty to England and its people, as well as to the king.

Political programmes to inculcate identity and nationalism in a people are largely a modern affair, and the image of a king such as Henry I sitting down with his advisors to map out a strategy to increase English patriotism will quite rightly strike readers as ludicrous. Occasionally, if one can trust Fitz Stephen's account of Becket's embassy, government officials may have consciously promoted the image of England, but not as an end in itself. Nonetheless the actions and ideologies of the government brought some of the same results, though of course on a much reduced scale, through raising a consciousness of England in people's minds and through supporting an ideology which linked king, country, and people, and promoted loyalty to all three. The process by which government inadvertently influenced people was subtle, so subtle that it was probably invisible to contemporaries, but that simply made it more effective. As I have argued before, identities and constructs are most powerful when they seem overwhelmingly obvious, even natural; the English government helped to create a situation in which both England and Englishness took on those apparent characteristics.

The process by which government affected geographic and eventually ethnic identities was, however, a slow one. No one picked up an English coin, or attended a crown-wearing, and felt an instant and deep loyalty to the *patria* of England. Only gradually would government activity help the immigrants to think of themselves as belonging to a place called England, and to transfer allegiance from Normandy or elsewhere to England. Only slowly, and only with the merging of legal practice, would the government help to foster a sense of unity with natives. Because of the ethnic divide between English and Normans, moreover, it was easier for government to instill a sense of attachment to England than to the English. Henry I was already trying to tap into it at the beginning of his reign, as we have seen. The author of the *Gesta Stephani*, in explaining the attempts of magnates to avoid a battle between the forces of Stephen and the future Henry II in 1153, wrote that fighting would be to the loss of the realm, and that leaders on both sides considered the war to be the destruction of the whole realm.[33] This suggests that the author's sense of England as a community or collective identity was in part political. By creating a political community within England, the royal government helped to set the stage for the triumph of Englishness. In the early thirteenth century, as we shall see, an early high point of the government's influence on geographic loyalties and identity was reached as Englishness, loyalty to England, and politics became thoroughly tangled up in the wars associated with Magna Carta.

---

[32] Salter, *Cartulary of Oseney Abbey*, 4, no. 20B; Eyton, 'The Staffordshire Chartulary, Series I–II', series 2, no. 24.

[33] Potter and Davis, *Gesta Stephani*, 238.

How important a factor was government in the unification of peoples and the anglicization of the Normans? This, of course, is impossible to quantify, but some comparisons may help to clarify the issue. The example of Scotland suggests that it was a very important factor indeed. Scotland had the one other powerful monarchy in the British Isles, and it is notable that not only the descendants of Continental immigrants to that region, but also of people who in the twelfth century were still considered English, ended up with a Scottish identity. On the other hand, the continuity of English identity among settlers in Ireland and Wales, even in times and places where the hand of the English government was very light, and the survival of Welsh and Irish identity after the firm imposition of English government in the early modern period, shows that there was no simple correlation. Even some of the most powerful modern states which have set out to create unified ethnic or national identities have failed to do so, and English medieval government, as precocious as it was, had much less power to influence people. English government clearly played a significant role in the unification of English and Normans and the revival of English identity, but it was only one among a number of institutions and factors involved in these complex processes.

17

The English Church, English Saints, England, and the English

A SECOND INSTITUTION that led immigrants to feel a part of England, and therefore promoted Englishness, was the English church. Like the English government, the English church acted in subtle but important ways to reshape geographic and ethnic loyalties. The fact that there was an English church, with its own growing bureaucracy, constantly reinforced the constructs of a place called England and a people called the English. As an institution with responsibility for the spiritual well-being of the inhabitants of England, the English church could foster a collective identity in the country. The church could also foster cultural unity, at least once some of the initial disputes, such as the confrontation at Glastonbury over liturgy, were healed. Obviously the church as an institution would have had the most influence on churchmen and nuns, but, as I have argued, these formed a particularly important group with regards to identity. Moreover, as the loyalty of immigrant laypeople shifted to local churches, which formed part of the overall English church, and as powerful members of the laity became involved in issues involving the English church, they too could have been drawn into a nexus of existing ideas and loyalties that would help to anglicize them.

As Z. N. Brooke has shown, references to the *Ecclesia Anglorum*, the *Ecclesia Angliae*, and later the *Ecclesia Anglicana* were common in the sources throughout the period.[1] This English church drew its existence from the cultural unity Bede described and from the strong connection between it and the royal government, for it corresponded to no precise institutional division within the church.[2] England was divided into two archbishoprics, and the primatial authority claimed by the archbishops of Canterbury extended to all of Britain and to Ireland. Nevertheless, for good practical and political reasons, the English church did function as a unit. The potential link between this institutional English church and the idea of England is best illustrated by William of Malmesbury's *Gesta Pontificum Anglorum*. William's work is essentially a series of histories of important churches within England, but collectively it acts as a history of the religious affairs of England and the

---

[1] Brooke did so in the context of an argument that the term 'Ecclesia Anglicana' in Magna Carta was not a sign of growing patriotism, but this does not invalidate my argument that the concept of the English church could subtly affect how people thought about geographic and ethnic identity: Z. N. Brooke, *The English Church and the Papacy from the Conquest to the Reign of John*, 2nd edn. (Cambridge, 1989), 3–22.　　　[2] Cheney, *From Becket to Langton*, 11, 103.

English, acting as a companion work to his *Gesta Regum Anglorum*. As William moved from church to church, he also created a verbal map of the sacred geography of the land. Any reader would come away from this work with a sense of England as a discrete and distinctive land.[3] On a more mundane level, councils of the English church by their very existence, and by issuing decrees such as the one in 1102 forbidding the practice of selling men *in England*, served to raise consciousness of England in the minds of people.[4] Indeed, every time even the simplest reference was made to the English church or the church of the English, it strengthened the two constructs and made their existence seem obvious and matter-of-fact. The existence of an English church may even have given an impression that England was a divinely sanctioned entity, part of God's ordering of the world.

The English church, like England itself, had to compete with local allegiances, for churchmen, monks, and nuns had fierce loyalties to their own churches. But just as regional loyalties could coexist with and even feed into attachment to England, so too could loyalties to individual churches exist within the framework of the English church. When Henry of Huntingdon wrote that the new church at Lincoln ceded to none within England, or the scholar William de Montibus preached, in a sermon in a church dedicated to St Andrews, that the church was one of the saint's principal churches in England, they were, in a minor way, raising the consciousness of England in people's minds even while addressing local loyalties.[5] William of Malmesbury devoted a disproportionate amount of time to his own monastery and its saint in his *Gesta Pontificum Anglorum*, but in doing so he placed loyalty to his own church in the context of loyalty to the English church.[6] Thus the effects of the English church on geographic loyalties and ethnic identities were not greatly dampened and may sometimes have been fostered by deep loyalties to individual churches. In this context it should be noted that Emma Cownie has shown how the immigrant nobility, which initially favoured Continental monasteries with their newly gained wealth, increasingly favoured foundations in England.[7] Both she and Brian Golding have shown the frequent burials of immigrant nobles in England.[8] Both of these indicate new-found attachments to individual English churches, and it is possible that such attachments could help to create attachment to or at least foster greater awareness of the English church and therefore of England. It is notable that the foundation charter of Lewes, from *c*.1089, speaks of monks of Cluny being given to William de Warenne and his wife, the founders, 'for England'.[9] Likewise, allegiance to the church as a whole could also coexist with

[3] *WMGP* 3–343.
[4] Whitelock *et al.*, *Councils and Synods*, vol. 1, part 2, p. 678.
[5] *HHHA* 748; Joseph Goering, *William de Montibus (c. 1140–1213): The Schools and Literature of Pastoral Care* (Toronto, 1992), 551.
[6] *WMGP* 330–443.
[7] Cownie, 'The Normans as Patrons of English Religious Houses', 57–60; id., *Religious Patronage in Anglo-Norman England, 1066–1135*, 185–206.
[8] id., *Religious Patronage in Anglo-Norman England*, 201–3; Brian Golding, 'Anglo-Norman Knightly Burials', in *The Ideals and Practices of Medieval Knighthood*, ed. Christopher Harper-Bill and Ruth Harvey (Woodbridge, 1986), 35–48.
[9] Salzman, *The Chartulary of the Priory of St. Pancras of Lewes*, 1: 3.

Englishness, as when John of Salisbury, in the *Metalogicon*, proudly claimed individual scholars and religious thinkers in Paris as English, or wrote that the death of Pope Adrian had 'saddened all Christian peoples and nations, but affected our England, the country where he was born, with sharper sadness, and washed it with more tears'.[10]

How did the English church create a sense of unity that crossed ethnic lines? Most importantly, the existence of an English church underscored the crucial fact that English and Normans shared the same religious beliefs. Moreover, immigrants and natives became members of the same unit within the wider Christian church. This not only gave immigrants a link with the English, but it also set them slightly apart from their relatives who were part of the Norman church or some other Continental unit, although of course continuing ties with Normandy and the movement of churchmen back and forth across the Channel limited the effects of any distinctiveness that was created.[11] The English church probably played less of a role than government in creating new, as opposed to underscoring existing, cultural unity. Nonetheless, councils of the English church did help to bring conformity between English and Normans in such matters as locating episcopal seats in cities. Thus the English church, like the English government, helped to bring a sense of unity to the two peoples.

The English church also added an important dimension to the whole set of linked loyalties to ruler, kingdom, and people. The church had strongly supported the king before the conquest, and naturally the new immigrant prelates continued the tradition. The council at Winchester in 1072 decreed that traitors against the king would be excommunicated, and ordered each priest to sing three masses and members of other orders to sing one psalter for the king.[12] But as we saw in the last chapter, loyalty to the king could be linked to loyalty to the kingdom. Thus, prior Odo of Canterbury could say to Henry II, after Becket's death, that a replacement was needed whose prayers would 'stabilize the kingdom and support the *patria*'.[13] Devotion to the *patria* and by extension to its people became, by the back door as it were, a religious duty.

Much of what the church did, no doubt, was to reaffirm in the minds of natives that they were English, but one can also catch glimpses of how the church might draw foreigners into the nexus of constructs and loyalties that would help to anglicize them. I will start with Lanfranc, who as archbishop of Canterbury stood at the top of the English church. The works of Osbeorn, Eadmer, and Nicholas reveal the kinds of expectations he faced from native monks about his relation, as archbishop, to the land and people of England. When Osbeorn wrote to Anselm to chide him for not yet giving up his abbacy at Bec to accept the position, he accused him of preferring 'a nest of narrow solitude to the breadth of the English', and although

[10] John of Salisbury, *Metalogicon*, ed. J. B. Hall and K. S. B. Rohan (Turnhout, 1991), 71, 114, 142, 183.

[11] David Spear, 'Norman Empire and the Secular Clergy 1066–1204', *Journal of British Studies*, 21, no. 2 (1982), 1–10

[12] Whitelock *et al.*, *Councils and Synods*, vol. 1, part 2, p. 606.

[13] *Becket Materials*, 4: 181.

this was written after Lanfranc's death it expresses the sort of attitude he would have heard earlier.[14] Osbeorn and Eadmer, following their models in their lives of Dunstan, strongly emphasized Dunstan's position as pastor or metropolitan of the English people. For both writers, the archbishop of Canterbury was by his position inextricably linked with the land of England and the English.[15] Most interestingly, Nicholas, writing to Eadmer during the latter's short stint as bishop of St Andrew's, though he spoke of Eadmer's new flock as a barbaric *gens*, also described them as 'your' *gens*.[16] To be the prelate of a people involved on a certain level identification with them. It is in this context that Lanfranc's description of himself as a *novus Anglus* should be read.

Lanfranc was rare in declaring himself English, even if of the newly minted variety, so early, but evidence relating to Henry I's nephew Henry of Blois, who was raised on the Continent, can reveal how the English church (along with the government) could help to create a link between an immigrant and England. Henry of Blois made a speech to a church council of England during the Empress Matilda's brief period of dominance after the battle of Lincoln, in his capacity as papal legate. William of Malmesbury, who was present, wrote that he spoke of the clergy of England coming together for the peace of the *patria*, and described England as formerly a land of peace. In other words, if William's version can be trusted, he both used and thereby promoted the image of England as a special place and as a *patria*.[17] One might dismiss this as 'mere' rhetoric, or an invention by William. However, in a set of enamel plaques on which Henry is depicted and which he obviously commissioned, the inscriptions request that an angel, also depicted, take the donor to heaven sometime after taking the gift, 'but not to hurry lest England rise in mourning for the one through whom there is peace or war, agitation or repose'.[18] Henry none too modestly linked England's fate to his own here, but in doing so he firmly linked himself to England. There is no sign that Henry identified himself as English, in this period when lingering ethnic divides still made that identity problematic, but like the author of the *Gesta Stephani*, he clearly identified with the community of England. Henry of Blois was a cosmopolitan figure, but the existence of the English church (and no doubt the English kingdom), helped him to develop an attachment to the land of England and its people. Clearly, the English church could act as an adjunct to the royal government in maintaining and propagating the concepts of England and Englishness.

One way the church played a key role in a way the government could not was through the cults of specific saints who had been connected to England.[19] The evidence that people often linked saints with England and Englishness after the conquest, as before, is cumulatively overwhelming. Most scholarly discussion of English cults after the conquest has to do with two issues. First, the writing of lives

---

[14] *S. Anselmi Opera Omnia*, 4: 9.

[15] Stubbs, *Memorials of St. Dunstan*, 108, 199.

[16] Wharton, *Anglia Sacra*, 2: 234–6.

[17] William of Malmesbury, *Historia Novella*, 90.

[18] George Zarnecki *et al.*, *English Romanesque Art, 1066–1200* (London, 1984), 261.

[19] See also Turville-Petre, *England the Nation*, 59–67, for a later period.

has been set in the context of the overall preservation of culture. Second, there has been a debate over whether or not the Normans looked down on English saints, to which I will return. Only Clark has argued, in passing, that saints' cults acted as a vehicle for the survival and spread of Englishness.[20] Here I wish to pursue her argument, and place it within the context of my general picture of the triumph of Englishness after the conquest.

The first step is to provide some illustrations of precisely how saints were associated with and raised the prestige of both England and the English. The most striking example of a link between a saint and the English in this period comes from a sermon on St Alban printed by Hearne and attributed to William of Newburgh, according to its editor, by 'certain erudite men'. The sermon begins by describing the Romano-British saint as 'our' St Alban, and goes on with: 'I say ours confidently, not fearing the false claims of the Britons. "What," they say, "has the Briton Alban to do with you? You are English, your fathers exterminated his people and occupied his [burial] place with his body. You persevere in the sin of your fathers to this very day, calling yours what you hold captive."' To the modern reader, or at least this modern reader, the attacks of the Britons on English claims to Alban carry devastating moral force, but the preacher will have none of it. 'Rather, there is much more between the admirable martyr and us English. What, O Britons, is there between him and you? Offended by the sins of his people, which came to his attention even in heaven, he crossed over to the English, and, I say, from a Briton became English, from yours became ours.' Thereafter, the sermon, clearly addressed to a self-consciously English audience, insistently refers to 'our' Alban.[21] This passage shows how a strong and aggressive sense of English identity could be closely intertwined even with a saint who was not self-evidently English. Unfortunately, since the manuscript of this sermon has not been located, Hearne's attribution of it to William of Newburgh cannot be confirmed, and we cannot even be certain that it dates from the period with which this book is concerned.[22] However, Alban was often described as the 'protomartyr of the English' in the period, and there is strong evidence for links between other saints and either England, the English, or both, that comes from unimpeachable sources.[23]

This evidence comes from a range of writers, some deeply concerned with Englishness and others less so. Some passages focus on the link between saints and England. William of Malmesbury declared his desire to praise the saints of his *patria* in the *Gesta Pontificum Anglorum*.[24] Eadmer wrote, in a passage drawing on images of England's fecundity: 'Britain, which the English (having defeated the Britons and settled) call England, has great native and imported riches . . . not only

[20] Clark, *Words, Names and History*, 37.

[21] William of Newburgh, 'Sermo de Sancto Albano', in *Guilelmi Neubrigensis Historia sive Chronica Rerum Anglicanum*, ed. Thomas Hearne, vol. 3 (Oxford, 1719), 819, 874.

[22] Richard Sharpe, *A Handlist of the Latin Writers of Great Britain and Ireland Before 1540* (Turnhout, 1997), 794.

[23] For St Alban see *EHOV* 2: 348; Alexander of Neckam, *De Naturis Rerum*, 460; Roger of Wendover, *Flowers of History*, 2: 112.

[24] *WMGP* 277. See also *WMGP* 5, 165–6; *WMGR* 182, 398, 576; *VW* 4; Stubbs, *Memorials of St. Dunstan*, 253, 254, 269, 285, 304, 317.

does it have quantities of worldly goods but it thrives with a great abundance of most holy men; as a result of their merits, God has adorned the island munificently and cults have multiplied.'[25] Similarly, William of Wycomb, in his *vita* of his friend Bishop Robert Bethune of Hereford (who died in 1148), writes the following about the arrival of the bishop's body at Dover: 'Happy England, undertake your priceless treasure to your rejoicing bosom and magnify God. The just judge did not wish to deprive you of the corporeal presence of one whom you raised, whom you had as a light on the road of justice.' William then goes on at some length in the same vein.[26] Many passages linking saints to England survive from a variety of sources, ranging from ones equally florid down to passing references to a saint as 'the light of England' or some similar construction.[27]

Saints were even more associated with the English as a people, and often enough with both people and country. Eadmer could depict Pope Gregory the Great, who had sent missionaries to England, as leading the English to God on the Day of Judgement, and William of Malmesbury wrote, in the beginning of a section on the saints of the English in his *Gesta Regum Anglorum*, that God had placed among them a larger number of miraculously preserved bodies than would be found in any other *gens*. Both believed that people were likely to pay more attention to saints from their own people. Eadmer felt he needed to explain why St Andrew mattered to the English, and William, in a preface dedicated to Henry of Blois, argued that although people would respect holy foreigners they would be still more inspired by the lives of holy 'compatriots'.[28]

William and Eadmer were by no means alone in linking saints and the English. Reginald of Durham wrote in his life of Godric of Finchale, in a passage drawing on a biblical parable, that after a pilgrimage to Jerusalem the saint returned to his 'natal land' because Christ did not wish 'to use the talent of the English by burying it in a foreign land, nor to take away the light of that people, lending it to a foreign people and taking it away from his own', and immediately thereafter spoke of him as coming joyfully to the borders of the English (*fines Anglorum*).[29] Even a saint such as Cuthbert, who was strongly connected with, and indeed helped to create, a regional identity in the 'land of St Cuthbert', could also be connected to England as a whole. Thus Reginald of Durham, who recorded Cuthbert's authority around Durham, also talked about Cuthbert's pre-eminence among English saints, described a murderer who came to his shrine as visiting all the regions of England and the saints

[25] *HCY* 1: 161. See also Eadmer, 'Opuscula de Sanctorum', 212; Stubbs, *Memorials of St. Dunstan*, 182, 200.

[26] William de Wycomb, 'De vita Roberti Betun, episcopi Herefordensis', in *Anglia Sacra*, ed. Henry Wharton, vol. 2 (London, 1691), 319.

[27] Folcard, 'Vita S. Botulphi', *AASS*, June, 4: 327; Blake, *Liber Eliensis*, 280; Alexander Penrose Forbes, ed., *Lives of S. Ninian and S. Kentigern* (Edinburgh, 1874), 209, 210; Jocelin of Furness, *Vita Sancti Waltheni*, 277; *Radulphi de Coggeshall Chronicon Anglicanum*, 19.

[28] *WMGR* 386; *Early History of Glastonbury*, 40; Eadmer, 'Nova Opuscula', 212; Stubbs, *Memorials of St. Dunstan*, 199. See also *WMGR* 114, 120, 232, 386–414, 590–2; *WMGP* 15, 186, 254; Stubbs, *Memorials of St. Dunstan*, 203; Eadmer, 'Nova Opuscula', 208–13; Eadmer, 'Vita S. Bregwini', 185–6; Eadmer, 'Vita Odonis', 86–7.

[29] Reginald of Durham, *Vita Sancti Godrici*, 58 (see also 406).

of that land, and spoke of a man choosing by lot among the chief saints of England 'Cuthbert, Edmund, and Thomas'.[30] Perhaps the most striking evidence of links between a saint and the English comes from a collection of miracles of St Edmund, in which an abbot from Anjou, giving thanks at Bury St Edmund's, wrote in a first-person account that the monks asked why he was so devoted to St Edmund, 'even though I am not English, but rather Angevin'.[31] Again, there survives a multitude of passages, ranging from the complex to simple references such as a saint being the 'flower of the English', that firmly linked the saints to the English.[32]

Saints could even be associated with the defence of England and the English. Roger of Howden wrote that when the earl of Leicester landed in England with a great army of foreigners during the 1173–4 revolt, the royal army, led by Richard de Lucy and Humphrey de Bohun, carried the banner of St Edmund against them and smote them with the virtue of God and the saint.[33] A miracle story from the Fifth Crusade in the Barnwell Chronicle shows that this was still remembered years later. According to the chronicler, after Damietta was captured an English knight dedicated two mosques that had been converted to churches to the English martyrs Edmund and Thomas. The miracle concerned a Fleming who mocked the former and was duly punished, and in the course of it the chronicler claimed that the Flemings (who had made up much of the earl of Leicesters's army) hated the saint for the misfortunes they suffered in England in Henry II's reign.[34] I have noted the importance of the idea of defending the *patria* of England, and though the precise language was not used, the concept of the saint as a defender of the realm was certainly present.

In considering the potential impact of the link between saints' cults and the constructs of England and Englishness, it is worth remembering the importance of the cults in the lives of religious houses and their popularity among the laity. Adoration of individual saints was worked into the liturgy of monasteries, and was often the subject of sermons and prayers, and through these mediums the links between saints and England or the English could be brought beyond saints lives and other written works into the services and prayers of monks, nuns, and clerics. For

---

[30] id., *Libellus Beati Cuthberti*, 38–9, 209, 260. See also *WMGP* 268; *WMGR* 182. For Cuthbert and local identity, see Aird, *St Cuthbert and the Normans*, 5, 231, 274–5.

[31] Arnold, *Memorials of St. Edmund's Abbey*, 1: 176–8. For other references in which Edmund is seen as a particularly English saint, see ibid., 1: 372; *Dialogi Laurentii Dunelmensis*, 69, and below.

[32] For examples not included in other notes, see Folcard, 'Vita S. Botulphi', 327–8; Rollason, *Mildrith Legend*, 111, 115, 120, 122, 127; 'De S. Wereburga Virgine', in *AASS*, Feb., 1: 391; *EHOV* 2: 324; Hugh the Chanter, *History of the Church of York*, 66, 88–90; *SMO* 1: 346, 348, 375; 'Les Mélanges de Mathieu préchantre de Rievaulx au début du XIIIᵉ siècle', ed. Andre Wilmart, *Revue Bènèdictine*, 52 (1940), 56–8; Raine, *Miscellanea Biographica*, 17. St. Augustine of Canterbury was linked to England with especial frequency: Goscelin of Canterbury, 'Libellus de Miraculis Sancti Augustini', 537–8, 541, 544–7, 550–1, 554–5, 558–9; 'Historia Translationis S. Augustini Episcopi', 13, 15, 18–19, 34; Wharton, *Anglia Sacra*, 2: 56, 59, 62, 70; Rodney Thomson, ed., *The Life of Gundulf Bishop of Rochester* (Toronto, 1977), 53; *WMGP* 5; Stevenson, *Chronicon Monasterii de Abingdon*, 2: 295; *Chronicle of Hugh Candidus*, 59; *Historical Works of Gervase of Canterbury*, 1: 43; *GCO* 8: 126; Forbes, *Lives of S. Ninian and S. Kentigern*, 209; Walker, *Cartulary of St Augustine's*, no. 71; Franklin, *Cartulary of Daventry Priory*, nos. 600, 609.

[33] [Roger of Howden], *Gesta Regis Henrici Secundi*, 1: 60–2.

[34] *Barnwell Chronicle*, 242–3.

instance, one prayer to St Cuthbert from a manuscript of the early twelfth century begins, 'O glory of the English', and a long poem to the saint from the early thirteenth century begins, 'O father of the English'.[35] Thus, churchmen and nuns would have been exposed to links between saints and England or the English not just through written material, but also through those aspects of cults that were integrated into prayers and festivals. As for the laity, we cannot know precisely what churchmen told them about saints when they made pilgrimages to cult sites or on other occasions, but it is hard to believe that the emphasis on links between saints and the English, which was so widespread in the written material on saints, did not also surface in oral discussions. Ideas about saints may have spread through sermons as well. Unfortunately, no sermon on English saints survives in English or French, but there does survive a Latin sermon on Gregory the Great, who was an honorary English saint because of his role in the conversion, by Odo of Canterbury, abbot of Battle, who was also noted for his preaching in French and English. Odo made a point of the debt of the English people to Gregory. 'The English people ought especially to exalt him,' wrote Odo, 'because through him, it was made a friend of the angels. To others he is generally an apostle, but he is our own apostle.'[36] If Odo could write a Latin sermon along these lines, he could equally write vernacular ones. Thus, ideas about the connections between saints and the land and people of England probably reached a very broad audience. A final point about the impact of saints cults on identity is that in the imaginations of the time saints were vivid and powerful entities, and one needed to take them and anything about them seriously, which may well have extended to their ethnicity. All in all, saints' cults were in a powerful position to influence the society around them.

Before turning to precisely how the Englishness of many saints influenced identity, however, it is necessary to turn to the debate over Norman attitudes to English saints. There survive a number of stories about immigrants doubting or even scorning English saints, many of which emphasized ethnicity as a factor.[37] I have already discussed Eadmer's passage on Lanfranc's doubts about certain saints established by the English. The first Norman abbot of Abingdon, according to the chronicle of that monastery, dismissed certain saints as 'English rustics'.[38] One version of a story about Warin, the first Norman abbot of Evesham, testing relics by fire refers to them as being held in honour by the English, and says that the abbot wondered 'how a people born from the kindred of so many holy men could be defeated by the French and subjected to them?'[39] Gerald of Wales, in his life of Ethelbert, included a story about a Norman who judged the saint unworthy of honour, 'because of the innate hatred between the English and Normans'.[40] Not surprisingly, a Norman monk

[35] Thomas H. Bestul, ed., *A Durham Book of Devotions* (Toronto, 1987), 75; Raine, *Miscellanea Biographica*, 91. For the date of the poem, see Rigg, *History of Anglo-Latin Literature*, 24.

[36] *The Latin Sermons of Odo of Canterbury*, ed. Charles de Clercq (Brussels, 1983), 241.

[37] For stories which do *not* emphasize ethnicity, see *WMGP* 421; Blake, *Liber Eliensis*, 211–12.

[38] Eadmer, *Life of St Anselm*, 50–4 Stevenson, *Chronicon Monasterii de Abingdon*, 2: 284. See above, pp. 49, 233–4.

[39] MacRay, *Chronicon Abbatiae de Evesham*, 335–7 (see also 323–4).

[40] *GCO* 3: 429.

challenged the cult of Waltheof on the grounds that the deceased had been a traitor.[41] Finally, according to the version of the *Gesta Abbatum Sancti Albanum* written by Matthew Paris in the thirteenth century, Lanfranc's nephew, Abbot Paul, scorned his predecessors either because they were English or out of jealousy for their high birth.[42] Thus, some writers certainly believed that the Normans had an attitude of hostility to English saints.

For a long time scholars accepted these stories at face value, and generalized from them to suggest a widespread Norman scorn for English saints.[43] In an article published in 1987, however, Susan Ridyard challenged this view on several grounds; some of the evidence is late or problematic, relics that were scorned or casually treated in some stories were not always of saints but sometimes of predecessors, and Normans quickly began embracing English cults.[44] Her argument was bolstered by an article by Richard Pfaff claiming that a purge by Lanfranc of English saints did not take place, as previously thought, and that although there was some pruning, it affected non-English saints as well as English ones.[45] But to some degree the pendulum is now swinging back. Recently, Jay Rubinstein has suggested that Lanfranc did make a purge, but for theological reasons, and places other tests of relics, such as Warin's, in a similar context. However, he also argues that Eadmer *perceived* Lanfranc's actions as an attack on English tradition and reacted accordingly.[46] Paul Hayward has argued that many of the post-conquest accounts of saints and their translations to new sites were designed to persuade potentially hostile and sceptical Norman churchmen of the validity of their saints, and therefore of the righteousness of their communities. He also suggests that their fears of Norman hostility may have been exaggerated, and that the Normans, from the 1090s, began appropriating English cults for their own purposes.[47]

What I have written here about the close connections between saints and ethnicity may cast light, though of an ambiguous sort, on this debate. On the one hand, the link makes it more plausible that the status of individual cults might be affected by ethnic hostility, and that some Normans might have been predisposed to doubt local saints simply because they were English. On the other hand, the link may have caused later hagiographers to simply presume that ethnic hostility lay at the root of

---

[41] *EHOV* 2: 348; Giles, 'Vita et Passio Waldevi Comitis', 3, 15.

[42] *Gesta Abbatum*, 1: 62.

[43] e.g. Knowles, *Monastic Order in England*, 118–19; Fuchs, *Domesday Book*, 157.

[44] Ridyard, '*Condigna Veneratio*', 179–206. See also Gibson, *Lanfranc of Bec*, 166, 171.

[45] Richard W. Pfaff, 'Lanfranc's Supposed Purge of the Anglo-Saxon Calendar', in *Warriors and Churchmen in the High Middle Ages*, ed. Timothy Reuter (London, 1992), 95–108. Heslop has argued that a purge did take place at Canterbury, though he does not emphasize the anti-English nature of it: T. A. Heslop, 'The Canterbury Calendars and the Norman Conquest', in *Canterbury and the Norman Conquest: Churches, Saints and Scholars, 1066–1109*, ed. Richard Eales and Richard Sharpe (London, 1995), 53–85.   [46] Rubinstein, 'Liturgy Against History', 279–309.

[47] Hayward, 'Translation-Narratives in Post-Conquest Hagiography', 67–93; Paul Antony Hayward, 'The Miracula Inventionis Beate Mylburge Virginis attributed to "the Lord Ato, Cardinal Bishop of Ostia"', *EHR* 114 (1999), 543, 553–63. See also David Townsend, 'Anglo-Norman Hagiography and the Norman Transition', *Exemplaria*, 3 (1991), 385–433, for the interesting argument that many hagiographers wrote with both natives and immigrants in mind, and set up their stories so that each group could interpret aspects of the cult in its own favour.

individual doubts in the period after the conquest. For instance, a fairly typical story in Herman's eleventh-century collection of miracle stories of St Edmund records that a French knight named William son of Asketil sought the saint's help. A twelfth-century version of the story states that William initially hesitated to do so, because 'many of the French were accustomed to impudently deride the virtues of the saints resting in England'. Herman had described the ethnicity of several figures who doubted or challenged the saint, and described one as doubting 'the English martyr', but at most ethnicity was an implicit issue, whereas the later writer made it explicit.[48] Thus, as Ridyard argues, we must be careful about later writers, who may merely have assumed that because of ethnic hostility Normans would scorn English saints.

On the whole, however, I am inclined to agree with the arguments of Hayward and Rubinstein for a strong English reaction to a mild Norman scepticism that was quickly overcome (at least for key saints) and was inspired by a variety of factors. I would certainly not rule out the possibility that ethnic hostility created a certain predisposition toward scepticism among Normans. Moreover, as I argued earlier, political hostility may have made certain cults politically problematic.[49] But there was certainly no systematic drive to eliminate English saints. As Rubinstein and Pfaff have argued, theological doubts and the increasing rigour associated with revived intellectual life may have had more of an influence on individual attacks.[50] I also wonder if in some cases new prelates, faced with an indiscriminate treatment of earlier abbots as saints, not only sought to distinguish true saints from others, but also to focus attention on one or two figures and thereby create more powerful individual cults in their churches that could attract wider attention. This might explain why, according to William of Malmesbury, Abbot Warin of Malmesbury treated many of the relics of his predecessors cavalierly but assiduously promoted the cult of Aldhelm.[51] As this suggests, however, and as both Ridyard and Hayward have argued, cults were very useful to churchmen, and this consideration may often have counterbalanced any general hostility immigrant prelates might have had towards English saints.[52] One benefit specific to the retention of local saints would have been harmony with the English in a religious house. Moreover, given the countless miracle stories about doubters being punished for disbelief in or disrespect for individual saints, a genre into which the stories discussed above fit, it is hard to believe that immigrants would not have felt nervous about challenging any reasonably well established cult. Thus, any Norman hostility to English saints (and, despite the problematic nature of the sources, I suspect that there was some) would in practice have been muted, and generally directed at obscure cults.

[48] Herman, 'De Miraculis', 58–9, 74–5, 77–8; Arnold, *Memorials of St. Edmund's Abbey*, 1: 141–2. The Evesham version which puts an ethnic spin on the abbot's tests of relics was also late, at least in its present form: Hayward, 'Translation-Narratives in Post-Conquest Hagiography', 91, n. 112.
[49] See above, pp. 48–9.
[50] Pfaff, 'Lanfranc's Supposed Purge', 103–4; Rubinstein, 'Liturgy Against History', 294–8.
[51] *WMGP* 421–31.
[52] Ridyard, '*Condigna Veneratio*', 205–6; Hayward, 'Translation-Narratives in Post-Conquest Hagiography', 93. See also Denis Bethell, 'The Miracles of St. Ithamar', *Analecta Bollandiana*, 89 (1971), 422–3.

Given the degree to which ethnic pride was linked to saints, however, it is not surprising that the English would react strongly to even the threat of scorn for their saints, as Rubinstein and Hayward have argued.[53] Indeed, the very point of many of the stories is that the Norman doubters were forced, by reason, miraculous proof, or miraculous punishment, to acknowledge the validity of the saints not just as saints (which was of course always the point of stories of doubters), but also as English saints. Whether true or not, and there is no reason to doubt Eadmer on Lanfranc's doubts about Alfeah, the stories served as further defence of English culture and pride. What better answer to doubts about the religious standing of the English than to have the Norman abbot of Evesham test relics with just those doubts in mind, and be proven wrong? What better way to defend Alfeah's status than to have Anselm as his advocate? What better way to prove Waltheof's sanctity than a story about a Norman monk criticizing him and subsequently being struck down and dying?[54] Most of these stories, by their very nature as miracle stories, provide problematic evidence for the doubts and attitudes of Norman churchmen, but they are excellent sources for the attitudes of the English writers who recorded them for posterity. As such, they provide evidence for the way in which cults of English saints anchored English identity in the hostile years after the conquest, and the manner in which they served as key sources of English pride.

Whatever the truth to stories of Norman hostility to English saints on ethnic grounds, or the extent of that hostility if it existed, Ridyard was quite right in claiming that the Normans as a group sooner or later embraced English cults.[55] The Normans did not establish vigorous and permanent cults of specifically Norman saints in England, perhaps because of the growing focus on international saints such as the Apostles and Mary, perhaps because of a paucity of relics in Normandy compared to the abundance in England.[56] There were a few churches devoted to Norman saints such as Ouen, but no major cults.[57] Whatever the reasons, the saints most closely associated with Normandy never came close to challenging the dominance of English saints. Instead, the Normans turned to the saints of their new homeland. Goscelin of Saint-Bertin depicted a joyous crowd of French and English at the translation of Augustine of Canterbury's companion Hadrian in the late eleventh century, with tears of joy streaming down their faces.[58] There also exist many stories, some of an early date, of immigrants turning to English saints for miracles or supporting their cults.[59] If belief in saints was widespread among the

---

[53] Rubinstein, 'Liturgy Against History', 298–307; Hayward, 'Translation-Narratives in Post-Conquest Hagiography', 90.

[54] *EHOV* 2: 348; Giles, 'Vita et Passio Waldevi Comitis', 3, 15. See also *CJW* 3: 26–8.

[55] Chibnall makes the point that some English saints came to be venerated in Normandy: *Debate on the Norman Conquest*, 145.

[56] For devotion to international saints, see Alison Binns, *Dedications of Monastic Houses in England and Wales, 1066–1216* (Woodbridge, 1989), 18–19.

[57] For some dedications to St Ouen, see Walker, 'Charters of the Earldom of Hereford', no. 60; *Mon. Ang.*, 2: 75. But see Brooke and Keir, *London 800–1216*, 142, for the relative paucity of dedications to Continental saints in London.

[58] Goscelin of Saint-Bertin, 'Historia Translationis S. Augustini Episcopi', 38.

[59] *SMO* 1: 256–7; *CJW* 3: 32; Blake, *Liber Eliensis*, 306; Richard of Hexham, 'History of the Church of

laity, as seems likely, then the shift in the patronage of immigrant aristocrats to English churches must surely signal a shift in attachment to the saints of those churches as well as the institutions themselves. Even kings were drawn to the native saints, though whether policy or piety was uppermost in their minds is hard to say. An account from around 1072 depicts William I paying a respectful visit to Cuthbert, and the *Liber Eliensis* records (and perhaps exaggerates) his respect for St Etheldreda.[60] Henry II gathered a crowd of churchmen and magnates for the translation of the pre-conquest saint Frideswide at Oxford, and Richard I sent the captured banner of the ruler of Cyprus to St Edmund and his monastery.[61] The devotion of John to Wulfstan of Worcester and of Henry III to Edward the Confessor are well known.[62] Whatever the doubts of some members of the first generation of immigrants, their descendants displayed widespread, public, and no doubt often genuine, devotion to saints associated with England and the English.

Moreover, certain immigrants themselves became saints who were associated with England after their deaths. Gilbert of Sempringham, whose mother was English but whose father was Norman, was canonized as part of a concerted effort in which King John and Archbishop Hubert Walter played a role. One of the letters in his support described how he had promoted religion throughout England, and the author of his *vita*, in a letter to the archbishop, stated that God had blessed 'us' (whom he goes on to describe as 'English by *natio*') with the saint, spoke of the saints and martyrs of 'our island', and criticized those who made him 'a prophet without honour in his own country'. According to the account of the translation, a chest with his relics was placed on the shoulders of some of the 'chief and greatest men of England'. Clearly, Gilbert was promoted in part as a specifically English saint, even though his father was Norman, in a co-ordinated effort involving powerful men of Continental descent.[63]

Gilbert was not alone, nor was the fact that he was half-English by ancestry necessarily a factor. The greatest English saint in this period was Thomas Becket, both of whose parents were Normans. Becket's martyrdom, it is true, was the occasion of some anti-Englishness, but quickly and repeatedly he became associated not just with Canterbury but all of England. Even before he was officially canonized there was an antiphon composed in English, supposedly drawn from a vision, in which he was described as the 'help of England'. He was said to have excited devotion to God, 'which for a long time had been tepid in the minds of the English', and

Hexham', 53; *VW* 34–5; *WMGP* 21–31; Bethell, 'The Lives of St. Osyth', 116; Paul Grosjean, ed., 'Translatio S. Swithuni', *Analecta Bollandiana*, 58 (1940), 196; Osbert of Clare, 'Édouard le Confesseur', 122; Thomas of Monmouth, *Life and Miracles of William of Norwich*, 129–32, 135, 174, 211–13, 222–3. See also Ridyard, '*Condigna Veneratio*', 183, 189–90, 192–8, 201–2, 205–6. Given the advantages mentioned earlier of having Normans validate English saints, some instances may be inventions: Rubinstein, 'Liturgy Against History', 286–9. But there is no reason to believe that all such instances were invented, and expressions of devotion such as Anselm's prayer to Dunstan must surely have expressed genuine feeling.

[60] Craster, 'Red Book of Durham', 528; Blake, *Liber Eliensis*, 194.
[61] Philip, Prior of St. Frideswides, *De Miraculis Sanctae Frideswidae*, in *Acta Sanctorum*, Oct., 8: 569.
[62] For the former, see Peter Draper, 'King John and St Wulfstan', *Journal of Medieval History*, 10 (1984), 41–50.
[63] Foreville and Keir, *The Book of St Gilbert*, 2, 6–8, 190, 194, 214, 226.

to have encouraged every inhabitant of England in pious practices.[64] Roger of
Howden recorded a vision in which the saint told a group of crusaders that he, St
Edmund, and St Nicholas had been appointed custodians of the fleet of the king of
England.[65] These are only a few of a large number of passages linking Becket to
England and the English.[66] In the minds of contemporaries, this second-generation
immigrant became the quintessential English saint.

The degree to which Becket was treated as a specifically English saint reflects the
degree to which immigrants had come to be seen and to see themselves as English
by the late twelfth century. But the cults of English saints played an important role
in that process, and in the intensification of English identity leading up to the wars
at the end of John's reign. The effects probably began very early. Reginald of
Canterbury spoke of 'our English people', in the context of a series of poems on
Canterbury saints, and Lanfranc wrote, in his monastic constitutions, that he
placed the feast of Gregory the Great among the greater feasts because 'he is our
apostle, that is, the apostle of the English people'.[67] How, precisely, did saints' cults
work, not only to preserve Englishness among the natives, but also to help make the
Normans think of themselves as English?

Saints' cults could promote English identity in several ways. They acted as yet
another reinforcement for the constructs of England and Englishness, and served to
keep them in people's consciousness. Allegiance to cults helped to draw immigrants
into the nexus of geographic and ethnic constructs and loyalties associated with
England and the English, and thus made it seem more natural for them to think of
themselves as English. The existence of individual saints and of a body of saints
linked to England and the English also helped to make the country and the people
distinctive; one thing that linked the English together and separated them from
other people was their devotion to such figures as Cuthbert, Dunstan, and Edmund.
Adoption by immigrants of English cults, in other words, was an important aspect
of cultural assimilation, and helped to distinguish them from their relatives on the
Continent. Moreover, English saints loaned their prestige to both people and
country. We have seen how William of Malmesbury and others used the figures of
English saints from before the conquest, and ethnically English ones such as
Wulfstan from after it, to counter Norman depictions of the English as religiously
backward.[68] On a broader scale, such saints made association with England and the
English more acceptable and desirable by creating a very positive image of a place
and people favoured by God with so many holy figures. This could help to overcome the mild ethnocentric scorn of the Normans, and make them more likely to

[64] *Becket Materials*, 1: 150–1; 3: 153.
[65] *Chronica Magistri Rogeri de Hovedene*, 3: 42–3.
[66] *Becket Materials*, 1: 399, 444; 2: 21, 23, 33, 35–6, 67, 86, 104, 122, 146, 195, 261, 357–8; 3: 77, 154, 202, 511;
4: 140–1, 155; 7: 547, 583; Watkiss and Chibnall, *Waltham Chronicle*, 64; *Historical Works of Ralph de
Diceto*, 2: 80–1, 165; *Historical Works of Gervase of Canterbury*, 2: pp. xliv, lxxix; Cornog, 'The Poems of
Robert Partes', 245–6, 249; William Stubbs, ed., *Chronicles and Memorials of the reign of Richard I*, vol 2.,
Epistolae Cantuarienses (London, 1865), 8, 18–20, 92; Peter of Blois, *Opera*, PL 207: 136.
[67] Liebermann, 'Raginald von Canterbury', 551; *The Monastic Constitutions of Lanfranc*, ed. David
Knowles (New York, 1951), 61.
[68] See above, pp. 253–6.

accept and acknowledge an English identity. The Norman or part-Norman English saints were probably particularly important in this respect, for the very fact that immigrants became English saints could help to bind other immigrants more closely and enthusiastically to an English identity. That one of 'theirs' was an English saint, in other words, could make Englishness more attractive and compelling.

Finally, saints' cults also supported the whole complex of loyalties to church, king, land, and people described earlier. Aelred of Rievaulx wrote in his life of Edward the Confessor that 'England was glorified above all cities and kingdoms by the sanctity of its kings, of whom some were martyred, some went abroad for Christ, preferring exile to the *patria*, and some became monks', thus glorifying royal power through association with sanctity.[69] Strikingly, in an earlier drive to have Edward canonized, a letter written in King Stephen's name to the pope stated that the example of holy kings profited the English church, went on to note Edward's kinship to William, 'the conqueror of England', thus drawing Edward's prestige to Stephen's own dynasty, and finally requested permission for the feast of the saint to be celebrated in the church of the English.[70] The pope, in a letter requesting broader support for the canonization before making a decision, spoke of the proposed feast as being for the honour and profit of the whole realm.[71] Thus, saints had a role in creating and fostering attachment and loyalty to English kings, the English church, and the English kingdom. In the early years after the Norman Conquest, the link between saints, politics, and the people presented dangers for the conquerors. But as Stephen's letter shows, once hostilities had died down even immigrant kings could turn to saints to bolster loyalty to the realm and by implication to themselves. As I have argued before, the complex of loyalties to church, king, land, and people may have helped the rulers, and for that matter the leaders of the church, but it also served to create a sense of loyalty to England and its people, and thus in the long run fostered not just the identification with but also the strong attachment of nobles to Englishness that would emerge in the early thirteenth century. Rituals such as the translation of Gilbert of Sempringham on the backs of some of the 'chief and greatest men of England', could help to reinforce the whole complex of loyalties to land and people as well as king in magnates who were slowly developing the enthusiastic embrace of English identity characteristic of so much of thirteenth-century politics. Naturally, the precise impact of saints' cults on the development of an attachment to England and of Englishness among immigrants is hard to measure, but given the importance of saints' cults in this society, and the strong ties between saints, land, and people, I am confident that it was a very important one. Christian institutions and cults may have been an ethnically neutral factor in the abstract, but the *Ecclesia Anglicana* and English saints were important aids to the survival and revival of English identity.

---

[69] Aelred of Rievaulx, 'Vita S. Edwardi Regis', 737. See also ibid. 744, 746, and Osbert of Clare, 'Édouard le Confesseur', 76, 78, 123, 128.

[70] *The Letters of Osbert of Clare, Prior of Westminster*, ed. E. W. Williamson (London, 1929), 85–6.

[71] Ibid. 88.

18

Stereotypes and the Image of the English

With what verse can I describe the English people?
Often the subject has drawn my doubtful mind.
Having made a pact of friendship, they are true.
The greater virtue is to safeguard possessions than to desire [them.]
They are strong in war, energetic, powerful in fighting,
Ever severe, but they grow mild when battles are put aside.
They are handsome; cultivated, they flourish with love of virtue.
But virtue is nothing, except with respect for duty.
The English people does not know the disease of avarice,
Love of giving grows as much as wealth itself does.
The youth that first studies to give generously grows up giving.
(Unless pure, the vessel makes whatever is poured into it sour.)
It is very praiseworthy to them [to be] refined with a rich table
Cheerful faces always enter no matter what . . .
A gracious nature is given to them and gracious ways,
Thus they know what is the sweet mixture of virtues.
Why are the English people the envy of every people?
Envy seeks the heights, winds blow over the highest points.

(poem attributed to Alexander Neckam)[1]

In this chapter I will explore the image of the English, with particular emphasis on stereotypes, just as in Chapter 15 I focused on the image of England. Whereas the

---

[1] 'Quo versu Anglorum possim describere gentem, | Saepe mihi dubiam traxit sententia mentem. | Sunt in amicitiae percusso foedere veri. | Major at est virtus, quam quaerere, parta tueri. | Sunt bello fortes, alacres, validique duellis, | Aspera sed positis mitescant secula bellis. | Sunt nitidi, culti florent virtutus amore, | Sed nihil est virtus, nisi cum pietatis honore. | Quid sit avaritiae pestis gens Anglica nescit, | Crescit amor dandi, quantu ipsa pecunia crescit. | Aetas prima studet, dare large, dando virescit. | Vas nisi sincerum quodcunque infundus acescit. | Lautior est illis cum mensa divite cultus, | Accedunt hilares semper super omnia vultus. | Non ibi Damaetas pauper dicit Meliboeo, | In cratere meo Thetis est sociata Lyaeo. | Gratius ingenium datur his, et gratia morum, | Sic norunt quam sit dulcis mixtura bonorum. | Anglorum cur est gens quaevis invida genti? | Summa petit livor, perflant altissima venti.' This version is found in W. Camden, *Remains Concerning Britain* (London, 1870), 18. A slightly shorter version may be found in M. Esposito, 'On Some Unpublished Poems Attributed to Alexander Neckam', *EHR* 30 (1915), 456–7. Hunt accepts the attribution to Neckam, though Gibson suggests that some poems credited to Neckam may be by contemporaries; R. W. Hunt, *The Schools and the Cloister: The Life and Writings of Alexander Nequam (1157–1217)*, ed. Margaret Gibson (Oxford, 1984), 62–3, 142, 145–6.

image of England discussed in that chapter was overwhelmingly positive, the image of the English was mixed. Alexander Neckam obviously thought as highly of the people as of the land, but many of the stereotypes about the English were damning. It is my contention that the image of the English was a crucial factor in sustaining the construct of Englishness, and that the positive stereotypes, and even to some degree the negative ones, helped to draw the descendants of the immigrants into an English identity.

This is true although individual stereotypes were simplistic at best and idiotic at worst. Obviously different peoples can have broadly different characteristics, because cultures differ. When medieval travellers encountered other groups, they experienced real differences in the way peoples acted. But then as now, it was easy to reduce complex and nuanced differences to simplistic stereotypes; to treat cultural characteristics as innate; and to substitute assumptions, abuse, and wishful thinking for observation. The English suffered their fair share of simplistic stereotypes, which have been discussed by a number of scholars.[2] As useful descriptions of English culture in this period, they should be taken with more than a grain of salt.[3] But, as Fuchs and Bernard Guenée have argued, stereotypes could play an important role in how people thought about ethnic identity, and in that context need to be considered very carefully.[4] After all, the many ridiculous ideas about so-called racial characteristics that dominated intellectual discourse into the early twentieth century (and which still have some proponents) have had dire effects. Simplistic characterizations of peoples, whether positive or negative, are in many ways more powerful precisely because they are simple, easy to remember, and easy to employ, whether in the service of self-praise or of abuse. The most outrageous distortions can be compelling when they cater to the way people wish to see themselves or others. The type of characterizations discussed in this chapter (and the next) were important in building group identity, in classifying people into groups, and in maintaining boundaries and barriers between peoples. Moreover, in assessing the impact of what to us may seem at best flattering or comic passages and at worst nasty but ridiculous invective, it is important to keep in mind that even leading intellectuals of the time could take them seriously. Some of the material I will discuss was meant to be humorous, and even the insults could be employed in a bantering way. Nonetheless, sophisticated intellectuals such as Stephen Langton could use crude stereotypes in the most serious of contexts, as we shall see. Most modern intellectuals tend to be on guard against stereotypes, even if not always successfully, because of the horrors such labels have helped to create in the modern world. The concerns of medieval intellectuals lay elsewhere, however, and they were all too prone to use simplistic stereotypes when it suited their purposes.

---

[2] P. Rickard, *Britain in Medieval French Literature 1100–1500* (Cambridge, 1956), 163–89; Clanchy, *England and its Rulers*, 117, 178–9; Knowles, *Monastic Order in England*, 463; Short, '*Tam Angli quam Franci*', 153–4; Southern, *Medieval Humanism*, 141, 145–7.

[3] Short, '*Tam Angli quam Franci*', 153–4.

[4] Fuchs, *Domesday Book*, 16–21; Bernard Guenée, *States and Rulers in Later Medieval Europe*, trans. Juliet Vale (Oxford, 1985), 65. See also Eriksen, *Ethnicity and Nationalism*, 22–5.

In talking about the image of the English in the period, I will begin with the positive, and specifically with some passages on their good character in general. These passages contained praise that was probably applied to any people an author might want to flatter, but they also contained elements that were particularly associated with the English and which helped to create a distinctive image of that people. The first passage is the poem, probably written by Alexander Neckam, quoted at the beginning of the chapter. To judge by this poem, the English were indeed a remarkable people; loyal, warlike or peaceful as circumstances required, good-looking, cultivated, gracious, virtuous, dutiful, devoted to good eating, and above all generous.[5] In short, they were paragons. The second passage is double-edged, for it comes from the influential English satirical work the *Speculum Stultorum*. In that story, when Burnellus the Ass got to Paris he decided to associate with the English scholars there. He did so, we are told, because of their subtle minds, excellent customs, pleasing looks and speech, intelligence, good council, generosity, hatred of misers, and feasting and drinking. Women, 'wassail and drink hale', the author informs us, were their only vices. Given the humorously moral slant of this work, the reader is probably meant to focus on the breezily dismissed vices, and the whole passage is no doubt meant to take self-satisfied English scholars down a notch, but by that very token, this passage undoubtedly gives a good picture of the type of praise the English in Paris might have received from a less caustic writer, and probably of their own self image.[6] The final passage, like Alexander Neckam's, is genuinely positive. Interestingly, it is a poem by a self described *Gallus*, probably Hugh of Montacute, who travelled to England and who was either a very generous soul who loved the people he met there or a shameless flatterer. Upon arriving in England, according to the poem, he found 'a distinguished genus of natives (*clarum genus indigenarum*), moral customs, elegant deeds, lively manners and faces, generous hearts, and hands you would think were born for giving'. He goes on to emphasize that everything about them was *liber*, a word that not only meant free but had implications of frankness, independence of manner, and generosity.[7] Obviously, in the eyes of some (and not least themselves, one suspects), the English were an extraordinarily fine group of people.

Though much of the praise in these three passages was of a general nature, two elements emphasized in them seem to have been particularly associated with the English, namely generosity and a devotion to eating and drinking. Both of these characterizations were originally applied to the native English. Goscelin of Saint-Bertin had his patron Herman, a Lotharingian who was made a bishop by Edward the Confessor, speak of the hospitality of the English to all, including foreigners, and of their generosity.[8] In the *Gesta Herwardi* a foreign knight who was captured and released by the defenders of Ely spoke positively of feasting 'English style'.[9] But

---

[5] Camden, *Remains Concerning Britain*, 18
[6] Nigel de Longchamp, *Speculum Stultorum*, 64–5.
[7] Scott, 'Some Poems Attributed to Richard of Cluny', 195–6
[8] Goscelin of Saint-Bertin, 'Historia Translationis S. Augustini Episcopi', 32. See also *VW* 17.
[9] Hardy and Martin, *Gesta Herwardi*, 381.

these stereotypes remained unaffected by the expansion of Englishness to incorporate immigrants. Gerald of Wales could write in his account of the invasion of
Ireland of how Irish princes visiting Henry II and Dublin admired the elegant
plenty of the 'English table', and in another context he recounted being part of a
party entertained 'in the splendid style of English sumptuousness', by the magnate
William son of Alan, who was of Continental descent.[10] Adam of Eynsham, speaking of the generosity of the Burgundians, wrote that it nearly outdid the prodigality
of the English, as if this was a remarkable accomplishment.[11] Richard of Devizes had
the same French Jew who spoke of England as a land of milk and honey refer to the
English as generous and hospitable.[12] It is quite interesting how closely related
the image of England as an abundant land was to images of ethnicity here.[13]

Another positive stereotype of the English, at least among the English themselves, was that they had a lively and discriminating intelligence. It is common for
people to think of their own group as smarter than everyone else, but several
writers make a particular point of English intelligence. Alexander Neckam, in his
description of England, wrote that nature had endowed its people with a discriminating talent (*genius subtile*) that allowed them to master the noble and mechanical
arts.[14] Geoffrey of Vinsauf, describing a particular rhetorical device, wrote that one
could use 'subtilis Anglia', in place of 'Anglici subtiles' (again showing the link
between constructs of place and ethnicity).[15] In a passage from a religious dialogue
written at Bridlington, the master rebukes his student at one point, saying, 'if you
were as English in the quickness of your mind (*anglus uiuicitate sensus*) as you are by
natio . . .', and goes on to say that the pupil is displaying a Teutonic intelligence
in his inability to grasp the master's point.[16] It is possible that these are isolated
expressions of ethnocentrism, but it seems likely that there was a broader stereotype
of the English as unusually intelligent in particular ways.

It is easy to see how positive images and stereotypes could play an important role
in shaping identity, and more specifically in promoting and reinforcing English
identity. Who would not want to belong to the ethnic group described by Alexander
Neckam and Hugh of Montacute? I argued earlier that the defence of English
honour and the related creation of a largely positive picture of that people was
crucial to making Englishness an acceptable identity.[17] Positive portrayals of the
English without reference to the natives, like these, would only maintain the attrac-
tiveness of English identity. In this respect, the stereotypes of English generosity,
hospitality, devotion to good living, and intelligence could be particularly effective,

[10] Gerald of Wales, *Expugnatio Hibernica*, 96; *GCO* 6: 142.
[11] Adam of Eynsham, *Magna Vita Sancti Hugonis*, 2: 164.
[12] *Chronicle of Richard of Devizes*, 64.
[13] See also Scott, 'Some Poems Attributed to Richard of Cluny', 195–7, and Alexander of Neckam, *De Naturis Rerum*, 456–7.
[14] Alexander of Neckam, *De Naturis Rerum*, 457.
[15] Faral, *Les Arts poétiques*, 291.
[16] Robert of Bridlington, *The Bridlington Dialogue*, ed. A Religious of C.S.M.V. (London, 1960), 66;
Paul Meyvaert, '"Rainaldus est malus scriptor Francigenus"—Voicing National Antipathy in the
Middle Ages', *Speculum*, 66 (1991), 751. For another example, see Gervase of Tilbury, *Otia Imperialia*, 286.
[17] See Chap. 14.

because they were easy to remember and broadly disseminated. They also helped to strengthen the construct of Englishness in people's minds by attaching it to specific traits and characteristics that could distinguish the English from others. Thus, one can see how positive stereotypes could make people who were wavering between English and Continental identities favour the former, and how they could reinforce pride in their identity among those who already thought of themselves as English, thus strengthening their Englishness.

However, negative stereotypes of the English appear far more commonly than positive ones. In some cases they were the same stereotypes, only with a disapproving twist. Great feasts and large-scale consumption could be a sign of wealth, nobility, and hospitality, but could also be treated as sinful. Even generosity could be taken too far. Peter of Blois wrote to one Englishman who had boasted of his people's generosity that he had confused generosity with prodigality, and that 'your people are, above all other peoples, drinkers, gluttons, and profligate wasters of all temporal goods'.[18] Not too many people complained about English generosity, but the stereotype of the English as gluttons, and above all as drinkers, was widespread. Gerald of Wales remarked that the Welsh do not waste their fortunes on the vices of gluttony and drunkenness, 'as we see among the English people'.[19] Geoffrey of Vinsauf, in another version of his treatise, substituted 'Potatrix Anglia' (drunkard England) for 'subtilis Anglia'.[20] John of Salisbury, in a letter to Peter of Celle thanking him for a treatise on bread in the Bible, wrote jokingly that 'indefatigable drinking has made the English famous among foreign nations', and requested a gift of wine, 'enough for an Englishman and a drinker'.[21] These are only some of the many passages and anecdotes in which being English was associated with excessive drinking and eating.[22]

It was not just the idea that the English drank a lot that distinguished them in the realm of stereotypes. They were also stereotyped as ale-drinkers, though it might be better to say that they were stereotyped for not drinking wine, since other English drinks such as cider and mead are sometimes mentioned. When a canon lawyer from England made an argument Pope Innocent III found ridiculous, and claimed that he had learned it in the schools from his masters, the pope commented: 'you and your masters had clearly drunk a lot of English ale when you learned this.'[23] Another stereotype was of the English exclaiming 'wassail and drink hale' when they emptied their cups. This appeared most prominently in Geoffrey of Monmouth's popular work, but can be found in other sources as well, including the

[18] *The Later Letters of Peter of Blois*, 159–60.
[19] *GCO* 6: 213.
[20] Faral, *Les Arts poétiques*, 228.
[21] *Letters of John of Salisbury*, 1: 56–8.
[22] Other instances are discussed below. See also *Jordan Fantosme's Chronicle*, 72; John de Hauville, *Architrenius*, ed. Winthrop Wetherbee (Cambridge, 1994), 48; B. Hauréau, 'Un poème inédit de Pierre Riga', *Bibliothèque de l'École des Chartes*, 44 (1883), 9; Walter Map, *De Nugis Curialium*, 154; Rigg, *History of Anglo-Latin Literature*, 139; Chardri, *Le Petit Plet*, ed. Brian Merrilees (Oxford, 1970), 42.
[23] MacRay, *Chronicon Abbatiae de Evesham*, 189. See also Walter Daniel, *Life of Ailred of Rievaulx*, 73; Stubbs, *Memorials of St Dunstan*, 175–6, 265–6; Rickard, *Britain in Medieval French Literature*, 169.

Speculum Stultorum, as we have seen.[24] Gerald of Wales even had a humorous story in which a Cistercian abbot, meeting Henry II who had separated from his retinue, mistook him for a knight whom he hoped could influence the king and tried to soften him up by offering many toasts, 'English style'. To speed up the process, he taught a one-syllable version of 'wassail and drink hale'.[25] By the late twelfth century, a very specific image had developed of the hard-drinking Englishman guzzling ale to the shouts of wassail.[26]

Two points may be made about the stereotype of the English drunk. First, like the more positive stereotype of the lavish English table, it was tied in to the image of England as a place of abundance. Richard Fitz Nigel, who wrote a poem on the richness of the island, elsewhere referred to 'the great riches of the kingdom and the inborn drunkenness of its natives'.[27] An anonymous English poet and moralist made clever play with 'England, the fertile land' and the *gens* that inhabited it, and was both 'drunk and a lover of a full stomach'.[28] The second is that the images of the English as excessive eaters and drinkers, as drinkers of ale, and particularly as shouters of 'wassail and drink hale', were originally associated with the native English. Richard Fitz Nigel seems generally to use the term *indigeni* for native English, and the same may be true in his passage on drunkenness. William of Malmesbury reported a story that Harold's troops drank all night on the eve of Hastings, and contrasted the excessive drinking and eating of the English with the abstemiousness of their conquerors.[29] Geoffrey of Monmouth placed the use of wassail and drink hale in the fateful scene in which Vortigern met the daughter of Hengist and decided to marry her, a decision that facilitated the Saxon invasion.[30] In short, the stereotypes of the English as gluttons and heavy drinkers were closely associated with the native English, and may have fuelled Norman feelings of superiority. Yet the stereotype came to embrace the descendants of immigrants when they became English. Roger of Wendover wrote how earls and barons, during a time of idleness on campaign, turned to feasting, devoting themselves to drinks and drunkenness 'according to English custom'.[31]

Another, possible, stereotype of the English was as flighty dreamers. I say possible, because this appears chiefly in one notable passage, which has been discussed by Southern and Paul Meyvaert.[32] In this passage, Peter of Celle, arguing in a letter to

[24] *The Historia Regum Britannie of Geoffrey of Monmouth I. Bern, Burgerbibliothek, MS. 568*, ed. Neil Wright (Cambridge, 1984), 67. For later versions of this story, see *Laȝamon: Brut* 1: 370–3; Gervase of Tilbury, *Otia Imperialia*, 416–18.

[25] *GCO* 4: 209, 213–15.

[26] Other references will be found below. See also John de Hauville, *Architrenius*, 48.

[27] 'Innumeras regni huius divitias et item propter innatam indigenis crapulam': Richard Fitz Nigel, *Dialogus de Scaccario*, 87.

[28] BL Burney MS 305, fol. 72ʳ.

[29] *WMGR* 452, 458. See also *Historical Works of Gervase of Canterbury*, 2: 62; *Annales Monastici*, 2: 27; Wace, *Le Roman de Rou*, 2: 156.

[30] *Historia Regum Britannie of Geoffrey of Monmouth*, 67.

[31] Roger of Wendover, *The Flowers of History*, 3: 7.

[32] Southern, *Medieval Humanism*, 146–7; Meyvaert, 'Rainaldus est malus scriptor Francigenus', 749–50.

Nicholas of St Alban's against the feast of the Immaculate Conception, which was being promoted by various English intellectuals, wrote of English *levitas*, which he contrasted to Gallic *maturitas*, and went on to speak of the English as greater dreamers than the French and more prone to take dreams and fantasies seriously.[33] It is possible that we are dealing simply with the views of one person, but there is a certain correspondence to Orderic Vitalis's story of William Rufus talking about excessive English faith in the dreams of old women.[34] Here again there may be a negative stereotype of the English that was originally directed against the natives but stayed around to haunt the descendants of the conquerors who became English.

The final, and most bizarre, stereotype of the English, one that emerged in Henry II's reign and lasted until the seventeenth century, was that they had tails.[35] This arose from a miracle story, first appearing in Goscelin of Saint-Bertin's account of St Augustine, in which the inhabitants of a town attached the tails of some rays to the saint's garment to drive him away.[36] Wace gave a version of this in which the saint prayed for vengeance and God cursed his persecutors with tails.[37] From there the image spread to the English as a whole, and, as Lawman wrote in his translation of Wace, Englishmen in foreign lands 'had red faces' as a result, and were called base when abroad.[38] As Lawman's passage suggests, this ridiculous idea soon gained widespread currency. It has been suggested that Nigel Wireker was playing with this stereotype when he wrote that the ass Burnellus, who wanted to lengthen his tail, desired to associate with the English in Paris to become more like them.[39] A French poet, Pierre Riga, made a pun on the English *causa* (cause or case) and the English *cauda* (tail), and Becket may have been playing with the idea in a letter to Gilbert Foliot.[40] Richard of Devizes wrote that the Sicilians called all who followed King Richard 'English and tailed'.[41] One has to wonder how many people took this idea that the English had tails seriously, but it clearly became a favourite vehicle for abuse.

Negative images undoubtedly had a more mixed influence on English identity than positive ones. Though I have no evidence of it, I suspect that during the transitional period people of Continental descent, and particularly those whose families still had interests on the Continent, when travelling abroad and confronted with slurs against the English sometimes downplayed or denied their Englishness. However, such people may have found Englishness ascribed to them whether they liked it or not. Continental writers, including Norman ones, began treating all the inhabitants of England, including immigrants, as unproblematically English even

---

[33] Peter of Celle, *The Letters of Peter of Celle*, ed. Julian Haseldine (Oxford, 2001), 578–80.

[34] *EHOV* 5: 288.

[35] For an overview of this myth, see George Neilson, *Caudatus Anglicus: A Mediæval Slander* (Edinburgh, 1896).

[36] Wharton, *Anglia Sacra*, 2: 67.

[37] Wace, *Le Roman de Brut.*

[38] *Laȝamon: Brut*, 2: 772.

[39] Nigel de Longchamp, *Speculum Stultorum*, 159.

[40] Hauréau, 'Un poème inédit de Pierre Riga', 11; *Correspondence of Thomas Becket*, 1: 446.

[41] *Chronicle of Richard of Devizes*, 19.

at a time when writers in England were still ambivalent about speaking of collective groups of nobles as English. Suger, writing in the 1140s, treated William Rufus's forces as simply English.[42] Norman members of the Young King's following who were trying to undermine William Marshal's standing did so partly by complaining, 'we are all humiliated because an Englishman outshines us'.[43] When Gerald of Wales, that intermittent Englishman, went out in Paris on the night Philip Augustus was born, he encountered some old women who told him and his companions that a king was born who would bring shame and confusion on their king. Gerald remarked that they knew that he and his companions were born in the English kingdom, though in Gerald's own case this involved a generous definition of England.[44] After a messenger from the English-born bishop of Poitou, John Blanchesmains, caused an uproar at the abbey of L'Etoile, the English-born abbot of the monastery, Isaac, apparently got an earful, for he wrote to the bishop saying 'would that I were not an Englishman or that I had never seen any English where I live in exile'.[45] William and Gerald, at least, were partly Continental in origin, and they and Isaac were all ambivalent about their English identity, but that made no difference; from the point of view of their abusers, they were English. The ethnic identity of an individual is only partly determined by his or her own self-identity; the views of others matter as well. One forum for this sort of shaping was the practice of bantering or exchanging insults, which is surely the context in which many of these comments must be seen, and in this arena denial may have provoked greater insistence on an immigrant's Englishness by opponents determined to get his or her goat.

But how could negative stereotypes support Englishness? Marketers sometimes say there is no bad publicity, because even negative publicity calls attention to a product and raises its profile. In the same way, even negative stereotypes helped to strengthen Englishness as a construct, because they made people more likely to think about and use the idea of English identity, and because they helped to maintain the image of the English as a distinctive group with distinctive characteristics. In doing so they also helped to make the English people seem like a natural phenomenon rather than a creation of history. One important factor here is that writers such as Nigel Wireker, Thomas Becket, John of Salisbury, and Richard of Devizes, who were from England and thought of themselves as English, employed these negative stereotypes, thus giving them a high profile in England as well as abroad. Often this took the form of self-deprecating humour, but because of the duty of moralists to see the worst in their own people, sometimes stereotypes could be discussed with the greatest seriousness. In a passage of biblical commentary Walter Daniel, best known for his life of Aelred of Rievaulx, stated that etymologically the term Philistine meant 'falling down from drinking', and used this to launch a diatribe against drinking in England. This term, he wrote, could apply to

---

[42] *Oeuvres complètes de Suger*, ed. A. Lecoy de la March (Paris, 1867), 12, 14.

[43] Meyer, *L'Histoire de Guillaume le Maréchal*, 1: 188.

[44] *GCO* 8: 292–3.

[45] Isaac de Stella, 'Epistola ad Joannem Episcopam Pictaviensem de Officio Missae', *PL* 194: 1896.

many in England, and 'no more Philistines may be found in Syria or Palestine than in this our *patria*', going on to add that they drank ale or cider rather than wine, and discussing the harmfulness of excessive drinking.[46] Thus, an attack on excessive drinking becomes a statement about the English people.

In an odd way, negative stereotypes could even foster a sense of unity among the inhabitants of England. When writers joked or preached about stereotypical English shortcomings, they were on some level inviting any English reader or listener to share their amusement or distress. The best illustration of this comes from a sermon Stephen Langton preached in London in 1213 to a powerful and influential crowd shortly after absolving King John from excommunication after the interdict. Politically this was an important sermon, for Langton had to justify the interdict to an audience that was partly hostile or sceptical (he even had a heckler). As one might imagine, he had to address the issue of relations between the king, the English church, and its flock, that network of institutions and loyalties I have noted before. But one of his main arguments was that the interdict had been brought on by sin, and above all by what he described as the two chief sins of the English, gluttony and drunkenness. Again and again he returned to the link between the English and these sins: 'it is the property of the English to drink to [the sound of] wassail . . . it shames me that you can be said to be mighty drinkers . . . these two, gluttony and drunkenness rule us English . . . we English betray our Lord through our gullets.' This is a fierce attack, as befits an ardent preacher, but note that it is 'we English' who are the subject. Langton calls on his audience, and by extension on the English in general, to reform these vices, and says that whereas the English are known for their lack of moderation and their gluttony and drunkenness, he wants them to become known for their moderation. This is a call to the English to reform *as a people*. As such it reflects but also reinforces English identity.[47]

Stereotypes were also important in maintaining ethnic boundaries. When John of Salisbury wrote to Peter of Celle about sending wine to him as an English drinker, he was making a sophisticated joke, but he was also underscoring, even if only incidentally, the ethnic distinctions between them. Peter himself did the same in his letter to Nicholas of St Albans commenting on English dreaminess. But perhaps the best examples come when stereotypes provoked a defensive reaction in people. Richard of Devizes, as a sound moralist, disapprovingly referred to the 'English custom' of downing cups to the sound of music and described the English as 'the greatest of drinkers', but he was not about to let the French get away with claims of superiority. Describing problems on the Third Crusade, he wrote sarcastically that the French and English feasted while the money lasted, and 'saving the reverence due the French, to the point of nausea'.[48] Ale could even become a flashpoint of ethnic contention. The letter in which Peter of Blois, a great champion of wine over

[46] C. H. Talbot, ed., 'The *Centum Sententiae* of Walter Daniel', *Sacris Erudiri*, 11 (1960), 326–7.

[47] George Lacombe, 'An Unpublished Document on the Great Interdict (1207–1213)', *Catholic Historical Review*, NS 9 (1930), 408–20.

[48] *Chronicle of Richard of Devizes*, 73–5.

ale, condemned English profligacy also discusses the opinions of a certain Thomas in defence of ale. Apparently Thomas, whose precise identity is unknown, had asserted that he must fight by a law of nature for his *patria* ('a lege nature pugnare pro patria'), but argued for ale instead, which he wanted to make 'the queen and lady not only of all drinks but all peoples' (punning on *poculum* and *populus*). According to Peter, Thomas had argued that ale 'made men liberal and generous', described the drink as 'the master of liberality and friendship, and the glory of his people', and 'imprudently and impudently ascribed all the glory of the soil of Great Britain to ale'. 'How glorious is this defender of the *patria*,' remarks Peter sourly, 'who impugns it when he praises it alone for its liberal drinking.'[49] I have quoted this letter at some length because it brings together so many themes: the idea of defending the *patria*, the generosity of the English, the abundance of their land (with Britain, as was not uncommon, substituted for England), and their excessive consumption of ale. I would be surprised if this exchange over the glories of ale and its English drinkers was meant very seriously. But it does show how cultural practices, stereotypes, and ethnic loyalties could all be mixed together. More specifically, it shows how debates over stereotypes could sharpen ethnic boundaries and thereby strengthen ethnic identities.

Scholars quite rightly tend to avoid taking medieval stereotypes seriously as accurate cultural descriptions, but the effects of stereotypes on ethnic identity should not therefore be ignored. Positive stereotypes could greatly strengthen an ethnic identity. Negative ones could undoubtedly harm a vulnerable identity, but could actually reinforce one that was already strong for other reasons. Stereotypes also helped to delineate ethnic boundaries, a point that will become even clearer in the next chapter, on the image of the Other in England after the conquest.

[49] *Later Letters of Peter of Blois*, 162–4.

19

The Image of the Other

THIS CHAPTER CONCERNS the ways in which views in England of other peoples helped to strengthen English identity and eliminate the boundaries between native and immigrant. Anthropologists have often stressed that ethnic identity is relational, in other words, that it is defined partly in contrast to other groups, and Fredrik Barth in particular has argued that peoples define themselves through what makes them different from other groups.[1] Similarly, Guenée has linked increasing awareness of distinctions between natives and foreigners and growing national identity in the later Middle Ages.[2] What the inhabitants of England thought about other peoples helped to shape how they thought about themselves. It also helped to create a sense of unity that overcame earlier divisions. In the decades after the conquest the English and Normans probably contrasted themselves mainly with each other. But as time went on comparison with other peoples made the conquerors and the conquered seem more alike. Exposure to other groups helped to make clear what the two peoples had in common from the beginning and, as cultural assimilation proceeded, underscored their growing cultural unity. As immigrants began moving toward an English identity, encounters and comparisons with other groups could help to intensify that identity, especially because ethnocentric contempt for other groups could help make English identity seem superior. In the long run this even led to anti-foreign sentiment and the politicization of Englishness.

English writers were remarkably free with their sneers at other peoples. Though hostility against Scandinavians had diminished greatly since the time of the Viking invasions, English writers still commonly referred to them as barbarians.[3] Less frequently, English writers also called the Germans or Saxons barbarians.[4] Gervase of Canterbury extended the label barbarian to the Sicilians in the context of Richard's visit on the Third Crusade, and Richard of Devizes regularly and contemptuously referred to the Sicilians as Griffons, depicting them as unwarlike and effeminate.[5] In some of these cases the peoples in question are implicitly or explicitly contrasted

---

[1] Eriksen, *Ethnicity and Nationalism*, 36–41, 111–13; Barth, *Ethnic Groups and Boundaries*.

[2] Guenée, *States and Rulers*, 63–5.

[3] WMGR 482; William of Malmesbury, *De laudibus et miraculis Sanctae Mariae*, 94–5; EHOV 2: 208; 4: 54; 5: 222–4; Mon. Ang., 5: 301; Adam of Eynsham, *Magna Vita Sancti Hugonis*, 2: 66–7; Reginald of Durham, *Libellus Beati Cuthberti*, 108; WNHA 111; Walter de Gray Birch, ed., *Vita Haroldi* (London, 1885), 28; Nancy F. Partner, *Serious Entertainments: The Writing of History in Twelfth-Century England* (Chicago, 1977), 100.

[4] *Letters of John of Salisbury*, 2: 70, 396; *Historical Works of Ralph de Diceto*, 2: 17.

[5] *Historical Works of Gervase of Canterbury*, 2: 87; *Chronicle of Richard of Devizes*, 17–25.

with the English, who are thereby portrayed as civilized and warlike. Thus, negative depictions of all kinds of groups could be used to bolster English pride and identity. However, I will focus on three groups, one of them made up in turn of a collection of peoples. The first group is the Jews, particularly the Jewish communities that were introduced into England after the Norman Conquest. The second group is made up of the Celts who inhabited other parts of Britain and Ireland. The third group is the French.

The Jews were separated from English and Normans by what was, in the Middle Ages, the nearly insuperable barrier of religion, yet were geographically inter-mingled with them. Their very existence posed what too many bigoted Christians considered to be an affront to their beliefs and values. Reaction to the Jews was probably exacerbated by the fact that they were new on the English scene, having been introduced to England after the conquest from Normandy, and slowly spread-ing out from London in the course of the twelfth century.[6] Even before the conquest the anti-Semitic strain in Christian writing had found its way to England in the form of passing comments.[7] After the conquest England had a sorry role in the intensification of bigotry against and oppression of the Jews that was characteristic of Western Europe in the central Middle Ages.[8] Two episodes stand out. The first was the claim that the boy William of Norwich had been killed by the Jews and sub-sequently became a saint, an invention that spawned a whole series of claims about ritual murders in England and elsewhere, and thereby strengthened medieval anti-Semitism. The second was the attack on the Jews of York associated with the Third Crusade, which was the worst attack on Jews in medieval England. In both of these episodes peoples of native and Continental descent can be found co-operating in the oppression of the Jews.

The episode of William of Norwich is well known, and has been carefully studied by Gavin Langmuir.[9] A young Christian boy disappeared under mysterious circumstances and his family accused the local Jews on the flimsiest of evidence. The sheriff of the county doubted the charges, but the boy's family, which included many clerics, received support from the bishop. Subsequently a monk named Thomas of Monmouth entered the scene and set out to turn the boy into a martyred saint. Despite lingering doubts, his claims eventually gained widespread accept-ance, and a cult with many miracles to its credit grew up around the boy. The success of this cult ensured that there would be many similar accusations from then on.[10] Unfortunately we do not know Thomas of Monmouth's background, though

---

[6] H. G. Richardson, *The English Jewry Under Angevin Kings* (London, 1960), 1–14; Stacey, 'Jewish Lending and the Medieval English Economy', 85–6.

[7] e.g. *Asser's Life of King Alfred*, ed. W. H. Stevenson, 2nd edn. (Oxford, 1959), 82.

[8] For some useful recent overviews of anti-Semitism in the period, see Robert I. Moore, *The Formation of a Persecuting Society: Power and Deviance in Western Europe, 950–1250* (Oxford, 1987), 27–45; Robert Chazan, *Medieval Stereotypes and Modern Antisemitism* (Berkeley, 1997).

[9] Gavin I. Langmuir, 'Thomas of Monmouth: Detector of Ritual Murder', in his *Toward a Definition of Antisemitism* (Berkeley, 1990), 209–36.

[10] For other English examples, see *Chronicle of Richard of Devizes*, 64–9; *Historical Works of Gervase of Canterbury*, 1: 296; William Henry Hart, *Historia et Cartularium Monasterii Gloucestriæ Sancti Petri Gloucestriæ*, vol. 1 (London, 1863), 20–1.

his name indicates that he came from the Welsh marches. But many of William's relatives had old English names such as Wenstan, Elviva, Wluuard, Godwin, and Livive, and were clearly of wholly or predominantly native background. A leading witness in the case, Aeluerdus Ded, also had a native name.[11] The bishop in question, Everard, however, was of Continental background. A monk of Norman background, Peter Peverel, was apparently devoted to the cult. Those who sought miracles from William, and who must therefore have accepted the anti-Semitic story behind his cult, included many people with English names, but also Reginald de Warenne, member of a leading Norman family, his wife, and daughter.[12] Thus, individuals of native and immigrant descent were united in building up a cult founded upon paranoid hatred of the Jews.

The massacre at York is also well known, and has been most fully treated by R. B. Dobson.[13] It was the most serious of a number of attacks in England at the beginning of Richard's reign. Various assaults on individual Jews or their houses led the Jewish community of York to take refuge in the castle. Mistrusting the royal castellan, they locked him out, prompting the sheriff to call a siege which soon became dominated by leaders intent not just on retaking the castle but also on slaughtering the people within. The Jews, realizing the hopelessness of their position, chose mass suicide. Those few who did not kill themselves offered to convert, but were instead murdered. The leaders of the killers identified by chroniclers, Richard Malebisse, Philip de Fauconberg, William de Percy of Bolton Percy, and Marmaduke Darel, were all prominent local gentry of Continental descent.[14] But the pipe rolls reveal many more people who were involved. These included Richard of Tong, son of Essulf and brother of the one person known to be the subject of Henry II's statute on the native English and landholding.[15] Also implicated were native members of York's urban elite as well as ordinary townspeople with English names.[16] Once again, people of native and Continental descent joined together to oppress the Jews.

These two episodes illustrate the shared intensity of anti-Semitic hatreds among both natives and immigrants, and suggest some ways in which a Jewish presence in England may have fostered the creation of a unified identity and therefore of assimilation. First, the presence of a religious minority within England underlined the shared religious identity of the two peoples. In particular, the coming of this group with its own distinctive rituals and practices may have made Christian immigrants seem a lot less alien to natives than they might otherwise have appeared, and may also have made the cultural and religious differences between

---

[11] Thomas of Monmouth, *Life and Miracles of William of Norwich*, 10–11, 16, 27, 40.

[12] Ibid., 43–9, 129–32, 211–13, 222–3.

[13] R. B. Dobson, *The Jews of Medieval York and the Massacre of March 1190* (York, 1974), 17–37.

[14] *WNHA* 321; Bond, *Chronica Monasterii de Melsa*, 1: 251. For Malebisse and his background, see Hugh M. Thomas, 'Portrait of a Medieval Anti-Semite: Richard Malebisse, *Vero Agnomine Mala Bestia*', *Haskins Society Journal*, 5, ed. Robert B. Patterson (Woodbridge, 1993), 1–15. For the others and their families, see *EYC* 1: 419; 3: 48–9; 11: 10, 104–12, 186–91, 336–7.

[15] *Pipe Roll 6 Richard I*, 161; *EYC* 3: 389–90. See above, p. 67.

[16] *Pipe Roll 4 Richard I*, 215–17.

English and Normans seem less significant. Second, the existence of Jews as a highly distinctive group meant that the sort of tensions and frustration that foster ethnic hostility could be channelled into anti-Semitism rather than reinforcing the early hostility between English and Normans. Third, anti-Semitism itself may have served as a bond between English and Normans. This discussion of the effects of shared anti-Semitism on relations between the conquerors and the conquered must necessarily be speculative, but there have certainly been many cases in history where a despised minority has inadvertently helped to unite other groups: not least is the example of how racism against African-Americans fostered the assimilation of European immigrants in the United States. I think it similarly likely that anti-Semitism in England helped to unify English and Normans. It is unlikely, however, that the Jewish Other favoured an English over a Continental identity for the unified people that emerged from the process of assimilation. What the Jewish presence was most likely to promote was Christian identity, and the constructs of Englishness and *Normanitas* both had a Christian component.[17]

Hostility to the Welsh, Irish, Scots, and Galwegians (who were often described as a distinct group in the English sources), and the image of the Celtic barbarian which was being developed in this period, promoted both unity and a specifically English identity. In the last couple of decades excellent work has been done on the relations between the English and their insular neighbors in the central and late Middle Ages, and on the ways in which Celtic peoples were depicted and stereotyped, particularly by the English. Scholars have shown how Celts were criticized for being economically and politically backward, for ignoring the rules of war and being militarily inferior, for political failings and disunity, for their marital and sexual customs, and for being barely Christian. More generally, they were depicted as barbarians. Understandably enough, modern scholarship has focused mainly on the impact of relations and stereotypes on the various Celtic peoples. Because of English expansionism and imbalances in power, the Scots, Welsh, and Irish were far more heavily affected by their encounters with the English in this period than were the English, or at least the English of England. Moreover, this modern work has been part of a widespread effort to counterbalance the past tendency to focus on English history to the detriment of the other peoples of the British Isles. Nonetheless, it is worth exploring the impact of the English–Celtic encounter on English identity, particularly in this period of threat to that identity. Davies has mentioned the element of disdain for the Celts in the triumphal Englishness of figures such as William of Malmesbury and Henry of Huntingdon, but only in passing.[18] I wish to pursue this connection and explore the role of the Celtic Other in the development of a unified and increasingly intense English identity more fully.

The anti-Celtic bias may have been stronger in Normandy than in England before the conquest.[19] In both it was relatively mild compared to what would

---

[17] See e.g. William of Newburgh's tendency to frame the opposition as between Jews and Christians, even in a specifically English context: *WNHA* 280, 308–22.

[18] Davies, 'Boundaries and Regnal Solidarities', 11–12.

[19] See above, p. 39.

develop in the course of the twelfth century. As Gillingham has written, even in the early twelfth century writers such as John of Worcester and Orderic Vitalis, in his early writings, could be mildly positive or at least neutral about Celtic peoples.[20] But from the 1120s hostility increased steadily, at the very time that hostility between English and Normans was slowly disappearing. Nicholas, the native prior of Worcester, writing to Eadmer about his attempts to fit in as bishop of St Andrews in 1120, spoke harshly about the barbarity of the Scots, though he thought a good bishop could help them to amend their ways.[21] William of Malmesbury, who began writing not long thereafter, was, as Gillingham noted, crucial in creating a negative image of the Celts.[22] Thereafter, negative characterizations of, and expressions of hostility toward, the insular neighbours of the English became common, though not universal, in English sources.[23] Even Gerald of Wales, though he identified partly with the Welsh, celebrated a victory over them in a letter to Archbishop Hubert Walter of Canterbury, saying they would have seized outlying parts of the kingdom if they could have, and slaughtered the English population. In his *Description of Wales* he described both how Wales could be defended and, speaking 'for the English', how it could be conquered. In one version he suggested that driving the Welsh out would be the best way to secure the land; in modern parlance, he advocated ethnic cleansing.[24]

I would argue that it is not entirely a coincidence that hostility between English and Normans decreased while hostility between those two groups and the Celts increased, for I believe that the latter process helped the former. Above all, this is because the various wars with the Scots, Galwegians, Welsh, and Irish created a common enemy for natives and immigrants. Norman landlord and English peasant alike suffered in the violent invasions from Scotland that periodically occurred throughout the period in question. Given the many political, cultural, and ethnic ties across the border, not least the presence of ethnically English people north of the border, reactions to invasions from Scotland evoked complex responses south of the border. But a theme that emerges again and again in the sources are atrocity stories whose villains are invariably Galwegians or Scots.[25] As for the Welsh, immigrants and natives may again have occasionally suffered from raids across the border, but it was the Normans and English who were primarily the aggressors. Norman nobles, of course, led the attack, but they brought English settlers and fighters with them. Some early burgesses of Brecon, Kidwelly, and Cardiff, including a reeve of the last town, had distinctively English names or

---

[20] Gillingham, *English in the Twelfth Century*, 26–8. But the passage about Queen Margaret improving the Scots and abolishing their evil ways in *ASC* D 1067 should be noted.

[21] Wharton, *Anglia Sacra*, 2: 234–6.

[22] Gillingham, *English in the Twelfth Century*, 9, 27–9.

[23] For the more moderate views of Roger of Howden, see ibid., 69–91.

[24] *GCO* 1: 291; 6: 225, n. 4, 226.

[25] *HHHA* 710; *EHOV* 6: 522; Aelred of Rievaulx, 'Relatio de Standardo', 181, 186–8; id., 'De Sanctis Ecclesiae Haugustaldensis', 177–8, 183; Potter and Davis, *Gesta Stephani*, 54; *SMO* 2: 190–2; *Jordan Fantosme's Chronicle*, 140; *Chronica Magistri Rogeri de Hovedene*, 2: 57; *WNHA* 72; *Historical Works of Gervase of Canterbury*, 1: 247; *Historical Works of Ralph de Diceto*, 1: 376; Richard of Hexham, *De Gestis Regis Stephani*, 151–3.

patronyms, and the castellan of Kidwelly in 1114 had the English name Eadmund.[26]
The English and Normans were not inevitably allied against the Welsh.[27] Nonetheless, it must normally have been a case of Welsh in one camp and invaders and
settlers of whatever origin in the other. As for the invasion of Ireland, by this time
the immigrant invaders had been subsumed into an English identity, but it is worth
noting that families of identifiably native descent in the male line, such as the
Audleys, Ridales, and Aylwards, participated alongside knights and nobles of
Continental ancestry in the invasion.[28] Thus, in general, the interests of English and
Normans were aligned together against those of the various Celtic peoples they
encountered.

In questions of assimilation and identity, what mattered was not just the fact but
also the perception of shared interests, not just alliance but also the feeling of unity
in the face of a common foe. Such perceptions and feelings can be found in several
sources. Orderic Vitalis wrote of both English and Normans mourning when
Robert of Rhuddlan was killed by the Welsh, of Earl Hugh of Chester summoning
French and English alike to fight a combined Scandinavian and Welsh raid, and of
English and Normans searching together for Hugh of Montgomery's body when he
was killed in the raid.[29] It is in the context of the battle of the Standard that Henry of
Huntingdon used his phrase *gens Normannorum et Anglorum*, which treats the
English and Normans as a united people.[30] The most compelling evidence of a sense
of English and Norman unity in the face of Celtic attack, however, comes in a speech
which a native, Aelred of Rievaulx, attributed to an immigrant, Robert de Brus, on
the eve of the same battle.

This speech illustrates how a complex web of loyalties and identities might be
reduced to a question of 'we English and Normans' versus 'those Celts'.[31] Both
Aelred and Robert had ties to the Scottish court; indeed, it was Robert's friendship
to King David that introduced the Bruce family to Scotland. Both would have been
aware of the complexities of political and ethnic allegiance in the border regions.
But according to Aelred, Robert, who was trying to persuade King David to desist
from battle, had a fairly simple message. Why, he asks, has the king raised an army
against the English and Normans, who had always been so useful to him? Does the
king really want to depend solely on the Scots, and reject the council of the English

[26] Golding, *Conquest and Colonisation*, 182; Davies, *The Age of Conquest*, 97–100; Patterson, *Earldom of Gloucester Charters*, no. 173; Kealey, *Roger of Salisbury*, 232. See also *GCO* 1: 310.
[27] See above, p. 63.
[28] Goddard Henry Orpen, *Ireland Under the Normans, 1169–1216*, vol. 1 (Oxford, 1911), 273–4; Robin Frame, *Ireland and Britain, 1170–1450* (London, 1998), 44–5; Smith, *Colonisation and Conquest*, 40, 43, 48; Brendan Smith, 'Tenure and Locality in North Leinster in the Early Thirteenth Century', in *Colony and Frontier in Medieval Ireland*, ed. T. B. Barry *et al.* (London, 1995), 33, 36; Seán Duffy, 'The First Ulster Plantation: John de Courcy and the Men of Cumbria', in ibid. 20. For the native ancestry of the Audleys, see Round, *Peerage and Pedigree*, 2: 29–33. For the Ridales, see *EYC* 2: 115–20. The Aylwards were descended from a merchant with that native English name.
[29] *EHOV* 4: 142; 5: 222–4.
[30] *HHHA*, 716.
[31] Aelred of Rievaulx, 'Relatio de Standardo', 192–5. See also Walter Daniel, *The Life of Ailred of Rievaulx*, p. xlii.

and the help of the Normans? Does he seriously want to rely on the Galwegians? Earlier, Robert continues, the king had received English help against the Scots, brought by Walter Espec and other nobles of the English (*proceres Anglorum*), and it was for that reason that the Scots hate 'us' and have committed atrocities. Obviously this speech is a tricky piece of rhetoric, trying to persuade the Scottish king that his interests lay with the English and Normans, not with the Scots and Galwegians, but the distinction between the two opposed pairs of peoples is strongly emphasized in it.[32]

The irony of an ancestor and namesake of Robert the Bruce having such a speech attributed to him is unmistakable. More important, this is a prime example of how comparison with and hostility towards Celtic peoples could create so strong a unity between English and Normans as to erase or nearly erase the distinctions between them. Of course, we cannot know whether Aelred accurately represented Robert's speech or opinions, just as we cannot know whether Robert of Rhuddlan was really mourned by the English, as Orderic asserts. At the very least, however, these passages show how hostility to the various Celtic peoples reduced the distance and the divisions between the English and Normans in the minds of writers. Exposure to Scots and Galwegians certainly made *Aelred* feel closer to the Normans. If Aelred's speech really does reflect Robert's mindset, and he obviously felt that such a speech was at least believable, it may also illustrate how such exposure made the Normans feel closer to the English, even on some level English themselves. The speech itself, moreover, and the other passages noted above, could foster as well as reflect a sense of unity between Normans and English. Whether Aelred invented this speech or adapted it from something Robert really said, it clearly fits into his wider message of unity and harmony between English and Normans. As this last suggestion indicates, Aelred, and perhaps Orderic and Henry of Huntingdon, may not have been entirely disinterested observers in remarking on English and Norman unity in the face of the Celts. But what is more likely than that hostility to a common foe could help to unite the two peoples?

Moreover, stereotypes about the Celts, as well as the real cultural differences they reflected and distorted, may have helped to make the English seem more civilized and culturally closer to immigrants in the minds of both natives and people of Continental background. Baudri of Bourgueil, in his *Itinerarium*, contrasted both England and Normandy very favourably to Britanny.[33] Similarly, William of Malmesbury could contrast the 'squalid multitude' of rustic Irish with the more cultivated English and French who inhabited towns and engaged in commerce.[34] In comparison to the 'barbaric' Celts, natives and immigrants in England may have looked a lot better to each other. It should be stressed again that William of Malmesbury, who was so concerned with English identity, was responsible for creating some of the earliest negative images of the Celts, and that such figures as Henry of Huntingdon and Aelred of Rievaulx, who were also concerned with

[32] See Ransford, 'A Kind of Noah's Ark', 138–9, for another analysis of this speech.
[33] Baudri de Bourgueil, *Itinerarium*, 1173–4.
[34] *WMGR* 738.

defending the English, likewise expressed negative views of various Celtic peoples.[35] No doubt there was genuine ethnocentrism involved, and real (if one-sided) outrage at the deeds of Scottish, Galwegian, and Welsh invaders. But one wonders if in their desire to defend the English, particularly from the charges of barbarism, they were not all too ready to depict other groups as the 'real' barbarians. In comparison, the English could be placed alongside the Normans and French as part of the cultivated, civilized world. In sum, the cultural differences of the Celts and, even more, stereotypes about them may have aided assimilation in two ways. First, by making the cultural differences between English and Normans look minor in comparison, comparison with Celtic cultures probably made it easier to bridge those differences. Second, by making English identity look more respectable in contrast, the Celtic Other could have made it more likely for immigrants to accept that identity.

Even peaceful and friendly encounters with people of another ethnic group can heighten awareness of one's own identity because of the relational nature of ethnicity. For the English and the Celts this is best illustrated by an exchange from Lawrence of Durham's *Dialogi*, between Lawrence, another English monk Philip, and a third monk Peter, who is described as *Brito*, meaning either Breton or, more likely, Briton.[36] In this brief passage the two English monks joke with Peter over their respective ethnicities, using the hoary *Anglicus/ angelicus* pun, alluding to the supposed descent of the Britons from Brutus, and referring to the seizure of *Britannia* and the change of name to *Anglia*. These passages form part of a sophisticated Latin poem, and do not represent verbatim dialogue, but their casual tone makes it seem likely that they reflect actual joking between Lawrence and his fellow, learned monks. Like John of Salisbury's bantering with Peter of Celle, though with a sharper edge, this kind of joking reinforced ethnic identities and boundaries even within a friendly setting.

Most encounters were more combative, and under the hostile conditions between the English and their neighbours ethnic identity did not just have an emotional draw, but practical consequences as well, in the form of discrimination. Gerald of Wales's account of his quest to be appointed to the see of St Davids reveals that there was a policy of discrimination against the Welsh that paralleled the earlier one against the English, in appointments to bishoprics. However, in this case the English were the beneficiaries. English by this time was defined to include immigrants such as Reginald Foliot, who was specifically described as an English candidate. It was, however, also defined somewhat narrowly, to exclude Gerald, who was lumped in with the Welsh, even though he was only part-Welsh by birth and to a large degree seems to have considered himself as English.[37] Gerald's disappointment caused him to emphasize his Welshness for a time, but earlier ambition caused him to focus on his Englishness, and the latter reaction was prob-

---

[35] *WMGR* 726, 738; *WMGP* 360; *VW* 42; *HHHA* 710, 714; Aelred of Rievaulx, 'Relatio de Standardo', 181, 186–8, 192–3; id., 'Genealogia Regum Anglorum', 714; id., 'De Sanctis Ecclesiae Haugustaldensis', 177–8, 183.
[36] *Dialogi Laurentii Dunelmensis*, 37–8.
[37] *GCO* 1: 43, 60, 94–5, 107, 121, 306–7, 332; 3: 121–2, 298–9, 302, 320–1.

ably most common for those who hoped for royal favour and advancement in the kingdom.[38] Unlike the earlier discrimination against the English, discrimination against the Welsh, and later the Irish, become more or less permanent. This was both a result and a cause of the stronger ethnic boundaries separating English from Celts than English from Normans. But it was also another reason why opposition to the Celtic Other reinforced English identity, in this case even for English settlers in Wales and Ireland.

Finally, the hostility towards the Scottish, Galwegians, Welsh, and Irish was often accompanied by an unpleasant triumphalism about English dominance over supposedly inferior foes. The best examples come from the conquest of Ireland. Gervase of Tilbury wrote that once the 'obscenae Hiberniensium gentes' who lived off their herds and neglected religion had been expelled, Henry II gave the land to the English in knights' fees, after which the land was cultivated and religion flourished.[39] Alexander Neckam, in his geographical work, said that Ireland would shine, if only its inhabitants were not barbarous and uncultivated, but wrote that the 'savage people' had been conquered and now served the English.[40] The English may have been outraged about attacks against themselves, but apparently felt quite secure about their right to conquer other, 'inferior' peoples. I argued earlier how favourable comparisons of the English to the Celts may have helped make English identity more respectable. Here I would remark that the sentiments of military and moral superiority found in these passages served to bolster English pride and thereby reinforce English identity in yet another way.

What of the effects of hostility to the Celts on English-versus-Norman identity? So far I have spoken about the Celts as a unified Other. This seems to me justified because the same sort of stereotypes were applied to Bretons, Welsh, Scots, Galwegians, and Irish alike, and no doubt the characterizations of these people influenced each other. But medieval authors had no similar collective terms, and wrote about each group individually. There was no common Celtic enemy. For the people of Normandy the Bretons were always a potential threat, but the Welsh, Scots, Galwegians, and Irish were not. The reverse was true for the inhabitants of England, some of whom were of Breton descent. After the attacks on Bretons stemming from the revolt of 1075, I have found no other evidence of anti-Breton sentiment in England.[41] But conflict with the Welsh, Scots, Galwegians, and Irish was something that the inhabitants of England, immigrant and native alike, did not share with the people of Normandy. Though appeals to the glorious tradition of the Normans may have been made before the battle of the Standard, in the long run, I suspect, hostility to the insular Celts was far more likely to make people think of themselves as English. Thus, I would argue that the Celtic Other served not only to draw Normans and English together, and to reinforce Englishness where it already existed, but also helped to make the former adopt the identity of the latter.

---

[38] Bartlett, *Gerald of Wales*, 50–7.
[39] Gervase of Tilbury, *Otia Imperiala*, 308.
[40] Alexander of Neckam, *De Naturis Rerum*, 461.
[41] *Letters of Lanfranc*, 124–6.

At various times in history the French have been the great Other for the English, and hostility towards them a key factor in strengthening English and, from the eighteenth century on, British identity.[42] The French Other was also fundamentally important in the period under review here, but in complex and unexpected ways. Attitudes toward the French were, to say the least, ambivalent. On the one hand there was great admiration for French culture and, from the late twelfth century, there was admiration for the French royal house, which culminated in the baronial invitation to Philip Augustus's son, the future Louis VIII, to seize the crown from King John after the repudiation of Magna Carta. On the other hand there was a continuing anti-French streak, inspired partly by resentment against claims of French superiority, but mainly by intermittent warfare and political conflict. As a result, attitudes to the French had complicated effects on identity in England. In many ways this anti-French sentiment had its fullest impact only with the French conquest of Normandy, and with the defeat of Louis in 1217, events I will discuss in the next chapter. But here I will lay some groundwork for this discussion, and describe some of the earlier effects of anti-French sentiment.

To understand the admiration for the French of many writers from England, it is important to remember that this was a time of enormous cultural vitality in Northern *Francia*, and that this area provided cultural leadership for other parts of Europe and particularly England. Indeed, Southern has described England as an intellectual colony of France in this period.[43] Rodney Thomson has argued, I think rightly, that this view goes too far.[44] But Laon, Orleans, and above all Paris were intellectual centres for a broad area that included England. French was developing as a key language of literature, and though, as we shall see, Anglo-Norman writers were in the forefront of this, the language originated in France and, by the end of our period, the French spoken in England was coming under criticism. As we shall also see, the French Gothic of Saint-Denis provided an inspiration for architects in England, as elsewhere, late in our period. As for chivalric culture, Northern France was the heartland of the tournament, and figures like the historical William Marshal and the fictional Hereward travelled there to prove themselves. In short, Northern *Francia* was extremely important as a source of cultural influence in England. Normandy played a role in this that was naturally crucial right after the conquest, but as time went on it became less so in relation to other areas of the French cultural sphere, particularly Paris and the Île de France.

Praise of the French can be found in a variety of sources. William of Malmesbury viewed the French as a fount of learning and civilization for the English, often re-interpreting his sources in the process.[45] Later in the century scholars who studied at Paris often came away with high praise for the city and its people. Alexander Neckam wrote at length about Paris and the people of the Seine (*gens Secana*), pre-

[42] Hilton, 'Were the English English?', 41–2; Colley, *Britons: Forging the Nation*, 24–5, 33–5, 88–90, 251–2, 368.
[43] Southern, *Medieval Humanism*, 158–9.
[44] Rodney M. Thomson, 'England and the Twelfth-Century Renaissance', *Past and Present*, 101 (1983), 3–21.
[45] Gillingham, *English in the Twelfth Century*, 5–6, 28–9.

sumably the Parisians or the people of the region, describing them as prompt in arms, a noble example to other lands, prudent, pious, learned, and powerful.[46] Herbert of Bosham, writing about his exile in the company of Becket, devoted a section to praising the French and 'sweet France'.[47] Gerald of Wales wrote of the great military might of the French, and William of Newburgh wrote that Richard introduced tournaments into England because of the superiority of Gallic knights.[48] There was no shortage of admiration for the French and their culture in England.

The French kings received a surprising amount of praise as well, at least in the Angevin period. Walter Map, whose picture of his own ruling house was somewhat mixed, depicted Louis VI and Louis VII in a very favourable light. French royal support for Thomas Becket brought forth reciprocal praise from the archbishop's supporters. Herbert of Bosham's passage on the French culminated in a tribute to their rulers. Herbert and Thomas himself both praised Louis VII in letters.[49] John of Salisbury also praised him for his humane welcome of the exiles, and even seems to have sympathized with the French forces and with Poitevin rebels in their battles against Henry II's forces.[50] A final figure whose dissatisfaction with the kings of England made him praise the Capetians enthusiastically was Gerald of Wales, who in his *De Instructione Principibus*, finished during the wars surrounding Magna Carta, castigated the Angevin rulers and exalted their rivals.[51] Thus, in the political as well as the cultural sphere, there was a remarkable amount of admiration for the French.

Nonetheless, there was a strong streak of anti-French sentiment throughout the period from 1066 to the civil wars at the end of John's reign. Partly this was inherited from Norman anti-French sentiment from before the conquest.[52] Norman hostility to the French continued to be expressed after the conquest in the strongest of terms, which is hardly a surprise considering the continuing warfare with the French, and this animosity could therefore continue to influence the inhabitants of England through contacts with Normandy.[53] The involvement of the inhabitants of England themselves in the many wars fought between the kings of France and England over Normandy and, after 1154, over the Angevin lands, either through active campaigning or financial support, helped to stoke up hostility in England towards the French kings and the French as a whole. Finally, French hostility against and scorn for the English, inspired by those same wars and Gallic ethnocentrism, also inspired anti-French feelings in England.

[46] Alexander of Neckam, *De Naturis Rerum*, 413–14.
[47] *Becket Materials*, 3: 407–8.
[48] *GCO* 8: 318; *WNHA* 422–3.
[49] *Becket Materials*, 3: 407–8; 6: 43, 330; *Correspondence of Thomas Becket*, 2: 946.
[50] *Letters of John of Salisbury*, 2: 6, 86, 134–6, 562–70, 638.
[51] *GCO* 8: 6–7, 141, 288–94, 302–3, 308, 310–11, 317–22, 326–9; Bartlett, *Gerald of Wales*, 94–100.
[52] See above, pp. 38–9.
[53] *EHOV* 3: 158; 4: 74–8; Étienne of Rouen, *Draco Normannicus*, 643, 686, 690–5, 722, 754–5; Peter of Blois, *Opera*, 96–8, 109–10, 447; William Stubbs, ed., *Itinerarium Peregrinorum et Gesta Regis Ricardi* (London, 1864), 140; Wace, *Le Roman de Rou*, 1: 3–5, 11–12, 164; 2: 64–72, 77–84; Blacker, *The Faces of Time*, 47, 103.

The attitudes of the French are important enough to warrant some attention. French hostility towards the English can be illustrated by a poem by Pierre Riga, written after Henry II outmanoeuvred Louis VII in the matter of some castles in the Norman Vexin. This poem is an attack on Henry himself, but is equally an attack on the English, despite the fact that Norman territory, and the old confrontation between Normans and French, was at issue. The poem is shaped as a debate over the merits of the case by representatives of the kings, but is filled with ethnic invective. Naturally the French get the better of this, and the English are described, as noted earlier, as having tails, and also as drinkers and better weavers than fighters.[54] As for other sources, I have already described Peter of Celle's condescending depiction of the English as dreamers.[55] The poem of William Marshal describes how the French arrogantly divided up the equipment of the English on the eve of one tournament, confident of their martial superiority.[56] French attitudes were, of course, more complex than these passages alone would indicate, with English scholars and knights being welcomed in the lands of the king of France during times of peace. Nonetheless, there was clearly an element of hostility and disdain towards the English among the French at this time.

Such attitudes could not help but provoke a response. I have noted William of Malmesbury's defensive comment about Gallic pride, and this may have been directed not just against immigrants but the French in general.[57] The passage in the poem of William Marshal was, as one might guess, a prelude to the discomfiture of the French. Geoffrey of Vinsauf, in his treatise on rhetoric, used the terms 'boastful *Gallia*', and 'womanly Gauls'.[58] Nigel Wireker, in his passage on the English in Paris, contrasted French stinginess with English generosity and, in what is probably another reference to French boastfulness, the French tendency to multiply threats with the English tendency to multiply cups of alcohol.[59] As usual with exchanges of ethnic insults, much of this was probably meant in a bantering way, but the joking reveals an undercurrent of ethnic hostility.

More important was the hostility aroused by war. As with the wars between the kings of Scotland and England, the wars between the latter and the kings of France were complicated affairs, involving many different groups. Contemporary writers were well aware of this. William of Newburgh wrote that war between the kings disturbed many peoples (*populi*).[60] But as Pierre Riga's poem indicates, it was easy for people to consider dynastic wars as ethnic or national ones, and to a surprising degree the wars were depicted as being between the French and English, even though Normans, Poitevins, Angevins, and others were not forgotten. Orderic could speak about English (and Norman) versus French armies even in the reign of

---

[54] Hauréau, 'Un poème inédit de Pierre Riga', 7–11.
[55] See above, pp. 302–3.
[56] Meyer, *L'Histoire de Guillaume le Maréchal*, 1: 95–6.
[57] *WMGR* 88; see above, p. 254.
[58] Faral, *Les Arts poétiques*, 275, 291.
[59] Nigel de Longchamp, *Speculum Stultorum*, 66.
[60] *WNHA* 248.

Henry I.[61] John of Salisbury, in a letter written about an early struggle between
Henry II and Louis VII, before he became bitter over Henry's treatment of Becket,
wrote hopefully that 'fortune, aided by justice, will give the French king and people
into our hands'.[62] William of Newburgh, in the same passage noted above, wrote
that each *gens* supported its king, and he clearly saw English–French hostility as one
part of the struggle, for he recorded that King Philip tried to stir up the Danes
against the English. He generally described the forces opposing the Angevin kings
as French, and in one place spoke of their cunning and in another described them
as 'both ferocious and arrogant by nature'.[63] Roger of Howden generally spoke of
fighting between the men of the two kings, but he too occasionally slipped into an
ethnic or national view of the wars. He spoke of how the French still considered
their king's flight from Richard in 1198 a source of shame, and had the earl of
Arundel refer to an 'evil act of the perfidious French'.[64] In sum, warfare and political rivalries inspired a fair amount of English hostility toward the French.

This hostility was not as pronounced as it would become in the context of Prince
Louis's invasion. Moreover, what I have said about admiration for the French
makes it clear that attitudes toward them were far more complex and ambiguous
than feelings about the Celts and Jews. But enmity towards them nonetheless
helped to shape the nature of identity in England. First of all, early on the French
represented one more shared enemy, as native English were brought into Continental wars even in the 1070s. English support for the Normans against the men of
Maine and the French supporters of William's rebellious son did not eliminate the
hatred between the two peoples but may have prevented it from becoming worse,
and subsequent support by natives such as Edward of Salisbury in the reign of
Henry I must have helped to knit the Normans and English together.[65] Of course,
the wars against the French helped to maintain ties between the inhabitants of
England and Normandy, and thus may have slowed the anglicization of immigrants. But in the long run hostility to the French meant that the fall of Normandy
in 1204 had even more dramatic influence on resolving ambiguity and hesitancy
among the nobility than it would otherwise have had.

Meanwhile, as English identity grew among the immigrants, and as enmity
between Normans and French created enmity between French and English,
hostility to France could reinforce that new-found identity, just as ethnic hatreds
against the Celts did. As William of Newburgh's comments about each *gens* supporting its king suggests, there was a general tendency for dynastic wars to be seen
in an ethnic light. Therefore, warfare against the French helped to solidify a network
of loyalty in which support for king, realm, and people became interlocked and thus
mutually reinforcing. The wars against the French probably were less effective in

[61] *EHOV* 1: 161; 5: 216; 6: 216, 236.

[62] *Letters of John of Salisbury*, 1: 21–2.

[63] *WNHA* 1: 93–4, 174–5, 248, 277, 367–8, 456, 484; Partner, *Serious Entertainments*, 98–9; Schnith,
'Von Symeon von Durham zu Wilhelm von Newburgh', 255.

[64] *Chronica Magistri Rogeri de Hovedene*, 4: 59; [Roger of Howden], *Gesta Regis Henrici Secundi*, 1: 53.

[65] *ASC* DE1073, D1079; *EHOV* 3: 110; 6: 236.

this regard than those against the Celts, for English interests were less thoroughly engaged in fights over the royal family's Continental possessions, but even the strains created by the divergence in interests would lead indirectly to an intensification of English identity.

Even aside from the effects of active war, the French Other was a powerful force for strengthening and reinforcing existing English identity. Naturally there were ways in which contrast with the French functioned in similar ways to the contrasts with other peoples I have discussed so far, but there were also differences, largely because of more favourable attitudes towards French culture and a greater engagement with that culture. By and large, Jews and Celts could be despised and shunned as inferior peoples by ethnocentric English. In contrast, English scholars and aristocrats, both key groups in establishing identity, often travelled among the French and were thoroughly engaged with French culture. Hostility toward the French was offset, to a large degree, by admiration and friendship. In many ways this only made the impact of the French Other stronger. The greater interaction made the effect of bantering and exchanged insults all the greater, since the opinions of the French had to be taken seriously and were more likely to be heard. Stereotypes were clearly disseminated and reinforced partly because of the strong Anglo-French intellectual ties. The English could largely ignore scorn directed at them by peoples they considered clearly inferior, but French arrogance was another matter, and provoked a strong backlash that could in the end reinforce English pride and solidarity. Moreover, an exploration of relations with the French shows that even the most positive relations with a people perceived as ethnically or nationally distinct could serve to underscore one's own identity. Herbert of Bosham's enthusiastic description of the French, their land, and their kings came in the context of the welcome to Becket and his fellow exiles. Herbert compared 'the cup of sweetness', with which the French 'inebriated' the exiles to 'the cup of sorrow, the cup of bitterness, which our own people made us drain'.[66] To be welcomed by a foreign people only underscored Herbert's sense that some sort of English solidarity should exist, and that his own people should act more correctly by treating the archbishop and his followers well. I have stressed that ethnicity is relational, but a comparison of the French Other with the Jewish and Celtic Others shows that different relationships affected ethnic identity in different ways.

What made the French Other, and hostility to the French, most important, however, was that it affected the Frenchness of the immigrants. As I noted earlier, the term *Franci* (and also the term *Galli*) had a range of political and cultural meanings, and pre-conquest English usage was not the same as later English usage. But because sharp distinctions were not made between different kinds of French, attitudes toward one could affect attitudes toward the other. The anti-French attitude inherited from the Normans introduced ambiguities into Continental identity from the very beginning. Anti-French Norman sentiment could coexist with a certain acceptance of the French label after the conquest by those immigrants who

[66] *Becket Materials*, 3: 408.

were specifically Norman, because the term French was so flexible. But the result was that to some extent the two ways of conceptualizing and naming Continental identity in England were at war with each other, and this must have weakened both from an early period. In particular, given the feelings of Normans about the French, especially when combined with native anti-French feelings, French identity was never likely to become the dominant one.

More important is the fact that anti-French feeling almost certainly undermined the influence of the many aspects of Continental culture brought to England by the conquest itself or through the continuing contacts with Northern *Francia* fostered by the conquest. Constructs are heavily influenced by cultural facts on the ground, even if the relations between the two are complex, and one might have expected that the introduction of so much Continental culture would have had a greater impact on questions of identity, and in particular would have strengthened the original, Continental identity of the invaders to a much larger extent. It did not in part because Norman culture was seen basically as French culture. Thus, when Orderic Vitalis, who was well aware of the traditional enmity between Normans and French, wrote of cultural influence after the conquest, he spoke of Gallic goods and merchants entering the market, and of the English adopting new styles of clothing because their native garb seemed shameful to the French.[67] Similarly, the immigrant Herman spoke of *French* customs rising and English affairs declining under William I.[68] One should not push individual anecdotes too far, given the fluidity of the terms involved, but there was in fact little to distinguish the Normans culturally from their neighbours on the Continent. The cultural influence the invaders brought with them was likely to be associated with all of *Francia* rather than just Normandy. This only increased as time went on and Paris became the greatest intellectual and cultural centre of northern Europe. Thus, cultural influence was far more likely to favour a French than a more narrowly Norman identity, but any such cultural influence was offset by hostility towards the French. As a result, a key potential prop for the Continental identities of the invaders was weakened throughout the period in question, making anglicization and the resolution of ambiguities about identity much easier. In Normandy, cultural similarity to surrounding regions mattered less, partly because there were no strong competing identities, and partly because there were political differences and the anchor of place to keep Norman identity intact. Obviously these latter factors could not succour Norman identity in England.

Images of the Other and hostility to other peoples demonstrate the strength of English identity. But these phenomena also reinforced that identity. Interaction with and comparison to other groups strengthened ethnic boundaries, fostered a sense of unity, and deepened the sense of Englishness. War, as so often, provided a tremendous impetus to unity and ethnic identity. Together, these factors helped to unify the inhabitants of England, promote English over Norman or French identity, and strengthen feelings of Englishness. The increasingly amicable relations

---

[67] *EHOV* 2: 256.   [68] Herman, 'De Miraculis', 58.

between Normans and English that developed in the twelfth century, and the peaceful assimilation between the two peoples, was no doubt extremely fortunate for England. But it should not be forgotten that this increasing amity was accompanied by wars and some ugly prejudices against other groups. The dissolution of ethnic division that was so positive for England was accompanied by the hardening of other ethnic hostilities, with sad consequences for the English, and even more for their neighbours.

20

The Intensification and Politicization of English Identity

ANY STUDENT OF thirteenth-century English politics is familiar with the importance of English identity and anti-foreign feeling in that period.[1] But this represents a radically different pattern of politics from that found for most of the twelfth century. The goal of this chapter is to study the transformation, largely concentrating on events in the reigns of Richard I and John. More specifically, I wish to trace five interrelated developments. The first was the intensification of English identity among the predominantly immigrant elites. The second was the increasingly strong focus on the realm of England as a community to which loyalty was owed. The third was the development of a politically based xenophobia, directed not only against potentially hostile or disruptive outsiders, but also against new immigrants who might compete for power and royal favour with the established and increasingly English elites. Fourth was the solidification of anti-French views during the civil war surrounding Magna Carta. Fifth was the increasing tendency to view politics through an ethnic or national lens. In tracing the politicization of Englishness, I will pay as much attention to the interpretation of events and the rhetoric surrounding them as to the events themselves, for when it comes to constructs, perception is at least as important as reality.

Before turning to the events of the reigns of Richard and John, it is important to examine the development of anti-foreign sentiment before 1189, a subject that has largely been ignored. Of course, the hostility towards the Celts, Jews, and French discussed in the last chapter was related to this. Here I am concerned with a more specific group and a more specific set of issues. The group consists of people from the Continent, and particularly areas from which William the Conqueror had drawn his forces. Hostility towards such groups as Celts and Jews would have been unproblematic in England throughout the period, but general hostility towards foreigners from the Continent was a different matter as long as that was a fair description of most of the elites. Thus, such hostility both marked and reinforced a

[1] Carpenter, *Minority of Henry III*, 261–2, 272–3, 324–5, 394–5; Clanchy, *England and its Rulers*, 128–31, 173–8, 184–98; H. MacKenzie, 'The Anti-foreign Movement in England, 1231–32', in *Anniversary Essays in Medieval History by Students of C. H. Haskins* (Boston, 1929), 183–203; J. R. Maddicott, *Simon de Montfort* (Cambridge, 1994), 291, 293–4, 297, 303, 334, 361–2; Reader, 'Matthew Paris and the Norman Conquest', 142–6; Nicholas Vincent, *Peter des Roches: An Alien in English Politics, 1205–1238* (Cambridge, 1996), 6–8, 28, 37–41, 201–5, 393–5, 414, 429.

major shift in identity for the descendants of the conquerors, though its development was both slow and complex. The specific set of concerns consisted of fear of invasion from the Continent, concern with Continental foreigners creating disruption, and a belief that offices and power in England should be reserved for its people.

David Crouch has found evidence of established immigrants closing ranks against new ones as early as the end of Henry I's reign, but expressions of anti-foreign sentiment directed against people from the Continent first appear in the context of Stephen's reign.[2] Stephen, like most kings, relied on mercenaries, particularly from Flanders, and these became the target for criticism. Even here, most such expressions come from later writers. But William of Malmesbury did single out foreign knights who entered England in Stephen's service, and particularly Flemings and Bretons, for blame in the plundering and atrocities in that reign, although he also attacked knights from England for being involved.[3] William thus stands as a bridge between a kind of pro-Englishness that was centred on natives, and one that could incorporate immigrants as well. But he was unusual for writers working in Stephen's reign. Later writers tended to focus on the Flemings under Stephen. The most vigorous example comes from William Fitz Stephen, who wrote in 1173–4 that during Stephen's reign the 'native' nobles had been disinherited and 'foreign Flemings and fighters had occupied Kent and a great part of the realm'. He went on to fulsomely praise Henry II's expulsion of the Flemings.[4] Gervase of Canterbury expressed similar sentiments.[5] Flemings had played an important role in the conquest, and some English nobles had Flemish ancestry. In providing the noble Flemings such as William of Ypres with land and power Stephen was not acting all that differently from William II and Henry I, who settled Continental favorites (albeit mainly Norman ones) in England.[6] But clearly attitudes had begun to change.

Anti-foreign sentiment also appeared during the dispute between Henry II and Thomas Becket. Henry had the borders watched for supporters of Becket, particularly foreigners, and expelled Welsh clerics from England.[7] When Henry and Thomas made their ill-fated peace, and the latter returned to England, the royal officials who met them, Gervase of Cornhill, Reginald de Warenne, and Ranulf de Broc, reacted negatively to the foreigners Thomas brought with him. According to one source, they complained specifically that he had brought French clerics. According to several sources, they tried to take oaths to the king from foreign clerics.[8] Not long thereafter, according to Benedict of Peterborough, when Thomas tried to meet the Young King, sparking a debate among the latter's advisors, Earl

[2] Crouch, 'Normans and Anglo-Normans', 57–8.
[3] William of Malmesbury, *Historia Novella*, 32, 72.
[4] *Becket Materials*, 3: 18–19.
[5] *Historical Works of Gervase of Canterbury*, 1: 105, 111, 158, 161; 2: 73. See also *WNHA* 101–2.
[6] See Amt, *Accession of Henry II*, 85–91, for a discussion of Stephen's Flemings.
[7] Barlow, *Thomas Becket*, 191; *Becket Materials*, 3: 103; 4: 66, 118–19; 7: 150; *Correspondence of Thomas Becket*, 2: 1024.
[8] *Becket Materials*, 1: 101; 3: 118–19; 4: 68–9; *Correspondence of Thomas Becket*, 2: 1350.

Reginald of Cornwall remarked that if the archbishop had brought troops of armed foreigners (*copiae armatorum alienigenarum*) he might be reasonably suspected by the natives, but since he had not the meeting should be allowed.[9] As far as the Becket controversy was concerned, the issue of his foreign support was minor, but these passages show how anti-foreign, and particularly anti-French, sentiment could creep into it.

Several sources also indicate a certain amount of nativism in the debate over who should succeed Thomas Becket as archbishop. Gilbert Foliot, in a letter to the king, discussed the failure of Henry's candidates, the bishop of Bayeux, the abbot of Bec, and the abbot of Cerisy, and suggested that he support someone from his realm, which, as the letter's editors argue, probably meant England.[10] A source from the circle of Odo, prior of Canterbury and later abbot of Battle, was more explicit, stating that the monks felt that a person of foreign birth (*persona natione alienigena*) would not be fitting, and later that, 'in England and among the English there were bishops and abbots, and religious and holy monks obedient to the church of Canterbury from whom a suitable person could be selected in a suitable manner, so that recourse to bishops and abbots from overseas was neither worthwhile nor appropriate'.[11] Such sentiment may not have been unique to this election. Adam of Eynsham recorded that a noble who recommended the Burgundian, Hugh, to be bishop of Lincoln, stated that because of his good character he 'would not be shunned as a foreigner (*alienigena*) but respected as a citizen and native (*cives* and *domestica*)'. Hugh did become bishop in 1186, but this passage suggests that there was concern about how he would be accepted as a foreigner.[12] A comparison with William of Malmesbury's account of the debate that led to the appointment of Archbishop Ralph in 1114 is instructive. There, opposition to foreigners referred to someone who was not Norman.[13] By Henry II's reign, it could be directed against Norman candidates, as Foliot's letter indicates. In Henry I's reign, the English were barred from bishoprics. Looking forward, these episodes are forerunners to the widespread opposition in the thirteenth century to the appointment of foreigners to important ecclesiastical (and secular) offices.

A certain amount of anti-foreign sentiment can also be found in accounts of fighting in England during the 1173–4 revolt against Henry II, not just in the context of invasion from Scotland. In England, as elsewhere in the Angevin lands, this was at heart a civil war, but the rebels received aid from the king of France and the count of Flanders. In particular, the earl of Leicester brought an army of Normans, Flemings, and French to England to support the rebel cause. Obviously there must have been local figures in the rebel forces but chroniclers preferred to celebrate the subsequent defeat of this army as a victory of natives, with the support of St

---

[9] *Becket Materials*, 1: 112.

[10] Morey and Brooke, *Letters and Charters of Gilbert Foliot*, 292–4.

[11] *Becket Materials*, 4: 177–8. See also, *Historical Works of Gervase of Canterbury*, 1: 244.

[12] Adam of Eynsham, *Magna Vita Sancti Hugonis*, 1: 48. See also, *Historical Works of Gervase of Canterbury*, 1: 494.

[13] *WMGP* 126.

Edmund, over foreigners and particularly over the Flemings.[14] For instance, Jordan Fantosme dismissed the invaders as weavers rather than fighters, and spoke of the vengeance of God in the defeat of 'the Flemings and the people of France'.[15] Writing at a later date, Gervase of Canterbury also rejoiced in the slaughter of the 'Flemish wolves [who] envying English abundance had left their "natural" endeavour, namely the business of weaving, and boasted of seizing England'.[16] It may be that the army was overwhelmingly from outside England, and that Flemish mercenaries were especially numerous, but one suspects that the chroniclers were influenced by anti-foreign sentiment to focus on the discomfiture of outsiders. Indeed, it is likely that the invasion itself fanned anti-foreign sentiment.

Clearly the anti-foreign sentiment of the thirteenth century, directed against people from the Continent, had roots in the twelfth century. Equally clearly, people from Normandy might be seen as foreigners even in Henry II's reign, which fits in with the completion of a shift by most immigrants to an English identity during that time. But compared to what one finds in the thirteenth century, particularly during times of crisis, the amount and vociferousness of anti-foreign language directed against Continentals was limited. This can best be seen from a comparison of accounts of events of 1173–4 with those of the wars surrounding Magna Carta, both situations in which civil war and foreign invasion were mixed. Anti-foreign rhetoric was simply on another level in the later period, as will become apparent. Another important point is that, although there was a definite sense of 'us' versus 'them' in anti-foreign passages, who 'we' were was often left vague before 1189 as a result of the general ambiguity about collective identity in this period. Writers often used ethnically flexible terms such as 'native' to describe the forces they saw as opposed to foreigners, or no term at all. Only occasionally, as in the passage cited above about choosing a successor to Becket, was 'we' clearly distinguished as meaning the English. Thus, collective identity remained an awkward subject even in the anti-foreign contexts that should have been most conducive to expressions of Englishness.

Another important point about anti-foreign sentiment before 1189 is that hostility to other peoples from within Henry II's extended empire was muted. Normans may sometimes have been considered foreigners, and some people in England may therefore have felt they should not receive English bishoprics, but it was the Flemings and French who were targeted for hostility. In their attacks on foreigners, chroniclers ignored the Normans whom Ralph of Diceto states Earl Robert of Leicester brought to England in 1173.[17] Given the Norman ancestry of much of the nobility, the continuing ties with Normandy, and the overwhelming probability that magnates and others with substantial cross-Channel landholdings still thought of themselves as Norman (even if some may also have started to think of themselves

---

[14] For instances not discussed below, see [Roger of Howden], *Gesta Regis Henrici Secundi*, 1: 60–2; *Becket Materials*, 1: 316, 365, 485–7.

[15] *Jordan Fantosme's Chronicle*, 70–80.

[16] *Historical Works of Gervase of Canterbury*, 1: 246.

[17] *Historical Works of Master Ralph de Diceto*, 1: 377–8.

as English), this is not surprising. What is more interesting is that the hatred of Poitevins, which was so prominent in the thirteenth century, was basically not an issue in the twelfth century. It is true that John of Salisbury, in a letter to John of Canterbury, the bishop of Poitiers, did speak of the 'unfaithfulness which I have heard said of your people', presumably meaning his flock.[18] But this is an unusual example, and it is striking that in twelfth-century accounts of the murder of Earl Patrick by Poitevin rebels, there is none of the sort of vituperation based on ethnicity common in later accounts of Poitevin activities.[19] Though fellow subjects of Henry II may have been targets of English desires to keep appointments in their own hands, real hostility seems to have been directed at people from beyond the Angevin empire.

Despite these caveats, the existence of anti-foreign sentiment, directed against people from the Continent, in the reigns of Henry II and perhaps Stephen, is significant. It provides further, if indirect, evidence for the rapid progress of assimilation in those reigns. It shows the rising solidarity within the kingdom of England, and the decline of connections between the immigrant elites of England and their ancestral lands. Moreover, like so many other factors discussed in this book, anti-foreign feeling served as a cause, as well as a symptom, of assimilation and the rise of English identity. Like the many hostilities analysed in the last chapter, the anti-foreign sentiment discussed here promoted unity within England.[20] Despite the ambiguity expressed in the sources, a sense that the Normans were a distinct people could not but help to foster an English identity, while hostility to the Flemish and the Bretons may have made any immigrants with roots in those areas more likely to embrace Englishness and to resolve any ambiguities about their own identity. Perhaps most important, however, the relatively mild anti-foreign attitudes found in the reigns of Stephen and Henry II helped to pave the way for the anti-foreign movements found in subsequent reigns.

The first political movement with a strong anti-foreign element, though one shot through with problems and ambiguities, was the drive to oust from power William Longchamp, whom Richard I had left as one of his two main surrogates when he went on crusade. After Richard left, a complex power-struggle ensued in which William outmanoeuvred a rival, but then sparked increasing resentment among the powerful men of the realm, led for a time by John. Longchamp's position collapsed when he tried to stop Richard's illegitimate brother, Geoffrey, archbishop-elect of York (who had sworn to stay out of England), from entering the country, and some of the chancellor's followers dragged Geoffrey out of a church in Dover where he had taken refuge.[21] Personal ambitions, factional fighting, and

---

[18] *Letters of John of Salisbury*, 2: 178–80.

[19] *Chronicle of Robert of Torigni*, 235–6; *Letters of John of Salisbury*, 2: 566; *Historical Works of Ralph de Diceto*, 1: 331; *Historical Works of Gervase of Canterbury*, 1: 205; *Chronica Magistri Rogeri de Hovedene*, 1: 273–4. The killing undoubtedly did influence the views of Patrick's nephew William the Marshal and those in his circle: Meyer, *L'Histoire de Guillaume le Maréchal*, 1: 58; 2: 71, 86–7.

[20] See also Fuchs, *Domesday Book*, 364–5.

[21] See Ralph V. Turner and Richard R. Heiser, *The Reign of Richard Lionheart: Ruler of the Angevin Empire, 1189–1199* (Harlow, 2000), 110–29, for a recent overview of the crisis.

political manoeuvring lay behind this conflict, but according to several sources, ethnic hostility also played a role. In particular, Longchamp was attacked for despising and hating the English, for being a foreigner, and for favouring foreigners.[22] I shall return to the question of how accurately the accounts depict the events and the role of ethnic hostility in them. The accounts themselves, written within a decade or so of the events, display a marked upsurge in anti-foreign rhetoric. Strikingly, this was directed towards a man who came from Normandy and was a royal favourite.

The first account of Longchamp's hostility toward the English appeared in a letter written by Hugh Nonant, bishop of Coventry, during the crisis. Hugh wrote that 'although England served him zealously on bended knee', he dismissed his knights and household and, 'spurning the English people, pompously went about accompanied by troops of French and Flemings'.[23] Gerald of Wales, in two works written in the 1190s, elaborated on this theme. According to Gerald, Longchamp would, 'through arrogance and the verbose boastfulness of the Normans' and 'because of the innate hatred of the Normans', preach to the English that they had once been praiseworthy in war and learning but were so no longer, because of excessive luxury and drunkenness. Gerald claimed that Longchamp and his followers would abuse the English by saying, 'I would be English if I did this; I would be worse than English if I admitted that', and that, when they prepared to carry out their 'natural needs', they would say, 'Let us go make English'. Gerald also spoke of Longchamp exercising tyranny over the English people and directing his malice against 'the English kingdom and the noble men of the realm'.[24] Gerald's claims should be taken with a grain of salt, but a more sober author such as Roger of Howden could write of Longchamp's threatening attitude toward the English people after he failed to regain power, and William of Newburgh stated that England had rejoiced at his death because of fears that he might attempt to avenge his expulsion.[25] Clearly, much of the hostility towards Longchamp was based on the belief that he himself was hostile towards the English.

The attack on Longchamp for being a foreigner was more complex. Bishop Hugh, attempting to portray Longchamp as an outsider, wrote that his grandfather had been a serf from Beauvais, and accused him, in turning aside from the English, of aspiring to the 'libertas' of the French.[26] The latter charge is unclear, but both were designed to exploit anti-French feelings in England, and in the former case class bias as well. Anti-foreign prejudice was echoed in a passage from Richard of Devizes, in which John upbraided the chancellor for introducing to the English the French manner of bending the knee.[27] Gerald repeated Hugh's story of Longchamp's grandfather and went one better by claiming that Longchamp himself had betrayed four strongholds to the king of France. But Gerald clearly identified him

---

[22] See also Southern, *Medieval Humanism*, 141–2, and Fuchs, *Domesday Book*, 14–15.
[23] *EEA* 17: 125–9.
[24] *GCO* 2: 348; 4: 413, 417, 424.
[25] [Roger of Howden], *Gesta Regis Henrici Secundi*, 2: 240; *WNHA* 490.
[26] *EEA* 17: 125.
[27] *Chronicle of Richard of Devizes*, 32.

as Norman. Gerald even linked Longchamp's sex life to his ethnicity. He created a picture of a household where only 'natural copulation' was reviled, and added stories of an outraged Longchamp casting out a beautiful young girl who had been smuggled into his bed, and of the chancellor pointing out, with a long rod, his favourites among the young nobles serving at table. In introducing this section, Gerald wrote: 'That unspeakable and horribly outrageous crime of the Normans, which they took from the French but made especially their own, was so strong in this particular Norman that he acted like the standard-bearer of all the rest in that abuse.'[28] On a less sensational note, William of Newburgh wrote that when Richard left the realm in Longchamp's hands, everyone was angry because he had acted negligently in entrusting it, against the counsel and desire of his magnates, 'to a foreign man of obscure name and little probity, faith, or industry'.[29] Finally, both Roger of Howden and Geoffrey of Wales record that when Longchamp tried to sneak out of England disguised as a woman, he was caught in Dover because he did not know the English language, thus prompting people to take a second look at him and become suspicious.[30] This story is part and parcel of a picture of Longchamp as an outsider in England.

Longchamp was also targeted for bringing in and supporting other foreigners. I have already quoted Bishop Hugh's passage on the matter. Gerald of Wales, Gervase of Canterbury, and William of Newburgh also commented on his habit of surrounding himself with foreign knights, particularly French and Flemish ones, and on his recruitment of foreign mercenaries.[31] Gerald wrote that he brought in French and Flemish knights not just to guard himself but to oppress the natives (*naturales*) of the kingdom.[32] Most important, however, Richard of Devizes wrote that when Longchamp tried to take custody of Lincoln Castle from one of John's followers, John told him that it was not fitting to take custodies of castles from free, law-worthy, and well-known men of the realm and turn them over to unknown newcomers.[33] Thus, the complaint of favouritism towards foreigners that was so often levied against kings in the thirteenth century was directed against the king's representative here.

How seriously can we take these characterizations of Longchamp and the anti-foreign sentiments expressed in them? There are good reasons for scepticism. Bishop Hugh Nonant, who was so outraged by Longchamp's spurning of the English, was every bit as Norman as his target, having been born and raised in Normandy.[34] That other great defender of the English, John, was noted by Roger of Howden for summoning French and Flemish soldiers for his rebellion against

---

[28] *GCO* 2: 348; 4: 418, 423–4.

[29] *WNHA* 306–7.

[30] *Chronica Magistri Rogeri de Hovedene*, 3: 146; [Roger of Howden], *Gesta Regis Henrici Secundi*, 2: 219–20; *GCO* 4: 410–12.

[31] *GCO* 4: 391, 402, 425, 427; *Historical Works of Gervase of Canterbury*, 1: 497–8; *WNHA* 338, 341; *Chronica Magistri Rogeri de Hovedene*, 3: 143.

[32] *GCO* 4: 425.

[33] *Chronicle of Richard of Devizes*, 31.

[34] *GCO* 4: 394. For an account of Hugh's career, see *EEA* 17: pp. xxvi–xxxiv, xli–xlvii.

Richard not long after Longchamp's defeat, and by Gervase of Canterbury for gathering with Philip a multitude of Flemings, 'who had long envied the delights and riches of England'.[35] John later became notorious for what was seen as excessive favouritism towards foreigners. Longchamp himself was not such an outsider as he was depicted, for David Balfour has cast strong doubt on claims about Long-champ's servile background, and shown that his father held some land in England and his mother almost certainly came from the Lacy family, which was among the most prominent in England.[36] Clearly, accounts of the struggle against Longchamp were heavily influenced by propaganda and invective.

Even if one should treat the accounts with scepticism, however, there is good reason to believe that ethnic hostility and offended English sensibilities were a factor in the downfall of William Longchamp. Enough different sources record some aspect of anti-foreign sentiment in this context to indicate that it was not simply invented by chroniclers, especially since the anti-foreign sentiments were hitherto rare enough to indicate that writers were not simply trotting out old clichés to explain Longchamp's fall. Moreover, the fact that Hugh Nonant's letter, written during the struggle, used anti-foreign propaganda indicates that he expected claims about Longchamp's spurning of the English and embracing of foreigners to strike a chord among the political elites. He and John may well have been manipulating anti-foreign sentiment for their own political ends, but that shows that there was sufficient hostility towards people from the Continent to make it worth exploiting. I doubt that anti-foreign sentiment and anger over slights, or perceived slights, to the English were the main factors in Longchamp's fall, but they were an important tool in the hands of his enemies, and therefore a contributing factor.

Moreover, the rhetoric itself is revealing. Taken together, the various attacks on Longchamp provide a wonderful window into attitudes about class, sexuality, gender, and gender-bending, as well as about ethnicity. Naturally I will focus on what they say about ethnicity, but it is worth noting that a number of 'bad' things, namely servile origins, 'unnatural' sexual practices, and the humiliation of being caught and roughed up when disguised as a woman, are all lumped together with being foreign. In other words, being foreign itself seems on some level to have been a source of shame from the perspective of Longchamp's attackers. In any case, these accounts mark the beginning of the fundamentally important habit of viewing internal English politics through an ethnic lens. One also sees in Richard of Devizes's account of John's speech on the custodies of castles the first claims in the surviving literature that secular offices should be reserved to the inhabitants of England. This view is also implicit in William of Newburgh's statement about wide-spread resentment over Richard entrusting the kingdom to a foreigner. William of Newburgh's statement not only links the welfare of the realm to internal control, but also depicts the king as harming that welfare against the good advice of its lead-ing men, providing the first intimation of the way in which the network of loyalties

---

[35] *Chronica Magistri Rogeri de Hovedene*, 3: 205; *Historical Works of Gervase of Canterbury*, 1: 514.

[36] David Balfour, 'The Origins of the Longchamp Family', *Medieval Prosopography*, 18 (1997), 73–92.

to state and people could turn against the king and his government instead of working to the royal advantage.

Finally, the attacks on Longchamp are interesting because of what they reveal about attitudes toward the Normans. Most commentators continued to avoid any attack on the Normans per se, despite the fact that Longchamp, the relatives who accompanied him, and presumably some of his followers were born and raised in Normandy, focusing instead on his grandfather's origins, his introduction of French bowing, and his habit of surrounding himself with those established villains, the French and the Flemish. I would suggest that these writers were purposely skirting the fact that Longchamp and some of his followers came from Normandy in order not to include the Normans in their anti-foreign rhetoric. This, however, had the effect of implicitly turning the Normans into the French. In contrast, Gerald of Wales, who was rarely shy about insulting anyone, firmly identified Longchamp as Norman and condemned what he claimed were Norman sexual practices. But in doing so, he linked the Normans explicitly to the French. The avoidance of attacks on the Normans in most of the accounts suggests that ties to Normandy and the Normans remained strong. But Gerald's account may indicate the beginning of strain in those ties, and all the accounts at least suggest that the Normans might suffer, in the minds of the English, from association with the French even before the fall of Normandy.

The movement against William Longchamp points, therefore, to a significant intensification of English identity, particularly among the politically powerful, by the beginning of Richard's reign. At the same time, the drive against Longchamp must have furthered that intensification. If nothing else, it rallied and raised consciousness of English identity. More important, it brought Englishness and anti-foreign feeling firmly into the realm of politics. Yet one should also avoid exaggerating the importance of Englishness and anti-foreign feeling in the drive against Longchamp. These themes do not appear in the admittedly brief accounts of Ralph of Diceto or Gervase of Canterbury.[37] Nor were they associated with other events in Richard's reign. Thus the attacks on Longchamp must be seen as an important step in the politicization of Englishness, but not the culmination of that process.

Before moving on, it is worth considering what the positioning of Hugh and John as members of the 'indigenous' camp, and of Longchamp as an outsider, can tell us about the nature of English identity and its role in politics. Hugh and John's championing of the English may simply be a lesson in cynical political manipulation, but I suspect that things were more complicated. The irony of Simon de Montfort's position as a leader of the self-consciously English and anti-foreign baronial movement of the middle of the thirteenth century has often been remarked on.[38] But in a society where English identity was not simply a matter of

---

[37] *Historical Works of Ralph de Diceto*, 2: 96–101; *Historical Works of Gervase of Canterbury*, 1: 497–8, 504–8.

[38] e.g. Maddicott, *Simon de Montfort*, 361–2; Clanchy, *England and its Rulers*, 192; Richter, *Sprache und Gesellschaft*, 168.

ancestry (since anyone important claimed to be descended from the Normans), what made someone English was bound to be complex. Place of birth, where one was raised, and cultural attributes all mattered, but ethnic identity and allegiance remained somewhat fluid. I suspect that once ethnicity began to intersect with politics, to be in the 'English' camp meant to support the established elites against newcomers, and was closely connected to the degree to which a person was integrated into the kingdom's power structure and political elite. Hugh Nonant had been in England in Becket's household as early as 1164, and was an established English bishop by the beginning of Richard's reign. Gerald of Wales described him as Norman in origin, but also included him among the noble men of the English kingdom whom Longchamp hated.[39] John, by his very position as a member of the royal house, had a place in the English power structure, and could plausibly act as the champion of the English elites. Similarly, Simon de Montfort, through his marriage and political connections, integrated himself enough into the English elite to act as its leader.[40] But Longchamp, whatever his maternal connections, was a political outsider when introduced by Richard, and as such could be perceived as a threat to traditional interests. A related point is that as ethnicity entered politics, to some degree Englishness became associated with political stances. Anyone who supported those stances, even if only temporarily, would get drawn into the 'English' camp. This is not to claim that John, Hugh Nonant, and Simon de Montfort became unambiguously English through politics; they did not. But I do hope that these suggestions, and the continuing ambiguity and flexibility of what it meant to be English, can help to explain why such figures can be found championing pro-English and anti-foreign forces.

For obvious reasons, there is a long tradition of seeing the loss of Normandy in 1204 as a turning-point in questions of assimilation and particularly identity, though the emphasis scholars have placed on it varies with the speed with which they think anglicization and the uniting of the two peoples took place.[41] Having placed the completion of assimilation in Henry II's reign, I can hardly count John's loss of Normandy as a causal factor in that process. Moreover, as Short has remarked, there is no reason to wait until 1204 for a shift in identity.[42] Nonetheless, the loss of Normandy was important to identity because it changed the political landscape in ways that would help to intensify Englishness, and it influenced anti-foreign and particularly anti-French feelings. Above all, it helped to resolve earlier ambiguities about the collective identities of the elites in England by radically diminishing their ties with Normandy.

The fall of Normandy presented most magnates with a clear choice of political allegiance that could not help but resolve ambiguities about identity in the long run. Before 1204 most magnates in England, and some lesser figures as well, still had

[39] GCO 4: 394, 417.

[39] *GCO* 4: 394, 417.

[40] Maddicott, *Simon de Montfort*, 361.

[41] Freeman, *History of the Norman Conquest*, 5: 349; A. L. Poole, *From Domesday Book to Magna Carta, 1087–1216*, 2nd edn. (Oxford, 1955), 431–3; F. M. Powicke, *The Loss of Normandy*, rev. edn. (Manchester, 1960), 303–7; Carpenter, *Minority of Henry III*, 261.

[42] Short, '*Tam Angli quam Franci*', 173.

property in Normandy. To those with extensive interests, the question of identity must have been complex. As we have seen, Jordan Fantosme depicted the countess of Leicester lumping the earl of Arundel in with the boastful, beer-drinking English in 1173, the same year in which Roger of Howden could depict him making a speech based on the Norman myth in Normandy.[43] Such figures could be perceived as having either English or Norman affiliation and may well have had split loyalties. Undoubtedly, the continuing strong Norman ties of many of the most important members of the landed elites, and their relatives in the church, contributed to the continuing reluctance of many writers to describe those elites as English. Philip's victory changed this situation. Those with cross-Channel holdings had to decide where their interests and allegiance lay, and those who were most attached to Normandy generally withdrew to their estates there, while those based largely in England gave up their lands in Normandy. There were exceptions, and no doubt many hoped the situation would be temporary, which would delay any impact on their identity, but effectively the Anglo-Norman baronage became divided permanently into an English nobility and a Norman one.

The speed with which those who chose to shift allegiance to Philip Augustus and give up their lands in England came to be known collectively as Normans in the royal records rather than, say, traitors, is remarkable. In the summer of that year various phrases, many of them focusing on the shift in political allegiance, were used to describe those whose land was confiscated for deserting John, but by the end of the year it had become standard to refer to the deserters as Normans.[44] By implicit contrast, those who had elected to give up their lands in Normandy and remain loyal to John were not Norman but English. This contrast was probably possible only because of the degree to which the English and Norman aristocracies were already seen as separate by 1204, but the shift from a variety of phrases to concentration on the geographic/ethnic term Norman indicates that the events of that year sharply accentuated the perceived differences. Of course, the separation of the two aristocracies was no simple matter. A case from 1220 demonstrates both the slowness with which this division took place, and the kind of process by which it occurred.[45] As another case from that year makes clear, the king and his council had instituted a policy that no one in England need respond to claims for land from people living 'under the power of the king of France' until the *Anglici* had that right in *Francia*.[46] In the case in question, Reginald and Robert de Courtenay tried to block a dower claim from Matilda de Courtenay on that basis, saying that she lived under the French king and had her land in Normandy. She retorted that she was 'de Anglia' and had land there, like the Earl Marshall and others. Unfortunately the outcome of her case remains unknown, but unravelling the interknit aristocracies of England and Normandy was obviously no easy process, and it was still, in 1220, hard to figure out how to classify someone like Matilda de Courtenay, who seems

[43] *Jordan Fantosme's Chronicle*, 72; [Roger of Howden], *Gesta Regis Henrici Secundi*, 1: 52–3.
[44] *Rot. Lit. Claus.*, 3–5, 7–9, 12–14.
[45] *CRR* 9: 37.
[46] *CRR* 8: 343. See also a later case, 15: 435–6.

to have been from England but who stayed in Normandy.[47] It is interesting that writers did not speak of Normans or French being excluded from the courts, but of those living under the power of the king of France: they were concerned primarily with political allegiance. But it is also interesting that they consistently spoke of the English making claims in Normandy. This clearly shows that any uncertainties about the identities of those who stayed in England disappeared rapidly. They did so in part because there was less and less to associate them with their Norman holdings as the years passed.

Warfare over Normandy, and over the other Continental lands of the Angevin kings, may also have served to focus attention on the interests of the realm of England, and how they might sometimes diverge from those of the king. Though magnates with interests in Normandy would have shared the desire of their kings to hold or, later, reconquer Normandy, other people from England, including any descendants of Normans who had few remaining ties, had no such interests. Very few indeed were deeply concerned about the fate of Anjou, Poitou, and Aquitaine, except insofar as they owed loyalty to their king. Ralph of Coggeshall, writing sometime later, lamented that Richard in his later years placed heavy exactions on the English, who had already paid so much for his ransom.[48] Ralph attributed this to greed, but the real reason was that Richard needed money for wars on the Continent, and many of his subjects in England may have resented paying for wars from which they and most of their compatriots derived no benefit. J. C. Holt has shown how John only increased financial pressure on his subjects in England after 1204 in order to finance his attempts to recover the lost lands, and has argued that this was an important cause of the Magna Carta revolt, which attempted to protect the interests of the English realm and its inhabitants against what were seen as the king's excesses.[49] This is a point to which I will return, but the wars surrounding Magna Carta, which set the pattern for a kind of English nationalism in the thirteenth century, to a large degree resulted from the pressures of Continental war.

The loss of Normandy and other provinces, and the related wars, also helped to alter relations with Continental peoples. Though Philip's victories no doubt increased respect for the political ability and power of the Capetian dynasty, and contributed to the decision of the rebel barons to call in Philip's son Louis, the wars also increased tensions with and hostility towards the French. Moreover, the threat of French hostility was no longer a distant one, restricted to the Continental lands, for after 1204 Philip was in a position to threaten England. Thus, the Barnwell Chronicle could record that in 1213 Philip threatened England 'with extermination', rejoice that the English destroyed his fleet, and claim that God had freed the country from its peril.[50] The increased French threat only reinforced attachment to an English identity.

The conquest did not radically change attitudes towards the Normans, but it is

[47] Matilda had clearly been involved in earlier negotiations for her land: *Rot. Litt. Pat.*, 44, 106, 122.
[48] *Radulphi de Coggeshall Chronicon Anglicanum*, 92.
[49] Holt, *The Northerners*, 143–74. See also Ralph V. Turner, *King John* (Harlow, 1994), 98–114.
[50] *The Barnwell Chronicle*, 209–11. See also *Annales Monastici*, 2: 274; 3: 35.

likely that the loss of ties with them removed a check to English xenophobia. It is true that Geoffrey of Vinsauf, writing during John's reign, like Gerald of Wales, characterized the Normans as boasters (elsewhere he applied the same term to the French), and Ralph of Coggeshall spoke of John's loss of 'stubborn' Normandy.[51] Falkes be Bréauté, of Norman origin, became a target of anti-foreign animosity in Henry III's minority, just as Longchamp had.[52] But there was nothing resembling the degree of hostility directed towards Poitevins. Still, even though no hatred against the Normans developed, the one group of foreigners with whom the English elites intermingled fairly easily, precisely because the nobilities were so intertwined, were cut off. Thus, a set of ties that must once have mitigated rising English xenophobia largely disappeared. The loss of ties with the Normans may have been particularly important in allowing a rise in hostility towards foreigners at the royal court. After the loss of Normandy, favourites at the royal court were generally complete outsiders to the old Anglo-Norman sphere, and therefore easy targets for hostility. The shifting political allegiances of many Poitevins, caught between two powerful royal houses, only exacerbated hostility towards that group in particular.[53] Thus, animosity towards other subjects of the kings of England, and especially towards those who received favour and reward in England, became much more pronounced in the thirteenth century than in the twelfth, when it barely mattered.

The next incident, or rather set of incidents, which marked the continuing politicization of English identity was the interdict, and John's subsequent decision to make the pope overlord of England as part of his effort to make peace.[54] These incidents revolved around issues of papal authority and church–state relations, but issues of Englishness, loyalty to the realm, and what the king owed the realm managed to insert themselves in this sphere. During the course of the twelfth century, as papal power and ability to influence England grew, a certain inevitable backlash developed against the papacy, even among pious churchmen. Criticism of the papacy was generally made independently of any expressions of English identity or loyalty, though Gervase of Canterbury remarked in one passage that the Roman curia was accustomed to English bribes, and in another that the archbishop of Canterbury sent to Rome large amounts of the relics of England, namely of Ruffinus and Albinus, which was a sarcastic way of referring to gold and silver.[55] There is a hint here of the later complaints made in England and elsewhere of wealth flowing from one's own country to Rome. But the real expressions of Englishness come only with the interdict.

It was John who, perhaps inadvertently, brought the role of Englishness into the whole affair by objecting to Stephen Langton, partly on the grounds that he was someone unknown to the king and was too closely associated with Paris. In doing so John echoed broader anti-French sentiment. John was speaking from his own

---

[51] *Radulphi de Coggeshall Chronicon Anglicanum*, 146; Faral, *Les Arts poétiques*, 228, 275, 291.

[52] Carpenter, *Minority of Henry III*, 261–2, 272–3.

[53] Clanchy, *England and its Rulers*, 128–31, 187–9; Vincent, *Peter des Roches*, 28.

[54] For a recent overview of these events, see Turner, *King John*, 155–74.

[55] *Historical Works of Gervase of Canterbury*, 1: 428, 560.

interests, not a sense of Englishness, but his concerns in this case meshed with those of people who were influenced by a strong English identity and a related xenophobia. Innocent III responded by saying that Stephen was from 'your land'.[56] Stephen Langton himself stressed his Englishness and love for England, both in a letter to all the 'faithful Christians of the kingdom of England', and in the sermon that he made after the affair was ended.[57] His feelings of devotion to the English people may well have been genuine, but they also played a role in his struggle to win the moral high ground and defend his actions. For one thing, his declarations of love for England and the English refuted one of John's major objections to his candidacy, and may have softened any concerns about his Parisian connections. Moreover, by stressing his Englishness, Stephen could more easily appeal to the good of the realm and its people in his opposition to the king. He argued, in his letter to the English, that the realm would suffer if it repeated the sins against Thomas Becket, and that in defending the rights of the church he was therefore acting in England's best interest.[58] He also argued that he was working in the king's best interests in opposing his demands, but obviously arguments of this sort were tricky, and Langton's professed love of the realm of England gave him another string to his bow. In his arguments, the network of loyalty to king, land, and people remained intact, but some of the emphasis was moving away from loyalty to the king and towards loyalty to land and people.

Ralph Turner, in his recent biography of John, argued that contemporaries did not have the hostile reaction to John's decision in 1213 to surrender his crown to the pope that later writers expressed. He points out that the anonymous Barnwell annalist described it as wise both for John and his people. Turner also dismisses the later claim that Stephen Langton opposed the decision.[59] But at least one contemporary writer and Langton supporter did so, with great emphasis on how the decision affected England and the English. This was Matthew, precentor of Rievaulx in the early thirteenth century, who wrote several relevant poems.[60] One was a poem in praise of the archbishop, in which he used the sort of language found so often linking saints to England and the English, describing him within a short space as 'angelic man and English flower', the 'radiance of the English', and the 'flower of the English', thus driving home the archbishop's claims to an English identity. A second poem contrasts John unfavourably with his ancestor William the Conqueror, comparing the latter's conquest of the English with the former's surrender of the crown, and goes on to attack the surrender in the harshest terms. Addressing Jesus, he says that the pope is powerful, 'but you are stronger', and calls on him to remove 'the deadly yoke that oppresses the English'. He stated that he

---

[56] C. R. Cheney and W. H. Semple, *Selected Letters of Pope Innocent III Concerning England (1198–1216)* (Edinburgh, 1953), 86–7.

[57] *Historical Works of Gervase of Canterbury*, 2: pp. lxxviii–lxxxiii; see above, p. 305.

[58] Ibid. 2: pp. lxxix–lxxxi.

[59] Turner, *King John*, 168–9.

[60] Wilmart, 'Mathieu préchantre de Rievaulx', 56–8, 61. William the Breton and possibly Philip Augustus also saw the decision as demeaning for England: Delaborde, *Oeuvres de Rigord et de Guillaume le Breton*, 2: 262, 272.

'who obstructed the rights of the English' had sinned, claimed it was better to die than lose liberty, and wrote that 'England was once a free Sara, but is made Agar, and serves as a bond-maiden'. A similar vehemence appears in the third poem, which urges England to lament the surrender, compares its former greatness to its present servitude, and calls on the country to throw off the yoke. It is striking that for a prominent monk and supporter of Langton, the papal appointee, English liberty was such a strong and emotional issue, and a 'servitude' that meant so little in practical terms could arouse such passion. Not everyone in England shared these passions, but Matthew's poems provide another example of how English identity was a rising force in politics and the interpretation of political events in the early thirteenth century.

The growth of ethnic politics reached a new peak during the baronial revolt at the end of John's reign, and the resulting struggle that lasted into the beginning of Henry III's.[61] During these events, both sides appealed to English solidarity and anti-foreign sentiment, writers consistently interpreted the events partly in an ethnic or nationalist light, and feelings of ethnic solidarity seem genuinely to have been one important political force. All five of the factors I described at the beginning of the chapter, the intensification of Englishness among the nobility, the strong focus on the realm of England, politically based xenophobia, the solidification of anti-French feeling, and the tendency to view politics through an ethnic or national lens, came together in these struggles. Though the events and interpretations I discussed earlier in this chapter began to bring Englishness and xenophobia into English politics, the wars surrounding Magna Carta made them central, and thereby set a pattern that would endure through Henry III's reign and beyond.

Anger against the foreign favourites of the king, which had reared its head during the dispute against Longchamp but thereafter quieted down, became a crucial issue at the end of John's reign. Even the Barnwell annalist, who was very even-handed in his treatment of John, criticized him for being 'generous and liberal to outsiders, but a plunderer of his own people, trusting in foreigners more than his own people, as a result of which they deserted him at the end'.[62] John's decision to bring in foreigners, some of them his subjects, against his rebellious English barons was a sensible military move, but produced particular anger among the chroniclers. The Waverley chronicler wrote in one passage that 'Foreign barbarians and a multitude of men of different tongues landed in England, obstinately supporting the error of the king', and in another passage described John savagely attacking the barons with foreigners and other supporters.[63] Roger of Wendover, describing how one group of foreigners coming to John's aid drowned, claimed that this 'genus of perverse men' were coming to England to 'expel and nearly exterminate the natives' in order to seize their land.[64] Ralph of Coggeshall wrote that after being forced to accept

---

[61] For overviews of these events, see Holt, *Magna Carta*, 105–268; Turner, *King John*, 225–57; Carpenter, *Minority of Henry III*, 1–49.

[62] *Barnwell Chronicle*, 232.

[63] *Annales Monastici*, 2: 283.

[64] Roger of Wendover, *The Flowers of History*, 2: 147–8.

Magna Carta, John summoned foreigners and forced the English from his court. He attributed the drowning of many of the foreigners at sea to divine intervention.[65] Magna Carta itself, and the related 'articles of the barons', shows that hostility toward foreigners was not just an invention of chroniclers but an integral part of the baronial movement. Clause 50 of the charter demanded the removal from office of a number of foreign favourites, along with their *sequela*, a contemptuous term generally reserved to describe the families of serfs. The following clause demanded the expulsion of foreign knights and soldiers, 'who have come, with horses and arms, to the harm of the realm'.[66] Xenophobia was certainly not the only motivating force behind the revolt of the barons, but it was an important one.

The baronial revolt and Magna Carta also reshaped how people thought about the network of loyalties to king, realm, church, and people. Ideally these loyalties formed a seamless web, but in their attempt to justify opposing the king, the rebels, like Stephen Langton during the interdict, had to focus on other allegiances within the network. In both the prologue to Magna Carta and the beginning of the clause concerning the powers of the twenty-five barons to constrain the king, two crucial passages in the document, reference is made to the 'emendation of the realm' (one might note the contrast to the foreigners who came to *harm* the realm in clause 51). The same phrase about the reform of the realm is found in the introduction to the Forest Charter of 1217. Nor was the English church forgotten: the first and last clauses of Magna Carta confirmed the rights of the *ecclesia Anglicana*.[67] One might object that no reference was made to the welfare or the rights of the English people, and that loyalty to the realm and its church does not necessarily constitute an ethnic loyalty. But, as noted in Chapter 6, one clause does refer simply to the English, and one should not overlook the fact that this document was not intended for all of John's subjects, only his English ones. A shift away from emphasis on personal loyalty to the king, which, after all, the English elites still shared with Poitevin and Gascon nobles, to an emphasis on the English realm and church in many ways implied a loyalty to the English people, especially since the elites had become unambiguously English.

Despite the xenophobic aspects of their movement and the widespread anti-French sentiment in England, the barons called in Louis, son and heir to Philip Augustus, after John repudiated Magna Carta. This is best seen as an act of desperation by John's enemies, who had been outmanoeuvred and feared the king's wrath. Militarily it was a sound move, and Louis attempted to blunt any xenophobia by claiming to act for 'the common good of England'.[68] But the invitation to Louis stepped up ethnic tension still more, and ultimately served to strongly reinforce English identity and loyalty. Ethnic or nationalist hostilities flared up in Louis's own ranks. The Dunstable annalist wrote that 'the French, growing proud and removing the nobles of England from their councils, began to call them traitors,

[65] *Radulphi de Coggeshall Chronicon Anglicanum*, 173–5.
[66] Holt, *Magna Carta*, 310–11, 328–30.
[67] Ibid. 316, 330, 332, 336, 359 n. 1.
[68] Rymer, *Foedera*, 1: 140.

and kept the castles which they captured, denying the English their rights . . .'.[69] Roger of Wendover made similar claims, and spoke of wavering among the rebel magnates because they were held in contempt by the French.[70] The Barnwell annalist wrote that Louis stayed near the coast for ease of escape, partly because he saw the English as fickle and inconstant.[71] According to Ralph of Coggeshall, when some French and English knights were captured at Colchester, and the latter were imprisoned while the former were freed on condition that they return to France, this aroused great anger among the English rebels. When the freed knights arrived in London, they were taken and accused by the 'native' barons of faithlessly betraying their English comrades when accepting different conditions from them. The French knights were nearly hanged, but the sentence was delayed and they were kept in chains until the arrival of Louis.[72] Obviously many of these disputes were not purely ethnic, a point David Carpenter has stressed.[73] The interests of the English rebels did not necessarily coincide with those of Louis and his followers, and suspicions and conflicts were bound to arise when the two parties joined together. Nonetheless, it is interesting how the chroniclers interpreted the conflicts in ethnic rather than political or factional terms, with a revival of the old image of the arrogant French.

Moreover, as a result of Louis's invasion, English identity and xenophobia became rallying-points for the royalist rather than the baronial forces, though not thanks to John. In his official correspondence John occasionally made appeals to the defence of the kingdom or the land of England in the same vein that Henry I had done more than a century earlier, but as king he did not champion Englishness in the way he had apparently done during the attack on Longchamp.[74] The language he used in his appeals to English subjects was little different from that in treaties with foreign lords to attract mercenaries.[75] Indeed, by the end of his reign John had become so alienated from his English subjects that he wrote to one of his foreign commanders: 'Take good care of your beloved body, for you cannot trust the English much.'[76] In contrast, the first scutage of Henry III's reign could be described in one royal record as being 'to deliver England from the French'.[77]

Outside the royal government itself, the reaction was still stronger. Even chroniclers who harshly condemned John had strong qualms about the invasion. Ralph of Coggeshall may have seen God's hand in the drowning of John's foreign supporters, but he also wrote of the French at the battle of Sandwich: 'Thus God smote the heads of his enemies who were coming to scatter the English people.' Roger of Wendover criticized the 'most evil plunderers from the kingdom of the

---

[69] *Annales Monastici*, 3: 47.
[70] Roger of Wendover, *The Flowers of History*, 2: 194–5, 200, 204.
[71] *Barnwell Chronicle*, 233.
[72] *Radulphi de Coggeshall Chronicon Anglicanum*, 179–80.
[73] Carpenter, *Minority of Henry III*, 29.
[74] Rymer, *Foedera*, 1: 110; *Rot. Litt. Pat.*, 55, 72b.
[75] e.g. *Rot. Litt. Pat.*, 98b; *Rot. Litt. Chart.*, 190b.
[76] *Rot. Litt. Claus.*, 273b.
[77] The passage was in a later addition to the Pipe Roll of John's last year: *Pipe Roll 17 John*, 14.

French' and the depredations of the 'foot soldiers of the kingdom of the French', who 'were like the filth and scum of that region'.[78] Royalist writers were happy to appeal to Englishness and xenophobia, particularly after the death of John. A remarkable poem about the battle of Lincoln, which tried to delicately balance support for John with condemnation of him, and which tried to rally support for John's young son Henry, drew heavily on these themes.[79] It began: 'A fourfold madness slithered up to the English people.' The first 'madness' was England's own pride, which of course called for divine punishment, as a result of which 'the honour of the English had bowed'. But God's anger, in the view of the poet, had been sated by John's death. The other three aspects of 'madness' were the French, the Scots, and the Welsh. The latter groups were also allied to the barons, which allowed royalists to bring anti-Celtic sentiment into play as well. The poet went on to write that the tears of the English for John would bring forth English strength, and that 'England drew victorious swords by the divine will. Standard-bearing troops, fierce in battle, fearsome to the enemy, poured forth from castles for the common good.' The poet also drew on other themes to garner support for Henry, but the appeal to English identity, the well-being of the realm, and the hatred of foreigners is unmistakable.

The practical impact of English loyalties and xenophobia on the resistance to Louis is hard to measure, but there are certainly indications that it mattered. The Waverley annalist wrote that many nobles took the sign of the cross, vowing to eject Louis and the French from England, preferring to have a king from their own land rather than from a foreign land.[80] The Dunstable annalist wrote of Willikin of the Weald and his supporters, a kind of guerilla band, killing the French wherever they could find them.[81] Hatred of the French may have extended far down the social ranks. The Dunstable annalist spoke of French foot-soldiers being slaughtered in the flight after the battle of Lincoln by local villagers, and Roger of Wendover made a similar claim about the French fugitives in general.[82] All these passages seem to indicate that the French were particular targets of hostility in a way that English rebels were not. In short, the strength of English identity and xenophobia were factors in the royalist victory over Louis and his English allies.

So strong was the force of English loyalty and hostility to the French as a result of Louis's invasion that they caught up even the least xenophobic. This at least is the impression given by *The History of William Marshal*, a poem that comes out of, and strongly reflects, a cosmopolitan milieu. William himself spent long stretches on the Continent, and his son William, the patron of the poet, was born in Normandy. When the elder William was expelled from the Young King's retinue at one point, he travelled to the French court. When Philip seized Normandy, William made a

---

[78] *Radulphi de Coggeshall Chronicon Anglicanum*, 185; Roger of Wendover, *The Flowers of History*, 2: 209, 211.

[79] Wright, *Political Songs*, 19–27.

[80] *Annales Monastici*, 2: 287.

[81] Ibid. 3: 46.

[82] Ibid. 3: 50; Roger of Wendover, *The Flowers of History*, 2: 219.

deal with him to retain his lands there, to John's dismay.[83] In the poem William was clearly identified as English in a tournament list and in the passage in which envious Continental courtiers complained about the renown he had gained. But very little emphasis is put on his Englishness.[84] Even during the struggle against Louis's invasion, the poet speaks in vague terms of 'ours', the army, or the people who were with the Marshal.[85] As for the French, they are regularly depicted as enemies in the many wars William fought under the Angevin kings, but in a fairly matter-of-fact tone.[86] We have seen that the poem contains one passage in which the arrogant French are humbled in a tournament, but generally there is little hostility towards them. Indeed, King Philip, along with one of the few Normans who had sided with him and gained his trust, are given practically the last words in the poem.[87] This is not a work that is committed to Englishness, nor possessed by hatred of other groups, except perhaps the Poitevins.[88]

Nonetheless, when it comes to the civil wars surrounding Magna Carta, the poem echoes many of the sentiments found in other sources. There is an un-favourable comment on the Flemings and other foreign knights and soldiers that John summoned for the siege of Rochester. Another passage describes the 'whore-mongers' of France boasting that the land was now theirs and that the English would have to leave, whereupon the author interjects a comment that he had seen a hundred that the English had killed being eaten by dogs. Other passages speak of the arrogance of the French and their desire to drive the English from England. As for the English, in one battle scene the poet describes how the royalists fought hard against the count of Perche, 'because they greatly hate those of France', and later on he ascribes a desire to 'eject the French from the land' to moderate royalists in a debate. William himself is made to speak about how the French, despite dominat-ing tournaments, were hiding behind the walls of Lincoln. In a subsequent speech, after the victory at Lincoln, the Marshal is recorded as saying that God had given a victory over the French who had come into England against God's will to claim the realm.[89] In short, even in a cosmopolitan source not notable for its dedication to the English, the complicated conflicts surrounding Magna Carta were reduced to a simplistic depiction of the English nobly defending their land against evil foreigners.

I noted earlier the contrasts between the role of ethnicity, and particularly Englishness, in the combined civil war and invasion of 1173–4 with those of

---

[83] Meyer, *L'Histoire de Guillaume le Maréchal*, 1: 238–40; 2: 101–7.

[84] Ibid. 1: 167, 188. See Carpenter, *Minority of Henry III*, 261–2, 273, and Clanchy, *England and its Rulers*, 186, for possible ambiguity in the identity of William's sons.

[85] e.g. Meyer, *L'Histoire de Guillaume le Maréchal*, 2: 204, 205, 221, 236.

[86] e.g. ibid. 1: 269, 279, 282, 284, 291, 310.

[87] Ibid. 1: 95–6; 2: 327–9; D. J. Power, 'Between the Angevin and Capetian Courts: John de Rouvray and the Knights of the Pays de Bray, 1180–1225', in *Family Trees and the Roots of Politics: The Prosopography of Britain and France from the Tenth to the Twelfth Century*, ed. K. S. B. Keats-Rohan (Woodbridge, 1997), 361–84.

[88] See above, n. 19.

[89] Meyer, *L'Histoire de Guillaume le Maréchal*, 2: 179, 180, 203, 227, 239, 247, 257, 261–2, 274.

1215–17.[90] Obviously the differences reflected the growing strength of both English identity and xenophobia in the intervening period. Both John and the rebels may have been surprised at how much controversy their employment of outside help aroused. But the events of 1215–17 themselves strengthened English identity. Whatever its shortcomings, Magna Carta radically altered English politics and made it much easier to conceive of and defend a loyalty to the community of England that was independent of loyalty to the king, and could possibly even trump it. The development of a political community that was defined as much by its allegiance to the realm of England as to the king himself could not help but foster English identity. Louis's invasion itself helped to strengthen English loyalties. Indeed, I believe that the shock of a foreign invasion, even if summoned by an English faction, powerfully galvanized English sentiment. Louis's army plundered and destroyed, as all armies of the time did, and this was bound to provoke a backlash. Moreover, Louis's invasion made hostility to foreigners a possible royalist as well as rebel stance, thus ensuring it a respectable future. In addition, the arrogance of Louis's French followers, at least from the English perspective, must also have served to dampen the enthusiasm for the French that had hitherto existed alongside hostility towards them. French mistrust also brought home to English nobles that they were very much outsiders from a Continental perspective, however much they may have admired Continental culture. Whether they liked it or not, they were English in Continental eyes, and as a result they were likely to embrace Englishness all the more firmly. Who knows what would have happened had Louis successfully gained the English crown? But the wrangling between his French and English followers, and his eventual defeat, only served to discredit Continental connections and strengthen English identity.

One of the great political issues of Henry III's reign was hatred of foreigners, whether in the attacks on Falkes de Bréauté and Peter des Roches, the movement against foreign clerics in 1231–2, or above all, the great baronial revolts of the mid-century. Though the opposition to Longchamp must be seen as the first appearance of this issue, the baronial revolt against John made it into a fixture in politics. The motives of the English barons were pragmatic; they wanted to limit competition for royal favour and thereby retain a greater share of royal benefits for themselves, and they were also distressed by the ability of the king to bring in foreign soldiers to oppose them. But the anti-foreign sentiment in itself strengthened the boundaries between the English nobility and other nobles, thereby strengthening the Englishness of the former group. Foreigners could still sometimes cross that boundary, as Simon de Montfort did.[91] But the hatred of foreign favourites helped to make the nobles of England much more firmly and self-consciously English.

One would certainly not want to reduce ethnicity to power politics, but there was an important relationship between the two, and once Englishness became politicized in the reigns of Richard and John it became more important. It is interesting

---

[90] See above, p. 326.
[91] Carpenter, *Minority of Henry III*, 261–2, 272–3; Maddicott, *Simon de Montfort*, 361; Vincent, *Peter des Roches*, 38–9.

in this context to look back to the politics of Edward the Confessor's reign, and especially the events of 1051–2 when the Godwines were exiled and forced their way back in. Then too, appeals to ethnic identity, English solidarity, and hostility towards foreigners had played a role. Rebels could use loyalty to the nation even against the king.[92] The conquest, of course, had put an end to such political scenarios by introducing an aristocracy to whom Englishness did not matter. With assimilation, and the gradual, cautious adoption of English identity by the descendants of the invaders, the stage was set for the revival of the kind of attitudes found in Edward's reign. The revival occurred not because those attitudes were well remembered, but because English identity more generally had been preserved, and because parallel circumstances had been created. As we have seen, the first tentative steps occurred in the reigns of Stephen and Henry II. But it was only in the reigns of Richard and John, and above all in the events of 1215–17, that Englishness re-emerged as a powerful force in English politics, even more powerful than before the conquest. The nobility had become thoroughly English in identity, xenophobia became entrenched, and loyalty to England and English solidarity could be effective calls to arms. English identity once again reigned unchallenged in England.

[92] See above, pp. 24–5, 30–1.

PART IV

Identity and Culture

21

History and Identity

CULTURAL ASSIMILATION, AS I sought to show in Part II, was strongly affected by the precise nature of the social interaction between the two assimilating peoples. Yet one cannot simply mechanically trace the relative contribution of each ethnic group and the shape of the new integrated culture from the numbers of individuals in each people, or even from the numbers of each people in various social groups. Many factors will influence the process of cultural assimilation. For instance, the idea that a group is tainted in some way, through being portrayed as barbaric, backward, or lower class, can cause the customs and culture of that people to be devalued. Once the English had decided that the Welsh and Irish were barbarians, even the most attractive elements of their cultures could be viewed with suspicion, which would hamper or prevent cultural assimilation. Moreover, just as personal interaction and constructs of identity affected cultural assimilation, so the melding of the two cultures affected questions of identity and relations between the English and Normans, a point that is no more than common sense. All of these considerations point to a need to focus on the contribution of culture to ethnic relations and identity.

In Chapter 4 I described the various cultural divides that served as ethnic barriers between the English and Normans in the immediate aftermath of the conquest. By the end of the twelfth century, and in most cases much earlier, these divides had disappeared, helping to unify the two peoples. Moreover, by the late twelfth century various cultural attributes had begun to distinguish the inhabitants of England, including those with Continental ancestry, from their contemporaries across the English Channel. Reginald of Durham tells how Parisian doctors, unable to heal a sick student from Durham, told him to return to his native soil and food, whereupon he returned to 'his own English territory'. Apparently French cuisine was notably distinctive and did not agree with this particular English cleric. Gerald of Wales shows how clothing and manner could betray Englishness, sometimes with serious practical consequences. On one occasion when the kings of England and France were at war, and the latter was seizing English travellers, Gerald tried to sneak through Artois, but the royal custodian of the town saw his servants and 'considering them to be English by their manner (or appearance) and clothes', seized Gerald, who subsequently had to be ransomed.[1] Equally, the French stood out in

---

[1] Reginald of Durham, *Vita Sancti Godrici*, 453. 'Per habitus ipsorum et vestes Anglicos esse perpendens', *GCO* 3: 240.

England; a miracle story of St Modwenna from the second half of the twelfth century says that Jordan, prior of Burton, upon seeing a French youth outside the monastery could tell by his speech and appearance (*loquela* and *cultus*) that he was foreign.[2] Thus, shifts in culture helped to strengthen Englishness by distinguishing the inhabitants of England from people on the Continent.

That there are important links between culture, ethnicity, and identity is relatively straightforward, but one must be cautious about simplistic or anachronistic assumptions about how the links function. For instance, cause and effect were obviously interlinked. Moreover, though ethnic identities depended heavily on distinctive cultural traits, existing identities could focus attention on or even distort the nature of specific cultural practices, at least in the way they were perceived. A good example of distortion is the way in which the massive imports of wine to England were ignored in discussion of the English as beer or cider drinkers. Cause and effect and truth and fiction are not always easy to sort out when it comes to the interaction of culture, ethnicity, and identity.

More important, one must be wary of anachronistic assumptions based on modern experience and scholarship about what precise areas of culture mattered when people thought about ethnicity and identity. It is easy to believe that the aspects of culture that matter most to us, or that we link most closely to ethnicity, would also be central to them. Differences in phenotype, which the racism of the modern period has caused to be of continuing and overwhelming importance even today, were simply not discussed in a post-conquest context, in part because any physical differences between the English and their conquerors were barely detectable, if detectable at all, but also because such differences did not assume the importance they would gain in later periods. Equally superficial differences in clothing and bearing, however, could matter, as Gerald of Wales's anecdote illustrates. We might see differences in warfare as merely technical, but they played an important role in medieval ethnic differentiation; even in the late twelfth century the link between the French and tournaments mattered to contemporaries.[3] Thus, in pursuing the influence of culture on ethnicity and identity, it is important to abandon preconceptions about which aspects of culture mattered most and which were likely to be tied to questions of identity.

I intend to further explore the complexity of relations between culture and identity, and to illustrate the arguments set out above, through three case studies. The first case study further investigates the telling of history after the conquest, showing more ways in which it influenced identity, but also showing the limitations of that influence and how identity shaped history. Historians, anthropologists, nationalists, and politicians have long recognized the tie between history and larger ethnic or national identities. A shared past, real or invented, can help to create and maintain the 'imagined community' by fostering a sense of unity.[4] I have already

[2] Geoffrey of Burton, *Life and Miracles of St Modwenna*, 216.

[3] *WNHA* 422–3.

[4] Some particularly pertinent or useful discussions include Davies, *Matter of Britain*; id., 'Language and Historical Mythology', 15–24; Guenée, *States and Rulers*, 58–63; Reynolds, 'Origines Gentium', 375–90; Smith, *Ethnic Origins of Nations*, 174–208.

discussed the importance of history (and myth) to English and Norman identity before the Norman Conquest and how English apologists used history to defend English pride and honour, and the cults of saints obviously had a strong historical element, but there are also other ways in which history contributed to the triumph of Englishness. In a sense this chapter can be seen as an extension of Part III, which explored the reasons why Englishness became the dominant identity in England by the early thirteenth century. In anthropological terms, government, religion, politics, stereotypes, and warfare are all aspects of culture. So too is the production of history, and thus this chapter describes one more way in which an aspect of culture shaped identity.

Yet after the conquest, as Peter Damian-Grint has recently pointed out, a choice of histories was available to the inhabitants and particularly the elites of England, most particularly English and Norman history. The conquest itself could be understood either as an event in the history of England and the English people, or as a notable achievement of the Norman people. In the middle of the twelfth century, after Geoffrey of Monmouth finished his popular work, a third, and potentially very enticing alternative emerged, namely British history, which could be tied into the potential geographic and political attractions of Britishness.[5] Obviously, in the end it was interest in English history (with Monmouth's vision of history incorporated into it) that dominated in England, but there was nothing foreordained about this, just as there was nothing foreordained about the triumph of English identity. The growing focus on English history was, of course, in large measure a result of the adoption of English identity by the descendants of the conquerors. The growing strength of Englishness also reshaped views of the conquest itself. Thus, while the cultural production of history shaped identity, identity also shaped the cultural production of history, illustrating the complex interaction of culture and construction that is an important theme of Part IV. This whole argument is complicated by the fact that historians, however conscientiously they try to reproduce the past faithfully, construct history, if only through the decisions they make about selection and omission. Thus, this chapter concerns the interactions of constructs as well as of construct and culture. This may reveal the conceptual limitations of the tripartite scheme of levels I have set out, but nonetheless the chapter can illustrate the complexity of ethnicity, and some ways in which two of the levels I have described interacted.

There is no need here to discuss in detail the rich Norman historical tradition before and after the conquest, or to stress again the strength of what Davis called 'the Norman myth'.[6] But it is worth looking at the availability and influence of Norman history in England. Various histories of the Normans, including those of Dudo, William of Jumièges, Robert of Torigni, and Wace were available in England.[7] The influence of Norman works can be found in writers working in

---

[5] Peter Damian-Grint, *The New Historians of the Twelfth-Century Renaissance: Inventing Vernacular Authority* (Woodbridge, 1999), 194–6.　　　　[6] Davis, *Normans and their Myth*, 49–68.

[7] Gameson, *Manuscripts of Norman England*, 63, 106, 132; Shopkow, *History and Community*, 38, 221, 238. The earliest MS of Wace's *Roman de Rou* was in an early thirteenth-century MS of Battle Abbey that was probably produced in England: *Roman de Rou*, 3: 19–21, 72.

England. For instance, John of Worcester and Henry of Huntingdon used a set of Norman annals, and the latter may also have used a vernacular version of Norman history.[8] William of Malmesbury drew from William of Poitiers, William of Jumièges, and other sources to add some pre-conquest Norman information to his history of the English kings.[9] Because of the close links, particularly in political terms, between England and Normandy after the conquest, historians in the former land naturally also recorded post-conquest Norman history in their works, though as we shall see, not always to the extent one might expect. Written Norman history was certainly available in England and considered of at least moderate interest by a number of historians working in England.

Norman traditions of oral history must also have existed, though by their nature these are hard to trace. Many family memories, especially of the most prominent noble lineages, would have encompassed events of broader Norman significance, and for those with continuing connections across the Channel these would have included incidents from after 1066 as well as before. Moreover, the accounts of speeches before the battle of the Standard and during the siege of Lisbon that contained aspects of the Norman myth, though likely to be literary creations, surely reflect continuing consciousness of Norman history among the elites of England.[10] Even the speech that Roger of Howden partly copied from Henry of Huntingdon but attributed to the earl of Arundel in 1173 suggests that he believed Norman history was important to Anglo-Norman magnates.[11] If van Houts is right about Wace's access to oral history about the Norman Conquest in Henry II's reign, then many magnates with ties to Normandy would have had similar access in the same period.[12] It seems, therefore, very likely that Norman history and a predominantly Norman view of the past remained available not just to literate churchmen but to the secular elites as well.

As a force to influence identity, moreover, Norman history had a number of advantages. It was a history of winners. It was an exciting historical tradition, filled with adventures, feuds, and, above all, warfare. The excesses of Dudo and the likely exaggerations of oral history would only have added to this quality of entertainment. Written vernacular versions of Norman history, which made them accessible to a wider audience than ones in Latin, were available in Wace and Benoît from Henry II's reign. Finally, a continuing cultivation of Norman history would have tied in neatly with interests in family history for most elite families.

Norman history, however, also had some serious disadvantages. Memories faded, and though oral history was probably more tenacious in a predominantly

---

[8] *CJW* 2: 306–7, 350–1, 372–3, 396, 508–9, 522; *HHHA* pp. xcviii, cv–cvi.

[9] *WMGR* 200–2, 232–4, 304–8, 426–40; R. M. Thomson, ed., *William of Malmesbury Gesta Regum Anglorum*: vol. 2, *General Introduction and Commentary* (Oxford, 1999), 110–11, 129, 162–3, 219–25, 227.

[10] *HHHA* 714–16; Aelred of Rievaulx, 'Relatio de Standardo', 185–9; David, *De Expugnatione Lyxbonensi*, 104–8.

[11] [Roger of Howden], *Gesta Regis Henrici Secundi*, 1: 52–3.

[12] Elisabeth van Houts, 'Wace as Historian', in *Family Trees and the Roots of Politics: The Prosopography of Britain and France from the Tenth to the Twelfth Century*, ed. K. S. B. Keats-Rohan (Woodbridge, 1997), 103–32.

oral culture than it is today, over time it would inevitably attenuate. The poetic history of William Marshal indicates that his family either had no knowledge about or no interest in his (English and Norman) ancestry beyond his parents.[13] The loss of memory meant that Norman history as a force in England would come to depend increasingly on those manuscripts of Norman history that existed in England. However, Albu has argued that most of the histories of the Normans presented them in an ambivalent fashion, emphasizing an almost bestial violence and a treacherous streak in their collective character.[14] As I suggested in Chapter 14, concern for sin could be compatible with histories that strongly supported a people, and I am not sure that Norman patrons would have been all that discomfited by a picture of themselves as extremely violent. Nonetheless, Albu is right to underscore the reservations of many of the writers of Norman history about the subjects of their work. As a result, the accounts of Norman history may have created a less than positive image, and therefore have been a weaker force for shaping identity, than older accounts of the Norman myth would suggest. Finally, within England after the conquest, no historian wrote a new work concerned primarily with Norman history, nor did any historian there place a major account of the Norman Conquest and the deeds of the conquerors and their descendants primarily within a Norman context. John of Worcester, William of Malmesbury, Henry of Huntingdon, and even the first-generation immigrant Simeon of Durham (to the extent that he was involved with the history of the kings of England later attributed to him) were all concerned primarily with English rather than Norman history, however much they may have written about the Normans in England. There was no work written in England that traced the deeds of Anglo-Norman kings and magnates in England in the twelfth century in a framework that went back to Rollo rather than the Anglo-Saxon kings. Whatever the oral traditions, there was nothing in writing quite like Gerald of Wales's *Expugnatio Hibernica*, which celebrated the exploits of the early English invaders of Ireland not as another episode in Irish history but as a subject in its own right, and could therefore act as something of an 'origin myth' for the English in Ireland.[15] Written histories of the Normans, which included some of their activities in England, may have been imported into England after the conquest, but they were not being generated there.

This may have been due primarily to chance and historiography rather than reflecting the ways most immigrants and their descendants viewed history, at least in the generations immediately following the conquest. It may be partly happenstance that the few scholars in England who were both interested in and had the skills to write broader 'national' histories were more interested in English than Norman history. But there were also good reasons why the writing of English history was a more urgent project. For anyone interested in Norman history,

[13] Georges Duby, *William Marshal: The Flower of Chivalry*, trans. Richard Howard (New York, 1985), 58.

[14] Albu, *Normans in their Histories*, 13–15, 41–6, 62–4, 73–7, 88–105, 113–15, 119, 125–44, 150–64, 175–9, 185–6, 191–210, 222–3, 234–5, 239.

[15] Gerald of Wales, *Expugnatio Hibernica*. See also Orpen, *Song of Dermot and the Earl*.

William of Jumièges's work, periodically updated by his redactors, was available, and oral history may have sufficed for more recent events. There was, in the generations following the conquest, no crying need for new work on Norman history, at least once the Normans had successfully disseminated their defence of William's invasion, which they did quickly. For the English, as William of Malmesbury stressed at the beginning of his work, nothing comprehensive and satisfying existed in Latin after the time of Bede.[16] As skill in Old English declined, and as the English needed to present their history to the conquerors, it obviously became important to transfer and translate the knowledge contained in vernacular sources to new Latin histories. Moreover, there was a psychological need to find out what had gone wrong for the English, and to use history to defend the English against the Normans. For the Normans in England these needs did not exist, at least not to the same degree. Nonetheless, however unrepresentative of elite thought the surviving histories may have been, once memories faded they had a disproportionate effect on how the past, including the Norman Conquest itself, was perceived by later generations. Had some immigrant cleric chosen to write a Normanocentric history of the rulers and elites of England after the conquest, the long-term impact of history on identity might well have been quite different. As it was, once oral tradition faded and the elites of England had to rely on written texts, there would have been no sources tying the deeds of their ancestors in England, after the Norman Conquest itself, into the whole tradition of *Normanitas*. Even the conquest itself, within the English historiographic tradition, would have been depicted primarily as a milestone in English, not Norman, history. This meant that their own broader sense of the past was more likely to be a primarily English than a Norman one, even though they might continue to hang onto the knowledge of their Norman ancestry.

In the middle of the twelfth century Geoffrey of Monmouth's *Historia Regum Britannie* radically altered the shape of insular historiography. Though there were doubts about the worth of the work in the twelfth century, it had a major impact on contemporaries, including historians. Henry of Huntingdon was influenced by it, and Geoffrey Gaimar translated it into French, though his version is lost. It is the only historical work, to my knowledge, that can be securely placed in the possession of great nobles, namely Robert of Gloucester and Walter Espec.[17] A number of manuscripts survive from twelfth-century England, and in the long term, judging by the survival of manuscripts, it became one of the most popular historical works in the European Middle Ages, outranking even Bede's history.[18] Whatever its faults as history, which seem to have been more apparent to some contemporaries than to others, it was tremendously entertaining and tailored to the interests of twelfth-century society. Any account of the effects of history on identity in England must take this popular work into account.

---

[16] *WMGR* 14.

[17] *HHHA* pp. ci–cii, 558–82; Gaimar, *L'Estoire des Engleis*, pp. liii, 204, 206.

[18] Julia Crick, *The Historia Regum Britannie of Geoffrey of Monmouth: IV. Dissemination and Reception in the Later Middle Ages* (Cambridge, 1991), 9, 216–17. As Damian-Grint notes, French versions of Geoffrey's history were much more popular than French versions of English or Norman history: Damian-Grint, *New Historians*, 194–6.

Geoffrey's own ethnic biases, and those of his history, remain disputed. Because the work focuses on the history of the Britons, several scholars have argued that he and his works favoured either the Welsh or the Bretons, and O. J. Padel has pointed out Geoffrey's interest in Cornwall and the Cornish.[19] Many others, pointing to Geoffrey's dedications to figures such as Robert of Gloucester, Waleran of Meulan, and King Stephen, have argued that he was pro-Norman, though by this they generally mean that he catered to the political and dynastic concerns of the ruling elites rather than a specific sense of Norman pride.[20] Davies and Michelle Warren have argued for ambiguous feelings on the part of this man from the borderlands.[21] Reynolds has argued that his history was popular in part because his emphasis on the Britons meant that his history transcended a historical past dominated by the division between English and Normans.[22] Given that much of the *Historia Regum Britannie* is dominated by war against the Saxons, no one has argued that this is an essentially pro-English book.[23] If nothing else, the widespread disagreement attests to Geoffrey's caginess as a writer. But whatever Geoffrey's intentions, his work could clearly be interpreted in theory to favour either some sort of 'British' identity, or possibly Norman identity. The question that matters here is whether it did so in practice, and whether Geoffrey's popular history had any discernable influence on ethnic identity within England.

Geoffrey's work manifestly failed to stem the shift from Norman to English identity in any measurable way. It may have had subtle effects that helped slow the decline of *Normanitas*, but no concrete evidence survives for this. Nor did his work create or sustain any substantial sense of Britishness as an ethnic or national identity in England, except in one area, namely Cornwall, where it did help to sustain an existing British identity. Within a couple of decades of Geoffrey's major work, John of Cornwall wrote his own version of the prophecies of Merlin, which contained independent material but was inspired and influenced by Geoffrey's version. John promised that he would explain the prophecies according to 'our Britannic [language]', by which he presumably meant Cornish, referred to the perfidy of the English against the Britons and Normans, and spoke of the devastation by the inhabitants of Devonshire 'among us', which he said had been discussed in Britannic. Clearly Geoffrey's work helped sustain this Cornish writer's sense of being a Briton, and distinct from the English.[24]

---

[19] J. S. P. Tatlock, *The Legendary History of Britain: Geoffrey of Monmouth's Historia Regum Britanniae and its Early Vernacular Versions* (Berkeley, 1950), 396–401, 443; Gillingham, *English in the Twelfth Century*, 19–39; Padel, 'Geoffrey of Monmouth and Cornwall', 1–20; Green, *Government of England*, 154–5; D. R. Howlett, *The English Origins of Old French Literature* (Dublin, 1996), 50–1.

[20] Tatlock, *Legendary History of Britain*, 399, 443–5; Stephen Knight, *Arthurian Literature and Society* (New York, 1983), 38–67; Francis Ingledew, 'The Book of Troy and the Genealogical Construction of History: The Case of Geoffrey of Monmouth's Historia regum Britanniae', *Speculum*, 69 (1994), 665–704; Maureen Fries, 'The Arthurian Moment: History and Geoffrey's *Historia Regum Britannie*', *Arthuriana*, 8 (1998), 88–99.

[21] Davies, *The Matter of Britain*, 6–7; Warren, *History on the Edge*, 25–59.

[22] Reynolds, *Kingdoms and Communities*, 267.

[23] See Michael J. Curley, *Geoffrey of Monmouth* (New York, 1994), 102–8, for anti-English sentiment.

[24] Curley, 'John of Cornwall's Prophetia Merlini', 231, 237–8.

More striking still, Walter of Coutances, who was from Cornwall despite his name, was considered and almost certainly considered himself a Cornish Briton. Walter's ultimate ancestry has not been traced, and he may well have been of insular origin, indeed from a Cornish-speaking family for all we know.[25] But his Britishness, as presented in the sources, is of a particularly Galfridian nature. Gerald of Wales described Walter as being from 'an old and true Briton lineage', and elsewhere as being from the house of Corineus, Geoffrey's founder of Cornwall, and from 'the noble people of the Britons'. Both Gerald and a later writer using the same source, derived from Lincoln, referred to his ultimate Trojan origins, further showing Geoffrey's influence at work.[26] More telling, John de Hauville, the author of *Architrenius*, which was dedicated to Walter and clearly sought to flatter him, made much of Walter's Cornish-British-Trojan background. He praised Cornwall in the context of praising Britain, recounted the deeds of Corineus, described the Trojan origins of the Cornish, and placed Walter's father, Reinfrey, alongside Arthur and Gawain in a war against avarice.[27] If these references are any indication, Geoffrey of Monmouth made Walter's Cornish-British ancestry, whether real or fictitious, a great source of pride to him. Apart from the examples of these two Cornish men, however, Geoffrey's work seems to have had very little impact on elite or other ethnic identity in England in the period of concern. British identity never became important in England (outside of Cornwall) in the period with which this book is concerned. Indeed, so strong was the sense of Englishness that Geoffrey's work, which was certainly on some level anti-English, could become anglicized and swallowed up into English history in certain traditions. Even Wace, who was not at all concerned with English identity, repeatedly and anachronistically referred to 'Engleterre' in his translation of Geoffrey's history into French, showing how the strength of the idea of England could distort his sense of Geoffrey's historical vision.[28] Davies has discussed how Geoffrey's 'Matter of Britain', became co-opted by the 'Matter of England', and he and others have shown how Geoffrey's work was incorporated into English historiography, to the point that Edward I could use it to promote English ambitions in Britain.[29] Thus, a strong identity could as easily reshape a powerful vision of history as the reverse, and even popular history might have only a limited influence on ethnic identity. Geoffrey's work, though extremely successful, did not make the English British, nor stop the Normans from becoming English.

Why did Geoffrey's work have so little impact on ethnic identity? There are a number of likely reasons. First, if Geoffrey was trying to support Welsh, Breton, or

[25] If Roger son of Reinfrey is to be identified with the Roger son of Reinfrey who attested Reading charters in the company of a brother named Edward, this might suggest an insular background, possibly from a native Cornish family that came under English and Norman influence in their naming patterns: Kemp, *Reading Abbey Cartularies*, 2, no. 1209.

[26] GCO 4: 408; 7: 38.

[27] John de Hauville, *Architrenius*, 10–12, 136–44.

[28] Rollo, *Historical Fabrication*, 110–13.

[29] Davies, *Matter of Britain*, 16–17; Warren, *History on the Edge*, 81–129; Clanchy, *England and its Rulers*, 11–13.

any other identity, he did so in a subtle fashion, perhaps so subtle that it had little impact. This is particularly true of Norman identity, since the Normans do not even feature in the work. Moreover, Geoffrey's work and the Arthurian cycle it popularized were the subject of some scepticism and opposition in the twelfth century. William of Newburgh's attack on Geoffrey of Monmouth is famous, as is Gerald of Wales's humorous account of demons flocking around a copy of the *Historia Regum Britannie*.[30] Aelred of Rievaulx chastised a monk for being more affected by Arthurian tales than by religious ones.[31] As David Rollo has pointed out, Aelred and William may have been influenced by their own English loyalties in their reaction to Arthur and Geoffrey, but the reactions also reflected reasonable doubts about the historicity of Geoffrey's work.[32] History that was treated sceptically was less likely to influence identity. Moreover, if Geoffrey was trying to build up 'British' pride, he faced stronger prejudices, particularly against the Welsh, than the English writers I have noted earlier faced from the Normans. The continuing warfare of the English and Normans against the Welsh may also have helped maintain ethnic barriers that would nullify the attractions that Geoffrey's history provided to a British identity. But the chief reason for its lack of influence is that a single history, no matter how popular, is unlikely to create identity where no other source for that identity exists.

Much has been made, particularly by modernists, of invented traditions and their effects on identity. Most historians would agree that Geoffrey of Monmouth's history largely consisted of invented tradition. But only in Cornwall, where there were linguistic and perhaps other cultural features that made British identity and a connection to Geoffrey's past believable, did Geoffrey have any influence on identity, by shoring up and reshaping an ethnic identity that already existed. In the face of a strong sense of English identity, and a well-established English historiography, Geoffrey of Monmouth's history was unlikely to have much impact. I have emphasized that constructs cannot influence identity or indeed operate independently of cultural and social realities. Geoffrey's historical construct, which put the Britons in a heroic light and helped prominent Cornish figures to rethink their identity, but had little influence in England, can help to dispel the idea that any set of images alone, however powerful or popular, can substantially reshape group identities in the absence of at least a reasonably strong affinity with reality.

This brings us to the effects of English history, and the extent to which English versions of history nurtured as well as resulted from the overall success of English identity. Southern's well-known argument that the burst of historical writing in England after 1066 was a response to the conquest has been noted before. Other historians have implicitly or explicitly noted a link between this historical material and the survival of Englishness.[33] The task here is to build on this work by discussing what made English history more effective than its 'competitors' in shaping identity, and to explore the mechanics of its influence to the extent possible.

[30] *WNHA* 11–18; *GCO* 6: 58.

[31] Ailred of Rievaulx, 'Speculum Caritatis', in *PL* 195: 565.

[32] Rollo, *Historical Fabrication*, 121, 309–10.

[33] Southern, 'The Sense of the Past', 246–56; Williams, *ENC* 164–86; Gillingham, *English in the Twelfth Century*, 135; Davies, *Matter of Britain*; id., 'Language and Historical Mythology', 15–24.

I start with the effects of pre-conquest history on identity. This sort of history was, by relative standards, widely available after the conquest. Gameson's work on manuscripts surviving from between the conquest and c.1130 suggests that Bede's history, which constituted the 'origin myth' of the English people, was one of the most popular books in the period, and by far the most important history. Gransden has also shown the great importance and influence of Bede in the late eleventh century and throughout the twelfth century. The antiquity of the work, and Bede's general reputation as a holy and learned scholar, gave his history an authority and prestige that neither the Norman historians nor Geoffrey of Monmouth could hope to match.[34] Pre-conquest 'national' history subsequent to Bede was preserved not only in the vernacular but also though translation and incorporation in the works of influential historians such as John of Worcester, William of Malmesbury, and Henry of Huntingdon, all of which survive in a number of copies from the twelfth and early thirteenth centuries, and which served as a basis for the writings of later historians. Gaimar's history even made large chunks of material from the Anglo-Saxon Chronicle available in the vernacular of the conquerors.[35] In addition to broad histories, there was a great deal of other written historical material available, including monastic histories, saints' lives, laws, and charters. More important still, there would have been a tremendous amount of pre-conquest oral history preserved in the early generations after the conquest, and at least some would have been available to immigrants through various contacts and relationships across ethnic lines.

Finally, the English too had their invented traditions or history which, to the extent they were believed, could help to shape identity and counteract the influence of other invented traditions. James Campbell rightly laments the flood of bad history from the middle of the twelfth century.[36] But as Geoffrey of Monmouth's work indicates, invented traditions could be particularly popular because they were designed to appeal to the taste of a contemporary audience. Gaimar's account of Havelok the Dane, which he added to pre-conquest history, gave it a certain romance quality that would have been appealing to his contemporaries, judging by the general popularity of such stories.[37] Even more interesting are some of the early romances in the 'Matter of England', written in the early thirteenth century when English identity was being consolidated among the aristocracy. One of these, the *Roman de Waldef*, probably written in the first decade of the thirteenth century, was set during the time of divided English kingdoms and claimed to be a translation and recovery of material lost through the Norman Conquest.[38] Though neither Waldef (Waltheof) nor his father, King Bede, corresponds in any way to their historical namesakes, the names are clearly designed to point the audience to a specifically English past. Though set in a time before the unification of England, the main

---

[34] Gameson, *Manuscripts of Norman England*, 32–3, 35–7, 42; Gransden, 'Bede's Reputation', 397–419.

[35] Gaimar, *L'Estoire des Engleis*, pp. liv–lv.

[36] Campbell, 'Twelfth-Century Views', 221–6.

[37] Gaimar, *L'Estoire des Engleis*, 2–25.

[38] A. J. Holden, *Le Roman de Waldef (cod. Bodmer 168)* (Cologny-Genève, 1984), 17–18.

characters are consistently identified as English. The poet described the only fault of Waldef's father, Bede, as excessive friendliness to foreigners, an echo of the anti-foreign sentiment that was rising in England.[39] Though the poem does mirror close ties between Normans and English, for Bede goes to rescue the Normans from the French, that very episode claims an English military superiority to both groups.[40] Throughout the poem the English are explicitly praised for various chivalric virtues.[41] Much of the story involves Continental warfare and conquests, and though this obviously would have had a contemporary resonance, there are also explicit comparisons made with Belinus and Arthur. In some sense Waldef and his relatives formed an English answer to Geoffrey of Monmouth's Briton heroes.[42] The *Roman de Waldef* was not particularly popular, and other romances set in England were less concerned with Englishness. But Gui de Warwick, hero of the popular romance of that name, was clearly described as English, and his adventures were set in the reign of Æthelstan who, besides being an important historical king, was depicted by Geoffrey of Monmouth as the king who united Loegria under the Saxons.[43] Here again was an English hero who could stand shoulder to shoulder with the heroes of Geoffrey's appealing and anachronistic work. Thus, there came to exist pre-conquest English 'history' that could appeal very much to lovers of romance and chivalry, that was accessible to those without any command of Latin, and that could compete with Geoffrey of Monmouth's popular work on its own turf.[44]

All in all, the pre-conquest English historical tradition had advantages lacking to its 'competitors' in influencing identity. It was anchored by the work of one of the most prestigious scholars of the Middle Ages. Pre-conquest history continued not only to be copied, but also to be translated and written in England after the conquest, and linked to post-conquest historical events. Judging by surviving manuscripts, it was the most widely available tradition in Latin, and it may have been nearly as available as British or Norman history in French (not to mention that it could still be read in English in the generations immediately following the conquest). English oral traditions were probably as strong as Norman ones after the conquest, and had the advantage of being linked to saints' cults, religious houses, and other institutions of continuing local relevance, which may have made them less likely to quickly fade and more likely to eventually be preserved in writing than Continental memories. The invented traditions of the English may not have been as successful or popular as Geoffrey of Monmouth's remarkable work, but they could help to counteract its influence, and in any case the relatively accurate and well-

---

[39] Holden, *Roman de Waldef*, 57.

[40] Ibid. 62–8.

[41] Ibid. 62–7, 79–80, 103, 191, 232, 235, 239, 245, 251, 253, 270.

[42] For references to Arthur and Belinus see ibid. 209, 237, 242, 279.

[43] Ewert, *Gui de Warewic*, 2: 16–21, 47, 57, 136, 151; *Historia Regum Britannie of Geoffrey of Monmouth*, 1: 147.

[44] See Susan Crane, *Insular Romance: Politics, Faith, and Culture in Anglo-Norman and Middle English Literature* (Berkeley, 1986), 15; Crane, 'Anglo-Norman Cultures in England', 40–1, 43; Legge, *Anglo-Norman Literature*, 139–75, for the appeal and importance of the pre-conquest romance heroes.

attested core of the English historical tradition was less likely to be doubted or ridiculed than the *Historia Regum Britannie*.

The effect of history on identity, like most other factors, was generally so subtle that few people remarked on it. For the people of native descent, most of whom already thought of themselves as English, pre-conquest English history could shore up that identity in a number of ways beyond those discussed in earlier chapters. History gave depth to the constructs of England and Englishness, and the fact that English history itself was of some antiquity only gave them more of a sense of unchanging reality. The very survival of the constructs depended on their transmission from generation to generation, and particularly across the potential historical rupture created by the Norman Conquest. History gave strength to other building-blocks of the concepts of England and Englishness as well. In a period when the old and traditional was highly respected, the long existence of an English government and an English church, enshrined both in written history and in the memories of those who lived at the time of the conquest, helped to ensure that these institutions would be respected and maintained. Even the strengthening of Englishness through the Welsh Other could be supported by history: I have already noted how the English monks Lawrence and Philip joked with the Briton monk Peter about the seizure of *Britannia* and its transformation into *Anglia*.[45] The idea of English history as part of the divine plan could help authors, and presumably much of their audience, to work through and explain the disasters the English had faced, and could help to assuage the trauma of being a conquered people.[46] Finally, the fact that so many of the histories of the English were written with an eye on the divine plan gave the existence of England and the English an aura of being ordained by God, and thus in some sense inevitable. God could, of course, cause the English to cease to exist, as Henry of Huntingdon put it, but in general, historical memory was what gave the two constructs their greatest appearance of solidity, and thus helped the English to preserve their identity.[47]

For the Normans to be influenced by pre-conquest English history, it not only had to be accessible to them but also of interest. It is certainly not inevitable that conquerors will take an interest in the history of those they have defeated. To take a modern example, American history in the United States has generally been treated as beginning with European exploration or the founding of Jamestown, not with the crossing of the Bering Straits, though Native Americans are citizens of the country, and though the United States itself only came into being long after the European arrival. In the European Middle Ages conquerors rarely bothered to learn much from non-Christians they had conquered. Even in the Christian country of Ireland, the Anglo-Norman conquerors showed little interest in the rich written historical traditions of the regions they overran or of the island as a whole. But in England the Normans were drawn into an interest in pre-conquest English history for a number of reasons.

[45] See above, p. 314.
[46] Van Houts, *Memory and Gender*, 128–9; Wormald, 'Engla Lond', 17.
[47] *HHHA* 412.

The most important of these was William the Conqueror's claim to be the legitimate successor of Edward the Confessor. This meant that the history of the reigns of Edward and his predecessors had to be known to some degree and accepted as legitimate and important subjects in their own right. Even Norman propaganda had to contain a certain amount of pre-conquest history.[48] Henry I's marriage to Edith-Matilda only made the history of the English kings, at least those of the West Saxon line, all the more important, which of course was the whole point of Aelred of Rievaulx's 'Genealogia Regum'.[49] The claims of the royal house to legitimate succession meant that histories of the pre-conquest kings could be treated as supportive of the monarchy rather than a sign of rebelliousness, and therefore gave them a legitimacy that histories of conquered rulers might not have had in a different situation, and made it more likely that at least some immigrants would take an interest in them.

The claim that the king and his nobles simply stepped into the shoes of their *antecessores* also meant that earlier documents and oral testimonials about rights and privileges were of intense practical interest, as were the existing laws of the kingdom. Not all of this would have had much effect on ethnic or national identity. But the review of charters would have drawn readers into the world of pre-conquest nobles, churchmen, and above all kings, and perhaps sparked the desire to understand something of pre-conquest political history in order to understand the circumstances and quality of grants. Forgery of charters, a common practice in the post-conquest period, would also have required a reasonable knowledge of pre-conquest history, and though the details could be drawn from natives, any Norman prelate (or secular landholder, if they engaged in the practice) would have been well advised to have the story more or less straight.[50] As seen in Chapter 16, some immigrant intellectuals made a serious effort to understand and unravel pre-conquest law.[51] This again drew them into broader English political history, as when the writer of 'The Laws of Edward the Confessor' included a dynastic history in his legal compilation.[52] Thus, the political, legal, and institutional continuity demanded by William's policies required the immigrants to take seriously pre-conquest history and historical documents.

The institutional continuity within the English church helped to create an even greater awareness of the pre-conquest English past among immigrants, especially churchmen and nuns. Monks, nuns, and clerics would have been most concerned about the history of their own specific institutions, but this often required delving into general works of pre-conquest history. Bishop William of Saint-Calais, in his *De Iniusta Vexacione*, described how he had replaced clerics with monks at Durham after reading the *vita* of St Cuthbert and Bede's *Ecclesiastical History*.[53] Archbishop

---

[48] e.g. *GGWP* 2–6, 18–20.

[49] Aelred of Rievaulx, 'Genealogia Regum Anglorum', 711–38.

[50] Howlett, *English Origins*, 19–20. For an overview of forgery in the period, see Clanchy, *From Memory to Written Record*, 318–27.

[51] See above, p. 278.

[52] O'Brien, *God's Peace and King's Peace*, 192–6. See also Howlett, *English Origins*, 23–5.

[53] Van Caenegem, *English Lawsuits*, 1: 91.

Ralph of Canterbury, in a letter to the pope defending the rights of his see against those of York, referred to 'old histories of the English people', and 'old chronicles of the English' to buttress his arguments.[54] Even lay patrons of refounded houses could be drawn into learning about the English past; an 1115 confirmation by Walter de Gant to Bardney Abbey, founded anew by Walter's father Gilbert under William I, refers to Bede's account of the house and notes its destruction by 'the cruel persecutions of foreigners'. Though a scribe would have composed the charter, it is likely that the Gants knew the history.[55] The cultivation of saints' cults naturally also involved a certain amount of interest in history. Perhaps the best example of how all these factors could come together is that of Simeon of Durham. Though an immigrant who oversaw the making of his own personal copy of William of Jumièges's Norman history, Simeon became more and more concerned with the production of both local and more broadly English history as a monk at Durham. He copied parts of Bede's historical works, was almost certainly responsible for an important history of his own house, and wrote a brief history of the archbishops of York. He was involved in the copying and probably compilation of annals, and there is good reason to think he had a hand in the *Historia Regum Anglorum* later attributed to him. In short, Simeon became involved first with the history of his own church and its saint, then with that of a neighbouring church, and eventually with the history of England as a whole.[56] Thus, the English church served the cause of English identity not only directly but also indirectly, by sparking interest in English history.

It is also likely that curiosity about their new home manifested itself among immigrants. This curiosity might often be local in nature, but could have broader implications, partly because of the strength of England as a geographic construct. According to an account of the foundation of Whitby, the Norman knight Reinfrid was struck by the story and site of an ancient monastery at Whitby in Yorkshire, the county where his family came to be based after the conquest. Moved by this, he joined the monastery of Evesham and subsequently met a native monk of Winchcombe, Aldwin, who had learned of the ruined monasteries of the north through reading Bede. These two, inspired by a story, a historical site, and a book, were crucial to the monastic revival in the north.[57] Reinfrid's story is unusual, but many other immigrants must have been equally curious about their home, and their descendants even more so. William of Malmesbury believed or at least hoped that Robert of Gloucester would be interested in his history of the English kings.[58] Henry of Huntingdon stated that his patron, Bishop Alexander of Lincoln, commanded him to write his history, and Gaimar said the same of his francophone and therefore probably at least partly immigrant patron Constance.[59] King John had a book of

[54] *HCY* 2: 230–1, 234, 240–1, 243.

[55] *Mon. Ang.*, 1: 628–9.

[56] *LDE*, pp. xlv–l; Michael Gullick, 'The Hand of Symeon of Durham: Further Observations on the Durham Martyrology Scribe', in *Symeon of Durham: Historian of Durham and the North*, ed. David Rollason (Stamford, 1998), 14–31; J. E. Story, 'Symeon as Annalist', in *Symeon of Durham*, 202–13.

[57] J. C. Atkinson, ed., *Cartularium Abbathiae de Whiteby*, vol. 1 (Durham, 1879), 1; *LDE* 200; *EYC* 11: 92–3.   [58] *WMGR* 10–12.

[59] *HHHA* 4–6; Gaimar, *L'Estoire des Engleis*, 203–5; Short, 'Patrons and Polyglots', 244.

English history in French brought to him at one point in the early thirteenth century.[60] There clearly was interest in English history, including pre-conquest history, on the part of many leading members of the Anglo-Norman elite.

The effects of pre-conquest history in helping to change the identity of immigrants were no doubt as subtle as they were in the case of maintaining existing identity. No one was likely to become English simply by reading English history. But for immigrants to learn the (sometimes exaggerated) pre-conquest nature of the laws they followed, the indubitably English origins of the ecclesiastical house in which many lived, or the pre-conquest history of the government they served placed them in a firmly English rather than Continental context, and thus made it easier for them to think of themselves as English. Pre-conquest history of all sorts forged links between the immigrants and their native predecessors, thus tying them into an English milieu in yet another way. In this process the tendency of so many historians to link pre- and post-conquest history was crucial, for it placed the actions of their contemporaries in a chronological line and a context that cut across the conquest. They made the deeds of the kings and nobles part of English history, thus making England and ultimately the English the proper setting for the immigrants. Put another way, those people whose history was English were more likely to come to see themselves as English. The impact of this would be slow, and therefore hard to trace, but it seems likely that the dominance of English history gradually helped to make immigrants or their descendants English, and once they came to see themselves as English, helped to maintain and strengthen that identity.

What of the history of the conquest itself? One would expect memory of that savage affair to divide English and Normans and help the latter to maintain their separate identity. Yet in the event memory of the conquest, though divisive at first, eventually may have become more of a help than a hindrance to the reconstruction of Englishness. Anderson, in his seminal work *Imagined Communities*, included a section with the intriguing title 'The Reassurance of Fratricide'. Anderson's argument is that earlier struggles, which occur before one could speak, in his view, of nations and nationalism, became incorporated into national biographies with the rise of nationalism. In doing so they become unifying rather than dividing factors, because national consciousness wipes out the divisive aspects of these conflicts. One of his main examples, interestingly, concerns the Norman Conquest.[61] My argument here is that a similar phenomenon could occur even before the emergence of modern nationalism. This phenomenon also illustrates how ethnic or national identity could influence the cultural production of history, reinforcing an important argument of this chapter.

As Chapter 7 showed, historians such as Gaimar and Aelred of Rievaulx could use history, including accounts of the conquest, to promote ethnic reconciliation. Meanwhile the conquest came to be more and more embedded in English history (although it never stopped being part of Norman history, as the works of Wace and Benoît attest). Indeed, the conquest became a major locus in English historical

[60] *Rot. Litt. Claus.*, 29b.
[61] Anderson, *Imagined Communities*, 199–203.

writing for the idea of fighting for the *patria*, despite the fact that most of the elite were descended from the invaders, or claimed to be. Historians in the century-and-a-half after 1066 again and again spoke of the English in the battles of that year, and in subsequent rebellions, fighting and dying for the *patria*, or for the *päis*, or for the liberty of England or the English.[62] Even Battle Abbey, the monument of Norman victory at the battle of Hastings, became the 'emblem of the crown of the king of England', as the *Chronicle of Battle Abbey* put it.[63] In some ways, the very fact that the Norman Conquest became domesticated, as it were, meant that even the invaders became anglicized in retrospect, which could help to influence the identity of their descendants.

Most striking are later histories of the conquest, written during the period in which Englishness became consolidated among the elites, that were pro-English and in some cases anti-Norman but in ways that were different from the works discussed in Chapter 14. The authors of these later works were not very concerned about defending the English, but they were willing to defend Harold and to attack William explicitly in ways that earlier writers did not dare or choose to do. The differences reflect the greater security of the ruling dynasty, the decline of English defensiveness due to assimilation, and growing English chauvinism. The first of these works was the Waltham Chronicle, written sometime after 1177. Here the author's attitude was shaped by the loyalties of his house, for Harold had been the greatest patron of Waltham, though it should also be remembered that since Henry II was the current patron, the writer had to be concerned not to offend him. For the Waltham chronicler Harold was a practically flawless hero, and he dealt with Norman charges against Harold and his family either by ignoring them or by changing the facts, as when he had Tosti fight with rather than against Harold at Stamford Bridge, thus avoiding the charge of fratricide sometimes levied against the latter. The author treated Harold as the legitimate and uncontested king, and reduced William's motivation for the invasion, with a comment on the perfidious tricks of the Normans, to Harold's refusal to marry his daughter. The author even described the miracle-producing cross at Waltham bowing in sorrow as Harold prepared to go to his death, and though he could not help but admit that God had refused Harold his support, he resorted to platitudes and lamentations, as well as practical explanations of the English defeat, to hurry the reader past this uncomfortable point. As the editors of the Chronicle note, the author maintained a careful and correct attitude toward the Norman regime, but he described the Normans in general as savage, and his support for Harold and critical view of the conquest is startling when compared to earlier accounts.[64]

The second work is the *Vita Haroldi*. Its author, who was probably writing around 1200, was one of many members of the Geoffrey of Monmouth school of

---

[62] *GGWP* 126; *WMGR* 422, 452, 454; *WMGP* 207; *VW* 23–4; *GND* 2: 168; *EHOV* 2: 172, 180, 206, 216; Gaimar, *L'Estoire des Engleis*, 164; Osbert of Clare, 'Édouard le Confesseur', 114–15; Hardy and Martin, *Gesta Herwardi*, 374; Étienne of Rouen, *Draco Normannicus*, 647; Blake, *Liber Eliensis*, 174, 179.

[63] Searle, *Chronicle of Battle Abbey*, 160.

[64] Watkiss and Chibnall, *The Waltham Chronicle*, pp. xiii, xxxiv, 44–50.

historical fiction; his whole work was based on the unlikely premiss that Harold escaped the battle of Hastings to become a hermit, and he had Harold's brother Gyrth (also, apparently, a survivor) provide substantiating evidence after 1177, making him at least 130 years old.[65] He too was careful to defend Harold's reputation. He admitted that Harold made an oath to William, wrote about a withered oak he had seen in Rouen that supposedly died immediately after Harold made his oath, and even related that many claimed Harold's perjury led to the downfall of English liberty, but then went on to rebut the traditional arguments. First of all, he stated that Harold was forced to swear and therefore it was licit not to fulfill his oath. Second, he said that the English were angry when they heard about the oath, crying 'let it not be that we serve the Normans', rejecting the 'barbaric Norman yoke', and refusing to permit the throne to be granted to William. Third, he argued that Norman behaviour after the conquest clearly justified Harold's refusal to turn England over to them. As for the withered tree at Rouen, the author made dark comments about tree worship and then offered explanations that exculpated Harold—perhaps the withered tree referred to those who forced Harold to take an oath against his will, as well as their descendants, or perhaps to those who diminished the ancient vigour of the church in England.[66] The author never explained why God allowed his hero to be defeated in battle, but one gets the impression that he believed it was to force Harold from the heroic status of king and warrior to the even more heroic status of hermit. In any case this work, like that of the Waltham chronicler, provides a remarkable attack on the legitimacy of the Norman Conquest.

More remarkable still was the attitude of a much more sober and responsible historian, William of Newburgh, writing between 1196 and 1198. William described his royal namesake as 'surnamed the Bastard', wrote that he invaded 'either out of lust for domination or the sake of avenging injuries', and recorded that Archbishop Stigand refused to consecrate as king 'a cruel man and usurper of the rights of another'. He viewed Archbishop Ealdred as being sensible and pragmatic for agreeing to crown the king and using his influence to soften this 'most ferocious man', but included the story, drawn from the anonymous York historian, of the archbishop cursing the king, who then had to humble himself. Most strikingly, he condemned William for killing so many Christians at Hastings, writing: 'in the place in the monastery [of Battle] where the greatest slaughter was made of the English struggling for the *patria*, if even a little rain wettens the ground it exudes real blood, appearing recently shed, and the evidence of the crime itself speaks, as if the voice of so much Christian blood still calls to God from earth.'[67]

With one last historical account, we move away from the attacks on William and the Norman Conquest but not from the celebration of the English. This account comes from a chronicle ending in 1219 written on the Continent by a

[65] Birch, *Vita Haroldi*, 85–6. Aelred alluded to the possibility of Harold having become a hermit: Aelred of Rievaulx, 'Vita S. Edwardi Regis', 766.

[66] He also disassociated Harold from his father's deeds: Birch, *Vita Haroldi*, 15–16, 50–65.

[67] *WNHA* 20–3. For the date, see Gransden, *Historical Writing in England*, 263.

Premonstratensian of English origin. William is described as the 'rex Anglie benignissimus', who tells surviving nobles after the battle of Hastings that he would preserve their nobility, liberty, and honour, and commands that those who do accept his offer be left in peace. But it also includes a celebration, clearly drawn from earlier lost sources combined with a certain amount of romance, of the deeds of certain English nobles who are 'affected by such grief over the loss of the kingdom', that they refuse William's offer, 'choosing rather to die or be driven from the *patria* perpetually than to see foreigners rule their people'. These exiles, after the failure of Danish assistance, travel to Constantinople, defeating hordes of Muslims on the way, and gain great renown and success there, even founding a 'New England' some distance from the city. I do not believe that the writer was aiming at conciliation between the two peoples here; that had already come about. Instead, the conquest was so far past that both sides could be 'the good guys' to this chronicler from England, without any sense of contradiction or need for partisanship.[68]

All of these later sources should probably be seen in the context of the increasing anti-foreign sentiments of the late twelfth and early thirteenth centuries, and the consolidation of Englishness in that period, just as the earlier conciliatory works should be seen in the context of the final stages of assimilation, and the earlier debates must be viewed in the light of the ethnic hostility that reigned in the decades after the conquest. Of course, responses to the conquest were complex in each of these periods; Rebecca Reader has shown that ambiguity and confusion continued even in Matthew Paris's work in the thirteenth century.[69] But overall, responses to the conquest were influenced by contemporary considerations about identity and ethnicity. At heart, the Norman Conquest became anglicized. Anderson argued that this took place only in the nineteenth century with the rise of nationalism, but in fact the process was basically complete by around 1200.

Finally, there are the effects of post-conquest history on identity to be considered. By the reigns of Richard and John the invaders and their descendants had been involved in English history for over a century. It is worth reiterating that their actions in England came to be depicted as part of English history, not Norman history, in most post-conquest historical works. It is true that some historians working in Normandy, such as Orderic Vitalis and Robert of Torigni, did write about Normans on both sides of the Channel. But in England historians were largely concerned with the Normans in England, and tended to pay little attention to Norman history, even when one might expect them to take an interest. A good example is Geoffrey of Anjou's seizure of Normandy during Stephen's reign. Modern historians have argued that this helped the Angevin cause in England by forcing any major cross-Channel landholder who supported Stephen to contem-

---

[68] Krijnie N. Ciggaar, ed., 'L'Émigration anglaise à Byzance après 1066', *Revue des Études Byzantines*, 32 (1974), 301–42 (quotations at p. 320); Christine Fell, 'The Icelandic Saga of Edward the Confessor: Its Version of the Anglo-Saxon Emigration to Byzantium', *Anglo-Saxon England*, 3 (1974), 179–96.

[69] Reader, 'Matthew Paris and the Norman Conquest', 118–47.

plate losing his or her Norman lands.[70] Yet the major historians of the reign in England paid little attention to this pivotal event. Henry of Huntingdon, John of Hexham, and the author of the *Gesta Stephani* ignored it altogether. The Anglo-Saxon Chronicle made a bare mention of it.[71] William of Malmesbury noted it only to complain that Geoffrey kept Robert of Gloucester away from England to help him in its completion.[72] In short, historians in England sometimes tended to divorce England and its inhabitants from Normandy and its inhabitants even more than events would warrant. Some later chroniclers in England, such as Ralph of Diceto, took a somewhat broader view, but one that did not particularly treat the Normans and English as a unit, and other historians, such as William of Newburgh, maintained an Anglocentric view.[73]

Did the Anglocentric view of the conquest and of post-conquest history presented by so many writers in England help to anglicize immigrants? It seems likely. When Thomas Becket described why Archbishop Ealdred of York rather than Archbishop Stigand of Canterbury crowned William I, and referred to his argument being clear 'from the celebrated history of our people' it is reasonably clear that by 'our people' he meant the English, though Becket himself was a second-generation immigrant.[74] The depiction as patriots of English defenders and rebels, eventually including even Harold, in works from around 1200 could help to promote a similar attitude towards defending England among contemporaries, and the presentation of William and the Normans as hostile invaders, long after the internal ethnic strife had disappeared, could bolster the growing anti-foreign sentiment that blossomed in the thirteenth century. Paradoxically, the fact that the conquest became anglicized in some sense also meant that the conquerors (and their descendants) became anglicized. Most important, when the barons tried to curb John, one of their abortive techniques was to make an appeal to English history based on a request that he honour the coronation charter which Henry I had granted to their predecessors.[75] By the early thirteenth century important points of historical reference and of tradition had long been centred on England for the elites, despite their Continental background. For most, their history, and the history of their ancestors, had for over a century largely been English history and had been told as English history. There are many ways in which the passage of time helped to anglicize immigrants, but one was the creation of a long English history that included the immigrants, and could therefore help them feel more English.

History and identity, as has long been recognized, are closely intertwined. There

---

[70] Marjorie Chibnall, *The Empress Matilda: Queen Consort, Queen Mother, and Lady of the English* (Oxford, 1991), 105–6, 116; Jim Bradbury, *Stephen and Matilda: The Civil War of 1139–53* (Stroud, 1996), 147–55.

[71] *ASC* E 1140.

[72] William of Malmesbury, *Historia Novella*, 124–6.

[73] Ralph of Diceto can in some senses be called a historian of the Angevin empire, since he took an interest in the history of all of Henry II's lineages, but this was not likely to favour Norman as opposed to English identity.

[74] *Correspondence of Thomas Becket*, 2: 1264.

[75] Holt, *Magna Carta*, 135–41, 150–1, 296–303.

is no doubt that history, and the way it is presented, affect the way people understand their own social identities. Yet it was not a given that after the Norman Conquest the telling of history would centre around Englishness rather than *Normanitas* or Britishness. It did so partly because historians who considered themselves English, and valued that identity, emphasized the Englishness of the past. The telling of history shaped identity, and identity shaped the telling of history.

22

High Culture, Religious Culture, and Ethnicity

THESE DAYS THE concept of heritage is one of the defining characteristics of the overlapping constructs of England and Britain. Though British heritage covers everything from Stonehenge to the Tate Modern, important aspects date to the period covered in this book. Castles are central to England's and Britain's heritage, and none is better known than the Tower of London, the origins of which date to William the Conqueror's attempts to secure the Norman Conquest. Cathedrals are also important heritage sites, and some of the greatest, including Canterbury Cathedral, date at least in part to the century-and-a-half after 1066. Beautifully illuminated manuscripts from the period are proudly displayed at the British Library and English objects at the British Museum. Campaigns are launched to keep 'national treasures' like the Becket Casket (though it was almost certainly made in France) from being sold out of the country. In general, past cultural achievements are celebrated as important sources for national identity. At the same time, the continuing production of high culture is considered important to national pride.[1] The question raised in this chapter is whether cultural achievements played a similar role in English or Norman pride and identity after the Norman Conquest.

Before answering this question I must provide a brief and necessarily over-simplified account of the cultural interaction between English and Normans in several important cultural arenas. Such an account, however, is complicated by the fact that the late eleventh and twelfth centuries formed a period of great cultural change throughout Western Europe. Scholars have sometimes attributed all changes between 1066 and 1100, or 1135, or even 1150 to the Norman Conquest, but regions that experienced no equivalent conquest also saw their art, architecture, music, and intellectual life change radically. It is often impossible to say, especially for later generations after the conquest, if a prelate made a change because he was an immigrant dissatisfied with English ways or simply because he was interested in recent intellectual and artistic trends. In many early cases the two may have been combined. Nonetheless, the dissatisfaction the Normans sometimes expressed, particularly with the English religious life, and the sweeping changes they made in some areas indicate that the Normans introduced cultural shifts that would not

---

[1] Smith, *National Identity*, 92–3.

otherwise have happened or would have happened quite differently. Moreover, even when changes occurred that would have taken place anyway, it was a hierarchy dominated by immigrants that presided over them.

I have already had cause to note one of the most important intellectual changes that came with the Normans, namely the increased emphasis on patristic scholarship which brought to England many works previously unknown there.[2] More generally, the Anglo-Norman period was a crucial one for the building up of libraries. Both changes were trends throughout northwestern Europe, and in some ways England was only a couple of decades behind in 1066 (although in this respect the individual monastery, nunnery, or cathedral was probably the more important unit, since churches within regions varied greatly in intellectual attainment and progressiveness). But in the event, it was the Norman Conquest and the reformers it brought that helped England to catch up over the Anglo-Norman period. On the technical level the Normans introduced a new style of script, which was distinctive from traditional English hands.[3] More broadly, the Norman Conquest brought England firmly into what Rodney Thomson has called a 'homogenous cultural region' with Northern France.[4]

The Normans also brought changes to liturgical practices and sacred music, as the painstaking research of David Hiley has shown.[5] This is not an area of culture that most modern people would place on the same level as art or architecture, but it was very important to the medieval religious and thus to intellectuals. It was precisely changes in worship that brought about the great Glastonbury riot, and when Gilbert Crispin wrote that Lanfranc had 'forbidden the vanity of barbarous rites', he may have been referring in part to *ritus* in its narrower sense of worship.[6]

In painting, most of which is now represented by manuscript illumination, the question of Continental influence is complicated by the pre-conquest influence of

---

[2] See above, pp. 251–2.

[3] Richard Gameson, 'English Manuscript Art in the Late Eleventh Century: Canterbury and its Context', in *Canterbury and the Norman Conquest: Churches, Saints and Scholars, 1066–1109*, ed. Richard Eales and Richard Sharpe (London, 1995), 96–9; id., *Manuscripts of Norman England*, 1–20; Ker, *English Manuscripts*, 7–8, 22–6, 32–4; Knowles, *Monastic Order in England*, 95–9, 124–6; Lawrence, 'Manuscripts', 103–4, 106–7; Anne Lawrence, 'Anglo-Norman Book Production', in *England and Normandy in the Middle Ages*, ed. David Bates and Anne Curry (London, 1994), 79, 89–91; Rodney M. Thomson, 'The Library of Bury St Edmunds Abbey in the Eleventh and Twelfth Centuries', *Speculum*, 47 (1972), 627–36; id., *Manuscripts From St Albans Abbey 1066–1235*, vol. 1 (Woodbridge, 1982), 13–18; id., 'Norman Conquest and English Libraries', 27–40; Waller, 'Rochester Cathedral Library', 237–50; Webber, *Scribes and Scholars*, 9–10, 31–7, 45–81; Teresa Webber, 'Script and Manuscript Production at Christ Church, Canterbury, After the Norman Conquest', in *Canterbury and the Norman Conquest: Churches, Saints and Scholars, 1066–1109*, ed. Richard Eales and Richard Sharpe (London, 1995), 150–1; id., 'Diffusion', 29–45; id., 'The Provision of Books for Bury St Edmunds Abbey in the 11th and 12th Centuries', in *Bury St Edmunds: Medieval Art, Architecture, Archaeology and Economy*, ed. Antonia Gransden (Leeds, 1998), 186–93.

[4] Thomson, 'England and the Twelfth-Century Renaissance', 4.

[5] David Hiley, 'The Norman Chant Traditions—Normandy, Britain, Sicily', *Proceedings of the Royal Musical Association*, 107 (1980–1), 1–33; id., 'Thurstan of Caen', 57–90; id., 'Changes in English Chant Repertories in the Eleventh Century as Reflected in the Winchester Sequences', *ANS* 16: 137–54; id., 'Post-Pentecost Alleluias in Medieval British Liturgies', in *Music in the Medieval English Liturgy: Plainsong and Mediæval Music Society Centennial Essays*, ed. Susan Rankin and David Hiley (Oxford, 1993), 145–74.

[6] *Works of Gilbert Crispin*, 201.

Anglo-Saxon art on artists in Flanders and Normandy.[7] Nonetheless, Continental and English styles remained distinctive, and strong Continental, and particularly Norman, influence can be found in many books created in England, as well as in the few surviving wall paintings. Judging by the surviving manuscripts, moreover, the Anglo-Saxon tradition of large narrative illustrations was abandoned for a time, and narrative scenes were shifted to historiated initials. Some scholars have linked this to a Norman emphasis on good texts rather than beautiful books.[8] Sculpture probably declined for a time, since the Normans had less interest in it and a less sophisticated tradition of carving. Here again, however, there was strong Norman stylistic influence, especially at first, including the introduction of elements such as chevron ornamentation and simplified Corinthian capitals. The Normans were also more skilled at integrating sculpture into architecture.[9]

The Normans brought the most radical change in the arena of architecture.[10] Though the English had had fortifications before the conquest, the Normans introduced the motte-and-bailey castle and the use of great stone keeps. More striking still was their influence on the architecture of great churches. Over the space of a couple of generations they replaced all the great abbeys, nunneries, and cathedrals with new ones. So thorough was this destruction of the old that, according to Eric Fernie, no undisputed standing masonry of pre-conquest origin survives in any major church.[11] The new churches were also in a markedly different style from traditional Anglo-Saxon ones, though Edward the Confessor's church at Westminster

[7] J. J. G. Alexander, *Norman Illumination at Mont St Michel 966–1100* (Oxford, 1970), 57–67; François Avril, *Manuscrits Normands XI–XIIème siècles* (Rouen, 1975), 6, 10–11, 17–20, 22–3, 25, 37–8, 63, 77; C. R. Dodwell, *The Pictorial Arts of the West* (New Haven, 1993), 191–203.

[8] T. S. R. Boase, *English Art: 1100–1216* (Oxford, 1953), 25–30, 41–2; C. R. Dodwell, *The Canterbury School of Illumination, 1066–1200* (Cambridge, 1954), 19–20, 30–2; id., *Pictorial Arts*, 193–5; Gameson, 'English Manuscript Art', 106, 116–17, 140–1; C. M. Kauffman, *Romanesque Manuscripts 1066–1190* (London, 1975), 19–20; Otto Pächt, *Pictorial Narrative in Twelfth-Century England* (Oxford, 1962), 12–13; David Park, 'The "Lewes Group" of Wall Paintings in Sussex', *ANS* 6: 222–7; Francis Wormald, *Collected Writings*, 2 vols., ed. J. J. G. Alexander *et al.* (New York, 1984), 1: 65–6, 69, 161–2; 2: 24–5; Zarnecki, *English Romanesque*, 17–18.

[9] Deborah Kahn, *Canterbury Cathedral and its Romanesque Sculpture* (London, 1991), 118–24; George Zarnecki, *English Romanesque Sculpture 1066–1140* (London, 1951), 10–14; id., *The Early Sculpture of Ely Cathedral* (London, 1958), 10–11, 13–14; id., '1066 and Architectural Sculpture', in *Studies in Romanesque Sculpture* (London, 1979), 1: 91, 96–7, 99–100; id., 'Romanesque Sculpture in Normandy and England in the Eleventh Century', *PBC* 1: 168–89, 233–5; id., *English Romanesque*, 18–20, 146–7; id., *Further Studies in Romanesque Sculpture* (London, 1992), 420.

[10] A. W. Clapham, *English Romanesque Architecture After the Conquest* (Oxford, 1934), 1–50; Eric Fernie, *The Architecture of the Anglo-Saxons* (New York, 1983), 163–4; id., *An Architectural History of Norwich Cathedral* (Oxford, 1993), 115–19, 153; id., *The Architecture of Norman England* (Oxford, 2000), 19–27, 50–2; Richard Gem, 'Bishop Wulfstan II and the Romanesque Cathedral Church of Worcester', in *Medieval Art and Architecture at Worcester Cathedral* (Leeds, 1978), 32–3; id., 'The Significance of the 11th-century Rebuilding of Christ Church and St Augustine's, Canterbury, in the Development of Romanesque Architecture', in *Medieval Art and Architecture at Canterbury Before 1220* (Leeds, 1982), 1–19. Eric Fernie has underlined the complexity and variety of influences in the shifts in architecture brought by the conquest: Eric Fernie, 'The Effect of the Conquest on Norman Architectural Patronage', *ANS* 9: 71–85 and 'Architecture and the Effects of the Norman Conquest', in *England and Normandy in the Middle Ages*, ed. David Bates and Anne Curry (London, 1994), 105–16.

[11] Fernie, 'Architecture and the Effects', 105–7; id., 'Saxons, Normans and their Buildings', *ANS* 21: 1–3; id., *Architecture of Norman England*, 24.

anticipated them. Many drew heavily on Norman models, though influences also came from other regions on the Continent. Though recent excavations at Canterbury may force us to revise upwards our belief about the size of at least one great Anglo-Saxon church, nonetheless the Normans generally built on a much greater scale; indeed, a number of their cathedrals were among the largest buildings in Christendom at the time.[12] According to Arnold Klukas, a number of prelates not only changed architectural styles in their rebuilding, but also designed the new churches to accommodate liturgical change.[13] Debate will continue about cultural change and continuity after the Norman Conquest, but there is no doubt that in the area of architecture the term 'revolution' is warranted.

The Norman Conquest brought, to borrow a useful phrase from Richard Gameson, 'a critical auditing of Anglo-Saxon civilisation'.[14] Self-confident, and with a mild ethnocentric feeling of superiority to the English 'barbarians', the Normans did not hesitate to sweep aside what they did not approve of, or thought they could improve on. They showed no compunction about tearing down venerable buildings, altering at will liturgical arrangements that had the sanction of tradition, and bringing in new artistic and intellectual traditions to supplement or replace old ones. Yet there was no wholesale rejection of Anglo-Saxon culture. As always, Norman ethnocentrism was tempered by pragmatism. The Normans were perfectly willing to treasure and admire those aspects of English culture that impressed them. William of Poitiers wrote of the splendour of the treasures William the Conquer brought back to Normandy with him, and praised the artistry of English women in textiles.[15] As David Dumville has shown, the diffusion of lavishly decorated English books through Normandy and other parts of the Continent, and their subsequent preservation, indicates that they were highly regarded cultural artefacts.[16] This openness of the Normans, along with the efforts and activities of English survivors, provide the context for artistic and intellectual survival from the Anglo-Saxon period into the twelfth century and in some cases beyond. This survival was just as important as Norman innovation for understanding cultural interaction in the Norman period.

We have already seen the successful efforts of many intellectuals of native or mixed backgrounds to preserve much of the English intellectual tradition. They were aided by the tolerance of immigrant prelates. In addition, the Normans made use of native scribes in a variety of tasks, including their campaigns to build up libraries and copy patristic texts.[17] Though both the Normans and changing fashion

[12] Kevin Blockley, 'Canterbury Cathedral', *Current Archaeology*, 12 (1993), 124–30. See John Harvey, *Cathedrals of England and Wales* (New York, 1974), 80, 85–7, 91, for a comparative look at the size of Anglo-Norman cathedrals.
[13] Arnold William Klukas, 'The Architectural Implications of the *Decreta Lanfranci*', ANS 6: 136–71.
[14] Gameson, 'English Manuscript Art', 95.
[15] GGWP 176.
[16] David N. Dumville, 'Anglo-Saxon Books: Treasure in Norman Hands?', ANS 16: 83–99.
[17] Gameson, 'English Manuscript Art', 102–3; id., *Manuscripts of Norman England*, 8; Ker, *English Manuscripts*, 19–20, 22–6, 32–4; Lawrence, 'Manuscripts', 101–8; Thomson, *Manuscripts from St Albans Abbey*, 1: 14; id., 'Norman Conquest and English Libraries', 36–7; Webber, *Scribes and Scholars*, 19; id., 'Script and Manuscript Production', 153.

transformed the liturgy, at some churches traditions were preserved. Winchester was a notable case in point, and there and at Ely, according to Klukas, the new churches, though radically different in style, were built to accommodate the traditional liturgy.[18] This may have been a concession to the native monks that mattered far more than architectural style, and is probably connected to Bishop Walkelin's attempts to win over his monks, and to the ties which he and his brother, the abbot of Ely, created with native monks. More generally, the eventual acceptance of many native saints may have outweighed liturgical change in the minds of many native religious.

In the artistic realm there was also survival of Anglo-Saxon traditions. Just as native and immigrant scribes worked side by side in scriptoria, so too did English and Norman artists. Illuminations in a very traditional style can be found into the twelfth century along with ones in Continental style. Anglo-Saxon art continued to have influence even as new styles and influences were adopted in the course of the twelfth century.[19] In sculpture too, the influence of Anglo-Saxon tradition was felt well into the twelfth century, whether through survival, revival, or both.[20] Even in architecture, where the greatest artistic and stylistic changes were made, Anglo-Saxon models continued to be something of an inspiration. In parish churches 1066 marked far less of a break than in great ones. But in the greatest churches too, the second generation of Norman building incorporated certain pre-conquest influences, albeit in a new context.[21]

This last point illustrates one of the most important aspects of cultural inter-

[18] Klukas, 'Architectural Implications', 151–3; id., 'The Continuity of Anglo-Saxon Liturgical Traditions as Evident in the Architecture of Winchester, Ely and Canterbury Cathedrals', in *Les Mutations socio-culturelles au tournant des XIᵉ-XIIᵉ siècles: Études Anselmiennes* (Paris, 1984), 111–23. For continuity as well as change in the liturgy, see Kristine Edmondson Haney, *The Winchester Psalter: An Iconographic Study* (Leicester, 1986), 66, 71; Hiley, 'Thurstan of Caen', 57–90; Hiley, 'Changes in English Chant Repertories', 54.

[19] Janet Backhouse, D. H. Turner, and Leslie Webster, *The Golden Age of Anglo-Saxon Art, 966–1066* (Bloomington, Ind., 1984), 194–5, 198–209; Malcolm Baker, 'Medieval Illustrations of Bede's *Life of St. Cuthbert*', *Journal of the Warburg and Courtauld Institutes*, 41 (1978), 19, 30; Boase, *English Art*, 39–41, 157–9; Dodwell, *Canterbury School*, 21–32, 57; Gameson, 'English Manuscript Art', 101–2, 116, 119, 122–3, 126; Haney, *Winchester Psalter*, 18–22, 27–9; Kauffman, *Romanesque Manuscripts*, 20, 28; Park, 'Lewes Group', 222–3; Wormald, *Collected Writings*, 1: 66–9, 154–68; 2: 23–4; id., *English Drawings of the Tenth and Eleventh Centuries* (London, n.d.), 53–8; Zarnecki, *English Romanesque*, 22, 26, 211, 232.

[20] John Beckwith, *Ivory Carvings in Early Medieval England* (London, 1972), 62, 75–6; Boase, *English Art*, 59, 73–4; Ewa Chwojko and Malcolm Thurlby, 'Gloucester and the Herefordshire School', *Journal of the British Archaeological Association*, 150 (1997), 21–2; Kahn, *Canterbury Cathedral*, 49–51; Zarnecki, *English Romanesque Sculpture 1066–1140*, 14–15, 17, 27; id., *English Romanesque Sculpture 1140–1210* (London, 1953), 5–6, 10; id., *Early Sculpture of Ely Cathedral*, 12–13, 30–3, 37; id., '1066 and Architectural Sculpture', 97–102; id., *Further Studies*, 250–6.

[21] Jean Bony, 'Durham et la tradition saxonne', in *Études d'art médiéval offertes à Louis Grodecki*, ed. Mc. K. Crosby *et al.* (Paris, n.d.), 79–93; Clapham, *English Romanesque Architecture*, 101; Peter Coffman, 'The Romanesque East End of Southwell Minster', in *Southwell and Nottinghamshire: Medieval Art, Architecture, and Industry*, ed. Jennifer S. Alexander (Leeds, 1998), 2–3; Fernie, 'Effect of the Conquest', 72–7; id., *Architecture of the Anglo-Saxons*, 162–3, 168–73; M. F. Hearn, 'Romsey Abbey: A Progenitor of the English National Tradition in Architecture', *Gesta*, 14 (1975), 27–40; Lisa Reilly, 'The Emergence of Anglo-Norman Architecture: Durham Cathedral', *ANS* 19: 335–51; Lisa A. Reilly, *An Architectural History of Peterborough Cathedral* (Oxford, 1997), 41–2, 77, 85–6, 126; Fernie, *Architecture of Norman England*, 20, 34, 208–9.

action in the Anglo-Norman period, namely the openness of both natives and immigrants to the influence of the other, and to outside influence as well. The selective receptivity of immigrants to Anglo-Saxon artistic traditions will already be clear. Even the seals of William II and Henry I, among the politically most important artistic expressions of the new Norman government, show Anglo-Saxon influence.[22] Bede's Englishness did not prevent immigrant prelates and scholars (such as Simeon of Durham) from embracing his work. Anselm, even before he moved to England, expressed interest in the monastic rule of the tenth-century reformers, the *Regularis Concordia*, and ultimately most immigrant prelates tended to be open to some of the traditions of their new churches.[23] On the English side there was defensiveness about English traditions, but this did not prevent even staunch defenders of English traditions or Englishness from embracing intellectual and artistic aspects of the new order. As precentors, Osbeorn and Eadmer were perforce involved with the liturgical and intellectual changes brought by Lanfranc and Anselm. Elmer was a very close imitator of Anselm's intellectual approach. Bishop Wulfstan, though in many ways an important preserver of Anglo-Saxon tradition, reluctantly followed the Norman lead by tearing down his cathedral and building a larger one in the new style.[24] Though Norman and English artistic taste and intellectual outlook was no doubt shaped, at least in the first generation, by the preconquest traditions of both lands, neither group clung so stubbornly to these traditions that it rejected new or foreign trends.

The openness of both groups resulted in a dynamic atmosphere of cultural and intellectual interchange and innovation that helped to forge a rich Anglo-Norman culture that was a full participant in the European mainstream of the time. The process began quite early. As Gameson has argued, the Bayeux Tapestry, with its Norman message and contents, its possible English subtext, its English and perhaps Continental artistic influence, and its English craftswomanship, is very much an Anglo-Norman cultural artefact.[25] So too were the many buildings, illuminations, and sculptures that combined English and Norman influences. As time went on other foreign influences continued to sweep into English art, including newer French styles but also Italian and even Byzantine ones.[26] For instance, Henry Maguire has shown that as late as the 1140s a Northampton sculptural workshop

[22] F. Saxl, *English Sculptures of the Twelfth Century* (London, 1952), 19. See also Zarnecki, *English Romanesque*, 300.

[23] *S. Anselmi Opera Omnia*, 3: 151.

[24] VW 52. See also C. M. Kauffman, 'Manuscript Illumination at Worcester in the Eleventh and Twelfth Centuries', in *Medieval Art and Architecture at Worcester Cathedral* (Leeds, 1978), 44–5, for Norman elements in manuscripts made for or under Wulfstan.

[25] Gameson, 'Origin, Art, and Message', 163, 173–4.

[26] Larry M. Ayres, 'The Role of the Angevin Style in English Romanesque Painting', *Zeitschrift für Kunstgeschichte*, 37 (1974), 193–223; Dodwell, *Canterbury School*, 39, 81–97; id., *Pictorial Arts*, 336, 341–7, 354–5, 359–62, 368; Lindy Grant, 'Architectural Relationships between England and Normandy, 1100–1204', in *England and Normandy in the Middle Ages*, ed. David Bates and Anne Curry (London, 1994), 116–29; Haney, *Winchester Psalter*, 22–34; Kahn, *Canterbury Cathedral*, 132–5; Kauffman, *Romanesque Manuscripts*, 27–8; Otto Pächt, C. R. Dodwell, and Francis Wormald, *The St. Albans Psalter (Albani Psalter)* (London, 1960), 115–25; Zarnecki, *Further Studies*, 444–5; id., *English Romanesque Sculpture, 1140–1210*, 16–19, 29–33.

drew on Anglo-Saxon models, but was also influenced by Romanesque Italian art.[27] In the intellectual sphere as well, Norman and English traditions clearly merged. English and Norman scripts fused to form a new English style of writing.[28] French culture continued to be tremendously important, but Southern has argued that Anglo-Saxon traditions lay partly behind English interest in mathematics and science in the twelfth century, and therefore behind the important role English scholars played in bringing Arabic learning into the Western European sphere.[29] Neither ethnic nor attendant cultural strife prevented England and its inhabitants from participating fully in what is often called the Twelfth Century Renaissance.

How do cultural developments after the conquest relate to assimilation and identity? The cultural melding described above formed an important part of the broader cultural assimilation that helped to unify the two peoples. In turn, personal interaction contributed to and increased the openness of the Normans and English to the ideas and traditions of the other group; it is probably no accident that it was in the second generation of post-conquest building that English influence began to be felt once more in large churches. No doubt the pragmatic willingness of most humans to borrow what they admire or find useful from their enemies, attested in the Middle Ages by the extensive borrowing by Christians of Muslim technology and learning, also played a role in the cultural interaction discussed earlier. But I believe that another factor, albeit a negative one, was the distant relationship between ethnic identity and some important cultural areas in the minds of people of the time.

In the modern period, as noted earlier, nationalists often make a point of emphasizing great thinkers, artists, or monuments, and sometimes of promoting new works, to enhance the national image. Scholars interested in minorities often look for impressive intellectuals, writers, or artists, in part to correct the biases of the past, but also often with the intention of promoting or instilling ethnic pride. Such ambitions do not prevent tremendous cultural and intellectual interchange between countries and ethnic groups in the modern world, but it does sometimes lead individuals or groups to actively resist outside cultural influences. National or ethnic pride also tends to make people and governments place a special value on achievements that emerged from their own group and sometimes to denigrate those of hostile peoples.

In one arena we have already seen a similar phenomenon in the post-conquest period. The conquerors were mildly dismissive of the intellectual and religious achievements of the English, while those who were pro-English sought successfully to rehabilitate their people through reference to the achievements of the past. However, the competition here was not between two clashing intellectual systems, one distinctively English and the other Norman. Instead, what mattered was the relative success in adhering to a shared intellectual and moral system, namely Christianity. What mattered was faithfulness to what was considered best practice

---

[27] Henry P. Maguire, 'A Twelfth Century Workshop in Northampton', *Gesta*, 9 (1970), 11–25.
[28] Thomson, 'Norman Conquest and English Libraries', 39.
[29] Southern, *Medieval Humanism*, 164–71.

by reformers, which in theory trumped tradition, whether English or Norman. It is true that writers such as Orderic Vitalis and William of Malmesbury associated ecclesiastical and intellectual reform with the Norman Conquest and therefore with the Normans and other immigrants, but from their point of view, and that of most English intellectuals, the correct response was to embrace, not reject, the reforms. By doing so natives did not become Normans, but instead transformed themselves into better Christians. They did not reject their Englishness but instead fulfilled its past promise. Thus, although intellectual differences did become intertwined with debates about ethnic worthiness after the conquest, the result was not that intellectual differences sustained ethnic ones, as often happens when intellectual systems clash, but rather that ethnic pride helped to close the cultural gap.

In other areas, such as art and architecture, the evidence suggests that medieval thinkers saw fewer connections between ethnic pride and culture than do modern ones. Certainly some casual connections were made between peoples and artistic skills. William of Poitiers describes the skill of English women at embroidery in gold, sometimes called *opus Anglicana*, and attributed the quality of English craftsmen to the Germans, *artium scientissimi*, who lived among them.[30] Ralph of Caen, in his life of Tancred, implied that the English were especially skilled as sculptors.[31] Loose connections were also made between ethnicity and styles. For instance, an anonymous York chronicler wrote of a crucifix and pulpit commissioned by Archbishop Ealdred as being made with 'Germanic work'.[32] But expressions of pride in such connections are harder to find. For instance, the chronicles are full of individual cases of rebuilding churches but surprisingly little comment was made on the collective architectural revolution brought by the Normans.[33] William of Malmesbury's comment on the Normans' preference for larger dwellings may refer to the secular side of the rebuilding, but covers neither style nor ecclesiastical architecture. Elsewhere William noted that Bishop Herfast transferred his see from Elmham to Thetford because 'he did not want to be seen to have done nothing, since the Normans strive hard for future fame'.[34] Here, it is true, the motive is couched in ethnic terms, but the accomplishment itself is described in personal ones. On the English side, Richard Gem has shown that there was a certain resistance to the Romanesque style by natives; perhaps one can speak of a critical auditing of Norman innovation. However, the resistance was on the basis of old against new, simple against elaborate, but not, in any of the surviving evidence, English against Norman.[35] Perhaps that was implicit, but among the many lamentations for the losses of the Norman Conquest, which included mourning for lost artistic treasures, there was no grief for changes in artistic or architectural *style*.[36] For us

---

[30] *GGWP* 176.

[31] *Recueil des Historiens des Croisades*, 3: 661.

[32] *HCY* 2: 354.

[33] See Ch. 13, n. 130, for references to individual prelates and rebuilding.

[34] *WMGR* 458; *WMGP* 150.

[35] Richard Gem, 'England and the Resistance to Romanesque Architecture', in *Studies in Medieval History Presented to R. Allen Brown*, ed. Christopher Harper-Bill *et al.* (Woodbridge, 1989), 129–39.

[36] See Chap. 14, n. 82, for references to the laments.

one of the great achievements of the Normans was their introduction of the Romanesque style, but judging by the surviving evidence contemporaries did not think in the same terms. Instead they thought of the achievements of individual prelates and churches. Scholars have sometimes viewed the huge Norman churches as a means of impressing the power of the conquerors upon the conquered, and this may well be so, but it is probably better to consider it the cumulative result of the efforts of individual prelates rather than any collective policy.[37]

One reason why intellectual, artistic, and architectural trends may have spread so easily in the medieval West is that they were more closely associated with individuals or local institutions on the one hand, and the Catholic church on the other, than with ethnic groups or nations. National and ethnic rivalries were not likely to stop the spread of scholastic thought or Romanesque or Gothic architecture, because even though the French may have held cultural leadership in these areas, these developments were not seen as intimately linked to Frenchness. When Canterbury, in the late twelfth century, adopted the Gothic style pioneered by Suger at Saint-Denis, two architects named William were involved. One was from Sens in France, but the other was specifically described as being born in England.[38] Gothic architecture, insofar as it was even considered a unity, was a Christian style, not a French one, in the minds of contemporaries.

One exception to the general rule of disassociation between intellectual or artistic change and ethnicity, however, comes from Orderic Vitalis's description of the riot and massacre at Glastonbury. According to him this came about when Abbot Thurstan forced the monks to give up the chant 'the English had learned from the disciples of the blessed Pope Gregory', and to learn new ones 'from the Flemings and Normans'.[39] This close link between chant at Glastonbury and larger ethnic issues, however, is not found in other sources. More important, it comes in a cultural arena that most modern people would not associate with feelings of ethnic or national solidarity. Post-conquest liturgical practices are not what come to the fore when most people think of Britain's or England's heritage.

This discussion reveals the dangers of bringing modern assumptions to a discussion of pre-modern solidarities. It is perfectly reasonable to discuss Norman, English, or Flemish styles of art and architecture, since they clearly existed and were occasionally acknowledged by contemporaries. But it is dangerous to assume that they made the same connections between artistic or architectural accomplishments and ethnic or national pride that we do. For us, great works of art might help to define group identity. For them, saints or styles of liturgy might perform these functions instead. To warn against making modern nationalist assumptions in the study of medieval art or architecture is, admittedly, to preach to the converted. Since the Second World War, scholars have recognized the dangers of modern nationalism and have shied away from repeating the mistakes of nationalist

[37] Fernie, 'Architecture and the Effects', 106; Dodwell, *Anglo-Saxon Art*, 234; Grant, 'Architectural Relationships', 120; Coffman 'Romanesque East End', 3.

[38] *Historical Works of Gervase of Canterbury*, 1: 6, 21.

[39] *EHOV* 2: 270.

scholars. But there is a corollary to my argument that will cut against the contemporary grain. That we do not find evidence of group solidarity where we expect it, based on modern assumptions, does not necessarily mean that it did not exist. We may simply be looking in the wrong places.

23

Language, Literature, and Ethnic Identity

'Sire,' ço li dit li burgois,
'Ne conisiez pas les Englois.
Ne dengnerunt del champ fuïr
Ne pur vivre ne pur murrir,
A lur seingnur ja ne faldrunt,
Occire ainz tuz se ferunt,
Ainz que el champ fussent vencu
Mult avrïez des vos perdu.'

'Sir,' thus spoke the townsman to him,
'You do not know the English.
They will refuse to flee the field,
Neither for life nor death,
Will they ever fail their lord.
They would rather be killed
Than leave the field defeated.
You will lose many of your men.'

(*Le Roman de Waldef*, ll. 4821–8)

For many nineteenth- and twentieth-century theorists and activists, language was crucial to nationalism. Nationalists were closely involved with the work of standardizing languages and creating dictionaries and treatises on grammar. Nationalist governments sought to create linguistic uniformity in order to strengthen national sentiment.[1] The many ethnic leaders or would-be leaders who wished to create new nations for their own people often used language, whether German, Italian, Basque, Gaelic, or Magyar, to take only a few examples, as a key argument for their politics. Though many aspects of modern nationalism have been discredited in academic circles, its influence remains strong, not least in shaping a common assumption that there will necessarily be a very close link between language and identity in all places and all times. This assumption is frequently warranted, but can also sometimes lead to a distorted view of the past.

The belief in a close link between language and national identity has certainly influenced literary and historical study of the period after the Norman Conquest,

---

[1] Anderson, *Imagined Communities*, 71–82.

and this includes important recent work by scholars whose opinions deserve to be taken very seriously. Michael Clanchy, in one of the best recent discussions of Englishness in the central Middle Ages, suggests that the linguistic effects of the conquest constituted an important though temporary blow to English identity, and that survival of English was important for survival of Englishness.[2] Adrian Hastings, in his overview of the English contribution to nationalism, concurs.[3] Short has posited an intermediate identity between English and Norman based on a combination of descent and language.[4] The close link made by scholars between language and identity has had an especially profound effect on literary studies. For years Anglo-Latin and Anglo-Norman literary works remained neglected, and although there were a number of reasons for this, it was partly because they were not felt to be properly part of the literary heritage of England. Only in the last generation has this neglect changed in any significant way.[5] One of the important early debates in the study of medieval English concerned continuity between Old and Middle English, and this debate was shadowed by nationalist concerns. Though the nationalism has dropped out, the debate continues to be important.[6] Moreover, the idea that one ought to find a link between language and identity continues to influence literary studies. This is most obvious in the study of Lawman's *Brut*, the first surviving monumental work in English from the post-conquest period, for scholars often wrestle with the fact that this English poem is a translation of Wace's translation of Geoffrey of Monmouth's anti-Saxon history.[7] The question is, to what degree did people in the period make a strong link between the English language and Englishness?

I follow the lead of an older, neglected article by Galbraith, and a more recent one by Davies, that downplay the overt link between language and identity, at least in England in the period under consideration.[8] I *do* think that the history of language

[2] Clanchy, *England and its Rulers*, 3, 173, 182–4.

[3] Hastings, *Construction of Nationhood*, 44, 46–8.

[4] See above, p. 72. See also, Damian-Grint, *New Historians*, 191–2.

[5] Elizabeth Salter, *English and International: Studies in Literature, Art, and Patronage of Medieval England*, ed. Derek Pearsall and Nicolette Zeeman (Cambridge, 1988), 1–100; Susan Crane, *Insular Romance: Politics, Faith, and Culture in Anglo-Norman and Middle English Literature*, 1–223; Pearsall, *Old English and Middle English Poetry*, 85–102. To be fair, Wilson, who was very concerned to trace continuity, also discussed Latin and French influence in early Middle English: Wilson, *Early Middle English Literature*, 23–85, 166, 216. But for a long time, M. Dominica Legge was a voice crying in the wilderness about the importance of Anglo-Norman literature, particularly in *Anglo-Norman in the Cloisters* and *Anglo-Norman Literature*.

[6] R. W. Chambers, 'The Continuity of English Prose from Alfred to More and his School', in Nicholas Harpsfield, *The Life and Death of Sir Thomas More, Knight, Sometymes Lord High Chancellor of England*, ed. Elsie Vaughn Hitchcock and R. W. Chambers (London, 1932), pp. lxxxi–c; Angus F. Cameron, 'Middle English in Old English Manuscripts', in *Chaucer and Middle English Studies in Honour of Russell Hope Robbins*, ed. Beryl Rowland (London, 1974), 218–29; Franzen, *Tremulous Hand*, 105–10; Howlett, *English Origins*, 18–22; Carolynn VanDyke Friedlander, 'Early Middle English Accentual Verse', *Modern Philology*, 76 (1979), 219–30; Pearsall, *Old English and Middle English*, 76–85, 150–7. See also the works cited below in nn. 12, 14.

[7] See below for further discussion of Lawman's *Brut*.

[8] V. H. Galbraith, 'Nationality and Language in Medieval England', *TRHS* 4th ser., 23 (1941), 113–28; Davies, 'Language and Historical Mythology', 1–9. See also, Armstrong, *Nations Before Nationalism*, 241–82.

played a fundamental role in assimilation. I also believe that there must have been at least some connection made between the English language and English identity, given the frequent reference to language in the medieval lists of what characterized different peoples. But I argue that the connection was fairly weak, with important consequences for our understanding not only of the history of identity, but also of language and literature in England in the central Middle Ages.

A brief overview of the linguistic situation following the conquest may be useful here.[9] For written language, the picture is relatively clear. After the conquest the use of English began to decline both in absolute and proportional terms. Old English works continued to be copied and even occasionally written, but the massive expansion of writing largely took place in Latin, and later also in French.[10] The paucity of new works in English made it very difficult to maintain a living literary tradition in English. The resulting lack of a widespread, unified English literary culture, and the disappearance of 'official' sponsorship, whether by the royal government or the ecclesiastical hierarchy, meant that the use of the standardized West Saxon form of Old English withered away. From the final entries in the Anglo-Saxon Chronicle onwards, written English came in a Middle English form, with regional variations, little or no standardization, and orthography and grammar that were radically different from Old English. This meant that within a few generations even English-speaking readers found it difficult to decipher Old English texts. The author of the *Gesta Herwardi* was already writing of the difficulty of reading his alleged vernacular source, and when the scribe and scholar known as the Tremulous Hand was glossing Old English works in the thirteenth century, he was involved in an antiquarian and not always successful enterprise halfway between interpretation and translation.[11] The lack of any strong continuing and unified school of writers in English, and the problems later writers faced in reading surviving Old English books, meant that there was an extraordinary rupture between the Old and Middle English literary traditions.

The rupture was not complete, but the long search for aspects of continuity between Old English and Middle English has yielded few results. There was surely some link between the Old English alliterative tradition and the Alliterative Revival of the fourteenth century, but it was probably no more than a tradition of oral alliterative poetry that may not have had the complex verse forms of the written poetry that came before and after. If there were written links, they may have come through the looser alliterative forms of the Old English homiletic tradition.[12]

[9] Georges Bourcier, *An Introduction to the History of the English Language*, trans. Cecily Clark (Cheltenham, 1981), 40–1, 119–59, provides a particularly good overview of the impact of the conquest on English, and for the general shift from Old to Middle English. For the influence of the Norman Conquest on orthography, see D. G. Scragg, *A History of English Spelling* (New York, 1974), 15–21.

[10] For the continuing use of Old English, see Franzen, *Tremulous Hand*, 27–8, 103–4; Pearsall, *Old English and Middle English Poetry*, 75–6; Wilson, *Early Middle English Literature*, 17–18, 106–7

[11] Hardy and Martin, *Gesta Herwardi*, 339–40; Franzen, *Tremulous Hand*, 84–102, 178–82, 186.

[12] For debate over continuity in alliterative poetry, or lack thereof, see N. F. Blake, 'Rhythmical Alliteration', *Modern Philology*, 67 (1969), 118–24; Thomas Cable, *The English Alliterative Tradition* (Philadelphia, 1991), 2–3, 41–65; Dorothy Everett, *Essays on Middle English Literature* (London, 1955), 34–41; Angus McIntosh, 'Early Middle English Alliterative Verse', in *Middle English Alliterative Poetry*

Lawman, working much earlier, may have been more influenced, whether directly or indirectly, by Old English writing, but even for him the tendency now is to see antiquarian sentiments and archaizing traditions, rather than any thorough and knowledgeable immersion in Old English literature.[13] Early Middle English devotional literature may have owed something to the works of Ælfric and others.[14] But overall, the discernible influence of Old English literature after the middle of the twelfth century is negligible.

To this must be contrasted the enormous influence that French and Latin works had on Middle English ones in a variety of ways, including subject, verse form, and even vocabulary.[15] Lawman was only the first of many Middle English writers to base his work on a French exemplar. The heroes of chivalric romance, such as Arthur and his knights, first introduced to a wider audience in Latin and French works, dominated secular literature, whereas Old English heroes like Beowulf were conspicuously absent. Key writers like Chaucer, translator of the *Roman de la Rose*, were steeped in Continental traditions. The vocabulary of later Middle English works was obviously drawn from the spoken English of the day, with its large admixture of French words, not from Old English. In sum, the Middle English literary tradition had its written roots not primarily in Old English but in Latin, and above all, in French.

This debt of Middle English literature to French raises a very important point, namely that during the period in which Englishness not only survived but triumphed, French remained a more common language of writing than English (and both were far behind Latin). Indeed, in the twelfth century England seems to have been a key region for the production of French writing, in some ways ahead of French-speaking areas on the Continent.[16] Equally surprising, some of the indi-

---

and its Literary Background, ed. David Lawton (Cambridge, 1982), 20–33; Douglas Moffat, *The Soul's Address to the Body: The Worcester Fragments* (East Lansing, 1987), 25–33; Oakden, *Alliterative Poetry in Middle English*, 1: 131–80; 2: 3–7, 85–6, 113–68, 199, 211–12, 233–5; Derek Pearsall, 'The Alliterative Revival: Origins and Social Backgrounds', in *Middle English Alliterative Poetry and its Literary Background*, ed. David Lawton (Cambridge, 1982), 34–53; Thorlac Turville-Petre, *The Alliterative Revival* (Totowa, 1977), 6–25; Wilson, *Early Middle English Literature*, 13–16.

[13] For work on Lawman, see below, nn. 52, 55.

[14] Dorothy Bethurum, 'The Connection of the Katherine Group with Old English Prose', *Journal of English and Germanic Philology*, 34 (1935), 553–64; Chambers, 'Continuity of English Prose', pp. xciv–c; Bertha Millet, '"Hali Meiðhad," "Sawles Warde," and the Continuity of English Prose', in *Five Hundred Years of Words and Sounds: A Festschrift for Eric Dobson*, ed. E. G. Stanley and Douglas Gray (Cambridge, 1983), 100–8. Franzen, *Tremulous Hand*, 104; Moffat, *Soul's Address*, 39–40; Moffat, *Old English and Middle English Poetry*, 82–3; Barbara Raw, 'The Prayers and the Devotions in the *Ancrene Wisse*', in *Chaucer and Middle English Studies in Honour of Russell Hope Robbins*, ed. Beryl Rowland (London, 1974), 260–71; Wilson, *Early Middle English Literature*, 106–27, 170–3. See, however, Cecily Clark, 'As Seint Austin Seith . . .' *Medium Ævum*, 46 (1977), 212–18.

[15] Salter, *English and International*, 1–100; Crane, *Insular Romance*; Pearsall, *Old English and Middle English Poetry*, 85–97.

[16] Clanchy, *From Memory to Written Record*, 18; Crane, 'Anglo-Norman Cultures in England', 44–7; Howlett, *English Origins*, 22–3, 63, 69, 105, 125, 130, 162–4; Legge, *Anglo-Norman Literature*, 362–5; Richter, *Sprache und Gesellschaft*, 18–20; Short, 'Patrons and Polyglots', 229–30. The relatively small amount of attention paid to Anglo-Norman literature by French scholars is another example of the possible distortions caused by modern nationalism or assumptions stemming from modern nationalist theory.

viduals linked with French works were English by descent. I have noted that Edith-Matilda, who considered her English ancestry important, was probably the first patron of the Anglo-Norman *Voyage of Brendan*.[17] The St Albans Psalter, given to and perhaps commissioned for Christina of Markyate, included an Old French *vita* of St Alexis.[18] A man named both William and Adgar translated a collection of miracle stories of the Virgin Mary from Latin into French; Adgar was perhaps a form of Edgar and may therefore suggest English ancestry.[19] Ian Short has emphasized the overall importance of multiculturalism and multilinguism for literature in this period.[20] This is clearly true, but what I would emphasize is just how tenuous the links between ancestry, language, identity, and political allegiance were in the history of writing and literature in England in the centuries following the conquest.

The history of spoken language in the period, not surprisingly, is murkier than that of written language, and for some time there has been debate about the degree to which French or English dominated in different social groups. The surviving evidence consists largely of a few dozen anecdotes, almost always without commentary or context, which reveal some individual speaking English or French. These anecdotes, as Dahood has pointed out, can be problematic, and are often susceptible to many different interpretations; as a result, I do not believe that we will ever have a very clear idea of what percentages of the population spoke French, either as a mother tongue or a learned one.[21] The current consensus seems to be that French was never spoken by more than a minority and that even the aristocracy (or most of it) adopted English as a native language in the course of the twelfth century.[22] I suspect that this consensus is right, but the argument remains unproven. In any case, French remained an important spoken as well as written language in certain social sectors at least into the fourteenth century. This is shown most notably by Michael Richter's study of the language used by those testifying in a canonization proceeding in 1307; a substantial minority both of the clergy and the townspeople who testified were willing and able to do so in French.[23] A final and very important point, to which I will return, is that there is widespread evidence of bilingualism or at least familiarity with the two languages among the elites, and even of trilingualism among the clergy.

Was French seen as superior to English or more cultivated, second to Latin in a hierarchy of languages, as some scholars have argued?[24] There is some evidence for

---

[17] See above, p. 142.

[18] Pächt *et al.*, *The St. Albans Psalter*, 5, 136–40.

[19] Adgar, *Le Gracial*, ed. Pierre Kunstmann (Ottowa, 1982), 11, 97; Legge, *Anglo-Norman Literature*, 187–91.

[20] Short, 'Patrons and Polyglots', 230, 245–9.

[21] Dahood, 'Hugh de Morville', 40–56.

[22] See, in particular, Rothwell, 'Teaching of French', 37–46; Rothwell, 'Role of French', 445–66; Short, 'On Bilingualism in Anglo-Norman England', 468; Ian Short, 'Patrons and Polyglots', 246; Wilson, 'English and French in England', 37–60.

[23] Richter, *Sprache und Gesellschaft*, 173–201.

[24] Bourcier, *History of English*, 120–1; R. A. Lodge, 'Language Attitudes and Linguistic Norms in France and England in the Thirteenth Century', in *Thirteenth Century England* 4, ed. P. R. Coss and S. D. Lloyd (Woodbridge, 1992), 79–83; Pearsall, *Old English and Middle English Poetry*, 86–8; Short, 'Patrons and Polyglots', 248–9.

this. Gervase of Tilbury, explaining Harold's trip to Normandy in an anachronistic fashion, said that the noblest English had the custom of sending their sons to be raised among the Gauls to study arms 'and to remove the barbarity of their native tongue', which probably refers to English, though it could conceivably refer to a polishing of Anglo-Norman.[25] Gerald of Wales, in a passage berating his nephew for what Gerald saw as a multitude of faults, criticized him for his ignorance of 'all languages, and chiefly two, Latin and French, which are most important among us'. The verb Gerald uses, *presto* or *praesto*, generally has connotations of superiority.[26] I am not sure that these two anecdotes should be taken too far in indicating a widespread sense that French was innately or culturally superior. Nonetheless there was certainly a linkage between speaking English and being lower class, as when Jocelin of Brakelond referred to the serf who could not speak French, or the *vita* of Hugh of Avalon referred to that immigrant bishop needing a translator to speak to a peasant woman.[27] At the same time there was also a connection between speaking French and being aristocratic, as indicated by a lawsuit in which doubt was cast on the status of four men as knights partly because one could not speak French.[28] Clearly French had a certain prestige, if for no other reason than for being linked to the upper classes.

By the standards of modern nationalist theories or assumptions about a necessarily close linkage between language and identity, something is badly out of joint with the histories of identity and language after the Norman Conquest. How can assimilation take place without linguistic unification? Why did assimilation not lead to linguistic uniformity? How could English identity make a full recovery while French remained more prestigious than English and a more important language of writing? Why did the triumph of English identity not bring a much stronger revival of English literature? In raising these questions, moreover, it is worth emphasizing that these conundrums exist not only for the period around 1200, but even into the fifteenth century. English identity grew still stronger during these centuries, but French remained an important literary and aristocratic language.[29] Indeed, as Clanchy has remarked, one of the most self-consciously English chroniclers of Edward I's reign, Langtoft, wrote in French.[30] Thus the puzzles noted here do not stem simply from the oddities of a transitional period, but are raised by more than two centuries of English history.

The questions about the links between language and assimilation are perhaps easier to answer. I have argued that language was an important social barrier between the two peoples. But if, as the current consensus argues, by the end of the twelfth century all except recent immigrants, and perhaps those aristocrats with

---

[25] Gervase of Tilbury, *Otia Imperialia*, 474.

[26] Gerald of Wales, *Speculum Duorum*, 132.

[27] *Chronicle of Jocelin of Brakelond*, 33; Adam of Eynsham, *Magna Vita Sancti Hugonis*, 2: 118. See also, Hardy and Martin, *Gesta Herwardi*, 385; Birch, *Vita Haroldi*, 32

[28] Van Caenegem, *English Lawsuits*, 2: 679.

[29] Helen Sugget, 'The Use of French in England in the Later Middle Ages', *TRHS* 4th ser., 28 (1946), 61–83

[30] Clanchy, *England and its Rulers*, 229.

extensive Norman holdings, spoke English as their native or 'maternal' tongue, then the survival of French as an important language would be no more harmful to assimilation and subsequent national unity than the even greater continuing importance of Latin. The shift to English as a first language by the descendants of immigrants would have been part and parcel of the process of assimilation.

But I would argue that bilingualism was also very important in facilitating the process. I would suggest that England fairly quickly developed into a bilingual society, at least in towns, the aristocracy, and perhaps among the middling sort. By this I do not mean a situation in which every individual was bilingual (or, in the case of clerics and Jews, trilingual), but one similar to that found in my own city of residence, Miami. Here there are many monolingual speakers of English, Spanish, Portuguese, and Haitian Creole. But there are also many bilingual and multilingual people as well. Society in Miami functions in several different languages, and though life is somewhat more difficult for the monolingual, there is almost always someone around to translate, and even essentially monolingual people know a smattering of English or Spanish or both. Many people grow up bilingual, and partly because of continuing ties to home countries, pass their bilingualism on to their children. Obviously drawing lessons from modern experience and applying them to the Middle Ages has its dangers, but I do so partly because I suspect that many assumptions made by English and American scholars about language use in the past are based on the relentlessly monolingual environment in which, until recently, most anglophone intellectuals in those countries were raised. It is all too easy for English and American scholars raised before the 1980s and 1990s to take a monolingual society as a given, and ignore the many multilingual societies that exist today and have existed in the past. Moreover, because language education has long been given a low priority in England and the United States, it is easy to associate it with very high levels of education that were rare in the Middle Ages, and to ignore the ease of language acquisition by children in a bilingual or multilingual society.

I should emphasize that the evidence for bilingualism and trilingualism, like the evidence for French-speaking or English-speaking, is anecdotal.[31] Though the anecdotal evidence for bilingualism and trilingualism is fairly large in proportion to the total evidence for the linguistic abilities of individuals, there is no way to know how representative this evidence is, and therefore no way to determine how extensive bilingualism was. But I would suggest that it was possibly quite widespread outside of the peasantry and that it was sustainable for many generations. I suspect that scholars sometimes place too much emphasis on the difference between 'maternal' or 'native' languages and learned ones. Someone who grew up with one anglophone parent and one francophone parent, with francophone parents and anglophone

[31] Searle, *Chronicle of Battle Abbey*, 306–8; *Chronicle of Jocelin of Brakelond*, 40, 128–9; Blake, *Liber Eliensis*, 316; *EHOV* 6: 488; Map, *De Nugis Curialium*, 36; Jocelin of Furness, *Vita Sancti Waltheni*, 261. See also Clark, *Words, Names and History*, 197–8; M. Dominica Legge, 'Anglo-Norman as a Spoken Language', *PBC* 2: 110; Wilson, 'English and French in England', 58–60; Short, 'On Bilingualism in Anglo-Norman England', 478. See Rothwell, 'Role of French', 449–50, for arguments against widespread bilingualism.

servants, or even with playmates who had a different language, could easily become fluent in both languages. The ability to become bilingual applied not just to the descendants of immigrants. Anglophone as well as francophone children could pick up second languages through play in integrated urban or even rural settings where French speakers had penetrated the middling levels of society. The anglophone children of servants in a francophone household could probably pick up a fair amount of French, especially if their parents encouraged them to do so in hopes that they could thereby prosper in the service of francophone aristocrats. Even adults could learn a fair amount in day-to-day interactions with speakers of other languages, as must often have happened between immigrant lords and native servants or estate officials. Though the country as a whole was undoubtedly largely anglophone, moreover, it was the peasantry that provided this majority. In other social sectors the anglophone majority may have been much less pronounced, which made easier the maintenance of French, at least as a second language that was nonetheless widely used.

In settings or social classes where both languages were used, moreover, it would not be too difficult for bilingual people to pass on both languages to their children. It is true that the slow shift to English in the aristocracy that probably took place over the course of the twelfth century would slowly have made bilingualism less easy to acquire in the home, but there were other means to train children in French. Whatever the shortcomings of medieval education by modern standards, educators had a great deal of practical experience with language training because of the need to train clerics, monks, and nuns in Latin. Not all religious learned Latin very well, as Gerald of Wales attested, but to the extent that formal education existed, language training was central, and the practical expertise gained thereby could be applied to French as well as Latin.[32] Parents could therefore make sure that their children learned French by hiring a tutor, as one knight did. They could also send children to an aristocratic francophone household to be raised, or even send them to the Continent, as Gervase of Tilbury's anachronistic belief about Harold suggests was common in his own day.[33] Certainly there were monolingual people in the period in question, including no doubt the vast majority of peasants, and there were members of the elite, such as Hugh of Avalon and Peter of Blois, who could not speak English. They could function fully in society (although Peter avoided preaching) because either English or French was common at the appropriate level, and because there was always someone around who could translate.[34]

This theory about the bilingualism of English society in the twelfth century, if it is correct, has several important consequences. Bilingualism meant that the language barrier was being broken down long before the majority of the aristocracy spoke English as their first language. Bilingualism could aid interaction and assimilation, without requiring that immigrants give up their ancestral tongue right away, or indeed at all. Bilingualism could ease the process of an entire new people gaining

[32] *GCO* 2: 341–8.
[33] *Becket Materials*, 1: 347–8; Gervase of Tilbury, *Otia Imperialia*, 474.
[34] Adam of Eynsham, *Magna Vita Sancti Hugonis*, 2: 7, 118; *Later Letters of Peter of Blois*, 195, 337.

command of English in the absence of any formal schooling in the language. The process would have been gradual, but so too was assimilation. At the same time, bilingualism meant that ethnic or national unity could be achieved without making society as a whole monolingual. Indeed, it was one of the reasons why the elites could become firmly English by the beginning of the thirteenth century without giving up French for another two centuries or more.

This last point raises the question, however, of why assimilation, the triumph of English identity among the elites, and the growth of anti-French sentiment did not end or at least sharply limit the use of French in England, especially given the general tendency for one language to push another out. Partly the answer has to do with the particular nature of elite Englishness. Aristocrats considered themselves English of Continental descent, and just as they came to see no contradiction between considering themselves English and taking pride in Norman ancestry, so they apparently viewed the extensive use of French as compatible with being English. There were also many advantages to be gained from the continuing cultivation of French. As we have seen, it was a prestigious language that associated one with the aristocracy.[35] For the aristocracy as a whole, it was one more cultural marker that set them apart from ordinary people. Anglo-Norman may also have served as a unified language that could circumvent the problems caused by mutually unintelligible dialects in English.[36] For aristocrats and clerics, the knowledge of French gave the potential for service and preferment in the king's Continental domains, and indeed beyond. Finally, for all the elites, knowledge of French opened up wide cultural horizons, just as Latin did for the clergy. The maintenance of French in England was neither easy nor automatic after a few generations had gone by from 1066, but it is easy to understand why many members of the elites made the effort.

A converse question is why the retention of French as a prestigious language did not seriously impede the revival of English identity and its triumph among the elites. There are several important reasons. First of all, it is not entirely clear what identity the language we call French would have supported. Nationalist movements, educational systems, and other factors have all tended to reify and standardize 'official' languages, sometimes making linguistically arbitrary distinctions between dialects and languages. There is some truth to the quip that a language is a dialect backed up by an army. In the Middle Ages the situation was much more fluid than in modern Europe. Sophisticated observers were certainly aware of the complexity of the linguistic situation, and of language or dialectical groupings. Goscelin of Saint-Bertin spoke of the French, Normans, and eight other groups speaking Gallic, and the English, Saxons, Flemings, and Danes speaking Teutonic.[37] However, there was no systematic method of classifying languages and dialects and no widely agreed-upon standard for identifying some of them. What we call French

[35] Clanchy, *From Memory to Written Record*, 199–200.
[36] Legge, 'Anglo-Norman as a Spoken Language', 115; Richter, *Sprache und Gesellschaft*, 161–2; Rothwell, 'Role of French', 455–6; W. Rothwell, 'Anglo-French Lexical Contacts, Old and New', *Modern Language Review*, 74 (1979), 292–3.
[37] Goscelin of Saint-Bertin, 'Liber Confortatorius', 86–7. See also *WMGR* 98; *GCO* 6: 77–8, 177–8; *Chronica Magistri Rogeri de Hovedene*, 2: 233.

was sometimes called *Franceis*, or the *lingua Francorum* or some equivalent phrase in Latin.[38] In the Latin sources from England in the twelfth century it was over-whelmingly called Gallic. More important, the language was occasionally referred to as Norman, and sometimes as Roman, what we would call Romance.[39] What group, then, did speaking Anglo-Norman French make one a member of? From Ælnoth of Canterbury's point of view, it made one Roman (or romance?), though he was unusual in this respect.[40] If one thought of the language as Norman then it could help make one Norman, but that was a limited usage. Maybe it made one Gallic, but that was perhaps not quite the same as being French, and in any case, the growing hostility against the French, as I have argued, would negate the possible influence of French culture, including language, on identity. Some of the same ambiguity applied to English—Gerald of Wales occasionally spoke of English as Teutonic.[41] But almost invariably English was called precisely that by the Latin, Anglo-Norman, or Middle English version of the term. To the extent that language affected identity, English was in a much better position to do so, because of the tight terminological link between the people and the language.

A related factor was the divergence of Anglo-Norman French from the French of Paris, and the scorn heaped on speakers of French from England. Several instances of this appear from as early as the second half of the twelfth century. A couple of authors apologized for their French, including the nun who translated the life of Edward the Confessor into Anglo-Norman, and spoke of knowing 'a false French' of England.[42] Walter Map's anecdote about a fountain at Marlborough that causes its drinkers to speak garbled French is surely a joking reference to Anglo-Norman French.[43] To what degree the jokes, which continued to be a staple of humour in later centuries, reflected poorly learned French and to what degree they reflected dialectical differences is not clear. What is important, however, is that the English and French elites, to paraphrase Churchill, came to be divided by a common lan-guage. Thus, from the later twelfth century on, the use of Anglo-Norman was nearly as likely as the use of English to foster English distinctiveness.[44]

Another, fundamentally important, factor was that French, or Anglo-Norman, turned out to be a perfectly acceptable vehicle for Englishness. We have already seen

---

[38] Marie de France, *Fables*, ed. Harriet Spiegel (Toronto, 1987), 258; Södergård, *Vie d'Edouard le Confesseur*, 109; Stubbs, *Memorials of Saint Dunstan*, 236–7; Gerald of Wales, *Speculum Duorum*, 56.

[39] For references to the Norman language, see *WMGP* 285; *CJW* 3: 96; *Historical Works of Gervase of Canterbury*, 2: 416. For references to Romance, see Hardy and Martin, *Gesta Herwardi*, 385; *Chronicle of Richard of Devizes*, 66. The terms 'Romance' and 'French' could sometimes be seen as synonyms: Reginald of Durham, *Vita Sancti Godrici*, 203–4; Marie de France, *Fables*, 256, 258. See also Clanchy, *From Memory to Written Record*, 216–17.

[40] Ælnoth of Canterbury, 'Gesta Swenomagni Regis', 96–7, 99. See also Grosjean, 'Translatio S. Swithuni', 196.

[41] e.g. *GCO* 6: 64.

[42] Södergård, *Vie d'Edouard le Confesseur*, 109. See also Thomas of Kent, *The Anglo-Norman Alexander*, ed. Brian Foster and Ian Short, 2 vols. (London, 1976–7), 1: 146; 2: 69.

[43] Map, *De Nugis Curialium*, 496. See also Gerald of Wales, *Speculum Duorum*, 56.

[44] Clanchy, *From Memory to Written Record*, 198; Crane, *Insular Romance*, 4–5; Legge, 'Anglo-Norman as a Spoken Language', 108–9; W. Rothwell, 'Stratford atte Bowe and Paris', *Modern Language Review*, 80 (1985), 39–43; Short, 'On Bilingualism in Anglo-Norman England', 469–73.

that much English history, real and fictitious, was recorded in French. In many ways the most strongly English work of all from the early thirteenth century was the *Roman de Waldef*, even though it was thoroughly 'French' in language and multi-cultural in its literary influences. I have discussed this poem in Chapter 21, but it is worth emphasizing here how the French language was used as a vehicle to praise the English; the passage quoted at the beginning of the chapter is only the most fulsome example. 'Deus! tant sunt Engleis beles genz!' exclaims the sister of the king of Normandy at one point. Elsewhere the English are described as 'vallanz', 'pruz', 'dur', 'forz', and 'hardiz e fiers e conqueranz'.[45] The *Roman de Waldef* is unusual in the degree to which it championed Englishness in French, but it was not unique. Chardri, in the *Petit Plet*, praised English ladies and knights, comparing them favourably to the French, and Angiers, in a translation into French of Gregory the Great's *Dialogues*, begins one chapter by saying: 'Now I will tell you about the English, to whom God grant victory and peace.'[46] There is no reason why writers should not praise the English in French (or Romance), and it is probably only our modern assumptions that make it seem surprising.

A final, and crucial, reason for the apparently limited links between language, assimilation, and identity, however, is that medieval people did not see those links as necessarily all that important. On a practical level, it is true, such links must have mattered; the use of English was obviously one thing that made the English distinctive. Almost certainly language issues became bound up with ethnic tensions. When the Norman elite in Henry I's reign sought a Norman rather than Italian to become archbishop of Canterbury, they made a reference to sharing the paternal language.[47] The glee some of Longchamp's opponents derived from describing how his attempt to flee from England failed because he could not speak English may reflect resentment at his refusal to learn the language.[48] But writers did not explicitly link the use of the English language with English pride or honour. Indeed, to writers such as William of Malmesbury the use of English rather than Latin in writing was something of an embarrassment. The only writer to protest the declining use of English in the church was the author of the Worcester Fragment, and although his concern was for the well-being of the English, for him preservation of the language was only a means to an end, namely effective preaching.[49] In general, no writer, to my knowledge, linked writing in English and English pride or honour. In this respect Englishness in the twelfth and early thirteenth centuries was quite different not only from modern Englishness, but also from Englishness in the fourteenth century, when issues of language and ethnicity or nationality came to be more closely linked.[50]

[45] Holden, *Roman de Waldef*, 63, 191, 232, 235, 239, 251, 253.

[46] Chardri, *Le Petit Plet*, pp. xxxi, 41–2; Legge, *Anglo-Norman Literature*, 198; id., *Anglo-Norman in the Cloister*, 61.   [47] WMGP 126.

[48] EEA 17: 128; [Roger of Howden], *Gesta Regis Henrici Secundi*, 2: 219–20; GCO 4: 410–12.

[49] Dickens and Wilson, *Early Middle English Texts*, 1–2.

[50] Crane, 'Anglo-Norman Cultures in England', 51–60; Galbraith, 'Nationality and Language', 124–7; Pearsall, *Old English and Middle English Poetry*, 88; Turville-Petre, *England the Nation*, 1–221; Richter, *Sprache und Gesellschaft*, 163–9.

This conclusion has important implications not only for our understanding of identity but also for our study of writing and literature after the conquest. There was clearly a salvaging effort designed to rescue much Old English culture after the Norman Conquest, and I have argued that this was linked to a desire to protect and defend the heritage and honour of the English. My argument here may help to explain what was salvaged and what was not. As much as possible was saved of the hagiographical tradition. The Old English poetic tradition was allowed to die. This was not only because the preservers of tradition were clerics, monks, and nuns; after all, much Old English poetry was religious in nature. It was certainly not because there was a lack of native clerics who could potentially carry on the tradition, although the lack of powerful patrons for Old English works no doubt made a difference. But it is also important to remember that what mattered in defending English pride and answering Norman claims were saints and learning in Latin. Because ethnic pride was linked closely to saints, but only very loosely to vernacular literary traditions, however sophisticated, the latter were far more disposable for anyone seeking to preserve English traditions. Moreover, what mattered was content, not the language in which it was written. An enormous effort went into preserving English culture and transmitting it to the Normans by translation into Latin. No concerted effort was put into preserving written English, because the essential job had been done by translation. I suspect that most modern people, like me, would be willing to trade a dozen translated (or invented) Latin saints' lives for another epic like *Beowulf,* or even for a minor masterpiece like *The Wanderer.* But our priorities are different from those of medieval intellectuals. On a more positive note, the lack of connection between ethnic or national identity and literature helped to leave Middle English writers open to the nourishing influence of Latin and French works. The greatness of the Middle English tradition depended heavily on its international roots.

My conclusion will, I hope, only reinforce the trend toward setting that tradition in a broader context. I also hope that my work in this chapter and elsewhere will influence how we look at early Middle English literature. Let me take the example of Lawman and his *Brut.* Lawman certainly had a consciousness of being English and a certain amount of English prejudice. He stated at the outset that he was concerned with the history of England and the English, and in a brief passage later in the poem about the Normans, referred to their 'nið craften' (malicious craftiness), and the ill effects of conquest in general.[51] These statements, and also a feeling that the first major poem in Middle English ought to be far more English in its inspiration and outlook than it is, have led scholars, as I noted earlier, to wonder why on earth he should have translated a French translation of a Latin work, especially one that devotes so much space to condemning the Saxon and Angle ancestors of the English. More broadly, the issue of the Englishness or otherwise of this work has been central in the scholarship devoted to it.[52]

---

[51] *Laȝamon's Brut,* 1: 2–3, 186–7.

[52] Everett, *Essays on Middle English Literature,* 28–45; Oakden, *Alliterative Poetry,* 2: 20–3; E. G. Stanley, 'Laȝamon's Antiquarian Sentiments', *Medium Ævum* 38 (1969): 23–37; Françoise H. M. Le Saux,

The puzzles of Lawman's Englishness and choice of topic can be explained by several factors discussed in this work. First, Lawman should not be placed in a context of virulent hostility between English and Normans and of deeply defensive Englishness, for by 1189, the earliest date at which the poem was possibly written, assimilation had basically been accomplished and Englishness was becoming firmly fixed and unproblematic even among the elites.[53] Lawman's attack on the Normans and the Norman Conquest may be seen as similar to those of such self-confidently English writers as William of Newburgh and the authors of the *Waltham Chronicle* and the *Vita Haroldi*. These seem to me patriotic responses to a past invasion of England, but ones that were inspired by the growing strength of Englishness in the time of the authors, rather than by any continuing effects of the conquest. Because Englishness faced no serious threat in Lawman's time, he could casually attack the Normans without making it central to his purpose. Indeed, Englishness was so strong (and views of the inferiority of the Britons so fixed), that Geoffrey of Monmouth's views of the English no longer represented much of a threat. Moreover, since the elites had come to accept the somewhat contradictory state of being English of Norman ancestry, Englishness had many sources other than ancestry alone, including a strong sense of place. Therefore it is not so strange that Lawman sometimes elided the Britons and English, for instance, in his discussion of the return of Arthur.[54] Working in an atmosphere that was not threatening to Englishness, Lawman could translate from French a fascinating and popular work about the land that had become England, and could attack the Normans in passing, without feeling the tension that seems so obvious to modern readers.

Most important in explaining the puzzles of Lawman, however, is the looseness of the link between identity and literature in this period. I suspect that the use of a French source dependent on a Latin one struck Lawman as no more a betrayal of Englishness than the poet of the *Roman de Waldef* considered the use of French to be unsuitable in a strongly pro-English work. One should not expect even a self-consciously English poet to place too much emphasis on the English poetic tradition at this time.[55] Moreover, the fact that the poem is in English should not lead one to expect that it will automatically be more explicitly pro-English than works in

---

Laȝamon's Brut: The Poem and its Sources (Cambridge, 1989), 59, 73–83, 162–75, 184–227; Pearsall, *Old English and Middle English Poetry*, 108–13; Salter, *English and International*, 48–69; I. J. Kirby, 'Angles and Saxons in Laȝamon's *Brut*', *Studia Neophilologica*, 36 (1964), 51–62; Daniel Donoghue, 'Laȝamon's Ambivalence', *Speculum*, 65 (1990), 537–63; Lesley Johnson, 'Reading the Past in Laȝamon's *Brut*', Neil Wright, 'Angles and Saxons in Laȝamon's *Brut*: A Reassessment', and James Noble, 'Laȝamon's "Ambivalence" Reconsidered', all in *The Text and Tradition of Laȝamon's Brut*, ed. Françoise Le Saux (Cambridge, 1994), 141–60, 161–70, and 171–82.

[53] For the date, see Le Saux, *Laȝamon's Brut*, 1–10.

[54] *Laȝamon's Brut*, 2: 750.

[55] See, however, P. J. Frankis, 'Laȝamon's English Sources', in *J. R. R. Tolkien: Scholar and Storyteller, Essays in Memoriam*, ed. Mary Salu and Robert T. Farrell (Ithaca, NY, 1979), 64–75; Blake, 'Rhythmical Alliteration', 120, 122–3; S. K. Brehe, '"Rhythmical Alliteration": Ælfric's Prose and the Origins of Laȝamon's Metre', in *The Text and Tradition of Laȝamon's Brut*, ed. Françoise Le Saux (Cambridge, 1994), 65–87, and Oakden, *Alliterative Poetry*, 2: 20–3, 250–1, for possible Old English influence on the poet. But see also Le Saux, *Laȝamon's Brut*, 178–83, 189–92, 195–222, for arguments against extensive influence.

Latin or in French. In fact, if one is searching for a strongly and self-consciously English literary work, one should look not to Lawman's *Brut* but to the *Roman de Waldef*.

As a historian, and in the brief space devoted to art, architecture, and literature in Part IV, I cannot hope to have fully unravelled the connections between culture and ethnicity in the medieval period. But I hope to have made two very important points. First, there were important connections between culture and ethnicity in this period, just as one would expect. Second, these connections are not necessarily the ones that modern experience or theory would lead us to predict. In looking at the effects of specific aspects of culture on group identities and the influence of identities upon particular areas of culture in the pre-modern period, it is best to approach the subject with as few preconceptions as possible.

Conclusion

WHEN THE ENGLISH barons of Norman descent began using Englishness in the political struggles at the end of our period, they were not acting all that differently from the magnates, some of them of Scandinavian descent, in Edward the Confessor's reign. Such similarities, along with the tremendous strength of Englishness in our own world-view, can make the survival of that identity across the conquest, and the absorption of their conquerors by the English, seem unproblematic, almost natural or foreordained. The reality, as I have argued, was quite different. Although there were strong forces favouring both assimilation and the triumph of Englishness, there were also strong impediments to these outcomes, and factors that favoured ethnic hostility and the survival of Norman identity. There are no simple explanations for either the merging of the two peoples or the survival and eventual dominance of English identity. Both emerged from a complex array of historically contingent factors.

As I remarked in the Introduction, one of my goals is to demonstrate the very complexity of ethnic relations after the conquest, and this makes it difficult to draw out broad theories that can be applied to other cases. Indeed, I would argue that the complexity of ethnic relations generally makes it difficult to create widely applicable models that can explain more than a small part of any given case. However, I do believe that the theoretical methodology developed in this work does have wider application and can be used fruitfully in the development of other case studies. Studying ethnic relations on the three levels of the personal, the cultural, and the constructed is not easy, but can provide a fuller and more rounded picture than a focus on any single level.

In the case of ethnic relations after the Norman Conquest, important developments (and not always ones that modern people might expect) occurred on each of the three levels. Investigation of personal interaction at different social levels goes far to explain how, and among what social groups, aspects of native or Continental culture could become dominant. It also shows where and how cultural assimilation was most likely to take place. As one might expect, Continental culture remained dominant within the aristocracy while cultural interaction was most likely in various groups of middling power and, most important, within the institutional framework of the church. Study of interaction on the ground shows that all groups played a role in assimilation, but that peasants and aristocrats were less important than the groups in between, such as townspeople, people on the middling level of rural society, and the religious, although all these groups were less numerous than the peasantry and less powerful than the nobility. Peasants and aristocrats also had less influence on identity than one would expect. Various groups contributed to the triumph of Englishness, but churchmen, and perhaps nuns, were the most important actors in this respect. However, this work also shows the limits of the study of interaction on the ground alone to explain assimilation and, still more, the triumph of English identity. Nothing about the personal interactions of the English and Normans, including intermarriage, necessarily forestalled the maintenance of an ethnically distinct Norman aristocracy. Some factors discussed on the personal level, particularly the social, political, and cultural dominance of the Normans and the continued emphasis of powerful families on their (sometimes fictitious) Norman ancestry, seemingly point to a counterfactual triumph of Norman identity. Thus, study of personal interaction between English and Normans explains much about assimilation and the triumph of Englishness after the Norman Conquest, but also raises important questions.

To fully understand these processes one must also study the way that people thought about ethnicity, assimilation, and the specific constructs of *Normanitas* and Englishness. The very lack of any strong ideology about ethnicity, and particularly about ethnic purity or superiority, coupled with a small bias in favour of ethnic harmony and intermarriage, helped along the process of assimilation. The pragmatism for which the Normans are famous fostered what I have called 'pragmatic prejudice' in the short term, but in the long term also favoured assimilation, as most scholars have believed. As for the triumph of English identity, this was aided by the staunch defence of English honour and pride by a number of writers who identified themselves wholly or partly with the conquered people and set out to combat the mildly ethnocentric criticisms of the conquerors. But no one, emphatically including the rulers of England, set out to foster Englishness or to make the Normans good English citizens. Instead, a broad range of ideas, images, and institutions slowly led the descendants of the conquerors to think of themselves more and more as English, albeit English of Norman descent. A powerful sense of England as a place played a strong but complex and by no means straightforward role. The existence of such institutions as the English government and English church subtly reshaped how people thought of themselves, as did less obvious factors such as saints' cults and national stereotypes. The development of images of the Jewish, Celtic, or French Other helped to reshape and reconstruct Englishness, and in the reigns of Richard and John politics once again became important in strengthening the construct of Englishness. The dominance of natives in the population as a whole obviously mattered greatly to the survival and eventual dominance of Englishness, but many other factors played crucial, albeit often subliminal, roles in the triumph of that identity.

Cultural differences and similarities between the two peoples also mattered, but sometimes in very unexpected ways. Cultural differences initially sharpened the strong politically based rift between the two peoples. But the broad similarity of the two cultures, particularly in the area of religion, eased the process of assimilation. A relatively rapid process of cultural assimilation, particularly within the confines of the church, was an especially important component of overall assimilation. But the maintenance of much Continental culture, including widespread use of French as at least a second or literary language, proved no bar to assimilation. Indeed, the French language could be used as a vehicle for works that were self-consciously English by the end of the period in question. Some artistic and cultural achievements that modern people would be likely to associate with ethnic or national pride had no such connotation in the post-conquest period. Other factors, such as the strength of English saints' cults, that few modern people would consider relevant turn out to have been very important in a medieval setting. In fact, it appears that saints' cults mattered more than language in allowing English rather than Norman identity to become dominant. No one doubts that culture matters tremendously to ethnic relations and identity, but this work has indicated that modern people should use caution when trying to determine what cultural factors were likely to have mattered in a pre-modern context.

As this last paragraph indicates, Englishness in the period under study differed radically from Englishness at the dawn of the twenty-first century. Indeed, Englishness changed radically within the period in question, moving from a secure and politically anchored identity embraced by the elites, to one under severe threat from a new elite, and back to an elite, politicized identity that nonetheless contained new elements, including new stereotypes and new, more powerful, and often strongly negative images of other peoples. In comparison to modern Englishness, the differences are even more profound. Within the British Isles there has been something of a geographic retreat of Englishness since the early thirteenth century, particularly from southeastern Scotland, but also from Ireland, where an English elite had established itself in many parts of the country. Symbols are important in the construction of identity, and many of the symbols familiar to modern people, including flags, anthems, or the figure of John Bull, simply did not exist in the medieval period. Though the construct of England merged into that of Britain in the post-conquest period, that of Englishness did not intermingle with that of Britishness, as is so common today. The intellectual and institutional underpinnings of Englishness, like those of other national identities, are much stronger today, even if one takes into account the backlash against earlier strident forms of nationalism. Although I have shown that Englishness was a much more powerful construct in the post-conquest period than many scholars of the last generation or two have been willing to allow, it was much less powerful than the combined constructs of Englishness and Britishness are today.

This comparison raises the question of the relationship between modern and pre-modern identities once more. In a recent work the Africanist Adrian Hastings has made the striking argument that nationalism was a pre-modern English invention with roots extending as far back as the Anglo-Saxon period.[1] As always, much will depend on one's definition of nationalism. But certainly, the idea that England

---

[1] Hastings, *Construction of Nationhood*, 4–8, 35–65.

was a pioneer in the creation of nationalism, or of a kind of proto-nationalism that paved the way for modern constructs, is an intriguing one and at least possible. Writers on identity in Italy in the medieval period have recently argued that there was nothing like the broader identity so obvious in medieval England from at least the late Anglo-Saxon period.[2] England's precocious royal government, and other factors, such as the strength of Bede's model, may have made England quite different from other European countries and regions (and those in other parts of the world as well), and an emerging prototype for what would become the modern nation state.

I have strong doubts, however. Hastings's theory will only be proven or disproven through rigorous comparative work on a variety of societies, not only in Europe but throughout the globe. Such a study obviously lies beyond the scope of this work, but there are certain factors that raise questions in my mind even about the precocity of England in a European setting, particularly when it comes to the realm of ideas. Some of the most important writers whose works revealed and promoted Englishness were among the most cosmopolitan English figures of the day. Were their ideas on identity likely to be so different from those of other scholars throughout Europe? Certainly the use of ethnic or national stereotypes was common in the schools, which suggests that one important aspect of Englishness was far from unique. Also telling is the *Philippide*, an epic poem by William the Breton written around the end of the period covered in this book. This work was primarily a panegyric for Philip Augustus, but it was hardly less a panegyric for the French, despite being written by a Breton (many Bretons sided with the French at this time against the kings of England).[3] I suspect that the English construct of Englishness was not out of the intellectual mainstream at the time. What may be different is that England, whose modern borders had largely become fixed by the second half of the twelfth century, has had more political and ethnic stability within those borders. The construct of Frankishness/Frenchness may have had as much of a continuous history as Englishness, but one that at various times incorporated far larger and smaller areas than does modern France. This is an important difference, but it is also important not to weigh the medieval versions of these constructs simply by their apparent conformity to modern nations.

It is not my intention to answer the fascinating questions raised by Hastings's hypothesis, nor the questions raised over the modernity of nationalism more generally, but rather to suggest two important areas of future research. More research needs to be done on various identities, and especially broader ones, throughout Europe in the central and late Middle Ages.[4] Such research needs to be aware of, but not restricted by, the debates of modern social scientists. Researchers should look at

---

[2] Teresa Hankey, 'Civic Pride versus Feelings for Italy in the Age of Dante', in Smyth, *Medieval Europeans*, 196–216, and Diego Zancani, 'The Notion of "Lombard", and "Lombardy" in the Middle Ages', in Smyth, *Medieval Europeans*, 217–32.

[3] Guillaume le Breton, *Philippide*, vol. 2 of *Oeuvres de Rigord et de Guillaume le Breton*, ed. H. François Delaborde (Paris, 1885), 1–385.

[4] There is, I should note, already a large amount of German-language scholarship on this subject.

medieval identities on their own terms, not simply as precursors of modern ones, and should not restrict themselves to identities that still matter in the modern world. Obviously scholars should avoid the nationalist approaches of earlier generations of scholars, many of whom were as interested in nation-building as in history. At the same time, historians should not throw the baby out with the bathwater, which was the reaction of a couple of generations of scholars, and ignore broader identities altogether, particularly when they seem too closely related to modern nationalisms.

A second area of research needs to be the study of particularly long-lived identities such as Englishness over the long term, and particularly across the (heavily constructed) divide between modernity and the pre-modern. This would require looking not only at continuity, but even more important, at the fluidity of, and changes within, individual identities. Such projects would almost certainly involve teamwork, but could help to shed light on the nature of broader identities as well as on the history of specific constructs and peoples. They would also shed light on the subject of modernity.

Englishness has returned to the realm of public discourse. This is because globalization is forcing a consideration of all broader identities, and because the European Union is raising still more challenges to existing identities within its area. Even more important is the pressure which devolution is placing on the easy equation between Englishness and Britishness. Among some groups there is much concern about the future of English (and even more, about British) identity. An American medievalist is not in much of a position to make predictions about the future of Englishness. But I would point out that Englishness (like many other identities) has proved quite fluid and therefore adaptable in the past. This is probably not much comfort to those most concerned with its survival, for these are most likely to have an image of Englishness as a timeless and unchanging phenomenon. Nonetheless, I strongly suspect that there is a great deal of life in the old construct yet.

Native English Landholders in the *Cartae Baronum*

THOSE LISTED INCLUDE individuals with clearly English names and those who can be traced as members of native patrilineages. I have restricted the list to those who held a quarter fee or more. Where possible, I have noted links to Domesday Book tenants and provided references to further information. Parenthetical references are to page numbers in Hall, *Red Book of the Exchequer*, vol. 1. Asterisks indicate individuals or families discussed in this book.

    1. Ailric of Orchaddone (p. 207) held 1 fee from the bishop of Winchester in the time of Henry I; his son Richard holds in 1166. This fee seems to have been a member of the manor of Taunton, where several natives had holdings in 1086.[1]

    2. Henry of Merriott (p. 211) holds ½ new fee of Abbotsbury. Grandson of Harding son of Eadnoth the Staller. The return explains that Henry obtained this through marriage of his father Nicholas with the niece of Roger of Salisbury, who held custody of the abbey.

    3. *Earl Patrick (pp. 213, 236, 239–41, 298) holds 1 old fee from Shaftesbury; 2 old fees and a third for castle ward at Salisbury from the Bishop of Salisbury; 60 fees from the king. Grandson of Edward of Salisbury.

    4. Richard son of Osulf (p. 215) holds ½ new fee from Alfred of Lincoln.

    5. Rembaldus Huscarl (p. 224) held 1 fee of Glastonbury in the time of King Henry I.

    6. *Nicholas son of Harding of Meriet or Merriott (pp. 230, 290) holds 2½ fees from the king; 1 old fee from Earl William Gloucester. Grandson of Eadnoth the Staller.

    7. *Robert son of Harding (pp. 243, 273, 298, 326) holds ½ old fee from Humphrey de Bohun, 1 new fee from William son of Alan, 5 fees from the king, ¼ new fee from Earl William of Warwick. Grandson of Eadnoth the Staller.

    8. *Jordan of Trecarrel (p. 249) holds ½ fee from the bishop of Exeter.[2]

    9. Edward of Wotolta (p. 249) holds ½ old fee from the bishop of Exeter.

    10. Ansgod son of Godwin (p. 260) holds 1 old fee from Henry de Pomerai.

    11. Richard son of Osulf (p. 262) holds 1 fee from Earl Reginald.[3]

    12. Godwin Dapifer (p. 270) holds ⅓ new fee from Gervase Painel.

    13. Gilbert Anglicus (p. 273) holds 1 old fee 'muntatoris' from William son of Alan.[4]

    14. Roger Anglus (p. 275) holds ¾ new fee from Geoffrey de Ver.[5]

    15. Alwin of Legam (p. 276) holds ½ fee from Guy Salvage.[6]

---

[1] See *EEA* 8, no. 93 for a charter of Henry of Blois confirming Ailric's land to Richard.

[2] Easting and Sharpe, 'Peter of Cornwall', 207, 209, 228–9, 247–8.

[3] One or more men named Osulf had held a large number of estates in 1066. Six of these were held by another native, Algar, in 1086, and one wonders if there is not a family connection: *DB* 1: 124b.

[4] Eyton, *Antiquities of Shropshire*, 11: 367–9.

[5] Ibid. 11: 246–8.

[6] Two holdings, Bourton, and possibly Hughley, were held of Much Wenlock Priory by Edric son of Aluric in 1086: *DB* 1: 252d. Williams has suggested that this may have been Eadric the Wild whom she sug-

16. Azo brother of Leomer (p. 291) holds ½ old fee from Earl William of Gloucester.

17. Roger son of Heming (p. 306) holds 1 old fee of Abingdon.[7]

18. Walter Canute (p. 309) holds 5 fees of the honour of Wallingford.

19. Gilbert Huscarle (p. 309) holds 3 fees of the honour of Wallingford.[8]

20. Ravening of Missenden (p. 317) holds ½ fee from Walter de Bolebec. Ulviet held ½ hide in Missenden and ½ hide in Amersham from Hugh de Bolebec in 1086.[9]

21. *Henry and Hugh of Arden (p. 325) hold 5 and 5⅓ old fees respectively from Earl William of Warwick. Grandsons of Thorkel of Warwick.

22. Gilbert of Segrave (p. 326) holds ¼ new fee from Earl William of Warwick. A minor royal official, son of Hereward, and father of the powerful royal servant Stephen of Segrave.[10]

23. *Robert son of Sawin (p. 334) holds 1 fee from Robert de Chokes.

24. Henry of Brailsford (p. 338) holds 1 new fee from the Earl Ferrers. Head of a prosperous local family that lasted into the fourteenth century, and grandson of Elfin, who held four estates from Henry de Ferrers in 1086.[11]

25. Ralph son of Hugh of Cromwell (p. 341) holds 1 old fee from the bishop of Lincoln. Ancestor of the baronial house of Cromwell and grandson of Alden the king's thegn, who held a number of estates in 1086.[12]

26. Odo of Cockfield (p. 348) holds 1 old fee from Walter son of Robert. Cadet member of the Cockfield family.

27. Robert Huscarl (p. 350) holds a share in 1 fee held from William de Montefichet.

28. Roger Anglicus (p. 351) holds 1 new fee in Fernham from William de Montefichet through wardship.

29. *Robert of Cockfield (pp. 352, 364, 393, 397) holds 3 fees from Earl Alberic de Ver; 1 old fee in Suffolk from Bishop Nigel of Ely; 1½ old fees from Bury St Edmund's; 1 new fee from Earl Hugh Bigod.

30. Robert son of Robert son of Elric (p. 353) holds 1 fee from Earl Alberic de Ver. A lawsuit of 1232 reveals that his sister Beatrice inherited from him land in Wilbraham in Cambridgeshire and Radwinter in Essex. No native tenant was recorded in either place in 1086, but an Aluric of Wilbraham served as a juror, and an Aluric had held land in Radwinter in 1066. Elric is probably to be identified with one or both of these figures.[13]

31. Roger son of Edmund (pp. 354, 366) holds 1 old fee from Roger de Raimes in Suffolk; 1 old fee from Hamo Pecche.

32. William son of Edmund (p. 357) holds ¼ fee from the demesne of Robert de Raimes.[14]

gests was an ancestor of the Savage or Salvage family: *ENC* 92. A family called the Leighs later held these manors, and so it is possible that Alwin fits somewhere into this picture: *VCH Shropshire*, 10: 340.

[7] Roger can be found attesting a charter of Henry d'Oilly and supervising work on the castle at Oxford: Salter, *Eynsham Cartulary* 1, no. 68; *Pipe Roll 19 Henry II*, 167; *Pipe Roll 20 Henry II*, 77.

[8] Turner, 'Roger Huscarl', 215.

[9] *DB* 1: 150b. See Jenkins, *Charters of Missenden Abbey*, 1, nos. 70, 181–2; 2, nos. 277, 283–4 for charters involving Ravening and his sons. Ravening is an unusual, perhaps unique, name but Raven and names with Raven as an element were common in insular nomenclature.

[10] Turner, *Men Raised from the Dust*, 121.

[11] *DB* 1: 274b–275a; S. P. H. Statham, 'The Brailsfords', *Journal of the Derbyshire Archaeological and Natural History Society* (1938), 66–80.

[12] *DB* 2: 292b–293a; *CRR* 10: 148–9; *VCH Nottinghamshire*, 1: 234; Barley, *Newark-on-Trent*, pp. xxix–xxx

[13] *CRR* 14: 480–1; *DB* 2: 78a; Hamilton, *Inquisitio Comitatus Cantabrigiensis*, 12.

[14] It is possible that either Roger or Walter son of Edmund was the ancestor of the Edmund of Tuddenham who held one knight's fee of the same honour in the early thirteenth century, and appeared as a knight on several occasions: *Book of Fees*, 1: 233, 357; *CRR* 7: 261; 12: 9, 172; 13: 71.

33. Albert Anglicus (365) holds 1 old fee in Hertfordshire from Bishop Nigel of Ely.

34. Geoffrey son of Swein (pp. 367, 370) holds 1¼ fees from Stephen de Scalariis; ¹⁄₁₂ old fee from Hugh de Scalariis. He gained some or all of this through marriage to the granddaughter of a Flemish landholder of 1086.[15]

35. Richard Anglicus (p. 374) holds ½ old fee in Wirham from William de Say.

36. Hugh son of Alger (p. 385) holds 1 old fee from Maurice de Craon. He was almost certainly a descendant of the Algar who in 1086 held 2 carucates in 2 estates from Guy de Craon. Hugh married Matilda, widow of Goscelin, the son of a minor tenant-in-chief, Heppo Balistarius, and they had a son named Herbert.[16]

37. William son of Edmund (p. 397) holds ¼ new fee from Earl Hugh Bigod.

38. Walter Hautein or Haltane (pp. 404, 406) holds 4 old fees from the honour of Clare. Almost certainly a descendant of the Godwin Haldein (or hall thegn) who held many of the same estates of the king in 1086. Connected by marriage to several Norman families.[17]

39. *William of Bulmer (pp. 417, 420, 428–9, 432) holds 5 old fees from the bishop of Durham; 1 old fee from Roger de Mowbray; just over 3 old fees from the king; ¼ fee from Everard de Ros. Grandson of Ansketil of Bulmer, sheriff of Yorkshire and likely a native.

40. Stephen of Bulmer (pp. 417, 439–40) holds 1 old fee from the bishop of Durham; 5 old fees and 1¾ new fees from the king. Son of Ansketil of Bulmer and heir to the Muschamp lands through his wife.[18]

41. Everard son of Lewin (p. 423) holds ½ fee from Henry de Lacy (Robert, his brother, has ⅕ fee).[19]

42. Elyas son of Essulf (p. 423) holds ¼ fee from Henry de Lacy.

43. Adam son of Peter (p. 424) holds 1 fee from Henry de Lacy. Grandson of Essulf and head of the Birkin family.[20]

44. Richard of Tong (p. 424) holds ¼ fee from Henry de Lacy.

45. Adam son of Norman (p. 425) holds with one other man 1 old fee from William de Percy. Norman's father Uctred may have been the son of an important pre-conquest thegn, Alwin.[21]

46. Peter of Meaux (pp. 425–6) holds ¾ new fee and a share in ⅓ new fee from William de Percy. Son of Gamel son of Uctred son of Norman.[22]

47. Nigel of Plumpton (p. 426) holds 1 new fee from William de Percy. Nephew of Orm and therefore a possible descendant of Eldred, the 1086 tenant of Plumpton and another family holding.[23]

48. *John son of Odard (pp. 427, 439, 441) holds 1 old fee from William de Vescy; a share in 1 old fee from Stephan of Bulmer; 3 fees from the king. Possible grandson of Ligulf of Bamburgh, one of Henry I's sheriffs of Northumberland.

49. Anschetil son of Gospatric (p. 428) holds 1 old fee from William of Bulmer. Ancestor of the Ridale or Habton family and of the Riddells of Scotland.[24]

---

[15] *VCH Cambridgeshire*, 5: 38; Keats-Rohan, *Domesday People*, 125.

[16] *DB* 1: 367b–368a; BL Add MS 35296, fols. 360ʳ–361ʳ; Keats-Rohan, *Domesday People*, 136.

[17] *DB* 2: 271a–b; Round, *Rotuli de Dominabus*, pp. xlvi, 47, 55; *EYC* 5, no. 326.

[18] Hedley, *Northumberland Families*, 1: 37

[19] *EYC* 3: 351–3.

[20] *EYC* 3: 358–9; Clay and Greenway, *Early Yorkshire Families*, 6.

[21] *EYC* 3: 478; 11: 243–5.

[22] *EYC* 11: 262; Clay and Greenway, *Early Yorkshire Families*, 59–60.

[23] *DB* 1: 322a; Bodleian Library, Dodsworth MS 148, fol. 1ᵛ.

[24] *EYC* 9: 220; Clay and Greenway, *Early Yorkshire Families*, 40.

50. Ralph of Wilton (p. 429) holds ½ old fee from William of Bulmer. Possible son of Ansketil of Bulmer.

51. *Ranulf son of Walter (p. 434) holds 3¾ old fees from the king. Great-grandson of Forne son of Sigulf and head of the Greystoke family.

52. Gospatric (p. 437) holds ⅓ new fee from Walter de Bolebec.[25]

53. Liulf son of Alwold (p. 439) holds 1 old fee from Stephen of Bulmer.[26]

54. William son of Siward (p. 440) holds 1 fee from the king.[27]

55. *William son of Aluric of Dilston (p. 441) holds ⅓ fee from the king. Son of one of Henry I's sheriffs of Northumberland.[28]

[25] Hedley, *Northumberland Families*, 2: 239.
[26] Ibid. 241.
[27] Ibid. 1: 54–5.
[28] Ibid. 1: 143–5.

Notable Native Patrilineages and Individuals of Southern England in the Twelfth Century

IN THIS APPENDIX I have included patrilineages that survived from 1086 into the twelfth century and other important native families or individuals absent from the *Cartae Baronum*. I have excluded families from Yorkshire, Lancashire, and further north for the sake of brevity (for native northern families, see above, pp. 112–15). I have named families found in the *Cartae Baronum* beside the county in which they were based, to give a better sense of the geographic distribution of known native patrilineages in the south. Asterisks indicate individuals or families discussed in the text.

Berkshire

1. A family descended from one Wolward held Inglesham in hereditary fee farm for £10, as a member of the manor of Faringdon, where Alfsi of Faringdon held 4 hides in 1086.[1] It is at least possible that Wolward was related to Alfsi of Faringdon. Certainly Alfsi left land-holding descendants, for Stenton discovered a charter from the late twelfth century by which one, Robert of Astrop, gave away a small manor that Alfsi's son had held in 1086.[2]

2. The land of the king's thegn Wigar who held 2 hides in Benham passed to his sons Hugh and Ralph, the elder of whom was alive in 1110.[3]

3. Several scholars have suggested that the father of William son of Alward, whose land and office William paid for in Henry I's pipe roll, may have been Alward the goldsmith who inherited 7 hides in Shottesbrook before 1086.[4]

Buckinghamshire (Ravening of Missenden)

1. In his introduction to the *Luffield Cartulary*, Elvey suggests that four prominent Buckinghamshire families, the Westburys, Wedons, Brocs, and Horwodes, were of native ancestry. His evidence for the Brocs seems to me basically nonexistent. For the Westburys it depends on descent from a man named Aldelm, and for the Horwodes, descent from brothers named Berner and Azur. These names may well indicate native ancestry, but unfortunately fall into the ambiguous category. The best case is with the Wedons, who were descended from an Alfred who possessed estates held by an Almar in 1086 from the count of Mortain and Miles Crispin, one of which he had held in 1066. Alfred is an ethnically ambiguous name, but it seems likely that Alfred of Wedon was a descendant as well as successor of the native survivor Almar.[5]

---

[1] *CRR* 5: 60–1; *DB* 1: 57b.

[2] *VCH Oxfordshire*, 1: 388; Stenton, 'English Families', 11.

[3] *VCH Berkshire*, 4: 120; Keats-Rohan, *Domesday People*, 466.

[4] *DB* 1: 63b; *Pipe Roll 31 Henry I*, 124; *VCH Berkshire*, 3: 164; Green, *Government of England*, 279; Keats-Rohan, *Domesday People*, 149.   [5] Elvey, *Luffield Priory Charters*, 2: pp. xlvii–l.

Cambridgeshire (Robert son of Robert son of Elric, Geoffrey son of Swein)

Cheshire

1. *Liulf of Twemlow, sheriff of the county under Earl Ranulf III.
2. A Waltheof son of Wulfric who attested a charter of Earl Ranulf II and whose daughter Margery married Gilbert Venables may be a son of the Uluric, or Wulfric, who held three small manors in 1086. Liulf of Twemlow may have some connection with this family.[6]

Cornwall *(Jordan of Trecarrel)*

1. Odmer, the brother and steward of Bishop Leofric of Exeter, who died in 1072, established a family that survived in a reasonably prominent position into the twelfth century.[7]

Derbyshire *(Brailsfords)*

1. In 1086 a king's thegn named Toli held Sandiacre. The pipe roll of 1131 shows a Robert son of Toli was in royal service in Derbyshire and Nottinghamshire and a Peter Toli received a Danegeld pardon under the same county rubric and received delivery of a falcon in the pipe roll of Henry II's second year. Two years later Peter of Sandiacre, who was a royal falconer and ancestor of the Sandiacre family, which held through a sergeancy of falconry, received a pardon from a county 'gift' for Derbyshire and Nottinghamshire. If Peter Toli and Peter of Sandiacre were the same, or father and son, this would indicate the survival of a native patrilineage from 1066 through the end of the twelfth century.[8]
2. In a charter from the middle of the twelfth century Earl Robert de Ferrers confirmed to Tutbury demesne tithes given by a number of lords, including the natives Elfin of Brailsford and Orm of Okeover, whose lordship of the estates in question is well attested. He also confirmed demesne tithes given by Ulsi in Twyford and Stenson, where Henry de Ferrers had held 5 carucates. It is likely that Ulsi was a moderately important local native landlord like Elfin and Orm, though there is no apparent link to any of the 1066 tenants.[9]

Devonshire

1. In the middle of the twelfth century a man with the English name of Aldred of Down or Rousdon, whose son Ralph was a knight, held land that had been held by a king's thegn in 1086. Aldred was also an inhabitant of Axminster.[10]

Dorset *(Henry of Merriott)*

1. Bishop Jocelin of Salisbury granted ¼ knight's fee to Walter son of Sweyn of Legha, dispensator.[11]

[6] *DB* 1: 267b, 265a; Barraclough, *Charters of the Earls of Chester*, no. 43; Tait, *Chartulary of St. Werburgh*, 1: 235; Ormerod, *History*, 3: 61, 210.   [7] *EEA* 11, no. 1; 12, no. 170.

[8] *DB* 1: 278b; *Pipe Roll 31 Henry I*, 7, 11; *Pipe Roll 2 Henry II*, 39, 46; *Pipe Roll 4 Henry II*, 153; *Pipe Roll 5 Henry II*, 59; *Pipe Roll 17 Henry II*, 99. See Darlington, *Cartulary of Darley Abbey*, 1: pp. xxx–xxxii, for the Sandiacre family.

[9] Earl Robert also confirmed a grant of tithes by Chetell in Sturston, where Henry had held less than 1 carucate in 1086, and by Toli in *Syrle*. *DB* 1: 275a–b; Avrom Saltman, ed., *The Cartulary of Tutbury Priory* (London, 1962), no. 52.   [10] *EEA* 10, no. 144; 11, no. 66; *Pipe Roll 14 Henry II*, 129.

[11] *EEA* 2, no. 209; 18, nos. 149, 188.

Essex (Robert son of Robert son of Elric)

1. *Ailward, royal official.
2. Henry II granted various lands to Alcher the hunter (who had an uncle named Orgar) and his sons, including ¼ knight's fee and the land of a man who committed adultery with Alcher's wife Edith, whom Alcher's son Richard managed to have falsely accused of robbery.[12]

Gloucestershire (Fitz Harding)

1. Keats-Rohan has shown that the Osward who held ½ hide in Trewsbury of Gilbert son of Turold in 1086 attested a charter of Osbern son of Pons in the reign of Henry I.[13]

Hampshire

1. A case of 1225 reveals that at some point in the twelfth century, possibly in Henry I's reign, a certain Godwin held 4 ploughlands in one of the villages called Worthy in the county.[14]
2. Uluric the Huntsman, who held land in Wiltshire as well as Hampshire, was succeeded by his son Walter, and in the pipe roll of 1131 the sheriff offered £100 and 3 marks of gold for the custody of Walter's heirs.[15]
3. The descent of the land of Aluric the Small, who held land in Wiltshire as well as Hampshire, is unclear, but it stayed in native hands. It was probably granted by Stephen to a grandson, also named Alvric, and then, by the future Henry II, to William Spileman, grandson of Edward Unnithing, whose family continued to hold by sergeanty.[16]

Hertfordshire (Albert Anglicus)

1. The Alden who retained Tewin through King William's intervention, for the soul of his son Richard, may have survived into Henry I's reign.[17]

Huntingdonshire

1. In Yelling, where a Suin, perhaps Swein, held 5 hides of Ramsey in 1086, an Alard of Yelling held 5 hides in 1166, and a Harold held the same amount for either ½ or a whole knight's fee late in Henry II's reign.[18]

Kent

1. A Walter son of Godwin had a wife and brother who proffered 100 marks for the custody of his land and heirs.[19]

---

[12] *Book of Fees*, 1: 121, 126; Ransford, *Early Charters of Waltham Abbey*, nos. 280–4; Conway, *Cartae Antiquae Rolls 11–20*, no. 533; *CRR* 13: 226.
[13] Keats-Rohan, *Domesday People*, 320.
[14] *CRR* 12, no. 51
[15] *DB* 1: 50a, 74a; *Pipe Roll 31 Henry I*, 37; Keats-Rohan, *Domesday People*, 437.
[16] *DB* 1: 51b, 73b; *Calendar of Charter Rolls*, 4: 442–3; *VCH Hampshire*, 4: 626–7; 5: 116–17; *VCH Wiltshire*, 2: 78; 9: 52, 56; 15: 269.
[17] *DB* 1: 141a–b; *RRAN* 2, no. 584 and n.
[18] *DB* 1: 204b; Hall, *Red Book of the Exchequer*, 1: 371; Hart and Lyons, *Cartularium Monasterii de Rameseia*, 3: 48; *VCH Huntingdonshire*, 2: 381.   [19] *Pipe Roll 31 Henry I*, 66.

Lincolnshire (Hugh son of Alger)

1. *Picot son of Colswein.
2. *The Ingoldsby family.
3. The Keals. This family, whose descent can be tracked in the Crowland Cartulary and the *Curia Regis Rolls*, is the most important of those whose history has not previously been traced.[20] The family was descended from Ketelbern of Keal, who had an estate of 9 small holdings and a mill in Domesday Book, held by three thegns in 1066, totalling slightly under 4 carucates and worth £5. 17s., possibly along with property in Lincoln.[21] He, or a successor of the same name, appeared, with at least his most important holdings, in the Lindsey survey of 1115–16, and gave the churches of West Keal and Sutton le Marsh to Crowland Abbey, a grant that was confirmed and later contested by various descendants. His wife was named Alexis of Chisy.[22] Ketelbern died sometime before the pipe roll of 1130, when his son Odo owed four falcons for his land. The demand for falcons may suggest that Ketelbern and his son were valued for procuring or training falcons, and that like other thegnly families they survived through ministerial service to the new royal family.[23] Odo attested a charter of the immigrant magnate William de Roumare, and other Keals, some of them certainly and others possibly members of the same family, witnessed charters of the Roumares and the earls of Chester.[24] Odo also made a grant to Kirkstead.[25] The family next appears in 1176, after Odo's son Alan died, when his sons were in royal custody, along with his land, worth £14 or £15 a year.[26] The land continued down through Alan's son William to William's son, who is named Ketelbern, as far as I know a unique example of a thirteenth-century native readopting a rare insular ancestral name. Sir Ketelbern, as he is called in some documents, can be found making deals concerning his land, and serving on a Lincolnshire jury in a politically sensitive case.[27] This Ketelbern was succeeded in turn by his son John and grandson Ralph.[28]

Middlesex

1. In a lawsuit of 1200 the manor of Bedfont was claimed on the grounds that Henry of Bedfont, who inherited it from Walter of Bedfont, was actually Walter's stepson and was really son of one Gospatric of Wilton. Henry naturally denied this.[29]

---

[20] *CRR* 14: 25; Spalding Gentlemen's Society, Crowland Abbey Cartulary, fols. 193ᵛ–194ʳ, 124ᵛ–125ʳ.

[21] This total ignores a holding of ½ carucate worth £1 immediately following, which was attributed to Ketelbern for 1066 but to no one for 1086; there is a good chance it was his as well, though this, like some other holdings, does not appear later in the family's hands. Ketelbern was involved in several suits over land at the time of the survey: *DB* 1: 336a, 370b, 375a–b.

[22] Foster and Longley, *Lincolnshire Domesday and the Lindsey Survey*, 252–4; Spalding Gentlemen's Society, Crowland Abbey Cartulary, fols. 193ᵛ–194ʳ, 124ᵛ–5ʳ; *EEA* 1, no. 100, n.; *CRR* 14: 25.

[23] *Pipe Roll 31 Henry I*, 113.

[24] Stenton, *Documents Illustrative of the Danelaw*, nos. 501, 507, 510–12, 515, 527, 529; Barraclough, *Charters of the Earls of Chester*, nos. 289, 299, 301, 302, 324.

[25] *Mon. Ang.*, 5: 420.

[26] *Pipe Roll 22 Henry II*, 86; *Pipe Roll 23 Henry II*, 116.

[27] See A. E. B. Owen, *The Medieval Lindsey Marsh: Select Documents* (Woodbridge, 1996), no. 76, and Stenton, *Danelaw Charters*, no. 493, for charters issued by William. For Ketelbern, see Owen, *Medieval Lindsey Marsh*, no. 37; *Book of Fees*, 1: 164; 2: 1057–8; *CRR* 16: 29–30.

[28] Spalding Gentlemen's Society, Crowland Abbey Cartulary, fols. 124ᵛ–25ʳ.

[29] *CRR* 1: 214; *RCR* 2: 115.

Norfolk (Hautein)

1. Ralph and Hubert, sons of Godric Dapifer, an important royal official in 1086, held his lands under William d'Aubigny. The lands subsequently passed to the Monte Canisio family.[30]

2. Keats-Rohan has traced several descendants of Alfred of Attleborough, who held 2 carucates of the king in 1086 and may have been an under-sheriff early in the twelfth century.[31]

3. A legal case from 1201 reveals the marriage of a sokeman of Bury St Edmunds named Peter son of Godwin to the heiress of a knight, William of Walton.[32]

Northamptonshire (Robert son of Sawin)

Nottinghamshire (The Cromwells)

1. The Arngrim who held land from Sibthorpe and its outliers from Ilbert de Lacy in 1086 had a grandson named Ralph of St Paul, though it is not clear if Ralph inherited through his father or his mother.[33]

Oxfordshire

1. Matthew, grandson of Sueting, who held 1½ hides in Wheatley from Abingdon in 1086, held part of a knight's fee from the abbey.[34]

Shropshire (Gilbert Anglicus, Roger Anglus, Alwin of Legam)

1. The powerful thegn Siward son of Æthelgar was succeeded by his son Ealdred, who survived into the twelfth century, but it is impossible to trace the family thereafter in Shropshire.[35]

2. Estates held by a Hunnit in 1086 passed to the Toret family. They may have been descendants of a Toret who held land in 1086 that subsequently passed to another family. Alternately, it is possible that the Hunnit and Toret of 1086 were related and that the former named an heir after the latter. In any case, the Torets, a prominent local family who developed close ties with the Dunstanvilles and later gained land in Yorkshire through marriage, were probably of native descent.[36]

3. The Sprenghose family, which gained a certain local prominence as a knightly family, was descended from one Ailric, who lived in the reign of Henry II.[37]

4. Williams has suggested that the Savage family was descended from Eadric the Wild.[38]

---

[30] *Mon. Ang.*, 3: 330; Hall, *Red Book of the Exchequer*, 1: 397–8.

[31] Keats-Rohan, *Domesday People*, 28–9, 140.

[32] *CRR* 2: 25–6; *RCR* 2: 253–4.

[33] Trevor Foulds, *The Thurgarton Cartulary* (Stamford, 1994), 227.

[34] *DB* 1: 156b; Stevenson, *Chronicon Monasterii de Abingdon*, 2: 4–6; Keats-Rohan, *Domesday People*, 424.

[35] Rees, *Cartulary of Shrewsbury Abbey*, no. 1.

[36] Eyton, *Antiquities of Shropshire*, 2: 48–9, 305–9; 6: 140; 7: 340; 8: 100, 114–15; 10: 180–6, 236–7, 326; Williams, *ENC* 90.

[37] Eyton, *Antiquities of Shropshire*, 6: 25–7, 49–61.

[38] Williams, *ENC* 91–3. See an additional piece of circumstantial evidence under Alwin de Legam in Appendix 1 above.

5. If Williams is right that the Alcher who held land only in 1086 was a native, then another important local family, the Aers, were of native descent.[39]

Somerset (*Ailric of Orchaddone, the Merriotts*)

1. As Stacy has shown, a Godwin, who held 2 hides from Glastonbury in Domesday Book, survived well into the twelfth century but was able to retain only a virgate for his successors.[40]

2. A king's thegn named Doda held 3 virgates in Dodington in 1086. Henry II confirmed to Baldwin son of Harding 3 virgates his father and ancestors held there of the Hospitallers, and it is at least possible that Harding was a descendant of Doda.[41]

Staffordshire

1. *The Audleys
2. The Okeover family.[42]
3. *The Ridware family. Descended from Atsor the Englishman, they rose to prominence under William, steward of the Earl Ferrers[43]
4. The Leigh family. This family, which later entered the knightly ranks, can only be traced back to Robert son of Ulviet, who received the manor of Leigh from Burton in fee farm in Henry II's reign, but they also held land from the Staffords which Woodman and Alsi held of Robert of Stafford in 1086, raising the possibility of earlier origins.[44]
5. Orm of Darlaston. He held Darlaston at farm from Burton Abbey, and married the daughter of Nicholas of Beauchamp. In 1131 he owed 40 marks for breaking the peace. The heiresses of two of his sons married into the Audley and Gresley families.[45]

Suffolk (*Cockfields, Roger son of Edmund*)

1. Ulward of Wangford, who held several estates from Bury St Edmund's in 1086 and farmed two others, apparently gained King Henry I's support by becoming his man, and was succeeded by his son Goscelin.[46]
2. Keats-Rohan has suggested that the Richard son of Stanhard who attested some Bury deeds was son of the Stanard who was a minor tenant-in-chief and mesne tenant as well.[47]
3. The Sibton cartulary reveals the existence of the Wenhaston/Malet family descended from one Ailwyn, who changed his name to Geoffrey. The family had close connections to the Bigods and a number of estates, part of which were held for ½ a knight's fee.[48]
4. An agreement of 1112 in which Ædricus Latimer placed lands in Fornham, Suffolk, and Harlow, Essex, in gage for 35 marks suggests that he was a modestly wealthy landholder.[49]

[39] Williams, *ENC* 91.
[40] *DB* 1: 90a; *EEA* 8: 210–11; Stacy, 'Henry of Blois', 26.
[41] *DB* 1: 99a; *VCH Somerset*, 5: 65–6.
[42] Wrottesley, 'Okeover of Okeover', 3–187.
[43] id., 'The Rydware Chartulary', 229–302.
[44] *DB* 1: 249a; Wrottesley, 'Staffordshire Cartulary, Series III', 227–8.
[45] Wrottesley, 'Burton Chartulary', 13, 35–6; *Pipe Roll 31 Henry I*, 73.
[46] *DB* 2: 357b–358b, 360b; Douglas, *Feudal Book*, 17, nos. 26, 38.
[47] Keats-Rohan, *Domesday People*, 422.
[48] Brown, *Sibton Abbey Cartularies*, 1: 69–73; 2, no. 303–5; 3, no. 817.
[49] Douglas, *Feudal Book*, no. 172; Tsurushima, 'Domesday Interpreters', 216.

Surrey

1. Though the lands of the powerful thegn Oswold passed to Normans in the twelfth century, he, or a relative of the same name, granted demesne tithes in one of his manors early in that century.[50]

2. A case in 1220 reveals that a father and son, both named Hemming, held 3½ hides in *Bagshet* at rent. The younger Hemming's son 'was led into Wales' at some point and was not present when Hemming died. Later a man named Geoffrey Aurifaber showed up claiming to be Hemming's son. The jurors were unsure but thought his claim was probably true.[51]

Warwickshire (Ardens)

1. The Le Notte family was descended from the daughter of Guthmund, brother of Thorkel of Warwick. Her husband's identity is unknown.[52]

2. Eddulf or Hadulf, who held two estates from Thorkel of Warwick in 1086, which he had also held in 1066, was the ancestor of a family that lasted into the thirteenth century.[53]

3. A Ralph son of Godwin de halla who owed 10 marks in Henry I's pipe roll may be the son of the Godwin who held 1 carucate in Hodnell (*Hodenhelle*) in 1086.[54]

Wiltshire (Salisburys)

Worcestershire

1. Bishop Teulf enfeoffed Oswin camerarius with ½ a knight's fee in Upton. Subsequently this was held by Peter of Upton, who may or may not have been a relative.[55]

[50] *VCH Surrey* 3: 323–4.
[51] *CRR* 9: 332–3.
[52] Williams, 'Vice-Comital Family', 288; *CRR* 6: 72; *VCH Warwickshire*, 4: 222.
[53] *DB* 1: 241a; *VCH Warwickshire*, 6: 35, 204.
[54] *DB* 1: 241a; *Pipe Roll 31 Henry I*, 107.
[55] Hollings, *Red Book of Worcester*, 4: 413.

Bibliography

MANUSCRIPT SOURCES

British Library

    Add MS 9822. Register of Ely Abbey.
    Add MS 35296. Register of Spalding Priory.
    Add MS 40,000. Thorney Liber Vitae.
    Add MS 47,677. Kenilworth Cartulary.
    Arundel MS 201 pt. 2. Poetry.
    Burney MS 305. Poetry.
    Cotton Caligula A xiii. Vol. 2 of Pipewell Cartulary.
    Cotton Claudius D xiii. Register of Binham Priory.
    Cotton Titus C viii. Register of Wymondham.
    Cotton Vespasian E xxiv. Evesham Abbey Register.
    Cotton Vitellius D ix. Cartulary of St Nicholas, Exeter.
    Harley MS 61. Shaftesbury Abbey material.
    Harley MS 236. Cartulary of St Mary's, York.
    Harley MS 491. Fragment of a mortuary roll, attached to a copy of William of Jumièges.
    Harley MS 662. Cartulary of Dunmow Priory.
    Harley MS 2110. Register of Castle-Acre Priory.
    Harley MS 3650. Kenilworth Cartulary.
    Harley MS 3763. Evesham Cartulary.
    Additional Charters 20415, 20580.
    Cotton Charter xi 7

Bodleian Library

    Dodsworth MSS 129, 148.
    Dugdale MSS 13, 15.
    MS James 23.
    Nottinghamshire charters, no. 2.

Cambridge University Library

    Add. MSS 3020–3021. The Red Book of Thorney.
    Peterborough D&C MS 1.

Spalding Gentlemen's Society

    Crowland Abbey Cartulary.

York Minster Library

    MS XVI.A.1. Cartulary of St. Mary's, York.

PRINTED SOURCES

ABBO OF FLEURY, *Life of Saint Edmund*, ed. Michael Winterbottom, Toronto Medieval Latin Texts (Toronto, 1972).

ADAM OF DRYBURGH, *De Tripartito Tabernaculo*, PL 198: 609–796.

ADAM OF EYNSHAM, *Magna Vita Sancti Hugonis: The Life of St Hugh of Lincoln*, ed. Decima L. Douie and David Hugh Farmer, 2nd edn., 2 vols (Oxford, 1985).

ADAM OF PETIT PONT, 'Adam of Petit Pont's *De Utensilibus*', in *Teaching and Learning Latin in Thirteenth-Century England*, vol. 1, ed. Tony Hunt (Cambridge, 1991).

ADELARD OF BATH, *Adelard of Bath, Conversations with his Nephew: On the Same and the Different, Questions on Natural Science, and On Birds*, ed. Charles Burnett (Cambridge, 1998).

ADGAR, *Le Gracial*, ed. Pierre Kunstmann (Ottowa, 1982).

AELFRIC, *Aelfric's Lives of Saints, Being a Set of Sermons on Saints' Days formerly observed by the English Church*, 4 parts in 2 vols., ed. Walter W. Skeat, EETS os 76, 82, 94, 114 (London, 1881–1900).

—— *The Homilies of the Anglo-Saxon Church: The First Part Containing the Sermones Catholici, or Homilies of Aelfric, in the Original Anglo-Saxon with an English Version*, ed. Benjamin Thorpe, 2 vols. (London, 1844–6; repr. 1971).

—— *Homilies of Aelfric: A Supplementary Collection*, ed. John C. Pope, 2 vols., EETS os 259–60 (London, 1967–8).

ÆLNOTH OF CANTERBURY, 'Gesta Swenomagni Regis et Filiorum eius et Passio Gloriosissimi Canuti Regis et Martyris', in *Vitae Sanctorum Danorum*, ed. M. C. Gertz (Copenhagen, 1908), 1: 77–136.

AELRED OF RIEVAULX, 'Vita S. Edwardi Regis et Confessoris', PL 195: 737–90.

—— 'Genealogia Regum Anglorum', PL 195: 711–38.

—— 'Speculum Caritatis', PL 195: 501–620.

—— 'Relatio de Standardo', in *Chronicles of the Reigns of Stephen, Henry II, and Richard I*, ed. Richard Howlett, Rolls Series (London, 1886), 3: 181–99.

—— 'De Sanctis Ecclesiae Haugustaldensis et eorum Miraculis Libellus', in *The Priory of Hexham*, ed. James Raine, Surtees Society, 44 (Durham, 1864) 1: 173–203.

AETHELWEARD, *The Chronicle of Aethelweard*, ed. A. Campbell (London, 1962).

ALEXANDER OF NECKAM, *De Naturis Rerum with the Poem of the Same Author, De Laudibus Divinae Sapientiae*, ed. Thomas Wright, Rolls Series (London, 1863).

ALEXANDER OF TELESE, *Alexandrini Telesini Abbatis Ystoria Rogerii Regis Siciliae, Calabriae, atque Apuliae*, ed. Ludovica de Vava, Fonti per la storia d'Italia, 112 (Rome, 1991).

ALFRED OF BEVERLEY, *Annales sive Historia de Gestis Regum Britanniae*, ed. Thomas Hearne (Oxford, 1716).

AMATUS OF MONTECASSINO, *L'Ystoir de li Normant et la Chronique de Robert Viscart*, ed. M. Champollion-Figeac (Paris, 1835; repr. New York, 1965).

Anonymous of Béthune, *Histoire des ducs de Normandie et des rois d'Angleterre*, ed. Francisque Michel, Société de l'Histoire de France (Paris, 1840).

ANSELM, *S. Anselmi Cantuariensis Archiepiscopi Opera Omnia*, ed. Francis Schmitt, 6 vols. (London, 1946–61).

ANSELM, *The Letters of Saint Anselm of Canterbury*, ed. Walter Fröhlich, 3 vols., Cistercian Studies Series, 96 (Kalamazoo, 1990–4).

ARNOLD, THOMAS, ed., *Memorials of St. Edmund's Abbey*, 3 vols., Rolls Series (London, 1890–6).

ASSER, *Asser's Life of King Alfred*, ed. W. H. Stevenson, 2nd edn. (London, 1959).

ATKINSON, J. C., ed., *Cartularium Abbathiae de Whiteby*, vol. 1, Surtees Society, 69 (Durham, 1879).

ATTENBOROUGH, F. L., ed., *The Laws of the Earliest English Kings* (Cambridge, 1922; repr. New York, 1963).

AUSTIN, DAVID, ed., *Boldon Book* (Chichester, 1982).

BARLEY, M. W., ed., *Documents Relating to the Manor and Soke of Newark-on-Trent*, Thoroton Society Record Series, 16 (Nottingham, 1956).

BARLOW, FRANK, ed., *The Life of King Edward Who Rests at Westminster*, 2nd edn. (Oxford, 1992).

The Barnwell Chronicle, in *The Historical Collections of Walter of Coventry*, ed. William Stubbs (London, 1873) 2: 196–279.

BARRACLOUGH, GEOFFREY, ed., *The Charters of the Anglo-Norman Earls of Chester c. 1071–1237*, Record Society of Lancashire and Cheshire, 126 (Gloucester, 1988).

BATES, DAVID, ed., *Regesta Regum Anglo-Normannorum: The Acta of William I (1066–1087)* (Oxford, 1998).

BAUDRI DE BOURGUEIL, *Les Oeuvres poétiques de Baudri de Bourgueil*, ed. Phyllis Abrahams (Paris, 1926).

—— *Itinerarium*, PL 166: 1173–82.

BEARMAN, ROBERT, ed., *Charters of the Redvers Family and the Earldom of Devon, 1090–1217*, Devon and Cornwall Record Series, NS 37 (Exeter, 1994).

BEDE, *Bede's Ecclesiastical History of the English People*, ed. Bertram Colgrave and R. A. B. Mynors (Oxford, 1969).

BELL, A., ed., 'The Anglo-Norman *Description of England*: An Edition', in *Anglo-Norman Anniversary Studies*, ed. Ian Short (London, 1993), 31–47.

BENOÏT, *Chronique des Ducs de Normandie par Benoit*, ed. Carin Fahlin (vols. 1–2) and Östen Södergård (vol. 3), 3 vols (Uppsala, 1951–67).

BESTUL, THOMAS H., ed., *A Durham Book of Devotions* (Toronto, 1987).

BETHELL, DENIS, ed., 'The Lives of St. Osyth of Essex and St. Osyth of Aylesbury', *Analecta Bollandiana*, 88 (1970), 75–127.

—— ed., 'The Miracles of St. Ithamar', *Analecta Bollandiana*, 89 (1971), 421–37.

BIDDLE, MARTIN, ed., *Winchester in the Early Middle Ages: An Edition and Discussion of the Winton Domesday* (Oxford, 1976).

BIRCH, WALTER DE GRAY, ed., *Vita Haroldi* (London, 1885).

—— ed., *Liber Vitae: Register and Martyrology of New Minster and Hyde Abbey, Winchester* (London, 1892).

BLAKE, E. O., ed., *Liber Eliensis*, Camden Society, 3rd ser., 92 (London, 1962).

BOND, EDWARD A., ed., *Chronica Monasterii de Melsa*, vol. 1, Rolls Series (London, 1866; repr. Nendeln, 1967).

The Book of Fees, Commonly Called Testa de Nevill, 3 vols. (London, 1920–31).

BOUTEMY, ANDRÉ, 'Notice sur le recueil poétique du manuscrit Cotton Vitellius A xii du British Museum', *Latomus*, 1 (1937), 278–313.

BRIDGEMAN, CHARLES G. O., 'The Burton Abbey Twelfth Century Surveys', *William Salt Archaeological Society Collections for a History of Staffordshire*, 3rd ser., 41 (1916), 209–300.

BROWN, P., ed., *Sibton Abbey Cartularies,* 4 vols. Suffolk Charters, 7–10 (Woodbridge, 1985–8).

[BYRHTFERTH], *Vita Sancti Egwini,* in *Vita quorundum Anglo-Saxonum,* ed. J. A. Giles, Caxton Society (London, 1854).

Calendar of Charter Rolls Preserved in the Public Record Office, vol. 2 (London, 1906).

Calendar of Charter Rolls Preserved in the Public Record Office, vol. 4 (London, 1912).

CAMDEN, W., *Remains Concerning Britain* (London, 1870).

CAMPBELL, ALISTAIR, ed., *Encomium Emmae Reginae,* Camden Society, 3rd ser., 72 (London, 1949).

CHARDRI, *Le Petit Plet,* ed. Brian Merrilees, Anglo-Norman Text Society, 20 (Oxford, 1970).

CHENEY, C. R., and W. H. SEMPLE, eds., *Selected Letters of Pope Innocent III concerning England (1198–1216)* (London, 1953).

CHIBNALL, MARJORIE, ed., *Charters and Custumals of the Abbey of Holy Trinity Caen,* British Academy Records of Social and Economic History, NS 5 (London, 1982).

CIGGAAR, KRIJNIE N., ed., 'L'Émigration anglaise à Byzance après 1066', *Revue des études Byzantines,* 32 (1974), 301–42.

CLAY, CHARLES, ed., *Yorkshire Deeds* 4, Yorkshire Archaeological Society Record Series, 65 (Leeds, 1924).

—— 'A Holderness Charter of William Count of Aumale', *Yorkshire Archaeological Journal,* 39 (1957), 339–42.

COLKER, MARVIN L., 'The Life of Guy of Merton by Rainald of Merton', *Mediaeval Studies,* 31 (1969), 250–61.

—— 'Latin Texts Concerning Gilbert, Founder of Merton Priory', *Studia Monastica,* 12 (1970), 241–70.

CONNOLLY, PHILOMENA, 'The Enactments of the 1297 Parliament', in *Law and Disorder in Thirteenth-century Ireland: The Dublin Parliament of 1297,* ed. James Lydon (Dublin, 1997), 139–61.

CORNOG, WILLIAM H., 'The Poems of Robert Partes', *Speculum,* 12 (1937), 215–50.

CRASTER, H. H. E., 'The Red Book of Durham', *English Historical Review* 40 (1925), 504–32.

CRAWFORD, S. J., ed., *The Old English Version of the Heptateuch,* EETS OS 160 (Oxford, 1922, repr. 1969).

CURLEY, MICHAEL J., 'A New Edition of John of Cornwall's *Prophetia Merlini*', *Speculum,* 57 (1982), 217–49.

DANIEL OF MORLEY, 'Philosophia', ed. Gregor Maurach, *Mittellateinisches Jahrbuch,* 14 (1979), 204–55.

DARLINGTON, REGINALD R., ed., *The Cartulary of Darley Abbey,* 2 vols. (Kendal, 1945).

DAVID, CHARLES WENDELL, ed., *De Expugnatione Lyxbonensi* (New York, 1936).

DAVIES, J. CONWAY, ed., *Cartae Antiquae Rolls 11–20,* Pipe Roll Society, NS 33 (London, 1960).

DAVIS, H. W. C., 'London Lands and Liberties of St. Paul's, 1066–1135', in *Essays in Medieval History Presented to Thomas Frederick Tout,* ed. A. G. Little and F. M. Powicke (Manchester, 1925), 45–59.

DAVIS, R. H. C., ed., *The Kalendar of Abbot Samson of Bury St. Edmunds and Related Documents,* Camden Society, 3rd ser., 84 (London, 1954).

'De S. Wereburga Virgine', *Acta Sanctorum* (Feb.) i. 391–4.

DELABORDE, H. FRANÇOIS, ed., *Oeuvres de Rigord et de Guillaume le Breton,* 2 vols. (Paris, 1882–5).

DELISLE, LÉOPOLD, ed., *Rouleaux des morts du IXe au XVe siècle* (Paris, 1866).

—— ed., *Recueil des actes de Henri II roi d'Angleterre et duc de Normandie,* 4 vols. (Paris, 1909–27).

DICKENS, BRUCE, and R. M. WILSON, eds., *Early Middle English Texts* (New York, 1951).

DOBBIE, ELLIOT VAN KIRK, ed., *The Anglo-Saxon Minor Poems* (New York, 1942).

DOUGLAS, DAVID C., ed., *Feudal Documents from the Abbey of Bury St. Edmunds*, British Academy Records of the Social and Economic History of England and Wales, 8 (London, 1932).

—— ed., *The Domesday Monachorum of Christ Church Canterbury* (London, 1944).

DOWNER, L. J., ed., *Leges Henrici Primi* (Oxford, 1972).

DUDO OF ST QUENTIN, *De Moribus et actis primorum Normanniae Ducum auctore Dudone Sancti Quintini Decano*, ed. Jules Lair (Caen, 1865).

DUGGAN, ANNE J., ed., *The Correspondence of Thomas Becket, Archbishop of Canterbury, 1162–1170* (Oxford, 2000).

DUMVILLE, DAVID, and MICHAEL LAPIDGE, eds., *The Annals of St Neots with Vita Prima Sancti Neoti*, vol. 17 of *The Anglo-Saxon Chronicle: A Collaborative Edition*, ed. David Dumville and Simon Keynes (Cambridge, 1984).

EADMER, *The Life of St Anselm Archbishop of Canterbury*, ed. Richard W. Southern (London, 1962; repr. Oxford, 1972).

—— 'Edmeri Cantuariensis Cantoris Nova Opuscula de Sanctorum Veneratione Obsecratione', ed. A. Wilmart, *Revue des Sciences Religieuse*, 15 (1935), 184–219, 355–79.

—— 'Vita S. Bregwini', in *Anglia Sacra*, vol. 1, ed. Henry Wharton (London, 1691), 184–90.

—— 'Vita Odonis', in *Anglia Sacra*, vol. 2, ed. Henry Wharton (London, 1691), 78–87.

—— 'Vita Wilfridi Episcopi', in *Historians of the Church of York*, vol. 1, ed. James Raine (London, 1879), 161–226.

——————, 'Vita Sancti Oswaldi', in *Historians of the Church of York*, vol. 2, ed. James Raine (London, 1886), 1–59.

EDWARDS, EDWARD, ed., *Liber Monasterii de Hyda*, Rolls Series (London, 1866).

ELMER, 'Écrits spirituels d'Elmer de Cantorbéry', ed. Jean Leclercq, *Studia Anselmiana*, 31 (1953), 45–117.

ELVEY, G. R., ed., *Luffield Priory Charters*, 2 vols., Northamptonshire Record Society, 22 and 26 (Welwyn Garden City, 1968–75).

ESPOSITO, M., 'On Some Unpublished Poems Attributed to Alexander Neckam', *EHR* 30 (1915), 450–71.

ÉTIENNE OF ROUEN, *Draco Normannicus*, in *Chronicles of the Reigns of Stephen, Henry II, and Richard I*, vol. 2, ed. Richard Howlett, Rolls Series (London, 1885).

EVERARD, JUDITH, and MICHAEL JONES, eds., *The Charters of Duchess Constance of Britanny and her Family, 1171–1221* (Woodbridge, 1999).

EWERT, ALFRED, ed., *Gui de Warewic*, 2 vols. (Paris, 1933).

EYTON, R. W., 'The Staffordshire Chartulary, Series I–II', *William Salt Archaeological Society Collections for a History of Staffordshire*, vol. 2 (Birmingham, 1881), 178–276.

FARAL, EDMOND, *Les Arts poétiques du XIIe et du XIIIe siècle* (Paris, 1924; repr. 1962).

FARITIUS, 'Vita S. Aldhelmi', *PL* 89: 63–84.

FARMER, HUGH, ed., 'The Vision of Orm', *Analecta Bollandiana*, 75 (1957), 72–82.

FARRER, WILLIAM, ed., *The Chartulary of Cockersand Abbey*, 7 vols., Chetham Society, NS 38–40, 43, 56–57, 64 (Manchester, 1898–1905).

—— ed., *The Lancashire Pipe Rolls and Early Lancashire Charters* (Liverpool, 1902).

FAUROUX, MARIE, ed., *Recueil des actes des ducs de Normandie de 911 à 1066*, Mémoires de la Société des Antiquaires de Normandie, tome 36, 4th series, vol. 6 (Caen, 1961).

Feet of Fines of the Reigns of Henry II and Richard I, Pipe Roll Society 17 (London, 1894).

FOLCARD, 'Vita S. Botulphi', *AASS* (June), iv. 327–8.

FORBES, ALEXANDER PENROSE, ed., *Lives of S. Ninian and S. Kentigern* (Edinburgh, 1874).

FOREVILLE, RAYMONDE and GILLIAN KEIR, eds., *The Book of St Gilbert* (Oxford, 1987).

FOSTER, C. W., and THOMAS LONGLEY, eds., *The Lincolnshire Domesday and the Lindsey Survey*, Lincoln Record Society 19 (Gainsborough, 1924; repr. 1976).

—— and KATHLEEN MAJOR, eds., *The Registrum Antiquissimum of the Cathedral Church of Lincoln*, 10 vols., Lincoln Record Society, 27–9, 32, 34, 41, 46, 51, 62, 67 (Hereford and Gateshead, 1931–73).

FOULDS, TREVOR, ed., *The Thurgarton Cartulary* (Stamford, 1994).

FOWLER, G. HERBERT, ed., *Cartulary of the Abbey of Old Wardon*, Bedfordshire Historical Record Society, 13 (Aspley Guise, 1930).

FRANKLIN, M. J., ed., *The Cartulary of Daventry Priory*, Northamptonshire Record Society, 35 (Northampton, 1988).

FRIEDBERG, EMIL, ed., *Corpus Iuris Canonici*, vol. 2 (Leipzig, 1879).

GEFFREI GAIMAR, *L'Estoire des Engleis*, ed. Alexander Bell, Anglo-Norman Text Society, 14–16 (Oxford, 1960).

GEOFFREY OF BURTON, *Life and Miracles of St Modwenna*, ed. Robert Bartlett (Oxford, 2002).

GEOFFREY OF COLDINGHAM, 'Vita Bartholomaei Farnensis', in *SMO* 1: 295–325.

GEOFFREY OF MALATERRA, *De Rebus Gestis Rogerii Calabriae et Siciliae Comitis et Roberti Guiscardi Ducis fratris eius*, ed. Ernesto Pontieri, Rerum Italicarum Scriptores, vol. 5, pt. 1 (Bologna, 1927–8).

GEOFFREY OF MONMOUTH, *The Historia Regum Britannie of Geoffrey of Monmouth I. Bern, Burgerbibliothek, MS. 568*, ed. Neil Wright (Cambridge, 1984).

GEOFFREY OF WELLS, 'Geoffrey of Wells, De Infantia Sancti Edmundi', ed. R. M. Thomson. *Analecta Bollandiana*, 95 (1977), 25–42.

GERALD OF WALES, *De Invectionibus*, ed. W. S. Davies, *Y Cymmrodor*, 30 (1920), 1–248.

—— *Speculum Duorum*, ed. Yves Lefèvre, R. B. C. Huygens, and Brian Dawson (Cardiff, 1974).

—— *Expugnatio Hibernica: The Conquest of Ireland*, ed. A. B. Scott and F. X. Martin (Dublin, 1978).

GERVASE OF CANTERBURY, *The Historical Works of Gervase of Canterbury*, ed. William Stubbs, 2 vols., Rolls Series (London, 1879–80).

GERVASE OF TILBURY, *Otia Imperialia: Recreation for an Emperor*, ed. S. E. Banks and J. W. Binns (Oxford, 2002).

GERVERS, MICHAEL, ed., *The Cartulary of the Knights of St. John of Jerusalem in England: Secunda Camera*, British Academy Records of Social and Economic History, NS 6 (Oxford, 1982).

GIBBS, MARION, ed., *Early Charters of the Cathedral Church of St. Paul, London*, Camden Society, 3rd ser., 58 (London, 1939).

GILBERT CRISPIN, *The Works of Gilbert Crispin Abbot of Westminster*, ed. Anna Sapir Abulafia and G. R. Evans, British Academy, *Auctores Britannici Medii Aevi*, 8 (Oxford, 1986).

GILES, JOHN A., ed., 'Vita et Passio Waldevi Comitis', in *Original Lives of Anglo-Saxons and Others Who Lived before the Conquest*, Caxton Society, 16 (1854; repr. New York, 1967), 1–31.

GOODMAN, A. W., ed., *Chartulary of Winchester Cathedral* (Winchester, 1927).

GOSCELIN OF SAINT-BERTIN, 'Libellus de Miraculis Sancti Augustini', *AASS*, 3rd edn. (Metz, 1935) 1: 535–9.

GOSCELIN OF SAINT-BERTIN, 'Historia Translationis S. Augustini Episcopi', *PL* 155: 13–46.
—— 'The Liber Confortatorius of Goscelin of Saint Bertin', ed. C. H. Talbot, *Studia Anselmiana*, 38 (1955), 1–117.
—— 'The Life of Saint Wulsin of Sherborne by Goscelin', ed. C. H. Talbot, *Revue Bénédictine*, 69 (1969), 68–85.
GRAINGER, FRANCIS, and W. G. COLLINGWOOD, eds., *The Register and Records of Holm Cultram*, Cumberland and Westmorland Antiquarian and Archaeological Society Record Series, 7 (Kendal, 1929).
GREENWAY, D. E., ed., *Charters of the Honour of Mowbray, 1107–1191*, British Academy Records of Social and Economic History, NS 1 (London, 1972).
GREENWAY, DIANA, and LESLIE WATKISS, eds., *The Book of the Foundation of Walden Monastery* (Oxford, 1999).
GROSJEAN, PAUL, ed., 'Vitae S. Roberti Knaresburgensis', in *Analecta Bollandiana*, 57 (1939), 364–400.
—— ed., 'Translatio S. Swithuni', *Analecta Bollandiana*, 58 (1940), 190–6.
GUY OF AMIENS, *The Carmen de Hastingae Proelio of Guy, Bishop of Amiens*, ed. Frank Barlow (Oxford, 1999).
HALE, WILLIAM, ed., *The Domesday of St. Paul's*, Camden Society, 69 (London, 1858).
HALL, G. D. G., ed., *The Treatise on the Laws and Customs of the Realm of England Commonly Called Glanvill*, 2nd edn. (Oxford, 1993).
HALL, HUBERT, ed., *The Red Book of the Exchequer*, 3 vols., Rolls Series (London, 1896).
HAMILTON, N. E. S. A., ed., *Inquisitio Comitatus Cantabrigiensis* (London, 1876).
HARDY, T. D., and C. T. MARTIN, eds., *Gesta Herwardi* and *La Lai d'Haveloc le Danois*, in *Lestorie des Engleis*, Rolls Series (London, 1889), 1: 535–59.
HARMER, F. E., ed., *Anglo-Saxon Writs* (Manchester, 1952; repr. Stamford, 1989).
HARPER-BILL, CHRISTOPHER, and RICHARD MORTIMER, eds., *Stoke by Clare Cartulary*, 3 vols., Suffolk Charters, 4–6 (Woodbridge, 1982–4).
HART, CYRIL, 'An Early Charter of Adam of Cockfield, 1100–1118', *EHR* 72 (1957), 466–9.
—— ed., *The Thorney Annals 963–1412 A. D* (Lewiston, 1997).
HART, WILLIAM HENRY, ed., *Historia et Cartularium Monasterii Sancti Petri Gloucestriæ*, 3 vols. (London, 1863–7).
—— and PONSONBY A. LYONS, eds., *Cartularium Monasterii de Rameseia*, 3 vols., Rolls Series (London, 1884–93).
HASSALL, W. O., ed., *The Cartulary of St Mary Clerkenwell*, Camden Society, 3rd ser., 71 (London, 1949).
HAURÉAU, B., 'Un poème inédit de Pierre Riga', *Bibliothèque de l'École des Chartres*, 44 (1883), 5–11.
HEARNE, THOMAS, ed., *Textus Roffensis* (Oxford, 1720).
HEMMING, *Chartularium Ecclesiae Wigorniensis*, ed. Thomas Hearne (Oxford, 1723).
HERBERT DE LOSINGA, *Epistolae Herberti de Losinga*, ed. Robert Anstruther, Caxton Society, 5 (London, 1846).
HERMAN, 'De Miraculis Sancti Eadmundi', in *Memorials of St. Edmund's Abbey*, ed. Thomas Arnold, Rolls Series (London, 1890), 1: 26–92.
HERMANN, 'De Miraculis S. Mariae Laudunensis', *PL* 156: 961–1018.
HERZFELD, GEORGE, ed., *An Old English Martyrology*, *EETS* OS 116 (London, 1900).
HILDEBERT OF LAVARDIN, *Hildeberti Cenomannensis Episcopi Carmina Minora*, ed. A. Brian Scott (Leipzig, 1969).
—— *Opera*, *PL* 171: 135–1158.

HILTON, R. H., ed., *The Stoneleigh Leger Book*, Dugdale Society, 24 (Oxford, 1960; repr. Nendeln, 1968).

HINDE, HODGSON, ed., 'Vita S. Margaretae Scotorum Reginae', in *Symeonis Dunelmensis Opera*, Surtees Society, 51 (Durham, 1868), 1: 234–54.

HODGETT, G. A. J., ed., *Cartulary of Holy Trinity Aldgate*, London Record Society, 7 (London, 1971).

HOFFMAN, HARTMUT, ed., *Chronica Monasterii Casinensis*, Monumenta Germaniae Historica SS 34 (Hanover, 1980).

HOLDEN, A. J., ed., *Le Roman de Waldef (cod. Bodmer 168)* (Cologny–Genève, 1984).

HOLDSWORTH, C. J., ed., *Rufford Charters*, 4 vols., Thoroton Society Record Series, 29, 30, 32, 34 (Nottingham, 1972–81).

HOLLINGS, MARJORIE, ed., *The Red Book of Worcester*, 4 parts (London, 1934–40).

HOLT, J. C., and RICHARD MORTIMER, Acta *of Henry II and Richard I*, List and Index Society, 21 (Richmond, Surrey, 1986).

HUGH CANDIDUS, *The Chronicle of Hugh Candidus a Monk of Peterborough*, ed. W. T. Mellows (London, 1949).

HUGH THE CHANTER, *The History of the Church of York, 1066–1127*, ed. Charles Johnson, rev. M. Brett, C. N. L. Brooke, and M. Winterbottom (Oxford, 1990).

HULL, P. L., ed., *The Cartulary of Launceston Priory*, Devon and Cornwall Record Society, NS 40 (Torquay, 1987).

HULTON, W. A., ed., *Documents Relating to the Priory of Penwortham*, Chetham Society, 30 (Manchester, 1853).

ISAAC DE STELLA, 'Epistola ad Joannem Episcopam Pictaviensem de Officio Missae', *PL* 194: 1889–96.

IVO OF CHARTRES, 'Letters', *PL* 162: 11–288.

JEAYES, ISAAC HERBERT, ed., *Descriptive Catalogue of the Charters and Muniments in the Possession of the Rt. Hon. Lord Fitzhardinge at Berkeley Castle* (Bristol, 1892).

—— ed., 'Descriptive Catalogue of the Charters and Muniments Belonging to the Marquis of Anglesey', *William Salt Archaeological Society Collections for a History of Staffordshire*, vol. 61 (Kendal, 1937), 1–195.

JENKINS, J. G., ed., *Charters of Missenden Abbey*, 3 vols., Buckinghamshire Record Society, 2, 10 (Twichells End and London, 1938–62).

JOCELIN OF BRAKELOND, *The Chronicle of Jocelin of Brakelond*, ed. H. E. Butler (London, 1949).

JOCELIN OF FURNESS, *Vita Sancti Waltheni*, in *AASS: Augusti Tomus Primus* (Paris, 1867), 249–78.

JOHN OF FORD, *Wulfric of Haselbury*, ed. Maurice Bell, Somerset Record Society, 47 (Frome, 1933).

JOHN DE HAUVILLE, *Architrenius*, ed. Winthrop Wetherbee (Cambridge, 1994).

JOHN OF ST OUEN, 'Translationes Audoeni', in *AASS August*, 4: 820–4.

JOHN OF SALISBURY, *The Letters of John of Salisbury*, ed. W. J. Millor, H. E. Butler, and C. N. L. Brooke, 2 vols., 2nd edn. (Oxford, 1986).

—— *Metalogicon*, ed. J. B. Hall and K. S. B. Rohan, *Corpus Christianorum Continuatio Mediaevalis*, 98 (Turnhout, 1991).

JONES, THOMAS, ed., *Brut y Tywysogion or The Chronicle of the Princes: Red Book of Hergest Version*, 2nd edn., Cardiff, 1973).

JONES, W. H. RICH, ed., *The Register of S. Osmund*, 2 vols., Rolls Series (London, 1883–4).

JORDAN FANTOSME, *Jordan Fantosme's Chronicle*, ed. R. C. Johnston (Oxford, 1981).

KEMBLE, J. M., ed., *Codex Diplomaticus Aevi Saxonici*, 6 vols. (London, 1839–48).

KEMP, B. R., ed., *Reading Abbey Cartularies*, 2 vols., Camden Society, 4th ser., 31, 33 (London, 1986).

KENNEDY, A. G., 'Cnut's Law Code of 1018', *Anglo-Saxon England*, 11 (1983), 57–81.

KING, EDMUND, ed., 'Estate Records of the Hotot Family', *A Northamptonshire Miscellany*, 1–58, Northamptonshire Record Society, 32 (Northampton, 1983).

KLUGE, F, 'Fragment eines angelsächsischen Briefes', *Englische Studien*, 8 (1885), 62–63.

LACOMBE, GEORGE, 'An Unpublished Document on the Great Interdict (1207–1213)', *Catholic Historical Review*, NS 9 (1930), 408–20.

LANCASTER, WILLIAM T., ed., *Abstracts of the Charters and Other Documents Contained in the Chartulary of the Cistercian Abbey of Fountains*, 2 vols. (Leeds., 1915–18).

LANDON, LIONEL, ed., *The Cartae Antiquae Rolls 1–10*, Pipe Roll Society, NS 17 (London, 1939).

LANFRANC, *The Monastic Constitutions of Lanfranc*, ed. David Knowles (New York, 1951).

—— *The Letters of Lanfranc Archbishop of Canterbury*, ed. Helen Clover and Margaret Gibson (Oxford, 1979).

LAPIDGE, MICHAEL, ed., *Anglo-Saxon Litanies of the Saints*, Henry Bradshaw Society, 106 (Woodbridge, 1991).

LAPORTE, J., ed., 'Inventio et Miracula Sancti Wulfranni', Société de l'histoire de Normandie, *Mélanges*, 14 (1938), 7–87.

LAWRENCE OF DURHAM, *Dialogi Laurentii Dunelmensis Monachi ac Prioris*, ed. James Raine, Surtees Society, 70 (Durham, 1880).

LAȝAMON, *Laȝamon: Brut*, ed. G. L. Brook and R. F. Leslie, 2 vols., EETS, 250, 270 (London, 1963–78).

LEES, BEATRICE A., ed., *Records of the Templars in England in the Twelfth Century*, British Academy Records of the Social and Economic History of England and Wales, 9 (London, 1935; repr. Munich, 1981).

LEYS, AGNES M., ed., *The Sandford Cartulary*, 2 vols., Oxford Record Society, 19, 22 (Oxford, 1938–41).

'Libellus de Revelatione, Ædificatione et Auctoritate Fiscannensis Monasterii', in *PL* 151: 699–724.

LIEBERMANN, F., 'An Early English Document of About 1080', *Yorkshire Archaeological Journal*, 18 (1905), 412–16.

—— ed., 'Raginald von Canterbury', *Neues Archiv der Gesellschaft für ältere deutsche Geschichtskunde*, 13 (1888), 517–56.

—— ed., *Die Gesetze der Angelsachsen*, 3 vols. (Halle, 1903–16).

LOUD, GRAHAM A., and THOMAS WIEDEMANN, eds., *The History of the Tyrants of Sicily by 'Hugo Falcandus' 1154–69* (Manchester, 1998).

LOVE, ROSALIND C. ed., *Three Eleventh-century Anglo-Latin Saints' Lives* (Oxford, 1996).

LOYD, LEWIS C., and DORIS MARY STENTON, eds., *Sir Christopher Hatton's Book of Seals* (Oxford, 1950).

LUARD, HENRY RICHARD, ed., *Annales Monastici*, 5 vols., Rolls Series (London, 1864–9).

LUCIAN, *Liber Luciani de Laude Cestrie*, ed. M. V. Taylor, Lancashire and Cheshire Record Society, 64 ([Edinburgh], 1912).

McNULTY, JOSEPH, ed., *The Chartulary of the Cistercian Abbey of St Mary of Sallay in Craven*, 2 vols., Yorkshire Archaeological Society Record Series, 87, 90 (Wakefield, 1933–4).

MACRAY, W. DUNN, ed., *Chronicon Abbatiae de Evesham*, Rolls Series (London, 1863).

—— ed., *Chronicon Abbatiae Rameseiensis*, Rolls Series (London, 1886).

MARBOD, *Opera*, *PL* 171: 1158–782.

MARIE DE FRANCE, *Fables*, ed. Harriet Spiegel (Toronto, 1987).

MASON, EMMA, ed., *The Beauchamp Cartulary Charters 1100–1268*, Pipe Roll Society, NS 43 (London, 1983).

—— *Westminster Abbey Charters, 1066–c. 1214*, London Record Society, 25 (London, 1998).

MATTHEW PARIS, *Chronica Majora*, ed. Henry Richards Luard, 7 vols., Rolls Society (London, 1872–83).

MAYR-HARTING, H., ed., *The Acta of the Bishops of Chichester, 1075–1207*, Canterbury and York Society (Torquay, 1964).

MEYER, PAUL, ed., *L'Histoire de Guillaume le Maréchal*, Société de l'Histoire de France, 3 vols. (Paris, 1891–1901).

MOORE, JOHN S., ed., *Domesday Book: Gloucestershire* (Chichester, 1982).

MOORE, STUART A., ed., *Cartularium Monasterii Sancti Johannis Baptiste de Colecestria*, 2 vols., Roxburgh Club (London, 1897).

MOREY, ADRIAN, and C. N. L. BROOKE, eds., *The Letters and Charters of Gilbert Foliot* (Cambridge, 1967).

MOZLEY, J. H., 'The Collection of Mediaeval Latin Verse in MS. Cotton Titus D. XXIV', *Medium Ævum*, 11 (1942), 1–45.

NICHOLS, FRANCIS MORGAN, ed., *Britton*, vol. 1 (1865; repr. Holmes Beach, 1983).

NIGEL DE LONGCHAMP, *Speculum Stultorum*, ed. John H. Mozley and Robert R. Raymo (Berkeley, 1960).

Ninth Report of the Royal Commission of Historical Manuscripts, Appendix (London, 1883; repr. Nendeln, 1979).

O'BRIEN, BRUCE R., *God's Peace and King's Peace: The Laws of Edward the Confessor* (Philadelphia, 1999).

ODO OF CANTERBURY, *The Latin Sermons of Odo of Canterbury*, ed. Charles de Clercq (Brussels, 1983).

OFFLER, H. S., ed., *Durham Episcopal Charters 1071–1152*, Surtees Society, 179 (Gateshead, 1968).

ORM, *The Ormulum*, ed. Robert Holt (Oxford, 1878; repr. New York, 1974).

ORPEN, GODDARD HENRY, ed., *The Song of Dermot and the Earl* (Oxford, 1892).

OSBEORN OF CANTERBURY, *Vita Sancti Elphegi* and *Eiusdem Sancti Translatio*, in *PL* 149: 371–94.

OSBERT OF CLARE, 'La Vie de S. Édouard le Confesseur par Osbert de Clare', ed. Marc Bloch, *Analecta Bollandiana*, 41 (1923), 1–131.

—— *The Letters of Osbert of Clare, Prior of Westminster*, ed. E. W. Williamson (London, 1929).

OWEN, A. E. B., ed., *The Medieval Lindsey Marsh: Select Documents*, Lincoln Record Society, 85 (Woodbridge, 1996).

PATTERSON, ROBERT B., ed., *Earldom of Gloucester Charters: The Charters and Scribes of the Earls and Countesses of Gloucester to A.D. 1217* (Oxford, 1973).

PELTERET, DAVID A. E., ed., *A Catalogue of English Post-conquest Vernacular Documents* (Woodbridge, 1990).

PETER OF BLOIS, *Opera*, *PL* 207.

—— *The Later Letters of Peter of Blois*, ed. Elizabeth Revell, *Auctores Britannici Medii Aevi*, 13 (Oxford, 1993).

PETER OF CELLE, *The Letters of Peter of Celle*, ed. Julian Haseldine (Oxford, 2001).

PETER OF CORNWALL, 'Peter of Cornwall: The Visions of Ailsi and his Sons', ed. Robert Easting and Richard Sharpe, *Mediavistik*, 1 (1988), 207–62.

PHILIP, Prior of St Frideswide's, *De Miraculis Sanctae Frideswidae, AASS* (Oct.), 8: 568–89.

PLUMMER, CHARLES, and JOHN EARL, eds., 'Acta Lanfranci', in *Two Saxon Chronicles Parallel* (Oxford, 1892; repr. 1972), 1: 287–92.

PONCELET, A., ed., 'Sanctae Catharinae Virginis et Martyris Translatio et Miracula Rotomagensia', *Analecta Bollandiana*, 22 (1903), 423–38.

POTTER, K. R., and R. H. C. DAVIS, eds., *Gesta Stephani* (Oxford, 1976).

PRESCOTT, J. E., ed., *The Register of the Priory of Wetherhal*, Cumberland and Westmorland Antiquarian and Archaeological Society (London, 1897).

RAINE, JAMES, ed., *Miscellanea Biographica*, Surtees Society, 8 (London, 1838).

—— ed., *Liber Vitae Ecclesiae Dunelmensis*, Surtees Society, 41 (London, 1841).

RALPH OF COGGESHALL, *Radulphi de Coggeshall Chronicon Anglicanum*, ed. Joseph Stevenson, Rolls Series (London, 1875).

RALPH OF DICETO, *The Historical Works of Master Ralph de Diceto*, ed. William Stubbs, 2 vols., Rolls Series (London, 1876).

RANSFORD, ROSALIND, ed., *The Early Charters of the Augustinian Canons of Waltham Abbey, Essex 1062–1320*, Studies in the History of Medieval Religion, 2 (Woodbridge, 1989).

Recueil des Historiens des Croisades: Historiens Occidentaux, vols. 3–4 (Paris, 1866–79; repr. Farnborough, 1967).

REES, UNA, ed., *The Cartulary of Shrewsbury Abbey*, 2 vols. (Aberystwyth, 1975).

—— ed., *The Cartulary of Haughmond Abbey* (Cardiff, 1985).

REGINALD OF CANTERBURY, *The Vita Sancti Malchi of Reginald of Canterbury*, ed. Levi Robert Lind, University of Illinois Studies in Language and Literature, 27: 3–4, (Urbana, Ill., 1942).

REGINALD OF DURHAM, *Libellus de Admirandis Beati Cuthberti Virtutibus*, Surtees Society, 1 (London, 1835).

—— *Libellus de Vita et Miraculis Sancti Godrici, Heremitæ de Finchale*, ed. Joseph Stevenson, Surtees Society, 20 (London, 1847).

Report on the Manuscripts of Lord Middleton, Historical Manuscripts Commission (London, 1911).

RICHARD FITZ NIGEL, *Dialogus de Scaccario*, ed. Charles Johnson, F. E. L. Carter, and D. E. Greenway, rev. edn. (Oxford, 1983).

RICHARD OF DEVIZES, *The Chronicle of Richard of Devizes of the Time of King Richard the First*, ed. John T. Appleby (London, 1963).

RICHARD OF HEXHAM, *De Gestis Regis Stephani et de Bello Standardi*, in *Chronicles of the Reigns of Stephen, Henry II, and Richard I*, vol. 3, ed. Richard Howlett, Rolls Series (London, 1886), 139–78.

—— 'History of the Church of Hexham', in *The Priory of Hexham*, ed. James Raine, Surtees Society, 44 (Durham, 1864), 1: 1–66.

RICHARDSON, H. G., and G. O. SAYLES, eds., *Select Cases of Procedure Without Writ under Henry III*, Selden Society, 60 (London, 1941).

RICHTER, MICHAEL, ed., *Canterbury Professions*, Canterbury and York Society, 67 (Torquay, 1973).

ROBERT OF BRIDLINGTON, *The Bridlington Dialogue*, ed. A Religious of C.S.M.V (London, 1960).

ROBERT OF TORIGNI, *The Chronicle of Robert of Torigni*, in *Chronicles of the Reigns of Stephen, Henry II, and Richard I*, vol. 4, ed. Richard Howlett (London, 1889).

ROBERTSON, A. J., ed., *The Laws of the Kings of England from Edmund to Henry I* (Cambridge, 1925).

ROBERTSON, A. J., ed., *Anglo-Saxon Charters* (Cambridge, 1956).

ROGER OF HOWDEN, *Chronica Magistri Rogeri de Hovedene*, ed. William Stubbs, 4 vols., Rolls Series (London, 1868–71).

[——], *Gesta Regis Henrici Secundi Benedicti Abbatis*, ed. William Stubbs, 2 vols., Rolls Series (London, 1867).

ROGER OF WENDOVER, *The Flowers of History*, ed. Henry G. Hewlett, 3 vols. (London, 1886–9).

ROMUALD OF SALERNO, *Romualdi Salernitani Chronicon*, ed. C. A. Garufi, *Rerum Italicarum Scriptores*, vol. 7, part 1 (Città di Castello, 1935).

ROSS, C. D., and MARY DEVINE, eds., *The Cartulary of Cirencester Abbey*, 3 vols. (London, 1964–77).

ROUND, J. H., ed., 'The Northamptonshire Survey', in *VCH Northamptonshire*, ed. W. R. D. Adkins and R. M. Serjeantson (Westminster, 1902), 1: 356–92.

—— 'Bernard, the King's Scribe', *EHR* 14 (1899), 417–30.

—— ed., *Calendar of Documents Preserved in France Illustrative of the History of Great Britain and Ireland* (London, 1899).

—— ed., *Rotuli de Dominabus et Pueris et Puellis de XII Comitatibus [1185]*, Pipe Roll Society Publications, 35 (London, 1913; repr. Vaduz, 1966).

ROYCE, DAVID, ed., *Landboc sive Registrum Monasterii Beatae Mariae Virginis et Sancti Cenhelmi de Winchelcumba in Comitatu Gloucestrensi Ordinis Sancti Benedicti*, 2 vols. (Exeter, 1892–1903).

RYMER, THOMAS, ed., *Foedera*, vol. 1, part 1 (London, 1816).

SALTER, H. E., ed., *Eynsham Cartulary*, 2 vols., Oxford Historical Society, 49, 51 (Oxford, 1907–8).

—— ed., *Cartulary of the Hospital of St. John the Baptist*, 3 vols., Oxford Historical Society, 66–9 (Oxford, 1914–16).

—— ed., *Facsimiles of Early Charters in Oxford Muniment Rooms* (Oxford, 1929).

—— ed., *The Cartulary of Oseney Abbey*, 6 vols., Oxford Historical Society, 89–91, 97–8, 101 (Oxford, 1929–36).

—— ed., *The Boarstall Cartulary*, Oxford Historical Society, 88 (Oxford, 1930).

—— ed., *The Thame Cartulary*, 2 vols., Oxford Record Society, 25–6 (Oxford, 1947–8).

SALTMAN, AVROM, ed., *The Cartulary of Tutbury Priory* (London, 1962).

SALZMAN, L. F., ed., *The Chartulary of the Priory of St. Pancreas of Lewes*, 2 vols., Sussex Record Society, 38, 40 (Lewes, 1932–4).

SCOTT, A. B., 'Some Poems Attributed to Richard of Cluny', in *Medieval Learning and Literature: Essays Presented to Richard William Hunt*, ed. J. J. G. Alexander and M. T. Gibson (Oxford, 1976), 181–99.

SEARLE, ELEANOR, ed., *The Chronicle of Battle Abbey* (Oxford, 1980).

SÖDERGÅRD, ÖSTEN, ed., *La Vie d'Edouard le Confesseur: Poème Anglo-normand du XIIᵉ siècle* (Uppsala, 1948).

SOMNER, WILLIAM, *Dictionarium Saxonico-Latino-Anglicum* (1659; repr. Menston, 1970).

SOUTHERN, RICHARD W. and F. S. SCHMITT, eds., *Memorials of St. Anselm*, British Academy, Auctores Britannici Medii Aevi, 1 (Oxford, 1969).

STACY, N. E., *The Surveys of the Estates of Glastonbury Abbey, c. 1135–1201*, British Academy Records of Social and Economic History, NS 33 (Oxford, 2001).

STAPLETON, THOMAS, ed., *Chronicon Petroburgense*, Camden Society, 47 (London, 1849).

STENTON, DORIS MARY, ed., *Rolls of the Justices in Eyre for Lincolnshire 1218–19 and Worcestershire 1221*, Selden Society, 53 (London, 1924).

—— ed., *Pleas before the King or his Justices, 1198–1212*, vol. 4, Selden Society, 84 (London, 1967).

STENTON, F. M., ed., *Documents Illustrative of the Social and Economic History of the Danelaw*,

British Academy Records of the Social and Economic History of England and Wales, 5 (London, 1920).

—— ed., *Facsimiles of Early Charters from Northamptonshire Collections*, Northamptonshire Record Society, 4 (Northampton, 1930).

STEVENSON, J., ed., *Liber Vitae Ecclesiae Dunelmensis* (London, 1841).

—— ed., *Chronicon Monasterii de Abingdon*, 2 vols., Rolls Series (London, 1858).

STEVENSON, W. HENRY, ed., *Records of the Borough of Nottingham*, vol. 1 (London, 1882).

STUBBS, WILLIAM, ed., *Itinerarium Peregrinorum et Gesta Regis Ricardi*, Rolls Series (London, 1864).

—— ed., *Chronicles and Memorials of the reign of Richard I*, vol 2, *Epistolae Cantuariensis*, Rolls Series (London, 1865).

—— ed., *Memorials of Saint Dunstan Archbishop of Canterbury*, Rolls Series (London, 1874, repr. Wiesbaden, 1965).

—— ed., *Select Charters and Other Illustrations of English Constitutional History*, 8th edn. (Oxford, 1900).

SUGER, *Oeuvres Complètes de Suger*, ed. A. Lecoy de la March (Paris, 1867).

SWEET, HENRY, ed., *King Alfred's West-Saxon Version of Gregory's Pastoral Care*, 2 vols., EETS, 45 and 50 (London, 1871).

TAIT, JAMES, ed., *The Chartulary or Register of the Abbey of St. Werburgh, Chester*, 2 vols., Chetham Society, NS 79, 82 (Manchester, 1920–23).

TALBOT, C. H., ed., *The Life of Christina of Markyate: A Twelfth Century Recluse* (Oxford, 1959; repr. 1987).

—— 'The *Centum Sententiae* of Walter Daniel', *Sacris Erudiri*, 11 (1960), 266–383.

THOMAS OF KENT, *The Anglo-Norman Alexander*, ed. Brian Foster and Ian Short, Anglo-Norman Text Society, 32–3 (London, 1976–77).

THOMAS OF MONMOUTH, *The Life and Miracles of William of Norwich*, ed. Augustus Jessopp and Montague Rhodes James (Cambridge, 1896).

THOMSON, RODNEY, 'Twelfth-Century Documents from Bury St Edmunds Abbey', *EHR* 92 (1977), 806–819.

—— *The Life of Gundulf Bishop of Rochester*, Toronto Medieval Latin Texts (Toronto, 1977).

THORPE, BENJAMIN, ed., *Diplomatarium Anglicum Aevi Saxonici* (London, 1865).

TIMSON, R. T., ed., *The Cartulary of Blyth Priory*, 2 vols., Thoroton Society Record Series, 27–28 (London, 1973).

TURNER, G. J. and H. E. SALTER, eds., *The Register of St. Augustine's Abbey Canterbury Commonly Called the Black Book*, 2 vols., British Academy Records of the Social and Economic History of England and Wales, 2–3 (London, 1915–24).

URRY, WILLIAM, *Canterbury under the Angevin Kings* (London, 1967).

VAN CAENEGEM, R. C., ed., *Royal Writs in England from the Conquest to Glanvill: Studies in the Early History of the Common Law*, Selden Society, 77 (London, 1959).

—— ed., *English Lawsuits from William I to Richard I*, 2 vols., Selden Society, 106–7 (London, 1990–1).

Vita Lanfranci, PL 150: 29–58.

WACE, *Le Roman de Rou*, ed. A. J. Holden, 3 vols., Société des Anciens Textes Français (Paris, 1970–3).

WALKER, DAVID, ed., 'Charters of the Earldom of Hereford, 1095–1201', in *Camden Miscellany* 22, Camden Society, 4th ser., 1 (London, 1964).

—— ed., *The Cartulary of St Augustine's Abbey, Bristol*, Bristol and Gloucestershire Archaeological Society, Gloucestershire Record Series, 10 (Bristol, 1998).

WALSINGHAM, THOMAS, *Gesta Abbatum Sancti Albani*, ed. Henry Thomas Riley, 3 vols., Rolls Series (London, 1867–9).

WALTER DANIEL, *The Life of Ailred of Rievaulx*, ed. Maurice Powicke (London, 1950; repr. Oxford, 1978).

WALTER MAP, *De Nugis Curialium: Courtiers' Trifles*, ed. M. R. James, rev. C. N. L. Brooke and R. A. B. Mynors (Oxford, 1983).

WALTHER, HANS, 'Scherz und Ernst in der Völker- und Stämme-Charakteristik mittel-lateinischer Verse', *Archiv für Kulturgeschichte*, 41 (1959), 263–301.

WARNER OF ROUEN, *Moriuht: A Norman Latin Poem from the Early Eleventh Century*, ed. Christopher J. McDonough (Toronto, 1995).

WARNER, GEORGE F., and HENRY J. ELLIS, eds., *Facsimiles of Royal and Other Charters in the British Museum* (Oxford, 1903).

WATKINS, AELRED, ed., *The Great Chartulary of Glastonbury*, 3 vols., Somerset Record Society, 59, 63, 64 (Frome, 1947–56).

WATKISS, LESLIE, and MARJORIE CHIBNALL, eds., *The Waltham Chronicle* (Oxford, 1994).

WEBB, A. N., ed., *An Edition of the Cartulary of Burscough Priory*, Chetham Society, 3rd ser., 18 (Manchester, 1970).

WEST, J. R., ed., *St. Benet of Holme, 1020–1210*, 2 vols., Norfolk Record Society, 2–3 (n.p., 1932).

WHARTON, HENRY, ed., *Anglia Sacra*, 2 vols. (London, 1691).

WHITELOCK, D., M. BRETT, C. N. L. BROOKE, eds., *Councils and Synods: With Other Documents Relating to the English Church*, vol. 1, pt. 1: *AD 871–1066*; pt. 2: *1066–1204* (Oxford, 1981).

WIGRAM, SPENCER ROBERT, ed., *The Cartulary of the Monastery of St. Frideswide at Oxford*, 2 vols., Oxford Historical Society, 28 and 31 (Oxford, 1895–96).

WILLIAM OF APULIA, *La Geste de Robert Guiscard*, ed. Marguerite Mathieu (Palermo, 1961).

WILLIAM OF MALMESBURY, *El libro 'De laudibus et miraculis Sanctae Mariae' de Guillermo de Malmesbury*, ed. José M. Canal, 2nd edn. (Rome, 1968).

—— *Historia Novella*, ed. Edmund King and K. R. Potter (Oxford, 1998).

—— *The Early History of Glastonbury: An Edition, Translation and Study of William of Malmesbury's* De Antiquitate Glastonie Ecclesie, ed. John Scott (Woodbridge, 1981).

WILLIAM OF NEWBURGH, 'Sermo de Sancto Albano', in *Guilelmi Neubrigensis Historia sive Chronica Rerum Anglicanum*, ed. Thomas Hearne (Oxford, 1719), 3: 874–902.

WILLIAM OF WYCOMB, 'De vita Roberti Betun, episcopi Herefordensis', in *Anglia Sacra*, ed. Henry Wharton (London, 1691), 2: 293–322.

WILLIAMS AB ITHEL, JOHN, ed., *Annales Cambriae*, Rolls Series (London, 1860).

WILMART, ANDRÉ, 'Les Mélanges de Mathieu préchantre de Rievaulx au début du XIIIe siècle', *Revue Bénédictine*, 52 (1940), 15–85.

WILSON, JAMES, ed., *The Register of St. Bees*, Surtees Society, 126 (Durham, 1915).

WOODCOCK, AUDREY M., ed., *Cartulary of the Priory of St. Gregory, Canterbury*, Camden Society, 3rd ser., 88 (London, 1956).

WRIGHT, THOMAS, ed., *Early Mysteries and other Latin Poems of the Twelfth and Thirteenth Centuries* (London, 1838).

—— ed., *The Political Songs of England from the Reign of John to that of Edward II*, Camden Society, 6 (London, 1839).

—— *Bibliographia Britannica Literaria* (London, 1846).

—— ed., *The Anglo-Latin Satirical Poets and Epigrammatists of the Twelfth Century*, 2 vols., Rolls Series (London, 1872).

WROTTESLEY, GEORGE, 'The Staffordshire Chartulary, Series III', *William Salt Archaeological Society Collections for a History of Staffordshire*, vol. 3 (Birmingham, 1882), 178–231.

—— 'An Abstract of the Contents of the Burton Chartulary', *William Salt Archaeological Society Collections for a History of Staffordshire*, vol. 5 (London, 1884), 1–101.

—— 'An Account of the Family of Okeover of Okeover, co. Stafford, with Transcripts of Ancient Deeds at Okeoever', *William Salt Archaeological Society Collections for a History of Staffordshire*, vol. 7 (London, 1904), 3–187.

—— 'The Rydware Chartulary', *William Salt Archaeological Society Collections for a History of Staffordshire*, vol. 16 (London, 1895), 229–302.

WULFSTAN, *Sermo Lupi ad Anglos*, ed. Dorothy Whitelock (New York, 1966).

—— *The Homilies of Wulfstan*, ed. Dorothy Bethurum (Oxford, 1957).

—— *Die 'Institutes of Polity, Civil and Ecclesiastical'*, ed. Karl Jost, Schweizer Anglistische Arbeiten, 47 (Bern, 1959).

WULFSTAN OF WINCHESTER, *Life of St Aethelwold*, ed. Michael Lapidge and Michael Winterbottom (Oxford, 1991).

—— *Frithegodi Monachi Breviloquium Vitae Beati Wilfredi et Wulfstani Cantoris Narratio Metrica de Sancto Swithuno*, ed. Alistair Campbell (Zürich, n.d).

SECONDARY SOURCES

ADIGARD DES GAUTRIES, JEAN, *Les Noms de personnes scandinaves en Normandie de 911 à 1066* (Lund, 1954).

AIRD, WILLIAM M., 'Northern England or Southern Scotland? The Anglo-Scottish Border in the Eleventh and Twelfth Centuries and the Problem of Perspective', in *Government, Religion and Society in Northern England, 1000–1700*, ed. John C. Appleby and Paul Dalton (Stroud, 1997), 27–39.

—— *St Cuthbert and the Normans: The Church of Durham, 1071–1153* (Woodbridge, 1998).

ALBU, EMILY, *The Normans in their Histories: Propaganda, Myth and Subversion* (Woodbridge, 2001).

ALEXANDER, J. J. G., *Norman Illumination at Mont St Michel 966–1100* (Oxford, 1970).

AMORY, PATRICK, *People and Identity in Ostrogothic Italy, 489–554* (Cambridge, 1997).

AMT, EMILIE M., 'Richard de Lucy, Henry II's Justiciar', *Medieval Prosopography*, 9 (1988), 61–87.

—— *The Accession of Henry II in England: Royal Government Restored, 1149–59* (Woodbridge, 1993).

ANDERSON, BENEDICT, *Imagined Communities: Reflections on the Origin and Spread of Nationalism*, Rev. edn. (London, 1991).

ARMSTRONG, JOHN A., *Nations Before Nationalism* (Chapel Hill, 1982).

AVRIL, FRANÇOIS, *Manuscrits normands XI–XIIᵉᵐᵉ siècles* (Rouen, 1975).

AYRES, LARRY M., 'The Role of the Angevin Style in English Romanesque Painting', *Zeitschrift für Kunstgeschichte*, 37 (1974), 193–223.

BACKHOUSE, JANET, D. H. TURNER, and LESLIE WEBSTER, *The Golden Age of Anglo-Saxon Art, 966–1066* (Bloomington, Ind., 1984).

BAILDON, W. PALEY, 'The Family of Leathley or Lelay', in Thoresby Society, *Miscellanea*, no. 11 (Leeds, 1904), 2–36.

BAKER, MALCOLM, 'Medieval Illustrations of Bede's *Life of St. Cuthbert*', *Journal of the Warburg and Courtauld Institutes*, 41 (1978), 16–49.

BALFOUR, DAVID, 'The Origins of the Longchamp Family', *Medieval Prosopography*, 18 (1997), 73–92.

BARELL, A. D. M., and M. H. BROWN, 'A Settler Community in Post-conquest Rural Wales: The English of Dyffryn Clwyd, 1294–1399', *Welsh History Review*, 17 (1995), 332–55.

BARLOW, FRANK, *The English Church 1000–1066: A Constitutional History* (Hamden, Conn., 1963).

—— *Edward the Confessor* (Berkeley, 1970).

—— *The English Church, 1066–1154* (New York, 1979).

—— *William Rufus* (Berkeley, 1983).

—— *Thomas Becket* (London, 1986).

BARROW, G. W. S., *The Anglo-Norman Era in Scottish History* (Oxford, 1980).

—— 'The Kings of Scotland and Durham', in *Anglo-Norman Durham 1093–1193*, ed. David Rollason, Margaret Harvey, and Michael Prestwich (Woodbridge, 1994), 311–23.

—— 'The Scots and the North of England', in *The Anarchy of King Stephen's Reign*, ed. Edmund King (Oxford, 1994), 231–53.

BARROW, JULIA, 'A Twelfth-Century Bishop and Literary Patron: William de Vere', *Viator*, 18 (1987), 175–89.

BARRY, T. B., ROBIN FRAME, and KATHARINE SIMMS, eds., *Colony and Frontier in Medieval Ireland* (London, 1995).

BARTH, FREDRIC, ed., *Ethnic Groups and Boundaries: The Social Organization of Culture Difference* (Boston, 1969).

BARTLETT, ROBERT, *Gerald of Wales, 1146–1223* (Oxford, 1982).

—— *The Making of Europe: Conquest, Colonization and Cultural Change, 950–1350* (Princeton, 1993).

—— 'Symbolic Meanings of Hair in the Middle Ages', *TRHS* 6th ser., 4 (1994), 43–60.

BATES, DAVID, *Normandy Before 1066* (London, 1982).

—— 'Normandy and England After 1066', *EHR* 104 (1989), 851–80.

—— 'The Rise and Fall of Normandy, c. 911–1204', in *England and Normandy in the Middle Ages*, ed. David Bates and Anne Curry (London, 1994), 19–35.

BECKWITH, JOHN, *Ivory Carvings in Early Medieval England* (London, 1972).

BERESFORD, M. W., and H. P. R. FINBERG, *English Medieval Boroughs: A Hand-List* (Totowa, 1973).

BERNSTEIN, DANIEL J., *The Mystery of the Bayeux Tapestry* (Chicago, 1987).

BETHURUM, DOROTHY, 'The Connection of the Katherine Group with Old English Prose', *Journal of English and Germanic Philology*, 34 (1935), 553–64.

BINNS, ALISON, *Dedications of Monastic Houses in England and Wales, 1066–1216* (Woodbridge, 1989).

BLACKER, JEAN, *The Faces of Time: Portrayal of the Past in Old French and Latin Historical Narrative of the Anglo-Norman Regnum* (Austin, Tex., 1994).

BLAIR, C. H. HUNTER, 'The Sheriffs of Northumberland 1076–1602', *Archæologia Æliana*, 4th ser. 20 (1942), 11–89.

BLAIR, JOHN, 'Frewin Hall, Oxford: A Norman Mansion and a Monastic College', *Oxoniensia*, 43 (1978), 48–99.

BLAKE, E. O., 'The *Historia Eliensis* as a Source for Twelfth-century History', *Bulletin of the John Rylands Library*, 41 (1959), 304–27.

BLAKE, N. F., 'Rhythmical Alliteration', *Modern Philology*, 67 (1969), 118–24.

BLIESE, John R. E., 'The Courage of the Normans: A Comparative Study of Battle Rhetoric', *Nottingham Medieval Studies* 35 (1991), 1–26.

BLOCKLEY, KEVIN, 'Canterbury Cathedral', *Current Archaeology*, 12 (1993), 124–30.

BOASE, T. S. R., *English Art: 1100–1216* (Oxford, 1953).

BOISSONNADE, M. P.,'Administrateurs laïques et ecclésiastiques Anglo-Normands en Poitou à l'époque d'Henri II Plantagenet (1152–1189)', *Bulletin de la Société des Antiquaires de L'Ouest*, 3rd ser., 5 (1922), 156–90.

BONY, JEAN, 'Durham et la tradition saxonne', in *Études d'art médiéval offertes à Louis Grodecki*, ed. Mc. K. Crosby, André Chastel, and Anne Prache (Paris, n.d), 79–93.

BOSWELL, JOHN, *Christianity, Social Tolerance, and Homosexuality: Gay People in Western Europe from the Beginnings of the Christian Era to the Fourteenth Century* (Chicago, 1980).

BOURCIER, GEORGES, *An Introduction to the History of the English Language*, trans. and adapted by Cecily Clark (Cheltenham, 1981).

BRADBURY, JIM, *Stephen and Matilda: The Civil War of 1139–53* (Stroud, 1996).

BRAND, PAUL, '"Time out of Mind"; The Knowledge and Use of the Eleventh- and Twelfth-Century Past in Thirteenth Century Legislation', *ANS* 16: 37–54.

BREESE, LAUREN WOOD, 'The Persistance of Scandinavian Connections in Normandy in the Tenth and Eleventh Centuries', *Viator*, 8 (1977), 47–61.

BREHE, S. K., '"Rhythmical Alliteration": Ælfric's Prose and the Origins of Laȝamon's Metre', in *The Text and Tradition of Laȝamon's Brut*, ed. Françoise Le Saux (Cambridge, 1994), 65–87.

BRETT, M., *The English Church Under Henry I* (London, 1975).

BRITNELL, RICHARD H., *The Commercialisation of English Society, 1000–1500*, 2nd edn. (Manchester, 1996).

BRITNELL, RICHARD H., and BRUCE M. S. CAMPBELL, *A Commercialising Economy: England 1086 to c. 1300* (Manchester, 1996).

BROOKE, C. N. L., 'The Composition of the Chapter of St. Pauls 1086–1163', *Cambridge Historical Journal*, 10 (1950), 111–32.

—— 'The Archdeacon and the Norman Conquest', in *Tradition and Change: Essays in Honour of Marjorie Chibnall*, ed. Diana Greenway, Christopher Holdsworth, and Jane Sayers (Cambridge, 1985), 1–19.

—— and GILLIAN KEIR, *London, 800–1216: The Shaping of a City* (Berkeley, 1975).

BROOKE, Z. N., *The English Church and the Papacy From the Conquest to the Reign of John*, 2nd edn. (Cambridge, 1989).

BROOKS, N. P., and H. E. WALKER, 'The Authority and Interpretation of the Bayeux Tapestry', *PBC* 1: 1–34.

BROWN, R. ALLEN, *The Normans and the Norman Conquest* (New York, 1968).

—— 'The Status of the Norman Knight', in *War and Governance in the Middle Ages: Essays in Honour of J. O. Prestwich*, ed. John Gillingham and J. C. Holt (Woodbridge, 1984), 18–32.

BRÜHL, CARLRICHARD, *Deutschland–Frankreich. Die Geburt zweier Völker* (Cologne, 1990).

BUDNY, MILDRED, and TIMOTHY GRAHAM, 'Dunstan As Hagiographical Subject or Osbern as Author? The Scribal Portrait in an Early Copy of Osbern's *Vita Sancti Dunstani*', *Gesta*, 32 (1993), 83–96.

BURNETT, CHARLES, *Adelard of Bath: An English Scientist and Arabist of the Early Twelfth Century*, Warburg Institute Surveys and Texts, 14 (London, 1987).

BURNS, ROBERT I., *Muslims, Christians, and Jews in the Crusader Kingdom of Valencia* (Cambridge, 1984).

BURTON, JANET, *Monastic and Religious Orders in Britain, 1000–1300* (Cambridge, 1994).

CABLE, THOMAS, *The English Alliterative Tradition* (Philadelphia, 1991).

CAM, HELEN M., *Liberties and Communities in Medieval England* (London, 1963).

CAMERON, ANGUS F., 'Middle English in Old English Manuscripts', in *Chaucer and Middle English Studies in Honour of Russell Hope Robbins*, ed. Beryl Rowland (London, 1974), 218–29.

CAMPBELL, ALISTAIR, *Skaldic Verse and Anglo-Saxon History* (London, 1971).

CAMPBELL, JAMES, 'Observations on English Government from the Tenth to the Twelfth Century', *TRHS* 5th ser., 25 (1975), 39–54; repr. in Campbell, *Essays in Anglo-Saxon History* (London, 1986).

—— 'Some Twelfth-Century Views of the Anglo-Saxon Past', *Peritia*, 3 (1984), 131–50; repr. in *Essays in Anglo-Saxon History* (London, 1986), 209–28.

—— 'Some Agents and Agencies of the Late Anglo-Saxon State', in *Domesday Studies*, ed. J. C. Holt (Woodbridge, 1987), 201–18.

—— 'The Late Anglo-Saxon State: A Maximum View', *Proceedings of the British Academy*, 87 (1995), 39–65.

—— 'The United Kingdom of England: The Anglo-Saxon Achievement', in *Uniting the Kingdom? The Making of British History*, ed. Alexander Grant and Keith J. Stringer (London, 1995), 31–47.

—— ERIC JOHN, and PATRICK WORMALD, *The Anglo-Saxons* (London, 1982).

CAROZZI, CLAUDE, and HUGUETTE TAVIANI-CAROZZI, eds., *Peuples du moyen âge: problèmes d'identification* (Aix-en-Provence, 1996).

CARPENTER, D. A., *The Minority of Henry III* (Berkeley, 1990).

CARR, A. D. 'An Aristocracy in Decline: The Native Welsh Lords after the Edwardian Conquest', *Welsh History Review*, 5 (1970–1), 103–29.

CASTILE, GEORGE PIERRE, and GILBERT KUSHNER, eds., *Persistent Peoples: Cultural Enclaves in Perspective* (Tucson, 1981).

CHAMBERS, R. W., 'The Continuity of English Prose from Alfred to More and his School', in Nicholas Harpsfield, *The Life and Death of Sir Thomas More, Knight, Sometymes Lord High Chancellor of England*, ed. Elsie Vaughn Hitchcock and R. W. Chambers. EETS os 196 (London, 1932), pp. xlv–clxxiv.

CHAPLAIS, PIERRE, 'William of Saint-Calais and the Domesday Survey', in *Domesday Studies*, ed. J. C. Holt (Woodbridge, 1987), 65–77.

CHAZAN, ROBERT, *Medieval Stereotypes and Modern Antisemitism* (Berkeley, 1997).

CHENEY, C. R., *From Becket to Langton* (Manchester, 1956).

CHENEY, MARY, *Roger, Bishop of Worcester, 1164–79* (Oxford, 1980).

CHIBNALL, MARJORIE, *Anglo-Norman England, 1066–1166* (Oxford, 1986).

—— *The World of Orderic Vitalis* (Oxford, 1984).

—— *The Empress Matilda: Queen Consort, Queen Mother, and Lady of the English* (Oxford, 1991).

—— '"Racial" Minorities in the Anglo-Norman Realm', in *Minorities and Barbarians in Medieval Life and Thought*, ed. Susan J. Ridyard and Robert G. Benson (Sewanee, 1996), 49–61.

—— *The Debate on the Norman Conquest* (Manchester, 1999).

—— *The Normans* (Oxford, 2000).

[CHRISTELOW], STEPHANIE L. MOOERS, 'Patronage in the Pipe Roll of 1130', *Speculum*, 59 (1984), 282–307.

CHRISTIANSEN, ERIC, *The Northern Crusades: The Baltic and the Catholic Frontier, 1100–1525* (Minneapolis, 1980).

CHWOJKO, EWA, and MALCOLM THURLBY, 'Gloucester and the Herefordshire School', *Journal of the British Archaeological Association*, 150 (1997), 17–26.

CLANCHY, MICHAEL T., *From Memory to Written Record: England 1066–1307*, 2nd edn. (Oxford, 1993).

—— *England and its Rulers, 1066–1272*, 2nd edn. (Oxford, 1998).

CLAPHAM, A. W., *English Romanesque Architecture After the Conquest* (Oxford, 1934).

CLARK, CECILY, 'As Seint Austin Seith . . .', *Medium Ævum*, 46 (1977), 212–18.

—— 'English Personal Names Ca. 650–1300: Some Prosopographical Bearings', *Medieval Prosopography*, 8 (1987), 31–60.

—— 'Onomastics', in *The Cambridge History of the English Language:* Vol. II, *1066 to 1476*, ed. Norman Blake (Cambridge, 1992), 542–606.

—— *Words, Names and History: Selected Papers of Cecily Clark*, ed. Peter Jackson (Woodbridge, 1995).

CLAY, CHARLES, 'The Family of Thornhill', *Yorkshire Archaeological Journal*, 29 (1929), 286–321.

—— and DIANA E. GREENWAY, *Early Yorkshire Families*, Yorkshire Archaeological Society Record Series, 135 (Wakefield, 1973).

COFFMAN, PETER, 'The Romanesque East End of Southwell Minster', in *Southwell and Nottinghamshire: Medieval Art, Architecture and Industry*, ed. Jennifer S. Alexander, British Archaeological Association Conference Transactions, 21 (Leeds, 1998), 1–12.

COKAYNE, G. E., and VICARY GIBBS, *The Complete Peerage of England, Scotland, Ireland, and the United Kingdom*, rev. edn., 12 vols. in 13 (London, 1910–59).

COLLEY, LINDA, *Britons: Forging the Nation, 1707–1837* (New Haven, 1992).

CONTAMINE, PHILIPPE, 'The Norman "Nation" and the French "Nation" in the Fourteenth and Fifteenth Centuries', in *England and Normandy in the Middle Ages*, ed. David Bates and Anne Curry (London, 1994), 215–34.

COSS, PETER R., *Lordship, Knighthood and Locality: A Study in English Society, c. 1180–c. 1280* (Cambridge, 1991).

—— 'Knights, Esquires and the Origins of Social Gradation in England', *TRHS* 6th ser., 5 (1995), 155–78.

COWDREY, H. E. J., 'Bishop Ermenfrid of Sion and the Penitential Ordinance following the Battle of Hastings', *Journal of Ecclesiastical History*, 20 (1969), 225–42.

COWNIE, EMMA, 'The Normans As Patrons of English Religious Houses, 1066–1135', *ANS* 18: 47–62.

—— *Religious Patronage in Anglo-Norman England, 1066–1135* (Woodbridge, 1998).

CRANE, SUSAN, *Insular Romance: Politics, Faith, and Culture in Anglo-Norman and Middle English Literature* (Berkeley, 1986).

—— 'Anglo-Norman Cultures in England, 1066–1460', in *The Cambridge History of Medieval English Literature*, ed. David Wallace (Cambridge, 1999), 35–60.

CRICK, JULIA, *The Historia Regum Britannie of Geoffrey of Monmouth: IV. Dissemination and Reception in the Later Middle Ages* (Cambridge, 1991).

CROUCH, DAVID, *The Image of Aristocracy in Britain, 1000–1300* (London, 1992).

—— 'The Hidden History of the Twelfth Century', *Haskins Society Journal*, 5, ed. Robert B. Patterson (1993), 111–30.

—— 'Normans and Anglo-Normans: A Divided Aristocracy?' in *England and Normandy in the Middle Ages*, ed. David Bates and Anne Curry (London, 1994), 51–67.

—— 'From Stenton to McFarlane: Models of Societies of the Twelfth and Thirteenth Centuries', *TRHS* 6th ser., 5 (1995), 179–200.

CUOZZO, ERRICO, 'Á propos de la coexistence entre Normands et Lombards dans le Royaume de Sicile: la révolte féodale de 1160–1162', in *Peuples du Moyen Âge: Problèmes d'identification*, ed. Claude Carozzi and Huguette Taviani-Carozzi (Aix-en-Provence, 1996), 45–56.

CURLEY, MICHAEL J., *Geoffrey of Monmouth*, Twayne's English Authors Series, 509 (New York, 1994).

DAHOOD, ROGER, 'Hugh de Morville, William of Canterbury, and Anecdotal Evidence for English Language History', *Speculum* 69 (1994), 40–56.

DALTON, PAUL, *Conquest, Anarchy, and Lordship: Yorkshire, 1066–1154* (Cambridge, 1994).

—— 'Scottish Influence on Durham 1066–1214', in *Anglo-Norman Durham 1093–1193*, ed. David Rollason, Margaret Harvey, and Michael Prestwich (Woodbridge, 1994), 339–52.

—— 'The Governmental Integration of the Far North, 1066–1199', in *Government, Religion and Society in Northern England, 1000–1700*, ed. John C. Appleby and Paul Dalton(Stroud, 1997), 14–26 .

DAMIAN-GRINT, PETER, *The New Historians of the Twelfth-Century Renaissance: Inventing Vernacular Authority* (Woodbridge, 1999).

DARBY, H. C., *Domesday England* (Cambridge, 1977).

DAVIES, R. R., *Lordship and Society in the March of Wales, 1282–1400* (Oxford, 1978).

—— 'Lordship or Colony', in *The English in Medieval Ireland*, ed. James Lydon (Dublin, 1984).

—— *Domination and Conquest: The Experience of Ireland, Scotland and Wales, 1100–1300* (Cambridge, 1990).

—— *The Age of Conquest: Wales 1063–1415* (Oxford, 1991).

—— 'The Peoples of Britain and Ireland 1100–1400: I. Identities', *TRHS* 6th ser., 4 (1994), 1–20.

—— 'The Peoples of Britain and Ireland 1100–1400: II. Names, Boundaries and Regnal Solidarities', *TRHS* 6th ser., 5 (1995), 1–20.

—— *The Revolt of Owain Glyn Dŵr* (Oxford, 1995).

—— 'The Peoples of Britain and Ireland 1100–1400: III. Laws and Customs', *TRHS* 6th ser., 6 (1996), 1–23.

—— 'The Peoples of Britain and Ireland 1100–1400: IV. Language and Historical Mythology', *TRHS* 6th ser. 7 (1997), 1–24.

—— *The Matter of Britain and the Matter of England* (Oxford, 1996).

DAVIS, R. H. C., *The Normans and their Myth* (London, 1976).

DAWTRY, ANNE, 'The Benedictine Revival in the North: The Last Bulwark of Anglo-Saxon Monasticism?' in *Religion and National Identity*, ed. Stuart Mews, Studies in Church History, 18 (Oxford, 1982), 87–98.

DE BOUARD, MICHEL, 'De la Neustrie carolingienne à la Normandie féodale: continuité ou discontinuité?' *Bulletin of the Institute of Historical Research*, 28 (1955), 1–14.

DE VOS, GEORGE and LOLA ROMANUCCI-ROSS, eds., *Ethnic Identity: Cultural Continuities and Change* (Palo Alto, 1975).

DOBSON, R. B., *The Jews of Medieval York and the Massacre of March 1190*, Borthwick Papers, 45 (York, 1974).

—— 'A Minority Ascendant: The Benedictine Conquest of the North of England, 1066–1100', in *Minorities and Barbarians in Medieval Life and Thought*, ed. Susan J. Ridyard and Robert G. Benson (Sewanee, 1996), 5–26.

DODWELL, C. R., *The Canterbury School of Illumination, 1066–1200* (Cambridge, 1954).

—— *Anglo-Saxon Art: A New Perspective* (Manchester, 1987).

—— *The Pictorial Arts of the West* (New Haven, 1993).

DOLLEY, MICHAEL, *The Norman Conquest and the English Coinage* (London, 1966).

DONOGHUE, DANIEL, 'La ʒamon's Ambivalence', *Speculum*, 65 (1990), 537–63.

DOUGLAS, DAVID C., *William the Conqueror: The Norman Impact upon England* (Berkeley, 1964).

—— *The Norman Achievement 1050–1100* (Berkeley, 1969).

DRAPER, PETER, 'King John and St Wulfstan', *Journal of Medieval History*, 10 (1984), 41–50.

DRELL, JOANNA H., 'Cultural Syncretism and Ethnic Identity: The Norman "Conquest" of Southern Italy and Sicily', *Journal of Medieval History*, 25 (1999), 187–202.

DU BOULAY, F. R. H., *The Lordship of Canterbury: An Essay on Medieval Society* (New York, 1966).

DUBY, GEORGES, *William Marshal: The Flower of Chivalry*, trans. Richard Howard (New York, 1985).

DUFFY, SEÁN, 'The Problem of Degeneracy', in *Law and Disorder in Thirteenth-century Ireland: The Dublin Parliament of 1297*, ed. James Lydon (Dublin, 1997), 87–106.

—— *Ireland in the Middle Ages* (New York, 1997).

DUGGAN, CHARLES, *Decretals and the Creation of 'New Law' in the Twelfth Century* (Ashgate, 1998).

DUMVILLE, DAVID N., 'Anglo-Saxon Books: Treasure in Norman Hands?', *ANS* 16: 83–99.

EKWALL, EILERT, *Early London Personal Names* (Lund, 1947).

ELLENBLUM, RONNIE, *Frankish Rural Settlement in the Latin Kingdom of Jerusalem* (Cambridge, 1998).

EMPEY, C. A., 'Conquest and Settlement: Patterns of Anglo-Norman Settlement in North Munster and South Leinster', *Irish Economic and Social History*, 13 (1986), 5–31.

ERIKSEN, THOMAS HYLLAND, *Ethnicity and Nationalism: Anthropological Perspectives* (London, 1993).

EVERARD, J. A., *Britanny and the Angevins: Province and Empire, 1158–1203* (Cambridge, 2000).

EVERETT, DOROTHY, *Essays on Middle English Literature* (London, 1959).

EYTON, R. W., *Antiquities of Shropshire*, 12 vols. (London, 1854–60).

FAITH, ROSAMOND, *The English Peasantry and the Growth of Lordship* (London, 1997).

FARRER, WILLIAM, *Honors and Knights' Fees*, vol. 1 (London, 1923).

FAULL, MARGARET L., and S. A. MOORHOUSE, eds., *West Yorkshire: An Archaeological Survey to A. D. 1500*, 3 vols. (Wakefield, 1981).

FELL, CHRISTINE, 'The Icelandic Saga of Edward the Confessor: its Version of the Anglo-Saxon Emigration to Byzantium', *Anglo-Saxon England*, 3 (1974), 179–96.

FELLOWS JENSEN, GILLIAN, *Scandinavian Personal Names in Linconshire and Yorkshire* (Copenhagen, 1968).

FERNIE, ERIC, *The Architecture of the Anglo-Saxons* (New York, 1983).

—— 'The Effect of the Conquest on Norman Architectural Patronage', *ANS* 9: 71–85.

—— *An Architectural History of Norwich Cathedral* (Oxford, 1993).

—— 'Architecture and the Effects of the Norman Conquest', in *England and Normandy in the Middle Ages*, ed. David Bates and Anne Curry (London, 1994), 105–16.

—— 'Saxons, Normans and their Buildings', *ANS* 21: 1–9.

—— *The Architecture of Norman England* (Oxford, 2000).

FINN, R. WELLDON, *An Introduction to Domesday Book* (New York, 1963).

FLANAGAN, MARIE THERESE, *Irish Society, Anglo-Norman Settlers, Angevin Kingship: Interactions in Ireland in the Late Twelfth Century* (Oxford, 1989).

FLEMING, ROBIN, *Kings and Lords in Conquest England* (Cambridge, 1991).

—— *Domesday Book and the Law: Society and Legal Custom in Early Medieval England* (Cambridge, 1998).

Foot, Sarah, 'The Making of *Angelcynn*: English Identity before the Norman Conquest', *TRHS* 6th ser., 6 (1996), 25–49.

Forssner, Thorvald, *Continental-Germanic Personal Names in England in Old and Middle English Times* (Uppsala, 1916).

Forster, R. H., 'Turgot, Prior of Durham', *Journal of the British Archaeological Association*, 63 (1907), 32–40.

Frame, Robin, *Colonial Ireland, 1169–1369* (Dublin, 1981).

—— *The Political Development of the British Isles, 1100–1400* (Oxford, 1990).

—— '"Les Engleys Nées in Irlande": The English Political Identity in Medieval Ireland', *TRHS* 6th ser., 3 (1993), 83–103.

—— *Ireland and Britain, 1170–1450* (London, 1998).

Frankis, P. J., 'Laȝamon's English Sources', in *J. R. R. Tolkien: Scholar and Storyteller, Essays in Memoriam*, ed. Mary Salu and Robert T. Farrell (Ithaca, NY, 1979), 64–75.

Franzen, Christine, *The Tremulous Hand of Worcester: A Study of Old English in the Thirteenth Century* (Oxford, 1991).

Freeman, Edward A., *The History of the Norman Conquest of England*, 6 vols., 3rd edn. (Oxford, 1877).

Friedlander, Carolynn VanDyke, 'Early Middle English Accentual Verse', *Modern Philology*, 76 (1979), 219–30.

Fries, Maureen, 'The Arthurian Moment: History and Geoffrey's *Historia Regum Britannie*', *Arthuriana*, 8 (1998), 88–99.

Fuchs, Rüdiger, *Das Domesday Book und sein Umfeld: zur ethnicschen und sozialen Aussagekraft einer Landesbeschreibung im England des 11. Jahrhunderts* (Stuttgart, 1987).

Galbraith, V. H., 'Nationality and Language in Medieval England', *TRHS* 4th ser., 23 (1941), 113–28.

Gameson, Richard, 'English Manuscript Art in the Late Eleventh Century: Canterbury and its Context', in *Canterbury and the Norman Conquest: Churches, Saints and Scholars, 1066–1109*, ed. Richard Eales and Richard Sharpe (London, 1995), 95–144.

—— 'The Origin, Art, and Message of the Bayeux Tapestry', in *The Study of the Bayeux Tapestry*, ed. Richard Gameson (Woodbridge, 1997), 157–211.

—— *The Manuscripts of Norman England (c. 1066–1130)* (Oxford, 1999).

Garnett, George, '"*Franci et Angli*": The Legal Distinctions Between Peoples After the Conquest', *ANS* 8: 109–37.

—— 'Coronation and Propaganda: Some Implications of the Norman Claim to the Throne of England in 1066', *TRHS* 5th ser., 36 (1986), 91–116.

Geary, Patrick, *Aristocracy in Provence: The Rhône Basin at the Dawn of the Carolingian Age* (Philadelphia, 1985).

—— 'Ethnic Identity as a Situational Construct in the Early Middle Ages', *Medieval Perspectives*, 3 (1988), 1–17.

Gellner, Ernest, *Nations and Nationalism* (Oxford, 1983).

Gem, Richard, 'Bishop Wulfstan II and the Romanesque Cathedral Church of Worcester', in *Medieval Art and Architecture at Worcester Cathedral*, British Archaeological Association Conference Transactions, 1 (Leeds, 1978), 15–37.

—— 'The Significance of the 11th-century Rebuilding of Christ Church and St Augustine's, Canterbury, in the Development of Romanesque Architecture', in *Medieval Art and Architecture at Canterbury Before 1220*, British Archaeological Association Conference Transactions, 5 (Leeds, 1982).

—— 'England and the Resistance to Romanesque Architecture', in *Studies in Medieval history Presented to R. Allen Brown*, ed. Christopher Harper-Bill, Christopher J. Holdsworth, and Janet L. Nelson (Woodbridge, 1989), 129–39.

GIBSON, MARGARET, *Lanfranc of Bec* (Oxford, 1978).

—— T. A. HESLOP, and RICHARD W. PFAFF, eds., *The Eadwine Psalter: Text, Image, and Monastic Culture in Twelfth-Century Canterbury* (London, 1992).

GILLINGHAM, JOHN, 'Richard I and the Science of War in the Middle Ages', in *War and Government in the Middle Ages*, ed. John Gillingham and J. C. Holt (Totowa, 1989), 78–91.

—— 'William the Bastard at War', in *Studies in Medieval History Presented to R. Allen Brown*, ed. C. Harper-Bill, C. J. Holdsworth, and J. L. Nelson (Woodbridge, 1989), 141–8.

—— 'Killing and Mutilating Political Enemies in the British Isles from the Late Twelfth to the Early Fourteenth Century: A Comparative Study', in *Britain and Ireland, 900–1300: Insular Responses to Medieval European Change*, ed. Brendan Smith (Cambridge, 1999), 114–34.

—— *The English in the Twelfth Century: Imperialism, National Identity and Political Values* (Woodbridge, 2000).

—— ' "Slaves of the Normans"? Gerald de Barri and Regnal Solidarity in Early Thirteenth-century England', in *Law, Laity and Solidarities: Essays in Honour of Susan Reynolds*, ed. Pauline Stafford, Janet L. Nelson, and Jane Martindale (Manchester, 2001), 160–71.

—— 'Civilizing the English? The English Histories of William of Malmesbury and David Hume', *Historical Research*, 74 (2001), 17–43.

GIVEN, JAMES, *State and Society in Medieval Europe: Gwynedd and Languedoc Under Outside Rule* (Ithaca, NY, 1990).

GLICK, THOMAS F., *Islamic and Christian Spain in the Early Middle Ages* (Princeton, 1979).

GOERING, JOSEPH, *William de Montibus (c. 1140–1213): The Schools and Literature of Pastoral Care* (Toronto, 1992).

GOLDING, BRIAN, 'Anglo-Norman Knightly Burials', in *The Ideals and Practices of Medieval Knighthood*, ed. Christopher Harper-Bill and Ruth Harvey (Woodbridge, 1986), 35–48.

—— *Conquest and Colonisation: The Normans in Britain, 1066–1100* (New York, 1994).

—— 'The Hermit and the Hunter', in *The Cloister and the World: Essays in Medieval History in Honour of Barbara Harvey*, ed. John Blair and Brian Golding (Oxford, 1996), 95–117.

GRANSDEN, ANTONIA, *Historical Writing in England c. 550 to c. 1307* (Ithaca, NY, 1974).

—— 'Bede's Reputation as a Historian in Medieval England', *Journal of Ecclesiastical History*, 32 (1981), 397–425.

—— 'Tradition and Continuity During the Last Century of Anglo-Saxon Monasticism', *Journal of Ecclesiastical History*, 40 (1989), 159–207.

GRANT, ALEXANDER, and K. J. STRINGER, eds., *Uniting the Kingdom? The Making of British History* (London, 1995).

GRANT, LINDY, 'Architectural Relationships between England and Normandy, 1100–1204', in *England and Normandy in the Middle Ages*, ed. David Bates and Anne Curry (London, 1994), 116–29.

GRAPE, WOLFGANG, *The Bayeux Tapestry: Monument to a Norman Triumph* (Munich, 1994).

GRAY, J. M., *The School of Pythagoras (Merton Hall), Cambridge*, Cambridge Antiquarian Society Quarto ser., NS 4 (Cambridge, 1932).

GREEN, JUDITH, 'The Sheriffs of William the Conqueror', *ANS* 5: 129–45.

—— *The Government of England under Henry I* (Cambridge, 1986).

—— 'Unity and Disunity in the Anglo-Norman State', *Historical Research*, 62 (1989), 115–34.

—— *The Aristocracy of Norman England* (Cambridge, 1997).

GREENWAY, DIANA, 'Conquest and Colonization: The Foundation of an Alien Priory, 1077', in *The Cloister and the World: Essays in Medieval History in Honour of Barbara Harvey*, ed. John Blair and Brian Golding (Oxford, 1996), 46–56.

GRIFFITHS, RALPH A., *Conquerors and Conquered in Medieval Wales* (New York, 1994).

GRUEBER, HERBERT A., and CHARLES FRANCIS KEARY, *A Catalogue of English Coins in the British Library: Anglo-Saxon Series*, vol. 2 (London, 1893).

GUENÉE, BERNARD, *States and Rulers in Later Medieval Europe*, trans. Juliet Vale (Oxford, 1985).

GULLICK, MICHAEL, 'The Hand of Symeon of Durham: Further Observations on the Durham Martyrology Scribe', in *Symeon of Durham: Historian of Durham and the North*, ed. David Rollason (Stamford, 1998), 14–31.

HADLEY, D. M., '"And they Proceeded to Plough and to Support Themselves": The Scandinavian Settlement of England', *ANS* 19: 69–96.

—— *The Northern Danelaw: Its Social Structure, c. 800–1100* (London, 2000).

HAMIL, FREDERICK COYLE, 'Presentment of Englishry and the Murder Fine', *Speculum*, 12 (1937), 285–98.

HANAWALT, EMILY ALBU, 'Scandinavians in Byzantium and Normandy', in *Peace and War in Byzantium*, ed. Timothy S. Miller and John Nesbitt (Washington, DC, 1995), 114–22.

HAND, G. J., *English Law in Ireland, 1290–1324* (Cambridge, 1967).

HANEY, KRISTINE EDMONDSON, *The Winchester Psalter: An Iconographic Study* (Leicester, 1986).

HANKEY, TERESA, 'Civic Pride versus Feelings for Italy in the Age of Dante', in *Medieval Europeans: Studies in Ethnic Identity and National Perspectives in Medieval Europe*, ed. Alfred P. Smyth (New York, 1998), 196–216.

HANNING, ROBERT W., *The Vision of History in Early Britain from Gildas to Geoffrey of Monmouth* (New York, 1966).

HARPER-BILL, CHRISTOPHER, 'John of Oxford, Diplomat and Bishop', in *Medieval Ecclesiastical Studies in Honour of Dorothy M. Owen*, ed. M. J. Franklin and Christopher Harper-Bill (Woodbridge, 1995), 83–105.

HARVEY, JOHN, *Cathedrals of England and Wales* (New York, 1974).

HARVEY, SALLY, 'The Knight and the Knight's Fee in England', *Past and Present*, 49 (1970), 3–43; repr. in *Peasants, Knights and Heretics*, ed. Rodney Hilton (Cambridge, 1976), 57–84.

HASTINGS, ADRIAN, *The Construction of Nationhood: Ethnicity, Religion and Nationalism* (Cambridge, 1997).

HAYWARD, PAUL ANTONY, 'Translation-Narratives in Post-Conquest Hagiography and English Resistance to the Norman Conquest', *ANS* 21: 67–93.

—— 'The Miracula Inventionis Beate Mylburge Virginis attributed to "the Lord Ato, Cardinal Bishop of Ostia."' *EHR* 114 (1999), 543–73.

HEARN, M. F., 'Romsey Abbey: A Progenitor of the English National Tradition in Architecture', *Gesta*, 14 (1975), 27–40.

HEDLEY, W. PERCY, *Northumberland Families*, 2 vols., Society of Antiquaries of Newcastle upon Tyne (Gateshead, 1968–70).

HESLOP, T. A., 'The Canterbury Calendars and the Norman Conquest', in *Canterbury and the Norman Conquest: Churches, Saints and Scholars, 1066–1109*, ed. Richard Eales and Richard Sharpe (London, 1995), 53–85.

HIGHAM, NICHOLAS, *Rome, Britain and the Anglo-Saxons* (London, 1992).

HIGOUNET, CHARLES, *Les Allemands en Europe centrale et orientale au moyen âge* (Paris, 1989).

HILEY, DAVID, 'The Norman Chant Traditions—Normandy, Britain, Sicily', *Proceedings of the Royal Musical Association*, 107 (1980–1), 1–33.

HILEY, DAVID, 'Thurstan of Caen and Plainchant at Glastonbury: Musicological Reflections on the Norman Conquest', *Proceedings of the British Academy*, 72 (1986), 57–90.

—— 'Changes in English Chant Repertories in the Eleventh Century as Reflected in the Winchester Sequences', *ANS* 16: 137–54.

—— 'Post-Pentecost Alleluias in Medieval British Liturgies', in *Music in the Medieval English Liturgy: Plainsong and Mediæval Music Society Centennial Essays*, ed. Susan Rankin and David Hiley (Oxford, 1993), 145–74.

HILL, J. W. F., *Medieval Lincoln* (Cambridge, 1948; repr. Stamford, 1990).

HILTON, RODNEY, 'Were the English English?' in *Patriotism: The Making and Unmaking of British National Identity*, ed. Raphael Samuel (London, 1989), i. 39–43.

HOBSBAWM, ERIC, and TERENCE RANGER, eds., *The Invention of Tradition* (Cambridge, 1983).

HOLDEN, BROCK W., 'The Balance of Patronage: King John and the Earl of Salisbury', *Haskins Society Journal*, 8, ed. C. P. Lewis and Emma Cownie (Woodbridge, 1996), 79–89.

HOLDSWORTH, CHRISTOPHER, 'Hermits and the Powers of the Frontier', *Reading Medieval Studies* 16 (1990), 55–76.

HOLLISTER, C. WARREN, *Monarchy, Magnates and Institutions in the Anglo-Norman World* (London, 1986).

HOLT, J. C., *The Northerners: A Study in the Reign of King John* (Oxford, 1961; repr. 1992).

—— *Magna Carta* (Cambridge, 1965).

—— 'Feudal Society and the Family in Early Medieval England: I. The Revolution of 1066', *TRHS* 5th ser., 32 (1982), 193–212.

—— 'Feudal Society and the Family in Early Medieval England: II. Notions of Patrimony', *TRHS* 5th ser., 33 (1983), 193–220.

HOOPER, NICHOLAS, 'Edgar the Ætheling: Anglo-Saxon Prince, Rebel and Crusader', *Anglo-Saxon England*, 14 (1985), 197–214.

HOWE, NICHOLAS, *Migration and Mythmaking in Anglo-Saxon England* (New Haven, 1989).

HOWLETT, D. R., *The English Origins of Old French Literature* (Dublin, 1996).

HUDSON, JOHN, 'Life Grants of Land and the Development of Inheritance in Anglo-Norman England', *ANS* 12: 67–80.

—— *Land, Law, and Lordship in Anglo-Norman England* (Oxford, 1994).

—— *The Formation of the English Common Law: Law and Society in England from the Norman Conquest to Magna Carta* (London, 1996).

HUNEYCUTT, LOIS L., 'The Idea of the Perfect Princess: The *Life of St Margaret* in the Reign of Matilda II (1100–1118)', *ANS* 12: 81–97.

—— 'Proclaiming her dignity abroad': The Literary and Artistic Network of Matilda of Scotland, Queen of England 1100–1118', in *The Cultural Patronage of Medieval Women*, ed. June Hall McCash (Athens, Ga., 1996), 155–74.

HUNT, R. W., *The Schools and the Cloister: The Life and Writings of Alexander Nequam (1157–1217)*, ed. Margaret Gibson (Oxford, 1984).

HYAMS, PAUL, *Kings, Lords, and Peasants in Medieval England: The Common Law of Villeinage in the Twelfth and Thirteenth Centuries* (Oxford, 1980).

—— 'The Common Law and the French Connection', *PBC* 4: 77–92.

INGHAM, NORMAN W., 'Has a Missing Daughter of Iaroslav Mudyri Been Found?' *Russian History/Histoire Russe*, 25 (1998), 231–70.

—— DAVID FARIS, and DOUGLAS RICHARDSON, 'The Origin of Agatha—The Debate Continues', *New England Historical and Genealogical Register*, 152 (1998), 215–35.

INGLEDEW, FRANCIS, 'The Book of Troy and the Genealogical Construction of History: The

Case of Geoffrey of Monmouth's *Historia regum Britanniae*', *Speculum*, 69 (1994), 665–704.

Jackson, Peter, 'The *Vitas Patrum* in Eleventh-Century Worcester', in *England in the Eleventh Century*, ed. Carola Hicks, Harlaxton Medieval Studies, 2 (Stamford, 1992), 119–34.

Jewell, Helen M., *The North–South Divide. The Origins of Northern Consciousness in England* (Manchester, 1994).

John, Eric, *Orbis Britanniae and Other Studies* (Leicester, 1966).

Johnson, Lesley, 'Reading the Past in Laʒamon's *Brut*', in *The Text and Tradition of Laʒamon's Brut*, ed. Françoise Le Saux (Cambridge, 1994), 141–60.

—— 'Imagining Communities: Medieval and Modern', in *Concepts of National Identity in the Middle Ages*, ed. Simon Forde, Lesley Johnson, and Alan V. Murray, Leeds Texts and Monographs, ns 14 (Leeds, 1995), 1–19.

Jones, W. R., 'The Image of the Barbarian in Medieval Europe', *Comparative Studies in Society and History*, 13 (1971), 376–407.

Kahn, Deborah, *Canterbury Cathedral and its Romanesque Sculpture* (London, 1991).

Kantorowicz, Ernst H., '*Pro Patria Mori* in Medieval Political Thought', *AHR* 56 (1950–1), 472–92.

Kapelle, William E., *The Norman Conquest of the North: The Region and Its Transformation, 1000–1135* (Chapel Hill, 1979).

Karras, Ruth Mazo, 'Friendship and Love in the Lives of Two Twelfth-Century English Saints', *Journal of Medieval History*, 14 (1988), 305–20.

Kauffman, C. M., 'Manuscript Illumination at Worcester in the Eleventh and Twelfth Centuries', in *Medieval Art and Architecture at Worcester Cathedral*, British Archaeological Association Conference Transactions, 1 (Leeds, 1978), 43–50.

—— *Romanesque Manuscripts 1066–1190*, vol. 3 of *A Survey of Manuscripts Illuminated in the British Isles*, ed. J. J. G. Alexander (London, 1975).

Kealey, Edward J., *Roger of Salisbury, Viceroy of England* (Berkeley, 1972).

Keats-Rohan, K. S. B., 'William I and the Breton Contingent in the Non-Norman Conquest 1060–1087', *ANS* 13: 157–72.

—— 'The Bretons and Normans of England 1066–1154: The Family, the Fief and the Feudal Monarchy', *Nottingham Medieval Studies*, 36 (1992), 42–78.

—— 'The Making of Henry of Oxford: Englishmen in a Norman World', *Oxoniensia*, 54 (1989), 287–309.

—— *Domesday People: A Prosopography of Persons Occurring in English Documents, 1066–1166* (Woodbridge, 1999).

Keefe, Thomas K., *Feudal Assessments and the Political Community under Henry II and His Sons* (Berkeley, 1983).

Ker, N. R., *Catalogue of Manuscripts Containing Anglo-Saxon* (Oxford, 1957).

—— *English Manuscripts in the Century after the Norman Conquest* (Oxford, 1960).

Keynes, Simon, *The Diplomas of King Æthelred 'the Unready' (978–1016): A Study in Their Use as Historical Evidence* (Cambridge, 1980).

—— 'Regenbald the Chancellor (sic)', *ANS* 10: 185–222.

Kidd, Colin, *British Identities before Nationalism: Ethnicity and Nationhood in the Atlantic World, 1600–1800* (Cambridge, 1999).

King, Edmund, 'Economic Development in the Early Twelfth Century', in *Progress and Problems in Medieval England: Essays in Honour of Edward Miller*, ed. Richard Britnell and John Hatcher (Cambridge, 1996), 1–22.

KIRBY, I. J., 'Angles and Saxons in Laȝamon's *Brut*', *Studia Neophilologica*, 36 (1964), 51–62.

KLUKAS, ARNOLD WILLIAM, 'The Architectural Implications of the *Decreta Lanfranci*', *ANS* 6: 136–71.

—— 'The Continuity of Anglo-Saxon Liturgical Traditions as Evident in the Architecture of Winchester, Ely and Canterbury Cathedrals', in *Les Mutations socio-culturelles au tournant des XIe-XIIe siècles: Études Anselmiennes* (Paris, 1984), 111–23.

KNIGHT, STEPHEN, *Arthurian Literature and Society* (New York, 1983).

KNOLL, PAUL, 'Economic and Political Institutions on the Polish–German Frontier in the Middle Ages: Action, Reaction, Interaction', in *Medieval Frontier Societies*, ed. Robert Bartlett and Angus MacKay (Oxford, 1989), 151–74.

KNOWLES, DAVID, *The Monastic Order in England: A History of its Development from the Times of St Dunstan to the Fourth Lateran Council 940–1216*, 2nd edn. (Cambridge, 1963).

—— C. N. L. BROOKE, and VERA C. M. LONDON, *The Heads of Religious Houses in England and Wales 940–1216* (Cambridge, 1972).

LANGMUIR, GAVIN I., 'Thomas of Monmouth: Detector of Ritual Murder', in *Toward a Definition of Antisemitism* (Berkeley, 1990), 209–36. Originally in *Speculum*, 59 (1984), 822–46.

LAPIDGE, MICHAEL, 'Byrhtferth and the *Vita s. Ecgwini*', *Medieval Studies*, 41 (1979), 331–53.

LAWRENCE, ANNE, 'Manuscripts of Early Anglo-Norman Canterbury', in *Medieval Art and Architecture at Canterbury Before 1220*, British Archaeological Association Conference Transactions, 5 (Leeds, 1982).

—— 'Anglo-Norman Book Production', in *England and Normandy in the Middle Ages*, ed. David Bates and Anne Curry (London, 1994), 79–93.

LAWSON, MICHAEL K., *Cnut: The Danes in England in the Early Eleventh Century* (London and New York, 1993).

LEGGE, M. DOMINICA, *Anglo-Norman in the Cloisters: The Influence of the Orders upon Anglo-Norman Literature* (Edinburgh, 1950).

—— *Anglo-Norman Literature and its Background* (Oxford, 1963).

—— 'Anglo-Norman as a Spoken Language', *PBC* 2: 108–17, 188–90.

LENNARD, REGINALD, *Rural England 1086–1135: A Study of Social and Agrarian Conditions* (Oxford, 1959).

LE PATOUREL, JOHN, *The Norman Empire* (Oxford, 1976).

—— 'The Norman Conquest, 1066, 1106, 1154?' *PBC* 1: 103–20, 216–20.

LEPELLY, RENÉ, 'A Contribution to the Study of the Inscriptions in the Bayeux Tapestry: *Bagias* and *Wilgelm*', in *The Study of the Bayeux Tapestry*, ed. Richard Gameson (Woodbridge, 1997), 39–45.

LE SAUX, FRANÇOISE H. M., *Laȝamon's Brut: the Poem and its Sources* (Cambridge, 1989).

—— ed., *The Text and Tradition of Laȝamon's Brut* (Cambridge, 1994).

LEWIS, C. P., 'The Domesday Jurors', *Haskins Society Journal*, 5, ed. Robert B. Patterson (Woodbridge, 1993), 17–44.

—— 'The French in England before the Norman Conquest', *ANS* 17: 123–44.

—— 'Joining the Dots: a Methodology for Identifying the English in Domesday Book', in *Family Trees and the Roots of Politics: The Prosopography of Britain and France from the Tenth to the Twelfth Century*, ed. K. S. B. Keats-Rohan (Woodbridge, 1997), 69–87.

LEWIS, SUZANNE, *The Rhetoric of Power in the Bayeux Tapestry* (Cambridge, 1999).

LIFSHITZ, FELICE, 'Dudo's Historical Narrative and the Norman Succession of 996', *Journal of Medieval History*, 20 (1994), 101–20.

—— *The Norman Conquest of Pious Neustria: Historiographic Discourse and Saintly Relics, 684–1090* (Toronto, 1995).

Liss, Peggy K., *Mexico Under Spain, 1521–1556: Society and the Origins of Nationality* (Chicago, 1975).

Lodge, R. A., 'Language Attitudes and Linguistic Norms in France and England in the Thirteenth Century', in *Thirteenth Century England*, 4, ed. P. R. Coss and S. D. Lloyd (Woodbridge, 1992), 73–83.

Lomas, Richard, *North-East England in the Middle Ages* (Edinburgh, 1992).

Loud, G. A., 'The "Gens Normannorum"—Myth or Reality?', *PBC* 4: 104–16.

—— 'How "Norman" was the Norman Conquest of Southern Italy', *Nottingham Medieval Studies*, 25 (1981), 13–34.

—— *Church and Society in the Norman Principality of Capua, 1058–1197* (Oxford, 1985).

—— *Conquerors and Churchmen in Norman Italy* (Aldershot, 1999).

Loyn, H. R., *The Vikings in Britain* (New York, 1977).

Lund, Neils, 'The Settlers: Where Do We Get Them From—and Do We Need Them?' in *Proceedings of the Eighth Viking Congress*, ed. Hans Bekker-Nelsen, Peter Foote, and Olaf Olsen (Odense, 1981), 147–71.

Lydon, F. J., *The Lordship of Ireland in the Middle Ages* (Dublin, 1972).

—— ed., *The English in Medieval Ireland* (Dublin, 1984).

—— 'Nation and Race in Medieval Ireland', in *Concepts of National Identity in the Middle Ages*, ed. Simon Forde, Lesley Johnson, and Alan V. Murray, Leeds Texts and Monographs, ns 14 (Leeds, 1995), 103–24.

McDermid, Richard T. W., *Beverley Minster Fasti*, Yorkshire Archaeological Society Record Series, 149 (Huddersfield, 1993).

McGuire, Brian Patrick, 'Love, Friendship, and Sex in the Eleventh Century: The Experience of Anselm', *Studia Theologica*, 28 (1974), 111–52.

McIntosh, Angus, 'Early Middle English Alliterative Verse', in *Middle English Alliterative Poetry and its Literary Background*, ed. David Lawton (Cambridge, 1982), 20–33.

MacKenzie, H., 'The Anti-foreign Movement in England, 1231–32', in *Anniversary Essays in Medieval History by Students of C. H. Haskins* (Boston, 1929), 183–203.

Maddicott, J. R., *Simon de Montfort* (Cambridge, 1994).

Maguire, Henry P., 'A Twelfth Century Workshop in Northampton', *Gesta*, 9 (1970), 11–25.

Mason, Emma, 'St Wulfstan's Staff: A Legend and Its Uses', *Medium Ævum*, 53 (1984), 157–79.

—— 'Legends of the Beauchamps' Ancestors: The Use of Baronial Propaganda in Medieval England', *Journal of Medieval History*, 10 (1984), 25–40.

—— *St Wulfstan of Worcester, c. 1008–1095* (Oxford, 1990).

—— *Westminster Abbey and its People, c. 1050–c. 1216* (Woodbridge, 1996).

Matthew, Donald, *The Norman Monasteries and their English Possessions* (London, 1962; repr. Westport, Conn., 1979).

Mayer, Hans Eberhard, 'Latins, Muslims and Greeks in the Latin Kingdom of Jerusalem', *History*, ns 63 (1978), 175–92.

Mayr-Harting, H., 'Functions of a Twelfth-Century Recluse', *History*, ns 60 (1975), 337–52.

Meyvaert, Paul, ' "Rainaldus est malus scriptor Francigenus"—Voicing National Antipathy in the Middle Ages', *Speculum*, 66 (1991), 743–63.

Miller, Edward, 'England in the Twelfth and Thirteenth Centuries: An Economic Contrast?', *Economic History Review*, 2nd ser., 24 (1971), 1–14.

—— and John Hatcher, *Medieval England: Rural Society and Economic Change, 1086–1348* (London, 1978).

Millet, Bertha, ' "Hali Meiðhad", "Sawles Warde", and the Continuity of English Prose', in *Five Hundred Years of Words and Sounds: A Festschrift for Eric Dobson*, ed. E. G. Stanley and Douglas Gray (Cambridge, 1983), 100–8.

MOFFAT, DOUGLAS, *The Soul's Address to the Body: The Worcester Fragments* (East Lansing, 1987).

MOORE, JOHN S., 'Prosopographical Problems of English *libri vitae*', in *Family Trees and the Roots of Politics: The Prosopography of Britain and France from the Tenth to the Twelfth Century*, ed. K. S. B. Keats-Rohan (Woodbridge, 1997), 165–88.

MOORE, ROBERT I., *The Formation of a Persecuting Society: Power and Deviance in Western Europe, 950–1250* (Oxford, 1987).

MORILLO, STEPHEN, *Warfare Under the Anglo-Norman Kings, 1066–1135* (Woodbridge, 1994).

—— ed., *The Battle of Hastings: Sources and Interpretations* (Woodbridge, 1996).

MORSE, RUTH, *Truth and Convention in the Middle Ages: Rhetoric, Representation, and Reality* (Cambridge, 1991).

MURRAY, ALAN V., 'Ethnic Identity in the Crusader States: The Frankish Race and the Settlement of Outremer', in *Concepts of National Identity in the Middle Ages*, ed. Simon Forde, Lesley Johnson, and Alan V. Murray (Leeds, 1995), 59–73.

—— 'How Norman was the Principality of Antioch? Prolegomena to a Study of the Origins of the Nobility of a Crusader State', in *Family Trees and the Roots of Politics: The Prosopography of Britain and France from the Tenth to the Twelfth Century*, ed. K. S. B. Keats-Rohan (Woodbridge, 1997), 349–59.

MUSSET, LUCIEN, 'Naissance de la Normandie', in *Histoire de la Normandie*, ed. Michel de Bouard (Toulouse, 1970), 75–130.

—— *The Germanic Invasions: The Making of Europe A.D. 400–600*, trans. Edward and Columba James (Philadelphia, 1975).

NANDY, ASHIS, *The Intimate Enemy: Loss and Recovery of Self Under Colonialism* (New Delhi, 1983).

NASH, MANNING, *The Cauldron of Ethnicity in the Modern World* (Chicago, 1989).

NEILSON, GEORGE, *Caudatus Anglicus: A Mediæval Slander* (Edinburgh, 1896).

NELSON, LYNN H., *The Normans in South Wales, 1070–1171* (Austin, Tex., 1966).

NIGHTINGALE, PAMELA, 'Some London Moneyers and Reflections on the Organization of English Mints in the Eleventh and Twelfth Centuries', *Numismatic Chronicle*, 142 (1982), 34–50.

—— *A Medieval Mercantile Community: The Grocers' Company and the Politics and Trade of London, 1000–1485* (New Haven, 1995).

NIRENBERG, DAVID, *Communities of Violence: Persecution of Minorities in the Middle Ages* (Princeton, 1996).

NOBLE, JAMES, 'Laȝamon's "Ambivalence" Reconsidered', in *The Text and Tradition of Laȝamon's Brut*, ed. Françoise Le Saux (Cambridge, 1994), 171–82.

Northumberland County History Committee, *A History of Northumberland*, 15 vols. (Newcastle-upon-Tyne, 1893–1935).

OAKDEN, J. P., *Alliterative Poetry in Middle English: The Dialectical and Metrical Survey*, 2 vols. (Manchester, 1930–5; repr. 1968).

O'BRIEN, BRUCE R., 'From *Morðor* to *Murdrum*: The Preconquest Origin and Norman Revival of the Murder Fine', *Speculum*, 71 (1996), 321–57.

OFFLER, H. S., 'Fitz Meldred, Neville and Hansard', in *North of the Tees*, ed. A. J. Piper and A. I. Doyle (Aldershot, 1996), 1–17.

ORAM, RICHARD D., 'A Family Business? Colonisation and Settlement in Twelfth- and Thirteenth-century Galloway', *Scottish Historical Review*, 72 (1993), 111–45.

ORMEROD, GEORGE, *History of the County Palatine and City of Chester*, 3 vols., 2nd edn. (London, 1882).

ORPEN, GODDARD HENRY, *Ireland Under the Normans, 1169–1216*, vol. 1 (Oxford, 1911).

ÖZKIRIMLI, UMUT, *Theories of Nationalism: A Critical Introduction* (New York, 2000).

PÄCHT, OTTO, *Pictorial Narrative in Twelfth-Century England* (Oxford, 1962).

——C. R. DODWELL, and FRANCIS WORMALD, *The St. Albans Psalter (Albani Psalter)* (London, 1960).

PADEL, O. J., 'Geoffrey of Monmouth and Cornwall', *Cambridge Medieval Celtic Studies*, 8 (1984), 1–28.

PAINTER, SIDNEY, *Studies in the History of the English Feudal Barony*, Johns Hopkins University Studies in Historical and Political Science, 61: 3 (Baltimore, 1943).

PALLISER, D. M., *Domesday York*, Borthwick Papers, 78 (York, 1990).

PALMER, J. J. N., 'The Wealth of the Secular Aristocracy in 1086', *ANS* 22: 279–91.

PARK, DAVID, 'The "Lewes Group" of Wall Paintings in Sussex', *ANS* 6: 200–35.

PARKER, CIARÁN, 'The Internal Frontier: The Irish in County Waterford in the Later Middle Ages', in *Colony and Frontier in Medieval Ireland*, ed. T. B. Barry, Robin Frame, and Katharine Simms (London, 1995), 139–54.

PARTNER, NANCY F., *Serious Entertainments: The Writing of History in Twelfth-Century England* (Chicago, 1977).

PATTERSON, ROBERT B., 'Robert Fitz Harding of Bristol: Profile of an Early Angevin Burgess-Baron Patrician and his Family's Urban Involvement', *Haskins Society Journal*, 1, ed. Robert B. Patterson (London, 1989), 109–22.

PEARSALL, DEREK, *Old English and Middle English Poetry* (London, 1977).

——'The Alliterative Revival: Origins and Social Backgrounds', in *Middle English Alliterative Poetry and its Literary Background*, ed. David Lawton (Cambridge, 1982), 34–53.

PELTERET, DAVID A. E., *Slavery in Early Mediaeval England: From the Reign of Alfred Until the Twelfth Century* (Woodbridge, 1995).

PETTIFER, ADRIAN, *English Castles: A Guide by Counties* (Woodbridge, 1995).

PFAFF, RICHARD W., 'Lanfranc's Supposed Purge of the Anglo-Saxon Calendar', in *Warriors and Churchmen in the High Middle Ages*, ed. Timothy Reuter (London, 1992), 95–108.

PHYTHIAN-ADAMS, CHARLES, *Land of the Cumbrians: A Study in British Provincial Origins, A.D. 400–1120* (Aldershot, 1996).

PLATELLE, HENRI, 'Le Problème du scandale: les nouvelles modes masculines aux xie et xiie siècles', *Revue Belge de Philologie et d'Histoire*, 53 (1975), 1071–96.

PLATT, COLIN, *Medieval Southampton: The Port and Trading Community, A.D. 1000–1600* (London, 1973).

POHL, WALTER, 'Conceptions of Ethnicity in Early Medieval Studies', *Archaeologia Polona*, 29 (1991), 39–49.

——'Ethnic Names and Identities in the British Isles: A Comparative Perspective', in *The Anglo-Saxons from the Migration Period to the Eighth Century: An Ethnographic Perspective*, ed. John Hines (Woodbridge, 1997), 7–32.

——'The Barbarian Successor States', in *The Transformation of the Roman World AD 400–900*, ed. Leslie Webster and Michelle Brown (Berkeley, 1997), 33–47.

——'Social Language, Identities and the Control of Discourse', in *East and West: Modes of Communication: Proceedings of the First Plenary Conference at Merida*, ed. Evangelos Chrysos and Ian Wood (Leiden, 1999), 127–41.

——and HELMUT REIMITZ, eds., *Strategies of Distinction: The Construction of Ethnic Communities, 300–800* (Leiden, 1998).

POLLOCK, FREDERICK, and FREDERIC WILLIAM MAITLAND, *The History of English Law before the Time of Edward I*, 2nd edn., with an Introduction by S. F. C. Milsom (Cambridge, 1968).

POOLE, A. L., *Domesday Book to Magna Carta, 1087–1216*, 2nd edn. (Oxford, 1955).

PORÉE, A. A., *Histoire de l'abbaye du Bec*, 2 vols. (Évreux, 1901).

POST, GAINES, 'Two Notes on Nationalism in the Middle Ages', *Traditio* (1953), 281–320.

—— *Studies in Medieval Law and Thought: Public Law and the State, 1100–1322* (Princeton, 1964).

POSTLES, DAVID, 'The Foundation of Oseney Abbey', *Bulletin of the Institute of Historical Research*, 53 (1980), 242–4.

—— '"Patronus et Advocatus Noster": Oseney Abbey and the Oilly Family', *Historical Research*, 60 (1987), 100–2.

—— 'Cultures of Peasant Naming in Twelfth-Century England', *Medieval Prosopography*, 18 (1997), 25–54.

POTTS, CASSANDRA, '*Atque unum ex diversis gentibus populum effecit*: Historical Tradition and the Norman Identity', *ANS* 18: 139–52.

—— 'When the Saints go Marching: Religious Connections and the Political Culture of Early Normandy', in *Anglo-Norman Political Culture and the Twelfth-Century Renaissance*, ed. C. Warren Hollister (Woodbridge, 1997), 17–31.

—— *Monastic Revival and Regional Identity in Early Normandy* (Woodbridge, 1997).

POWELL, JAMES M., ed., *Muslims Under Latin Rule, 1100–1300* (Princeton, 1990).

POWER, D. J., 'Between the Angevin and Capetian Courts: John de Rouvray and the Knights of the Pays de Bray, 1180–1225', in *Family Trees and the Roots of Politics: The Prosopography of Britain and France from the Tenth to the Twelfth Century*, ed. K. S. B. Keats-Rohan (Woodbridge, 1997), 361–84.

POWICKE, FREDERICK M., *The Loss of Normandy*, rev. edn. (Manchester, 1960).

PRAWER, JOSHUA, *The Latin Kingdom of Jerusalem: European Colonialism in the Middle Ages* (London, 1972).

—— *Crusader Institutions* (Oxford, 1980).

RANSFORD, ROSALIND, 'A Kind of Noah's Ark: Aelred of Rievaulx and National Identity', in *Religion and National Identity*, ed. Stuart Mews, Studies in Church History, 18 (Oxford, 1982), 137–46.

RAW, BARBARA, 'The Prayers and the Devotions in the *Ancrene Wisse*', in *Chaucer and Middle English Studies in Honour of Russell Hope Robbins*, ed. Beryl Rowland (London, 1974), 260–71.

READER, REBECCA, 'Matthew Paris and the Norman Conquest', in *The Cloister and the World: Essays in Medieval History in Honour of Barbara Harvey*, ed. John Blair and Brian Golding (Oxford, 1996), 118–47.

REILLY, LISA, 'The Emergence of Anglo-Norman Architecture: Durham Cathedral', *ANS* 19: 335–51.

—— *An Architectural History of Peterborough Cathedral* (Oxford, 1997).

REUTER, TIMOTHY, 'The Making of England and Germany, 850–1050: Points of Comparison and Difference', in *Medieval Europeans: Studies in Ethnic Identity and National Perspectives in Medieval Europe*, ed. Alfred P. Smyth (New York, 1998), 53–70.

REYNOLDS, SUSAN, 'The Rulers of London in the Twelfth Century', *History*, NS 57 (1972), 337–57.

—— 'Medieval *Origines Gentium* and the Community of the Realm', *History*, 68 (1983), 375–90.

REYNOLDS, SUSAN, 'What Do We Mean by "Anglo-Saxon" and "Anglo-Saxons?"' *Journal of British Studies*, 24 (1985), 395–414.

—— 'Towns in Domesday Book', in *Domesday Studies*, ed. J. C. Holt (Woodbridge, 1987), 295–309.

—— 'Eadric Silvaticus and the English Resistance', *Bulletin of the Institute of Historical Research*, 54 (1989), 102–5.

—— *Kingdoms and Communities in Western Europe, 900–1300*, 2nd edn. (Oxford, 1997).

RICHARDS, MARY P., 'The Manuscript Contexts of the Old English Laws: Tradition and Innovation', in *Studies in Earlier Old English Prose*, ed. Paul E. Szarmach (Albany, 1986), 171–92.

—— *Texts and Their Traditions in the Medieval Library of Rochester Cathedral Priory*. Transactions of the American Philosophical Society, NS 78, pt. 3 (1988).

RICHARDSON, H. G., *The English Jewry under Angevin Kings* (London, 1960).

RICHTER, MICHAEL, *Sprache und Gesellschaft im Mittelalter: Untersuchunger zur Mündlichen Kommunikation in England von der Mitte des elften bis zum Beginn des vierzehnten Jahrhunderts* (Stuttgart, 1979).

—— 'Bede's *Angli*: Angles or English', *Peritia*, 3 (1984), 99–114.

RICKARD, P., *Britain in Medieval French Literature 1100–1500* (Cambridge, 1956).

RIDYARD, SUSAN, '*Condigna Veneratio*: Post-Conquest Attitudes to the Saints of the Anglo-Saxons', *ANS* 9: 179–206.

—— *The Royal Saints of Anglo-Saxon England: A Study of West Saxon and East Anglian Cults* (Cambridge, 1988).

RIGG, A. G., *A History of Anglo-Latin Literature 1066–1422* (Cambridge, 1992).

RITCHIE, R. L. G., 'The Date of the *Voyage of St. Brendan*', *Medium Ævum*, 19 (1950), 64–6.

ROBINSON, J. ARMITAGE, *Gilbert Crispin, Abbot of Westminster: A Study of the Abbey Under Norman Rule* (Cambridge, 1911).

ROLLASON, DAVID, 'Lists of Saints' Resting-Places in Anglo-Saxon England', *Anglo-Saxon England*, 7 (1978), 61–93.

—— *The Mildrith Legend: A Study in Early Medieval Hagiography in England* (Leicester, 1982).

—— 'Relic-Cults as an Instrument of Royal Policy c. 900–c. 1050', *Anglo-Saxon England*, 15 (1986), 91–103.

—— *Saints and Relics in Anglo-Saxon England* (Oxford, 1989).

ROLLO, DAVID, *Historical Fabrication, Ethnic Fable and French Romance in Twelfth-Century England* (Lexington, NY, 1998).

ROOSENS, EUGENE, *Creating Ethnicity: The Process of Ethnogenesis* (Newbury Park, 1989).

ROTHWELL, W., 'The Teaching of French in Medieval England', *Modern Language Review*, 63 (1968), 37–46.

—— 'The Role of French in Thirteenth-Century England', *Bulletin of the John Rylands Society*, 58 (1976), 445–66.

—— 'Anglo-French Lexical Contacts, Old and New', *Modern Language Review*, 74 (1979), 287–96.

—— 'Stratford atte Bowe and Paris', *Modern Language Review*, 80 (1985), 39–54.

ROUND, J. H., 'Odard the Sheriff', *Genealogist*, 5 (1889), 25–8.

—— *Geoffrey de Mandeville: A Study of the Anarchy* (London, 1892).

—— *Feudal England* (London, 1895).

—— *The Commune of London and Other Studies* (Westminster, 1899).

—— 'Helion of Helions Bumpstead', *Transactions of the Essex Archeological Society*, NS 8 (1900–2), 187–91.

Round, J. H., *Peerage and Pedigree: Studies in Peerage Law and Family History*, 2 vols. (London, 1910).

—— *Family Origins and Other Studies* (New York, 1930).

Rubinstein, Jay, 'The Life and Writings of Osbern of Canterbury', in *Canterbury and the Norman Conquest: Churches, Saints and Scholars, 1066–1109*, ed. Richard Eales and Richard Sharpe (London, 1995), 27–40.

—— 'Liturgy against History: The Competing Visions of Lanfranc and Eadmer of Canterbury', *Speculum*, 74 (1999), 279–309.

Rumble, Alexander R., 'The Palaeography of the Domesday Manuscripts', in *Domesday Book: A Reassessment*, ed. Peter Sawyer (London, 1985), 28–49.

—— 'The Domesday Manuscripts: Scribes and Scriptoria', in *Domesday Studies*, ed. J. C. Holt (Woodbridge, 1987), 65–77.

Sahlins, Marshall, *Historical Metaphors and Mythical Realities: Structure in the Early History of the Sandwich Islands Kingdom* (Ann Arbor, 1981).

—— *Islands of History* (Chicago, 1985).

Salter, Elizabeth, *English and International: Studies in the Literature, Art, and Patronage of Medieval England*, ed. Derek Pearsall and Nicolette Zeeman (Cambridge, 1988).

Saltman, Avrom, *Theobald, Archbishop of Canterbury* (London, 1956).

Sanders, I. J., *English Baronies: A Study of their Origin and Descent, 1086–1327* (Oxford, 1960).

Sawyer, Peter, *The Age of the Vikings* (London, 1962).

—— 'Conquest and Colonization: Scandinavians in the Danelaw and in Normandy', in *Proceedings of the Eighth Viking Congress*, ed. Hans Bekker-Nelsen, Peter Foote, and Olaf Olsen (Odense, 1981), 123–31.

Saxl, F., *English Sculptures of the Twelfth Century* (London, 1952).

Schnith, Karl, 'Von Symeon von Durham zu Wilhelm von Newburgh, Wege der englischen 'Volksgeschichte' im 12. Jahrhundert', in *Speculum Historiale; Geschichte im Spiegel von Geschichtsschreibung und Geschichtsdeutung*, ed. Clemens Bauer (Munich, 1965), 242–56.

Scragg, D. G., *A History of English Spelling* (New York, 1974).

Searle, Eleanor, *Lordship and Community: Battle Abbey and its Banlieu 1066–1538* (Toronto, 1974).

—— 'Women and the Legitimization of Succession at the Norman Conquest', *PBC* 3: 159–70, 226–9.

—— *Predatory Kinship and the Creation of Norman Power, 840–1066* (Berkeley, 1988).

Sharpe, Richard, *A Handlist of the Latin Writers of Great Britain and Ireland Before 1540* (Turnhout, 1997).

Shopkow, Leah, 'The Carolingian World of Dudo of Saint-Quentin', *Journal of Medieval History*, 15 (1989), 19–37.

—— *History and Community: Norman Historical Writing in the Eleventh and Twelfth Centuries* (Washington, DC, 1997).

Short, Ian, 'On Bilingualism in Anglo-Norman England', *Romance Philology* 33 (1980), 467–79.

—— 'Patrons and Polyglots: French Literature in Twelfth-Century England', *ANS* 14: 229–49.

—— 'Gaimar's Epilogue and Geoffrey of Monmouth's *Liber vetustissimus*', *Speculum*, 69 (1994), 323–43.

—— '*Tam Angli quam Franci*: Self-definition in Anglo-Norman England', *ANS* 18: 153–75.

Smith, Anthony D., *The Ethnic Origins of Nations* (Oxford, 1986).

—— *National Identity* (Reno, 1991).

SMITH, ANTHONY D., 'National Identities: Modern and Medieval?' in *Concepts of National Identity in the Middle Ages*, ed. Simon Forde, Lesley Johnson, and Alan V. Murray, Leeds Texts and Monographs, NS 14 (Leeds, 1995), 21–46.

—— 'Culture, Community and Territory: The Politics of Ethnicity and Nationalism', *International Affairs*, 72 (1996), 445–58.

SMITH, BRENDAN, 'Tenure and Locality in North Leinster in the Early Thirteenth Century', in *Colony and Frontier in Medieval Ireland*, ed. T. B. Barry, Robin Frame, and Katharine Simms (London, 1995), 29–40.

—— *Colonisation and Conquest in Medieval Ireland: The English in Louth, 1170–1330* (Cambridge, 1999).

SMITH, MARY FRANCES, 'Archbishop Stigand and the Eye of the Needle', *ANS* 16: 199–219.

SMYTH, ALFRED P., 'The Emergence of English Identity, 700–1000', in *Medieval Europeans: Studies in Ethnic Identity and National Perspectives in Medieval Europe*, ed. Alfred P. Smyth (New York, 1998), 24–52.

SOUTHERN, R. W., *Saint Anselm and His Biographer: A Study in Monastic Life and Thought 1059–c. 1139* (Cambridge, 1963).

—— *Medieval Humanism and Other Studies* (Oxford, 1970).

—— 'Aspects of the European Tradition of Historical Writing: 4. The Sense of the Past', *TRHS*, 5th ser., 23 (1973), 243–63.

—— *Saint Anselm: A Portrait in a Landscape* (Cambridge, 1990).

—— *Scholastic Humanism and the Unification of Europe* (Oxford, 1995).

SPEAR, DAVID, 'The Norman Empire and the Secular Clergy 1066–1204', *Journal of British Studies*, 21: 2 (1982), 1–10.

SPIEGEL, GABRIELLE M., *Romancing the Past: The Rise of Vernacular Prose Historiography in Thirteenth-Century France* (Berkeley, 1993).

Stacey, Robert C. 'Jewish Lending and the Medieval English Economy', in *A Commercialising Economy: England 1086 to c. 1300*, ed. Richard H. Britnell and Bruce M. S. Campbell, 78–101 (Manchester, 1995).

STACY, N. E., 'Henry of Blois and the Lordship of Glastonbury', *EHR* 114 (1999), 1–33.

STAFFORD, PAULINE, *The East Midlands in the Early Middle Ages* (Leicester, 1985).

—— *Unification and Conquest: A Political and Social History of England in the Tenth and Eleventh Centuries* (London, 1989).

—— 'Women and the Norman Conquest', *TRHS* 6th ser., 4 (1994), 221–49.

—— 'Political Ideas in Late Tenth-century England: Charters as Evidence', in *Law, Laity and Solidarities: Essays in Honour of Susan Reynolds*, ed. Pauline Stafford, Janet L. Nelson, and Janet Martindale (Manchester, 2001), 68–82.

STANLEY, E. G., 'Laȝamon's Antiquarian Sentiments', *Medium Aevum*, 38 (1969), 23–37.

STATHAM, S. P. H., 'The Brailsfords', *Journal of the Derbyshire Archaeological and Natural History Society* (1938), 66–80.

STENTON, DORIS M., *English Justice Between the Norman Conquest and the Great Charter 1066–1215* (Philadelphia, 1964).

STENTON, F. M., *Anglo-Saxon England*, 3rd edn. (Oxford, 1971).

—— 'English Families and the Norman Conquest', *TRHS* 4th ser., 26 (1944), 1–12.

—— *et al., The Bayeux Tapestry: A Comprehensive Survey*, 2nd edn. (London, 1965).

STEVENSON, W. H., 'A Contemporary Description of the Domesday Survey', *EHR* 22 (1907), 72–84.

STORY, J. E., 'Symeon as Annalist', in *Symeon of Durham: Historian of Durham and the North*, ed. David Rollason (Stamford, 1998), 202–13.

STRAYER, JOSEPH REESE, *The Administration of Normandy under Saint Louis* (Cambridge, Mass., 1932).

STRICKLAND, MATTHEW, 'Slaughter, Slavery or Ransom: The Impact of the Conquest on Conduct in Warfare', in *England in the Eleventh Century*, ed. Carola Hicks, Harlaxton Medieval Studies, 2 (Stamford, 1992), 41–59.

—— *War and Chivalry: The Conduct and Perception of War in England and Normandy, 1066–1217* (Cambridge, 1996).

—— 'Military Technology and Conquest: The Anomaly of England', in *ANS* 19: 353–82.

STRINGER, KEITH J., *Earl David of Huntingdon 1152–1219: A Study in Anglo-Scottish History* (Edinburgh, 1985).

—— 'State-building in Twelfth-century Britain: David I, King of Scots, and Northern England', in *Government, Religion and Society in Northern England, 1000–1700*, ed. John C. Appleby and Paul Dalton (Stroud, 1997), 40–62.

SUGGET, HELEN, 'The Use of French in England in the Later Middle Ages', *TRHS* 4th ser., 28 (1946), 61–83.

TABUTEAU, EMILY ZACK, *Transfers of Property in Eleventh-Century Norman Law* (Chapel Hill, N.C., 1988).

TAKAYAMA, HIROSHI, *The Administration of the Norman Kingdom of Sicily* (Leiden, 1993).

TATLOCK, J. S. P., *The Legendary History of Britain: Geoffrey of Monmouth's Historia Regum Britanniae and its Early Vernacular Versions* (Berkeley, 1950).

TATTON-BROWN, TIM, 'The Beginnings of St Gregory's Priory and St John's Hospital in Canterbury', in *Canterbury and the Norman Conquest: Churches, Saints and Scholars, 1066–1109*, ed. Richard Eales and Richard Sharpe (London, 1995), 41–52.

THOMAS, HUGH M., 'A Yorkshire Thegn and his Descendants after the Conquest', *Medieval Prosopography*, 8 (1987), 1–22.

—— *Vassals, Heiresses, Crusaders, and Thugs: The Gentry of Angevin Yorkshire, 1154–1216* (Philadelphia, 1993).

—— 'Portrait of a Medieval Anti-Semite: Richard Malebisse, *Vero Agnomine Mala Bestia*', *Haskins Society Journal*, 5, ed. Robert B. Patterson (Woodbridge, 1993), 1–15.

—— 'The *Gesta Herwardi*, the English, and their Conquerors', *ANS* 21: 213–32.

—— 'The Significance and Fate of the Native English Landholders of 1086', *EHR*, forthcoming, 2003.

THOMPSON, SALLY, *Women Religious: The Founding of English Nunneries after the Norman Conquest* (Oxford, 1991).

THOMSON, RODNEY M., 'The Library of Bury St Edmunds Abbey in the Eleventh and Twelfth Centuries', *Speculum*, 47 (1972), 617–45.

—— *Manuscripts from St Albans Abbey 1066–1235*, 2 vols. (Woodbridge, 1982).

—— 'England and the Twelfth-Century Renaissance', *Past and Present*, 101 (1983), 3–21.

—— 'The Norman Conquest and English Libraries', in *The Role of the Book in Medieval Culture*, vol. 2, ed. Peter Ganz (Turnhout, 1986), 27–40.

—— *William of Malmesbury* (Woodbridge, 1987).

—— 'Some Collections of Latin Verse from St. Albans Abbey and the Provenance of MSS. Rawl. C. 562, 568–9', in *England and the 12ᵗʰ-Century Renaissance*, ed. Rodney M. Thomson (Aldershot, 1998), chap. 4, pp. 151–61.

THORMANN, JANET, 'The *Anglo-Saxon Chronicle* Poems and the Making of the English Nation', in *Anglo-Saxonism and the Construction of Social Identity*, ed. Allen J. Frantzen and John D. Niles (Gainesville, Fla., 1997), 60–85.

TIPTON, C. LEON, ed., *Nationalism in the Middle Ages* (New York, 1972).

TOWNSEND, DAVID, 'Anglo-Norman Hagiography and the Norman Transition', *Exemplaria*, 3 (1991), 385–433.

TRUAX, JEAN A., 'Winning Over the Londoners: King Stephen, the Empress Matilda, and the Politics of Personality', *Haskins Society Journal* 8, ed. C. P. Lewis and Emma Cownie (Woodbridge, 1996), 43–61

TSURUSHIMA, H., 'The Fraternity of Rochester Cathedral Priory about 1100', *ANS* 14: 313–37.

—— 'Domesday Interpreters', *ANS* 18: 201–22.

—— 'Forging Unity between Monks and Laity in Anglo-Norman England: The Fraternity of Ramsey Abbey', in *Negotiating Secular and Ecclesiastical Power*, ed. Arnoud-Jan A. Bijsterveld, Henk Teunis, and Andrew Wareham (Turnhout, 1999), 133–46.

TURNER, RALPH V., 'Roger Huscarl, Professional Lawyer in England and Royal Justice in Ireland, c. 1199–1230', in *Judges, Administrators and the Common Law in Angevin England*, ed. Ralph V. Turner (London, 1994), 215–23. Repr. from *Irish Jurist*, NS 16 (1981), 290–8.

—— *Men Raised from the Dust: Administrative Service and Upward Mobility in Angevin England* (Philadelphia, 1988).

—— *King John* (Harlow, 1994).

—— and RICHARD R. HEISER, *The Reign of Richard Lionheart: Ruler of the Angevin Empire, 1189–1199* (Harlow, 2000).

TURVILLE-PETRE, THORLAC, *The Alliterative Revival* (Totowa, 1977).

—— *England the Nation: Language, Literature, and National Identity, 1290–1340* (Oxford, 1996).

VAN CAENEGEM, R. C., *The Birth of the English Common Law* (Cambridge, 1973).

VAN HOUTS, ELISABETH M. C., 'Scandinavian Influence in Norman Literature of the Eleventh Century', *ANS* 6: 107–21.

—— 'Historiography and Hagiography at Saint-Wandrille: The *Inventio et Miracula Sancti Vulfranni*', *ANS* 12: 233–51.

—— 'The Memory of 1066 in Written and Oral Tradition', *ANS* 19: 167–79.

—— 'Wace as Historian', in *Family Trees and the Roots of Politics: The Prosopography of Britain and France from the Tenth to the Twelfth Century*, ed. K. S. B. Keats-Rohan (Woodbridge, 1997), 103–32.

—— *Memory and Gender in Medieval Europe, 900–1200* (Toronto, 1999).

VAUGHN, SALLY N., *Anselm of Bec and Robert of Meulan: The Innocence of the Dove and the Wisdom of the Serpent* (Berkeley, 1987).

—— 'Eadmer's *Historia Novorum*: A Reinterpretation', *ANS* 10: 259–89.

Vincent, NICHOLAS, *Peter des Roches: An Alien in English Politics, 1205–1238* (Cambridge, 1996).

VON FEILITZEN, OLOF, *The Pre-Conquest Personal Names of Domesday Book* (Uppsala, 1937).

WALLER, KATHERINE M., 'Rochester Cathedral Library, An English Book Collection Based on Norman Models', in *Les mutations socio-culturelles au tournant des XIᵉ–XIIᵉ siècles: Études Anselmiennes* (Paris, 1984), 237–50.

WARD-PERKINS, BRYAN, 'Why Did the Anglo-Saxons Not Become More British?', *EHR* 115 (2000), 513–33.

WARREN, ANN K., *Anchorites and their Patrons in Medieval England* (Berkeley, 1985).

WARREN, MICHELLE R., *History on the Edge: Excalibur and the Borders of Britain, 1100–1300* (Minneapolis, 2000).

WARREN, W. L., 'The Myth of Norman Administrative Efficiency', *TRHS* 5th ser., 34 (1984), 113–32.

WASHINGTON, GEORGE, 'The Anglo-Scottish Lords of Leitholme and Great Strickland',

Transactions of the Cumberland and Westmorland Antiquarian and Archaeological Society, NS 60 (1960), 46–51.

—— 'The Parentage of William de Lancaster, Lord of Kendal', *Transactions of the Cumberland and Westmorland Antiquarian and Archaeological Society*, NS 62 (1962), 95–100.

WATT, JOHN A., *The Church and the Two Nations in Medieval Ireland* (Cambridge, 1970).

WEBBER, TERESA, *Scribes and Scholars at Salisbury Cathedral, c.1075–c.1125* (Oxford, 1992).

—— 'Script and Manuscript Production at Christ Church, Canterbury, After the Norman Conquest', in *Canterbury and the Norman Conquest: Churches, Saints and Scholars, 1066–1109*, ed. Richard Eales and Richard Sharpe (London, 1995), 145–58.

—— 'The Diffusion of Augustine's Confessions in England during the Eleventh and Twelfth Centuries', in *The Cloister and the World: Essays in Medieval History in Honour of Barbara Harvey*, ed. John Blair and Brian Golding (Oxford, 1996), 29–45.

—— 'The Provision of Books for Bury St Edmunds Abbey in the 11th and 12th Centuries', in *Bury St Edmunds: Medieval Art, Architecture, Archaeology and Economy*, ed. Antonia Gransden, British Archaeological Association Conference Transactions, 20 (Leeds, 1998), 186–93.

WENSKUS, REINHARD, *Stammesbildung und Verfassung, Das Werden der frühmittelalterlichen Gentes*, 2nd edn. (Cologne, 1977).

WERNER, KARL FERDINAND, 'Les nations et le sentiment national dans l'Europe médiéval', *Revue Historique*, 244 (1970), 285–304.

WICKHAM, CHRIS, *Early Medieval Italy: Central Power and Local Society, 400–1000* (Totowa, 1981).

WIGHTMAN, W. E., *The Lacy Family in England and Normandy, 1066–1194* (Oxford, 1966).

WILLIAMS, ANN, 'A Vice-Comital Family in Pre-Conquest Warwickshire', *ANS* 11: 279–95.

—— '"Cockles Amongst the Wheat": Danes and English in the Western Midlands in the First Half of the Eleventh Century', *Midlands History*, 11 (1986), 1–22.

—— *The English and The Norman Conquest* (Woodbridge, 1995).

—— 'The Anglo-Norman Abbey', in *St Augustine's Abbey*, ed. Richard Gem (London, 1997), 50–66.

—— 'The Abbey Tenants and Servants in the 12th Century', in *Studies in the Early History of Shaftesbury Abbey*, ed. Laurence King (Dorchester, 1999), 131–60.

WILSON, DAVID M., *The Bayeux Tapestry* (New York, 1985).

WILSON, R. M., 'English and French in England, 1100–1300', *History*, 28 (1943), 37–60.

—— *Early Middle English Literature*, 3rd edn. (London, 1968).

WISSOLIK, RICHARD DAVID, 'The Saxon Statement: Code in the Bayeux Tapestry', *Annuale Mediaevale*, 19 (1979), 69–97.

WOLFRAM, HERWIG, *History of the Goths*, trans. Thomas J. Dunlap (Berkeley, 1988).

—— *The Roman Empire and its Germanic Peoples*, trans. Thomas Dunlap (Berkeley, 1997).

—— and WALTER POHL, eds., *Typen der Ethnogenese unter besonderer Berücksichtigung der Bayern*, 2 vols., Österreichischen Akademie der Wissenschaften (Vienna, 1990).

WORMALD, FRANCIS, *Collected Writings*, 2 vols., ed. J. J. G. Alexander, T. J. Brown, and Joan Gibbs (New York, 1984).

—— *English Drawings of the Tenth and Eleventh Centuries* (London, n.d).

WORMALD, PATRICK, 'Bede, the *Bretwaldas* and the Origins of the *Gens Anglorum*', in *Ideal and Reality in Frankish and Anglo-Saxon Society*, ed. Patrick Wormald, Donald Bullough and Roger Colllins (Oxford, 1983), 99–129.

—— '*Engla Lond*: The Making of an Allegiance', *Journal of Historical Sociology*, 7 (1994), 1–24.

WORMALD, PATRICK, *The Making of English Law: King Alfred to the Twelfth Century*, Vol. 1: *Legislation and its Limits* (Oxford, 1999).

WRIGHT, NEIL, 'Angles and Saxons in Laʒamon's *Brut*: A Reassessment', in *The Text and Tradition of Laʒamon's Brut*, ed. Françoise Le Saux (Cambridge, 1994), 161–70.

YOUNG, CHARLES R., *The Making of the Neville Family in England 1166–1400* (Woodbridge, 1996).

YVER, JEAN, 'Les Premières Institutions du duché de Normandie', in *I Normanni e la loro espansione in Europa nell'alto medioevo*, Settimana di studio del Centro italiano di studi sull'alto medioevo (Spoleto, 1969), 299–366.

ZANCANI, DIEGO, 'The Notion of "Lombard", and "Lombardy" in the Middle Ages', in *Medieval Europeans: Studies in Ethnic Identity and National Perspectives in Medieval Europe*, ed. Alfred P. Smyth (New York, 1998), 217–232.

ZARNECKI, GEORGE, *English Romanesque Sculpture 1066–1140* (London, 1951).

—— *English Romanesque Sculpture 1140–1210* (London, 1953).

—— *The Early Sculpture of Ely Cathedral* (London, 1958).

—— '1066 and Architectural Sculpture', in *Studies in Romanesque Sculpture* (London, 1979), 173–84.

—— 'Romanesque Sculpture in Normandy and England in the Eleventh Century', *PBC* 1: 168–89, 233–5.

—— *Further Studies in Romanesque Sculpture* (London, 1992).

—— *et al.*, *English Romanesque Art, 1066–1200* (London, 1984).

ZIENTARA, BENEDYKT, 'Nationality Conflicts in the German–Slavic Borderland in the 13th–14th Centuries and their Social Scope', *Acta Poloniae Historica*, 22 (1970), 207–25.

Index